The Life of Henry Fielding

BLACKWELL CRITICAL BIOGRAPHIES

General Editor: Claude Rawson

The Life of
HENRY FIELDING

A Critical Biography

Ronald Paulson

Copyright © Ronald Paulson 2000

The right of Ronald Paulson to be identified as author of this work has been asserted in accordance with the Copyright, Designs and Patents Act 1988.

First published 2000

2 4 6 8 10 9 7 5 3 1

Blackwell Publishers Ltd
108 Cowley Road
Oxford OX4 1JF
UK

Blackwell Publishers Inc.
350 Main Street
Malden, Massachusetts 02148
USA

British Library Cataloguing in Publication Data

A CIP catalogue record for this book is available from the British Library.

Library of Congress Cataloging-in-Publication Data
Paulson, Ronald.
    The life of Henry Fielding: a critical biography / Ronald
Paulson.
        p.   cm. – (Blackwell critical biographies)
    Includes bibliographical references (p.   ) and index.
    ISBN 0-631-19146-1 (alk. paper)
    1. Fielding, Henry, 1707–1754.   2. Authors, English – 18th century –
Biography.   I. Title.   II. Series.
    PR3456.P38   2000
    823′.5—dc21
    [B]   99-43635
                                                                      CIP

Typeset in 10 on 11½ pt New Baskerville
by Best-set Typesetter Ltd., Hong Kong
Printed in Great Britain by MPG Books Ltd, Bodmin, Cornwall

This book is printed on acid-free paper

Contents

Illustrations

Preface

For what, I pray is the principal Part of a Learned Man's Life, but the exact History of his Books and Opinions, to inform the World about the occasion of his Writing, what it contain'd, how he perform'd it, and with what Consequences or Success? (John Toland)[1]

The method adopted in this biography calls for a word of explanation. It does not pretend to the encyclopedic coverage of Martin Battestin's *Life* (1989) or the swift, gripping narrative of Donald Thomas's biography (1990), which is also especially interesting and evocative on the topography of Fielding's life.

My procedure is to begin each chapter with an annotated chronology of the known facts and follow with analyses of the important issues. The genre is more an extended "character" than a biographical narrative. To some extent, of course, this involves (as in Fielding's own practice) a reconstruction into sequences of circumstantial evidence, primarily in the attempt to understand his character in relation to his conduct. When Fielding writes a series of pamphlets on a variety of different subjects, they reflect his circumstances of the time, they expose his real concerns, and they explain as they feed into a major work of art he is writing. *Tom Jones* is *the* major work of art, among other reasons because it follows the most significant facts of Fielding's mature years: privately the death of his wife Charlotte, and publicly the Jacobite Rebellion of 1745. These particular circumstances, along with many others, join to enable the configuration that is *Tom Jones*.

Fielding's life, centered on the writings for which he is chiefly remembered, was organized according to his shifting senses of career, his engrossment in different professions. Each was in its own way, for its own period, determining. When he was a playwright and theater manager he thematized the theater in his writings, and he carried the trope on into his later works, though modifying it against the experience of a journalist, barrister, and magistrate.

I use "career" because in Fielding's case it is not sufficient to say that he moved inexorably from one literary genre to the next, from drama to essay, from satire to novel. His sense of career was very different from that of the dominant literary figure when he arrived upon the scene. Alexander Pope's singleminded career was as poet, and he consciously followed the model of the Virgilian poet from pastoral to georgic to epic. Being a Virgilian writer as well as a writer of his time, he wrote no poems that were not political; but he adjusted the poet's career to the un-Virgilian times, replacing the epic with mock epics and translations of epics, and going on to write Horatian satires and epistles that, given his opinion of the 1730s, were less Horatian than Juvenalian.

Fielding was never a professional poet, though he churned out enough competent verse, nor was he exactly a man of letters; he was a gentleman seeking a livelihood and a place in society outside the army (his father's profession) or the clergy (about which he felt extreme ambivalence). The quickest way to earn money was as a successful playwright, and so initially he wrote plays, as Congreve had done (another writer who insisted he was a gentleman). His success and the theatrical system in London of the 1730s led him eventually to take upon himself the profitable role of manager as well as playwright. In 1737 when the theater was closed to him by the Licensing Act, he turned to the law and, to meet his immediate needs, to journalism; but his periodical essays reflected as well as supported his career as a barrister. The general outlines of Fielding's life maintain a congruence between the career of dramatist and the writings of 1728–37, of lawyer and the writings of the late 1730s and the 1740s, and of magistrate and the writings of the 1750s.

There is no doubt that, as some writers continue to insist, much of Fielding's writing was expedient, compelled by mere need and therefore influenced by the market. But he guided as well as followed the market and was never (or seldom) what he ironically referred to as a "hackney writer." The individuating characteristics of all his writings probably followed from an aristocratic idea of himself, of his own status, education, and abilities, which never abandoned him, only changing registers with changing circumstances.

His characteristic *modus operandi* was the counter-reaction. His breakthrough innovations were all responses – to *Hurlothrumbo*-like farces, to Walpolean politics, to Samuel Richardson's *Pamela* and *Clarissa*. Out of these responses (like Cervantes's to chivalric romance) he created the English comic novel.

He also invariably engrossed his writings with the personal problems that he was at the time trying to work out for himself. It is impossible to overlook the directly autobiographical elements of his writings, recognized by contemporaries – for example the figure of Tom Jones as a self-projection

of some sort, seen from the perspective of a barrister, an advocate for the
defense; of Billy Booth as a conflation of himself and his father, seen now
from the perspective of a grim but just magistrate. The professional phases,
in short, were informed by the period of marriage, and prior to that by the
time when he was a rake around London (with the stories of his attempted
abduction of one woman, his brawls and scraps with the law), and after his
wife's death by his grief for her, and shortly after that, his remarriage to
her maid.

Fielding does not let us forget his friendships and his loves, to which he
constantly refers. Although he was widely read and thought in terms of
ideas (Greatness, Good Nature, Good Breeding), Fielding was decisively
influenced by people, or personalities; thus, for example, the importance
of Plutarch's *Lives* or Plato's *Dialogues* over discursive philosophical or religious tracts. Professionally he existed and performed in relation to the
artist William Hogarth, the actress Kitty Clive, the actor David Garrick, and
the politician George Lyttelton – who were also his close friends; and he
reacted to and incorporated into his art the contemporary figures of
"Orator" Henley and Edmund Curll, the literary figures of Pamela and
Clarissa, and Colley Cibber's "Cibber," the public counter-symbols of his
age.

Each of his careers also elicited the strong opinions of his contemporaries, much of it abusive, and these personal caricatures, political and
moral, elicited defensive responses from Fielding which influenced in
various ways the structures of his major works.

For Fielding "storytelling" in the most general sense (in play, essay,
novel) is a covert means of dealing with these experiences; and the cultural
medium, the literary genre, in which he recounts his memories derives
from the givens of his time. We dramatize and elaborate in order to evoke
the emotion we wish or are taught that our audience should feel, or to
moderate or modulate trauma, making it comprehensible or bearable. The
poems, essays, and narratives of our contemporaries provide models with
which to formulate our own stories. Fielding had not only satires (of Swift,
Pope, and Gay) and histories (of Plutarch, Suetonius, Gilbert Burnet) but
spiritual autobiographies, criminal biographies, and the sentimental comedies of reformed rakes with their vestiges of the older comedy of unre-
formed libertinism. He had Shaftesbury's deism, Hogarth's version of
critical deism, and current models of physiological explanations for human
behavior. Indeed, Fielding's progress from fictions to what he calls history,
ending with the *Journal of a Voyage to Lisbon* and a projected history of
Portugal, shows that for him there was little difference between narrative
truth and historical truth.

I understand Fielding's biography in terms of the tensions between experience and representation, between the projects and struggles of a human
agent, distinct from the roles he found it expedient to play, the fictions he
utilized. The remarkable aspect of Fielding's story was his construction

(dependent on these shifting professions, on the historical situations that prompted the shift from profession to profession) of a new fictional form out of his plays, essays, political satires, and legal arguments. The careers from posterity's viewpoint proved incidental to the development of the new literary form, a strain of the English novel that continued in the comic works of Sterne, Austen, Dickens, and Thackeray, but also such encyclopedic social surveys as Eliot's *Middlemarch* and Conrad's *Nostromo*. Fielding's basic argument was that his "comic epic in prose" was new, never-before attempted, and that it was preferable, both morally and aesthetically, to the fictional narrative being developed by Richardson. From the biographer's viewpoint each profession signifies so far as it contributed to the literary construction that eventuated in *Jonathan Wild, Joseph Andrews, Tom Jones,* and *Amelia*. Fielding wrote three great books, one the ultimate Swiftean satire, one arguably the greatest comic novel in the language, and finally *Tom Jones* – *sui generis,* the culmination of all his experiences, experiments, and thoughts in his other works and careers. In one sense, this book is less a biography of Fielding than of his masterpiece, its conditions of composition (beginning with his brilliant comedies of the 1730s) and its sentimental afterlife (in *Amelia* and the works of the 1750s).

It is important to account for Fielding's particular moral sense, which included his appreciation of religion and his shifting relationship to freethinking. Richardson and his followers, hardly well-wishers, transmitted Fielding to the nineteenth century as a debauched skeptic whose novels were low, immoral, and possibly blasphemous, and Arthur Murphy's essay introducing the 1762 *Works* only abetted the Richardsonian image. But since James Work's corrective essay, "Henry Fielding, Christian Censor" (1949), and Battestin's book-length *Moral Basis of Fielding's Art* (1959), Fielding has been generally accepted as a pious latitudinarian Anglican. Although in Fielding's day latitudinarian meant to many no more than a safe deist, Battestin and other scholars have emphasized his orthodoxy to the distortion of his actual position vis-à-vis the church. They also have too little patience, or understanding, of deism, whether ethical or critical, which, in Battestin's words, "infect[ed] the air with still stronger emissions of infidelity," "poisons" that readers were liable to "swallow."[2] I try to see the phenomenon of deism more sympathetically and Fielding's position more accurately. Indeed, I do not believe that Fielding could have read *Pamela* as he did or written his responses without the deist way of reading which made it no longer possible to construe a *Robinson Crusoe* or a *Pamela* as its pious author had intended.

This biography has been, inadvertently, the work of 40 years. It began when I was asked by Maynard Mack to collect the essays for the *Twentieth-Century Views* volume on Fielding (1962), then by Brian Southam to gather the contemporary views of Fielding for the *Critical Heritage* volume (1969). Over the years, as I turned to questions of satire, popular culture, religion, and aesthetics in a variety of books, Fielding kept cropping up.[3] In retrospect I see I have written as Tristram Shandy wrote his *Life and Opinions*, by a process of infinite regress, which I have now forcibly brought to closure.

Besides the biographies of Fielding, it is a pleasure to acknowledge, most useful of all, the volumes of the Wesleyan edition of Fielding's works with their excellent introductions and annotation.

In particular I wish to thank Claude Rawson for asking me to write this book and for his attentive reading of the manuscript; Ruth Mack and Rachel Cole for assistance with research and bibliographical matters; Helen Rappaport and Alison Dunnett for copy editing and guiding the book through the press; Marie Lorimer for compiling the index; and Andrew McNeillie for his patience and personal concern throughout all aspects of the enterprise.

Frontispiece. William Hogarth, *Fielding*, 1762, etching and engraving by James Basire, frontispiece of *Works of Henry Fielding*, ed. Arthur Murphy; courtesy of the Trustees of the British Museum.

1

Student, 1707–1730

CHRONOLOGY

1707   Apr. 22. HF is born to Lieutenant-Colonel Edmund Fielding and his wife Sarah at Sharpham Park, Glastonbury, Somersetshire, the home of his maternal grandparents, Sir Henry and Lady Gould.[1] Sister Catherine b. July 16, 1708, Ursula b. Oct. 3, 1709.[2]

1709   Aug. Edmund pays £2,800 for a regiment of foot soldiers and the rank of colonel.

1710   The Fieldings settle in a farm at East Stour, mostly (but not entirely) provided by Sir Henry Gould.[3] April, Edmund fills his regiment and prepares for embarcation for Portugal, but arrives in Lisbon only to learn that his regiment has been ordered home.

1712   Aug. Edmund's regiment disbanded; in Sept. returns (aged 33) to East Stour as a half-pay colonel and learns that he owes the difference between the £3,000 in Judge Gould's will and the £4,750 actually paid for the East Stour farm.[4] HF's sister Sarah b. Nov. 8, 1710, Anne in June 1713, Beatrice in June 1714, and brother Edmund in April 1716. In Aug., Anne dies.[5]

1714–16   Edmund sinks into debt.[6] Spending much of his time in London, during the Jacobite Rebellion of 1715–16 he is commissioned colonel of a newly raised regiment (Feb.) and, among other follies, permits himself to be cheated of £500 at cards.[7]

1718   ca. Apr. 14. HF's mother dies (age 35).[8]
Dec. (?). Edmund returns to London, seeking a new commission; takes a house in Blenheim St., near Great Marlborough St.[9]

1719   Jan. (?) In London Edmund marries a Roman Catholic widow, Anne Rapha.[10]

Mar. 11. He is commissioned colonel of a "Regiment of Invalids" of the Chelsea Royal Hospital, including veterans of Marlborough's campaigns.[11]

June. Brings his new bride to East Stour, to "govern the Family."[12]

Aug. HF accompanies his father to his house in London.

Oct. He is enrolled by his father at Eton. His sisters are entered at Miss Mary Rooke's boarding school in the Cathedral Close at Salisbury by their grandmother, who has moved there after the death of Sir Henry. 18th, Edmund's first child by Anne Rapha is born.[13]

1720   Aug. 5–6. Edmund sells his part of the West Stour property, investing it in South Sea stocks; by Oct. sustains heavy losses in the crash.[14]

1721   Feb. 10. Lady Gould initiates an action in the Court of Chancery against Edmund, charging him with dissipating the children's inheritance and intending to convert them to Roman Catholicism. Apr. 7, she withdraws Henry from Eton in order to keep him near her (or he runs away from Eton, returning to her) in Salisbury.[15] May 18, Edmund sends his servants, Henry Halstead and Frances Barber, to recover his children from Lady Gould. The testimony shows Henry barricaded with his grandmother in her house and Edmund's servants outside shouting: "Damn the old bitch. I hope to see her gray hairs brought with sorrow to the grave. – Damn the old bitch, body and soul!" Their attempt is unsuccessful, but Henry returns to Eton in the autumn term. Edmund is successfully sued for £600 by his East Stour housekeeper Mary Bentham.[16]

June 30. Edmund lodges a complaint against Lady Gould.[17]

1722   May 28. The case is heard in Chancery and decided against Edmund. The Lord Chancellor decrees that Henry is to continue at Eton "till further orders" and spend holidays with Lady Gould; the other children are to remain with her.[18]

1724   summer(?). HF leaves Eton for good and shuttles between London and a house in Upton Grey, rented for him by his father, at which he seems to have spent part of his summers at least through 1728. Edmund himself moves to a more expensive house in Great Poland St.[19] Hogarth's popular prints, *The Lottery, Masquerades and Operas*, etc., are appearing in London.

1725   Sept. 21. Not happy at Upton Grey, HF travels south to Lyme Regis, is assaulted by bruisers, quite possibly hired by the guardian of the heiress, Sarah Andrew.[20] He is actively courting

Sarah and on Nov. 14 attempts unsuccessfully to abduct (or elope with) her.[21]

1726 Nov. In St. James's Parish, London, he is indicted for assaulting Joseph Burt, one of his father's servants (charges dropped).[22] In Feb., Hogarth's *Hudibras* prints are published; in Oct., Swift's *Gulliver's Travels*, followed in Dec. by the opposition journal *The Craftsman* and anti-Walpole prints by Hogarth.

1727 Mar. 16. Edmund Fielding is promoted to Brigadier General; pays HF a small allowance.[23] This spring HF shows his cousin, Lady Mary Wortley Montagu, three acts of a first play, *Love in Several Masques*; in Sept. shows her the finished comedy. He is also writing poetry.
Oct. 11. Coronation of George II.
Hogarth's *Masquerade Ticket* is published.
Nov. 10. HF publishes *The Coronation. A Poem. And an Ode on the Birthday. By Mr. Fielding. Printed for B. Creake in Jermayn-street; and sold by J. Roberts near Warwicklane.* Price 6d., no copies surviving.[24]

1728 Jan. 10. Cibber's *Provok'd Husband* opens at Drury Lane; 29th, Gay's *Beggar's Opera* at Lincoln's Inn Fields. Hogarth undertakes the first of several paintings of *The Beggar's Opera*.
30. HF publishes *The Masquerade, A Poem*, a general satire, publ. by James Roberts.[25]
Feb. 16. *Love in Several Masques. A Comedy. Written by Mr. Fielding*, a 5-act comedy, produced at Drury Lane; four nights, one benefit; publ. 23rd by John Watts.[26] He has enrolled at the University of Leiden to study law, but his play, delayed by the long run of Cibber's *Provok'd Husband*, has put off his departure.
Mar. 16. Arrives at Leiden after the term has begun and lives in the Castle of Antwerp, an inn near the university.[27]
May 18. Pope's *Dunciad* published.
July 20. Back in England, HF contributes (?) "The Norfolk Lantern," a satire on Walpole, to *The Craftsman*; and Aug. 3, "On the Benefit of Laughing" to *Mist's Weekly Journal*.[28]

1729 Jan. Edmund marries again (Eleanor Hill, a well-to-do widow of Salisbury).[29]
Feb. 22. HF returns to the University of Leiden, living in the house of one Jan Oson and running up debts. By Apr. 30 he has decamped, and his Italian tutor has seized his possessions in Oson's house. Battestin thinks he may have travelled on the continent (perhaps planning to return to Leiden to reclaim his possessions). During 1728–9 he has drafted new plays, *The Temple Beau, Don Quixote in England,* and *The Wedding Day*.[30]

Apr. *Hurlothrumbo,* the popular burlesque by Samuel Johnson of Cheshire, opens at the Little Theatre in the Haymarket.

During the summer HF collaborates with Lady Mary on a parody of Pope's *Dunciad,* probably in Twickenham where she is staying while her husband Sir Edward is in Bath and Yorkshire.[31]

Sept. Offers his new plays to Drury Lane; they are rejected.[32]

1730 Jan. 26. *The Temple Beau. A Comedy. Written by Mr. Fielding* is produced at the new theater in Goodman's Fields; first run of nine nights plus four more, three benefits; publ. Feb. 2 by Watts with prologue by James Ralph.[33]

EARLY LIFE

Family

In a letter to his friend James Harris, Fielding semi-facetiously refers to the Empress Maria Theresa as "My Cousin of Hungary."[34] Fielding's father, Edmund (1680–1741), was descended from the earls of Denbigh and Desmond, who thought themselves descended from the Hapsburgs; it was Basil, the second earl of Denbigh, who had forged the paper connecting the family with the Hapsburgs.[35] Edmund's father, John Fielding (1650–98), was a clergyman, canon of Salisbury and archdeacon of Dorset; opposing James II's Declaration of Indulgence for the Catholics, he was rewarded by William and Mary, after the Glorious Rebellion, with a royal chaplaincy. From his father's side Fielding inherited an aristocratic lineage, a tradition of Whig antipopery, and the fate of cadet branches of noble families.

Edmund Fielding chose one of the professions open to younger sons of his class, the army. In 1704 he distinguished himself at the battle of Blenheim (his son consistently praised the duke of Marlborough, even defending his indefensible widow). Eventually rising to the rank of lieutenant general, Edmund Fielding was one of the most successful professional soldiers of his time; but he achieved his summit of military glory in his early twenties and spent the rest of his career, bathetically, in the peacetime role of administering units while living on half-pay.[36] His son represents repeatedly in his plays and novels the soldier who in peacetime is neglected by his government. This soldier, however, is most often an aged lieutenant who serves under officers young enough to be his children or grandchildren, hardly the case of Edmund Fielding, who was himself commissioned ensign at 16 (1697).[37] This aged soldier never rises above the rank of lieutenant because he cannot afford to buy a higher rank and will not prostitute his wife to his superior officers. Henry seems to be concerned with both the unrewarded virtue and the libertine excess, assigning one to the old lieutenant and the other to the youthful colonel, in an odd way conflating them.

In *Joseph Andrews* (3.3.207, references here and throughout are to the editions of Fielding's works cited in the Bibliography) Mr. Wilson (whose life in certain particulars echoes Henry's) meets "a beautiful young Girl," whose father is "a Gentleman, who after having been forty Years in the army, and in all the Campaigns under the Duke of *Marlborough*, died a Lieutenant on Half-Pay; and had left a Widow with this only Child, in very distrest Circumstances" – whom Wilson proceeds to debauch. This vignette, with its dismaying conclusion, may reflect what Henry suspected (or heard) of his father's life in London, or it may confuse father and son, as he was to do years later in *Amelia*.

On one side of the family was the glamorous profession of the soldier, supplemented, one generation back, by the sober learning of the clergyman. On the other side was the more substantial profession of the law, another respectable calling for second sons of the aristocracy. In a sense the Westminster magistracy with which Fielding was rewarded in 1748, and not the novel he published in the same year, was the goal toward which his lineage pointed – though he doubtless would have preferred a judgeship of King's Bench.

His mother's father, Sir Henry Gould (1644–1710), was a judge of the Court of Queen's Bench; he had married Sarah Davidge in 1677, and with her came the estate of Sharpham Park near Glastonbury. This was strongly Protestant country, center of support for the duke of Monmouth's unsuccessful attempt to topple the popish James II. The Goulds' daughter Sarah (1682–1718) married Major Edmund Fielding in 1706, and their first born, Henry, arrived on April 22, 1707 at Sharpham (according to tradition, in the Harlequin Chamber, which had beneath a window the stone figure of a cross-legged harlequin playing a fiddle) and was named after his maternal grandfather.[38]

In the later Chancery suit over the custody of the children after Sarah's death, her family claimed that the marriage had been "contrary to their good liking," while Edmund claimed that he had been subsequently "well approved of and received" by Sir Henry Gould.[39] The fact is that six weeks before the younger Henry's birth Sir Henry made a new will in which he left Sarah £3,000 to be held in trust by his son Davidge Gould and his attorney, who were to see to it that Edmund "should have nothing to do nor intermeddle therewith." The money was invested and the interest paid to Sarah. In the case of her death, the money was to be used for the support of her children.[40]

Henry remained at Sharpham Park with his grandparents the Goulds until 1710 when he was three. In the spring of that year Judge Gould bought a farm for the Fieldings at East Stour, outside Shaftesbury and just across the border into northwest Dorset. Edmund Fielding believed that he had by this time made up personal differences with Judge Gould, who intended to cover the whole cost of the farm, but Gould died before he could adjust his will. Edmund was mistaken; he had to pay the difference between the £3,000 in Judge Gould's will and the £4,750 actually paid for the East Stour farm. He had already paid out £2,800 for a regiment of foot soldiers and the rank of colonel, but his regiment was disbanded. The farm was not a success and Edmund's financial situation worsened.

Nevertheless, with his East Stour farm he was a country gentleman and lived in the style of one with several servants and a French governess for the children (as Henry always did, even in the worst of times). He served as justice of the peace and was a figure of authority in the area, one who celebrated the Hanoverian calendar with drinks to the health of the royal family, bonfires, and mugs of beer and cider for the bell-ringers of the church.[41]

From three years old to 11 Henry lived on the farm at East Stour, with a father trying to operate a farm and survive as a gentleman on half-pay, obviously living beyond his means, and dashing back and forth between the farm and the flesh-pots of London; a father who ran up debts from both loans in Dorset and from gambling in London. One debt that appears to have been the result of play with sharpers directly anticipates the troubles of Captain Booth in *Amelia*, while Edmund's refusal to pay offers a precedent for his son's own later highhanded treatment of creditors.

From his French governess, Anne Delaborde, Henry received a grounding in French, and from John Oliver, the curate of nearby St. Mary's, Motcombe, a grounding in Latin.[42] If his father's farming and carelessness returned in the figure of Billy Booth, Parson Oliver gave his name to the sensible clergyman in *Shamela* who exposed the fraud of *Pamela*.

The first fact of Fielding's childhood then was his father's unsuccessful attempt to live up to his blood line and the prestige of his rising career in the army. The second fact was his mother's death, in the spring of 1718 when he was 11. His father's removal to London and his remarriage less than a year later was at best indecently hasty and at worst raised suspicions that the woman had been his mistress in London prior to his wife's death. That was a cliché of life in London; and Sarah, in the country, had been pregnant most of the time. The new wife was, moreover, a Roman Catholic; worse, she had daughters "in a Monastery beyond the Sea" and sent ahead to "govern the Family" her dairy-maid Mary Howard, a woman who claimed she was a Presbyterian, but "some Beads being discovered on her she owned herself to be of the Romish Church"; and when the new Mrs. Fielding herself arrived in East Stour she left "her own Romish Prayer Books in the Windows of the Roomes where the said Children used to go."[43] Her religion focused the subsequent tug of war over the children – and we must assume in particular over the son – between father and maternal grandmother. There is no doubt that the Gould side of the family, with which

Henry and his sister Sarah apparently felt more comfortable, demonized the stepmother and her Roman Catholicism.

In the subsequent Chancery case over the custody of the Fielding children, the chief issue, and the one that turned the case against Edmund, was religion. If the popery of the step-mother was the deciding issue, other factors that were emphasized were the quality of the food she served the children and the rebelliousness of Henry, the eldest son. It was alleged by the governess Anne Delaborde, who remained in the household, that

> in about six weeks after the said Papist Wife and servant came they made or caused such bread to be made that the said Children could not eat it but [Mrs. Fielding] made better bread for themselves which the said Children were not admitted to eat but gave them stinking whey butter which no person could well eat & then caused their Father to beat & abuse them for not eating it & the Small beer was so intolerably bad that the Children nor this Deponent could not drink it nor had they any other Beer or other sort of Liquor allowed them to drink but were forced to drink water for several days together.[44]

(Drinking water, it should be noted, was often a health hazard.) A witness for Edmund Fielding replied that "there was a very good table kept . . . where never was less than 2 very good dishes thereat often times 3 or 4 or more besides desserts or fruit & other things & plenty of Strong Beer."[45] Wherever the truth lay, the emphasis on food and its quality and quantity remained a subject of great importance for Fielding, as well as a metaphor of central significance in his works; in *Tom Jones* it figures the process of his novel, and in *The Journal of a Voyage to Lisbon* it represents a final norm of social life to which he clings in a collapsing world.

Here were reported the first signs of Henry's intransigence. The house was filled with women who doted on him, in particular his great aunt (his mother's aunt) Katherine Cottington, who apparently spoiled him as she propagandized against his father and the Roman Catholic religion. According to Anne Delaborde, the Fielding children became "so very much indulged and so unruly" that "she could not govern them," and Henry, according to the nursery maid, was encouraged by Mrs. Cottington "to be rude and do mischief" to the extent of spitting "in the servants' faces," and turning on "the whole family in general," even Mrs. Cottington – for which, we are told, his father gave him "one stroke or two with a whip."

His misbehavior appears to have gone beyond abuse of the papist "enemy" to include his siblings. One he called a "Shitten Bratt," and with his sister Beatrice he was "guilty of committing some indecent actions . . . all of which Mrs Cottington had due notice given her notwithstanding which she rather seemed to encourage than to correct him for so doing."[46] All we need conclude is that he was spoiled and high-spirited, with a tendency toward "indecent actions," which refer to foul deeds somewhere this side of sibling incest (Battestin's suspicion, based on references to hypothetical incest in *Joseph Andrews* and *Tom Jones*). Although there were apparently interbred families in the Glastonbury area, they were well below the social level of the Goulds and Fieldings.[47]

Eton

In October 1719, Edmund entered Henry at Eton College and the other children were turned over to Lady Gould, now living in Salisbury. At Eton, where Sir Robert Walpole had studied a generation earlier, Henry rubbed shoulders with William Pitt, George Lyttelton, Charles Hanbury Williams, and others who would govern England in the 1740s and 1750s.

Besides the friendships he garnered at Eton, from these three or four years he emerged with an excellent classical education, which he made constant use of in each of his careers. He was trained, like most of his educated contemporaries, by memorizing, translating, and imitating Latin texts and using Latin syntax as the model for his prose style. In *Tom Jones* he compliments his classmate Pitt, by this time the renowned parliamentary speaker, by asserting that all his "Imagination, Fire, and Judgment" could not have produced those orations "if he had not been so well read in the Writings of *Demosthenes* and *Cicero*, as to have transferred their whole Spirit into his Speeches, and with their Spirit, their Knowledge too" (14.1.740). As Pitt spoke, so Fielding wrote, whether essays or *Tom Jones*, and he did not conceal the fact.

Fielding never let his contemporaries forget his classical training. In the 1730s, in a letter to the *Daily Post*, "Philalethes" (Fielding himself) expressed amazement that Henry Fielding, a "Man so well born as this Author," should be maligned by Grub Street critics: "the Education which the Author of the Debauchees [*The Old Debauchees*] is known to have had, makes it unlikely he should err in those, or be able to write such wretched Stuff as [examples follow]." These are solecisms, he adds, "a Boy in the second form at Eaton would have been whipt for."[48] And when he launched *The True Patriot* in 1745, at the time of the Rebellion of Forty-Five, he began with the fact that "I am a Gentleman" and "my Intercourse [is] with People of Condition," stressing his "Learning, Knowledge, and other Qualifications for the Office I have undertaken" of True Patriot Historian in this time of crisis.[49]

His conceit was part of the caricature developed by his opponents, political and professional; but something more than conceit was at stake. Being an Etonian as well as the son of an arms-bearing gentleman explains more of the sense of responsibility Fielding felt than the role of poet or man of letters into which circumstances, as well as inclination, first directed him. In all of his undertakings, including plays that are more than commonly focused on the subject of their maker and making, and above all in his novels, Fielding represented himself in a position of authority, perhaps modelled on the justice of the peace which his father was, as chief gentleman of the area around his seat at East Stour, but also drawing on the authority of a scholar. However much he reflected himself in the lives of his characters (often misguided like those of Mr. Wilson and Tom Jones), he associated himself primarily with his "author."

As well as Latin and Greek texts, the students were made to memorize the New Testament and the liturgy of the Church of England, and recite prayers and attend chapel daily. At one point in April 1721, when he returned to his grandmother's house in Salisbury, Henry momentarily (perhaps only to shock) professed popish views, arguing "in defence of the Church of Rome, alleging it was the ancient church and that the Church of England was only since the Reformation"; principles which Mrs. Cottington believed he had absorbed from his stepmother. On the other hand, the piety inculcated in him at Eton could have raised an impressionable boy to high church opinions and higher. In 1720, however, a new headmaster had been installed – Henry Bland, "a Whig in politics and, by reputation, an Arian in religion," and, though apparently a beloved figure, perhaps one whose views led Henry to begin to question troubling doctrines.[50] The issues that would plague him were the immanence or transcendence of the deity and, it followed, the unequal distribution of rewards and punishments in this life (and in the next).

One retrospect on his schooling appears in the conversation between Joseph and Parson Adams in *Joseph Andrews* (3.5.230). Adams's view is that "Public Schools are the Nurseries of all Vice and Immorality. All the wicked Fellows whom I remember at the University were bred at them." "Joseph," he says, "you may thank the Lord you were not bred at a public School, you would never have preserved your Virtue as you have." But the context is Mr. Wilson's story, and Adams attributes all Wilson's folly, including his deism, to his education in a public school: he would rather a boy should "be a Blockhead than an Atheist or a Presbyterian," meaning by "Atheist" deist.

But Joseph responds that his late master Sir Thomas Booby "was bred at a public School, and he was the finest Gentleman in all the Neighbourhood. . . . It was his Opinion, and I have often heard him deliver it, that a Boy taken from a public School, and carried into the World, will learn more in one Year there, than one of a Private Eduation will in five"; and he told Joseph that "great Schools are little Societies, where a Boy of any Observation may see in Epitome what he will afterwards find in the World at large." Adams, who wants a boy to "be kept in Innocence and Ignorance," is expressing a naive opinion, and Joseph speaks for Fielding, who presumably thinks of himself and reflects his view of "good breeding" laid out in his "Essay on Conversation" and perhaps, as well, the seeds of his own religious skepticism in the 1730s.[51]

Country and city

At the age of 12 Henry had three homes among which he divided his time
– three symbolic and geographical areas: Eton, across the Thames from
Windsor Castle, with its classical curriculum and its elite cadre of boys from
the leading families of England; the country life of East Stour and Salisbury; and London with its particular lures and temptations, embodied in
the life-style of his father – seen no doubt by the Eton humanist in the light
of Juvenal's Third Satire, but also that of the Restoration rakes, Milton's
"sons of Belial," and in particular the notorious earl of Rochester.

What Harry Fielding would have seen in London in the 1720s was above
all plays – but besides the plays at the two patented theaters, the popular
arenas of Bartholomew and Southwark Fairs, the puppet and raree shows,
the rope-dancers, and the conjurors. He would have read the latest works
of Swift, Pope, and Gay; skimmed the popular "novels" of Defoe, Manley,
Heywood, and others; and absorbed the strikingly original graphic satires
of the young Hogarth.[52]

It is easy to think of him adrift in London, but he was quantitatively as
much in the country as in the city, constantly returning for part of each
year to the area south and west of London. From his boyhood in Dorset
and Somerset, though doubtless refined and directed by his classical
reading at Eton, he carried with him the assumption that the country was
a source of integrity and energy. The Virgilian and Horatian topos *beatus
ille* predicated the gentleman's wise retirement from the city to the country.
Henry's introduction to London at the end of his teens carried with it a
sense of country virtue submitting to urban corruption, supported by the
experience of a whole family with father and mother, broken by the death
of the mother and the departure of the father to London and the arms of
another woman.

The visits to Salisbury were to a fragment of a family – a grandmother,
four sisters and a small brother, and no father, in short a household of
women with the imperious young master, Henry. From the absconding
father and the step-mother in London, however, soon followed several half-
siblings. There is little doubt of the tensions between the two families at
the time. Fielding's favorite sister Sarah (born 1710) would devote much
of her fiction to the subject of fragmented families and their reconstruction, and Henry defined his major protagonists in relation to lost and
found, putative and surrogate, trustworthy and untrustworthy fathers. Tom
and Blifil, the half brothers in the Allworthy family, sum up the sort of
anxiety he and his sisters must have felt in relation to a patrimony – and
in particular Henry, shuttling back and forth between households, each of
which demonized the other.

Horace Walpole told a story of Fielding returning to Eton from holiday
without having done his lessons but with a comedy he had written instead

"in which he had drawn the characters of his Father and Family."[53] It is significant, at the least, that it was a comedy, surely Plautine. Laughter was one way to deal with an impossible situation, though, as he would show, there were other less socially acceptable ways as well.

In short, Fielding's remembered life in the country was at least as important as the life of London that came to predominate yet be judged by the norm of a country life remembered with nostalgia. Both *Joseph Andrews* and *Tom Jones* are vitalized and revitalized by the country: London actually takes up a relatively small and constricted space in these novels about the countryside, and this fact may explain some of the gloom of his last most urban novel *Amelia*, as well as the appropriation of Fielding in the nineteenth century when England came to associate its nationhood with the rural ethos.

Before the classical *beatus ille* he was brought up on the local superstitions and folklore of Somersetshire, from Glastonbury the folk memories of King Arthur, the stories of Joseph of Arimathea, the flowering thorn that grew from his staff, and the search for the Holy Grail that he brought with him – indeed, the repeated place name (and surname) of Paradise, recovered in *Tom Jones*, which also recalls the battle of Sedgemoor and its bloody aftermath in which the Protestant claimant was defeated by the popish king and beheaded, followed by the "Bloody Assizes" of Judge Jeffreys.[54]

Fielding tells us that Joseph Andrews was brought up on Sir Richard Baker's *Chronicle of the Kings of England* (1643), a "history" which was in fact a collection of horrors and wonders, a model that Fielding may never have forgotten for the theatrical power of its executions, carried out in the context of religious controversy. The drawing and quartering of Catholic traitors described with such relish by Baker was reflected in Henry's father, who according to his nursery maid, Frances Barber, said "he would as soon suffer his said Children's legs and arms to be cut off as he would suffer them or any of them to be brought up in the Popish Religion."[55] Edmund, however, spoke these words to prove that he was not himself a papist, though married to one.

Molly Apshones, in *The Welsh [Grub-Street] Opera* (1731), seeking similes to express her distress at her master Owen Apshinken's sexual advances, delves into country experience and superstitions:

> Henceforth I will sooner think it possible for butter to come when the witch is in the churn – for hay to dry in the rain – for wheat to be ripe at Christmas – for cheese to be made without milk – for a barn to be free from mice – for a warren to be free from rats – for a cherry orchard to be free from blackbirds – or for a churchyard to be free from ghosts, as for a young man to be free from falsehood.[56]

The city would have been revitalized and reimagined for Fielding by Joseph Addison's *Spectator* – a city of spectacle and spectators, governed by a metaphor of life-as-theater, and embodied in his aesthetic of the Novel or Uncommon (the here and now), with which he supplemented the Great and Beautiful in his "Pleasures of the Imagination" essays. But Addison's Novel was one end of a spectrum of curiosity and surprise that led, as he moved with Sir Roger de Coverley from London to his country estate, to the Strange, the realm of *faerie* in folklore, ballads, the comedies of Shakespeare, and the discourse of Molly Apshones.

Over the next few years we can presume that Henry followed the general itinerary he was to follow later, spending winters in London and summers in the south, in the vicinity of Salisbury, with his grandmother and his sisters, returning to town at the start of the "season" in October and then to the country again in June or July. He never gave up this schedule.

Rake

The next record of Henry is in the summer of 1725: he is 18 and living in a house in Upton Grey, Hampshire (north of Winchester, halfway between Basingstoke and Farnham), rented for him by Edmund, perhaps (given its isolation from both London and Salisbury) to keep him out of mischief. In September, however, he was in Lyme Regis, the port south of the Fielding farm in East Stour. One might suppose that, bored by the exile in Upton Grey, he had returned to Salisbury or further to East Stour, and thence wandered down to the coast, where the social life might be more exciting. He was travelling with a servant named Joseph Lewis, a fact which aligns him with both the status of a gentleman and the conventions of the comedies he would have been seeing in London: Aimwell has his Archer, Dicky his Brass, in Farquhar's *Beaux's Stratagem* and *Recruiting Sergeant*; and of course he was also familiar with all the servant–master pairs in the comedies of Plautus and Terence.

Another theatrical conceit: He was courting a local 15-year-old heiress, Sarah Andrew, whose guardian intended her for his own son. She was a family connection, sister of Honora Gould, the wife of Henry's uncle Davidge (the lawyer who would later help him secure admittance to the bar). Pretty and rich, she was immured by her guardian, and on September 22 Fielding swore an information that he had been set upon by the servants of Andrew Tucker (Sarah's guardian) and had suffered "two several blows in the face and other parts of his body."[57] Tucker claimed that he was "opposed to a connection with so dissipated, though well born and well educated a youth."[58] Therefore, on Sunday the 14th Fielding and Joseph Lewis attempted to intercept her on the way to church, presumably with the intention of eloping, but the attempt failed. Joseph Lewis was apprehended, and the next day Fielding departed Lyme Regis with a flourish, posting a first but paradigmatic literary effort:

November 15 1725
This is to give notice to all the World that Andrew Tucker and his son John
Tucker are Clowns, and Cowards
                Witness my Hand
                Henry ffeilding[59]

Again in November 1726 he cropped up in St. James's Parish London,
when he "shook, wounded and manhandled" Joseph Burt, one of his
father's servants.[60] Nor will this be the last such assault.

James Harris, who knew Fielding from the late 1720s and was perhaps
his closest friend, in his memoir repeats three times the observation that
"his Passions [were] vehement, and easily passing into excess" ("his Passions, as we said before, were vehement in every kind"); to which he adds:
"his person strong, large, and capable of great fatigues in every way; his
Face not handsome, but with an eye peculiarly penetrating and quick, and
which during the Sallies of Wit or anger never failed to distinguish it self."[61]
Arthur Murphy, who knew Fielding toward the end of his life, described
him as "in stature rather rising above six feet; his frame of body large and
remarkably robust, till the gout had broke the vigour of his constitution."[62]
His chief features were height, bulk, a long chin, and a Roman nose; all of
which he distributed among characters in his fictions.

LITERARY APPRENTICESHIP

By spring 1727 Fielding had begun to write. He showed the first three acts
of a comedy, *Love in Several Masques*, to his cousin, Lady Mary Wortley
Montagu, considered by Pope and others to be the wittiest woman of the
day; and (to judge by his dedication to her of the published play) he
received encouragement. The dedication also implies that she used her
influence to interest the managers of Drury Lane. What probably attracted
Cibber, Wilkes, and Booth were the roles he created that showed off their
particular talents.

Lady Mary, 18 years older than Fielding but no doubt taken with this
tall and strikingly clever young man, reported many years later an example
of his wit: he had informed her that he had no choice "but to be a Hackney
Writer or a Hackney Coachman."[63] He would have hoped that she could
open for him the doors of patronage. She was at this time on close terms
with a young woman named Maria Skerritt, and through her with Maria's
lover Sir Robert Walpole, the first minister of the king.[64] Lady Mary was
strongly Walpole, strongly Hanover, and by this time her friendship with
Alexander Pope was a thing of the past.

Fielding sent her a copy of the finished play (one of "my unworthy Performances") in September 1727, reminding her that she had read three

acts of it "last spring," and adding that "it will be entirely from your Sentence that they will be regarded as disesteemd by Me." The formality of the address recalls Gulliver's speech to the queen of Brobdingnag showing how easily a proud man can slip into the style of a courtier:

> I shall do my self the Honour of calling at your Ladyships Door to morrow at eleven, which if it be an improper Hour, I beg to know from your Servant what other Time will be more convenient. I am with the greatest Respect and gratitude, / Madam, / Your Ladyships most obedt, / most devoted humble Servant, / Henry ffielding.[65]

The dedication to the play is equally stylish, apologizing for "prefixing to this slight work the name of a lady, whose accurate judgment has long been the glory of her own sex, and the wonder of ours." However, Fielding strikes a note that will become a refrain: He knows his work is "not free from faults, not one of which escaped your immediate penetration," as contrasted with Lady Mary's "own perfection [which is] very visible to all who are admitted to the honour of your conversation," and which he associates with "those perfections and softer graces, which nature has confined to the female" (8:7). He will never fail to defend the flawed person or literary work against the paragon.

He visited Lady Mary at her Twickenham house, not far from Pope's, and talked about comedy and satire, the latter pro-Walpole and anti-Pope. Their friendship (or this combination of friendship and patronage) may be reflected in the publication on November 10, 1727 of Fielding's first book, a pair of poems on George II's coronation (October 11) and birthday (October 30). No copy of the book survives, but the advertisement included Fielding's name and that of the publisher, James Roberts, a publisher associated with the Court party. The poems were presumably panegyrics, but on January 30, 1728 Roberts also published another poem by Fielding called *The Masquerade,* a satire written in Swiftean hudibrastics and signed "Lemuel Gulliver, Poet Laureat to the King of Lilliput."[66]

This poem does not take a party position, but its title page aligns it with Swift, the English satirist Fielding most admired, and with a satire that was claimed by the opposition to Walpole. Fielding's feelings were not so engaged on the political issues that, though his cousin was a Walpole supporter, he would not have appreciated the brilliance and comic effect of Swift's satire. He supposes Gulliver visiting as a sort of fifth voyage one of John Jacob Heidegger's masquerades, notorious as the popular locus for shifting identities and arranging assignations. He writes in iambic tetrameter, acknowledging Swift's characteristic verse form, but once into the poem "Gulliver" encounters a "lady in a velvet hood" who instructs him in the masquerade (at l. 80), and reveals his fundamental debt to the earl of Rochester's dramatic poems, "Artemesia to Chloe," "Timon," and

"Tunbridge Wells." These poems, based on the conventions of formal verse satire, played off libertine assumptions against a lost ideal of pre-Restoration, Cavalier courtly love.[67] It is well to remember that the master genre of the period in which Fielding launched his writing career was satire, and a young man of his background may have been inspired by the mixed satire and eroticism of Rochester as well as by the more elevated Augustan satire of Dryden and Swift. The politics of Rochester – Old Whig, anti-court, oedipal, and deeply subversive – would prove the more sympathetic.

Although Fielding starts by invoking the satiric persona of Gulliver, and then the Rochester courtier rake, he settles on the persona of a struggling poet; this permits him to joke, as he had with Lady Mary, about the poet's poverty (as against the clergyman's wealth) and yet claim that beneath the disguise he is in fact a "young, smart, dapper man of quality." All of this is already most characteristic. At the outset of his career, and in the manner of Rochester, he mingles satiric convention and rakish self-display, which he carried over directly into his stage comedies. He often gives the impression of not wanting his reader to forget that even beneath the guise of the hackney poet is the close relative of Lady Mary and the earl of Denbigh.

The controlling metaphor in the poem is life-as-masquerade: "Cardinals, quakers, judges dance; / Grim Turks are coy, and nuns advance . . . / Known prudes there, libertines we find, / Who masque the face, t' unmasque the mind" (ll. 69–74). These are whores dressed as nuns, roles reversed, and the world turned upside down, a situation both comically incongruous and morally unsettling. "Grave churchmen here at hazard play," he writes (l. 71); it is difficult to miss the association of disguise and hypocrisy, of clergymen (by which he would have meant popish priests and their Church of England equivalents) and the grave affectation of virtue, which will distinguish all of his early works, and which he may by this time have encountered in the *Characteristicks* of the third earl of Shaftesbury.

The Masquerade could have been an offshoot of the play Fielding was writing, *Love in Several Masques*, in which both literal and figurative masking dominate. One of Fielding's favorite analogies is between men and actors. To think of living as acting is a natural way to express a concern with fashion and/or hypocrisy, the attempt to appear in society what one is not. The metaphor would have accompanied, and was perpetuated by, his primary interest in the stage; but it may have reflected also, as in the play he is supposed to have written while at Eton, the sudden transformations and revelations of and by his father, step-mother, aunts and uncles following his mother's death. But the evidence suggests that at this time the injunction to properly play your part implied both a historical moment and, for Fielding, a personal situation in which one's place in society was uncertain – in terms of manners, in terms of finances – in the flux of the move of politics from the exercise of a virtue guaranteed by landed property to a mechanism of management brought about by new mobilities of property and status. A vulgar pleb might play a perfect gentleman as convincingly as the gentleman himself and so pass as morally and socially what he or she is not – ultimately the problem Fielding addressed in his major works concerning a Walpole or a Shamela.

Love in Several Masques

From the testimony of Lady Mary Wortley Montagu, Fielding's chief motive for writing was cash, and so he produced entertainment gauged to satisfy the current market. Robert Hume, in the fullest study of Fielding's plays, sees *Love in Several Masques* as a rewriting of Christopher Bullock's popular *Woman in a Riddle* of 1716. The two plays, he shows, share the "double gallant" convention, a wealthy fop, "an Old Rich Litigious Stock-jobber" type, a rich young widow, another beautiful young lady, and a scheming maid.[68] Hume's categories, into which he invites us to fit Fielding's plays, are farce, satiric comedy, humane comedy, and reform comedy. *Love in Several Masques* would be humane comedy; more significant, however, is the fact that among Merital's humane progenitors the best known are William Congreve's Valentine and Mirabel, in *Love for Love* or *The Way of the World* (1695, 1700).

Fielding's tendency was to look up not down. Drury Lane was the most respectable of the patent theaters, the last upholder of classical English theater (by which Fielding, like Hogarth in his print *Masquerades and Operas* of 1724, meant Shakespeare, Jonson, Wycherley, Congreve, and Vanbrugh) against the incursion of John Rich's harlequinades at Lincoln's Inn Fields Theatre and the raree shows of Bartholomew Fair which, as Pope was at the moment showing, were supplanting the classical repertoire.

Fielding, the young, inexperienced playwright, like an apprentice poet who starts by writing the most "literary" of forms, the pastoral, had only his knowledge of the London stage repertory and the classic texts of the dramatists and satirists to draw upon. In his preface to the 1734 edition of *Don Quixote in England* he admits that in 1728 when he wrote it, "my too small Experience in, and little Knowledge of the World," had made it impossible for him to show Quixote "in a different manner from that wherein he appears in [Cervantes'] romance" (11:9). What experience he had so far (as opposed to the extraordinarily wide range he was to acquire) can be briefly summarized: Besides the obvious (and it will prove paramount) example of Cervantes' *Don Quixote*, there was a great deal of study of Latin and Greek, the classical texts of Plautus and Terence he studied at Eton (he also shows himself thoroughly familiar with the theoretical doctrines of Aristotle and others), and the classics of English drama as both read and seen in performance.

The current success at Drury Lane that delayed the production of *Love in Several Masques* was Colley Cibber's *Provok'd Husband,* Cibber's senti-mental revision of an unfinished play by Vanbrugh, the latest in a series of comedies focused on marriage, the married couple, and their problems. Drury Lane's current reputation was for the kind of play Cibber had intro-duced in *Love's Last Shift* (1697), a sentimental comedy that Fielding point-edly does not copy in his play (though he was astute enough to include a good part, the fop Rattle, for Cibber, whose greatest fame was for playing fops). Instead Fielding's play looks back to the pre-marital comedies of rakish courtship, primarily of Wycherley and Etherege. (Indeed, Cibber's play would serve as a negative example of comedy 20 years later in *Tom Jones.*)[69]

Fielding had personal experience of both kinds of comedy in London and in Wiltshire, but he chose the Plautine–Terentian plot of courtship, which reflects the young single man in search of amorous experience. The shadow of his adventure with Sarah Andrew and his posted insult to her guardian is visible in Merital's story, summarized by Lady Matchless in her concluding song, "Old Bromio's ranked among the beaus: / Young Cynthio solitary goes, / Unheeded by the fair!" Sir Positive Trapp, who says, "I hope to see the time, when a man may carry his daughter to market with the same lawful authority as any other of his cattle" (8:37), is the father who sells his daughter to the highest bidder.[70]

The Latin epigraph, which introduces the published play, draws atten-tion to his theme, as well as his classical learning. It is from Juvenal's Sixth Satire, on women, which in Fielding's free translation runs: "[Cesennia] brought [her husband] twice ten thousand Pounds, / With all *that* Merit she abounds. / *Venus* ne'er shot at him an Arrow" (i.e., it was not love but her "Fortune [that] darted through his marrow"). In the play that follows Fielding shifts the blame from the woman onto her father or guardian.

The moral structure of the play is based on the contrast of country and city. Wisemore, Lady Matchless (the widow), and Helena are all from the country and virtuous. Wisemore is a satirist on the order of Wycherley's Manly in *The Plain Dealer,* modelled on Juvenal's Umbricius (the last Roman, about to leave Rome for the country), who uses the honesty of the country to expose the corruption of the city.[71] He juxtaposes country, retirement, and the classics (Cicero, Epictetus, Plato, and Aristotle) with coffee-houses and tea-tables ("scandal, lies, balls, operas, intrigues, fash-ions, flattery, nonsense"). With "the habit of a country 'squire, with the sen-timents of an Athenian philosopher, and the passion of an arcadian swain" (in Marital's words, 8:42), Wisemore *and* Marital sum up what was most likely Fielding's self-fashioning at this moment.

The major characters, of course, even when speaking *for* the country, are London-based, and their discourse is the discourse of wit after the

example of Congreve, in particular his *Old Batchellor*, whose Bellmour
and Vainlove serve as the closest models for Fielding's Merital and Malvil.
Presumably from the classical tradition of comedy from Dryden to
Etherege, Wycherley, and Congreve, Fielding inferred that high comedy of
the five-act sort was defined by its wit.

Everything, from Lady Mary's interest in the young man to his earliest
writings, indicates that Fielding had a witty frame of mind – a basic love of
the incongruity of similitude that easily became, one can imagine in conversation, especially with ladies, charming nonsense. Wit, appropriately,
had its roots in the libertine ethos of the cavaliers and the materialist philosophy of Hobbes. Wit was the mark of social distinction, the epitome of
a secular discourse based on an empirical epistemology rather than inspiration, specifically on the discovery of resemblance in apparent difference.
For both Hobbes and Locke wit, based exclusively on the senses, was a corrective to the claim of religious knowledge to inhabit a position prior to
other forms of knowledge.

First associated with rakish seduction and irreverence, political and religious skepticism, wit became, in the 1670s, the satiric discourse of the exclu-
sionist Whigs, directed at court and high church. Attacked in the 1690s as
immoral by Jeremy Collier and Sir Richard Blackmore, wit could be corrected (in Locke's terms) by judgment, which distinguished the differences
in far-fetched similitudes, and in 1711 Addison refined the opposition of
judgment and wit into true and false wit, the one basing similitude on
nature, the other on mere word play.

Dryden had defined high comedy as witty conversation, that is, between
cavalier rakes. Repartee, "as it is the very soul of conversation, so it is the
greatest grace of Comedy, where it is proper to the Characters: there
may be much of acuteness in a thing well said; but there is more in a
quick reply": "the business of the Poet is to make you laugh: when he
writes humour he makes folly ridiculous; when wit, he moves you, if
not always to laughter, yet to a pleasure *that is more noble*" (emphasis
added). The valorizing of the comedy of witty conversation relies
upon Dryden's valorizing of wit itself, as a sort of epistemology that
leads to discoveries and a higher understanding, somewhere above mere
satire.[72]

In *Love in Several Masques* Fielding gives his wit to a pair of rakes but distinguishes them, one libertine and the other romantic lover. Malvil's similes
link lovers and madmen, courtship and a chancery suit, whose consequences are respectively marriage and imprisonment. Merital's link love
and happiness; but he also describes his love Helena as "kept as close as a
jealous Spaniard keeps his wife, or a city usurer his treasure," and this is
picked up by Lady Matchless and applied to her late husband. Merital's
simile degrades not the tenor, love, but the vehicle, Helena's guardian Sir
Positive Trapp.

Fielding's witty similitudes pursue this general reference outward – from the guardian to parliament and parliamentary elections, to the tyrannous cruelty of the king of France, the humorlessness of a Dutchman (even before Fielding visited the Netherlands), all threatening to love, courtship, or marriage. Also, however, are similes that refer to Fielding's experience as a playwright: Merital describes Wisemore as looking "as melancholy, as ill-natured, and as absurd, as I've seen a young poet who could not outlive the third night." To which Rattle adds, " —— Or an old bridegroom who has outlived the third night" (8:43).

Fielding's play ran four nights, a not unsuccessful run, long enough to give him a benefit performance – the primary source of income for a playwright – before he left to take up residence at the University of Leiden. The success was sufficient to earn publication, another significant fact. He was at this time just 21, and he informs the reader in his dedication to Lady Mary that "none ever appeared so early upon the stage" (8:9).

While *Love in Several Masques* is nothing special as a theatrical event, it is an ambitious attempt at witty writing – a series of set pieces on the subjects of women, virtue, and the classical topoi; a veritable commonplace book of aphorisms based on parallel and contrast, zeugma, and the other structures to be found in Congreve's comedies, and perfected in the couplets of Pope. Not easy to keep up with in a theater, they are more effectively mulled over and enjoyed on the page. Bookweight's remark to Luckless in *The Author's Farce*, "there are your acting plays, and your reading plays" (8:208), had its serious side. When in 1698 Vanbrugh, in his *Short Vindication of the "Relapse" and the "Provok'd Wife" from Immorality and Prophaneness*, wrote that he conceived his audience to consist both of playgoers and of readers, he was echoing a commonplace. Dryden's opinion was that only in print can the reader "find out those beauties of propriety in thought and writing which escaped him in the tumult and hurry of the stage"; and in his dedication to *The Spanish Friar*, he noted that "as 'tis my Interest to please my Audience, so 'tis my Ambition to be read: that I am sure is the more lasting and nobler Design."[73]

From the evidence of *Love in Several Masques* it appears that Fielding, while he had obviously had opportunities to familiarize himself with the current London theater, intended to make his name as a man of letters, and his models were Wycherley and, in particular, Congreve, whom he cites in his preface. As a man of the theater he stood to make, if successful, larger profits than any other sort of writer, and part of that profit was in sales of the book.

Fielding, who will use his prefaces, prologues, and epilogues to defend and therefore theorize his innovations, presents only the most conventional position in the prologue to *Love in Several Masques*. He invokes the comic muse and claims to have written humor free of indecency or of particular satire. The only point of interest is that he closes with an epilogue that distinguishes the different parts of his theater audience (gallery, boxes, pit). The issue is the judgment of his work – the apprentice works of a very young man – and apparently concerns Fielding greatly.

Leiden

Fielding had decided – or his father decided for him – to study law at the University of Leiden. Following his benefit night, he set off for Leiden, but while officially studying the law, in practice he was also improving his knowledge of the classics. Leiden was the great center of classical scholarship, with the celebrated Pieter Burmann its professor of History, Eloquence, and Greek. Most attention, however, was devoted to Latin – in particular to the study of ancient texts, which meant to a large extent to their style.

One other aspect of Leiden, however, was its reputation as a center of freethinking – deist, atheist, Socinian, or whatever. The Netherlands had long been recognized as a refuge for heterodox religious critics from throughout Europe. Hugo Grotius, the noted biblical scholar who was a particular hero of Anthony Collins, taught at Leiden, and John Toland had attended some 30 years previously. Fielding's time at Leiden could have made him aware of a long tradition of religious radicalism from a number of sources. James Harris described Fielding in those days: "Leaving School, he went to Leyden, whence returning soon to England, he fell into that Sort of Life, to which great Health, lively Witt, and yt flow of juvenile Spirits, so copious at this period, naturally lead every young man, unchecked by graver authority."[74] Harris may only be reflecting the date of his first intimacy with Fielding, but he regards the visit to Leiden as a watershed.

Fielding was back in England for the summer of 1728. It is a plausible hypothesis that, returning by way of Harwich (Mrs. Heartfree's route in *Jonathan Wild*), he visited Walpole's country seat Houghton and wrote the verses called "The Norfolk Lantern," on the huge ceiling lamp in the entrance hall (published in *The Craftsman*, July 20).[75] This brief satire, which uses the lantern as an emblem of Walpole's prodigality and power, was effective enough to produce an immediate response from the ministerial press.[76] This may be the poem referred to in an attack on Fielding in the 1740s that claims that Walpole

> once generously reliev'd him by sending him a considerable Supply of ready Money when he was arrested in a Country-Town some Distance from *London*, and must have rotted in Prison had it not been for this Generosity in the Minister. Soon after he libelled him personally in a satyr, and next Week had the Impudence to appear at his *Levee*. Upon Sir *R*[ober]*t*'s taxing him with

his Ingratitude, and asking him why he had wrote so and so; he answered very readily, *that he wrote that he might eat.* However Sir R[ober]t still continued his Generosity to him, till he grew quite abandon'd to all Sense of Shame. He then set up for a Play-Writer.[77]

Walpole was at Houghton during part of July that year and could have gotten Fielding out of a scrape of the sort to which he was prone.[78] The conclusion must follow that he did not intend Lady Mary to see this satire, which must either have reflected a need for quick money (even if it worked against the longer-term benefits of patronage) or, perhaps, an application of the skeptical discourse he had learned from the freethinkers of Leiden. The friendship with Lady Mary would explain the early courting of Walpole – and so the stories of Walpole's getting him out of trouble – and leaves the "Norfolk Lantern" attribution, if true, a first sign of a tendency to talk out of both sides of his mouth – a sort of expediency on the one hand or a suiting of his rhetoric to his audience on the other, both of which were Addisonian traits he later elaborated in his "Essay on Conversation" on the pragmatism of politeness; on the other hand, it was perhaps also an aristocratic recklessness, the pleasure taken in wit for its own sake.

"The Norfolk Lantern" shows a writer familiar with the satire of Nicholas Amhurst's opposition journal, *The Craftsman* – his use of analogy and irony, his disingenuous claim to be talking of stockjobbers, or Cardinal Wolsey, or Sir John Falstaff when in fact his referent was Walpole. The brilliance and comic effect of Amhurst's satire would have been more important to Fielding than the political affiliation; though Amhurst's villains, the papist ideologues he detected behind Walpole's bishops, were very much Fielding's own.

In an essay on "the Benefit of Laughing," which appeared in *Mist's Weekly Journal* August 3, 1728, Fielding introduces the physiological theory of laughter that will inform his mature work.[79] It relies on Aristotle's cathartic theory of tragedy, probably supplemented by a reading of Shaftesbury's *Sensus Communis*, proposing "to cure all Diseases incident to the Mind and Body of Man by a *Laugh.*"[80] He describes a sick man and a comic scene which "occasioned so much Laughter, and so diverted his Melancholy," that he immediately recovered and lived a productive life. The significant example is a cardinal "dying of an Imposthume," whose monkey puts on his cardinal's hat: "The odd Ambition of Pug to be made a cardinal [what Fielding will later call affectation], so tickled his Eminence, that he burst into a loud Laugh, which broke the Imposthume, and he recovered."[81]

To judge by a poem dated 1728, addressed to Rosalinda, Fielding spent part of the summer at Upton Grey.[82] At the same time as he was idealizing country values in his early plays he apologizes for the shabby surroundings, so different from London. He may be writing of one spot only, the farm where he is trapped, "This side a house . . . and that a shed":

On the house-side a garden may be seen,
Which docks and nettles keep for ever green.
Weeds on the ground, instead of flowers, we see,
And snails alone adorn the barren tree.

Another poem, "To Euthalia, Written in the Year 1728" ("Burning with love, tormented with despair"), suggests that this young lady has eclipsed both Rosalinda and "Sappho" (Pope's name for Lady Mary: her "wit each envious breast alarms," Fielding explains).

The *Anti*-Dunciad

In May 1728 Pope published *The Dunciad*, and a year later the expanded *Dunciad Variorum* with prefaces, essays, apparatus, and elaborate pseudo-scholarly annotation by "Martinus Scriblerus." In the long run this would be an event of the greatest importance for Fielding: Pope attacked the demotic discourse of the London subculture, of the fairs, harlequinades, and puppet shows, whose popularity both attracted and repulsed Fielding, and, at the same time, he showed how this "nonsense" could be absorbed and adapted to the end of true poetry. In the short run, Fielding was called upon by Lady Mary to attack *The Dunciad*.

In March 1728 while he was in Leiden, she had suffered Pope's attack in the third volume of his *Miscellanies* with a poem "To a Lady who father'd her Lampoons upon her Acquaintances," and in May *The Dunciad* included a scurrilous innuendo on her relationship with the Frenchman Nicolas-François Rémond. She was involved at this time in legal battles over the custody of her insane sister, and she felt that Pope's satire compromised her reputation.[83] The *Dunciad Variorum* retained the reference: It was probably at this point, in the summer of 1729, that she persuaded the gallant Fielding to join in her campaign against the Scriblerians, and the two friends, to amuse each another, collaborated on the composition of a mock-*Dunciad*. Two different sets of verses survive among Lady Mary's papers, Fielding's amounting to over 600 lines. The project was brought to a close by Lady Mary's serious illness in the autumn, and the events of the following year made it impossible that Fielding would ever look back on this apprentice work, which was understandably not published.

There are drafts of three cantos in Fielding's hand and endorsed by Lady Mary with her initials. Cantos 2 and 3 are so marked, and a fragment without a beginning appears to be Canto 1. The last is an address by the Goddess Dulness to her son – whom Fielding designates not Lewis Theobald but, turning the tables, Pope himself; and now George II (Pope's Dunce the Second following Dunce the First) and Caroline are "Wit's brightest Patrons." Dulness complains to Pope that

Never shall England more my God head own
While such a race expect the british Throne
Never to wear my hevy Chains submit
Till on it's Throne some Drowsy Monarch sit.
(ll. 73–80)

The shrewd Lady Mary, if not Fielding, has recognized Pope's *Dunciad* to be a political satire on the female line of succession in the House of Hanover and felt the need to correct the Jacobite myth. There is, nevertheless, no way to overlook the pragmatism of Fielding's lines on the royal family (very like the "praise is scandal in disguise" of Pope's *Epistle to Augustus*). They have to have been written with patronage as their object, whether Lady Mary's, or Walpole's, or the royal couple's.

Once past the preliminaries, Fielding takes as his model not Pope's own in *The Dunciad*, the action of Virgil's *Aeneid*, but the council in Pandemonium from Milton's *Paradise Lost*, Book II (Pope himself, of course, alluded to *Paradise Lost* in the openings of Books II and III). This permits him, reflecting Lady Mary's current feelings about Pope, to figure the Scriblerus group (including Gay, Swift, and Amhurst [Caleb Danvers]) as the fallen angels and Pope as their leader, Satan. His comments are those of hostile contemporaries – on Pope's Roman Catholicism, his Jacobitism, and his mercenary strain ("Let Wits be caught with Baits of empty Praise / Give me the Gold, ye Gods! – and them the Bays"; ll. 196–7). But they are also personal. For Fielding Pope was "Pope Alexander," the Great Poet just as (in the opposite political camp) Walpole was the Great Man, the Prime Minister. It is not difficult for a young poet to both internalize his art and attack the figure of the bad father.

Fielding also faults Pope for his shaky Greek and his sub-Etonian (or sub-Leiden) learning. In Codrus-Pope's meager two shelves of books one finds "such Books as pretty Fellows read / No Latin sham'd the courtly Shelf, no Greek / Which Obsolete tongues Pedants only speak" (ll. 24–6; again, ll. 107–8). This, with the literal translation of Gay and Swift into Greek (Ilar and Ochistes), is Fielding's way of reminding the reader of his own superior learning. He addresses Pope's tutelary deity Rhime:

Let English Criticks Milton's Strength commend
But mayst thou ever be thy Codrus [Pope's] Friend
Still to my Muse thy Influence impart
For Sense and Wit are needless where thou art
By thee almost the Realm of wit's undone
Oh aid the greatest Efforts of thy Son.
(ll. 167–71)

Fielding's disvaluing of Popean rhyme will return when, justifying his own "comic epic in prose," he takes Milton's side of the argument, claiming the liberty of blank verse or prose over the jingling, confining couplet.[84]

His preference for Addison, shared with Lady Mary and her Whig circle, follows from his attack on the Scriblerians. In the long run, he will owe more to the prose of the *Tatler* and *Spectator* than to Pope's verse, and he will learn more about constructing his novels from their essays than from the baroque allegories of *The Dunciad*, which he will associate with farce and nonsense. Fielding's parody of the Popean mode satirizes the emblematic fable, to which his novels will serve, among other things, as a "modern" corrective.[85]

Nevertheless, his most popular plays of the 1730s are built around dramatizations of the *Dunciad* allegory; and, as George Sherburn pointed out, Pope himself will copy Fielding's dramatization of the *Dunciad* fiction in his Fourth Book added in 1742.[86] Pope's satire of popular forms, which include farce and harlequinade, came to serve as the "farce" of his most successful plays. And the *Dunciad Variorum*, with its prefaces and notes of Scriblerus, showed him how to frame and interpret the subculture "farce" in texts he signed "H. Scriblerus Secundus."

Fielding's preference for Swift marks the liveliest scene of the poem, where he treats Codrus-Pope as a Lilliputian and anticipates the formula he will explore less than a year later in *Tom Thumb*:

> More had he spoke – but then Ochistes [Swift] laid
> A mighty Hand beneath his Shoulder Blade
> And grasping fast, high lifted him in Air
> (Then Dulness, say, how great was thy Despair)
> So have I seen some Boy a Squirrel take
> And spight of Grandmother's Entreaty shake.
> So Gulliver in Lilliput would rear
> The Pigmy Race half-dead with Shivring Fear
> And sure Ochistes was as Strong as Gulliver
> Now the vast chief, the Lilliputian Bard
> To Squeeze to Death between his Thumbs pepar'd.
> (ll. 229–39)

Fortunately for Pope the goddess interposes at this point, but the scene is followed by yet another simile from common life, in this case based on Swift's "Description of a Morning" or "of a City Shower":

> So in the Play-House Passage once I knew
> A Fight twixt swinging Moll and little Sue
> Sue bawl'd and curs'd in Dialect so bad
> Tis possible she'd read the D——
> At length Gigantick Moll began to twist
> The swelling Sinews of her Manly Fist
> Till Fear did Sue, Scorn greater Moll appease
> And both retir'd to cry their Oranges.
> (I, ll. 246–53)

The most characteristic and interesting parts of the poem are the Swiftean descriptions of everyday life in London, which will reappear in the sublime nonsense of the epic similes of *Tom Thumb*. Swift is only satirized for what he cannot help – the comic discrepancy between his ambition and his notable failure to rise in the Church of England.

The *Dunciad* fragments, in the perspective of Fielding's later work, set out his priorities, his general assumptions, and do not distort very much (except in the passage about the royal family) his system of values. He did not share the politics of the Scriblerians, but he did learn almost everything about writing from the great trio of Pope, Swift, and Gay, together with their antagonists in the *Spectator*.

These apprentice works offer evidence, first, that Fielding adapts himself to his audience, especially if we accept as his the "Norfolk Lantern," which expresses a view exactly contrary to that of the *Dunciad* parody;[87] second, that he must have enjoyed an extreme facility in writing – whether verse or prose – to have produced all those mock-*Dunciad* lines, probably within a week or so. He was alarmingly fluent at cranking out couplets, from poetic epistles of the Popean sort to prologues and epilogues of the sort Dryden wrote. Soon to follow was confirmation in the rapidity with which he wrote his plays.

Gay's Beggar's Opera

The other major event of the year of Fielding's introduction to the literary scene was also Scriblerian – the production of Gay's *Beggar's Opera* at Rich's Lincoln's Inn Fields Theatre. The subject of Gay's ballad opera (and its sequel *Polly*) takes up a disproportionate part of the *Dunciad* fragments. Fielding stresses, as most writers did, its phenomenal success, which he must have felt overshadowed *Love in Several Masques*. In the ambience of Lady Mary, he equates *The Beggar's Opera* with farce. He is repeating Rochester's aristocratic disdain of Dryden for wooing the public by writing for the theater rather than for the elite who read his own poems. Yet his lines focus on just the qualities he will himself find a place for and enlarge upon in his most successful plays, reaching the same broad audience. Even in *Love in Several Masques*, although the role of Rattle attracted Cibber, Fielding's talent lay less in the portrayal of fops, the fashionable Tattle or Rattle or Lord Formal, than in the demotic country discourse of Sir Positive Trapp and his "old English" family and its "antiquity." In this he reveals, besides his country roots, his familiarity with the rural comedies of George Farquhar, *The Recruiting Sergeant* and *The Beaux's Stratagem*.

He uses the enchanting Polly Peachum, as he will continue to use women, to epitomize his immediate reaction:

> A Bundle see beneath her arms she brings
> New Ballads that to former Tunes she sings
> You too might hear the Soft enchanting Sound
> Were not it's murmurs in applauses drown'd.

Her sin is to

> charm with Ribaldry, the great, the Fair.
> While Beau and Footman by the same applause
> Too true confess the Parallel she draws

– that is, between the high and the low in society (ll. 63–6, 70–3).

The Beggar's Opera opens with Mr. Peachum, the fence, singing that "the Statesman, because he's so great, / Thinks his Trade as honest as mine," adding: "A Lawyer is an honest Employment, so is mine." Gay's robbers, pimps, and whores sound and act as if they were lawyers, merchants, courtiers, and politicians. The characters are aping the manners of their superiors (Peachum as a "respectable" merchant, whores as ladies, Polly as a romance heroine, Macheath as a gentleman), and the result is a powerful social satire.

A witty young playwright could regard these analogies (essentially *Craftsman* analogies) as comparisons of the ostensibly dissimilar. At the end the Beggar, the author of the play, explains the similitude and (supplementing it with judgment) the difference:

> Through the whole Piece you may observe such a similitude of Manners in high and low Life, that it is difficult to determine whether (in the fashionable Vices) the fine Gentlemen imitate the Gentlemen of the Road, or the Gentlemen of the Road the fine Gentlemen. – Had the Play remain'd, as I at first intended, it would have carried a most excellent Moral. 'Twould have shown that the lower Sort of People have thier Vices in a degree as well as the Rich: And that they are punish'd for them.

The inference is that opera heroes and politicians, underneath their rhetoric and respectability, have the same cutthroat values as Macheath and Peachum, the highwayman and the fence, but (and this is the difference) only the latter "are punish'd for them." Gay's picture of the robbers does not stop with the realization that they are essentially the same as the prime minister and his cohorts, but goes on to suggest the contrast.

One or two even emerge as a sort of ideal against which to judge the rest. The "love" represented by the faithful Polly is contrasted with the brutal ledger-book pragmatism of the Peachums and Lockits, as well as with Macheath's "love" (Polly's own is compromised because she has admittedly learned about "love" by reading romances fed her by Macheath for purposes of seduction). Even the whores, though also with traitresses in their number, "are always so taken up with stealing hearts, that [they] don't allow [themselves] time to steal any thing else" (2:4). There is a passion driving them that is totally lacking in the calculating world of the counting house.

Before he can have seen Gay's play Fielding was already pitting love against commerce in *Love in Several Masques*, and Sir Positive Trapp (though speaking from the perspective of a family-proud rustic) remarks that we "upbraid the son whose father was hanged; whereas many a man, who deserves to be hanged, was never upbraided in his whole life" (8:85). The motif was also at hand in many of the Jonathan Wild pamphlets written before *The Beggar's Opera* (itself another version of the Wild story) appeared.[88] *The Beggar's Opera*, however, introduced the young Fielding to this topos in the theater, where imitation equaled impersonation.

Gay's lawyer, clergyman, courtier, and politician analogues naturalize the heroic level of a mock-heroic satire in which a dunce or a fishwife speaks as if aspiring to the status of an Aeneas or a Dido, or a hack writer to the status of Pope. Pope, however, had parodied Virgil's *Aeneid* in order to suggest an ideal against which the present-day Trojans who have sunk to dunces can be measured. He used the heroic level as a classical and religious ideal and thus suggested how different Theobald and the dunces are from Aeneas and the Trojans. Gay conveys the heroic level in a style similar to that of the *Dunciad*, but he conflates the high and the low. His purpose is to suggest the correspondence, not the divergence, between the heroic (or, for him, "great") world and the squalid world of contemporary London. The diction and mock-heroic similes in the mouths of Gay's robbers and whores do not allude to an ideal but rather show a correspondence between the activities of robbers and the debased-heroic (or ruling-class) activities their words evoke.

Gay's sequel of a year later, *Polly* (1729), which takes the characters to Jamaica, was a more conventional satire: the noble Indians act as a norm against which the representatives of European civilization make a sad showing. As John Loftis says, "We are compelled in *Polly* to take on the attitudes of the Indians, rational attitudes, and having done so we are too censorious of the colonists and pirates to enjoy their misdeeds."[89] In *The Beggar's Opera*, on a stage, impersonated by actors, Macheath and Peachum and Lockit are experienced as humor characters (would-be "gentlemen" or "respectable merchants"), and the effect is – as it obviously was on the stage of Lincoln's Inn Fields – more comic than satiric. The audience was more pleased than upset, and thus – another lesson for Fielding – made the play a phenomenal success.

The Beggar's Opera proved to be crucial for William Hogarth as well as Fielding. Attending an early, if not the first, performance, Hogarth sketched and then painted (at least six times) the scene in which Macheath is having difficulty choosing between his two "wives," Polly and Lucy, and they, in turn, are trying to mediate between their lover and their angry fathers, intent on hanging Macheath. Hogarth gives likenesses of the actors, showing them in their roles of Macheath, Polly, Peachum, and those characters in *their* equally theatrical roles of gentleman, romantic lover, holier-than-thou respectable merchant. Like Gay, he shows Macheath, as played by the actor, striking the pose of a Hercules at the Crossroads – the mock-heroic allusion. In the final version (see plate 4 on 82) he extends the theatrical analogy outward to the audience and to the duke of Bolton himself, who was in fact, by the end of the first season, the lover of Lavinia Fenton (Polly Peachum) and who appears as part of a separate play-within-the-play consisting of himself and Lavinia, whose eyes are on him instead of her father, with whom she is pleading for the life of Macheath.[90]

The Leiden plays

Fielding may have planned to matriculate at Leiden with a scholarly career in mind – one not unlike that of his Salisbury friend James Harris, an even better classicist than himself. Once in Leiden, however, he began to write plays in a more systematic way than he studied Latin and Greek and returned at the end of the 1729 spring term with three new plays of different types and styles, *Don Quixote in England*, *The Wedding Day*, and *The Temple Beau*, which he presented to the patentees of Drury Lane in September. They were rejected by the patent theaters, but *The Temple Beau* found a home at a new theater. In October 1729 Thomas Odell converted a workshop in Ayliffe Street, Goodman's Fields, into a theater which would draw more heavily upon a City audience than the West End audience of the other playhouses. The clergy's prompt attack on this theater as a corrupting force on respectable London citizens (apparently more vulnerable than the gentlemen of the West End) could have contributed to Fielding's hostility to the clergy which had already begun to mark (Battestin would say, mar) his work.

Valentine and Veromil, the two lovers of *The Temple Beau*, are once again respectively a London libertine and an idealizing country type who invokes courtly love. The country is associated with Veromil and Bellaria, the hero and heroine, as it will be associated with the heroes of *Joseph Andrews* and *Tom Jones*.

One suspects that in Veromil and Valentine Fielding was dramatizing two aspects of himself which he was later to combine in Tom Jones. Veromil makes Fielding's first statement of the unity of pleasure and virtue: "The innocent, the perfect joy that flows from the reflection of a virtuous deed far surpasses all the trifling momentary raptures that are obtained by guilt" (8:164); a sentiment that is summed up in the closing verses which contrast the libertine chase with true love. As in *Love in Several Masques*, the chase of several women is narrowed to the love of one, but now the libertine is bracketed as a villain, his values those of an ethical deist who betrays his friend as well as the woman who loves him. Fielding's Veromil and Valentine could derive from Congreve's Valentine and Scandal, or even Mirabel and Fainall, except that Fielding, writing ostensibly for Cibber's theater, felt he must add Valentine's reformation.

Fielding is exploring this contrast between romantic lover and libertine, working it out for himself, or simply regarding it with comic detachment. Libertinism (reflected also in the poems he was writing at the time) held an obvious attraction for him: he would have inherited it as an aristocratic counter to Interregnum religious hypocrisy, joined with ideals of courtly love (if not romance), personal and sexual freedom, as well as honesty, sincerity, wit, free and mutually satisfying sexual pleasure, and naturalness. All of this would have included the psychologizing of romances and the deconstruction of religious or religio-moral texts.[91]

With the replay of the contrasting rakes, however, Fielding begins to shift attention to the family, and the model is Congreve's *Love for Love* with its father-sons and brothers. *The Temple Beau* focuses on the relationship of fathers and sons; secondarily on sisters who are contrasted as prude and coquette; and ambivalently on scholarship – a pseudo-pedant (Young Pedant) and a pretended law student (the title character, Young Wilding) who is in fact a rake.

Arthur Murphy claimed that Fielding returned to London to write plays because his father had discontinued his £200 allowance.[92] If true, this could explain both why he returned for good in 1729 (as in 1728, he registered late; but this time he withdrew early, pursued by bill collectors) and also the choice of subject in *The Temple Beau*: the young rake, Wilding, whose high living is concealed under the ostensible study of law, and whose law books are replaced by Rochester's *Poems*, a book we have seen to be much in Fielding's mind. The case of Young Pedant in *The Temple Beau* shows the other side of the coin, the "Obsolete tongues Pedants only speak."

The Temple Beau would appear to be a rehearsal of various self-roles, scholar, hack writer, and possibly rake-suitor, and occupation is one of its subjects. In Young Pedant Fielding exorcises the discourse of Eton and Leiden[93] – but in the context of other students, Valentine and Veromil down from Oxford–Cambridge and Wilding studying law in the Temple. One subtext of the play is that without courtly patronage for a young writer, that is Fielding, now only the "stage may be the road to fame."

The second play written in Leiden, *The Wedding Day*, once again employs the two rakes, but this time the libertine Millamour (a thousand loves) is a Dorimant or Horner who is set off by his friend Heartfort (strong-heart). They are another version of the Valentine and Veromil pair, except that the emphasis falls on the lustful Millamour and, still more emphatically bowing to the sentimental Cibber mode, on his eventual reform, a convention Fielding will find it difficult to avoid in his mature fictions.

The emphasis also shifts, as in *The Temple Beau,* from the lovers (with the theme of love / friendship or honor) to the family. Fielding plays against each other the lovers on the stage and the projected configuration of a family, either patriarchal or (based on love) conjugal, depending on the outcome of the plot, which will unite both father and son and their wives – though in fact, as it turns out, the father has married his own daughter by an earlier liaison. Although he has not had time to consummate the marriage, at the end of the play incest is the subject that lingers in the reader's (and presumably the spectator's) memory.[94]

The Wedding Day is the earliest and crudest version of Fielding's use of a potential incest situation. Whatever we may wish to make of it, the incest does draw attention to itself as something more than a joke. But the incest is focused not on a sibling relationship (Battestin's argument for the incest of Fielding and his sister Sarah) but on a father and daughter. It is most likely the extreme example of the collapse of a family, a subject whose interest for Fielding was more pervasive and understandable than the hoary dramatic convention of incest. Incest is also, I suspect, one of the devices the libertine Fielding uses to *épater* his bourgeois audience.

Don Quixote in England is the most significant of the plays Fielding wrote in Leiden. Cervantes' *Don Quixote* was on Fielding's mind already in *Love in Several Masques,* where it receives four allusions. Helena herself is presented as a Quixote in that she knows the city only through books she read in the country. The next step was to write a play about Quixote that transplants him to England in the 1720s, and adapts him as a device for satiric comment.[95]

In its original form we must suppose that it was a short farce, an afterpiece, a first thought for *The Author's Farce.* Fielding's account, written when the play was produced and printed in 1734 (it now included the theatrical frame he had introduced in *The Author's Farce*), was that the play "had been sketched out into a few loose scenes" only, was put by, and later shown to Booth and Cibber, who were unenthusiastic, and so put by again until a play was needed in 1734 (11:9). Given the other two plays, we can assume that the original *Don Quixote in England* included the love intrigue of Fairlove and Dorothea, her father Sir Thomas Loveland, and his enforcement of a mercenary marriage with Squire Badger. The relatively extraneous election elements (Don Quixote for M.P.) were doubtless added in 1734.

Don Quixote meant to contemporaries the madman who sees giants in windmills – that is, in ordinary contemporary reality – and who, mistaking the illusion of a puppet show for reality, destroys it. Fielding eventually recovered Quixote's puppet show in a puppet version of *The Provok'd Husband* and in Garrick's *Hamlet* encountered by Tom Jones and his Sancho, Partridge. In a more general way, he materialized the scene in *The Author's Farce* and each of his rehearsal plays.

In this first trial run the play ends with Quixote's summation, which says that all the foregoing has been based on the metaphor of madness. When Dr. Drench calls him a "madman," Quixote replies: "Who would doubt the noisy boisterous squire, who was here just now, to be mad? Must not this noble knight here [Sir Thomas] have been mad, to think of marrying his daughter to such a wretch? You, doctor, are mad too, though not so mad as your patients. The lawyer here is mad" (11:69–70). Quixote indicates that we have witnessed a satiric anatomy of madness from Sancho's remark at the beginning of Act II that they "are looked on here to be neither more nor less, better nor worse, than a couple of madmen" to his own exclamation about Sir Thomas: "The usual madness of mankind!" (31, 65). Badger is a sort of alter Quixote, riding his hounds toward the lady he is to court, being diverted at an inn, mistaking John (Fairlove's servant) for a lord because of his livery, mistaking Sancho for a country squire, in short, betraying all the classic quixotic symptoms. Likewise Sir Thomas sees Badger through his madness for money as a good mate for his daughter (Quixote makes the analogy explicit, 3.14; 11:65), when any normal person sees that Badger is a fool.

Fielding has taken the conventional comic romance situation of his first comedies – the father wants his daughter to marry X while she wants to marry Y – and, by placing Don Quixote in the midst of it, creates a wholly satiric picture: madness becomes the common denominator of all actions. As Sir Thomas concludes, "I don't know whether this knight, by and by, may not prove us all to be more mad than himself" (11:70). "Madman" will be the model for the "nonsense" or "farce" (or burlesque) that Fielding uses as the ambiguous centerpiece of his next play, *The Author's Farce.*

As in *The Masquerade,* but now bolstered by Gay's *Beggar's Opera,* Fielding implies that the prevailing evil in England is play-acting, vanity, and hypocrisy. When Sancho Panza and we see "a country squire at the head of his pack of dogs," Quixote sees (mock-heroically) the giant "at the head of his army, that howl like Turks in an engagement." The latter is the burlesque or farce that, seen by Quixote, symbolizes the fact that he is the leader of the country who abandons his responsibility for his pleasure, who at the head of an army would be the same as at the head of his pack of dogs. He too has something in him of the evil giant who hunts women "like hares." If the squire were to be taken literally he would be a "dog-boy" or a gamekeeper. So the lawyer and doctor appear to be mere quacks and rogues, but Quixote sees them as "the prince of Sarmatia, and . . . of the Five Mountains," implying the similarity between the lowest and the highest, the merely annoying and the powerfully dangerous. When informed who they really are, he responds: "Monstrous enchantment! what odd shapes this Merlin transforms the greatest people into!" (11:481).[96]

The other side of the satire in *Don Quixote in England* is the reaction of fools and knaves to Quixote himself. When a coachload of people debouch in the innyard, in spite of his efforts to prevent them, the problem offered them is Don Quixote, who thinks their coach is a giant. Mr. Brief the counselor advises the landlady to see a justice of the peace to get the knight thrown out, and Dr. Drench the physician recommends physic. In fact, the whole play works on this general principle: what will be X's, Y's, and Z's reactions to Don Quixote? Squire Badger sees him as a rival for the hand of Dorothea; Sir Thomas Loveland sees him as "a philosophical pimp"; the politicians try to use him as an opposition candidate for parliament so that the other candidate will have to offer bribes; in short, each character interprets Don Quixote's motives in his own image. Presented with an apparently inexplicable action, each looks for a motive and in the process reveals himself. This will be Fielding's model for plot and action in *Joseph Andrews*, where, as we might imagine, it works better than on an actual stage.

Finally, *Don Quixote* showed, by placing a knight errant in a contemporary setting, one way to accommodate the high art of epic and romance to the low, comic, indeed farcical, in particular local, which would form the basis for Fielding's "comic epic in prose."[97] The intention, shared by ambitious artists (primarily Hogarth, but also John Vanderbank and Francis Hayman), was to find a way to raise the level of the local and actual, to heroicize it while critiquing the heroic. Quite simply, as he acknowledged a decade later, *Don Quixote* was the single most important fiction for him, the one from which his version of the English novel emerged.[98]

2

Playwright, 1730–1737

CHRONOLOGY

1729 April. Samuel Johnson's *Hurlothrumbo* draws crowds at the Little Theatre in the Haymarket.

1730 Jan. 26. *The Temple Beau* opens at Goodman's Fields. HF seems to have been living at this time with his father and his latest wife Eleanor in Dover St.[1]

Mar. 30. Begins his association with the Little Theatre in the Haymarket, where, just 23, he launches his first great success, *The Author's Farce; and the Pleasures of the Town. Written by Scriblerus Secundus*, 42 performances (revived, 17 performances Oct.–June 1731). 31st, publ. by John Roberts; in July a second (Watts), and before year's end a pirated Dublin edn.[2] "[T]he usual price paid to authors for plays which met with uncommon success" came to between £100 and 100 guineas.[3]

Apr. 24. He adds *Tom Thumb. A Tragedy* as afterpiece to *The Author's Farce*; 41 performances before July 24;[4] April 25, publ. by Roberts.[5]

May 1. Adds to *Tom Thumb* a new prologue and epilogue; 6th, with further additions.

June 6. Publishes 2nd edn., *Tom Thumb. A Tragedy. Written by Scriblerus Secundus*.[6]

June 23. *Rape upon Rape; or, The Justice Caught in his Own Trap. A Comedy*; publ. same day (Watts); eight performances, two benefits.[7]

Sept. Circulates a 5-act comedy, *The Modern Husband*, in MS., in particular to Lady Mary Wortley Montagu.[8]

Comes to an understanding with John Rich at Lincoln's Inn Fields Theater to launch a production of *Rape upon Rape*, calling it *The Coffee-House Politician; or, The Justice Caught in his Own Trap. A Comedy*.

Nov. 30. *Rape upon Rape* revived at the Little Haymarket (without HF's consent) as *The Coffee-House Politician* with *Tom Thumb*; an extra scene, "The Battle of the Poets; or, The Contention for the Laurel," apropos the selection of a poet laureate, is not by HF; only one performance.[9]

Dec. 4. *The Coffee-House Politician* is produced with HF's approval at Lincoln's Inn Fields (a benefit), but runs only four nights; publ., 4th by Watts (*Rape upon Rape* with a new title page, "Written by Mr. Fielding").[10]

1731 Mar. 24. Back at the Little Haymarket, the expanded *Tragedy of Tragedies; or The Life and Death of Tom Thumb the Great. With the Annotations of H. Scriblerus Secundus* is performed throughout the season; as afterpiece, *The Letter-Writers; or, A New Way to Keep a Wife At Home. A Farce in Three Acts. By Scriblerus Secundus* survives only four performances; both publ. by Roberts, the 24th (*Tragedy of Tragedies* with frontispiece by Hogarth).[11]

Apr. 3. HF Contributes a commendatory epilogue to Theobald's *Orestes*, publ. 10th with Theobald's dedication to Walpole.[12]

22. *The Welsh Opera*, a ballad opera, replaces *The Letter Writers* as afterpiece to *Tragedy of Tragedies*; four performances, and then on May 19, renewed with "several Alterations and Additions," six performances, and from the 26th five more performances with the anon. *Fall of Mortimer*, an unabashed attack on Walpole (same actor plays Robin and Mortimer);[13] publ. June 26 as *The Welsh Opera; or, The Grey Mare the better Horse. Written by Scriblerus Secundus, Author of the Tragedy of Tragedies* by E. Rayner, presumably from an actor's copy, without HF's authorization.[14]

June 11. Renamed *The Grub-Street Opera*, enlarged to three acts (and from 31 to 65 songs), the play is scheduled for performance but at the last minute withdrawn by HF. The *Daily Journal*, Aug. 12, includes the information that the company "know no more than that the Author desired it might not be performed." Its suppression by HF himself and an attack by Orator Henley in his pro-ministerial *Hyp-Doctor* of June 15–22, 1731 suggest a bribe.[15]

Aug. 18, publ. without authorization as *The Genuine Grub-Street Opera. Written by Scriblerus Secundus* by Rayner(?).[16]

Oct. 6. The Little Haymarket announces (*Daily Post*) it will open its new season on the 16th with *The Author's Farce*; but instead there is prize-fighting, tumbling, and rope dancing.

1732 HF (with other members of the Little Haymarket troup) moves up to Drury Lane, the government's own theater (1732–35). This could be related to his withdrawal of *The Grub-Street Opera*.

Jan. 1. He furnishes *The Lottery. A Farce*, a ballad opera (a collaboration with the musician "Mr. Seedo"), as afterpiece to Addison's

Cato and later Shakespeare's *Henry VIII;* 15 performances; revived Feb. 1, 15 more performances; publ. Jan. 7 (Watts).[17]

Feb. 1. *The Lottery,* revised with a new scene of the drawing of the lottery at the Guildhall; many more performances.

Feb. 14. At last, Drury Lane presents *The Modern Husband. A Comedy. Written by Henry Fielding, Esq.* with a stellar cast (Cibber playing Lord Richly, Robert Wilks as Bellamont, Theophilus Cibber as Captain Bellamant, and his wife Susannah as Lady Charlotte Gaywit); 13 consecutive performances plus an additional night (Mar. 18); at least four benefits. 21st, publ. by Watts, dedicated to Walpole.[18]

Mar.–Aug., HF is attacked in the opposition journal *The Grub-Street Journal,* presumably for his association with the ministry.[19]

May 3. A spectacular new production of *The Tragedy of Tragedies,* one night.[20]

Hogarth's *Harlot's Progress* is published.

June 1. *The Old Debauchees. A Comedy. By the Author of the Modern Husband,* six performances, one benefit; and (afterpiece) *The Covent-Garden Tragedy* ("a Farce"), a single performance; publ. June 13 and 24 (Watts).[21]

June 23. *The Mock Doctor; or, The Dumb Lady Cur'd. A Comedy. Done from Molière* (afterpiece to the *Old Debauchees*), 12 performances during the summer, seven in Sept., and six in the autumn; publ. July 11 (Watts).[22] More attacks by the *Grub-Street Journal;* the publication of *Covent-Garden Tragedy* on the 24th includes "A CRITICISM on the *Covent-Garden Tragedy,* originally intended for the *Grub-Street Journal.*" July 31, HF ("Philalethes") publishes a defense in the *Daily Post.*[23]

Sept. 8. The new season opens with *The Mock Doctor* as afterpiece to Buckingham's *The Rehearsal.*[24]

Nov. 16. Revised version of *Mock Doctor,* HF's benefit.[25] Again, on the 30th (at the king's command), and a second edn. publ. "With additional Songs and Alterations."[26]

1733 Jan. 3. More Molière: *The Miser* in rehearsal; opening postponed.[27]

Feb. 17. *The Miser. A Comedy. Taken from Plautus and Molière. By Henry Fielding, Esq.*; approx. 23 performances, four benefits;[28] publ. Mar. 13 (Watts).[29]

HF writes an "Epistle to Mr. Lyttleton[sic] occasioned by two Lines in Mr. Pope's Paraphrase on the first Satire of the 2d Book of Horace" defending Lady Mary Wortley Montagu following Pope's attack ("poxed by her love, libelled by her hate"). The poem is anti-Pope *and* anti-opposition and remains unpublished.[30]

Apr. 6. *Deborah; or, A Wife for You All,* a ballad opera, afterpiece to *The Miser,* one performance. A burlesque of Handel's *Deborah* (Mar. 17) with political overtones that can be interpreted as anti-court, it is suppressed and never published.[31]

Also this season: revivals of *The Lottery* and *The Tragedy of Tragedies*; at the Little Haymarket, a musical version called *The Opera of Operas* and a revival of *The Old Debauchees.*

May. Colley Cibber having sold his shares in Drury Lane, his son Theophilus, feeling betrayed, decamps with most of the actors; HF tries to carry on with the new patentee, John Highmore, and the rump company. 29th, *Daily Post*: "there will be no more Plays acted this Season."

June 7. Lady Gould dies in Salisbury; HF has her body carried from Salisbury to East Stour to rest beside his mother's.[32]

Sept.–Oct., Cibber institutes an ejectment suit against Highmore in Chancery.[33]

Oct. 27. *The Miser* is performed before king, queen, duke of Cumberland, "all the Princesses," and "a great Concourse of Nobility."[34]

Dec. 8. *The Universal Gallant* is in production (but put off until Feb. 1735) and a new production of *The Author's Farce* announced.[35]

1734 Jan. 15. *The Intriguing Chambermaid. A Comedy in Two Acts. Taken from the French of Regnard. By Henry Fielding, Esq.*, as afterpiece to the revised *Author's Farce. In which will be introduc'd an Operatical Puppet Show, call'd The Pleasures of the Town. With great Additions, and a new Prologue and Epilogue*; only six performances, one benefit; publ. by Watts.[36] Includes a poem "Sent to the Author by an unknown Hand," "To Mr. *Fielding*, occasioned by the Revival of the *Author's Farce*," full of praise. Referring to *The Modern Husband*, the author hopes that Walpole will respond to the dedication and extend patronage – and, "studious still of *Britain*'s Fame, / Protect thy Labours, and prescribe the Theme, / On which, in Ease and Affluence, thou may'st raise / More noble Trophies to thy Country's Praise."

HF's favorite actress Kitty Raftor (Clive) plays Charlotte, the name of the young lady he is courting.

By the end of the month Highmore and the Drury Lane actors have sold out to Charles Fleetwood.[37]

Feb.–Mar. HF plans to present *Don Quixote in England* but encounters obstacles: the popularity of the Dutch giant "Cajanus" in *Cupid and Psyche* between Feb. 5 and 12, commitments to actors for their benefits, and, Mar. 9, the triumphal return of Theophilus Cibber to manage Drury Lane.[38]

Apr. 5. Back at the Little Haymarket, HF opens the season with *Don Quixote in England. A Comedy. By Henry Fielding, Esq.* (written, 1728–9, with as afterpiece, *The Covent-Garden Tragedy*; 10 performances, one benefit. 17th, publ. by Watts, with a dedication to the earl of Chesterfield (who has recently gone into opposition).[39]

The dedication to the opposition leader, Chesterfield; the addition of the election satire to the original *Don Quixote in England*; and its performances at the dissident Little Haymarket rather than the establishment Drury Lane: all suggest a political orientation. About this time HF begins to contribute to the opposition journal, *The Craftsman.*[40]

Summer and autumn, in East Stour and Bath.[41]

Nov. 28. In Bath, marries Charlotte Cradock of Salisbury, who brings a £1,500 dowry; they return to Salisbury.[42] Edmund Fielding is promoted to major general.[43]

Dec. Now in London, with Charlotte's ill mother, HF and Charlotte live in York Buildings (Buckingham St.).

1735 Jan. 6. Back with Fleetwood at Drury Lane, HF produces *An Old Man taught Wisdom: or, The Virgin Unmask'd. A Farce*, a ballad opera starring Kitty Clive as Lucy (afterpiece to Otway's *Venice Preserved*); after a shaky first night, HF successfully revises and enjoys 11 more performances; publ. soon after (without the revisions) by Watts.[44] (*Miss Lucy in Town. A Sequel to The Virgin Unmasqued. A Farce; with Songs* is probably drafted soon after, but not produced until May 6 1742 at Drury Lane.)[45]

Feb. 10. *The Universal Gallant; or, the Different Husbands. A Comedy. By Henry Fielding, Esq.* fails with the first-night audience, ekes out two more performances, one benefit. 19th, publ. by Watts (*LDP*); dedication to the third duke of Marlborough, another opposition politician.

20. Mrs. Cradock buried, St. Martin-in-the-Fields, in an extravagant funeral.[46] HF, missing the funeral, is back at the farm in East Stour, in fact in nearby Shaftesbury assaulting Thomas Bennet (who claims his "life was greatly despaired of"), over a debt.[47]

25. Charlotte inherits her mother's estate; as executrix, proves her mother's will and probably joins him in East Stour. The rest of the year is spent at the East Stour farm, to which (Murphy recalled) he "retired . . . with a resolution to bid adieu to all the follies and intemperances to which he had addicted himself in the career of a town-life."[48]

This may be the time when he becomes intimate with William Young (1702–57), the prototype of Parson Adams, master of the nearby Gillingham Grammar School: Curate at East and West Stour, he officiated at Lady Gould's burial in June 1733.

Mar. George Lyttelton publishes *Letters from a Persian in England, to his friend at Ispahan*, largely opposition propaganda; Letters IX, XXIV, LV, and LXXIX on bribery and corruption will be rendered by HF in *Pasquin*, as Battestin puts it, "in dramatic form" (198). HF's friends at Eton (Lyttelton, Pitt) enter Parliament and join the opposition. During the summer they meet with Lord Cobham, the Grenvilles, Pope, and others at Stowe.

1736　Jan. 1. At Dorchester, HF sues Bennet, who "openly, publickly, falsely & malitiously spoke, asserted, pronounced and with a loud voice published . . . those false, feigned, scandalous and reproachefull English words following (that is to say) 'Mr. Fielding is not worth a farthing. He will go quickly off and cheat his Creditors.' " HF argues that this slander destroyed his credit and caused his creditors to sue him and seize his goods.[49]

Returns to London and offers a play (*The Good Natured Man?*) to Rich for his new Covent-Garden Theatre; it is declined.[50] He now sets up his own company, "the great Mogul's Company of English Comedians, Newly Imported," at the Little Theatre in the Haymarket, both writing plays and managing the theater. He is assisted in the management by his friend James Ralph.

N.B. His association with Drury Lane coincided with his most obvious gestures toward Walpole; in 1735 he is badly in need of more money, his friends form an opposition party, and he returns to the Little Haymarket and writes "farces" that satirize the ministry.

Feb. 24. In the *London Daily Post*, he announces "PASQUIN, / A Dramatic SATYR on the Times. / Being a Rehearsal of two Plays, viz. a Comedy, called The ELECTION; and a Tragedy, called The Life and Death of COMMON SENSE. . . . / N.B. Mr. Pasquin intending to lay about him with great Impartiality, hopes the Town will all attend, and very civilly give their Neighbours what they find belongs to 'em. / N.B. The Cloaths are old, but the Jokes intirely new."

Mar. 5. *Pasquin* produced, a great success with 43 consecutive performances, more than 60 for the season, and 12 benefits. Publ., April 8 by Watts as *Pasquin. A Dramatick Satire on the Times: Being the Rehearsal of Two Plays, viz. A Comedy call'd, The Election; and a Tragedy call'd, The Life and Death of Common-Sense. By Henry Fielding, Esq.*[51] By the 24th Edmund Fielding is serving as acting military governor of the Island of Jersey.[52]

Apr. 27. Daughter Charlotte born. Living in Charing Cross, perhaps to be within the Verge of the Court, safe from bailiffs.[53]

Apr. 29. *Tumble-Down Dick; or, Phaeton in the Suds. A Dramatick Entertainment of Walking, in Serious and Foolish Characters: Interlarded with Burlesque, Grotesque, Comick Interludes, call'd Harlequin A Pick-Pocket, Being ('tis hop'd) the last Entertainment that will ever be Exhibited on any Stage. Invented by the Ingenious Monsieur Sans Esprit. The Music compos'd by the Harmonious Signior Warblerini. And the Scenes painted by the prodigious Mynheer van Bottom-Flat* (afterpiece to *Pasquin*); 22 performances, after May 27 afterpiece to *Fatal Curiosity*; no benefits; publ. same day by Watts, dedicated to "Mr. JOHN LUN," i.e., John Rich.[54] A satire on Rich's harlequinades, *Tumble-Down Dick* directly burlesques a "New Pantomime Entertainment," *The Fall of Phaeton: or, Harlequin a Captive,* playing at Drury Lane (Feb. 28).

May 27. First season ends with HF's production of Lillo's tragedy, *Fatal Curiosity,* to which he contributes a prologue.[55]

June–Dec. Presumably in the country. Dec., despite the success of the season, he is borrowing money again, and involved again in Shaftesbury with Bennet.[56]

1737 Feb. 4. Announces plans for building a new theater, accommodating some 900 people, presumably located in the West End to compete with the patent theaters.[57]

19. At Drury Lane, produces *Eurydice, or The Devil Henpeck'd* (afterpiece to *Cato*), one performance, an author's benefit, disrupted by a riot.[58] The reception is so disastrous that Watts does not publish the text; later published by HF, *Eurydice, a Farce; As it was d-mned at the Theatre-Royal in Drury-Lane,* in his *Miscellanies,* vol. 2 (1743).[59]

24. Announces that a new play, *A Rehearsal of Kings; or, of Macplunderkan, King of Roguomania, and the ignoble Fall of Baron Tromperland, King of Clouts* (author unknown), will be performed at the Little Haymarket, beginning Mar. 9. He has also at "extraordinary Expence" furnished new costumes for the company and raised the price of tickets; offers "his Caveat against all (by what Names soever distinguish'd) who may *hire* and *be hired* to do the Drudgery of *Hissing, Catcalling, Ec.*" (as the week before at Drury Lane).[60]

Mar. 8. Concludes an agreement with John Potter to rent the Little Haymarket for the season.[61]

9. The first performance of *A Rehearsal of Kings,* presumably an attack on king and ministers, is prevented by a riot – "several hundred Persons were turn'd away."[62] It is performed from the 11th to 14th and finally on the 17th.

19. Successful revival of *Pasquin.*

21. *The Historical Register for the Year 1736,* another great success (afterpiece to a revival of Lillo's *Fatal Curiosity*); 34 performances, 16 benefits.[63]

Apr. 13. *Eurydice Hiss'd, or, A Word to the Wise* (afterpiece to *Historical Register,* now mainpiece); 21 performances; May 12, publ. by Roberts together as *The Historical Register for the Year 1736. To which is added a very merry Tragedy, called, Eurydice Hiss'd, or, A Word to the Wise. Both written by the Author of Pasquin.*[64] HF's dedication shows that he has abandoned plans to build a theater and is circulating a public "Subscription for carrying on that Theatre, for beautifying and enlarging it, and procuring a better Company of actors."

May 7. Print, *The Festival of the Golden Rump*, published; Walpole reads part of a farce of this name (anonymous) before Commons to demonstrate the scurrility of the stage.

May 20. Act before Commons to close all but the two patent theaters, thereby eliminating the Little Haymarket; 21st, HF publishes a letter from "Pasquin" in *Common Sense* protesting the bill. 23. Final production of *Historical Register* and *Eurydice Hiss'd*. Other clearly subversive plays are scheduled (including an "improv'd" version of Gay's *Polly*, which Walpole had suppressed in 1729), but John Potter, being "against all scandall & defamation," dismantles the sets, removed the decorations, and fills the house with lumber, bricks, and cartloads of lime.[65]

May 28 and July 2. Two *Craftsman* essays, possibly by HF, attacking the Licensing Act; the second educes scurrilous references to minister and monarch in the "old plays" of Shakespeare, Jonson, and Dryden. 13th, Amhurst, the editor, is arrested, confined for ten days; Henry Haines, the printer, spends two years in prison.[66]

June 21. Licensing Act passed, putting an end to HF's theatrical career.[67]

AUTHOR OF FARCE AND COMEDY

The Author's Farce

While Fielding was away in Leiden the success of *The Provok'd Husband* and *The Beggar's Opera* had created a market for new plays, loosening the stranglehold of the repertory.[68] Ballad operas were now being produced at Drury Lane, and Rich's Lincoln's Inn Fields Theatre, where the original *Beggar's Opera* played, was continuing to produce its popular harlequinades. Moreover, a third theater, the Little Theatre in the Haymarket, had opened in competition with the two licensed theaters. With no regular management, it served as a clearing house for (in Battestin's words) "an unconventional variety of new irregular and experimental pieces, often with risky political implications."[69] With the encouragement of new plays came the curiosity for novelty and "irregularity," especially (like *The Beggar's Opera*) with a burlesque edge. In the shadow of *The Dunciad* these farces appeared to be of Dulness's brood and a fulfillment of her prophecy that Bartholomew Fair was moving to the West End.

A case in point was the notoriously successful *Hurlothrumbo*, written and performed by a dancing master from Cheshire, Samuel Johnson, produced at the Little Haymarket in April 1729, which ran for over 30 nights and attracted fashionable audiences. Its popularity was due (according to one contemporary) to "the imperturbable conceit of the author," who, playing the part of Lord Flame, combined dancing master and madman, "sometimes in one key, sometimes in another, sometimes fiddling, sometimes dancing, and sometimes walking on high stilts."[70] Whatever Johnson's intention (which remains obscure), the effect was a burlesque of Dryden's heroic plays and their offshoots which, in Pope's terms, was pure *dulce* without *utile*. A Hurlothrumbo society was formed and the words "mere Hurlothrumbo" became proverbial for nonsense.[71]

Hurlothrumbo was the first of the stimuli that elicited Fielding's most original works. There was something gentlemanly about merely responding to a foolish play, as Buckingham had to Dryden's *Conquest of Granada* or Vanbrugh to Cibber's *Love's Last Shift*. Buckingham's *Rehearsal* (1671) was parody, Vanbrugh's *Relapse* (1696) was parody plus an alternative – just the procedure Fielding would use when he responded to *Pamela* with *Shamela* and then with *Joseph Andrews*.

Confronted with the phenomenon of *Hurlothrumbo*, however, his response was ambivalent. The classical scholar, the admirer of Swift's *Battle of the Books*, followed the line of *The Dunciad*, castigating such a corruption of classical ideals; but the struggling professional playwright was drawn to exploit the farce's popularity, and a strain of Fielding's genius happened to lie in the path of nonsense.

So, having failed to place his conventional five-act comedies, Fielding wrote *The Author's Farce*, within which appears a puppet play with elements of ballad opera, "The Pleasures of the Town"; this was produced, like *Hurlothrumbo* at the Little Haymarket, on March 30, 1730. But Fielding covers himself by embedding the nonsense in a fiction that explains and justifies it as, on one hand, expediency and, on the other, satire (another dramatization of Juvenal's Third Satire, "Rome," rendered "London").

The play is no longer, like *The Temple Beau*, about students but about professional writers, primarily, like himself, a playwright, essentially the author of the rejected comedies he wrote in Leiden. In terms of those plays, the important departure was *Don Quixote in England*, which shows a madman who sees the world as what we would call nonsense; in *The Author's Farce* the writer Luckless is told by his friend Witmore, "who but a madman would write in such an age?"

> If you must write, write nonsense, write operas, write entertainments, write *Hurlothrumbos*, set up an *Oratory* and preach nonsense, and you may meet with encouragement enough. If you would receive applause, deserve to receive sentence at the Old Bailey; and if you would ride in your coach, deserve to ride in a cart. (I.vi; 9:16)

The first sentence projects the puppet play which Luckless writes and which, in the Quixotic sense, turns out after all to be true; theatrical illusion proves to be truer than reality. The second sentence employs a particular kind of wit, which notes the resemblance between ladies in coaches and in carts, fine ladies on the way to parties and whores being whipped. This wit, in the manner of *The Beggar's Opera* and *The Dunciad*, extends the subject of bad writing to bad morals, the microcosm of Grub Street to the macrocosm of London.

Pope's *Dunciad*, like *Don Quixote*, authorized the subject of writing. Pope's self-defense (for that was largely the purpose of his *Dunciad*) turned Fielding's attention from scholarly and legal studies to the profession of writing and permitted him to write from his own experience, at this time still narrow, of books and the writing trade. (It also offered him the mode of the great poet's apologia which becomes a prominent aspect of his own writing.) In the first half of the play Luckless is the poverty-stricken poet whose search for survival brings him into conflict with the forces of commercial control over writing in London – not only, most pointedly, Marplay the theater manager (Cibber) but also Bookweight the bookseller (Edmund Curll) and the hacks whom they control and exploit. But the crucial and defining role is that of the playwright himself, with which Fielding opens the major phase of his dramatic career. The Christian name of Luckless, the impecunious hack who in his fantasy becomes King Henry I of Bantom, is Fielding's (he gives his heroine Harriot another form of it). Luckless is a gentleman, who, outraged by his treatment at the hands of the bourgeois Bookweight, has his servant kick the bookseller downstairs – an act not unlike some attributed to Fielding in these years.

Fielding divides *The Author's Farce*, the first half dramatizing the *Dunciad's* assumptions about commodification in the exempla of Luckless's struggles; the second half the *Dunciad's* fable of Dulness, presented as not epic but, in theatrical terms, tragedy. Paraphrasing the action of *The Dunciad*, Luckless reports: "My Lord Mayor has shortened the time of Bartholomew Fair in Smithfield, and so they are resolved to keep it all the year round at the other end of the town." In Fielding's dramatic "Dunciad" actors imitate puppets of allegorical figures that allude to, besides Cibber and Curll, the castrato opera star Senesino, the *Dunciad's* hero Lewis Theobald, John "Orator" Henley, the theatrical producer John Rich, and the "novelist" Eliza Haywood.

Witmore's proposal serves as introduction to the second half, Luckless's farce, as Pope's "Variorum," with its prefatory essays, served as an explanation of his *Dunciad*. Luckless's commentary on the action materializes the footnotes of the *Dunciad Variorum*. In the printed text, in order to underline his identification with Pope and his circle, and to distance himself from the farce, Fielding ascribes the play to "Scriblerus Secundus."

The Beggar's Opera had burlesqued the romance plot of Dryden's heroic plays and their imitators: Macheath, caught between his two rival "wives," recalls Antony between Cleopatra and Antony's wife Octavia in Dryden's

All for Love. But for whatever reason, as he had done in *Love in Several Masques*, Fielding shows the women of two generations both in love with the hero. His triangle of Luckless, Harriot, and her mother Mrs. Moneywood goes all the way back to Dryden's *Indian Queen* with Montezuma, the young Inca princess Orazia, and the motherly Mexican Queen Zempoala; the friendship of Luckless and Witmore, who selflessly pays his friend's bills, echoes Dryden's Montezuma and Acacis (son of Zempoala). Then in the farce the relationship of Luckless, Harriot, and Moneywood is transmuted into the allegory of Signor Opera, Mrs. Novel, and her mother Queen Nonsense.

The first is a contemporary, bourgeois setting that is, however, revealed to be after all romantic – in the pleasing fiction of "The Pleasures of the Town" and then, in reality, revealed as the truth beneath the "borrowed dress" of heroic tragedy. Luckless, the poet who has been fighting an uphill battle for recognition in a London of Bookweights and Marplays, turns out to be the heir to the throne of Bantom, with prospects of living happily ever after.

In one sense the farce contaminates the "real" world of the first half, imposing on it a happy ending. As in the heroic plays in which such lucky discoveries are made, the burlesque ending only says to the audience: You *like* this sort of thing, so here it is; it echoes the ending of *The Beggar's Opera*, where the Beggar, who is supposed to have written the play, gives up his poetically just ending (Macheath's hanging) for a happy one that will satisfy the people both inside and outside the play (actors and audience, who do not want to see themselves hanged), and by doing so further equate the two groups.[72]

As satire, the happy ending reifies the nonsensical world of the farce in contemporary London; farce has extended from the puppet play Luckless writes to the relatively realistic world of the frame action, which is now made over into a romance of lost princes and hidden identities. And to prove the point, as soon as Luckless succeeds to the throne of Bantom, he reverts to the very standards he has resisted and lampooned in the first half of the play. He takes Don Tragedio, Signor Opera, Marplay, and the rest along with him to entertain his subjects, the Bantomites. Under the disguise of a happy ending, with the comic feast to which even the bad characters are invited, Fielding the satirist shows that the forces of nonsense are indestructible. For the first but not the last time, he parodies the concept of the comedic happy ending, or the tragic convention of Poetic Justice (or the religious doctrine of equal Providence in the afterlife), in order to suggest that one may have to accept such a myth in order to survive. Gay showed Fielding, among other things, how the happy ending is merely a device of human contriving.

Another feature of Fielding's satire is to have it both ways, which takes the form of a mock recantation. At the end of *Love in Several Masques*

Wisemore took back all he had said: "And now ladies, I think myself bound to a solemn recantation of every slander I have thrown upon your sex: for I am convinced that our complaints against you flow generally (if not always) more from our want of merit than your want of justice" (8:99). And to his early translation of Juvenal's Sixth Satire, on women, Fielding added a note gallantly explaining that "to the honour of the English ladies, the Latin is by no means applicable to them."[73] Fielding lacks the uncompromising satiric conclusion of Swift, as if to say: I don't really mean it, *or do I?*

Seen from this perspective, at the end it is the hack writer's fantasy that is realized. If first we are shown the real corrupt world of London business, and second its allegorical representation in a farce, there is a third element: The Kingdom of Bantom, which returns to London the puppet world of "The Pleasures of the Town," is a dramatic transmogrification of the Luckless plot, as it is a happy rewriting of Fielding's own experience in literary London. Luckless-Fielding turns out to be more Sancho than Quixote, revealing his willingness to go along with his "master's" delusion by decking out a Jezebel as Dulcinea and theatricalizing her. In short, *The Author's Farce* is about someone who is willing to be pragmatic ("prudent" is Fielding's word, obsessively repeated in his works) but specifically in order to survive. Luckless even says first, only half-jokingly, that he is prepared to marry Mrs. Moneywood; but primarily he writes a *Hurlothrumbo* and goes back to Bookweight, as if he had not had him thrown downstairs, in order to peddle the text. This will be one paradigm of Fielding's life, adapting provisional structures or discourses, even while not under ordinary circumstances believing in them. But in the case of farce, or rather at the interface of farce and real life, he also finds himself a brilliant adept.

Farce/nonsense and wit

Dryden had declared that "popular applause" is surest with the employment of "the Zany of a Mountebank" who draws in the audience, "without wit on the Poets part, or any occasion of laughter from the Actor, besides the ridiculousness of his habit and his Grimaces," and this Dryden designated "Farce; which consists primarily of Grimaces." "Comedy," by contrast, "consists, though [as Aristotle had noted] of low persons, yet of natural actions, and characters . . . to be found and met with in the world. Farce, on the other side, consists of forc'd humours and unnatural events." Farce "performs by hazard," comedy "by skill." "Farces more commonly take the people than Comedies. For to write unnatural things, is the most probable way of pleasing them, who understand not Nature."[74] Dryden demonized farce, and in the *Spectator* Addison perpetuated the distinction favoring comedy over burlesque, character over caricature.[75]

Like Dryden Fielding associates wit with high discourse and five-act comedies of the sort written by Congreve (and, indeed, cites Congreve's essay on comedy, which supplemented Dryden's);[76] he contrasts comedy disparagingly with farce and nonsense in the opening lines of his prologue to *The Temple Beau*:

> Humour and wit, in each politer age,
> Triumphant, reared the trophies of the stage.
> But only farce, and show, will now go down,
> And HARLEQUIN's the darling of the town.

Wit survives, he says, at the new theater in Goodman's Fields, where his play (rejected by Drury Lane) is playing: "this refuge," "this infant stage" aims "to wake a dreaming age" (deluded by "farce") with the "comic muse" that will "scoff at vice, and laugh its crimes away" (103). In *The Author's Farce* the prologue ridicules the tragedies and heroic plays that reveal under the fustian mere farce. But why not, Fielding asks, replace the gravity of the stoic's discourse with the laughter of the "merry jester" who in "days of yore" "reformed my lord"?

> The aim of Farce is but to make you laugh.
> Beneath the tragic or the comic name,
> Farce and puppet-shows ne'er miss of fame.
> Since then, in borrowed dress, they've pleased the town,
> Condemn them not, appearing in their own.

– that is, here is honest, true farce; by which he means that he will replace tragedies that are bathetically farcical with farces that are at least true farces. In *The Author's Farce* he begins to explore the possibilities of the genre.

The aspect of *Hurlothrumbo*'s nonsense that attracted him was the crazy similitude, or wit carried too far, until it becomes nonsense:

Sementory. They gave upon a Woman, as they do upon a Bill of Fare after Dinner.
Seringo. The Simile is good.
Sementory. Oh *Seringo*! where shall I find a vertuous Man, like such a one that I have seen, chaste, and full of Rapture? Rapture is the Egg of Love, hatched by a radiant Eye, that brings to Life a *Cupid* in his breast.[77]

Nonsense poetry, from Sir John Hoskyns to Dryden and Pope (and on to Lewis Carroll and Edward Lear) is to a large extent an extreme subset of parody and burlesque. Parody and burlesque, at which Fielding happened to have a particular knack, were an integral part of the schoolboys' retaliation against the drilling of the classics into their unwilling heads.[78]

While Fielding associates wit with high discourse, in his farces (and increasingly also in his comedies) he narrows the range of wit to an equivalence of farce. Not without precedents: While in the wit of Etherege, Wycherley, and Congreve the subject (tenor) of the similitudes varied but tended to be love, woman, sex, or marriage, and sometimes gaming (all objects or enterprises that occupy the rake and define the parameters of his social identity), in more recent comedies such as Farquhar's *Beaux's Stratagem* (1707) the similitudes focused on one area: criminals are like respectable people and vice versa; the low are like the high (and specifically in respect to x, y, and z).[79] Then in *The Beggar's Opera*, the low *imitate* the high (Polly "loves to imitate the fine ladies"; 1.4.535), or, an aspect Fielding especially develops, the low or criminal may be *mistaken for* the high or respectable. The narrowing tendency corresponds to the topos of the world-turned-upside-down ("the world's turned topsey-turvey," as Young Pedant notes [7:108]), in which criminals have become respectable and "honest," and vice has become, or is regarded as, virtue: virtue now suffers scandal, rags, and poverty, and vice enjoys wealth and reputation, and in "The Pleasures of the Town" the Goddess Nonsense is told by Charon that she is "to be declared Goddess of Wit."[80] One of the features of nonsense is, of course, the inversion of ordinary values.

In the action of a farce events are presented solely for amusement and literally have no meaning; actions do not necessarily follow from character, and reality is distorted to the point of sheer nonsense. This is the form Fielding parodies and ridicules as a symbol of a pervasive moral laxity, of life itself become meaningless. He shows, however, that farce can be sheer nonsense or its meaning can proceed through the higher logic of analogy or allegory. He utilizes both possibilities; his play within a play is at the same time farce and parody of bad farce, so that he can call upon both ends of the farcical spectrum for the response of his audience – or, we might say, both low and high segments of his audience. In *Hurlothrumbo* the action is unlifelike, illogical, and meaningless. But in Fielding's imitation, which on one level can be taken as similarly nonsensical, the details are actually meaningful, and a higher (allegorical) reality emerges.

Farce was for Fielding the radical extreme of theatricality. His characters are always saying, "Why, what a farce is human life," or referring to "the grand pantomime played on the stage of life."[81] Farce, however low a form in itself, becomes Fielding's metaphor for contemporary life; that is, it is *true* to say that life is a farce.

But for Fielding nonsense cannot be left to speak for itself: it requires some sort of a commentator to draw attention to this meaning. Medley in *The Historical Register* (1737) says, "Sir, this scene is writ in allegory, and though I have endeavoured to make it as plain as possible, yet all allegory will require a strict attention to be understood, sir" (11:251). Fielding's classical training told him allegory must be reclaimed by a superimposed significance in the form of a moral, gloss, or commentary in which the reader takes an equal, if a different, pleasure. Like (or with) Pope, he is drawn to the farce; as a moralist he must attack it, but his pleasure lies in imitating and celebrating it. Pope uses it as the material out of which he makes his own poetry. Flowers in the snow, fish swimming in the branches of trees sum up the particular nonsensical beauty Pope produces from what he calls "dulness."[82] Pope's lines, "How Tragedy and Comedy embrace; / How Farce and Epic get a jumbled race" (*Dunciad* I.69–70), indicate a source of imaginary energy, a new way of writing poetry by poeticizing (while judging) the low, ugly, and transgressive.

Fielding incorporates the farce into a larger structure of evaluation and assessment. First wit is engaged in finding similitudes between the wildly dissimilar, and then judgment (commentary) supplies the distinctions that save it from slipping into nonsense. In *The Author's Farce*, following upon *The Dunciad*, wit is directed *at* the farce and yet takes its imaginative fire from its object of attack. As Gay showed in *The Beggar's Opera*, when seen and heard on the stage, the objects of satire become comic humor characters.

Tom Thumb: *farce/greatness*

As an afterpiece to supplement *The Author's Farce* Fielding wrote the most brilliant of his burlesques, *Tom Thumb*, a mixture of mock blank verse and heroic couplets. The point of origin was probably Swift's "Voyage to Lilliput" with its contrast of great and small: It must have been the rumor that Gulliver was having an affair with Flimnap's minuscule wife that stimulated Fielding's imagination.

Fielding, however, replaces Swift's satire of fantastic voyages with English folklore, probably carried with him from Glastonbury in the stories of King Arthur.[83] The English chapbook story of Tom Thumb takes place in King Arthur's court and Tom Thumb is a knight.[84] As a child he falls into a Christmas pudding his mother is making "and could not be / For some time after found, / For in the blood and batter he / Was lost and almost drowned." His mother, while milking a cow, ties Tom to a thistle to keep him safe, but the cow eats the thistle and with it Tom. His mother recovers Tom when the cow excretes him. He is also eaten by a fish, in whose belly he is conveyed to King Arthur. Again he is recovered and charms both king and queen; he becomes a knight and "none compar'd to brave Tom Thumb / In arts of Cavalry."[85] He emerges the martial Tom – so much so that he becomes ill, dies, and is buried with splendor and, most significantly perhaps, is resurrected. This is the first part; the second and third parts simply add more japes, suggesting Tom's decline – vaguely recalled perhaps in *Gulliver's Travels* and in something of the undercurrent of decadence Fielding suggests in his version.

The two characters of popular culture, celebrated in ballads and chap-books, to whom Fielding refers throughout his writings are the tiny Tom Thumb and the hulking Tom Hickathrift. He seems to associate himself with the other Tom, Hickathrift, because of his size – with Hickathrift's youth, which was difficult until he discovered and demonstrated his great strength. All of these Toms tended to be mischievous and get themselves into trouble (ending in Tom Jones), but Tom Thumb carries with him the associations of "Greatness"; spouting Marlovian bombast, played by a diminutive actress, he fascinates Fielding as he did Fielding's audience.

The preface to the expanded *Tom Thumb, The Tragedy of Tragedies*, makes it plain that "farce" equals "greatness" in the particular form of reputation (Tom's reputed feats) contrasted with the empirical data of his physical size.[86] The classical source of the topos is the figure of Alexander the Great found in the lives of Plutarch and the satires of Lucian. From his absorption in the classics Fielding carried the subject of greatness into the epistles and orations of *The Champion* and the *Miscellanies*, but it also dominated his plays and early prose narratives. Already in *The Temple Beau* Lady Lucy said to Bellaria: "Your eyes should first conquer the world, and then weep, like Alexander's, for more worlds to conquer" – and Bellaria responded: "I rather think he should have wept for those he had conquered. He had no more title to sacrifice the lives of men to his ambition than a woman has their ease" (8:124).

In *Tom Thumb* the topos of greatness takes the form of public versus private performance, domestic and sexual. Tom, clearly "great" in war, is, by the very nature of his Flimnapian size, inadequate to the requirements of the Amazonian giantess or even the normal-sized princess. Tom, for all his famous feats after all is only a few inches high, is manifestly incapable of having a woman, and at the end is casually swallowed by a cow. The jealous Grizzle advises Huncamunca that Thumb is "One fitter for your pocket than your bed! / Advised by me the worthless baby shun, / Or you will ne'er be brought to bed of one" (2.5; 9:42). If there is Thumb's reputation, which leads the giantess Glumdalca to cry: "Oh! stay, Tom Thumb, and you alone shall fill / That bed where twenty giants used to lie" (2.7; 9: 46–7), there is also Thumb's obvious sexual inadequacy. There are his own worries on the subject ("Yet at the thought of marriage I grow pale" [2.2; 9:34]), which suggest that he has simply fooled people, that his reputation is false. However, all of this can be answered by the fact that he did defeat giants, as he later defeats Grizzle's rebellion. The subject of reputation will be of primary interest to Fielding as he approaches *Tom Jones*, but the gist of his satire at this point is to oppose the "great man's" potency in political and economic spheres (which gives him his false reputation) to his powerlessness in the more commonplace world of the barnyard animal who makes a meal of him.

This notion of impotent greatness carries with it something of the Satanic villain of Dryden's satire. A sense of farcical evil arises from Tom's hypothetically inseminating Huncamunca, which is played upon until it reaches the height of absurdity in the parson's benediction over their wedding: "Long may they live, and love, and propagate, / Till the whole land be peopled with Tom Thumbs." Then in a bathetic simile the parson develops *Dunciad* imagery:

> So when the Cheshire cheese a maggot breeds,
> Another and another still succeeds:
> By thousands and ten thousands they increase,
> Till one continued maggot fills the rotten cheese.
> (2.9; 9:51)

This is the typical apparently nonsensical similitude (love-propagation is like a cheese breeding maggots) that in fact carries a higher, satiric sense. Through a monstrous relationship with Tom Thumb, the full-grown Huncamunca has become a breeder of mites, and the nation has been taken over by the busy, energetic, mindless little breed that Pope celebrated in *The Dunciad*.[87]

Fielding expresses wonder (and this is part of his celebration, as it is Pope's of the dunces) that something so diminutive could accomplish so much, however dubious the result. (The only sign of wickedness is the peremptory slaying of the bailiff and his followers who try to arrest Noodle – which was added in the revision.) The subtext is what happens to love in the wake of greatness. Against the world turned upside down of the "Newgate Pastoral," Gay offered the glimmering hope of love, a human ideal (though somewhat shopworn) against which to judge the "great" assumptions of the Peachums and Lockits.[88] In *Tom Thumb* Fielding, as he begins to analyze the subject of greatness, associates love with goodness, embodying the ideal of human interdependency in the character's adequacy in domestic situations.

Walpole

With the motif of the "great man," the topos of greatness, Fielding implicitly connected Tom Thumb with Walpole, the "Great Man": "The great Tom Thumb, / The little hero, giant-killing boy, / Preserver of my kingdom," says the king (1.2; 9:23). There has been a reaction among scholars against the view that all Fielding's references to greatness and great men are attacks on Walpole. Bertrand Goldgar, carefully delimiting the sense in which they are "political" or "attacks on Walpole," has argued that they can only be identified with certainty by the ministry's response to them in the late 1730s.[89] That Fielding's earlier plays offended no one, however, proves only that he was generalizing, examining "greatness" and not overtly or unmistakably Walpole.

Fielding did not become an active propagandist for the opposition until around 1734 when his Etonian friends entered Parliament. But his references are always political, in the same sense that Dryden and Pope, when they wrote about art, also wrote about politics and religion. This was part of his literary (Scriblerian) inheritance, though it was also an aspect of ordinary educated discourse. If you spoke of literature you were speaking of politics, and if you spoke of politics you were speaking of religion.

Although abstract "greatness" would have been the sort of theme Fielding wrote on at Eton, my opinion is that he came at it through the concrete figure of Walpole and specifically through Gay's amusing and relatively safe generalization of it in *The Beggar's Opera*.[90] His works of the 1730s reflect the prominent public figures whose careers and life-styles seemed paradigmatic: those of Cibber in the theater, Walpole in politics, both of whose lives were examples of the bourgeois success story of the rise from humble beginnings, a story of Christian advancing through conversion to self-understanding or, seen from a different perspective, of a toadstool rising from a dunghill.

Whether personal friends or significant outsiders (looked upon in a sense as news-items, read of in the journals and thus shared with his theater audience), all of whom he specifically cites at various points, these are people rather than literary or rhetorical topoi, and for that reason they are less conventional and stereotyped. This is not to deny that he begins with a theme or topos of "greatness." But he compares the classical idea of "greatness" with the people he knows (or the public contemporaries he knows); for example, the Walpole figure he reads about, who *is* symbolized, made *more* than he is – and so also with Cibber and then Pamela, who try to symbolize themselves. They ask to be demystified, compared with an ideal of greatness, by means of the techniques of the satirist Lucian as well as the historian Plutarch. These are people rather than literary and rhetorical topoi, and for that reason less conventional and stereotyped.

For a man with Fielding's aristocratic ethos but financial insecurity, it may have been the "progressive narrative" of Walpole (Michael McKeon's phrase)[91] that irritated, attracted, and intrigued him most: the story of the rise of the parvenu, the country squire, who climbs in effect to the rule of England and to the sobriquet of Great Man. The general outline is apparent in a contemporary Walpole ballad:

Good people draw near
And a tale you shall hear
A story concerning one *Robin*
Who, from not worth a groat
A vast fortune has got
By politicks, Bubbles, and Jobbing.[92]

Walpole represented unexampled power and "greatness" of a sort that was based on bribery and vast expenditures of money. But Walpole (another Eton man) was also the model, the exemplum, of the greatness that worried Fielding, the penniless aristocrat in a London dominated by Walpolean values (for which read: commercial, consumer, stockjobbing success).

The figure of Walpole-Greatness lies at the center of English national literature in this age of transition between royal and private patronage and the open market. Drama and poetry of the seventeenth century had been imaginatively conditioned by, and centered on, the monarch.[93] The poet's subject, directly or indirectly, was the character and myth of the ruler or ruling family. The watershed, separating heroic (or pseudo-heroic) from satiric modes, was the fall of Charles I (the last mythologized monarch) and the accession of Charles II, a saturnalian travesty of his martyred father. Though defended bravely by Dryden and others, Charles served as the focus for a new image, which was deflected into the safer image of the rakish anti-heroes of Restoration drama (Dryden's in heroic, Etherage's and Wycherley's in comic).

With the queens, Mary and Anne, we see an increasing focus on heroic female protagonists real and fictional, such as Calisto and Jane Shore. After the death of Queen Anne, the last Stuart, the new Hanoverian king was no longer accessible or viable as a plot-center. The magic had gone out of the political icon, itself originally a substitute for the religious icon. The Jacobite king was himself a rebel abroad, and the Hanoverian at home was a remote, German-speaking prince who preferred living in Hanover. As an apparent figurehead, his role was taken over by his "steward" or "prime minister," Walpole.

In the 1720s, until his fall in 1742, Walpole assumed (or, in the *Craftsman* idiom, usurped) the place of the monarch in the political imagination, of Drawcansir (the mock-hero of Buckingham's burlesque, *The Rehearsal*) in the literary. Walpole is in fact the figure to whom the poet or painter must go for the career of his "hero." Implicit is the shift from a ruler who is a synecdoche for the state, symbol of the body politic, to a peripheral figure, a low, parodic version. He is in some sense a "burlesque" of the king, or greatness; also, it goes without saying, more appropriate as a subject for writers of prose fiction than for the practitioners of epic or romance.

Fielding, from Tom Thumb to Jonathan Wild until Walpole's fall and replacement in his imagination by Richardson's Pamela (from Fielding's perspective a female Walpole), used the Walpolean career as an imaginative center.[94] In classical terms, Walpole elicited the subject of "greatness" because he represented false as opposed to true greatness, now to be found only in the circle of Fielding's friends who opposed Walpole in parliament. Pope set up against this figure the good aristocrat (a Cobham or Bathurst) and poet (himself or Swift). Fielding also accompanied his analyses of greatness with alternatives – not only the secular ruler but the heavenly providential power and, at some distance, the literary power of an author. He realized that when the monarch goes (as when the father goes), a prime minister is no replacement for the spiritual center of a kingdom, and concludes that the only other center is the artist, the creator of great public fictions like *Tom Jones*.[95]

In April 1731 Fielding added another afterpiece to *The Tragedy of Tragedies*, called *The Welsh Opera*, in which he develops Gay's situation of the "Newgate Pastoral," moving the "criminals" out of London to the countryside and portraying them as a country family with their servants – which, among other things, has the effect of rendering them (hardly "great") strange, quaint, and harmless.[96] The farm is plainly Fielding's England.[97] The Apshinken family suggests George II and Queen Caroline, and their servants, Robin the Butler, William the coachman, John the groom, and Thomas the gardener, recalling their "prime minister" Walpole and his rival William Pulteney. The strongly patriotic strain in the second half takes the form of the praise of country life, tobacco, and roast beef (all particular favorites of the author's) against the foreign taste in food and Mrs. Apshinken's Welsh-German meanness.

The popularity of the farce led Fielding to expand it into a mainpiece and call it *The Grub-Street Opera* (at the beginning of the third act it is explained that the lying letters, forged by Owen Apshinken, symbolize Grub Street productions). This version was never performed: Fielding appears to have been either paid or warned off performing the play, indeed from publishing it as well (though a pirated edition appeared). The reason was presumably the satire on the German royal family as the Welsh Apshinkens. The allegory is comic as concerns the king and queen (though probably to them offensive), but Owen, the prince of Wales, is Fielding's villain – lecherous, a seducer of women, but impotent. Both father and son are shown in their different ways to be subservient to the "petticoat government" of women.

The farce is the dysfunctional family, but the plot concerns another pair of contrasted lovers, one a master and the other his servant, but, more important, as in the earlier comedies, one a libertine and the other a romantic lover. Robin the butler, like Tom Thumb or earlier Gay's

Macheath, is the protagonist-hero, but Thumb's impotence has been transferred with the libertine's villainy to the egregious master, Owen Apshinken. Owen is, in fact, the libertine rake graduated to ethical deist. "All nature tells you what to do," he sings, and: "Nature never prompts us to a real crime: it is the imposition of a priest, not nature's voice, which bars us from a pleasure allowed to every beast but man" (9:238–9). And his friend, Parson Puzzletext, is the first of Fielding's corrupt priests; he and Owen continue the characteristic libertine topos with the similitude of the chase (of "a puss") and the seduction of a female (218–19).[98]

It is of interest, though, that "greatness," insofar as it is the implicit subject, applies not to the impotent Owen but to the virile, romantic lover, Robin. The opposition caricature of Walpole had two complementary aspects, both alluded to in *The Beggar's Opera*: In Macheath, his amorousness, infidelity, and adultery; in Peachum, his management skills, his control of parliament through bribery and threats. In *The Welsh Opera* Fielding emphasizes the rakish aspect and reduces the Peachum aspect to a butler's skimming a bit for his own benefit while being generally useful to his masters. Thus Robin can say, like Peachum: "O Sweetissa, Sweetissa! well thou knowest that, wert thou true, I'd not have sold thee for five hundred pounds" (232). But he can also conclude his soliloquy: "What avails it me that I can purchase an estate [the public aspect], when I cannot purchase happiness [the private]?" (262).

Though a roguish butler, and part of the reductive allegory, Robin is presented primarily as a lover, and not, as in *The Beggar's Opera* or *Tom Thumb*, a lover with more than one woman (which inevitably invokes Fielding's own father). The plot is essentially the romance of the boy losing the girl and then regaining her. This is not part of the allegory of the royal family; nor is Owen's trickery, which causes the misunderstanding, nor his motive, which is to get Robin's Sweetissa to himself. Fielding aims his satire primarily at the royal family and only secondarily (and showing sympathy, if not flattery) at Walpole. It would appear that he was still, at this time, hoping to attract Walpole's patronage.

The afterpiece

Fielding starts with an afterpiece, a short burlesque, and when it succeeds he develops the idea, expanding the farce and then adding framing devices. In *The Author's Farce* the original farce, "The Pleasures of the Town," began as a response to *Hurlothrumbo*, but it was presented as a supplement to a story about bad writing in London; it was then supplemented by another farce, *Tom Thumb*, to further examine the nature of farce, and this then has to be explained by forms of textual commentary, whether in the play itself or in its published form.

The great popularity of *Tom Thumb. A Tragedy* led Fielding to expand the text and publish the second edition as "Written by Scriblerus Secundus"; he opened the new year by further expanding the afterpiece into a mainpiece, which was first performed on March 24, 1731, calling it *The Tragedy of Tragedies; or, The Life and Death of Tom Thumb the Great*, and, as always, this was accompanied by its publication. But in this case publication added to the playtext both introduction and annotations (attributed now to "*H*. Scriblerus Secundus"). The dichotomy of acting and reading takes a more emphatic form here, where the reading version supplements the acted version with annotations and scholarly apparatus and includes the opportunity for a close reading of the lines themselves not permitted in oral delivery. The scholarly apparatus is part of a Scriblerian parody, but it and all the untranslated Latin tags draw attention once more to the author's learning. Part of Fielding's wit, or his chutzpah, lies in his citing all of these obscure lower level plays while in fact expecting his audience to recognize that he is invoking Shakespeare himself – indicating that *these* are pale shadows of Shakespeare, but also that he is capable of laughing at the Bard himself: For "O Tom Thumb! Tom Thumb! Wherefore art thou Tom Thumb?" he cites Otway's "Oh! Marius, Marius, wherefore art thou Marius" rather than "O Romeo, Romeo, wherefore art thou Romeo?"

We see something here of Fielding's method of composition when he writes a farce. Not only the farce but, as significantly, the afterpiece, a shorter burlesque along the lines of the ancient satyr play that followed the tragedy, was Fielding's contribution to English drama. The principle of the afterpiece, for Fielding at least, derived from the Scarron/Cotton *Virgile Travesty*, which presupposed the relation of piece and afterpiece, the *Aeneid* and its burlesque. Some of his afterpieces did originally follow a tragedy but by no means all.

When it followed one of his own farces, the tendency was toward elaboration, as he was probably taught in the rhetoric classes at Eton. *Tom Thumb* follows *The Author's Farce*, and so expands upon, and further exemplifies, "The Pleasures of the Town" as burlesque, that is, what he *meant* by "burlesque." Then *Tom Thumb* is expanded into its own independent farce and then further expanded with commentary and notes into a literary text. In fact, the basic Fielding paradigm is here: from stage play to dramatic text to fictional text, that is, from *The Author's Farce* to *Shamela* to *Joseph Andrews*. The point of origin, however, is the inflated, overly pompous *tragedy*; and then he leaves the original tragedy behind but depends on other texts, more immediate and personally involved "tragedies" that have to be explained or, in the case of his own farces, made acceptable.

The nucleus or basic building block, the piece of nonsense, is the allegory of Queen Nonsense, Signor Opera, and Mrs. Novel, the story of a courtship-marriage parallel to the story in the framing play, with one man and two women (Macheath and Polly and Lucy), ultimately Tom and

Sophia and Molly, Booth and Amelia and Mrs. Matthews. Returning to his source, in some cases he makes one of the women older than the hero, even motherly (Lady Booby, Jenny, Lady Bellaston, even Bridget); which may only indicate the origin in the conventional comic conflict of the generations, but may raise the question of why always a younger and an older woman.

Writing a comedy

Swift claimed that he had laughed only twice, once at the trick of a mountebank's Merry Andrew, and the other "at the Circumstance of Tom Thumb's killing the Ghost."[99] There is no question that Fielding's farces succeeded as entertainments – they made him the most successful English playwright of the 1730s. The ambivalent critical response to *The Author's Farce* and *Tom Thumb*, however, led him to reconsider his position. *Tom Thumb*, partly because of its great popularity, lent itself to different interpretations.[100] A political stick for both sides, it was read by some as an attack on Walpole, by others as an example of Walpolean taste.[101] It served the hostile *Grub-Street Journal* as another example of *Hurlothrumbo* farce, of the degenerate "Pleasures of the Town," and so of Walpole's taste for debased literature (as opposed to the poetry of Pope).[102] Another critic included *The Dunciad* itself along with *Tom Thumb* and *Hurlothrumbo* as proof of the "corrupted" judgment of "That stupid *Ass, the Town*."[103] Some regarded *Tom Thumb* as an attack "on all the Great Geniuses *England* has produced," not only Elijah Fenton, Nathaniel Lee, and Nicholas Rowe, but Dryden, Congreve, and Addison, a case of throwing out the baby with the bath.[104] This opinion was prevalent enough for Fielding to be defensive on the subject and wish to prove his ability to write the more respectable five-act comedy.[105]

As if to balance the popularity of the farces he had produced with his left hand, on June 23 of that same spectacular 1730 season Fielding produced *Rape upon Rape; or, The Justice Caught in his own Trap. A Comedy*, invoking in his title "comedy" and in his prologue "the heroic Muse," who "combats with her pen" "Vice, clothed with power."

Comedy, by contrast to farce, was the five-act form defined by Dryden as a pleasant mixture, "neither all wit, nor all humour, but the result of both," that is, partaking of both Jonsonian humor comedy (with humor characters) and Dryden's own comedy of witty conversation. Jonsonian humor comedy, however, was in fact satire and could, as Dryden noted, verge on farce: "to entertain an Audience perpetually with Humour, is to carry them from the conversation of Gentlemen, and treat them with the follies and extravagances of *Bedlam*."[106] Fielding's *Rape upon Rape*, which invokes the heroic muse of satire, is essentially Jonsonian; even the wit is restrained in the discourse of the lower orders, the denizens of a prison and magistrate's court. In some ways *Rape upon Rape* is another conventionalized version of the farcical microcosm of *The Welsh Opera*, the family replaced by the magistrate's court. Justice Squeezum's similes repeat the Beggar's conclusion about the difference between high and low: "Well, sir, if you cannot pay for your transgressions like the rich, you must suffer for them like the poor." Squeezum is an example of power unlimited except by the remote possibility of the countermand by a good justice (named Worthy).

The subject is (as the prologue says) "vice clothed with power," but Justice Squeezum is like Tom Thumb, while eminently successful in the world of his corrupt court jurisdiction, suffering when his wife appears or when he steps back into the domestic world. Like Squeezum, Fielding's men of power are usually older men; and older men, whose wives are invariably younger, are cuckolds. With the calculating but cuckolded Squeezum Fielding contrasts the faithful young lovers.

When he finished *Rape upon Rape*, Fielding was writing another, more ambitious comedy; in 1732 he offered *The Modern Husband* at Drury Lane, as the mature transcendence of the farces and burlesques of his youth. He wrote to Lady Mary Wortley Montagu that *The Modern Husband* was "written on a Model I never yet attempted."[107] He fills the play with witty Congrevian conversation, but the similes once again gravitate toward the *Beggar's Opera* analogies: Lord Richly reports that Mrs. Bellamant, whom he has allowed to beat him at cards, accepts his over payment "With the same reluctancy that a lawyer or physician would a double fee, or a court-priest a plurality" (10:62). In fact, though its subject is different, the play's form, focused on a villain and his plots, corresponds closely to the Jonsonian satire of *Rape upon Rape*. The difference is that in *The Modern Husband* the center is not a figure, Squeezum, but a group – Mr. and Mrs. Modern and Lord Richly, and closely entwined with them, the unfortunate Bellamants. The center of attention is no longer courting lovers but a married couple, and the model, therefore, is Vanbrugh's comedies of unhappy marriage (a kind of play associated with Drury Lane, to which he logically returned for its production).

Mrs. Modern supports herself and her husband by sleeping with affluent lords and cheating at cards. When Lord Richly tires of her and finds an attraction elsewhere, and when she loses at cards, Mr. Modern encourages her to help Richly to secure his new woman, the virtuous wife of Mr. Bellamant (another of Mrs. Modern's conquests who contribute to her support). But he also hatches a scheme of his own: to trap Lord Richly and Mrs. Modern in criminal conversation.

At the center of the power structure is Lord Richly, who exploits a society of equally corrupt types:

Death [exclaims Capt. Merit, another of Fielding's unpatronized soldiers, pointing to Col. Courtly], there's a fellow now – That fellow's father was a pimp; his mother, she turned bawd; and his sister turned whore: you see the consequence. How happy is that country, where pimping and whoring are esteemed public services, and where grandeur and the gallows lie on the same road! (10:20)

Such scenes, and the play as a whole, represent dramatic equivalents of Juvenal's satires, with the one good justice setting off the otherwise total corruption of the judicial system. All of these are set against a single not altogether virtuous family, the Bellamants. Mr. Bellamant is an adulterer and his son is a wasteful fop; only Mrs. Bellamant is an unmixed character of virtue. Lord Richly is the central knave who elicits and exploits the folly (which leads to knavery) of his clients, the Moderns and virtually all the other characters, with the single exception of Mrs. Bellamant.

What characterizes Fielding's adaptation of Jonson and Wycherley, and relates it to Juvenal, is the figure of the "great man" of wealth, power, patronage, who uses his power to seduce and discard the wives of less fortunate men, whether bad like Modern or good like Bellamant. A Lord Richly or a Justice Squeezum is the "great man," with the negative aspects of Mr. Peachum or Owen Apshinken, no longer the gallantry of Macheath or Robin the butler.

The play is dedicated to Sir Robert Walpole. The dedication is followed by references within the play to "great men" like Richly, but so generalized as to have passed by Walpole. One unmistakable irony, however, was that at Drury Lane Fielding uses Cibber, the most accomplished actor of fop roles of his generation, to represent the foppish center of evil in this society. And so the dedication of the play to the central symbol of the Moderns' world, Walpole himself, at least invites comment – a dedication that opens with unmistakable echoes of Horace's "Epistle to Augustus" (which Pope parodied a few years later). Battestin notes these "delicious ironies" but strangely concludes: "But Fielding's prose has no such ironic intent," and "With *The Modern Husband* Fielding meant to make his peace with Walpole" (128). It seems to me that Fielding is having it both ways. The coincidence of Walpole's Poet Laureate playing Lord Richly, which would not have registered with Cibber, corresponds to Walpole's acceptance of the dedication without applying the play to himself. But that does not mean that Fielding did not appreciate the significance of these two situations, or that this was not an example of his characteristic address to slightly different audiences, ostensibly embracing both.

Fielding tended to cover himself when he addressed Walpole, leaving open the hope of rewards from the Great Man. In his poem "To the Right Honourable Sir Robert Walpole" ("Written in the Year 1730") he introduced a version of the subject of "greatness," playing at the time in *Tom*

Thumb at the Little Haymarket. He, the poet ("your great Bard"), is literally "a greater Man than you" because

> We're often taught it doth behove us
> To think those greater who're above us.
> Another Instance of my Glory,
> Who live above you twice two Story,
> And from my Garret can look down
> On the whole Street of *Arlington*

– on which Walpole lived.[108] Battestin notes that Fielding's father and latest
step-mother (Eleanor) were at this time living on the east side of Dover
Street, from the upper floors of which Henry could have looked down on
Walpole's house in Arlington Street; which suggests that somewhere
behind Walpole was also Fielding's sense of dependence on his father's
"patronage."[109]

The name "Modern" implies both the decline of classical standards and
the reporting of a contemporary case of criminal conversation, that is, the
latest news, which had furnished the nucleus for *Rape upon Rape* as well as
Hogarth's *Harlot's Progress* of 1732. Setting off the newspaper reality,
however, the names are personifications: Mrs. Modern and Mrs. Squabble,
Lady Ever-play, and Mrs. Ruin shun the unpopular Mrs. Worthy; again,
at Lord Richly's, Lord Lazy is admitted while Capt. Merit (another
unpatronized soldier, who wants a command in Col. Favourite's regiment)
waits.

Beginning with these names Fielding establishes a set of opposing terms,
based once again on the farce of a world turned upside down: on the side
of virtue he lists poverty, merit, substance, and soul; on the side of vice,
roguery, wealth, reputation, and greatness (low greatness leading to the
gallows, high to grandeur); as a subtext, the British soldier in the battle
field is associated with heroism, in London with poverty. *The Modern
Husband* is an anatomy of London society, and part of the context of the
Moderns' plot is Mr. Modern's losses (like Edmund Fielding's) in the South
Sea Bubble; once again, the unspoiled country appears in the Bellamant
family that cannot wait to return to their country seat.

The high claim Fielding makes for the play in the prologue is the same
he will make in the preface to *Joseph Andrews*. This is plainly a "comedy"
into which he has put as much attention as he will into his first novel. It
was, however, for him the wrong model – he had not yet found the model
out of which to create a new genre suitable to his particular genius. Neither
the old satiric form of Jonson and Wycherley nor the new marital comedy
of Vanbrugh was finally congenial. He did take from Vanbrugh, and especially Farquhar, the dubious hero, and in that sense combined the
Malvin-Merital and Valentine-Veromil characters of the early comedies in

Mr. Bellamant; to this "mixed" figure he added, this time in the dedication to Walpole, his own Harry Luckless, the playwright and stage manager. The combination of rake and prudential farceur, autobiographer and master of ceremonies, character and commentator, is the end toward which Fielding is moving.

One problem in *The Modern Husband* may be that Fielding has limited himself to one social class, and to one discourse, the witty. The farces had covered the middling, professional types – authors, booksellers, stage managers – and *Joseph Andrews* will introduce servants as well as their masters. The country also exists in *The Modern Husband* but as only a remote ideal. The result looks forward to Fielding's final novel, *Amelia*, and so to the sort of novel Thackeray and Trollope would write 100 years later. But it was not a work that could eventuate in *Tom Jones*.

Molière

Fielding's farces had so far been burlesques of literary texts or plays in performance. In March 1730/1 as an afterpiece to the new *Tragedy of Tragedies* he added *The Letter-Writers; or, A New Way to Keep a Wife At Home*, a straight farce of the sort represented by Edward Ravenscroft's *The London Cuckolds* (originally produced in 1681, the most popular of early eighteenth-century farces, produced annually on Lord Mayor's Day). Ramble and Sotmore in *Rape upon Rape* owed something to the lustful and imbibing rake in *The London Cuckolds*. Now Fielding presents two London husbands (Ravenscroft had three), who have devised a scheme for keeping their wives at home, and two rakes involved with the two wives, slipping easily from one house to the other, constantly surprised by prematurely returning husbands. There are many closets and other hiding places into and out of which the lovers move.

On June 1, 1732 *The Modern Husband* was followed by *The Old Debauchees* and *The Covent-Garden Tragedy*, which failed; Fielding quickly recovered with his first adaptation of Molière, *The Mock Doctor*, added on June 23 as an afterpiece to shore up *The Old Debauchees*, and this proved a great success. He notes in his preface that Molière's *Misanthrope* owed its success chiefly to the adding of *Le Médicin malgré lui* – his own procedure during these hectic years. *The Mock Doctor* is the prototypical farce, based on a misunderstanding (Gregory is taken for a physician) from which everything else follows; but the misunderstanding is willed by the squabbling couple, Gregory and his wife Dorcas, who are a low (farcical) version of Mr. and Mrs. Modern. One suspects that Fielding chose this play because of the country setting and the resemblance between Gregory and Dorcas and Fielding's favorite comic couple, Punch and Joan. Besides being called "Mr. Drama" Fielding also earned the sobriquet of "England's *Moliere*."[110]

The success of *The Mock Doctor* led him to prepare a translation of Molière's *The Miser*, another full-blown comedy, ready for production by February 17, 1732/3, which was equally successful. The revised version of *The Author's Farce* was produced in December 1733, with a new Molière-influenced farce, *The Intriguing Chambermaid* added in January 1733/4 as afterpiece – the first of three pieces Fielding wrote especially for Kitty Clive, his favorite actress. The other two, which followed in 1735, were *An Old Man taught Wisdom* and (though not produced until 1742) *Miss Lucy in Town*. These are all Molière plays. They remind us that the chief attention of *The Letter-Writers*, despite the elaborate gymnastics of the farce, was focused on Mrs. Softly, the beleaguered wife who exclaims: "Where's the difference, whether one be locked up in one's own grave, or one's own house? – My soul is such an enemy to confinement, that if my body were confined, it would not stay in it" (9:189). She is the first of the vocal and central young women who emerge from Fielding's Molière plays.

In *An Old Man taught Wisdom* Old Goodwill, the father, is essentially Arnolphe, the husband of *L'Ecole des femmes*, and Lucy is Agnès – or Wycherley's version of her, Marjorie Pynchwife ("The girl I have bred up under my own eye; she has seen nothing, knows nothing, and has consequently no will but mine" [10:327]). But Fielding turns this situation into his own characteristic form of satiric farce, the most primitive form in which Jonson transferred formal verse satire to the stage.[111] He presents a naive girl interviewing prospective husbands, types who pass in review – an apothecary, a dancing master, a singing master, and a lawyer; after their follies have been exposed, she marries her true love the footman.[112] She is not a chastising or vituperative Juvenalian satirist but a Lucianic commentator who coolly leads on her various beaux to reveal their particular follies. She knows all along what she wants, and her constant standard is Mr. Thomas the footman, against whom she judges these pretentious fools.

As a sequel to *An Old Man taught Wisdom*, Fielding wrote *Miss Lucy in Town* (another star vehicle for Kitty Clive), which takes Lucy and Thomas to London. Although probably begun in 1735, the play was not produced until 1742. It may have, among other things, celebrated his own marriage of November 28, 1734 to Charlotte Cradock; the three preceding farces (*The Mock Doctor*, *The Intriguing Chambermaid*, and *The Old Man taught Wisdom*) could also be pre-nuptial comedies of predictably apprehensive projections.

Molière's major comedies, *Tartuffe* and *Le Misanthrope*, have villain-centered plots corresponding to those of Jonson's *Volpone* and Wycherley's *Country Wife*, but with the important difference that Molière was interested in obsession (related in some degree to Don Quixote), a character trait Fielding only picked up on after he began to translate his plays. Justice Squeezum in *Rape upon Rape* may have recalled the hypocrite Tartuffe, but not Tartuffe's dupe, Orgon, who served as the obsessed figure in *Tartuffe*.

The miser Harpagon, in his translation of *L'Avare*, is Fielding's first such figure. The surest sign of Molière is in Fielding's final Drury Lane play, another five-act comedy following upon the success of *The Modern Husband*, launched with great hopes on February 10, 1734/5: *The Universal Gallant; or, The Different Husbands*. If *The Modern Husband* was a Jonsonian comedy about a central figure of vice that draws out the vices and follies of the various social types around him, *The Universal Gallant* is a Molière comedy of obsession. The central characters are the two contrasting married couples, or more particularly the husbands. The play is in fact about the jealous husband, the Molière madman, his fixation being on his wife's supposed infidelity. Sir Simon Raffler, however, is actually more concerned about his image of himself as a cuckold: his scheme is not, finally, to try to make his wife unfaithful but to make people believe that he *is* a cuckold. He is mad about that image (as, from a different perspective, Fielding the satirist has been; now that he is married, he may be seeing it from the husband's point of view). His brother, Colonel Raffler, is equally mad (but more pleasantly) in his image of himself as the husband with faith in his wife (again a situation Fielding would have known from Ravenscroft's *London Cuckolds*). The "Universal Gallant" Captain Spark, a parallel figure to Sir Simon, would appear to be the great lover, while his pretensions to this are as empty as Sir Simon's to cuckoldom; and their pretensions are both exploded in parallel scenes at the end of the comedy.

The play presents a completely (or largely) innocent group of characters surrounded by a penumbra of guilty longings, hints, accusations, and various sinful hypotheses. The hypocrisy which is, in a sense, the object of the play's satire, is embodied in the opposite types of the innocent who would be thought a great lover and the husband who would be thought a great cuckold. They add a crucial ingredient missing from the earlier comedies – a delusion that is grounded in vanity rather than hypocrisy. The emphasis on what Fielding would come to call "affectation" in the preface to *Joseph Andrews* is evident in this, his final five-act comedy. It signals with Fielding's departure from Drury Lane the break with respectability, before his return to the Little Haymarket and the more congenial form of the farce.

The play was not a success, and its failure was celebrated by Fielding's enemies.[113] The defensive tone that appears for the first time in both his "Advertisement" and "Prologue," indicating financial need, may begin to reflect his feelings about the plight in which he has placed his new wife.

Lucianic burlesque

In 1736 Fielding returned to the Little Haymarket as both manager and playwright, and his first play was *Pasquin, A Dramatick Satire on the Times*, a five-act farce consisting of two plays. Following the model of Buckingham's *Rehearsal*, he presents plays in rehearsal on an obvious stage; the author is present and harangues the actors – Bayes-Dryden, the author, and a pair of critics (one naive, the other ironic). The actors are often rebellious – one of the parallels Fielding invokes between the literary and political levels of the action.

The first play is Trapwit's three-act comedy (defined as a comedy but plainly a farce, and set in the country), the second Fustian's three-act tragedy.[114] And, as *Pasquin* shows, the ultimate, embracing "farce" is the story of the playwright himself, of which the rehearsal forms only one stage – of, if not farce, then, as Sneerwell adds, tragedy.

Trapwit characterizes his comedy as un-witty, depending only on humor, nature, and simplicity, and invoking Molière (11:171). In fact, redefining "joke" and "wit" as bribe, "farce" as an election, and "comedy" as "an exact representation of nature" (that is, "nothing but bribery in this play"), the result is "a dramatick Satire."

Fustian's play, the murder of Queen Commonsense by the usurping Queen Ignorance, is the "tragedy" that Fielding chooses as the ironic genre for his dramatization of *The Dunciad*'s fiction of decline and apocalypse (204–5). As usual, the tragedy is turned to comedy by the ending in which, after Queen Common Sense has been murdered, her ghost returns to haunt Queen Ignorance. But in *Pasquin* the death and resurrection of Common Sense, and at the hands of Firebrand the priest, owes less to Pope's *Dunciad* than to a very un-Popean strain of anticlericalism. Priest-craft, Law, and Physic make up the evil trinity, but led by Priestcraft. Fire-brand is a safe name, suggesting fanaticism and the radical left; but his statements stress the power of priestcraft – which, again, is safely attributed to popery, but was part of the Old Whig polemic against the Walpole min-istry and the deist demystification of Scripture.

A contemporary satiric print shows Fielding – vaguely a portrait – on a stage offering Queen Common Sense a paper inscribed "Pasquin," and accompanied by Harlequin, Pierrot, as well as priest, lawyer, and physician (see plate 1).

Tumble-Down Dick; or Phaeton in the Suds was added on April 29 as an after-piece to *Pasquin*. It takes off where Fustian's tragedy ended, adding an "entertainment" by Machine, a parody of John Rich (the published text is dedicated to Lun, Rich's impersonation of Harlequin), a manifestation of the duncical train of Queen Ignorance. *Tumble-Down Dick* travesties Ovid's story of Phaeton's disastrous attempt to take over the chariot of the sun from his father, Apollo – the sun is a watchman's lantern, the Palace of the Sun a roundhouse; Aurora is delayed from going out to meet the sunrise because her linen is not washed; she is accompanied on her walk by girls carrying farthing candles to represent the stars; and Neptune is a waterman. Fielding introduces a magistrate, once again (as in *Rape*

Plate 1 Unknown artist, *The Judgment of the Queen o' Common Sense, Address'd to Henry Fielding Esqr.*, 1736, etching and engraving, courtesy of the Trustees of the British Museum.

upon Rape) apparently based on the notorious Westminster "trading justice" Thomas De Veil, and in close proximity songs about gin and allusions to the Gin Act of 1736, which he had enforced with rigor. As a consequence of his own imbibing, the justice ends the play as a merrily singing Harlequin, the hypocrite exposed. There is also a cuckolded cobbler quarreling with his wife, and other scenes take place in Tom King's coffee-house and a barber shop. The method of Fielding's burlesque is explained by Machine: "Does not a squib represent a thunderbolt in the rape of Proserpine? And what are all the suns, sir, that have ever shone upon the stage, but candles? And if they represent the Sun, I think they may very well represent the stars" (12:24).

Farce, enacted in (or in fact brought about by) the commentary of Trapwit, Fustian, or Machine, becomes satire. The ancient who provided Fielding with his commentators, more than either Horace or Juvenal, was the cynical Lucian, who, in the form of dialogues, showed that man's mind is for seeing through frauds and lies imposed on us by our fathers and grandfathers, by judges and lawyers, philosophers and priests. Fielding's persona of the 1730s derives from the Lucianic protagonist (a Menippus, Cyniscus, Damis, Diogenes, or Lucian himself) who asks questions, probing appearance, idealization, myth, and custom. Lucian depends on the surprise of exposure, on showing the apparently guilty to be innocent, the apparently noble ignoble. Perhaps partly for this reason, Lucian has no strong bias to a particular good as Juvenal does and no desire to map a subtle spiritual course for the reader as Horace does. His aim is double – to expose the real, however deep he must go under the illusions man weaves for himself; and to discomfit his reader, shake up his cherished values, and disrupt his orthodoxy. The typical Lucianic fiction has a markedly mobile protagonist who travels up to Olympus to question the gods or down to Hades to question the dead, always probing appearances, idealization, myth, and custom. He is very different from the Horatian observer, within society looking out, or the Juvenalian, a last fragment of the true society that has been isolated or expelled. He is not even necessarily a good man since his value is only as disrupter of orthodoxy and questioner of long-held assumptions. In the *Dialogues of the Dead* Diogenes, whom Lucian elsewhere attacks as merely another false philosopher, acts as a disruptive agent whose questioning, probing, and railing serve a useful corrective function.

Lucian is a young man's satirist – a young man who does not have a particular agenda of his own. More to the point, he was a freethinker's satirist. Lucian notoriously held up all religions and philosophies, including that of the early Christians, to a standard of reason and common sense; in the 1700s he was particularly unpopular with the Anglican clergy, evoking the sort of impious skepticism associated with deism. The Rev. Edward Young commented that "Some Satirical Wits, and Humorists, like their Father *Lucian*, laugh at every thing indiscriminately."[115] Fielding's advertisement in the 1750s for his and William Young's translation of Lucian argued that Lucian was helpful to the Church Fathers who used his satire against the heathen gods. But of course Lucian's satire was a two-edged sword, applicable as well to Christian mythology.[116]

The mythological stories of the underworld in the pantomimeharlequinade permitted Fielding to introduce a strong trace of Lucian in "The Pleasures of the Town" – from the scene at the river's edge with Charon, with the catalogue of passengers, to the scene laid in the afterlife. The effect of the last is not only the Lucianic one of turning things upside down for a clearer appraisal but, for Fielding, to suggest the moribund quality of the court of Nonsense and remove it from the world of actuality to the land of death where it belongs – and where it is also harmless, a comic rather than satiric fiction.

Fielding's use of Lucian extended to the theatrical adaptations of *Tumble-Down Dick* and the unlucky *Eurydice* and directly into the prose narrative,

A Journey from this World to the Next, both included, with such Lucianic imitations as "An Interlude between Jupiter, Juno, Apollo, and Mercury," in the *Miscellanies* (1743).[117]

In *Pasquin* Fielding creates two independent actions, one blatantly farcical and unreal, the other – though still stylized – representing the real world of moral and aesthetic judgment.[118] For the second he employs a series of commentators who, in the frame action, sit around and watch the farce being played. One is the playwright, another the critic, and another perhaps an aristocratic member of the audience or a beau. These interpreters are not always normative; the truth may be arrived at obliquely through simple ironies, but they do in one way or another tell us how to take the farce. This structure also gives Fielding a device with which to catch the maximum number of people gathered around the central object, the farce; they illuminate both it and themselves. But the structure also emphasizes Fielding's interest in the problem of understanding and interpretation, for which in time he will conclude that there *is* no single normative point of view focused on a moral problem.

On the other hand, one of the commentators is always the author of the play, and in the last climactic plays he becomes increasingly prominent and normative. In *Pasquin* there is still a discrepancy between the playwright as bad writer and as satiric commentator, between the heroic bombast of his play, which is ridiculed, and its subject, the defeat of Queen Common Sense by Queen Ignorance, which is exemplary. As the play proves, Fustian himself (the tragic playwright), attacked by the comic playwright Trapwit, attacks his own play. In the sequel to *Pasquin, The Historical Register for the Year 1736* (1737), the author Medley has the pragmatic awareness of Luckless in *The Author's Farce*, his play's purpose, he explains, is "to divert the town and bring full houses" (Medley as hack playwright), while at the same time its "design is to ridicule the vicious and foolish customs of the age" (Medley as satirist).

The ode to the new year, with which he opens the play, is a parody of Cibber's effusions as poet laureate and serves as a way of showing how insipidly the year opens in Walpolean England. "There, sir," he says, "there's the very quintessence and cream of all the odes I have seen for several years last past" (11:242–4). The scene without Medley's explanation is comic; with it, satiric. We have to be told by Medley that "this, sir, is the full account of the whole history of Europe, as far as we know it, comprised in one scene" in order to understand the pointless scene; it serves as a correlative to Medley's explanation of the briefness of his whole play considering that it is the record of a whole year (11:246). At other times his function is to generalize. In the second scene, showing that ladies are now the arbiters of taste, Medley's comment is explicit: "if we go on to improve in luxury, effeminacy and debauchery, as we have done lately, the next age, for ought I know, may be more like the children of squeaking Italians than hardy Britons" (11:249). Later, in the scene in the theater, Medley again explains so that no one will miss the point: there is "a strict resemblance between the states political and theatrical" and, when Apollo advises, "Let them hiss . . . as long as we get their money," he adds, to underline the identification with Walpole, "There, sir, is the sentiment of a great man" (11:257, 263). The other commentators – the critics Sneerwell and Sourwit – do not express divergent points of view so much as contribute ironically to a single interpretation of an event. The event itself is not allowed ambiguity.

What we see in these plays, anticipating issues in Fielding's writings of the 1740s, is a contradiction between a problematics of interpretation on the one hand and an effort to make the meaning absolutely clear on the other. *The Historical Register* shows Fielding narrowing his focus to express the evil of the Walpole ministry (or perhaps any ministry), and this both invited repression by the beleaguered ministry and prepared Fielding for the single normative perspective of his *Champion* essays.

The Novel or New

Like Trapwit and Fustian, Medley derives from Buckingham's Bayes, wanting "to have every thing new," by which he means simply *out of himself* (echoing also Swift's hack in his *Tale of a Tub*). But now, with the *newness* of his subject, the year 1736, and his "Ode to the New Year," he modulates into a sense of *new* that has changed for him, by way of Addison, to be descriptive if not honorific.

The literary context of "greatness" in *Tom Thumb* and Fielding's other studies of the topos, included Addison's "Pleasures of the Imagination" essays of 1712 in which he supplemented the aesthetic categories of the Beautiful/Ugly with others: the Great, which extends the pleasure of beauty to areas previously thought by aestheticians as ugly or terrifying (oceans, mountain ranges, and storms), and, a third category, the Novel, New, or Uncommon. The latter Addison associated with curiosity, surprise, the pursuit of knowledge, and variety – those qualities that were summed up negatively for the Scriblerians in the *Hurlothrumbo* farce. For Addison this was not a transgressive term but the source of "an agreeable Surprise." Preferable to the Great, the Novel "*gratifies* its Curiosity, and gives [the soul] an Idea of which it was not before possest." "It is this," he wrote, "that recommends Variety, where the Mind is every Instant called off to something new, and the Attention not suffered to dwell too long, and waste it self on any particular Object."[119] When asked for the "main design" of his play, Medley replies: "To divert the town" (11:242). The focus is plainly on the new, the present, and no longer the present in relation to the classical past. *The Historical Register* simply reports the events of the year past.

Life-as-theatre

The privileged aesthetic term in *The Spectator* is the Novel or New, and its formal attributes are the spectacle and its spectators. The "Fraternity of Spectators who live in the World without having any thing to do in it" is defined as "every one that considers the World as a Theatre, and desires to form a right Judgment of those who are the Actors on it" (no. 10, 1:45–6). In the essays which lead up to the climactic essays on "The Pleasures of the Imagination" the favored subject is "spectatoring," the favorite metaphor life-as-theater. In *Love in Several Masques* Wisemore began his satiric tirade with Addison's metaphor: "I have been a spectator of all its scenes," and continued: "I have seen hypocrisy pass for religion, madness for sense, noise and scurrility for wit, and riches for the whole train of virtues" (8:19–20).

Wisemore continues at length, but the basic elements are here, and they add up to the topos of the world turned upside down, which becomes Fielding's definition of farce and nonsense (synonymous with "the folly, foppery, and childishness of your diversions"). Medley, when asked if there is a connection between the political and his theatrical scene, responds by connecting "politics" with "farce," which he associates with a "playhouse, where, let me tell you, there are some politicians too, where there is lying, flattering, dissembling, promising, deceiving, and undermining, as well as in any court in Christendom" (11:242). He is, in short, summing up the strands that have developed in Fielding's plays over the last several years, all of which tended toward the genre of satire, and the metaphor of life as theater. (Medley, whose name is an English equivalent of the Latin *satura*, reproduces on the stage the mixture of scenes, speeches, poems, and allegories that characterize the variety and novelty of that form.)

The Historical Register is dominated by the politics-theater analogy.[120] Fielding demonstrates in his burlesque farces how similar the wretched piece of play-writing is to the wretched piece of politics or religion. A bill in parliament, the activities of great men, a village election with heroic speeches as well as bribery – all of these are symbolic farces, analogous in various ways to a puppet show or pantomime. The metaphor is implicit in all the rehearsal plays and explicit in the last of them, *Eurydice Hiss'd.*

The implications for Fielding's plays are that in society manners are manipulated from above – by an auctioneer (Mr. Hen) as well as a clergyman (Firebrand) or a politician (Walpole); that society and the cosmos also exist in a similar state of theatricality. Thus the writer is associated with the playwright and stage manager vis-à-vis his cast, with chance ever present to waylay the actor or misplace the script. Fielding's own theatrical experience shaped his particular understanding of the metaphor. He found the way to survive economically in the theater by being manager as well as playwright (as Hogarth, in the same years, was publisher and distributor as well as painter and engraver of his works). Thus his characteristic dramatic form was the rehearsal in which the unit of narrative is the scene as observed by spectators, critics, actors, and the author himself. There is already a script, but in the rehearsal situation the author and his audience can collaborate and make changes even at this point, aware as they are of the characters as actors in and out of their roles.

The Little Haymarket offered Fielding the opportunities of an ad hoc situation of a sort that was ideal for his improvisational genius. He had a theater, "the smallest and worst of the London theatres with a barely competent troupe of actors,"[121] in which he could try out not only his own new plays but those of others; and could experiment with staging[122] – dropping a curtain between acts and sometimes scenes, improving the lighting effects, reviving the rehearsal play, all devices that framed and highlighted scenes and permitted commentary on the scenes.

One of the advantages of being manager as well as dramatist at the Little Haymarket was that Fielding could choose the plays that shared the bill with his own. He ended his first season of the Mogul's Company with George Lillo's *Fatal Curiosity*, a *tragedy* of everyday people, and though specifically laid in Elizabethan times, one that is not distanced by style from contemporary speech (and in that sense is novel or new). In terms of tragic "greatness," he writes in his prologue that the play is no *Tragedy of Tragedies*:

> No fustian Hero rages here to Night;
> No Armies fall, to fix a Tyrant's Right:
> From lower Life we draw our Scene's Distress;
> – Let not your Equals move your Pity less!
>   (ll. 9–12)

He defended Lillo's earlier tragedy, *The London Merchant* (1731), against those who had dismissed it "because the subject was too low";[123] *Fatal Curiosity* extended his idea of a moral and activist theater from the comic into the tragic register.

In his second season these supplementary plays were primarily political, underlining the messages of his own farces. During that last spectacular but dangerous season, he produced not only his own satiric plays but those of others – *The Rehearsal of Kings, Sir Peevy Pet, The Lordly Husband, The Sailor's Opera* ("Macheath turn'd Pyrate: or, Polly in India"), and *The King and Titi* (about George II's abuse of Prince Frederick), with passing references to Walpole in Henry Carey's *The Dragon of Wantley* and Lillo's *Fatal Curiosity*.

Improvisation in 1736–7, however, also meant turning up the heat. Fielding's arrogance, already noted by unsympathetic commentators, may have grown in proportion to his success. His increasingly daring behavior in his two final seasons at the Little Haymarket was doubtless the result of over-confidence. In *Pasquin*, while the satire was quite general, and no mention was made of Walpole, the comedy was biased toward the country and against the court party, and the tragedy, focused on the continuity (or status quo) of religion, law, and medicine between the governments of common sense and ignorance, carried the conventional anti-Walpole innuendo. The *Historical Register* was another matter. This was, and was regarded as, particular satire – which to opponents meant lampoon and scandal – and was levelled at all parties. At the end the patriot opposition appears, only to be shown to be equally susceptible to Walpole's (Quidam's) bribes.

The popular success of the plays intensified the hostile criticism: *The Historical Register*, the *Gazetteer* wrote (May 7), was going a stage further from satire to scurrility: *Pasquin*, though it "laid the Foundation for introducing POLITICKS on the Stage," was "general in his Satyr", but now, having "gone so far with Impunity," in *The Historical Register* Fielding has carried this "Vein further" into personal satire, and finally, in *Eurydice Hiss'd*, he insinuates "to the *Vulgar*, who must ever be *led*, that *all Government is* but a *Farce (perhaps a damned one too)*. . . . There are Things which, from the Good they dispense, ought to be Sacred; such are *Government* and *Religion*. No Society can subsist without 'em: To turn either into Ridicule, is to unloose the fundamental Pillars of Society, and shake it from its *Basis*." The author refers to the Opposition who, "were they in the Administration, would be the first to discountenance" such satire and agree that "No Society can subsist without" government and religion.

Years later Harris recalled:

> How those Performances were received, those who saw them, may well remember. Never were houses so crowded, never applause so universal, nor the same Peices so often repeated without interruption, or discontinuance. Tis enough to say that such was ye force of his comic humour and poignancy, that those in power in order to restrain him, thought proper by a Law to restrain the Stage in ye general, bearing even by this act of Restriction the highest testimony to his abilities. The Legislature made a Law, in order to curb one private man.[124]

Fielding's two seasons at the Little Haymarket were so successful, his position as both dramatist and manager so extremely profitable, that he might have continued indefinitely developing the possibilities of a proto-Shavian comedy had it not been for the Licensing Act of 1737, which closed all but the two patent theaters. While it has been shown that the theater riots played a large part in the passage of the bill, the facts remain that Walpole's reading of an obscene and seditious farce, *The Golden Rump*, before Parliament was the determining factor, and the expectation was that this piece would be performed at the Little Haymarket.[125]

Chesterfield attacked the bill in a speech to the Lords, which Lord Hervey admired as "one of the most lively and ingenious speeches . . . full of wit, of the genteelest satire, and in the most polished, classical style that the Petronius of any time ever wrote."[126] "This Bill," Chesterfield said, summing up Fielding's decade of writing for the theater,

> is not only an encroachment on liberty, but it is likewise an encroachment on property. Wit, my lords, is a sort of property: the property of those who have it, and too often the only property they have to depend on. It is indeed but a precarious dependence. . . . by this Bill wit is to be delivered out to the public by retail, it is to be excised, my lords.[127]

His own wit links "wit" and Walpole's Excise Bill, which draws on Fielding's final example of wit in *Eurydice Hiss'd*, his analogy of his damned farce *Eurydice* and Walpole's failed Excise Bill. And so his writing for the *Craftsman* in the months following the closing of the theater included, not surprisingly, the one satire that went over the edge and led to prosecution of the editor and the printer.[128]

LIBERTINE AND FREETHINKER

The libertine ethos

Rape upon Rape again features the pair of rakes to which we have become accustomed: Ramble and Constant are the libertine and courtly rakes, new copies of Fielding's Malvil and Merital or Valentine and Veromil. Most interesting is the careless Ramble ("my thoughts have ever succeeded my actions" [127]), who carries the basic desideratum of the Fielding hero – spontaneous actions, grounded in good nature rather than calculation, lacking either prudence or hypocrisy.

In the context of the 1730s, the classical figure of the improvident young lover was supplemented by Fielding's personal situation. He was himself more than once hailed before a magistrate, and he writes *Rape upon Rape* from the point of view of Luckless and Ramble, the needy writer and the innocent gentleman without money, at the mercy of the power of the law – essentially a personalization of the high-low inversions of Justice Squeezum's similes.

One observer, attending the first performance of *Tom Thumb* as afterpiece to *The Author's Farce*, was much amused by both plays but added that the author was "in a very low condition of purse."[129] He referred to the author as "one of the sixteen children of Mr. Fielding," suggesting that Edmund too had reason to be pitied. Fielding referred in *Rape upon Rape* to the plight of the half-pay soldier, recalling his father: Ramble's friend Constant is the first of the soldiers who fought for England "till the reduction, when I shared the fate of several unhappy brave fellows, and was sent a begging with a red coat on my back" (9:126).

And yet Fielding's earnings from his plays were not inconsiderable. After *The Lottery* and *The Modern Husband,* another observer commented that "he has made little less than a thousand Pounds, but," he adds, "the poor Author has fall'n into the Jaws of *Rattle-snakes*. His Elbows have destroy'd the Off-spring of his Brain; and in Spight of all his good Sense he has been stript at Play by Sharpers."[130] Like his father before him.[131] His friend Lady Mary recalled after his death that his only rival in prodigality was Richard Steele: "They both agreed in wanting money in spite of all their Freinds [sic], and would have wanted it if their Hereditary Lands had been as extensive as their Imagination."[132]

In the same year as the observation on Fielding's "low condition of purse" the author of *The Candidates for the Bays* noted his addiction to snuff and alcohol as well as an excessive self-confidence in his own abilities:

Bedaub'd o'er with Snuff, and drunk as a drum,
And mad as a *March* Hare Beau F[ielding] does come;
He staggers, and swears he will never submit
To correction of (a) Friends, or the Censure of *Pit*;
He says what is flat shall for ever be so,
Who tells him a Fault he esteems as a Foe . . .
   (a) This Gentleman is so self-conceited that he quarrels with everyone that shews him a Fault.[133]

The Dramatick Sessions: or, The Stage Contest, an anonymous satire of July 1734, which notes his long legs ("With a Stride of three Yards") and his predilection for snuff ("Took a large punch of Snuff"), depicts him as a gambler and whoremaster, adding that he was too free with his language ("and then call'd her a B-tch").[134] Fielding's reputation during his years in the theater, at least among the unsympathetic, was as a *"foul mouth'd Farmer"* whose youth was spent in wrestling, quarrelling, and hard drinking.[135] The stories reveal a sense of status and empowerment combined with an aristocratic, indeed libertine carelessness which included as little concern about repaying debts as about his physical habits and appearance.

But there was worse – the passionate nature described by his friends Harris and, later, Arthur Murphy. The Bennet affair in February 1735, on the streets of Shaftesbury, the largest town near East Stour, just after Fielding's wedding, reveals the same violence that was recorded a decade earlier; the subject now is debt. The violence was apparently done for Fielding by hired bullies – the gentleman's refusal to sully his own hands on an opponent of the lower orders. The episode was repeated in 1736.

The accounts of his gambling led to the opinion of Arthur Murphy and others that Fielding's plays were only a convenient way to make enough money to lose in style.[136] The gentlemanly pose of an Etherege, Wycherley, or Congreve was Fielding's as well. He was a gentleman seeking a livelihood and a place in society outside the army or the clergy. The quickest way to earn money was as a successful playwright, and so initially he wrote plays. But his success and the theatrical system in London of the 1730s – and perhaps his prodigality – led him to write more than the gentlemanly play or two and eventually to take upon himself the profession of manager and entrepreneur as well as writer, which in fact earned him a great deal of money, beyond which he continued to live.

The libertine pose included the incredible facility and speed with which he wrote: As the player says to Scriblerus at the beginning of *The Welsh Opera,* "you write Plays, (or something like Plays) faster than we can act them, or the Town damn them"; and, looking back from *Eurydice Hiss'd,* Fielding recalls what it was like "To write nine Scenes with Spirit in one Day." And there was no denying his success in the theater: One "Scriblerus Scribleri" refers to him ("my very *negligent* friend," one who fails "to revise and correct his said Works") as "Henry Drama, Esq."[137]

An important aspect of the libertine life-style was amorousness. One of the love poems he wrote in these years was on a halfpenny owned by Gloriana, made precious by her touch, redeemed by the poet when she gives it to a beggar. He merges her act of charity and his erotic love: "What, parted with, gives Heav'n to me; / Kept, is but Pain and Grief to thee." This is a seduction song, but the vehicle is monetary exchange, and his poverty is contrasted with her wealth. The poem is on a continuum with his begging poems to Walpole. The *donnée* of these early poems is Fielding's poverty and need, sexual as well as financial. The subjects are love and patronage, sometimes joined; and these lead him into the subject of "greatness," which unifies the epistolary poems and occasionally finds an echo in the love poems. The poems document his loves and display his learning (his Latin imitations, his allusions to Martial and other Roman poets) and do not conceal his roots in libertinism.

However, one thing Fielding was not was an unthinking libertine, an unconsidered rake. In his earliest plays he balanced the aristocratic libertine code embodied in, for example, Valentine, against the essentially Christian code of Veromil, and while Veromil is preferred, Fielding implies a *concordia discors* if not a Horatian middle way. He seems to associate himself with Rochester, who epitomized the deist libertine ethos but was converted on his deathbed, as described by Bishop Burnet (Fielding's favorite English historian), to the Christian religion.

Deism

Valentine's discourse of libertinism is based on the Law of Nature (8:144). Mrs. Softly, we recall, echoes Addison's repudiation of confinement: "The

Mind of Man naturally hates everything that looks like a Restraint upon it . . ."[138] Similarly, the third earl of Shaftesbury's belief that if one tries to confine natural impulses, they will find an outlet elsewhere, his assumption of the precedence of nature over divine providence, will stay with Fielding. For all the lip service paid to divine providence, it is nature (with or without the capital) that can be counted on to right wrongs and to correct evil actions, not the conventional Judeo-Christian god. And Nature was the god of the deists.

It would appear that Fielding had both libertine and, with it, deist leanings in this period, and by balancing libertine against Christian heroes he explored the possibilities of ethical deism.[139] With each play, however, the ethical deist becomes increasingly unsatisfactory, leading down to the villainous Owen Apshinken in *The Welsh [Grub-Street] Opera*.

Fielding seriously considered the matter. Ethical deism was one consequence of the view that God created the world and, having set it going, abandoned it. In Fielding's own disapproving words in *The Champion*, without an immanent God "then Mankind might be left to pursue their Desires, their Appetites, their Lusts, in a full Swing and without Control."[140] Nevertheless, in religious thought his deepest doubts centered, unsurprisingly, on the immanence of the deity, the question of his miraculous intervention in the lives of his offspring (divine providence) – and, as he showed in his rehearsal farces, the question of just where authority lies.

One of the chief sources of the theatrical metaphor, as Addison notes, was religious. He related it in *Spectator* no. 219 to the operation of divine providence on the distribution of rewards and punishments. According to one metaphor, from Scripture, men are "Strangers and Sojourners upon Earth, and Life is a Pilgrimage," but according to the other, Epictetus' metaphor, the world is "a Theatre, where everyone has a Part allotted to him" and is judged by how well he plays his part.[141] The pilgrimage stresses teleology: whether the Christian pilgrimage or the epic journey, whether the travels of Adam or Odysseus or Aeneas, it must have a destination and follow the road or cut across fields. The aspects of providence Addison stressed in the theatrical metaphor were its apparent arbitrariness, inscrutability, and incalculable distance from our everyday concerns.

Because of its pragmatic and provisional quality this was a metaphor appropriated by the deists. "Hesiod" Cooke, for example, opened his deist argument by introducing the metaphor: "I shall look on the whole World as the Scene of Action on which a continual tragic-comedy is represented."[142] The provisional religion acceptable to Shaftesbury (the custom of belief in rewards and punishments) was often represented by him in a theatrical metaphor.

What remains when the deity is gone is the playwright. When, as in *The Author's Farce*, a play has a happy ending, and rewards and punishments are distributed, it is plainly the work of the playwright, who is demonstrating the discrepancy between his and the real world. In Fielding's last, strongly political plays of 1736–7 a prime minister (Walpole), surrogate for an ineffectual king, writes a political farce, manipulates his actors, and deceives his audience; and Fielding, the author of the play, associates himself with the minister as another surrogate and farceur. He explores the discrepancy between what is shown and what is hidden behind the scenes, between actor and role, but also between the playwright's "providence" and the actual performance, marred by "chance" (another crucial Fielding term). The bailiff who intercepts the actor before he can get to the theater, or even the audience that, for extraneous reasons, hisses the play, projects a world without a king, without a god.

It is easy to imagine Fielding confusing his natural father and his Father in heaven; if the one is absent or unwilling to intervene, so probably is the other. It is even easier to imagine him associating his father with popery and priestcraft as usurping and perverting the teachings of Jesus. The basic deist assumption was that Jesus, though not a superhuman agent, was a profound moralist.

But to see deism as simply a version of "God is dead and so everything is permitted," which Fielding repudiated, is to miss the real impact of deist thought on Fielding in the forms of rationalism which contributed to critical deism.[143] As an extension of anti-popery, deists questioned any priestcraft, and as an extension of empiricist reason, they questioned the authority of readings imposed on Scripture by the clergy, the evidence of the Scriptures themselves, and doctrines that flew in the face of reason.[144] While believing in God and his original providential order, deists regarded the Bible and the Church as purely human inventions; while subscribing to Christianity's moral principles, they could not believe they were mysteriously revealed in Scripture. While believing in a transcendent deity, their reason told them that miracles were inventions of an interested priesthood.

The essence of deism for Fielding was not ethical, which he tests and repudiates, but critical. He had a copy of Collins's *Discourse of the Grounds and Reasons* (1724) and Toland's *Christianity Not Mysterious* (1696), two of the foundational tracts of critical deism, in his library, as well as the works of Spinoza, Richard Simon, and Grotius, major influences on the early deist writers.[145] He took from critical deism a reading habit. What deism did for him and many of his contemporaries was to make it impossible to read innocently; if he read a spiritual autobiography he automatically applied reason to the story and asked questions about the authority of the text.

James Harris and other friends

The friendship between Fielding and James Harris dates from "as early as 1733–4 when Fielding was courting Charlotte Cradock, Harris's neighbor in Salisbury Close."[146] Especially significant is the fact that Harris, probably Fielding's closest friend from his Salisbury days onward, was associated with the third earl of Shaftesbury and not only in all probability acted as a conduit of Shaftesburian thought to Fielding, for whom the *Characteristicks* was of the utmost importance, but was himself in his writings a deist in the Shaftesbury mold. His mother, née Lady Elizabeth Ashley, was the younger sister of the third earl, especially close to Shaftesbury's younger brother Maurice, and dedicatee of his translation of the *Cyropoedia* with its strongly deist preface.[147] Harris, though he would have called himself, with Shaftesbury, a "theist," was correctly regarded during his lifetime as a "disciple" and "guardian and interpreter of Shaftesbury's reputation and moral philosophy."[148]

Fielding's deism was of the relatively respectable Shaftesburian sort. Shaftesbury did not demystify the New Testament texts as the more maligned deists Toland and Woolston did; rather, he ignored them, replacing them with classical texts. His ill-fame was due rather to his disparagement of the clergy and the Christian religion as predicated on a bad god and a morality of rewards and punishments in the afterlife. While Shaftesbury condemned such a religion, however, he allowed that it could serve a social function for the lower orders; for the aristocratic elite (the Whig oligarchy that ruled England) he projected another, higher conception of deity based on a mathematical order. We should emphasize the twofold sense of religion in Shaftesbury – the foundation for Fielding's double standard, one for the sophisticated aristocrat and the other for the childlike plebeian; one for himself in good times and the other to fall back upon after suffering repeated losses.

Shaftesbury associated the "divine example," a benevolent deity who can be loved and admired, with the neoplatonic "idea" – disinterested virtue with balance and harmony; even benevolence can become a vice if it is disproportionate with the other affections of the mind.[149] The Shaftesburian divine creation is figured as order (beauty is to deformity as regularity is to irregularity) of both the world and of man's individual mind, which as a religion can improve the already benevolent man. Therefore "God" is the great artist whose chief principle is the revelation of unity in apparent variety (politically, the subordination of the many to the few). And so this balanced system, in its perfection, must serve as a mental substitute for the world as we have it, inevitably marred by contingencies – by social contracts and the doctrines of clergymen (or, worse, atheists) that we are fallen, depraved, and in need of control by a doctrine of rewards and punishments.

In a world that may require, but whose elite at any rate is better off without, a legalistic religion, Shaftesbury believes that a work of art is the only proper substitute for the real world – as aesthetics is for religion. This is one interpretation (among several) of Fielding's way of ending *The Author's Farce*, where the mental construct of "The Pleasures of the Town" is reified.

Fielding employed both of Shaftesbury's senses of religion; especially the latter, as "divine example," in the palladian structure of *Tom Jones* and the role of the human surrogate "artist." He shared with Shaftesbury a strong, particularized distrust of the clergy. The rake Commons plans to become a priest and is having his final fling before taking orders. His friend Rakel asks him if he has "the Impudence to pretend to a Call." Commons: "Ay, Sir; the usual Call: I have the Promise of a good Living." Owen Apshinken's crony is the priest Puzzletext and whenever the reference is political the queen or minister is accompanied by a bad clergyman, as Queen Ignorance is by Firebrand. The anticlericalism, which probably began with the hatred of popery instilled in him as a child, was reinforced by the anticlericalism of the Old Whig satire aimed at Walpole's ministry; the latter may explain why Fielding had to distance his official self from deism in *The Champion*, as he later distanced himself from the opposition itself.

It seems likely that both Harris and Fielding would have come at their benevolist ideas through deist writers rather than latitudinarian Anglican clergymen. There was a significant overlap: The agency of reason was the premise of both Latitude Men within the Church of England and deists without. Shaftesbury, as well as the latitudinarian clergy, believed in conscience, an internal moral light; both justified religion by the standard of pragmatism: religious belief serves to make one happy. The deist, of course, went further, believing in a transcendent god only, the moral teachings of Jesus, their corruption by priestcraft, and religion based on mere custom (as Hume would argue, on belief and faith, not reason). Fielding, like Hume and Gibbon, had the excuse that his deism was only anticlericalism directed against popish superstition. This is not to say that Fielding did not read and enjoy sermons, but it does mean that Battestin's singleminded focus on sermons is in general a poor guide to the understanding of Fielding's theology.[150]

Harris's comment in his biographical sketch on Fielding's experience at freethinking Leiden is followed by a comment on his return to London, where he "conversed not only with persons the first in fashion and quality, but with infinite others of indiscriminate rank and characters, with whom either by chance or choice he was associated." By the latter the fastidious Harris may have meant Fielding's circle of friends in London in the 1720s–1730s, which included such known deists as Thomas Cooke and James Ralph.[151]

Cooke (1703–56) was about Fielding's age, but came of Muggletonian stock, and by 1722 was surviving as a hack writer.[152] He was known as "Hesiod" Cooke because of his best known work, his edition of Hesiod's works (1727/8), to which Hogarth contributed a frontispiece of Hesiod's bust. As a deist, Cooke focuses on the *Theogeny* (in vol. 2) and contributes "A Discourse on the Theology and Mythology of the Antients," that is, on ancient wisdom and the mythology of Nature, all of which he traces back to Egypt (as the Freemasons were doing at the same time).

Cooke's major deist tract, *A Demonstration of the Will of God by the Light of Nature* (a collection of his periodical essays in *The Comedian*, published in 1733), which Battestin sarcastically designates a "noble enterprise" (156), is plainly set forth in the terms of Christianity, with none of Thomas Woolston's satiric thrust or Amhurst's obvious disrespect for the Fathers or the New Testament itself. Cooke urges that instead of the institutional deity of the clergy and the biblical texts man should "cast his Eye into the Book of *Nature*, which the bounteous Hand of *God* has opened to him" (xiii). But Cooke sets out "to prove that God, requires no more of us than *Nature* requires" (5) – thus he critiques the observance of the Sabbath and offers "some Cases in which we ought to break it" (14–17), concluding that one ought "not to offend God hereafter by neglecting to gather in his Harvest on the sabbath day when he cannot on another Day" (17).[153] As in Fielding's works, Cooke's emphasis falls more often on the priest, who masks nature with his doctrine, than on the libertine ethical deist. A characteristic comment is that "the Animositys and Obstinacy of some of the Clergy have, in all Ages, been the greatest Obstacle to the Clemency, Prudence, and good Intentions, of Princes, and Establishment of their Affairs" (17).[154]

James Ralph was another friend. His association with Fielding began in 1728 when Ralph published *The Touch-Stone: or, Historical, Critical, Political, Philosophical, and Theological Essays on the reigning Diversions of the Town* – another attack on the spectrum of popular entertainments, a prose version of Hogarth's *Masquerades and Operas* of 1724 and Pope's *Dunciad* of the same year as Ralph's publication. Among other things, Ralph proposed to correct the "reigning Diversions" by burlesque and ironic praise (anticipating Witmore's advice to Luckless). In particular he recommended drawing upon English folklore, his example being the story of Tom Thumb.[155] In 1730 both Ralph and Fielding wrote plays that followed from the formulae of *The Touch-Stone* with the rehearsal formula of burlesqued farces: On March 30, Fielding produced *The Author's Farce* with "The Pleasures of the Town," and on April 2, Ralph followed with *The Fashionable Lady: or, Harlequin's Opera* (the latter the equivalent of Fielding's "Pleasures") at Goodman's Fields. The relationship with Ralph continued through the 1730s; in 1736 he joined Fielding as his assistant at the Little Haymarket and in 1739 in the writing and editing of *The Champion*.

A reputed deist, Ralph was sufficiently discreet that the evidence is mostly indirect. His deism can be extrapolated from the little pamphlet Benjamin Franklin wrote, *A Dissertation on Liberty and Necessity, Pleasure and Pain*, addressed to Ralph, which argues that without an immanent deity, good and evil are meaningless words, and man can merely obey his reflexes to escape pain and cannot, therefore, be judged, not even by the First

Mover himself. Ralph's poem, *The Tempest* (1727),[156] is equally indirect: he has the antithetical speaker, Lycas, attack those who

> fond of a *New* Belief,
> Distrust the Notion of a future State,
> And tremble to resign their Pleasures here,
> Or sleep for ever in Oblivion's Arms. . . .

On his deathbed Lycas finds himself unable, after all, to take comfort from the conventional religious beliefs. This is probably Ralph's closest approach to a doctrine of ethical deism,[157] but he is more open in his criticisms of the clergy, the area he would have shared with Fielding.

Nicholas Amhurst, "Caleb Danvers" of *The Craftsman*, was also primarily associated with deism through his anticlericalism; he was, indeed, expelled from Oxford for this impiety and wrote several tracts accusing the high church party of popery. He makes a complimentary reference to Fielding in the *Craftsman* for September 19, 1730, most likely an indication that Fielding was close to the Hogarth-Amhurst group, even though he may not have declared himself yet against Walpole; and by the mid-1730s they had become associated on *The Craftsman*.[158]

Hogarth

The most important of these friends, a close associate of Amhurst's as well as Ralph's, was William Hogarth. While Pope and Gay were of the generation of Fielding's father, Hogarth (born 1697) was only a decade older; he had established his engraving business in 1720 and by 1724 was a strikingly original graphic satirist. In a period that (owing much to Newton's *Optics*, Locke's *Essay*, and the *Spectator*) privileged the spectator's eye, Hogarth's combination of the visual and verbal permitted both the most vivid and the most nuanced, even subversive, communication. Fielding's frequent pleas for the pencil of Hogarth to render likeness and character more effectively than words give some idea of his importance to writers.

Fielding, upon his arrival in London in the 1720s, would have experienced Hogarth's early satires at first hand: *Masquerades and Operas* and *A Just View of the British Stage* (1724) showed the "Pleasures of the Town" trashing the works of Shakespeare, Jonson, and Congreve, directly anticipating Pope's *Dunciad* of 1728. By 1726 Hogarth, in league with Amhurst, was issuing anti-Walpole prints – *Cunicularii* and *The Punishment of Lemuel Gulliver*, as well as the *Large Masquerade Ticket* of 1727 (see plate 2), which appears to have inspired Fielding's earliest surviving poem. From the emblematic satire of the early prints Hogarth was in the process of turning to reportorial scenes – of Mary Toft's "miraculous" birth of 17 rabbits and of a Heidegger masquerade, both as if scenes on a stage. (At the same time, with his knack for catching likenesses, he was painting portraits of contemporaries, grouping them together in interiors with their characteristic possessions, furniture, and paintings.)

The metaphor shared by these two satirists, who would shortly become friends, was theatrical. In Fielding's *Masquerade* (1728) "Cardinals, quakers, judges dance; / Grim Turks are coy, and nuns advance . . . / Known prudes there, libertines we find, / Who masque the face, t' unmasque the mind" (ll. 69–74). "Grave churchmen here at hazard play" (l. 71) sounds like a memory of Hogarth's clergymen casting dice for Christ's robe in his *South Sea Scheme* (1724), but the general model for the poem was his *Large Masquerade Ticket*.[159] Fielding has suppressed Hogarth's satire on the coronation of George II, but he follows the central placement of Heidegger's grotesque face, the sequence of masked figures (as in the lines quoted), and even the sign "Supper Below," Hogarth's rude pun which he characteristically softens from fellatio or cunnilingus to "Below stairs hungry whores are picking / The bones of wild-fowl, and of chicken" (ll. 191–2).

Hogarth and Fielding were physically and socially an unlikely pair, one short and terrier-like, the other tall and burly; one from the lower orders, the other from the nobility. They shared their literacy – Fielding's training in the classics at Eton, Hogarth's at the foot of his father, a Latin teacher. Both flaunted their learning. Fielding's writings, heavily dependent on classical allusions and quotations, usually untranslated, required an audience that reached from the most highly educated down to the merely literate who were familiar with general allusions to the classics. Hogarth's graphic images uniquely offered something to all, from the educated down to the barely literate and the illiterate. The difference between a play seen on a stage and a text read in one's closet was a principle that applied equally to the plays of Fielding and the theatrical designs of Hogarth's prints, which (as he made clear in the subscription ticket for the *Harlot*) were intended for both a common audience that would grasp their general import and readers of greater penetration who could lift the "veil of allegory."[160]

The conscious association of the two artists began with Hogarth's frontispiece to *The Tragedy of Tragedies* (see plate 3), published in February 1731, just as he was launching his subscription for *A Harlot's Progress*.[161]

In mid-1730, Hogarth was beginning work on the *Harlot*, his first independent series of prints. Before, he had illustrated satiric texts, in particular the burlesques of Samuel Butler and Charles Gildon.[162] Now in the *Harlot* he used his images to project his own text, six engraved scenes, as if taking place on a stage. He employed the emblems and burlesque forms of his graphic satires, as well as contemporary likenesses of the sort

Plate 2 Hogarth, *Large Masquerade Ticket*, 1727, etching and engraving, courtesy of the Trustees of the British Museum.

he had painted in his conversation pieces. His paintings of Gay's *Beggar's Opera* (1728–9; see plate 4), where the contemporaries were actors playing roles in a play, were the transitional works between the reportorial prints and the *Harlot's Progress*. Indeed, his illustration for Fielding's *Tragedy of Tragedies* reiterates the scene he had illustrated in his paintings of *The Beggar's Opera*: the Macheath-Tom Thumb figure, cross-armed between his two "wives," Polly and Lucy, or Huncamunca and Glumdalca, who in this case tower over him.

Hogarth announces with his subscription for *A Harlot's Progress* that his satires were not equal to the seriousness of history painting, that he is progressing as an artist from his 1720s theatrical burlesques to the "nature" represented in the *Harlot's Progress*. He does so by way of the "heroic muse," celebrated in his subscription ticket by the figures of Nature, putti, and a faun, and by Latin inscriptions from Virgil and Horace. In the same way, in mid-June of 1730, Fielding produced *Rape upon Rape; or, The Justice Caught in his own Trap* and announced *The Modern Husband*

Plate 3 Hogarth, Frontispiece, *The Tragedy of Tragedies: or The Life and Death of Tom Thumb*, 1731, etching, courtesy of the Trustees of the British Museum.

for September (though it was delayed until February 1731/2). In these ambitious five-act comedies he acknowledges that the burlesque *Tom Thumb* was a lesser work than a "regular comedy" and announces *his* new genre, "heroic" comedy.

Both artists are attempting a new, serious art form based on but transcending farce. In the prologue to *Rape upon Rape* Fielding says that his subject is now Vice, which "hath grown too great to be abus'd" and requires "the Heroick muse who sings To-night, / Through these neglected Tracks attempts her Flight," and "combats with her Pen" a Vice that is "cloath'd with Pow'r." The central image of evil in the play is rape by the very magistrates who should be administering justice. Vice "cloath'd with Pow'r" directly connects Fielding's "heroic" comedy and Hogarth's *Harlot.*[163] Magistrates not only believe that "It is better for the public that ten innocent people should suffer, than that one guilty should escape," they commit the very crimes for which they punish the innocent (9:99).

Rape upon Rape alludes to the notorious Charteris case on which Hogarth based his first plate of the *Harlot.* Charteris, a Walpole supporter, had been pardoned after being capitally convicted of raping a servant girl, hired, as

Plate 4 Hogarth, *The Beggar's Opera*, 1729, painting, London, Tate Gallery.

the Harlot is, upon arrival in London from the country. Fielding alludes to Charteris's pardon for his rape conviction (9:146), which is an essential element of the contrast between the successful "great" and the unsuccessful *imitation* of "greatness." He underlines Charteris's association with Walpole by including among the Harlot's exploiters a clergyman who, instead of protecting her, is seeking preferment from the bishop of London and the magistrate Sir John Gonson, both associates of (and therefore surrogates for) Walpole. By attacking Walpole's supporters, Hogarth plainly implicates their master.[164]

Fielding's heroes, while victims of the ruling order, are all gentlemen and ladies (Hillaret only has to be proved the daughter of Politic to be freed from Justice Squeezum's court). Hogarth singles out a déclassé figure, a girl from the country who in London quickly descends into prostitution. The characters who exploit and destroy her (in this case successfully) are magistrates, prison warders, priests, physicians, close to the characters in *Rape upon Rape*. But the Harlot is quite outside the social order, and Hogarth avoids the happy, traditionally comic ending of *The Author's Farce*, as well as the mock-tragic ending of *The Tragedy of Tragedies*.

The salient features of the *Harlot's Progress* are (1) its theatrical, stage-like quality. Fielding described the effect a few years later in a *Champion* essay on Hogarth, "one of the most useful Satyrists any Age hath produced": "In his excellent Works you see the delusive Scene exposed with all the Force of Humour, and, on casting your Eyes on another Picture, you behold the dreadful and fatal Consequence."[165] The delusive scene describes his own procedure; but the second picture shows how different is Hogarth's final effect, which is uncompromisingly satiric (or, a contemporary might even have thought, tragic); the "comedy" of Hogarth's scenes lies rather in the witty comparisons and contrasts with which he reveals plot and character – the reading structure of the print.

The backstage view of *Strolling Actresses* (1738, see plate 5), actresses half in and half out of costumes surrounded by stage props, conveys precisely the effect of Fielding's rehearsal plays.[166] And *The Laughing Audience* (1733, see plate 6) expresses the segmented response of the audience, which Fielding put into words in his epilogue to *The Author's Farce*.

> The audience is already
> Divided into critic, beau, and lady;
> Nor box, nor pit, nor gallery can show
> One who's not lady, critic, nor beau.
> (ll. 18–21)

Fielding constantly gives us the playwright viewing and classifying the audience. It is easy to see why he will later invoke David Garrick (most notably in *Tom Jones*) as he does Hogarth, both "my friends," creating a sort of Fielding-Hogarth-Garrick trinity based on their rendering of character in a specifically theatrical way. He carried the model of the actor, the playwright, and the farce with him throughout the rest of his life.

(2) Anticlericalism. The priest in plate 1 of *A Harlot's Progress* should be protecting the young girl, M. Hackabout, from the bawd and Col. Charteris but is prudently studying the address of Edmund Gibson, bishop of London. In Plate 6 the priest, instead of officiating at the Harlot's wake, is groping under the skirts of the nearest whore, and in the picture on the wall of Plate 2 a bishop is stabbing Uzzah in the back for having saved the Ark of the Covenant from falling.

(3) The denial of an immanent god. In effect, the bishop has taken the place of the deity who, in the Old Testament story, strikes Uzzah dead. In every representation of a religious painting in his prints Hogarth removes the figure of God. His deletion of the deity could be related to the strong strain of iconoclasm in English Protestantism, but the *Deus absconditus* of the deists seems more consonant with Hogarth's intentions.[167] In social

Plate 5   Hogarth, *Strolling Actresses Dressing in a Barn,* 1738, etching and engraving, courtesy of the Trustees of the British Museum.

Plate 6 Hogarth, *The Laughing Audience*, 1733, etching, courtesy of the Trustees of the British Museum.

terms, what he portrays is not the Protestant's iconoclasm but God's withdrawal from man. God's role has been usurped by the ruling order, representatives (in successive plates of the *Harlot*) of the church, law, and medicine. The priesthood has, as the deists claimed, appropriated the role of God and metes out his religion of rewards and punishments.

The denial of an immanent god would have been taken as a shocking sign of deism, which Hogarth softens by shifting the emphasis onto the usurpation of the deity's function in the bishop and the other ministerial associates. Society's police are always present, whereas a benevolent god and social and civil mercy are absent.

(4) More shocking than the deletion of the deity is the fact that each plate of the *Harlot* burlesques the story of the Life of the Virgin and Christ's Passion, reducing them to the story of the decline and death of a harlot. Hogarth's plate 1 is a parody Visitation, plate 3 an Annunciation (see plates 7 and 8), 4 a Flagellation, 5 "soldiers" casting dice for Christ's robe *and* a mourning Virgin at the foot of the cross, and 6 a Last Supper with the dead Harlot in the place of the Host – the Body, with the Blood in the chalice nearby plainly a parody Eucharist.[168] But then Hogarth replaces the New Testament figures of Mary, Elizabeth, and Zacharias with recognizable living Londoners (Kate Hackabout, Elizabeth Needham, Francis Charteris) – the sort of contemporary portraits he used in his conversation pieces.

Plate 7   Hogarth, *A Harlot's Progress*, Plate 3, 1732, etching and engraving, courtesy of the Trustees of the British Museum.

Hogarth takes his model from the deist Thomas Woolston, a follower of Toland and Collins whose *Discourses on the Miracles of Our Saviour* (1727–30) had shocked respectable Londoners. Woolston's procedure was to test Jesus' miracles (i.e., the evidence of divine revelation) against historical fact and probability, demonstrating that he did not perform miracles; rather that his actions must be taken as allegories, and invariably allegories about not Jesus' divinity but the opposing corruption of the clergy who out of self-interest censure his (not miracles but) good works.[169] Woolston's portrait is on the wall in some versions of plate 2.[170] Woolston's reading of the miracle of the Virgin Birth was that Mary must have cuckolded Joseph; which Hogarth echoes in the Harlot's cuckolding of the Jew in plate 2.[171]

But if, in plate 1, the Harlot, bawd, and Charteris burlesque a Visitation, there is a second gestalt: The priest, Harlot, and bawd burlesque Virtue, Hercules, and Pleasure, the model for history-painting in Shaftesbury's *Tablature of the Judgment of Hercules* (1713), which recommended to the painter as his most promising subject matter the classical Choice of

Plate 8 Albrecht Dürer, *The Annunciation* (detail) woodcut, from *The Life of the Virgin* (1511).

Hercules, embodiment of civic-humanist "heroic virtue" (Shaftesbury was a deist who substituted Plato for Jesus). By substituting for Virtue, Hercules, and Pleasure, a self-centered clergyman, a young girl soon to be seduced into prostitution, and a bawd, Hogarth deflates the Choice of Hercules (a topos Gay used in the same way in *The Beggar's Opera* and Hogarth included in his paintings of the scene). Primarily he substitutes a young woman – a protagonist neither heroic nor male – for Hercules. He makes a woman the center of his story and, furthermore, substitutes for Shaftesbury's classical the Christian gestalt and its demystification in contemporary Londoners.

The emblems of the early prints he displaces from the characters to the paintings they hang on their walls and the poses of the characters who emulate them. This acts as a naturalization of the mock heroic irony of the Augustan satirists: the Harlot *thinks* she is the Virgin Mary and strikes that pose; her Jewish keeper thinks he is Jonah cursing Nineveh in the painting above his head (though in fact, he is revealed to be the cuckolded Joseph). This produces, among other things, a more "realistic" mode that replaces the old allegorical one. But also, in deist terms, the Harlot, M[ary?] Hackabout, is the human, everyday (in Addison's term, new or novel) reality of the so-called Incarnation, whether of the Church or the Renaissance artist, a Raphael or Michelangelo. If the deist *deus absconditus* leaves only people playing roles on a stage, the contemporary Incarnation is imagined as the actor assuming roles: essentially Hogarth's notion of character and, as we have seen, to a large extent Fielding's.

Some idea of the parallel between Hogarth's graphic scenes and Fielding's stage can be inferred from Aaron Hill's description of a performance of *Pasquin:*

> The ingenious Author of *Pasquin,* conscious how dangerous it might be, to venture *Common Sense* in the Stile of *Corregio* at first, has, in Imitation of some of the best of Painters, form'd to himself a Manner, out of different Stiles, which (tho' the Particulars may be traced) is, in the whole, *Original.* Thus in the Tragedy we see the bold, daring Pencil of *Michael Angelo.*[172]

I take this to mean that the lines were spoken and the figures gestured in an actorly equivalent of Michelangelo's *terribilitas:* "Even when they [the actors] *smile,* they look *terrible,* and *strike* with *Force.*" "He has here and there," Hill continues, "given them a *Flemish* Touch, for the sake of the *Vulgar*"; Hill would prefer a bit more of the sentimental Correggio manner. Hill may be putting into words the effect an educated viewer would have felt looking at Hogarth's *Harlot's Progress* with its mixture of sublime religious compositions and Flemish detail; he also suggests that Fielding followed a similar procedure. Fielding may have imitated Hogarth or both may have imitated Gay's *Beggar's Opera,* in which a character's pose evoked a Choice of Hercules or even, perhaps, a Last Supper.[173]

Looked at from the direction of the basic metaphor of the stage, Hogarth has based his "modern moral subjects" (as he called them) on role-playing. Looked at from the direction of an English painter attempting the highest painterly genre, history-painting, he has modernized the old religious subjects and, while retaining the signs of the old stories and compositions, replaced the miracle (or the heroic virtue) with a living woman. Seen in one way this is blasphemy, in another it is the humanizing of an idol, making it viable for contemporaries. And this will be the basis for Fielding's creation of character in his novels.

Blasphemy

It is unlikely that Fielding would not have understood Hogarth's New Testament burlesque. But what Hogarth carried off in the visual medium, as Woolston's conviction for blasphemy showed, was far more dangerous in the verbal. He demonstrates that images are more indeterminate than words, in shrewd hands an invitation to subversion, a fact that he exploits outrageously and successfully.

Fielding responded on June 2, 1732, less than a month after *A Harlot's Progress* was delivered to its subscribers, with *The Old Debauchees* and *The Covent-Garden Tragedy*.[174] They were presented as a pair, one "a farce" and the other "a Tragedy." Throughout the *Tragedy*, a burlesque taking place in a brothel run by Mother Punchbowl (Hogarth's Mother Needham), Fielding demonstrates the impact and the popularity of Hogarth's prints.[175] The harlot Stormandra sums up plate 1 when she cries, "dost think I came last week to town, / The waggon straws yet hanging to my tail?" And Love-girlo recalls plate 2:

> I'll take thee into keeping, take the room
> So large, so furnish'd, in so fine a street,
> The mistress of a Jew shall envy thee;
> By Jove, I'll force the sooty tribe to own
> A Christian keeps a whore as well as they.
> (10:120)

Kissinda is connected with the Harlot and her Jewish keeper, and much is made of whores being beaten in Bridewell (122, 128). Stormandra alludes to the Harlot and the watch she has filched (plate 3, fig. 7) when she reminds Bilkum of all she has done for him: "Did I not pick a pocket of a watch, / A pocket pick for thee?" And plate 4 is evoked when Mother Punchbowl observes that "The very hemp I beat may hang my son" (with whom the Harlot is pregnant in Bridewell). Even the Harlot's funeral is in the air when news is brought in of Stormandra's "Death": "Stormandra's gone! / Weep all ye sister-harlots of the town . . ." (122, 128).[176]

The plot, a parody of a heroic play, owes nothing to Hogarth: as usual, the hero Lovegirlo is loved by both Kissinda and Stormandra, the latter of whom is also desired by Capt. Bilkum. But the fragility of the characters, central to Hogarth's message, is endowed with pathos, as when Gallono threatens Mother Punchbowl: "Ill give a crown / To some poor justice to commit thee thither / Where I will come and see thee flogged myself" (131) – as had been the fate of Mother Needham, Punchbowl's prototype, earlier in the year.[177] These characters, like Hogarth's, are always in the shadow of the pillory, the prison, or the gallows, and their end is always contrasted to "the fate of greater persons."[178]

The Covent-Garden Tragedy was a failure, probably due to its unseemly brothel setting.[179] Although the subject of the *Harlot* is a whore, the variety of interiors Hogarth represented does not include one. Hackabout maintains her pseudo-aristocratic affectation by her independence. Calling himself "Philalethes," Fielding responded to his critics with John Dennis's defense of Etherege and Wycherley against the attacks of Jeremy Collier: "for why should any Person of Modesty be offended at seeing a Set of *Rakes* and *Whores* exposed and set in the most *ridiculous Light?*"[180]

But Fielding has also begun to touch gingerly upon Hogarth's scandalous materials. In *The Old Debauchees*, the mainpiece, a bad priest, Father Martin, poses as a heavenly spirit in order to enjoy the beautiful Isabel; he promises her that "Great things are design'd for you, very great things are designed for you . . . such Promotion, such Happiness as will attend you" – to which she replies with her own fiction: "I dreamt I was brought to bed of the Pope" (9:300). All of this is presented as an anti-papist satire, based on the story of Catherine Cadière and Father Girard, safely distanced to France. Isabel: "for none but the Church can contradict our Senses"; Old Laroon: "Nothing's impossible to the Church you know"; and Father Martin himself: "You are to believe what the Church tells you, and no more" (306–15). But the satire on priestcraft extends far enough to follow Hogarth and Woolston into the realm of miracles and the hint of a Virgin Birth.

"Miso-Cleros" (Richard Russel) in *The Grub-Street Journal* recognized the attack on the popish clergy as an attack on "priests and priestcraft in general": "since he makes so free with the Bible, no wonder if the Priests are splashed with his mud."[181] But Russel, a non-juror, made the mistake of referring to slighting remarks about purgatory in Scripture, and Fielding (writing as "Philalethes") riposted that, of course, Purgatory only exists for papists: No one "*but a Nonjuring Parson, would be asham'd* to represent a Ridicule on Purgatory as a Ridicule on the Bible, or the Abuse of *Bigotted Fools* and *Roguish Jesuits* as an Abuse on Religion and the English Clergy."[182]

In the context of the mainpiece, the afterpiece, *The Covent-Garden Tragedy*, offers a suspicious play on "Mother," in the *Prolegomenon* as well as the play proper, as bawd and as nurturing mother to her "sons" and "daughters." Mother Punchbowl is Fielding's burlesque of Andromache, the mother in Ambrose Philips's *The Distrest Mother* (1712), but she inevitably invokes Hogarth's Mother Needham, the *magna mater of* deist Nature in *Boys Peeping at Nature*, and therefore, in some sense, the parody of M[ary]. Hackabout, the "mother" in Hogarth's six plates.[183] The denouement is Bilkum's death in a duel and Stormandra's suicide, followed by what, in Woolston's terms, would have been a Resurrection, though in Fielding's a stage convention.[184] Characteristically, Fielding, tricking and trapping the priest, having him doused and tossed in a blanket, writes comedy; whereas in the *Harlot* priestcraft (statesmen, lawyers, doctors) destroys the girl.

Demystification of the sort practiced in *A Harlot's Progress* returns in Fielding's final stage farces of 1736–7. The question, by this time, is where among the overdetermined sources for these plays does Woolston's critique of Christ's miracles fit? The resemblance between Lucian's heterodoxy and Woolston's deism would have been obvious to Fielding. Both brought common sense (that is contemporary, domestic, new) reality to bear on false prophets: for Lucian most notably in the story of Peregrine, for Woolston in the story of Jesus. Although Fielding travesties only the safe classical myths of Lucian, neither Old nor New Testament stories,[185] he does share with Woolston the subject of bad critics and exegetes, often associated with clergymen (Puzzletext or Tickletext). In the second part of *Pasquin* he associates priestcraft with the stories priests tell (the miracles they claim) and tests Ignorance's "miracles" (nonsense) by Common Sense. This is a soft version of what Hogarth does more radically in images.

In his final seasons at the Little Haymarket, Fielding's increasing daring reached to the religious innuendo we have noticed, and this included flouting the prohibition against performing plays. Critics accused his company of "a want of common decency" for failing to "pay a due Observance to the *Wednesdays* and *Fridays* in *Lent*": "these Heathens had no respect to these Days, but play'd on, and would continue so to do (even in the *Passion* Week) had not they been expressly forbid by the Lord *Chamberlain*."[186] True, Fielding kept *Pasquin* running straight into Passion Week, and the riot at the Little Theatre at the opening of *A Rehearsal of Kings* (Feb. 1736/7) could have been due to its politics (which had worried Aaron Hill) or, as Battestin suggests, because "Fielding had once again flouted convention by scheduling the performance for a Wednesday in the Lenton Season," which led to the Lord Chamberlain's prohibition of all four theaters from doing so.[187] (We recall Cooke's critique of the observance of the Sabbath and his suggestion of "some Cases in which we ought to break it.")

The attacks on irreverence (ridicule) of church *and* state recall the element of critical deism that led to Woolston's conviction. "Ridicule" was sufficiently transgressive to bring down the government on Fielding's head, close his theater and many other theaters.[188] Corbyn Morris, a Walpole supporter, a few years later pointed out the special danger of theater, greater than any other medium. Hogarth's *Harlot* displayed Walpole surrogates and got away with it; it questioned the efficacy of the Church and got away with it; which may have contributed to Fielding's ever more daring experiments on the stage in the years following. But Hogarth's theatrical scenes, Morris would have pointed out, lack the immediacy of a theatrical experience – the interplay of the actors on the stage and the audience as both live individuals and as volatile mob.[189]

Hogarth's deism was iconoclastic; Fielding's, after some testing of the water in his comedies, was social and pragmatic. The immanence of the deity and the immortality of the soul were problems that worried him and that he never resolved; he brought them to an arbitrary conclusion in his practical legal writings of the 1750s, but this was by way of the assumptions of the deist Shaftesbury rather than any latitudinarian divine.

Polly, M[ary?], Kitty, and Charlotte

Fielding's *The Lottery*, first performed in January 1731/2, was immediately inspired by the State Lottery of 1731, the drawings for which lasted from October through November, and may, given Fielding's references to lotteries thereafter, have had a personal dimension.[190] Fortune was a female figure he continually invokes and tries to find ways to control (not surprisingly given the stories of his gambling losses). In his early print, *The Lottery* (1724, see plate 9), Hogarth had exploited the fact that the emblem of Fortune's wheel in the Renaissance iconologias (ever turning, raising to the top those soon to be cast to the bottom) was replicated in the lottery wheels, which actually operated on a stage. Hogarth filled the scene with emblematic figures, but they could as well be actors and actresses in emblematic rotes.

The aspect of Hogarth's *Harlot* that Fielding picks up is Hackabout's aspiration to be a fashionable lady, which leads to her disaster. She takes a lover behind the back of her keeper, affects fashionable dresses, which she is mocked for wearing in prison, and even hangs pictures on her wall as her Jewish keeper (a more successful example of upward aspiration) collects old master paintings. The "aping" of both Hackabout and her keeper is emphasized by the emblematic figures of monkey, mirror, and mask.

In Fielding's play Chloe, though she has not in fact fallen in with Charteris and Needham, is as deluded by the lottery as Hackabout is by the idea of being a London lady: "People of quality have indeed privileges, they say, beyond other people; and I long to be one of them" (285); and she surrounds herself with "milliners, mantua-makers, dancing-masters, fiddlers, and the devil knows what" (as, in fact, Hogarth's next hero, Tom Rakewell, will do in *A Rake's Progress*). "An't I strangely altered in one week, Jenny? Don't I begin to look as if I was born and bred in London?" could have been spoken by Hackabout (and Lovemore intends to fill the role of the "gallant" required by a "lady") in plate 2.[191] But Chloe claims to have £10,000 – she means a lottery ticket by which she hopes to win that amount; and so she attracts Tom Stocks, who poses as a lord, proposes marriage ("O how charming my life will be / When marriage has made me a fine lady!"), and they gull each other, ending in the scene of the lottery that would have recalled Hogarth's print. Fielding has rewritten Hogarth's *Harlot* as, to quote his subtitle, "A Farce," whose plot is allegorized by the lottery into the message that "the world's a lottery" (8:296), and given it a happy ending.[192]

In the first play of *Pasquin*, the comedy, the character's obsession (previously with "honor" or "greatness") is now focused, as it was with Chloe in *The Lottery*, on fasion or what he will later call "affectation." Ready to set out for London, the mayor's wife is asked by her daughter:

Plate 9 Hogarth, *The Lottery*, 1724, etching and engraving, courtesy of the Trustees of the British Museum.

"But must I go into keeping, mamma?"
"Child, you must do what's in fashion."
"But I have heard that's a naughty thing."
"That can't be, if your betters do it; people are punished for doing naughty
    things; but people of quality are never punished; therefore they never do
    naughty things." (2.1; 11:181)

These same words could have been spoken in *Harlot* plate 1 by Mother
Needham to young Hackabout. There are two parties to the same obsession, teacher and student. Though greatness was Fielding's primary theme
in the 1730s, in *Pasquin* it becomes the *imitation* of greatness, which was
Gay's version of the subject in *The Beggar's Opera* and Hogarth's chief subject
in both his *Harlot* and *Rake*.[193]

And it is embodied in a woman. In *The Lottery* Fielding first began to use
the central figure not of a villainous Squeezum or Modern but a young
woman, and the resemblance in that play between Chloe and M. Hackabout suggests that Hogarth's *Harlot* was a part of his model. Shamela
would be a completely realized character.

The Intriguing Chambermaid of 1734, originally an afterpiece for a revival
of *The Author's Farce*, is about another rake, the prodigal Valentine vis-à-vis
his father – a striking parallel to Tom Rakewell and his father in the sequel
to the *Harlot* that Hogarth was announcing at this time, *A Rake's Progress*;
but, of course, with a happy ending and a single female object, perhaps
significantly named Charlotte. (Fielding was courting Charlotte Cradock,
soon to be his wife.) Nevertheless, the figure of the chambermaid Lettice,
played by Kitty Clive, is the agent of the play's action; she also delivers the
epilogue, and the play is dedicated to her. She is, in fact, the first of Fielding's strong young women. Although she coincides with Hogarth's more
lugubrious Sarah Young (Rakewell's guardian angel, endeavoring to
mediate between him and the harsh world), she derives from the crafty
servant of the Plautine tradition. It may be no coincidence that following
this comedy Hogarth begins to present his own young mediating woman
in a comic context – a poet's wife, a musician's "muse," and ultimately his
own Comic Muse.

In *Miss Lucy in Town* (probably begun in 1735, not produced until 1742)
Fielding once again rewrites the plot of Hogarth's *Harlot*, now marrying
her. Lucy's single object (like Chloe's in *The Lottery* and Moll Hackabout's)
is to be a "fine lady." Like Hackabout, she is "a girl just arrived out of the
country" wishing to learn "all that a fine lady ought to be" (12:43, 37). She
unwittingly takes lodging in Mrs. Midnight's brothel, saying she is "lucky
to meet with this civil gentlewoman and this fine lady, to teach me how to
dress and behave myself" (48). She attends masquerades and is bought by
both Lord Bawble and the Jewish lecher Mr. Zorobabel; the latter, recalling the Jew of *Harlot* plate 2, tells her he will "make you the first of ladies"

and "furnish a house for you in any part of the town" (48). She is instructed that "a fine lady may kiss any man but her husband" – that is, like Hackabout in plate 2, she takes a beau (40). Lucy is totally won over to London fashion; but she has arrived accompanied by a husband *and* a father (the Harlot was not even met by her London cousin) and is capable of being returned safely to the country whence she came. This is another correction of the Harlot's story, the supplying of a happy ending.

In the theater of the 1700s women had come to the fore, partly as a result of Collier's attack on the comedy of libertine rakes, partly because of the presence of such brilliant actresses as Elizabeth Barry and Ann Bracegirdle – and so not only a Millamant in comedy but a Monimia, Ann Bullen, Calista, and Jane Shore in tragedy. In his theater Fielding had a remarkable group of actresses to work with and wrote brilliant female roles. For Kitty Clive he created hoydenish roles such as Miss Lucy, characters roughly on the model of Wycherley's Marjorie Pynchwife, country-bred but shrewd, simple but naturally virtuous; Gay's Polly Peachum was not far away.

There was no female equivalent to Walpole, the Great Man; unless perhaps Queen Caroline (d. 1737), a woman who dominated her husband, affected learning, and had strong (somewhat suspect) opinions on religion. She appears in person in *The Welsh [Grub-Street] Opera*, and there and elsewhere Fielding inveighs against "petticoat government."[194] Increasingly he turns his wit against "learned ladies." In his personal life, however, he had been close to Lady Mary Wortley Montagu, his cousin, a genuinely learned and witty woman, and a mover and shaker among men. She may have left traces on the women of Fielding's comedies (particularly Lady Matchless), but so far as I can see none on his fiction.

Femininity began as a corrective to male greatness, Fielding's chief topos in the 1730s; Gay's Polly vis-à-vis her father and Macheath made this point, and Hogarth had carried Polly's vulnerability to its logical conclusion in *Harlot* 1 when he replaced the figure of Macheath-Hercules (in a "Choice of Hercules") with a young woman whose choices are radically limited in a London of rakes, self-centered clergy, prostitute-chasing magistrates, and quack doctors. The Harlot, a female and vulnerable Polly Peachum in a satire that attacked the men who destroyed her, had been transformed by Hogarth in the late 1730s into a more positive figure who mediated between extremes of art and nature, as in *The Distrest Poet* and *The Enraged Musician*.[195]

If Fielding got something of the centrality of the heroine from Hogarth's prints, the turning of his attention from the rake to the young woman also corresponded to his interest in Kitty Clive in the theater and, in life, Charlotte Cradock.

Charlotte began as the object of the rake's attention. Fielding, who seldom wrote letters, claimed to Harris that he had written many love letters: "I solemnly declare, I can never give Man or Woman with whom I have no Business (which the Satisfaction of Lust may well be called) a more certain Token of a violent affection than by writing to them" (Sept. 8, 1741, *Corresp.*, 11). None, however, have survived; only the poetic epistles.

Many of the amorous poems, datable between the late 1720s and Fielding's marriage in 1734, are addressed to Charlotte aka Celia. These are conventional libertine lyrics treated wittily but with little distancing. One turns the "imperfect enjoyment" poem on its head: The poet is at a loss for words but demonstrates his love for Celia by his erection: "You need not tell; / Oh! Strephon, oh! I feel how well." But this poem will also prove paradigmatic for Fielding: it falls into the pattern of actions as a better gauge than words, or nature revealing the truth, or if words fail nature will find an outlet. Another poem wittily explains his hatred of mankind (which echoes Rochester's *Satyr against Mankind*) because all his love is possessed by Celia, leaving everyone else therefore the object of his hatred.

With the Celia poems comes the particularity of the Salisbury setting, the nymphs of New Sarum contrasted with Celia. The wittiest is the Lilliputian fancy (with the line, "Now on the rosy bud I'd rest, / Which borrows sweetness from thy breast"). "Celia," to judge by the poetic rebus ("Char," "a very good Fish,"; "lot," a way of Selling"; and "te," for "tea," a "very bad thing," presumably because Fielding prefers stronger drinks), is Charlotte Cradock. But Battestin thinks such "unabashedly erotic poems" as "An Epigram" and "The Question," also to Celia, could not have been addressed to Charlotte, especially when Fielding published them in the *Miscellanies*; so Celia must have been "his name for any number of young women he was enamored of" (96). But Charlotte was still alive in 1743 when the *Miscellanies* were published; and if she knew she was Celia, how would she react to other Celias who obviously were not? While "The Epigram" is innocent, "The Question" might have raised a blush to a virgin's cheek. But Fielding has Joseph Andrews sing a song similar to "The Question" thinking of Fanny, though they are both virgins; in *Tom Jones* and the erotic works leading up to it he goes to great lengths to show that "love" includes physical hunger.

He vacillated between the two Cradock sisters, Charlotte and Kitty; and in the summer of 1732 he appears to have fallen in love with a "Miss D. W." whom he called "Dorinda," eclipsing "Celia." He writes, and furthermore publishes in his friend Cooke's *Comedian*, in what Battestin describes as "an uncharacteristically maudlin vein that suggests how much in love he was,"

> And far, alas! by cruel Fate remov'd,
> (Too lovely Nymph! and O! too much belov'd!)
> Here, in the slightest Sketch, I fondly trace
> All the dear Sweetness of *Dorinda*'s Face:
> Tho Parents, Fortune, and tho she, conspire
> To keep far from me all my Soul's Desire,
> Still shall my ravish'd Eyes their Darling see,
> If not so beauteous, look more kind thro thee.[196]

He is writing "to Mr. [John] Ellys the Painter," his friend and collaborator at Drury Lane (and a colleague of Hogarth's), who began but never finished a portrait of Miss D. W.; he apparently alludes to her withdrawal by parents or by her own whim. (This is a poem in which he also praises such public figures as Hoadly and Walpole [without irony: "how wise, humane, and great"], whom he was courting at the time.) In 1733 he was back in pursuit of Charlotte, who combined beauty and an "accomplish'd Mind" nicely complemented by a dowry of £1,500; and in November of 1734 they were married. Miss D. W., however, might not augur well for a monogamous marriage. With Fielding's marriage to Charlotte in 1734 he begins to put his libertine phase in question, but he never becomes a platonic lover.

3

Hackney Writer and Barrister, 1737–1741

CHRONOLOGY

1737 June 21. Licensing Act passed.

Sept. 1. HF and Amhurst seen in converse as they stroll about Spring Garden (an area within the Verge of the Court, safe from duns).[1] HF is writing sporadically for Amhurst's *Craftsman*.

Nov. 1. Admitted as a "special" student to the Society of the Middle Temple (his address still East Stour).[2]

1738 Mar. Is ordering law books from John Nourse, bookseller.[3]

Aug. HF's uncle, Lt.-Col. George Fielding, dies leaving generous legacies to HF and Charlotte; but the will is contested by his widow and the case is not settled until June 1749.[4]

1739 May 14. The sale by himself and his siblings being formally completed (six shares of £250 each), HF takes leave of the farm at East Stour.[5] It seems likely that Peter Walter, the usurer and estate steward HF satirizes in *Joseph Andrews* and elsewhere, is involved in this transaction, perhaps in lending HF money at an extravagant rate.[6]

June. Borrows more money while promisory notes come due (both notes signed over to third parties to whom he already owes money).[7] Rest of the summer probably spent in Bath.[8]

July. Edmund Fielding promoted to lieutenant general.

Aug. HF and his family take up residence in Essex St., near the Middle Temple where he is studying law.[9]

Nov. 15. Launches *The Champion; Or, British Mercury. By the celebrated Capt. Hercules Vinegar, of Hockley in the Hole*, of which he is two-sixteenths proprietor; writes lead essays, assisted by James Ralph.[10]

Nov. Brings a suit against the toyman and pawnbroker William Deards in King's Bench, apparently to avoid repaying another loan.[11]

Dec. 11. Responding to criticisms, Vinegar moves from Hockley in the Hole to the more genteel Pall Mall (noted on the masthead). The next week he announces that the journal will now deal "in serious Politics."

1740 Feb. Cold London winter, with hardship for the Fieldings; HF is in debt to, among others, one Robert Henley of Milford Lane (near Essex St.), a coal merchant, for £20, which he has not paid by year's end. 6th, daughter Penelope buried (no record of her birth).[12]

Mar. He owes John Nourse, the bookseller, £45 for books, mainly law, and agrees to translate for him Gustave Adlerfeld's *Histoire militaire de Charles XII, roi de Suède* (Amsterdam, 1739), perhaps assisted by others, e.g., his friend the Rev. William Young, who has left the free School at Gillingham and settled in London.[13] In the same month he is sued for failure to repay a debt from 1739; between 1740 and 1742 he is successfully sued for three promisory notes to the value of £78.[14]

Apr. 7. Cibber's *Apology* published; satirized by HF in the *Champion* (Apr. 15, May 3).

10. With no. 64 the paper's title is changed to *The Champion; Or, Evening Advertiser*, its format from two to four pages: to keep the evening papers from stealing the *Champion*'s morning news and to allow more space for advertising.[15]

June. The *Daily Gazetteer* responds to the political content of *The Champion* with attacks.

20. Called to the Bar at the Middle Temple after only two and a half years, with the assistance of his uncle, Davidge Gould, a Master of the Bench at the Temple; pays £48.4s.10d. "Duties" and a "Fyne" of £2 on admission to chambers.[16] His writings for the *Champion* sharply decrease. His half-brother John (who will assist him in Bow Street and the Register Office) is blinded as the result of a three-month "cure" by the bungling of a surgeon, James Wilkie.[17]

July 15. HF is in Winchester, riding the Western Circuit.[18] While away, *The Champion* publishes his *Job Vinegar* papers.

Oct. 10. His translation of *Charles XII* published; it had been optimistically advertised as "Speedily" to be published Dec. 1739.[19]

Nov. 1. Beginning on this day, HF publishes a series of *Champion* papers, *An Address to the Electors of Great Britain* (his last contribution), reprinted in Edinburgh.

6. Richardson's *Pamela; or, Virtue Rewarded* published.

11. General Fielding unsuccessfully applies for the vacant governorship of Jersey (he has been acting governor), partly, he says, in order to "lay the foundation of a secure provision for my 4 daughters."[20] In fact, Sarah and her sisters remain spinsters, presumably not provided by Edmund with enough money to attract husbands from their own class. Edmund, having returned to England from Jersey (where he was safe from creditors), is arrested and committed to the Fleet Prison for an outstanding debt of over £2,000; remains, unable to pay, within the Rules of the prison until his death in June 1741.[21]

24. Judgment found against HF for the money he owes Henley the coal merchant; which he delays for a few more months by filing a Writ of Error. On Dec. 1 another creditor, Hugh Allen, demands payment for £200, and in Jan. takes him to court.[22]

Between June 1740 and Jan. 1741, HF presumably drafts *Journey from This World to the Next* and *Jonathan Wild.*

1741 Jan. 1. Undertakes *A History of Our Own Times* (semi-monthly magazine), in collaboration with Young.

7. *Of True Greatness. An Epistle to The Right Honourable George Dodington, Esq; by Henry Fielding, Esq.*, publ. by Charles Corbett (*DA*).

22. *ΤΗΣ ΟΜΗΡΟΥ VEPNON-IAΔOΣ, ΡΑ ΨΩΙΔΙΑ ἢ ΓΡΑΜΜΑ Α′ The Vernon-iad. Done into English, from the orignal Greek of Homer. Lately found at Constantinople. With Notes in usum, Ec. Book the First*, publ. Corbett (*DA*), a mock epic (both poems attack Walpole, contributing to a concerted effort to unseat him).

Feb. 13. Walpole survives the motion to remove him, scattering his opponents in disarray.

14. Second edition of *Pamela*, with puffs; 3rd edn., Mar. 12 (*DP*). By this time HF has severed connections with *The Champion.*[23]

27. A warrant is issued by Hugh Allen for HF's arrest (for £28.16s.), and a week later he is lodged in a bailiff's sponging house.[24]

Mar. 6. Last issue of the *History* (nothing in it by HF).

Mar. 9. Edmund, still in the Fleet, marries his servant, Elizabeth Sparrye.[25]

16. HF appears before the Palace Court, Southwark, and is bailed by his sister Catherine and his current publisher, Corbett. Freed on 20th; avoids paying the £35.9s.8d he owes Allen for another year.[26] He is depicted in the *Gazetteer* (Mar. 11) as Sisyphus, who has given up trying to get the opposition boulder to the top of the hill; it is suggested that Hercules Vinegar has left the *Champion* to join the *Gazetteer* (30th).

Between Feb. and Apr., presumably mostly while in the sponging house, HF writes *Shamela*.

ESSAYIST

The Champion

King John *[Cibber's revision of Shakespeare's play] no more provokes thy dreaded Rage,*
Despis'd for Magna Charta'*s Sacred Page:*
Th'unwieldy Law employs thy vaster Mind;
The Subject Act where Treason is defin'd,
The Habeas Corpus, *and the* Bill of Rights
Are now preferr'd to past Poetick Flights.[27]

So he, tho' haply as a Poet dead,
Shall teem more dreadful, with a Lawyer's Head,
Which all the former's venom shall retain,
And hiss and spit to vex Mankind again.[28]

I was bred up to Letters, *have been educated in a* good School, *and was then sent to a* foreign University, *where I kept close to my Books, and was well esteem'd by all the* Professors, *under whom I studied. But my Learning went no farther than* Humanity, History *and* Poetry. *My imagination was too fertile, and my Parts too volatile, for any of the grave Professions. My Inclination tended most towards* Poetry, *and chiefly* dramatick Poetry, *in which I gave Way to my Fancy.*

But now Fielding is prevented from using the stage as an outlet for his "Fancy" by "a Law made to regulate the STAGE." Thus in a *Craftsman* of December 1738, in a letter to Caleb D'Anvers, he sketches an autobiography.[29] The preceding verses for and against him are from 1738 and 1739 respectively.

The Licensing Act that closed his theater left Fielding one moment quite prosperous (though living beyond his means), the next looking for a way to earn a living. Though the chief reason for the closure had been his delving into politics, that was where the most lucrative employment lay; he continued writing the same anti-Walpole satire for *The Craftsman*.[30] But with a longer view toward security and respectability he simultaneously turned to the study of the law.

The essays he wrote for *The Craftsman* do more than satirize the ministry: they often start out with a moral issue that is gradually – sometimes only in a stinger at the end – given a political application. In them Fielding explores the possibilities of irony, allegory, and analogy, and in particular the interpretation and misinterpretation of texts, legal and literary.

These essays demonstrate his learning, his hermeneutics, and his maturity (he was now in his thirties); but he permits them also to reveal his particular, sometimes personal, thoughts on moral issues.

By the autumn of 1739 he had come to an understanding with a group of booksellers, including John Nourse, from whom he bought most of his law books, and probably with backing from Dodington and other opposition politicians who felt that *The Craftsman* and *Common Sense* needed supplementation.[31] His share, as a part proprietor, was two-sixteenths of the profits of the journal, with the promise from his political patrons of future rewards – neither of which, if we are to believe *The Opposition: A Vision*, lived up to expectations. He apparently wrote the lead essays (or most of them), including many "letters." The editorial work was handled by his assistant Ralph, who brought to *The Champion* almost a decade of journalistic experience. Ralph had written miscellaneous essays for *The Weekly Register* on all manner of subjects (exclusive of religion, where his opinions were scandalous); his politics had shifted with the winds, first for Walpole, then against, now supporting Dodington. He had joined Fielding at the Little Haymarket just when Fielding launched his anti-Walpole plays in the 1736 season – a collaboration that continued until Fielding quit *The Champion* in 1741 (after which Ralph presided until 1743). Ralph sometimes contributed essays but more often filled in the "Index to the Times" and the lesser departments of the journal. In general (with some exceptions), Fielding's essays were signed "C" and Ralph's "**"; C is probably for Clio, the muse of history (perhaps also for Charlotte).

Though the *Champion* was launched in November 1739, coincidental with the opening of parliament, politics was at first relatively muted; by December 18 Fielding announced that the journal was in such dire straits that, "though it was not, at first, my Intention to deal much in serious Politics in this Paper," he is now changing the policy. Subjects "of a more humerous [sic] Kind" were originally his aim, and *The Champion* was advertised as "Containing Essays on various Subjects," yet this was followed by the revealing Virgilian motto, "Quod optanti Divum promittere nemo / Auderet Volvenda dies en attulit." Dryden's translation, which includes the name of the addressee, reads: "What none of all the Gods cou'd grant thy Vows; That, *Turnus*, this auspicious Day bestows" (*Aeneid*, IX.6–7).[32] The sense, that while Aeneas is away Juno (enemy of the Trojans) urges Turnus to attack, sounds political; but the meaning can also be that Fielding's blockage on the stage has had the happy consequence of giving him a more respectable outlet in these essays. His plays had come to an end surrounded by the accusations of scurrility, obscenity, and impiety which dogged Fielding into the 1750s. He felt the need to defend himself against the attacks on his plays, and this took the dignified form of formulating positions that clarified the issues raised by those earlier works – primarily issues of politics, religion, and morality.

His first concern was to establish the ethos of the paper, the mask that was its basic fiction. He speaks through a person he calls Captain Hercules Vinegar, the classical "Heroic Virtue" of Hercules with local setting and satiric edge – incidentally a figure like Tom Hickathrift, with Fielding's physique:

> I have now determin'd to lay aside the Sword [he tells us], which, without Vanity, I may boast to have us'd with some Success, (though few Captains now living, can say the like) and take up the Pen in its Stead, with a Design to do as much Execution with the one, as I have already done with the other; or, in other Words, to tickle now, as I before bruised Men into good Manners. (Nov. 15, 1739; 1:1)[33]

But he also keeps Hercules' club on his wall, and the image on the front page is of Hercules wielding his club against the many-headed Hydra, who threatens London. In the background are the new Westminster Bridge, the London Monument, and St. Paul's Cathedral (plate 10). I would not want to rule out the possibility that the woodcut was based on a drawing by

Plate 10 After Hogarth (?), Headpiece for *The Champion*, 1739, woodcut, courtesy of the Trustees of the Bodleian Museum, Oxford.

Hogarth; a similar woodcut, for which Hogarth's drawing survives, was used by Fielding as headpiece for *The Jacobite's Journal* in 1748 (see plate 16, 241). Two of the three symbols of London dominated Hogarth's *South Sea Scheme* of 1724 (the Fire Monument recalling the fire allegedly caused by papists). The third, Westminster Bridge, was regarded by the opposition as a sign of Walpolian folly and corruption.[34] Hercules' Roman nose leads one to suspect that a portrait of Fielding may have been intended.

Vinegar, while localized in 1730s London, is a "champion," and as such he recounts the pedigree of his magic club: the "very strange and almost incredible Quality belonging to it, of falling, of its own Accord, on every egregious Knave who comes in its Way." An equivalent of Juvenal's automatic indignation ("difficile est saturam non scribere"), it has taken after Cardinal Wolsey, one of the *Craftsman* analogies for Walpole: "The Club is, in this Reign [of Henry VIII], reported to have beaten 100 Lawyers, 99 Courtiers, 73 Priests, 8 Physicians, and 13 Beaux, (whereof 12 died of the first blow) besides innumerable others." Gallantly it has cudgeled no women, though "It hath indeed sometimes expressed very odd Motions at the Sight of particular Women" (Dec. 8, 1739, 1:69–72).

Hercules' violence is complemented by the "prudent Coolness" of his wife Joan. Fielding begins with the unit of the family – the Vinegar family, adapted from the Bickerstaff family of Steele's *Tatler* but with professions that have personal significance for himself.[35] There is Hercules' uncle the lawyer, "the only Man of our Family," he writes hopefully, "who ever was rich," who will hold forth on legal matters. His son Tom, while training for the law, "hath given more of his Time to *Shakespeare* and *Dryden*, than *Coke* and *Littleton*."[36] His brother Nol is an "Adept in Classic Learning," and Fielding begins the second *Champion* (Nov. 17) with an untranslated quotation from Juvenal and by his second page is citing Silius Italicus, Sallust, and again Juvenal.

The subject is pride in ancestry – ironic and deprecatory, but a subject of interest, as if Fielding felt it important to set off false from true pride, as he had false from true learning. Hercules disclaims all interest in his own ancestry, blaming this affectation on his wife Joan (who claims that his descent is from *the* Hercules), but he quotes Addison's *Cato*, which could have carried a reference to Fielding's own case: "Thy Father's Greatness / Hath set thee in the fairest Point of Light, / To make thy Virtues or thy Faults conspicuous" (1:10). Indeed, Captain Hercules Vinegar assumes the role in his family of Fielding's father – "all Affairs relating to the Army, Militia, Trained-bands, and other the fighting Part of this Kingdom" (1:5).

Vinegar presides over a family with a variety of interests and points of view. As the papers proceed, however, Fielding does surprisingly little with the family or the Vinegar persona. He finds it difficult to get involved in a dramatic situation in the periodical; he tends to let Vinegar speak through

the length of an essay and, more often than not, simply forgets his crotch-
ety characteristics. Partly perhaps as a result of his legal studies, he develops in the *Champion* a persona that begins to move in the direction of the
detached, fair-minded judge whom he will later equate with the historian
in the figure of the Fielding narrator. It is no coincidence that one of his
larger preoccupations in the *Champion* is establishing a public ethos, one
distinct from the man who wrote the plays. In his later plays, action was
increasingly dependent on a commentator, and Medley, with the almost
newspaper-like potpourri of his *Historical Register*, leads naturally into the
Champion.

This is the conscientious citizen, the thoughtful husband and friend, the
Christian censor described by Wilbur Cross, James Work, and followed by
Battestin. He talks to his readers of subjects ranging from the relation
between fools and knaves to the defense of the clergy. His aim is to lead
men into a decent mode of behavior, not the bullying of Hercules with his
club; a descendant of the Horace of the *epistolae* rather than the *sermones*
and no relation to Juvenal; and a lawyer or a judge first, a satirist second.
He is no longer a Rochester libertine but a balanced, attractive person who
explores the extremes of the strategies he will use in his fictional works –
for example, "roasting" people (Mar. 13) or "good nature" (Mar. 27). In
one issue he presents a sermon on virtue in which he plays the moralist;
in the next he introduces a letter in which an antimask treats the same
subject satirically, expressing the opposing point of view. He shows sympathy for his fellowmen, as when a letter writer confesses that he is a hypocrite and Vinegar replies that a man who can write such a letter, so
revealing and self-aware of his own character, has already taken the first
step toward reformation. The *Champion* showed Fielding the close relation
between the periodical essay and what will become the discursive chapter
that punctuates a prose narrative.

Law student

At the same time he was writing these essays Fielding was serving his seven
years' apprenticeship as an "inner barrister," a period of intensive study
before being admitted to the bar. Although the study of law was not based
on classical texts (it was the antithesis of the codified Roman law), the
approach was much the same – memorization of writs and pleas, examination of transcriptions of cases, and, most strikingly parallel, the study of
Coke upon Littleton, Coke's voluminous commentary on Littleton's *Tenures*,
another version of the texts of Homer and Virgil. There were no classes,
no teachers; the basic principle was self-help, to which was added attendance at court to observe live trials.[37] James Harris recalled that Fielding
"took to ye Study of ye Law with indefatigable industry," copying, abridg-

ing, abstracting, and absorbing.[38] There are also stories of Fielding's ability to concentrate, poring over the law books, even after a night of heavy eating and convivial drinking. At the same time, he would have noted a tendency in these works to digest authorities rather than deduce principles; he would have been bemused by the extreme formality and the use of elaborate and, on the face of it, arbitrary "legal fictions."[39] As noted by one of the contemporary commentaries on the phenomenon of "Henry Drama" becoming a lawyer,

> While Others feel the drowsy Pow'r of *Coke*,
> Thy Antidote shall be some well-tim'd joke. . . .
>
> * * * * * * *
>
> Canst thou behold the Statutes monstrous Size,
> And feel no ludicrous Emotion rise?
> Canst thou look forward to a Hundred Year,
> Compute their Growth, and yet the Smile forbear?[40]

Such "fictions" kept before his eyes the notion of the world as theater, and the practice he observed recalled the nonsense of a world turned upside down.

The theater retains some of its authority in *The Champion*, especially when Fielding is dealing with politics. In an essay of May 10, 1740 he argues that if men and women are players, the satirist is the stage manager. He has the Moon explain that he is like the "Man behind the scenes at your Play-Houses . . . who, tho' he may behold Objects in the truest, sees them at the same time in the most odious Light, and is not so agreeably deceived as those to whom the painted Side of the Canvas represents a beautiful Grove or a Palace." In life, as in Rich's productions, the audience sees only "the Sights of Serpents, Dragons and Armies, whereas indeed those Objects are no other than Pieces of stuff'd Cloth, painted Wood, and Hobby-horses" run by "several Strings, wires, Clock-work &c." In the world Fielding explores "every Person . . . disguises his Mind, as much as Masque would his Countenance."[41]

This is a description that could equally fit a satirist and an officer of the court. With his legal training, the theatrical metaphor begins to shift into the judicial: "A Judge, on his Circuit, would not receive half the Respect that is usually offered him by the Populace, was he to travel without those attractive Ornaments [of his office] with which he is inclosed"; Fielding then turns more briefly to divines and physicians, who completed his trio of villains in *Pasquin*.[42]

There is the character of the barrister in the Vinegar family; there are references to judgment and punishment and the employment of legal terms; and as early as the December 22, 1739 issue Fielding introduces a mock court, Hercules Vinegar's "Court of Judicature" (sometimes called a

"Court of Censorial Enquiry"). This court, following the traditional claim of the satiric tribunal, is for those criminals not covered by the laws of the land – "Invaders and Destroyers of our Lives and Fortunes, and of the Persons and Honour of our Women, whom no Laws in being can any way come at." Vinegar presides at a mock trial to determine such questions as which of the London fops should be chosen "Prince of the Coxcombs" (Apr. 8, 1740) or what is the nature of Colley Cibber's violation of the English language in his *Apology* (May 17, 1740).

Coincidentally, the court Vinegar describes – and its officers and duties – corresponds not to the courts of King's Bench and Common Pleas in Westminster Hall but to the Westminster Magistrate's office in Bow Street. "I have set apart a large Room in my own House," Vinegar writes,

> at the upper End of which is a great Elbow-Chair, raised on several Steps, with a Desk and Cushion before it. In this Chair, I shall sit in Judgment; below is a Table, at which my Family are to be placed as Council: behind is the Bar, where the prisoners are to be arraigned, and on one Side is a Stool for the Evidence. As for Juries, I have no need of them, as I reserve to myself the full Power of convicting or acquitting as I think just. (December 22, 1739; 1:118)

This is the court of Justice Squeezum in *Rape upon Rape* and after 1748 of Fielding himself, which judged offenders prior to committing them to gaol and to a full trial with jury (his assistants "shall be thereto impowered by Warrant under my Hand and Seal, and convey them to the Prison aforesaid").

Creating a kind of composite magistrate's and criminal court, perhaps as an author must, Fielding envisions punishment as well as judgment. Here he joins court and theater: Executions are to be carried out on the stage of Drury Lane, he proposes, doubtless recalling his own less happy experiences with the reception of his plays by pit and galleries, but also foreshadowing the serious proposals he will make for public executions when he becomes Westminster Magistrate.

This composite court involves incidentally a modified definition of the satirist – a more legal, even social, interpretation with less sense of urgency; a transition from a prosecuting attorney to an impartial judge with a more or less even balance of alternatives before him, who often acquits or forgives. The metaphor that makes the satirist and, later, the reader, a magistrate and every character or action a case for judgment, will become a central one in *Tom Jones* and, in a somewhat different way, in *Amelia*.

The legal profession was the first "settling down" of Fielding, but another was his marriage. It was the profession of the law and his wife Charlotte – or only the idea of a wife – that led him in the *Champion* essays to present an official position on such crucial subjects as love, duty, friendship, and religion. At the same time they show him, as in the plays, working out his feelings about such subjects; and they are, in some ways, as self-incriminating as the speech he attributes to the hypocrite and, later, the letters he will give Shamela.

Subjects of particular interest

The *Craftsman* essays set the model for the *Champion*. Fielding's essay in *Craftsman* no. 600 (Jan. 7, 1737/8) is a genuinely learned exegesis of a passage in *Aeneid* II, which quotes the various translations, therefore interpretations, of Dryden, Pitt, and Trapp in order to offer his own reading. His question is why would Virgil present Ripheus as a virtuous man and yet, when he is killed, conclude, "Diis aliter visum," "the gods thought otherwise"? The question is "what Idea must We form of the Omniscience of *such Deities*, as make an Estimate of Persons directly contrary to their *true Character*? They must be no better than *Epicurian Gods*, intirely unacquainted with all *sublunary Affairs*, who pass so wrong a Judgment upon the Conduct of Mankind" (275). This is the old question of the justice of God, the inequality of rewards and punishments, strongly suggesting the deist conclusion that the deity is transcendent, and it draws attention to Fielding's abiding interest in the role of the deity in human affairs. He offers what is probably Virgil's own sense – that there is an awful chasm between our idea of virtue and the decrees of the gods; but, turning it into a joke, he concludes that Ripheus must have been a hypocrite, whose evil was seen only by the gods, and therefore: "*Ripheus* was *Prime-Minister of State* to old King *Priam*; by whose unconscionable Oppressions, Mal-Administration, and wrong-concerted Measures, his Countrymen had severely smarted" (277). The sting is in the political application, but the subject draws attention to, or is a cover for, the critical deist tradition of Collins and Woolston (or, in *The Craftsman*, Amhurst himself). At the least Fielding's ironic hermeneutics demonstrates a subtlety, slightly subversive and deconstructive, that supports the subtlest readings of his own works (as we shall see in the case of *Jonathan Wild*).

For the final application to Ripheus the prime minister, attributed to "the *Scholia* of one *Belchandwheezius*," he says he has been instructed by "an *honest, jovial Country Parson*" who has stopped by "to quaff a Bottle with me," and this is certainly his neighbor and friend, William Young, who was beginning to pose for the character of Parson Abraham Adams.

The subjects Fielding dealt with in *The Craftsman* he further developed in *The Champion*, where he was his own master. In the third issue (Nov. 20) he is concerned with the "Study of our own Minds," in the mistakes the actor makes in assuming roles (comic actors want to be tragedians), with personal references to his memories of the "Triumvirate" of Drury Lane, which lead him naturally into the theatricality of national politics. But he is also thinking about the problem, the danger of misdirecting "the Strength and Bent of [one's] genius," in particular the successful comic playwright (Wycherley or Congreve) who writes indifferent poetry or tragedy (1:15–16). He could be thinking of himself when he compares the "excellent Orator" with "a very indifferent Poet." He was beginning at this time to explore the generic possibilities of poetry and narrative fiction as well as the essay. Already he uses the theatrical metaphor in a way he will carry beyond the literary into the philosophical in *Tom Jones*: Men are often liable to assume "Characters for which Nature hath rendered them utterly unfit" (1:14–15).

In this and the following essays he shows himself to be concerned above all with appearances, dress, and costume belied by reality; false gravity (which he connects with Shaftesburian doctrine [1:21–2]) and even virtue without the clothing of decency; above all, hypocrisy. In the essay of December 11, 1739 the problem of words versus actions – which will come to a head for him with Richardson's *Pamela* – is illustrated by the letter of a hypocrite. Fielding's obsession with hypocrisy may suggest some concern about the doublethink of the writer who can write for either side and speak out of either side of his mouth (Ralph was a case in point, but he had himself both courted and satirized Walpole).

Fielding explores turncoats, taking the correct (official) position, but his irony is double-edged: "It must be granted, that no Man is so good a judge of the true Merits of a cause, as he who hath been on both Sides of it" (Jan. 12, 1739/40; 1:180). First, this is the turncoat's rationalization for his disgraceful behavior; but second, there is a sense in which a turncoat has earned an objectivity denied to his more faithful friends. He lives in a dangerous world in which "What is Loyalty in one Reign, is High-Treason in the next," and so calls for a reasonable pragmatism. On the contrary, Fielding concedes, one reason to "stand firm to your principles" is that "you may be assured that the Party you adhere to will one time or other get the Ascendent" (182). He leaves himself an opening, suggesting that money is another factor: "Any ill Usage from his Party, any Refusal of what he thinks himself entitled to, no doubt sufficiently justify this Exchange." But primarily his irony shows that the turncoat is a subject that worries him, related as it is to hypocrisy.

A decade later in the *Jacobite's Journal* (Mar. 26, 1748) he dropped the irony and explained why in "a Time . . . of profound Tranquillity" (unlike the present crisis) writers produce scurrilous writing for pay:

In a country where there is no public Provision for Men of genius, and in an Age when no Literary Productions are encouraged, or indeed read, but such as are season'd with Scandal against the Great; and when a Custom hath prevailed of publishing this, not only with Impunity but with great Emolument, the Temptation to Men in desperate Circumstances is too violent to be resisted; and if the Public will feed a hungry Man for a little Calumny, he must be a very honest Person indeed, who will rather starve than write it.

This he links to the plight of the turncoat: "[In such a time,] when the Consequence, at the worst, can probably be no greater than the Change of a Ministry, I do not think a Writer, whose only Livelihood is his Pen, to deserve a very flagitious Character, if, when one Set of Men deny him Encouragement, he seeks it from another, at their Expence." These words are without a doubt a sign of the continuing guilt he was accused of, and may have felt (or boldly not felt), for his own practice of turning from ministry to opposition and back in the 1730s.

A subject that preoccupies him in *The Champion* is the malicious attack on an author's work, especially when he is needy. In the printed text of *The Universal Gallant*, he had responded to the failure of the play with a defensive "Advertisement": "he must be an inhuman Creature indeed, who would out of sport and wantonness prevent a Man from getting a Livelihood in an honest and inoffensive Way, and make a Jest of starving him and his Family."[43] In the *Champion* he associates half-pay or discharged soldiers and authors as equally unrewarded for their endeavors (implicitly both are patriotic endeavors), and he pleads with critics whose wanton attacks deprive writers of their livelihood.[44]

On February 16, 1739/40 Fielding wrote an essay on charity, a subject of centrality for a man whose ethic is based on the "faith, hope, and charity" passage of Corinthians. Here he turns from the subject of charity to its object, and he begins by disqualifying indigent beggars, who "deserve Punishment more than Relief, and are a Shame not to the Legislative but the Executive Power of our Laws." What he was rather thinking of as objects of charity was a case such as himself:

> Distrest Circumstances are, not being able to support the Character in which Men have been bred, and the Want of Conveniencies to which they have been accustom'd, and therefore the first and chief Objects of our Charity are such Persons as, having been educated in genteel Life with moderate Fortunes, partly through Want of Resolution to quit the Character in which they were bred, and partly for Want of duly considering the Consequences of their Expences, have, by following their Superiors into Luxury, in order to support, as they call it, the Figure of Gentlemen, reduced themselves to Distress and Poverty. (1:277)

He refers to younger sons, children educated "in a Condition of Life far beyond what they will afterwards be able to support," and in particular the debtors who are hounded and locked up in prison: They are "snatch'd away from their poor Families, from the little Comforts of the Conversation of their Relations and Acquaintance, from a Possibility of employing their

Faculties for the Service of themselves, their Wives or their Children, from the Benefit of wholesome Air in common with the Brute-Creation" (278).[45] He singles out men ruined "by the noblest Acts of Friendship" such as signing for another's loan.

There is remarkably little irony in the essay. Later Fielding will add, with sentimental flourishes, the daughters of clergymen to his list of those who cannot "support the Character in which [they] have been bred."[46] He places the blame on "the Rapaciousness, Impatience and Unmercifulness of Creditors, more savage than Wolves, and the impious Severity of our Laws." Battestin notes "the self-serving tone of these remarks, whereby a degree of improvidence and self-indulgence verging on the vicious (certainly Charlotte and the children might be excused for thinking so, not to mention the tradesmen whose bills went unpaid) is applauded as the natural effect of innate generosity" (268).[47]

A week before the essay on charity Fielding wrote one of the strongest of the essays (Feb. 2, 1739/40). It treats the temptation of uncontrollable passion, whether (we may suppose) for drink or gambling or, as he makes quite clear in the essay, for women. The object of the essay is to indicate "by what Means we may best resist the Impulse of these dangerous Enemies, and arrive at that Perfection," which is prudent restraint; but his solutions (he dismisses both the grace of divines and the stoicism of the philosophers) are facile and the power of the essay lies in its description of the passion itself: "But in this War of the Mind, if Reason once lose a Battle, once suffer an absolute Overthrow, we seldom, if ever, see her exert herself again . . . The severest Slavery imposed by men on one another is light, in Comparison of that under an overbearing Passion" (1:233–4).

While there is "an Army of obstinate Passions," and he mentions revenge, pride, and fear, the passion that concerns him is lust. The effect is

> to dazzle our Eyes by the immediate Glare of the Object before us, so as to hurry us on to action, without giving our Understanding Leisure to consider and weigh the Consequence. Lust especially acts in this Way. . . . Indeed, if a Man would set before his Eyes the Ideas of Pain, Disease, Dishonour, Poverty, Death, and all the frightful Ideas of those Miseries, which the least Indulgence of this Passion will almost certainly bring upon him, he must be very fool-hardy to give way to it; but he is allured and charmed with the Hopes of the immediate Possession of a desirable Object, with the Satisfaction of the most violent of all Desires; he looks not beyond the present Moment which promises him perfect Happiness. (1:236–7)

This is the first stage of Fielding's explanation for Tom Jones's falling into the arms of Molly Seagrim and Jenny Waters (he will later find others). But another point is worthy of note: "It is easier to . . . drive [a foe] successfully out of the first Trench than out of the last": To describe all this primarily in the metaphor of warfare leads one to balance the conventionality of the topos against the association of these divagations with his father, the general.[48]

The personal strain of the *Champion* essays recalls his conflation of himself in *Eurydice Hiss'd* with Walpole, both failures, one at a Bill and the other a farce, but both "theatrical"; both also tyrants over their "companies" and, implicitly, operators who, successful over a long period of time, have come a cropper in this one instance.[49] The fact is that Fielding, in moments of dejection, tended to expose himself without the protection of irony. There are times when he transmutes his experience into comedy. The *Champion* essay on the dangers of passion reemerges in *Joseph Andrews* as a long, funny account of love concluding: "In short, thou turnest the Heart of Man inside-out, as a Juggler doth a Petticoat, and bringest whatsoever pleaseth thee out from it" (1.7.37). At other times – moments in his dedications and prefaces, in advertisements, and in his periodical essays – he resorts to pathos.

Most significant, because most public, was the subject of religion. In a sequel to the essay on charity (Feb. 19) Fielding invokes Christian rewards and punishments to pass judgment on the creditor who demands payment: "so surely as he forgives not his Neighbour his Trespasses, so surely will his Father in Heaven deny to forgive him his; nor," he adds, "do I know any [other] Crime in this World which can appear to a finite Understanding to deserve infinite Punishment." For Shaftesbury, we recall, rewards and punishments in the afterlife were the religion of a monstrous deity, though a regrettably necessary support for society. The hard winter of 1739–40 reveals Fielding changing from the libertine of the playhouse days to the sober citizen willing to invoke religion and the fear of punishment here or hereafter.

In 1740 he published a series of essays specifically attacking ethical deism and defending the clergy. At the same time, he let slip his prejudices and, above all, the problems he seems to have had with religious dogmas. These began with two on January 22 and 24, 1739/40, continuing with four more (essays "defending" the clergy) on March 29, and April 5, 12, and 19, 1740. Fielding criticizes deism in its three aspects: (1) the deletion of an immanent God (or, as he puts it, the desire to "believe the deity a lazy, unactive being" who will not intervene on our behalf); (2) the subsequent opening up of a libertine ethics; and (3) the denigration of the clergy (the climactic and most extended argument, clearly the most important for Fielding).

(1) While ostensibly condemning deism, however, Fielding retains the deist strategy of shifting attention from the question of revealed religion to the observable facts of human virtue and happiness in a social situation. The validity of religion is based less on whether it is true or false than on whether it fulfills a social function. The compartmentalization of religious

belief – rendering it part of a social compact – enabled him to set it off, in particular its form of providential design, as an aspect of manners.

The argument of the opening essay, against the deist assumption that the deity does not interfere in human events, is couched in the subjunctive, as if a wild hypothesis: "even *supposing* these Allegations were true, and Religion as false as they would have it imagined," and: "Was there no future state, it would be surely the *interest* of every virtuous Man to *wish* there was one . . ." (emphasis added). Instead of a theological argument, Fielding offers a pragmatic one:

> What a rapturous Consideration must it be to the Heart of Man to think the Goodness of the Great God of Nature concerned in his Happiness? How must it elevate him in his own opinion? How transported must he be with himself? What extatic Pleasure must he feel in his Mind. . . . If this be a dream, it is such a one as infinitely exceeds all the paultry Enjoyments this Life can afford. It is such a Delusion as he who undeceived you might be well said *Occidere & non servare*, to destroy, not preserve. How cruel woud it be in a Physician to wake his Patient from Dreams of purling Streams, and shady Groves, to a State of Pain and Misery? How much more cruel then is this pretended Physician of the Mind [the deist], who destroys in you those delightful Hopes, which, however vain, would afford such a Spring of Pleasure during the whole Course of your Life.[50]

This passage could pass for latitudinarian discourse, interpreted by the unsympathetic as carrying a self-interested and prudential emphasis – on the happiness and the easiness of the Christian life; on the belief that heaven is both rational and self-interested and that the practice of religion will make us happy.

But the passage unmistakably recalls Swift, for example his account in "The Digression on Madness" of "Happiness" "convey'd in the Vehicle of Delusion" ("How shrunk is every Thing, as it appears in the Glass of Nature?"), which is the "sublime and refined Point of Felicity, called, *the Possession of being well deceived*; The Serene Peaceful State of being a Fool among Knaves."[51] Fielding modulates Swift's savage irony into Addison's more sedate story in *Spectator* no. 413 of the romantic knight errant wandering in a world of primary qualities:

> our souls are at present delightfully lost and bewildered in a pleasing delusion, and we walk about like the enchanted hero of a romance, who sees beautiful castles, woods and meadows; and at the same time hears the warbling of birds, and the purling of streams [all of these, secondary qualities]; but upon the finishing of some secret spell, the fantastic scene breaks up, and the disconsolate knight finds himself on a barren heath, or in a solitary desert.

Addison's "purling of streams" and Fielding's "Dreams of purling Streams, and shady Groves" recall that "purling streams" and "shady groves," as a conventional image for romantic dreams of love, appeared, for example, in Eliza Heywood's dedication to *The Fatal Secret; or, the Lucky Disappointment: A Novel* (1724).[52]

But Fielding's passage also recalls his own dialogue between Queen Ignorance and Queen Common Sense in *Pasquin*, in which the former (whose chief adviser is the cleric Firebrand) argues that

> thinking only makes men wretched;
> And happiness is still the lot of fools.
>
> *   *   *   *   *   *
>
> While the poor goose in happiness and ease,
> Fearless grows fat within his narrow coop,
> And thinks the hand that feeds it is its friend.
>   (11:219–20)

Fielding's invocation of "happiness," and in particular the vocabulary of *rapture, ecstasy,* and *transportation,* probably owes most to Shaftesbury.[53] In his *Inquiry concerning Virtue and Merit* (1699, 1711) Shaftesbury denied Hobbes's view that virtuous behavior does not produce happiness, arguing that only the virtuous individual can experience true happiness, which consists in the ability to share the joy of benevolent acts. In the sequel he sums up a benevolent god and his providential design:

> For 'tis impossible that such a divine order should be contemplated without ecstasy and rapture, since in the common subjects of science and the liberal arts, whatever is according to just harmony and proportion is so transporting to those who have any knowlege or practice in the kind.[54]

There is a delicate irony in Shaftesbury's writing, which says that if religion in its Anglican forms proves conducive to happiness, he is willing to tolerate the orthodoxy necessary to preserve virtue and order, especially among the lower orders which need good examples. This is an aristocratic irony Fielding would have found elucidated in Shaftesbury's writings on enthusiasm and ridicule, which came to be known as deist irony ("esoteric" discourse vs. "exoteric"). Fielding's words in the *Champion* come very close to echoing Shaftesbury's "'Tis real Humanity and Kindness to hide strong Truths from tender eyes," by which he means both the ecclesiastical authorities and the lower orders.[55]

Fielding follows Shaftesbury in not presuming to assert (with Anglican clergymen) that this providential order corresponds to reality. The distinction is between the providential assumptions of the clergy, attributed to Fielding by Battestin and Williams, and the deists' view that providential design, however essential to our happiness and social stability, is a human fiction.[56] This is not so much to claim that Fielding is necessarily himself a deist as that he accepts the consequences of deism; he recognizes the providential order as having been rendered no longer valid by the deists except as a fiction – as "Dreams of purling Streams, and shady Groves" (in the *Champion*) or "poetic justice" and a happy ending.

(2) The second subject of the *Champion* essays attacking deism is virtue (Jan. 24, 1739/40). Fielding recalls Shaftesbury's figure of Virtue, projected by Theocles in *The Moralists* (Theocles' version of Prodicus and Cebes), leading a Roman triumph over "monsters of savage passions . . . ambition, lust, uproar, misrule, with all the fiends which rage in human breasts . . . securely chained" (2:44). But to this the skeptical Philocles opposes "an authentic picture of another kind," in which Virtue is the captive and "by a proud conqueror triumphed over, degraded, spoiled of all her honours, and defaced, so as to retain hardly one single feature of real beauty" (2:45). While Philocles' picture is characterized by his more pious companions as libertine and atheist, Theocles recognizes that the "proud conqueror" is not the atheist but "religion itself" – those who, pretending to expose "the falsehood of human virtue, think to extol religion," but "strike at moral virtue as a kind of step-dame, or rival to religion." These are the clerics who "would value virtue but for hereafter" – the advocates of rewards and punishments in the afterlife. Virtue, in short, even Theocles admits, is better without religion of *this* sort.

But Fielding goes beyond Shaftesbury. As if recalling Hogarth's *Harlot* 1, he summons up Shaftesbury's Choice of Hercules but rejects both the harlot Pleasure *and* Virtue, seen as "disagreeable," "rigid," with "intolerable penances," "thirst and hunger, whips and chains." To get at true Virtue he must strip both women. He begins with the mistranslation of Plato which he will use again in the dedication to *Tom Jones*, "That could Mankind behold Virtue naked, they would all be in Love with her."[57] Under the "tawdry, painted Harlot," Pleasure will prove to be "within, all foul and impure," and under Virtue's clerical-puritanical demeanor she will prove not "of that morose and rigid Nature" but alluring. "Virtue forbids not the satisfying our Appetites," he writes, "Virtue forbids us only to glut and destroy them. The temperate Man tastes and relishes Pleasure in a Degree infinitely superior to that of the voluptuous." Fielding keeps her within Shaftesbury's ascending scale of aesthetics to ethics, body to mind, and his two women look forward to the figures of lust and love, Molly and Sophia, in *Tom Jones*. Nevertheless, orthodox Christian virtue as a humanized, sexually desirable young female is a surprisingly provocative metaphor for a warning against deist libertinism. The metaphor involves not only dressing and undressing Virtue but her "embraces," the "pursuit," and the "possession" of her.

(3) A greedy, power-hungry clergy that interprets Scriptures in order to control their congregations was the basic myth accepted by a fairly wide spectrum, with latitudinarians and atheists at the extremes. Fielding's climactic essays defending the clergy against deist attack (beginning March

29, 1740) make a strange defense, one that devotes most of its time to out-
lining the reasons for the contempt in which its individual members, as distinct from the "order," are held.[58] Fielding's censures are of the privileges
bestowed on the clergy by the civil law, their honors, revenues, and immu-
nities from the law – in sum (using his favorite term), their "greatness."[59]
A preponderance of space is given to the lurid stories of Guinandus de
Briland and other clergymen who murdered and raped and used the law
to escape punishment. The third and the fourth essays, which are separated by an essay on vanity, define "clergyman" simply as a good shepherd
whose task is to "feed his Flock with Meat, Precept, and Example," who is
"entrusted with the care of our Souls, over which he is to watch as a Shepherd for his Sheep . . . To live in daily Communication with his Flock, and
chiefly with those who want him most (as the Poor and Distressed), nay,
and after his blessed Master's example, to eat with Publicans and Sinners."
When he asks "Can such a Man as this be the Object of Contempt?" he is
anticipating Parson Adams (in particular at the hands of the roasting squire
in book III): "perhaps indeed Boys and Beaus, and Madmen, and Rakes,
and Fools, and Villains, may laugh at this sacred Person; may shake those
ridiculous Heads at him." The final essay then concludes with another vivid
description of what the good clergyman is *not*, rendered in great and savage
detail.[60]

Clergymen are twice distinguished from deists and atheists, and Fielding, the public spokesman and (by this time) respectable barrister, wants
to dissociate himself from the name of deist. But he makes it quite clear
that his sense of the clergy is not unlike the bugbear of the deists: the
authoritarian interpreter of the law, scripture, and doctrine.

Critical, as opposed to ethical, deism focused on the corruption of
priestcraft; Fielding's feelings on this issue appear in the importance he
places on interpreting and largely discrediting clerical texts. "Learning" he
divides into false and true, with the first being largely that of religious commentators and the latter his own knowledge of classical texts. In the *Champion* for December 25, 1739 he divides the study of divinity into three
branches, "the *Credenda*, the *Agenda*, and the *Habenda*." He dismisses the
first, "Matters of Faith, regarding Doctrinal and Ceremonial Points,"
amounting to "about six Waggon-Loads of Books," and the third, tithes and
church profits; he accepts only the second, the actions of morality, and adds
(with irony), "I know some Persons have thought that the excellent and
divine Sermon on the Mount, contains all that can be said or thought on
this Subject," yet "there is scarce one Word which hath not been explained
in more Pages than have been written on all the abstruse and dark Passages of the ancient Philosophers" (1:126). He goes on, as usual, to the law
and medicine, and the message is the same: ignore the books, the formulations and protestations, for the actions which alone determine virtue. He
believed, with the deists, that the teachings of Jesus, summed up in the

Sermon on the Mount, had been obscured by the learned commentary and interpretation of self-serving priests.

Earning a living from 1740

The sharp decline of Fielding's writing for *The Champion* in June 1740 coincided with his completion of his legal studies; he tapered off his contributions partly at least in order to practice his profession. The series of essays on "The Voyages of Mr. Job Vinegar," though they may have been written during his leisure hours as he rode his first Western Circuit, could also have been written at a run before he launched his legal career and then printed piecemeal. The first paper appeared on March 20, 1739/40, but the remainder only began to appear on June 28, followed by eleven more beginning July 17 (the last essay is in October).[61] They sound as if Fielding was writing hastily, off the top of his head, but for this reason they shed some light on his immediate situation. The attacks on Walpole have increased in frequency and intensity in the spring, and now, on the model of Swift's Lilliput, Fielding produces an anatomy of Walpolean society. Nevertheless, the satire is plastered over a recital of the full range of Fielding's personal concerns.

The society's religion, for example, is the Walpolean worship of MNEY, but the churches are theaters, the services diversions and entertainments (March 20). Fielding balances the country's religion with its law, which he sums up as a game, another public diversion, "which our Men mistook for Law," rather like tennis. The players with rackets called briefs knock back and forth balls called Plt and Dft (plaintif and defendant): "young, robust Gamesters sometimes strike them away immediately, but those who are more experienc'd will keep them up till they are beaten to Pieces." The essay of July 17, then, published just as Fielding began to ride the Western Circuit, is exclusively about the law and gives some idea of how he, or any law student of the time, looked back on his legal education: the law books, which he had to memorize and annotate, consist of "no less than two hundred and seventy-three thousand, six hunded and nineteen Volumes in *Folio*" – by now, he notes, probably many more, as well as the statutes. The impossibility of such a task as reading all of these is mitigated by the use of abridgments.[62]

The next essay, on the 22nd, carries the subject of law into the criminal code and is, not surprisingly, most feeling on the punishment of debtors: The magistrate

takes a little Scrip of the Skin of a Person, to whom they give the Appellation of a BLFF [bailiff]: This BLFF then lies in Wait for the suspected Person, and, as he walks the Streets, leaps upon him, and rubs his Shoulder with this Skin:

> Hence follows an Infection, which, unless the poor Wretch can immediately meet with a Medicine very difficult to be found, called BALLLIUM [bail], presently contaminates the whole Mass of Blood to such a Degree, that he is locked up in a Dungeon all his Life-time, as unfit for human Society.[63]

Theater is, once again, equated with hypocrisy ("every Person in this Country disguises his Mind, as much as Masque would his Countenance"), and churches are theaters, worship entertainment.

As these essays appeared, he was riding the Western Circuit, looking for cases to plead, which would have meant scraping attendance upon solicitors. Earning a living at law was not easy for new barristers. Two years later he complained to Harris that he was spending his days in court where "I was *Auditor tantum*," i.e., a listener only.[64] One wonders if Mr. Wilson's attempt to make a living as a "Hackney-writer to the Lawyers" reflects Fielding's experience as a barrister: "instead of furnishing me with any Business," the attorney "laugh'd at my Undertaking, and told me 'he was afraid I should turn his Deeds into Plays, and he should expect to see them on the Stage.' "[65] If we replace scrivener with barrister we could have Fielding's experience with the attorneys from whom he sought employment to plead their clients' cases.

From this point Fielding's yearly schedule can be assumed: during term he attended the courts in Westminster Hall; in the spring and summer he rode the Western Circuit – from Winchester, Salisbury, and Dorchester down to Bodmin. He ended each circuit at Bath, and we can place him there during the late summer and autumn of the year when he devoted himself to his writing. That he was writing as he practiced law is also a reasonable presumption: "At his Lodgings, upon ye Circuit," Harris writes, "he was often working on his Peices of Humour, which when Business was approaching, soon vanished out of Sight, while ye Law Books and the Briefs with their receptacle ye Green Bag lay on ye Table ready displayed, to inspire the Client with proper Sentiments."[66] By October 16, 1740 he had finished with a translation of Adlerfeld's *Histoire militaire de Charles XII, roi de Suède* (the purest hack work to which he ever committed himself), and he must have been writing prolifically to staunch the hemorrhage of money caused by his extravagant life style.

What we see in the records of the courts, to which his debtors were forced, is aristocratic high-handedness after the example of his father. Drink was contributing to the first signs of gout, which would cripple him in his forties, gambling ate into his dwindling funds, but above all the style to which he was accustomed required endless small loans. He apparently borrowed whenever he felt the need and was slow and litigious in repaying, as he was easy at lending and quick to go to court to recover. (His attack on demanding creditors in *The Champion* applied to himself as much as his defense of debtors.)

The case of his father, however, must have shaken him. General Fielding had signed a note for one of his officers, who reneged, leaving him to repay the debt himself in 1736. He eluded the creditors while beyond the reach of bailiffs as governor of Jersey, but when he returned to London in the autumn of 1740 he was arrested for a debt of over £2,000 and remained, unable to pay, in the Rules of the Fleet Prison (where Hogarth's father had spent five years, 1708–12, when his son was 11–15 years old) until his death in 1741; at which time it became clear that there was no patrimony awaiting Henry or any of his younger siblings.

Fielding's own arrest took place in February 1741, coincidentally soon after publishing attacks on Walpole in his *History of Our Own Times* and *The Vernoniad*. His extravagance exposed him to the pressures of his political enemies. When he needed money he signed a note for a loan; endorsed by his creditor, this could pass from hand to hand until bought up by someone who called in the loan.[67] This made it possible for an enemy to buy up the debt, call in the loan, and consign him to prison, effectually silencing him, as Donald Thomas puts it, "as effectively as by prosecuting him for seditious libel."[68] The only trouble is that the records of the P.R.O. do not substantiate this interesting thesis. No connection is discernible between the debtors and Walpole when in 1741 Fielding was finally arrested. Moreover, it is difficult to imagine confinement in a sponging house curtailing Fielding's writing.

A year later, in 1742, despite the success of *Joseph Andrews*, he found it expedient to move from the Essex Street house (an expensive £50 a year lease) to Spring Garden, near enough to Whitehall and St. James's Palace to be within the "Verge of the Court," where he was safe from arrest. He was also beyond the jurisdiction of bailiffs riding the Western Circuit, outside the jurisdiction of Middlesex writs, and in Bath, where he spent the remaining months before returning to London for the term of the Westminster courts: another example, as he would have seen, of the chicanery available to him in his new profession.

EXPERIMENTS IN PROSE AND POETRY

One expedient was the short-lived *History of Our Own Times*, of January–February 1741, which was essentially a political journal Fielding invented, oversaw, and to which he contributed two or three essays. This was a magazine, along the lines of the monthly *Gentleman's Magazine* but appearing fortnightly, thus supposedly more distanced than a daily, tri-weekly, or weekly, but less so than a monthly. The first issue opens with Fielding's essay on "history" applied to current events (historians are, of course, actors – ignorant "of what is acted by others, while we ourselves are on the

Stage" [1]), surveying the other "histories" of the ministerial *Gazetteer,* the opposition *Craftsman* and *Champion,* and the differently prejudiced advertising journals, and proposing the corrective of a true history: "To instruct our Cotemporaries therefore, a little better in the *History of Their Own Times,* this Pamphlet is instituted."[69] For his title he echoes the strongly Protestant *History of his Own Times* of his favorite historian, Bishop Burnet, who wrote what Fielding took to be the authoritative account of the Old Whig ascendancy.

In the second issue of the *History* he contributed an essay on shame. Pure Swift, it shows him playing with a combination of satiric fictions – the clothes metaphor of *A Tale of a Tub,* the punning on different senses of "shame" as Swift played with the term "Christianity" in his *Argument against Abolishing Christianity.*[70] Before beginning to elaborate on Swiftean satire, however, he makes some exploratory statements about the relationship between vanity and shame, public and private forms of punishment, that dealt with issues close at hand. Finally, in the third issue he concocted a dream vision – an allegory – in which he rewrites the story of Aeneas and the golden bough as an allegory of Walpole passing out favors to his followers and the bribable members of the opposition, ending with the Great Man as Milo, caught in his own tree of corruption, the prey of wolves. But Fielding writes his allegory in his own way, meditating on the primitive worship that transferred authority from the deity to his "Chief Priest," the "goodly fat Man with an insinuating Face."

These pieces served another end, fitting into a sequence of generic experiments that began in *The Champion.* The essay on vanity and shame may have served as a nucleus for the more elaborate essays on conversation and character he subsequently wrote for his *Miscellanies.* The allegory extended the experiments with that form in *The Champion.* Elaborating allegory evidently gave Fielding a sort of pedantic pleasure, especially in the baroque exfoliation of detail. The result is too intricate, often tedious, a mode of writing unsuited to him and, as he must have realized, to the times as well.

In the first issue he advertised his poem *Of True Greatness,* in the second *The Vernoniad. Of True Greatness* praises George Bubb Dodington, the immensely wealthy politician who had recently gone into opposition. False greatness is embodied in the man-in-power, Walpole, and while the Walpolean favorite "hails Himself the Great," Dodington retires to the country, where "True Greatness lives but in the noble Mind." A supplementary form of greatness-in-retirement is Fielding himself: "Thus the great tatter'd Bard, as thro' the Streets / He cautious treads, least any Bailiff meets," disdains his enemies who wish "to drive out Greatness from his Mind."

The form is that of the Horatian epistle as practiced in the 1730s–1740s much more skillfully by Pope. If this is Fielding's serious attempt at the career of a poet, as well as the assiduous search for patronage, it falls short, finding a final resting place in the first, most conventional, and least interesting part of the *Miscellanies*, where it fits thematically into the dominant topos of these years, the problematics of the Great Man. By "True Greatness lives but in the noble Mind," however, Fielding means in the integrity of opposition – not, as he reformulates it in the preface to the *Miscellanies*, in a Horatian middle way of greatness and goodness.

In *The Vernoniad* Fielding returns to the *Dunciad*, now not a parodic attack but a direct and laborious imitation; and not a denigration of contemporary dunces contrasted with Roman epic but an attempt to combine the denigration of Walpole and the elevation of the heroic victor of the battle of Porto Bello, Admiral Vernon. The classical model is, as in the *Dunciad*, a conflation of the plot of the *Aeneid* and, for the religious dimension of damnation, *Paradise Lost*. The conclusion combines the apocalypse of *Dunciad* III and Pope's anti-Walpole satire *One Thousand Seven Hundred and Thirty Eight* ("Pale honour sickens with a yellow mien, / And infamy in scarlet robes is seen," etc. [15:57]). Satan instructs Mammon (Walpole) to persuade Aeolus to release his winds on the fleet of Admiral Vernon, who following his great victory had received no further support from Walpole, thought to be jealous of Vernon's triumph. Aside from the association of the Walpole ministry with Satan's legions and Walpole himself with money and bribery (hardly new subjects),[71] it is hard to see how the poem could have much worried Walpole. It primarily shows off the poet's virtuosity (which was of course also true of Pope's *Dunciad*), suggesting perhaps that Fielding still thought he might become the Pope of his generation. *The Vernoniad* is an ambitious poem that must have taken some time to write and annotate. It suggests that Fielding is running through the Popean repertoire, despite the evidence apparent to him in his *Dunciad* parody of 1729 that this is no longer a viable literary mode. We have to suppose him at this point in his career trying various genres in search of the one best suited to his talents, most profitable as a way to supplement his fees as a barrister.

I am presuming that these experiments, primarily the *Journey from this World to the Next* and *Jonathan Wild*, were conceived and drafted in part at least during this period, though they were not finished and published until they appeared in the *Miscellanies* of 1743 – by which time they were marked by the more recent events of the fall of Walpole and the death of Fielding's daughter Charlotte. Otherwise we must suppose (as the editors of the Wesleyan Fielding do) that he wrote them during the year between the publication of *Joseph Andrews* in February 1742 and the publication of the *Miscellanies* in April 1743. This was possibly enough time for Fielding to have written both narratives as well as the essays (which are much more elaborate and formal exercises than the essays of *The Champion*). It is, however, difficult to imagine that he could have regressed from *Joseph*

Andrews, a wholly new conception in response to Richardson's *Pamela*, to the primitive picaresque of the *Journey from this World to the Next* or the Swiftean satire of *Jonathan Wild*.

Although *The Vernoniad* did not make the cut in the *Miscellanies*, it shares with *Of True Greatness* the subject of greatness, which figures in both text and notes: Charles XII, whose life Fielding had recently translated, appears as one example who, having "their bowels from vast empires tore, / Now sleeps, and plagues the northern world no more" (Marlborough, a truly "great" man, is predictably complimented), and the accompanying note refers to "the honours in all ages paid to conquerors (alias robbers) tyrants (alias murderers) and prime ministers (alias plunderers)" (15:42–3), words that echo the farces and suggest that he was at the same time writing *Jonathan Wild*. The topos is developed in Mammon's speech to Aeolus:

> "Nature 'twixt men no other bounds hath set
> Than that of sums – the little and the great.
> Nor is it reckoned scandalous, to be
> A rogue. The scandal lies in the degree;
> A little robber meets my disregard,
> A great one my embraces and reward."
>
> (15:43)

Hidden in the classical myth and the cynical words of Mammon is a momentary glance at the deist cosmology:

> " . . . And as for Jove, he troubles not his head;
> But on his throne sips nectar, and then nods,
> And leaves the earth to us, his demy-gods:
> Cares not the affairs of wretched men to know,
> Indifferent where I plunder, or you blow,
> As some rapacious heir, with eager eyes
> Sees on the board the golden heaps arise."
>
> (53–4)

This is followed by its corollary, the puppet show, in Aeolus' reply to Mammon-Walpole, the puppet master, the "demy-god" or demiurge who takes God's (the monarch's?) place (in *The Champion* Walpole was himself a puppet):

> " . . . The world's thy puppet-shew, and human things
> Dance, or hang by, as thou dost touch the strings.
> In gay and solemn characters they shine,
> In robes or rags: for all the skill is thine.
> Behind the curtain in a various note,
> Thou bawlest or thou squeakest through each throat.
> Each puppet's drest, as to thy will seems good,
> The robes thou giv'st them – and the rest is wood."
>
> (57–8)

The world view that emerges from the subject of greatness is the familiar one of the farces – the puppet master and the world as a stage.

The theater, however, was no longer a viable option – and with it the theatrical metaphor. Now Fielding's riding of the circuit, and the precedents available to him in prose narrative, predicated the metaphor of life-as-a-journey. Besides the picaresque tales and *Don Quixote* he also had, of course, those *Champions* with their discrete units of essays and exempla; with his legal experience he had his reading of legal texts and briefs, preparation of pleas for plaintifs and defendants.

"The Voyages of Job Vinegar" implied a narrative, but these essays never progress beyond Job's first stop, the land of the PTSGHSIUSKI, and his account of their society is a conventional satiric anatomy along the lines of Gulliver's "Voyage to Lilliput," pointing out the analogies with England.[72]

The *Journey from this World to the Next* was a picaresque narrative (the form of *Lazarillo de Tormes* and *Guzman de Alfarache*), a more primitive form than the *Don Quixote* narrative on which Fielding was to base *Joseph Andrews*. The picaro as an observer is simply a mirror, a standard (however smudged) by which to judge what he encounters. Quixote stands out as an ideal and/or scapegoat of society, the protagonist of an anti-romance (for example, an anti-Pamela). As a picaresque narrative, the longest part of the *Journey* is focused on Julian the Apostate. Like Jonathan Wild, he is an evil man, but as a picaro his soul passes through dozens of metamorphoses (as the picaro does from master to master), each presenting another facet of folly or knavery; instead of changing masters he changes bodies, each with its particular vices – of a shifty slave, a miser, a spendthrift, a flattering courtier, a fop, and various kinds of hypocrite such as the pretender to gravity. Julian, however, is trying with each new body to live a decent life so that he can get to heaven. One noteworthy aspect of the *Journey* is that it presents a sense of justice in which just one good or bad action can either save a person from hell or prevent him from entering Elysium. But Julian is also related to the protagonists of spiritual autobiographies – the hungry soul seeking redemption; and one result is a series of brief biographies. The *Journey* also draws on the Lucianic dialogue, presenting the journey to the underworld (tried out in *The Champion*), but the structure of a survey has nowhere to go except to one more reincarnation, and so trails off; indeed the final story of Ann Bullen was written by Fielding's sister Sarah.

Once again Julian the Apostate's journey is framed by commentary. Julian's memory serves as an almost authorial awareness; he is looking back and judging his own actions. Now that he is finally purged and in heaven, he says of Zeno's court, "nothing could be more gay, *i.e.*, debauched"; or, as a general: "SEVERAL Poets, likewise, addressed Verses to me, in which they celebrated my Military Achievements; and what, perhaps, may seem strange to us at present, I received all this Incense with most greedy Vanity, without once reflecting, that as I did not deserve these Compliments, they should rather put me in mind of my Defects" (1.12.56–7). There is Fielding the author on the outside, the "I" of the narrative on the inside, Julian in heaven, Julian in each of his metamorphoses, and finally the other people involved in each metamorphosis. As in the rehearsal plays Fielding's basic form is the presentation of a brief epitome in action, followed by an explanation of its meaning.

By far the most interesting part of the *Journey* is the opening, in which Fielding explores the relationships among the characters in a coach and develops the contemporary and local settings through which they pass: the dark city recalls London and the canaled city of diseases Leiden, both as experienced by Fielding. Life is a coach-ride and a walk, following certain paths, being checked through by customs inspectors (of death). The speaker has enough of the characteristics of Fielding himself (a recently dead child, fear of venereal disease, feelings of guilt) to appear anchored in some sort of contemporary reality beyond the satiric conventions.[73] One wonders at the detail of his friends and relations all deserting his bedside, being heard "quarreling below stairs about my will," and leaving him with a drunken old woman to watch after his body. "Imagine me dead," Swift had written in his "Verses on the Death of Dr. Swift," and Fielding has done the same.

The editor of the *Journey* begins by posing the critical deist explanation for the historicity of the manuscript: was it a dream vision of "some very pious and holy Person" or "really written in the other World and sent back to this"? – an explanation "inclining to superstition." Or was it, "as infinitely the greatest Part imagine, . . . really the Production of some choice Inhabitant of *New Bethleham*"? One wonders, for that matter, what is the significance of Fielding's choosing Julian the Apostate – the Roman emperor who outlawed Christianity – as his example of the transmigration of souls?

Jonathan Wild

Jonathan Wild continues the progression of Fielding's experiments in genres of prose narrative. In *Wild* he again takes up biography, now as a totality, a single life beginning with birth and ending with death at the end of a rope; but with "greatness" he invokes the biographies of Plutarch. Within the biography he introduces a mélange of genres, suggesting how unstable the generic situation had become by the 1730s: a disquisition on hats, another listing proverbs; classical orations and a *consolatio*; a scene of "matrimonial dialogue," something between a Lucianic dialogue and a scene in *The Modern Husband*; and chunks of romance – all of these parodies. They add up to the sort of mixture of genres and tones identified with menippean satire on the prose model of Petronius' *Satyricon* (which Fielding may also have read at Eton).[74]

Satire is the master genre, or the satiric anatomy, unified by the subject of greatness; biography is the genre to which it parasitically attaches itself. The result is different from a Swift narrative like *Gulliver's Travels* or even a *manual* on greatness on the order of his *Instructions to Servants*, with which *Wild* has something in common. Swift's narratives go off in different directions, while *Wild* remains thematically unified, vigorously focused; the variety is in the variations on the theme of greatness. The reason for the unity is that, given all the possible biographical forms, *Wild*'s basic structure is the argument (or the essay as argument), derived from Plutarch's history rather than the wandering informal essay.

Wild is Fielding's first experiment with a novelistic, as opposed to a theatrical, "character." Wild begins as a "Walpole." The parallels between Wild and Walpole went back in opposition polemics to 1725 when Wild's career ended on the gallows: Both plundered the public, both worked by bribery and the bending of laws, both had "gangs," but only Wild was hanged for his crimes. In 1740 there were hopes (disappointed in early 1740/1) that Walpole's fall was imminent. It was in the latter half of 1740 that Fielding wrote *True Greatness*, dedicated to Dodington (publ. Jan. 1740/1), contrasting his "true greatness" with Walpole's false greatness. *Jonathan Wild* was a work Dodington liked to read aloud to his guests at Eastbury.[75] As *The Champion* increased its political pressure, the references to Wild began to appear, and this seems the most likely dating of *Wild*'s composition.[76]

Wild begins as a surrogate or analogical figure for Walpole, or the "great man," which means that he is not the evil agent himself. The aspirant Walpole is always implicitly related to the true Walpole not only as low to high but as unsuccessful to successful; which has the effect of saying that bad as these highwaymen and dishonest servants are they are not nearly so bad as their superiors, if for no better reason than that they do not get away with it. The Wild-Walpole analogies in *The Champion* included the verses:

> Nor *Wild*, great Man! who had his Day,
> And kept the lesser rogues in Pay,
> Can live in *Newgate*'s Rolls so long
> As thou, thou greater R[ogue]! in Song.[77]

The surrogacy of Wild can be traced to his remotest ancestors:

> O shame o' Justice, Wild is hang'd,
> For that'n he a Pocket fang'd,
> While safe old Hubert, and his Gang,
> Doth Pocket of the Nation fang.
> (*Misc.* 3:1.2.11)

The idea was not limited to Walpole-Wild. In *Tumble-Down Dick* Clymene's song about the great and low ("Somebody and Nobody") had picked up the theme from Hogarth's *Harlot*:

> Great whores in coaches gang,
>   Smaller misses
>   For their kisses
> Are in Bridewell banged;
>   While in vogue
>   Lives the great rogue,
> Small rogues are by dozens hanged.[78]

In these poor, rustic, underworld types Fielding shows us not pure evil itself but, in a way, the effects of evil, perhaps more specifically the social effects. These people ape evil and so are, in that sense, victimized by it as much as is the good citizen.[79] Our detestation is directed at the general target of those "greater persons" beyond, while our immediate attention rests, with the ambivalence of comic response, on the particular case of failure.

In *Jonathan Wild* Fielding once again invokes the image of the puppet master as the "great man," contrasting him with the audience (and the readers of romances) who "know the whole to be one entire fiction, [but] nevertheless agree to be deceived" (3.11.124). The playwright is a Walpole-Wild who manipulates Heartfree and others as if puppets. But now, while Wild himself is almost always on stage, front and center, it is Walpole, or the great gentleman, who is backstage, in the sense of directing Wild, his imitator: and this application of the stage metaphor is the chief innovation of the prose narrative *Jonathan Wild*.[80]

Like Swift in his best-known satires, Fielding uses as his narrator an advocate of greatness who praises Jonathan Wild and, like Plutarch, indicates the standards by which he is judged. The fiction consists of the Plutarchian speaker and his example, Wild, whom we see trying to live up to his instructor's high standards. Swift and other conservative satirists employed such a figure with its dark side turned toward us as a symbol of modernity, a madness based on the reading of modern rather than classical books. As Quixote imitated romance heroes, so Wild imitates modern statesmen and prime ministers and ends, as Quixote ended at the foot of the windmill, on the gallows.

The narrator as an advocate of greatness, perhaps Fielding's equivalent of the priest and his religion, consistently holds Wild up to an ideal, a model of behavior or deportment, which poor Wild (an aspect of the comedy of the figure) never quite attains. Walpole and Charles XII, let alone Alexander and Caesar, are *not* the subject of this new type of writing, any more than, in Hogarth's *Harlot*, Jesus and Mary the Mother are. One consequence is that Fielding's subject is an ordinary contemporary of the lower orders, a criminal and *not* a statesman, a god, or hero.

A corollary is a certain sympathy at the failure of the Quixotic upward aspiration, and a kind of verisimilitude. Despite the extreme stylization of the narrative, some human characteristics distinguish Wild from "greatness" (though Fielding's irony presents these as qualifying him for the "true" greatness of the surrogate, who hangs). Wild is another Fielding character, like Tom Thumb, whose success in business strikingly contrasts with his unluckiness in love. His victory over Bagshot, from which he retires with three-quarters of the loot, is immediately followed by his amatory defeat at the hands of Laetitia Snap. Wild's trouble with women extends even to business: that other lady, Fortune, causes him to lose "every farthing in his pocket," and a little later he is cheated of his loot by Moll Straddle. He is not, like Thumb, afraid of women, but he is unable to cope with them (and is presumably unattractive to them); at any rate, as soon as he has beaten his retreat, the fop Tom Smirke emerges from hiding to enjoy Laetitia's favors.

In both cases love stands as a norm of ordinary human activity. The "great man" can be successful in swindling fools and innocents, in securing Heartfree's execution, but his true frailty appears in ordinary human affairs. He is even momentarily touched by pathos when Heartfree's death warrant arrives, crying, "I may yet prevent this Catastrophe. It is not too late to discover the whole"; however, "GREATNESS instantly returned to his Assistance, checked the base Thought, as it first offered itself to his Mind" (4.4.148). It is such "a Weakness in Wild of which we are ourselves ashamed," "some Spark of Humanity," a "Blemish," that sets him off from the ideal of the great: "BUT, in Vindication of our Hero, we must beg Leave to observe, that Nature is seldom so kind as those Writers who draw Characters absolutely perfect" (149). This may already be a reference to Richardson's Pamela; but here his "weaknesses," deviating from the straight line of satiric allegory, are small humanizing traits.

Wild is, like Julian the Apostate, bad with a few traces of good; his perfect greatness (evil) is marred by one or two flaws (resembling goodness). Wild is, in fact, what Fielding will call in *Tom Jones*, a "mixed" character; but reversed, Tom will pose the question how despite one bad act a character can be basically good; and in any case both serve as correctives to the notion of a paragon, of good or evil.[81]

Like Hogarth's Harlot, Wild is another poor "redeemer" for the vices of the great. But now Fielding, covering himself, also introduces a truly Christlike figure, as Hogarth had introduced Sarah Young in *A Rake's Progress* to supplement Tom Rakewell. Fielding had another precedent as well. While at the Little Haymarket he defended Lillo's earlier tragedy, *The London Merchant* (1731), against those who had dismissed it "because the subject was too low"; he admired the simplicity and honesty of Lillo himself ("the Spirit of an old Roman, join'd to the Innocence of a primitive Christian," he wrote in his obituary),[82] who was a jeweler by profession; and a few years later he brings these together in *Jonathan Wild* in the figure of Heartfree, who is constantly referred to with praise-by-blame irony as "low" (as opposed to Wild's greatness) and is a City jeweler.[83] Lillo's contrast of the good and bad apprentice in *The London Merchant* turns into Heartfree versus Wild.

Following the Plutarchian model, Fielding presents "parallel" (contrasting) lives – of Wild and of Heartfree, of greatness and goodness, and their consequences. Wild's deficiency is pointed up by his opposite. Each has a "fides Achates" – Wild has Fireblood; Heartfree, Friendly – and each has a wife, Letitia and Mrs. Heartfree. At the end of book 4, chapter 10, Mrs. Heartfree, recounting her stout defenses of her virtue, is interrupted by a clamor proceeding from Wild's discovery of Laetitia in the arms of Fireblood.

Irony

Fielding's mind was not focused in the *Journey*; but it is, as never before or after, in *Jonathan Wild*. One focus is the consistency of the ironic discourse, but in one respect he is quite unlike Swift: He bolsters his irony with commentary. He explains in the preface what he is going to do in *Jonathan Wild*, and he even translates his ironies as he nears the end of his story: "completely GREAT, or completely low" (4.4.149).

More than in the plays (perhaps because of the reputation of the plays), Fielding is reluctant to leave the reader or spectator to see the connotations for himself; he consistently informs the reader that this *is* a farce and what its significance may be. An important difference between Swift's and Fielding's satire is that, while both use the irony of the obtuse speaker who damns his own cause without realizing it, Fielding uses the device much more sparingly and will not let him stand alone but surrounds him with Lucianic frames. In the periodicals a self-damning letter was usually followed by Vinegar's commentary on it. Only once does Fielding leave his ironic persona to speak for itself without any frame; in *The Jacobite's Journal* (1747–8) John Trott-Plaid, a Jacobite, explains the mysteries of popery and Jacobitism, and only the exaggeration lets the reader know that he does not express Fielding's own views. Still, the result was not altogether what Fielding wished. He switches to a conventional persona shortly and comments:

> I have observed that tho' Irony is capable of furnishing the most exquisite Ridicule; yet as there is no kind of Humour so liable to be mistaken, it is, of

all others, the most dangerous to the Writer. An infinite Number of Readers
have not the least Taste or Relish for it, I believe I may say do not understand
it; and all are apt to be tired, when it is carried to any Degree of Length.[84]

Fielding seems always to a have been somewhat unsure of the device. Swift's
use of the ironic persona leaves open the possibility that some Whig or
Dissenter *did* write his pamphlet, that Whigs really are mad; but Fielding
bolsters his ironies with translations and commentaries. He feels that the
directing hand of a playwright or a barrister is necessary to impose order
on the chaos which satire describes and to make perfectly certain the
meaning of the action.

He shows less interest in his commentators as "characters" (Swift's
Gulliver, Bickerstaff, Grub Street Hack) than as devices for establishing
the objective meaning of an action. The clear reality of the external world
is his arena, not reality as it looks, feels, or smells to the individual. He
remains throughout his career more concerned with the problem of understanding, of fixing meaning, than with the problem of conveying the sense
of felt reality – with the reader's, as opposed to his character's, understanding. It is revealing that he thought of Swift himself as the ironist in *A
Modest Proposal*, the Lucianic rhetorician who assumes various poses without
losing his own identity.[85] While Swift merged the satirist and the satiric
object in a single character whose perception was of prime interest, Fielding once again separates them, producing essentially the same commentator–scene relationship that characterized the satire of Lucian.

There is, however, one aspect of Fielding's irony that, abundantly shared
with Swift, he carries from his early practice of libertine wit, complicating
the problem of meaning. Jeremy Collier, Sir Richard Blackmore, and many
divines referred to the dangerous implications opened up by wittily
drawing similitude out of difference, comparison out of contrast. In
Jonathan Wild the reader comes to expect the play of contrast (based, presumably, on Plutarch's contrasting biographies). Heartfree's *consolatio* in
book 3, chapter 2, contrasts as good to bad with Wild's soliloquies in book
1. But the reader, accustomed to Fielding's wit, may wonder when Heartfree's *consolatio* is followed in the very next chapter by Wild's pragmatic
defense of murder. The reader may be tempted to see a parallel, interpreting Heartfree's defense as perhaps equally pragmatic.

The most striking example is the structural contrasts and parallels
between the chapter on proverbs in book 2 and Mrs. Heartfree's romantic
narrative in book 4. The first, seemingly an authorial digression, in fact
concludes the long catalogue of proverbs with the one proverb that
matters: that someone born to be hanged need not fear drowning. This
proverb supplements the providential or supernatural explanation for
Wild's escape from a watery grave, offered in the preceding chapter; the
proverbial is then demystified by the pragmatic explanation, which proves

his escape to have been due to his ability to swim: he is simply afraid of drowning and is able to swim back to the boat. Both serve as a secular, demotic, popular answer to the providential explanation for his escape. But even the explanation of providence has replaced divine intervention with that of Nature, a female figure (Wild's nemesis elsewhere), who supposedly saves him for (not from) the gallows.

The title of book 4, chapter 9, "A Very Wonderful Chapter indeed; which, to those who have not read many Voyages, may seem incredible . . . ," indicates that Mrs. Heartfree's narrative is a parody of travellers' tales of the sort Shaftesbury had ridiculed.[86] All the generic characteristics of a romance are present: encounters with a monster the size of Windsor Castle, a snake a quarter of a mile long, the phoenix, and pumpkins the size of Stonehenge, but primarily the pursuit of a maiden by rapists. (This is the romance that would be focused for Fielding by *Pamela.*)

The explanation of both Mrs. Heartfree and the native chief for her safe and prosperous emergence from her adventures (with jewels intact in both senses) is providence. The narrative, however, asks to be balanced against the *other* case of supposedly providential escape – Wild's escape from drowning. In the context of Wild's swimming to safety we see Mrs. Heartfree scheming to circumvent and exploit her seducers; at best it is a more positive and more successful version of Wild's pragmatism. On the face of it, romance conventions applied to Mrs. Heartfree's narrative (or, more precisely, *by* Mrs. Heartfree to her narrative) suggest, on a realistic level, that she is "romancing" the facts for the delight of her audience; the parallel with the gilding of Wild's facts with providential and proverbial interpretations implies her own pragmatic cunning, if not, carrying the joke further, a cover for her sexual adventures.

The romance of the faithful wife's miraculous (providential) escapes from seduction is interrupted by the sudden, comic explosion of Wild's discovery of his *un*faithful wife, Laetitia, a wife whose word *cannot* be believed. The interruption can be read as a contrast between Mrs. Heartfree's constancy and Tishy's betrayal, but also as a contrast between Heartfree's and Wild's reactions – credulity for the one and angry realization of the truth for the other. But the second contrast draws attention to the witty parallel between the two wives. We may wonder, in the context of the *Champion* essays on deism, and especially the *Miscellanies* essays on "Conversation" and "Affliction," whether Heartfree is a case of the husband being able to remain happy because he can believe in romance, providence, and a god who intervenes in man's affairs.

Mrs. Heartfree's romance narrative also asks to be related to all the places in the text where innuendo implies an unmentioned sexual act and to Fielding's general use of irony to contrast words and actions. The effect of this irony is to destabilize, to work against Fielding's glosses and explanations, and to herald the double irony that will distinguish *Tom Jones.*

The formal similitudes ask the reader to interpret Mrs. Heartfree's story this way. The alternative is to conclude that Fielding grew tired and was hurrying to complete his narrative; that he had not yet reached the sophisticated control and craftsmanship of *Joseph Andrews*.[87] The corroborating evidence for the view of a slack Fielding would be the *Journey* with its interesting opening sections trailing off into a tedious series of reincarnations. Even if we were to conclude that the effect may not have been caught by a reader, the confusion of providence and prudence, of romance and truth, shows that Fielding was himself of two minds. Fielding's test of Mrs. Heartfree's romance contaminates the religious belief in divine providence.

Earlier, we are invited to compare Heartfree's soliloquy on rewards in the afterlife (3.2) with the speech of the Ordinary of Newgate, who is the spokesman for religious orthodoxy. He replies to Heartfree, who (like Parson Adams in *Joseph Andrews*) believes that a sincere Turk stands a good chance of heaven, that the Turk will be damned, as will deists and dissenters (4.1.136). Finally (4.13), the Ordinary discourses to the condemned Wild, to whom he should be giving comfort, condemning him to hell fires – which are reserved for "all Revilers of the Clergy" (182).[88]

Jonathan Wild is in some ways Fielding's most radical work, politically as well as aesthetically;[89] but it marks a dead end. The combination of an unstable wit and Swiftean irony will become, in the hands of Fielding the barrister, an epistemological tool that is developed most fully in *Tom Jones*.

Why was *Jonathan Wild* not published in 1740, following *Of True Greatness* and *The Vernoniad*? A series of references that appear personal strongly suggest that Fielding was being offered money by Walpole to hold back publication of an attack, and that, perhaps because of his sinking finances, the bribe was ultimately successful. Battestin speculates that as early as January 12, 1739/40 the *Champion* essay on turncoats could have directly reflected Fielding's dilemma; by February 14, in debt and hardship in one of London's coldest winters, Fielding published a letter from a "no Politician" who is being solicited by both parties; while sympathetic to the patriots' cause, he is tempted out of concern for his family to accept the protection and support of the ministry. Another allusion to offers of bribery to curtail the attacks on Walpole appeared in the June 5 issue; after which Fielding went on the Western Circuit, publishing only the "Job Vinegar" papers. But in the October 4 issue Fielding printed an allegory of Walpole the mountebank who is distributing his pills (bribes):

[He] is one whose Pills I formerly refused on the like Conditions now offer'd, tho' I own, being in an ill state of Health, I accepted a few to stop the Publication of a Book, which I had written against his Practice, and which he threaten'd to take the Law of me, if I publish'd: These Pills, tho' a mere Matter of Bargain, he was pleas'd to consider as a great Obligation: But I can tell him, his Nostrums have now done so much Mischief, that whoever takes any Reward of him to secure his Practice any Longer, deserves more to be hang'd, and is a more infamous VILLAIN than any on the Records of the *Old Bailey.*

This is not only a transparent allegory of the author's unfortunate dealings with Walpole, the last clause establishes that the "Book, which I had written against his Practice" must have been *Jonathan Wild.*[90] And to round off the story, in January 1740/1, in the preface to *True Greatness*, Fielding tells Dodington that

> tho' I have been obliged with Money to silence my Productions, professedly and by Way of Bargain given me for that Purpose, tho' I have been offered my own terms to exert my Talent of Ridicule (as it was called) against some Persons (dead and living) whom I shall never mention but with Honour, tho' I have drawn my Pen in Defence of my Country, have sacrificed to it the Interest of myself and Family, and have been the standing Mark of honourable Abuse for so doing; I cannot yield to all these Persuasions to arrogate to myself a Character of more Consequence than (what in spite of the whole World I shall ever enjoy in my own Conscience) of a Man who hath readily done all the Good in his little Power to Mankind, and never did, or had even the least propensity to do, an Injury to any one Person.

As Battestin points out, the Wild-Walpole parallel was at its most potent in the years leading up to Walpole's fall; the analogy was "stale and irrelevant after February 1742," when at last Walpole did fall.[91] Once Walpole had fallen, he would have felt free to publish, not for the polemic but for the literary quality of which he must have been well aware.

The law

The ambivalence and skepticism Fielding attached to the immanence of the deity, as to the authority of the playwright/manager, is finally corrected at the climax of *Jonathan Wild* by the one good magistrate. He justifies the judicial model (as at the end of *Rape upon Rape*) by the existence of this magistrate. It is worth noting that while one good magistrate is found there is *no* example of a good clergyman – not until Fielding introduces Parson Oliver in *Shamela*. The fact that the magistrate is the only model who provides a good and viable example suggests that the court is now emerging as the privileged model for Fielding.

This is reasonable since the judicial metaphor invokes British common law – precedent, empirical evidence, interrogation of witnesses, and the sort of search for consistency of narration, as opposed to all the false witnesses, the perjured evidence of Wild and Fireblood against Heartfree – that equates Mrs. Heartfree's narrative with romance and puts both it and her providential explanation in question. In judicial terms, the providential, mythological, proverbial, *and* existential accounts of Wild's escape from drowning and, by extension and parallel, Mrs. Heartfree's from attempted rapes, are not providence but cunning lies. The difference, however, is that the "good Magistrate," who sees through Wild's falsehoods, hears Mrs. Heartfree's implausible narrative and accepts it: Fielding the clarifier makes this distinction, as against Fielding the irresponsible wit who cannot let pass the opportunity for similitude.

With the study of law Fielding began to supplement, and finally replace, the theatrical with the legal model of experience, civil society, and the world. Life as theater was replaced with life as a court of law. In Fielding's case the author, play, actors, and audience become a barrister pleading for a plaintif or a defendant; the defendant and the witnesses who testify as to the facts of the crime; with a jury to decide the facts of the case, a judge to decide the law. The author, who in Fielding's rehearsal plays had a relatively prominent part vis-à-vis the play and actors, now, as barrister, becomes dominant. Indeed, William Blackstone in his *Commentaries of the Laws of England* (1765) will refer to the plaintiff or defendant as an "actor," and traditionally the barrister's declaration was referred to as a *narratio* or *counte* or *tale*. He in fact grew out of the medieval profession of counters or narrators. His job was to focus on the "circumstances of time and place, when and where the injury was committed,"[92] his main object to amplify the matter outlined in the writ, to reveal a full cause of action.

The barrister's pleading could be for a plaintif or for a defendant. While Fielding obviously pored over the cases and commentaries in the digests and case collections, he would also have drawn upon Cicero's classic defenses. *Jonathan Wild*, for example, recalls Cicero's defense of Sextus Roscius, which became an attack on Magnus and Capito, and demonstrated both aspects, defense and prosecution in "a charge supported by a host of convincing circumstances," that is, most prominently a *narratio* rather than the testimony of witnesses.[93]

The law was either what Fielding had been looking for – perhaps what had been instilled in him by the Gould side of the family – or the expedient that he found when he was cast out of the theater and when it became necessary to repudiate deism. What Blackstone called "[t]hat ancient collection of unwritten maxims and customs, which is called the common law", "not committed to writing, but only handed down by tradition, use, and experience" (as opposed to the rigid written codification of Roman canon law, "so heartily relished by the foreign clergy"), satisfied Fielding's distrust of the written word, which informs *Joseph Andrews* and is summed up in Parson Adams's casting of his *Aeschylus* into the fire.[94]

He would have agreed, probably at this point but certainly by the time he was writing *Tom Jones*, with Blackstone's claim that England, governed by the common law, was "[a] land, perhaps the only one in the universe,

:h political or civil liberty is the very end and scope of the constitution. This liberty, rightly understood, consists in the power of doing whatever the laws permit . . . by which the meanest individual is protected from
the insults and oppression of the greatest."[95] The law could, moreover, be
distinguished from the lawyers, the magistrates, barristers or solicitors,
sergeants or attorneys, who were often (as he repeatedly shows) corrupt.
The law and its lawyers become, in his discourse, a more salvageable equivalent of religion and its priests, but decidedly more reliable in ordinary circumstances, perhaps because English Common Law, however fictitious, is
to be preferred to the myths promulgated by priests.

Nevertheless, Fielding himself was not above utilizing the law as a lawyer.
We cannot overlook the way he was led (by his extravagance and fecklessness) to exploit the legal fictions and formalities of escape and legal repair,
a game that he may have related to that of the politeness and contrivance
he advocated in his "Essay on Conversation," which he wrote in 1742 or
1743. His modus vivendi reflected what we have already noted of his pride
in his learning, once classical and now also legal. It is not surprising to see
him deploying all of his legal knowledge to foil his debtors and sometimes
succeeding.

The law was the substitute Fielding adapted for the immanent deity he
found it difficult to accept in a world of chance (or, like a father in a world
of broken families). The law represented a great world of mutual relations
based most happily on "good breeding" or forms of politeness, including
religion and the "legal fiction" of God. It harkened back to the natural law
of the model of the world created by a wise transcendent deity and put into
the hands of the motley human race, for whom He serves best as a "legal
fiction."

It follows that the English common law also substantiated Fielding's
nationalist and religious orientation, symbolized by his song "The Roast
Beef of Old England." The glory of the English common law was
exemplified in the independence of the judiciary: the crown delegates
justice to independent and objective surrogates in courts; personal loyalty
to the king is replaced by "a more objective form of loyalty to an imper-
sonal Crown and to the king's common law."[96] As Coke had argued, and
the civil war verified, law "existed independently of the royal authority and
prescribed its own rules for the operation of society"; but in England this
sense of "law" found its real and proper center and authority in parliament
rather than in the law courts.[97]

Historically English Common Law was seen as a corrective to the Roman
law or canon law, the codified law of the emperors that was transmitted
through the popish church. Fielding accepts and propagates, most elabo-
rately in *Tom Jones*, the myth – as formulated by Richard Bale, Matthew
Parker, and especially John Foxe's *Book of Martyrs* and Baker's *Chronicle*, and,
following the triumph of the Whigs, Gilbert Burnet's *History of His Own*

Times – of England as an elect nation free of popish absolutism, based on an ancient Church of England founded by Joseph of Arimathea (of Glastonbury, Fielding's birthplace), independent of Rome in both ecclesiastical and royal pedigree but constantly threatened by a foreign papacy.[98] In retrospect, we can see that this legal fiction of a Whig England was already at hand in the opposition satire of *The Craftsman* and the model Amhurst and his friends (including Hogarth the artist) offered for writing (and painting) in a distinctively English way in an English nation.

Even geographically the law signified for a Londoner. The lawyers studied, dined, and slept in the Inns of Court, halfway between the City and Westminster, the commercial and political capitals of England; a geographic position that dramatized the English law's political function as mediator between Crown and people. (This law, of course, was the English Common Law; canon law, Roman and church-oriented, continued to be taught at Oxford and Cambridge.) Of further significance for Fielding, the Inns of Court were adjacent to the theater district where he had distinguished himself in the earlier 1730s.[99]

4

Author of *Joseph Andrews*, 1741–1742

1740 Apr. 7. Cibber's *Apology* published; satirized by HF in the *Champion* (Apr. 15, May 3).

Nov. 6. Richardson's *Pamela; or, Virtue Rewarded* published.

1741 Feb. 14. Second edition of *Pamela*, with puffs; 3rd edn., Mar. 12, (*DP*).

Apr. 2. *An Apology for the Life of Mrs. Shamela Andrews. In which, the many notorious Falshoods and Misrepresenttions of a Book Called Pamela, are exposed and refuted; and all the matchless Arts of that young Politician, set in a true and just Light. Together with a full Account of all that passed between her and Parson Arthur Williams; whose Character is represented in a manner something different from what he bears in Pamela. The whole being exact Copies of authentick Papers delivered to the Editor. Necessary to be had in all Families. By Mr. Conny Keyber*, publ. by A. Dodd (*DP*); 2d edn., publ. Nov. 3 (*Champion*).

16. *The Crisis: A Sermon. By a Lover of his Country* (anti-Walpole prose pamphlet in the form of a sermon), publ. by A. Dodd, E. Nutt, and H. Chapelle.[1]

Spring–summer. HF begins *Joseph Andrews*.

June 18. Edmund Fielding dies within the Rules of the Fleet; buried on the 25th, St. Bride's.[2]

29. Meeting of the partners of *The Champion* at the Feathers Tavern to auction the collected edition (publ. 25th) of the *Champion* (Nov. 15, 1739 to June 19, 1740); bought by Chapelle. Only HF opposes, probably a sign (as B supposes [308–9]) that he did not

want to be associated with the anti-Walpole essays (predominantly by Ralph).

July 7–Aug. 8. Rides the Western Circuit.

Aug.–Oct. Stays in Abbey Green, Bath; becomes acquainted with Ralph Allen; enjoys the company of Hanbury Williams and Sir Thomas Burnet, and corresponds with Harris.[3]

Oct. 30. The *Daily Gazetteer* urges Hercules Vinegar (HF) to come over to the ministry; again, Nov. 13.

Dec. 1. The new parliament meets.

Dec. 15. *The Opposition: A Vision* (anti-Opposition, pro-Walpole), anonymous, publ. Thomas Cooper, ministerial printer, and advertised in the *Gazetteer*).[4]

1741–2. HF's son Henry born.[5]

1742 Jan. 12. *Joseph Andrews* has been bought by Andrew Millar for £183.11s., and is announced as "In the Press," being printed (1,500 sets) by Henry Woodfall (*DA, Champion*); printing finished by Feb. 15.[6]

Feb. 2. Fall of Walpole. HF issues proposals for his *Miscellanies*; one subscriber is Walpole, now (following his resignation) earl of Orford, who orders ten sets on royal paper.

22. *The History of the Adventures of Joseph Andrews, and of his Friend Mr. Abraham Adams. Written in Imitation of the Manner of Cervantes, Author of Don Quixote*, 2 vols.; 2nd edn., "Revised and Corrected with Alterations and Additions by the Author," June 10; 3rd edn., ill. by J. Hulett, Mar. 21–8, 1743, with HF's name now added; by which time, as B comments, to "dignify the work by owning it publicly suggests that he understood what he had achieved" (326). Further edns. in 1748, 1751.

ANTI-*PAMELA*: CHARACTER AND ACTION

Cibber's Apology

Early in 1740 *An Apology for the Life of Mr. Colley Cibber* introduced Fielding to another sort of hero, another aspect of "greatness," which, as it happened, immediately preceded his encounter with Richardson's *Pamela*. The *Apology* was published on April 7, and promptly Fielding began to satirize it in *The Champion*. His response may have been initially prompted by a personal attack on himself: Cibber describes him as one who, short of money, found that it was more profitable to be "intrepidly abusive" than "decently entertaining"; "to make his Poetical Fame immortal," he "set Fire to his Stage, by writing up to an Act of Parliament to demolish it."[7] In the *Cham-*

pion for April 22, however, Fielding draws attention to the parallel between actors and politicians, stage managers and ministers, and Cibber and Walpole, both Great Men.

Cibber fitted, as the cultural (and in that sense central) manifestation of the time, into the pantheon of bugaboos of Fielding's early years. In his first decade of writing, Cibber and the "Triumvirate" of the "Great Moguls" of Drury Lane stood out from the Harlequin of Lincoln's Inn Fields. Rich, the theater manager who carries on the enthusiastic displays of Swift's *Tale of a Tub*, had been summed up in the third book of *The Dunciad*. In his first characteristic play, *The Author's Farce*, Fielding – more than a decade before Pope – turned his spotlight on the Walpole of Drury Lane, who symbolized the "great man" of the theater, embodied in the control of one of the two licensed theaters, a monopoly on productions, and who had the temerity to rewrite Shakespeare, reject quality plays (such as his own), and lord it over unfortunate playwrights. Cibber, as Fielding saw, represented a form of greatness, especially after 1730 when he was chosen poet laureate, that was parallel to the political.

On November 6 Richardson's *Pamela; or, Virtue Rewarded* was published. It would have been obvious to Fielding that Cibber's self-portrait was of a comic Pamela; written in a totally self-engrossed style, it was the memoir version of Pamela's letters and journal. *Pamela*'s immense popularity must have attracted Fielding's attention; it embodied all the issues Cibber's *Apology* had exemplified and more; and at some point it became apparent to him that Richardson was offering a solution to the problem of a viable literary genre in the post-romance, post-satire age which had to be responded to and corrected – for a range of reasons from the moral and (to a classically trained mind) literary to the personal (a way of earning money on which to survive).

The difference is that Cibber, in his *Apology*, exposes the "Strings, Wires, and Clock-work" behind the "stuff'd Cloth, painted Wood, and Hobby-Horses" of the stage.[8] This was an admittedly self-serving account of his life that goes beyond stage performance to its backstage reality and its materialization as a text, with all the authority and exemplary power that a text has, an issue that linked Cibber's *Apology* with Pamela's letters. That Cibber was describing the life of an actor helped, of course. The theatrical metaphor is at the center of the *Apology*:

A Man who has pass'd above Forty Years of his Life upon a Theatre, where he has *never appear'd to be Himself*, may have naturally excited the Curiosity of his Spectators to know *what he really was*, when *in no body's Shape but his own*; and whether he, who by his Profession had so long been ridiculing his benefactors, might not *when the Coat of his Profession was off*, deserve to be *laugh'd at himself*; or from his being often *seen in, the most flagrant and immoral Char-*

acters; whether he might not *see as great a Rogue, when he look'ed into the Glass himself,* as when he held it to others. (emphasis added; 6)

The metaphor is of the actor who is also manager, who can assign his own role, and can now show off the discrepancy, make it public, without shame. Indeed, the book "shall likewise include with them ['the various Impressions of my Mind'] the *Theatrical History of my Own Time,* from my first Appearance on the Stage to my last *Exit*" (7). "Exit" also connects the *Apology* with Fielding's *Champion*s predicting the fall of Walpole.

Cibber shows himself playing the poet, the writer, the lover, and the stage manager – all the roles of the Fielding scenario. And the result is frank, unabashed self-exposure. But he also shows the portraits of a whole range of actors and their acting styles – the life of the London theater in the first four decades of the century. Primarily it is the two sides of the coin that must have intrigued Fielding. "But why," Cibber asks, "make my Follies publick? Why not? I have pass'd my Time very pleasantly with them, and I don't recollect that they have ever been hurtful to any other man living" (5). Cibber, all blatant affectation, plays the Restoration fop who is more interested in the reputation than the reality of his trivial sins; whereas Pamela must be read as a hypocrite, declaring virtue while acting out a scenario of subterfuge, feigned fainting spells, and seduction for monetary gain. Above all, a false gentility (now having replaced the other aspects of greatness) which conceals "Vartue" as "Virtue" as it conceals the true lower-class name Shamela as the romance heroine's Pamela. Appropriately, Shamela's *Apology* is edited by Conny Keyber, a conflation of Colley, cony, *cuniculus,* and *cunnus,* plus the Dutch (Cibber's father's) pronunciation of Cibber.

In the *Champion* for May 17 Fielding shifted from the theatrical to the legal metaphor, charging Cibber with the murder of the English language before Hercules Vinegar's Court of Censorial Enquiry.[9] Fielding's Cibber testifies that any wounds he inflicted were "from Accident only," since he understood so little of the language, and the jury acquits him of murder, bringing in a verdict of Chance-Medley. (On June 20 Fielding was called to the bar.)

Responding to Cibber's *Apology,* Fielding may have recalled Vanbrugh's response to Cibber's first success, *Love's Last Shift,* with *The Relapse,* the case (in Laura Brown's words) of being "inspired by [a] specific, inadequate antecedent."[10] In this case *Love's Last Shift,* as well as the *Apology,* in many ways anticipated *Pamela,* as Vanbrugh's response anticipated Fielding's, by playing the social/pragmatic world against the internalized moral world of Lovelace and Amanda, Pamela and Mr. B. From the start Cibber had represented to Fielding (as he had to Vanbrugh) a kind of writing that clapped a happy ending on a play not because it was plausible but because it pleased the audience.[11]

Shamela

The reception of Richardson's *Pamela* was astonishing. Published in November 1740, it was reviewed in the *History of the Works of the Learned*, unusual attention for a "novel," and recommended by the Rev. Benjamin Slocock from the pulpit of St. Saviour's, Southwark; Pope claimed it would do more good than many volumes of sermons. In January 1741 the *Gentleman's Magazine* wrote that it was "judged in Town as great a Sign of Want of Curiosity not to have read *Pamela*, as not to have seen the *French* and *Italian* dancers."[12] In February the second edition appeared with preface, introduction, and "letters" praising and explaining *Pamela*. Fielding would have been particularly struck by the letter that says the book "will infallibly be looked upon as the hitherto much-wanted Standard or Pattern for this Kind of Writing," and that its story is "true," making "no Alteration in the facts" (vii, ix). Another letter assures us that *Pamela* was written "for the Benefit of Mankind" and "will become the bright Example and Imitation of all the fashionable young Ladies of *Great Britain*" (xiv). Already praised by the clergy, *Pamela* was presented in the second edition as if it were a sacred text.

These effusions, framing the letters of Pamela, forcing on readers the interpretation that her story is one of "Virtue Rewarded," appear to have been the immediate stimulus that led Fielding to write *Shamela*; if so, he had only the month of March in which to compose it, but time enough for someone who wrote with the speed of Fielding.[13] Like the rehearsal plays, *Shamela* consists of two parts – the burlesque and the commentary of the "editor," Conny Keyber, and two clergymen, Parsons Tickletext and Oliver. The first was equivalent to the "farce," the second to the commentary of the playwright, critics, and actors that framed it. The fit was perfect in the case of *Pamela*, whose problem was the discrepancy between words and actions.

On the face of it Fielding's *Shamela* was written from the point of view of Mr. B., the expression of a libertine, which ignored the sensibility of the underclass girl. So Pamela becomes Shamela, the designing slut that Mr. B. suspected her of being and that she also appeared to be to the aristocratic sometime-rake Harry Fielding in such slips as when, with her pursuer close upon her, she recalls: "I found his hand in my bosom; and when my fright let me know it, I was ready to die; and I sighed and screamed, and fainted away. And still he had his arms about my neck."[14] Fielding uses burlesque, the rake's weapon of aggression against his servant girl, giving us the words of the *true* Pamela: "I thought once of making a little Fortune by my Person. I now intend to make a great one by my Vartue."[15] As a burlesque *Shamela* is the simplest kind of anti-romance, the "true history" that travesties romance by revealing the real schemer, "Shamela," beneath the pious phrases and coyness of the pseudonymous

"Pamela." Thus Mrs. Jervis is revealed to be a bawd, Parson Williams to be Pamela's lover, and "our old friend Nanny Jewkes" to be a rival for the love of Parson Williams. And from the Fielding perspective (that of the *success-ful* rake), Mr. B. becomes the Booby he appeared to be in his bungling attempts to seduce Pamela.

Fielding also burlesques the servant girl's writing style, her breathless prolixity, piled up minutiae, circumstantial lists of wearing apparel and books, and furious scribbling "to the moment": "Odsbobs! I hear him just coming at the door," she writes of Mr. Booby. "You see I write in the present Tense, as Parson *Williams* says. Well, he is in bed between us, we both sham-ming a sleep; he steals his hand into my bosom." To which she adds, "I counterfeit a Swoon" (27).

The "writing to the moment" of Pamela's letters and the formal inno-vations of Richardson's fiction only serve to intensify the "erotic novel" pop-ularized by Eliza Haywood, whom Fielding had allegorized as the flagitious Mrs. Novel in *The Author's Farce*.[16] The action of the puppet play was the marriage of Mrs. Novel with Signor Opera, followed by her seduction of the Presbyterian parson Murdertext – an Addisonian allegory of the degen-erate "novel" which conceals its erotic intent under moralizing.

With the extraordinary support the clergy gave *Pamela*, Fielding sensed the peculiar danger of Richardson's hold over readers. The effect of *Pamela*'s "writing to the moment" was to draw the reader as close as pos-sible to the heroine's thought processes, to immerse an innocent reader in Pamela's immediate experience.

Immersion (Ortega y Gasset's term describing the effect of the modern novel)[17] may lead to a sinister titillation in *Pamela*'s erotic scenes, but more seriously it allows the reader to identify so much with the character that she tends to lose a sense of relationships, the wholeness of the moral design, and a moral perspective on the character.[18] I use the feminine pronoun because, while Fielding would have appreciated the danger to readers of both sexes, he was drawn to this novel by its particular danger to women, in his opinion the readers most susceptible because most inex-perienced. The reader becomes uncritical, a "friend" of the character, and having accepted Pamela's rationalizations as completely as she would her own, emerges from the experience ready to modify her own conduct accordingly, and become another Pamela; with two possible consequences: She can end as Hogarth's Harlot did, an unsuccessful Pamela destroyed by men; or she can successfully seduce rakes and raise her own social status to theirs.

The personal application is not far to seek: Fielding himself, as reader, was the rake who only avoided Mr. B's folly by a strict control of his passions, as described in a *Champion* essay and not always achieved. He would be worried by the besotted B. – and indeed may have feared, as he had good reason to, that he was destined to relive Mr. B's experience himself one day. The more general application, as Fielding the satirist saw it (remembering his plays), was the danger of fashion and the conventions of "greatness" and "great men," all of which hindered not only the judgment of other people's actions but the decisions by which one takes one's own actions.

Fielding the barrister saw yet another issue, that of evidence in a court of law. In *Joseph Andrews*, considering the case of Tom Suckbribe, Fielding writes, "I am sufficiently convinced of his Innocence; having been positively assured of it, by those who received their Information from his own Mouth; which, in the Opinion of some Moderns, is the best and indeed only Evidence" (1.16.72). Alexander Welsh has argued that a change was taking place in this period in the presentation of evidence from the dependence on witnesses, whose credibility could be questioned on the basis of interest or simple error of perception, to the convincing narrative constructed on circumstantial evidence that was presented by the barrister (Welsh cites the well-known Blandy case of 1752).[19] Blackstone questions the credibility of witnesses "such as are *infamous*, or such as are *interested* in the event of the cause," as opposed to "the proof of such circumstances which either *necessarily*, or *usually*, attend such facts; and these are called presumptions, which are only to be relied upon till the contrary be actually proved" (though still "next to *positive* proof").[20] The germ of the contrast between witness's testimony and barrister's narrative was already present in ancient common law, and in the 1740s Fielding would have been well aware of the distinction between the unreliable witness and the convincing *narratio* of circumstances in the case of Pamela, the prototypical unreliable witness.

Pamela was an example not only of the unreliable witness but of the assumption of supernatural proofs; whereas the judicial system of testimony and circumstantial evidence represented a traditional secularization (another aspect of the separation of church and state) of supernatural proofs of just the sort Fielding does invoke a few years later, in a different context, for a less sophisticated audience, in *Examples of the Interposition of Providence in the Detection and Punishment of Murder* (1752).[21] Fielding's youthful attraction to critical deism may have joined the rules of legal evidence as he entered the case of *Pamela* in *Joseph Andrews* and, more definitively, *Tom Jones*.[22] But he would also, and as the skeptical thinker he was earlier in the 1730s, have carried the assumption that "*positive* proof" is seldom established. This, the judicial or judicious narrative, addressed to a jury, with the author pleading, is the new form that Fielding offers as a corrective to Richardson's "witness."

Fielding's response in *Shamela* is the Swiftean (or Lucianic) one, letting the witness condemn herself with her own words. But even when he has made the dramatic irony unmistakable, and simplified the action by burlesquing it, he must supplement Shamela's letters with the brief of Tickletext cancelled by that of Oliver, which places her actions in a clear per-spective. In *Joseph Andrews* he will drop the Tickletext figure (or incorpo-rate him into his text), leaving only a Parson Oliver to produce a convincing circumstantial narrative as a corrective to the whole Richardsonian enterprise.

The paragon

The second problem Fielding saw in *Pamela* was the apotheosis of the heroine into a "paragon," to which he responded with not its opposite, a villain, but a "mixed" character. From Pamela he educes an alternative way of constructing character. She is Richardson's personification (as the title page shows) of Virtue, and so Shamela is an anti-Pamela, which means a humanization of Pamela – or even a sign that Fielding believes that the personification of Virtue in Pamela includes particulars that, beyond Richardson's awareness, contradict the idealization.[23] Thus in good characters Fielding shows flaws and in bad characters reveals hypocrisy – Pamelian protestations contradicted by natural instincts (for Richardson, flaws). Fielding's procedure is essentially the opposite of personification, which was an agent of the sublime and so more appropri-ate for Richardson.

Fielding constructs Shamela in the same way he created Jonathan Wild. Besides the commentary of Oliver, he adds to the univocal letters of Pamela the letters from Shamela's mother, who treats her as her apprentice. In this sense she descends from the characters of *The Beggar's Opera*, Hogarth's Harlot, and, in particular in this case, Don Quixote, the imitator of romance. She acts according to a romantic ideal ("greatness," "fashion") that is external and not entirely appropriate to her. She reads her mother's letters which continually exhort her to pursue her (in fact her mother's) calculating end of capturing Mr. Booby, and listens to Parson Williams' Methodist sermons which advocate faith over works. Fielding's point is not only that these sermons are used as hypocritical masks but that they contain the code of hypocrisy that Shamela is teaching herself to follow. She is shown stretching to reach a mark held up to her by a hard taskmaster; her mother keeps urging her on and she, in her own way, like Jonathan Wild, always falls a little short.

Fielding's Shamela is, given her source in Pamela, a hypocrite, but her hypocrisy is learned from her models; her essential characteristic is passion for Parson Williams (because he is so well-hung and such a "jolly Parson"). Shamela's trouble is that she cannot control her passion for Williams, and in spite of her mother's warnings, this precipitates her downfall. Mr. Booby catches them in bed together and the whole scheme collapses. Though, as with Wild (and going back to Tom Thumb), the area of inadequacy is sexual, Shamela's is a positive passion she cannot control, while Wild's was a passion (first associated with physical hunger) that was not reciprocated and so ended not, as with Shamela, in a sexual explosion but in failure and disgrace, the old image of the cuckold. In Shamela Fielding is making his first move toward a protagonist who will supplant Pamela – not another Wildean villain. Love as a lack, Fielding says, helps to characterize the bad man and foretell the collapse of his schemes; but love as a positive force, even in so crude a form as Shamela's lust, will destroy hypocrisy and calculation.

He must have realized that Richardson's personification permitted Pamela to feel no physical attraction to Mr. B. and that her love came only with her realization of his conversion to virtue. This is the pious reading, which would have been Richardson's and Dr. Slocock's; not the psychological, which was Fielding's. The pious reader would have read Pamela's delaying her departure from Mr. B. as disobedience of her father's letter; Fielding would have read it as attraction to Mr. B. (as well, perhaps, as fear of returning to her parents and losing status), which leads her to continue finding excuses to stay. So he gives us Shamela, definitely attracted to – in love with – Parson Williams. Clearly this is lust, not love, as Fielding presents it.[24] But it also descends from the "love" of Polly Peachum in *The Beggar's Opera*, a romance convention against which we judge (however flawed and secondary, or "learned," her "love" was, derived from romances fed her by Macheath) the mercantile values of the parents and clergymen.

Fielding's reading of *Pamela* saw the danger of immersion in the plausible testimony of a witness, a young woman speaking in her own behalf, and so the acquittal of the culprit; but in *Shamela* he also offers evidence partially exculpatory because she is only a student, an imitator, herself immersed in her social milieu, and thus less guilty than the teachers and the fashionable code they expect her to follow.

For Fielding the major female symbol, the one who replaced Walpole, was Pamela, a paragon who tests both virtue and truth (sexual ethics and authenticity of text and voice), a challenge to which Fielding responded with great vigor and imagination. Initially, in his studies of greatness, Fielding's focus was not on women (as Angela Smallwood thinks) but on the constrictive forms of society that oppress women. This was a conventional view of women that Fielding held (and shared with Hogarth) based on the stories of Calista, Jane Shore, and the other tragic heroines. Twice in his *Craftsman* essays he refers to "the Protection of *distress'd Virgins*" as "the peculiar Business of . . . *Knights*"; which suggests, first, the oppression of women and, second, his own protective feelings, most likely focused on his wife Charlotte.[25]

We should accept everything he tells us, in letters and in his literary works, about his love for her. With her his attention had begun to shift from the object of satire to the ideal against which it is judged, from greatness to love. The secondary theme of love moves to the forefront in *Shamela* and *Joseph Andrews*. *Pamela* challenged his notion of a woman, outraging Fielding, a man who, infatuated with his wife, felt he knew what a virtuous woman really was; it challenged his assumptions of love, sexuality, and liberty, or rather offered him a foil against which to test his attitudes and analyses. With Charlotte love becomes a subject of primary interest, replacing the topos of greatness; love loses the compromising elements it carried with it in Polly Peachum and is raised to a primary level of importance, which *Pamela* in crucial ways questioned by opposing principle to inclination.

Perhaps at this point he had also to justify to himself his rakish past and his continuingly roving eye. Shamela's passion, recalling as it does Fielding's account of uncontrollable passion in *The Champion*, exposes and yet partially explains away the guilt usually associated with the male predator – but, oddly, in the shape of the woman he pursues. In her passion he, like her, may have seemed less culpable.

What is certain is that *Pamela* made Fielding conclude that a hero could be as interesting as a villain. His moral essays, though assisting him, could not have shown him the way. His reaction against *Pamela* led him to see that if the ordinary evil man is a mixed lot, so is the ordinary good man. With *Pamela*, and simultaneously his own married life, goodness became the problem for Fielding. The relative complexity of the evil man is transferred to the good man who is hereafter in the center of the narrative.

Joseph Andrews: *the ironic narrator*

As *Tom Thumb* grew into *The Tragedy of Tragedies*, *Shamela* was rethought and expanded into *Joseph Andrews*, in which Fielding expounds the larger issues of a new genre, defining it in contrast to Richardson's and to his own earlier work as well. He goes about it in the same way he did in *The Modern Husband*, claiming to replace burlesque, this time with comic "character." His solution, more successful than in the five-act comedies, is to supplement the directly imitated voices of the heroine and the commentators (Parsons Oliver and Tickletext) with one normative voice which controls and conveys the whole action. This is where Fielding's wit finds its appropriate venue: rather than in the conversation of rakes, in the form of a sustained ironic voice. But unlike the narrator of *Jonathan Wild*, whose irony was simple blame-by-praise, his irony now gives the impression of neutrality and authority, a corrective to the prejudiced testimony of a Pamela. It implies a contrast between a limited and conventional view and a more generous, inclusive one. This inclusiveness is very different from Richardson's, which gathers a great mass of minutiae and particulars within a narrow compass in order to submerge the reader. Fielding's irony holds the reader at some distance from the action in the old poet–audience relationship assumed and fostered by Dryden, Swift, and Pope.[26] With their authority, Fielding accepts the assumption that irony's air of artifice is compensated for by the sanity of the exposition. The "reality" generated by Fielding's irony in *Joseph Andrews* is a kind of control or discrimination, a depth of understanding – what Ian Watt has called "realism of assessment," as opposed to Richardson's "realism of presentation" or "formal realism."[27] If Richardson's "realism" is one of plenitude, Fielding's is one of larger and opposite reference.

If Richardson achieves an unprecedented verisimilitude by an oppressive intimacy, Fielding's irony polarizes his views of people, his kinds of people, and their experiences and motives. The ironic analogues he introduces have the effect of suggesting both the complexity and the interrelations of life. Ironic similes connect Slipslop and a tiger, Adams and Colley Cibber, Lady Booby and Cupid, Joseph and the Biblical Joseph.[28] The effect is like that of Fielding's earlier satires, to extend the behavior of a Lady Booby to the outside world of art, politics, religion, and the reader's own behavior. When Fielding wants to show how passion transforms sensible people, he compares it to Rich transforming (in his pantomimes) men into monkeys or wheelbarrows and to Cibber transforming the English language into something new and strange (1.7.36). The referents are clear: The implications involve not only the theatricality of Lady Booby's passion but the irrationality that is at the bottom of Rich's and Cibber's theatrical "fictions."

Fielding distinguishes between reality as the placement of something in a proper or "true" relationship to everything else in the world, and (Richardson's) reality as an expression of the authenticity of something. It follows that by reality Fielding means moral or factual truth apprehended by the reader, whereas he sees in *Pamela* the accurately reported workings of a character's mind, without any concern for their truth or falseness in relation to the external world.

Affectation

In his preface Fielding defines his sense of "character" against burlesque, "the exhibition of what is monstrous and unnatural." This was Addison's definition, for whom burlesque represented monsters as comedy represented living "characters"; thus a Pistol in *The Author's Farce*, a Queen

Ignorance in *Pasquin*, or, more recently, a Shamela was a burlesque. But Fielding defines burlesque as "appropriating the manners of the highest to the lowest, or *e converso.*" When the fishwife speaks as if she were Dido, the effect is more dignified than when Dido speaks as if she were a fishwife. This is the mock heroic, the form that praise-by-blame irony took for Fielding's models, the Augustan satirists; used consistently and applied to a character, the mock-heroic takes the form of the character's "affectation." This creation of an "affected" character permits Fielding to redefine the transgressive term "burlesque" and argue that one form of it, a character's "affectation," is the only true source of the "ridiculous," at the same time that he characterizes Richardson's Pamela.

The embodiment of the mock heroine in the affectation of a character was ready to hand in *Don Quixote*.[29] Fielding invokes Cervantes' novel on his title page not only for its plot but for its hero, a modern who reads romances and believes himself to be a knight errant – a madman whose delusions are tested by contact with the real world; in Fielding's terms, the prime case of affectation and the ridiculous.

As his friend Arthur Murphy noted, analyzing the scene in which Adams assures a stranger that he is rich by showing his half-guinea, the reader experiences "an Emotion of Laughter attended in this Instance with a Contempt for *Adams*' Want of Knowledge of the World."[30] We may not totally agree with "contempt," but the point is that Adams' innocence is accompanied by the affectation that he *is* knowledgeable, for example, in the world of the books he has read.

Fielding's irony serves as a controllable equivalent of Richardson's presentation of the workings of a mind. As *Jonathan Wild* showed, irony is essential to Fielding's definition of a character. A character exposes himself by assuming an elevated diction that does not fit, or is not earned, whether in terms of education (Mrs. Slipslop) or morality (Lady Booby). Fielding puts mock-heroic speeches in his characters' mouths: Lady Booby cries, "Whither doth this violent Passion hurry me! What Meanness do we submit to from its Impulse!" and reveals that she sees herself as a tragedy queen and her lust for Joseph as a grand passion.[31] But the narrator's ironies, in the manner of Dryden and the mock-heroic satirists, also expose Lady Booby's mind. As soon as she is alone, "the little God *Cupid*, fearing he had not yet done the Lady's Business, took a fresh Arrow with the sharpest Point out of his Quiver, and shot it directly into her Heart: in other and plainer language, the Lady's Passion got the better of her Reason" (1.7.36). This passage tells how Lady Booby would describe her feelings about Joseph (in terms of Cupids and hearts) and what actually happened ("Passion got the better of her Reason"); the passage not only sets her lust in perspective but also demonstrates her self-delusion, revealing an unhappy, misguided woman who rationalizes her petty affair into a great, theatrical Didoesque love. Its effect in the larger context of Lady Booby's character is to suggest that her hypocrisy (calling her lust virtue) may be only a means to an end that is beyond her control.

Mrs. Slipslop sees herself as the desirable (and literate) lover of Joseph; in this sense she is "like" a tiger in the simile used to describe her. We are told that she "at last gave up Joseph and his Cause, and with a Triumph over her Passion highly commendable" went off to get drunk. The ironic praise is obvious, but what it says in context is that she *felt* that she had triumphed and should be commended. Fielding's irony consistently, whether in speech or the author's comment, suggests the character's rationalization, just as Pamela's moral interpretations of her actions do (less self-consciously) in the novel he is critiquing. Whether from the character's own lips or from those of the commentator, the irony tends to become an expression of the character's psychology – or at least the character's manners in the particular sense of self-justification and exculpation. Lady Booby wants to think that her attack upon Joseph is *something else.*

Although *Don Quixote* is the literary paradigm, Fielding also draws on his experience in the theater of the criminals who spoke the discourse of gentlemen and merchants in *The Beggar's Opera* and in some of his own plays. From art he takes his example of burlesque monsters, distinguishing Hogarth's native English representation of character from Italian caricature (the nationalism is an important element of the arguments of both Fielding and Hogarth). "He who should call the ingenious Hogarth a burlesque painter," Fielding writes, "would in my Opinion do him very little Honour; for sure it is much easier, much less the Subject of Admiration, to paint a Man with a Nose, or any other Feature, of a preposterous Size, or to expose him in some absurd or monstrous Attitude, than to express the Affections of Men on Canvas" (6).

Hogarth reciprocated Fielding's compliment a year later with his subscription ticket to *Marriage A-la-mode*, called *Characters and Caricaturas* (see plate 11), which advised the reader to consult for further information the preface to *Joseph Andrews*. This print was, among other things, a comment on the construction of character in Fielding's novel. At the bottom center of the cloud of faces representing "character" are, grinning at each other, likenesses of Hogarth the "comic history-painter" and Fielding the "comic epic in prose" writer, who epitomize character (see plate 12).[32]

Underneath appear the idealized heads of St. John and St. Paul and, between them, what would ordinarily have been considered a "caricatured" or burlesqued head of a beggar. But all three are copied from the Raphael Cartoons, the generally accepted example of the highest reach of history painting. With these Hogarth juxtaposes caricatures by Ghezzi, Carracci, and Leonardo. Above them the mass of different, individualized faces expresses the variety of character – based on Raphael's beggar rather than

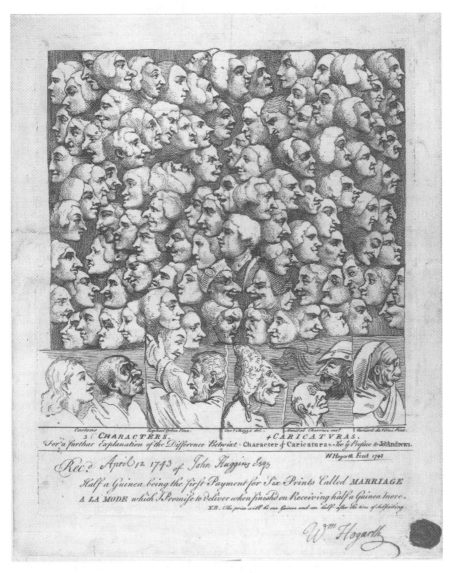

Plate 11 Hogarth, *Characters and Caricaturas*, 1743, etching, subscription ticket for *Marriage A-la-mode*, 1745, courtesy of the Trustees of the British Museum.

Plate 12   Hogarth, *Characters and Caricaturas*, detail, 1743, etching, courtesy of the Trustees of the British Museum.

either the caricatures or the idealized faces; "surprising" "variety" in the sense of Addison's aesthetics of the Novel. The subscription ticket announces that his new series of prints, *Marriage A-la-mode*, will be about "character," defined in the relation of the persons to the old master paintings and other art objects they collect (of martyrdoms or the Loves of the Gods), which define their affectation. This is an elaboration of the *Harlot's Progress* in which Hackabout was defined by her relation to a classical Hercules and a New Testament Virgin Mary, and then by her collection of a print of *Abraham Sacrificing Isaac* (in this case, she is Isaac) and portraits of her models, Macheath and Dr. Sacheverell. Her Jewish keeper was defined by the paintings of Old Testament scenes of harsh eye-for-an-eye judgment he collected (above, plate 7).

Models

Joseph Andrews begins with a discussion of examples (1.1) and a comparison of the exemplars of worldly wisdom, Pamela and Cibber, with the exemplars of simple goodness, Joseph and Adams. Besides contrasting good and evil, the examples also function as Fielding's way of defining character – in terms of contrasting images of themselves, the multiplicity of facets inherent in the notion of affectation. In one of the many epic similes attached to Parson Adams, we are told that

> he did, no more than Mr. *Colley Cibber,* apprehend any such Passions as Malice and Envy to exist in Mankind, which was indeed less remarkable in a Country Parson than in a Gentleman who hath past his Life behind the Scenes, a place which hath been seldom thought the School of Innocence; and where a very little Observation would have convinced the great Apologist, that those Passions have a real Existence in the human Mind. (1.3.23)

Adams' inability to detect malice and envy is compared to Cibber's, and the reader notes the irony – that Adams is unable (from simplicity and goodness) to recognize malice when it appears, while Cibber (all too aware of it) is unwilling to admit that it *is* malice. The parallel continues to be enforced from time to time, as in the chapter heading, "A curious Dialogue which passed between Mr. *Abraham Adams* and Mr. *Peter Pounce*, better worth reading than all the Works of *Colley Cibber* and many Others" (3.13.274).

In much the same way, Slipslop, whose pretended gentility and literacy recall Pamela's, is contrasted with Adams, whose shabbiness hides his true learning; a high churchman is contrasted with a low, a bad with a good. Whenever Fanny is in trouble at least two people come along, one to react selfishly and one (for either good or bad motives) to save her. When Adams asks a favor of two men, the first is rude, the second kindly.

Although Richardson presents an unromantic, bourgeois milieu, Fielding detects beneath the psychological and sociological realism the old outlines of the stereotypes of romance heroine, knight, and dragon. The heroine, taken at her own and her author's valuation, is much too good, and the villain much too bad; moreover, the subject is the pursual of the angelic by the diabolic (Mr. B. is frequently associated by Pamela with Lucifer). This Fielding takes to be an equivalent to the romance world of Quixote's reading.

He starts, in chapter 1, with Richardson's *Pamela* and Colley Cibber's *Apology*, just as Cervantes started with the romances of chivalry; here, says Fielding, we are shown an "ideal" male and female, models for their respective sexes. But they, like those knights and ladies, are neither real people nor real ideals; *Joseph Andrews* will show what a true ideal is and what real people are like. This involves, first, an adjustment of values. Self-seeking that uses chastity as a means to an end (Pamela) and vanity that calls unchastity a virtue (Cibber) are offered their opposites, true chastity and natural goodness (Joseph and Parson Adams). Second, it involves stripping off what appear to be virtues in most people and revealing the self-interest underneath. The latter, only half of the intention, corresponds to the travesty of *Shamela*.

But *Joseph Andrews* agrees with *Shamela* in treating the "romances" of *Pamela* and Cibber's *Apology* not as the reading of an isolated Quixote but as a pernicious ideal to which most people aspire. Fielding shows that ironically the romance world is the real (in the sense of practical) world. The Quixote parallel is enforced from time to time, as when Adams and his friends have difficulty getting away from an inn where they owe the reckoning: "they had more Reason to have mistaken [this inn] for a Castle than Don Quixote ever had any of those in which he sojourned, seeing they had met with such difficulty in escaping out of its Walls" (2.16.171).

The imaginary world of Quixote is quite real here: As was true in *Don Quixote in England*, these innkeepers and clergymen *are* monsters.

In the romance world characters' virtues are miraculously synchronized with their surroundings, and so Pamela saves her virtue and wins a fortune. Joseph and Adams, put into the real world where Pamela's virtues are as inappropriate as Quixote's delusions about chivalry, are notably unsuccessful. The explanation, Fielding insists, is that Pamela's virtue is feigned out of self-interest; this accounts for the strange synchronization of her "Virtue" and her world. Appear virtuous and act viciously: this is the Pamelian formula for success. Neither vice nor virtue can finally succeed, only pseudo-virtue.

The romance in the old Quixotic sense then is embodied in Joseph and Parson Adams. They have a true ideal that does not agree with the world around them, which behaves according to the code of the Cibbers and Pamelas. The romance values are chastity and charity, Christian virtues, all ironically exposed as inappropriate to eighteenth-century England. In short, Fielding has adopted the interpretation of *Don Quixote* (quite the opposite of Swift's, for example) that it attacks the accepted morality of contemporary society and criticizes it by the standard of an outmoded ideal.

Once the contrast of the examples of worldly wisdom, Pamela and Cibber, and the examples of simple goodness, Joseph and Adams, has been set up, Fielding takes the examples he has presupposed into the world of experience as Richardson and Cibber took theirs. By inference, Pamela and Cibber would have come through far differently. When Joseph maintains his virtue against Lady Booby's advances he is discharged; Pamela, for neither surrendering nor protecting hers, receives her master's hand in marriage. Adams is hardly an example for ambitious young Cibbers to follow: at 40 he is still a curate; when he had the influence of his nephew at his disposal he did not know how to use it. We are told from time to time what a different sort would have done in the same circumstances: the men who have captured him and Fanny, thinking them robbers, are so busy arguing among themselves over the reward "that a dextrous nimble Thief, had he been in Mr. *Adams*'s situation, would have taken care to have given the Justice no Trouble that Evening" (2.10.143).

True virtue seems to be, for Fielding, equated with the unfeigning and unaffected, with verisimilitude. As such, the unaffected person is repeatedly rewarded by abuse, blows, or even imprisonment in place of the vicious. Joseph is beaten by robbers and left naked in a ditch and is then subjected to equally brutal treatment at the hands of several respectable citizens who pass him in a coach. These are people whose respectable discourse is exposed as concealing acts as brutal as those of the outright robbers who left Joseph for dead. They are, once again, those rogues who die in their beds rather than on the gallows. The progress of

Joseph and Adams from London to Booby Hall is one long succession
of such violent encounters: Adams is brained with a blood pudding, chased
(as a substitute hare) by a pack of hounds, tormented with practical jokes,
and dropped into a tub of water. Throughout this section punishment
of the innocent acts as the central structural device. The persecutors, it
is made abundantly clear, in this world according to the theological
doctrine of rewards and punishments, are rewarded up to the comic
denouement.

In the opening chapter Fielding means by moral "examples" the literary models of Richardson's Pamela and Cibber's "Colley Cibber," both
as characters and as written narratives that allegorize experience. The issue
of Richardson's *Pamela*, greeted as it was by clerical praise, is closely linked
to the clerical authority of texts. The locus is, of course, Pamela's own text,
the letters by which the servant girl controls her betters and raises her social
status.[33] Like the accounts of New Testament miracles, they are in themselves nonsense, but tested against history and human psychology, they
reveal human desire.[34] In *Shamela* Fielding brought in Parson Oliver to
demystify the text as if he were Thomas Woolston. In *Joseph Andrews* he connects *Pamela* to the Old Testament.

History

From the classical historians Fielding took the topos of greatness, the compared and contrasted lives of Caesar and Alexander, and the "true history"
of Lucian. His contemporary historiographers, following the precedent of
classical models, tended to blur the distinction between the function of the
historian and that of the satirist.[35] The historian must be a judge, "shewing
the Rod to Tyrants, and advertising them of the Punishment [history] prepares. . . . Their future Fame keeps them more in awe than their Conscience." Thus in a history "Judgment follows the Narration of things." The
historian's claim was, in fact, very like the satirist's:

> He is Judge, and Judgment reaches the bad as well as the Good: His Func-
> tion is a publick witness, and 'tis the part of a Witness to conceal nothing.
> And in fine, 'Tis the publick Interest, that great Men and Princes to whom
> the *Laws* are but *Cobwebs*, should have some Bridle to stop them. and to a
> People that take *Religion* for a *Fantasm*, and *Hell* for a *Bugbear Eternal Infamy*
> is prepared for them in History.[36]

But Fielding's novels suggest that he was also sensitive to the changing cur-
rents of historiography in his time. The new developments were French
and evolved from Pierre Bayle's *Dictionary* (1690), of which Fielding owned
a copy.[37] The very formlessness of his *Dictionary* was Bayle's answer to the

over-formalized myths of earlier history, particularly ecclesiastical. For Fielding Bayle's test of myth by fact must have represented a historical counterpart to the Lucianic–Shaftesburian doctrine of ridicule; it was, as he must have been aware, one point of origin for the demystifications of the critical deists.

Typology was the ecclesiastical form of history – every character and action in the New Testament is foreshadowed by one in the Old – that was demystified by the critical deists. Battestin pointed out long ago that, on the evidence of many sermons, Abraham Adams and Joseph Andrews would have been regarded as the types of charity and chastity respectively.[38] What he failed to see was that typology was prescriptive and the character bursts out of it. Adams is an Abraham manqué: he can profess the conviction that Abraham was right to sacrifice his son Isaac but, when his own son is reported drowned, he forgets all of his professions and breaks the constricting type in which his Bible-reading has confined him. In the same way, "Joseph" (no longer Joey) rejects Lady Booby (Potiphar's wife), ostensibly because he acts according to the examples of the chaste Pamela's letters, and Parson Adams' sermons, but in reality because he is in love with a buxom young maid, Fanny Goodwill.

In 1740 in the third volume of his deist tract *The Moral Philosopher*, Thomas Morgan had treated Joseph and Abraham much as Woolston had treated Jesus; and Fielding similarly corrects the implausibilities of the biblical stories, revealing the historical Joseph and Abraham under the biblical paragons.[39]

If the first phase of the new development in history writing involved the questioning of accepted history as myth, the second demanded *l'histoire de l'esprit humain*, of manners, social institutions, and the forms of society. Voltaire is the great name associated with this phase, but Fontenelle and Fénelon as well as Bayle had advocated such history before him.[40] Their attack on heroes, like Fielding's, was supported by reference to facts and to factual accounts of customs. They advocated the study of "manners" as a corrective to the mere accumulation of facts – exactly Fielding's view in opposition to such writers as Richardson: Facts alone only confuse; they must be ordered so that the reader can reach a detached judgment.[41] The historical shift from political to cultural history, from battles to the conditions of society, family life and the like, parallels the general change in Fielding's work from satire to the novel, from the novel as satire to the novel as a study of manners and customs, and from a concern with the public realm to a concern with the social and the private. When Fielding uses the word "manners" in the introductory chapter to book 3 ("I describe not Men, but Manners; not an Individual, but a Species" [189]), he is equating it with species, meaning the depiction of character, disposition, and temperament. In practice his use of the mock heroic depicts manners in the sense of customs – customary modes of acting, fashions, or affectation.

Joseph is Fielding's working out of the "characters" of both Wild and Shamela – characters who attempted to live up to a standard but fell short; in that sense both were "mixed" characters, that is, human and flawed. They were related types, but Shamela, out of Pamela, was the more interesting because the more human. Pamela was "sainted" by Richardson and the clergy; and so Shamela was, by contrast, a harlot, but also in that sense a real, passionate woman. Joseph then *appears* to be a Shamela following the teachings of his sister Pamela and his priest Adams but in fact is motivated by his love for Fanny (as Shamela was for Williams). In both cases Fielding's is a demystifying, humanizing (and in that sense reactive) way of creating a character, parallel to Hogarth's treatment of M[ary?]. Hackabout, which began with the miracle of Mary and Jesus, the divine sacrifice and the Eucharist, and ended with the human sacrifice of a London prostitute. Both base this "character" on a preference for the human, the local and particular, over the heroic. As Hogarth, with the model of Woolston's demystification of religious texts, reacts to the priests' stories of miracles and the sacramental view of Jesus with a human version he regards as more real, so Fielding reacts to the canonization of Pamela by replacing her "virtue" first with a whore's passion in the real world and then, seeking a genuinely "good" protagonist, with a young man's.

In the scene where Joseph defends Parson Adams from the Squire's hounds, no simile, no figure from literature, says Fielding, is "adequate to our Purpose."

> For indeed, what Instance could we bring to set before our Reader's Eyes at once the Idea of Friendship, Courage, Youth, Beauty, Strength, and Swiftness; all which blazed in the Person of *Joseph Andrews.* Let those therefore that describe Lions and Tigers, and Heroes fiercer than both, raise their Poems or Plays with the Simile of *Joseph Andrews,* who is himself above the reach of any Simile. (3.6.241)

The simile transcended is only another way of saying what Hogarth said of the contemporary artist's model: "Who but a bigot, even to the antiques, will say that he has not seen faces and necks, hands and arms in living women, that even the Grecian Venus doth but coarsely imitate?"[42] When Hogarth wrote these words in 1753 he may have remembered Fielding's words in *Joseph Andrews*: Fanny's breasts are so beautiful "that Joseph hath declared all the Statues he ever beheld were so much inferior to it in beauty, that it was more capable of converting a Man into a statue, than of being imitated by the greatest Master of that Art" (4.7.239).

In *Joseph Andrews* Fielding has begun the practice of citing Hogarth for his mastery of likeness: If he only had the pen of Hogarth, he says he would show his reader how this or that character really looked. But when he attempts to convey Joseph's expression when accused by Lady Booby, after dismissing the sculpture of Phidias and Praxiteles, he concludes: "no, not from the inimitable Pencil of my Friend *Hogarth*, could you receive such an Idea of Surprize" (1.8.41).

Joseph Andrews ends with Joseph's refusal to make himself into a literary model like Pamela, declaring that he will never "be prevailed upon by any Booksellers, or their Authors, to make his Appearance [as Pamela had done] in *High-Life*." In between, Fielding shows Parson Adams trying to live according to books alone, but in a moment of great feeling throwing his book into the fire. There is a point at which a literary creation (Fielding never denies that either Joseph or Adams is this) can become mere fiction, by which he means mere model. When at the end Joseph refuses to be made a literary model, Fielding is demonstrating that his perception of the complexity of the real world would be only an exercise in bad faith if Joseph were to end as a new incarnation of the hero, engendering yet another set of maxims. Instead, he brings his story to a close by sending Joseph to bed with Fanny, an experience and not a demonstration.

Jesus' parable of the Good Samaritan

If Old Testament models are bad for the characters to follow – and the novel is about Joseph's (or at least the author's) breaking away from them and creating an identity of his own – one model from the New Testament, or rather from the parables of Jesus, is normative. The parable of the Good Samaritan stands firmly behind the episode of Joseph, the robbers, and the coachload of Pharisees and Levites with its one Good Samaritan (the postillion, later transported for robbing a hen roost), and its memory remains as an armature supporing patterns of social behavior in the rest of the journey to Booby Hall. The allusion to the Good Samaritan, Jesus' exemplum of charity (acts over faith), shows the reader how he is to take each encounter when there may not be a disinterested postillion present but only a chambermaid named Betty (lusting after Joseph).

The Good Samaritan was a popular subject of sermons; Bishop Hoadly's interpretation contrasted "the great Duty of universal Charity, and a most comprehensive Compassion" with the Levites who are "never so orthodox in their faith" but uncharitable.[43] Besides the sanction of Hoadly's sermons, the parable had a far more visible and public one after 1737 in the painting by Hogarth for the great staircase of St. Bartholomew's Hospital (see plate 13). In 1736–7 Hogarth executed two larger-than-life scenes, *The Good Samaritan* and *The Pool of Bethesda*, one illustrating human charity and the other

Plate 13 Hogarth, *The Good Samaritan*, 1737, painting, staircase, St. Bartholomew's Hospital, London; by permission of the governors of the Royal Hospital of St. Bartholomew.

divine; his pictures carry precisely the emphasis of Hoadly's sermon and of Fielding's scene in *Joseph Andrews*. When they were finished and in place, these pictures were part of the London landscape and the popular consciousness. Detached from the New Testament context, as indeed the deists detached the teachings of Jesus from the context of priestcraft, Hogarth offered visual images that trumped the stereotypes of the literary, printed text.[44]

For Hogarth chose to represent in both canvases the wounded or sick, a ministering figure of charity, and some Levites and Pharisees who, in the Good Samaritan parable, as Hoadly explained, are "in the Service of God, and devoted to the external Offices of their *Religion*," and so ignore the injured man.[45] The verses in the story of the Pool of Bethesda that connect the two stories are these (John 5.10, 16): "The Jews therefore said unto him that was cured, It is the sabbath day: it is not lawful for thee to carry thy bed"; "And therefore did the Jews persecute Jesus, and sought to slay him, because he had done these things on the sabbath day." Both Jesus and the lame man carrying his mat toward the curative waters of the pool are violating the Old Testament law; thus an act of charity transcends faith, the law, and orthodoxy.[46]

Hogarth and Fielding shared a distrust of scriptural authority, which Fielding safely embodied in the Old Testament story of Potiphar's wife, an obviously inappropriate model for Joseph facing Lady Booby. "Abraham Sacrificing Isaac" was the picture Hogarth affixed to the Harlot's wall (see above, plate 3), which summed up the patriarchal family, filial obedience, and arbitrary justice of a sort that was denied by Jesus' attempt to bring man back to the undefiled source of religion in love, in the face of the opposition of the scribes, Pharisees, and Levites – those who repeat by rote, who go by the written, the inscribed law, and who associate Christ with publicans, sinners, and harlots. The stories both Hogarth and Fielding chose were precisely those in which the ethos of Jesus comes into conflict with the scriptural law.

The encounter on the road is followed by one with the Tow-wouse family in the inn where Joseph is taken for treatment; the Good Samaritan is in this case a servant girl Betty, who is later discharged for going to bed with her master, Mr. Tow-wouse. There are other occasions, such as the unpaid inn reckoning, when the Levite Parson Trulliber refuses to help his fellow clergyman Adams, and a poor pedlar gives his mite. The Good Samaritan echoes build to unmistakable echoes of the trial and punishment of Jesus – Adams and Fanny condemned, the real criminal released.

Satire: words and actions

With the issue of Pamela the paragon went a second issue. When Pamela writes that she must escape the lecherous advances of Mr. B. but finds excuses to stay on in his house, she asks the reader to judge her words against her actions.

Fielding enters the construction of a new prose genre with the inclination and training of a satirist. As a satirist he was overwhelmingly interested in actions, and his aim was to distinguish profession from performance. In his rehearsal plays and in *Shamela* he placed commentators around actions so that both could be readily understood.[47] In *Joseph Andrews*, where he moves beyond the satire of *Shamela* to a formal alternative to Richardson's novel, he makes the important formal elements of his fiction the scene and the juxtaposition of a word and an action, a profession and a performance that exposes its falsity. To show that appearances or professions like Pamela's can be misleading, he fills his novel with situations in which a character speaks in high-flown (mock-heroic) terms, such as Lady Booby rationalizing her passion for Joseph (1.8–9) or the gentleman discoursing "on Courage, and the Infamy of not being ready at all Times to sacrifice our Lives to our Country" (2.9). Shortly thereafter Lady Booby's self-control dissolves and her lecherously leering face appears; the gentleman runs away at the first sound of a woman's cry of rape. A conventional pose (also what Fielding means by "affectation") gives way to reveal the real person through his actions – whether it be a worse person or occasionally a better. A third element is often present, which makes satiric judgment obligatory – an Adams, a quiet sort who makes no professions, but who rescues the girl who is being attacked or translates the Latin correctly, and thus gives us a norm by which to judge the other performers.

With the most important unit of satiric exposition established, Fielding launches into the elaboration of the central part of the novel – the adventures of the road. The parable of the Good Samaritan is his model for this simple satiric structure. Joseph is the prototypical touchstone, suffering humanity stripped of everything, but instead of stimulating charity, he reveals various forms of selfishness in the passengers: prurient prudery in the lady; greed in the coachman who wants his fare; in the lawyer, fear that the passengers will be called to account if Joseph dies; and in the old gentleman, fear that the robbers may still be near but eagerness for an opportunity to show off his wit in front of the lady. The ideal is indicated by the poorest, most un-Pamelian of the group, the postillion who lends Joseph his coat.[48]

This structure can be discrete, as in the stagecoach episode, or it can spread over several chapters. Joseph continues as a touchstone when he is taken to the Tow-wouses' inn, and reactions follow in quick succession – Doctor, Mr. Tow-wouse, Mrs. Tow-wouse, the servant girl Betty (like the postillion, the one charitable act), Mr. Barnabas the clergyman, and so on. Each new inn, each new encounter, presents a new "stagecoach" and a new set of characters to be met, tested, and judged.

The profession-performance and touchstone forms support the initial and sustaining argument of the novel about Pamelian appearance and reality. Beyond satire, however, these forms represent Fielding's notion of the way life operates, and they demonstrate his concern, doubtless growing with his career as a lawyer, with the meaning of an action. Pamela says she wants to escape from Mr. B., but if her actions are examined by themselves it becomes obvious that she really does not. Even at the outset action with Fielding is a way of dramatizing motive. But inevitably he must also ask himself: what of those undeniably pious actions such as Pamela's resisting Mr. B.'s lecherous advances and fleeing at his approach? Here the action by itself cannot be interpreted without reference to Pamela's motives. How much is it her virtue of chastity and how much her mercenary desire to substitute the role of wife for the less profitable one of mistress?

If Richardson is interested in Pamela's professions and actions, Fielding is forced back to her motives. Richardson claims that her professions and actions tell us her motives; Fielding suspects a radical discrepancy. The satirist ordinarily makes much the same claim as does Richardson (he admits that motives are slippery and thus relies only on concrete examples of conduct), but he is never accused of hypocrisy because he keeps an external and firm control on his characters. There is never a question of a discrepancy between action and motive in Swift's satire, only between words and motives or actions. But in the coach scene of *Joseph Andrews* character is judged as much through motive as action: the lawyer would take Joseph into the coach, but for the wrong reason (he is afraid, being among the last people in Joseph's company, that he will be legally held responsible for his death). Betty the chambermaid is kind to Joseph but her motive is at least partly sexual attraction. Again, landladies of inns refuse Joseph service because they think him a peasant, and other equally bad landladies lavish service on him thinking him a lord.

Charity is an objective action and so far does not depart from the criteria of the Augustan satirists. But, Fielding discovers, it is the motive of charity or love, already encountered in the Heartfrees who were foils to Wild (even perhaps the lust of Betty), that makes it good. Parson Adams, although he stresses works ("What signifies knowing your duty, if you do not perform it?"), is often prevented from carrying them out, despite his good intentions. When he offers the Catholic priest money, he finds he has none to give, and when he tries to comfort Joseph over the loss of Fanny, he in fact increases Joseph's grief. Although objectified in Adams' attempt to help the priest, and to some extent censured in his treatment of Joseph, the inwardness toward which Fielding is pointing can become in certain instances very difficult to prove; it could be related to the Quaker's inner light and the Puritan's conscience, both more concerned with private salvation than public welfare and both venerable targets of the Augustan satirists.

The touchstone structure is one logical development of the multiple commentators of Fielding's satiric farces. The normative aspect of these commentators led to the Fielding narrator. Their apparently different points of view in the farces resolved into a single one that unambiguously explained the action they observed. But the suggestion of multiple opinions and their reflection back on the commentators remained to some extent in the multiple reactions to a character or action that is itself unambiguous (perhaps made so by the normative narrator) and by which the spectators are judged. Already the device begins to imply the difficulty of judging an action, but as yet the difficulty lies in the observers, not in the action itself. The device may also, in the generally epistemological context of the anti-*Pamela*, suggest a range of attitudes rather than a group of different kinds of vice, or a comedy of manners. As part of an anti-romance situation, it brings together a number of people from different professions and social classes and records their differing reactions to a social situation or crisis, something out of the ordinary routine that will reveal their true selves, and (the crucial element), juxtapose the social appearance with the animal reality. In short, it suggests that revelation of character through an action is the point in question rather than merely the proof of a satiric theorem.[49]

The question a biographer poses, though cannot necessarily resolve, is how much of the word-action-motive structure is satiric convention and how much the author's choice among conventions and an expression of his particular way of thinking about and explaining himself. What is somewhat easier to assay is his transmutation of ugly experience into comic and satiric situations. The *Champion* essays showed what worried him and *Joseph Andrews* shows how he dealt with these on the level of comic art.

The Man in the Work

Journey and theater

Fielding saw Richardson's "new" literary form as dangerous because of its aggressive abandonment of classical models or any formal standards of excellence, its exaltation of the new and disordered, and its effect of raising the ego to an unprecedented prominence. Like the *Hurlothrumbo* farces and pseudo-tragedies of the 1720s, *Pamela* represented the culmination of the forces of bad writing and fraudulent morality that Swift had satirized in *A Tale of a Tub* and Pope in *The Dunciad*.

By the term "novel" was meant a contemporary romance, relatively short, usually a love story, which Richardson had expanded into something new and rootless – though, obviously, invoking the tradition of the spiritual autobiography and diary, which pretends to document the writer's conversion, salvation, and apotheosis, and serves as a Puritan tract. In the preface to *Joseph Andrews* Fielding claims to have developed the novel's affinities with the classical genres and in particular those genres associated with broad scope and objectivity of attitude. He specifies three models for his new form: on his title page *Don Quixote,* and in his preface the Homeric epic,[50] the "comic epic in prose" (a possibility recommended by Cervantes in *Don Quixote*), and his friend Hogarth's "comic history-painting."

In all of these acknowledgements Fielding is placing in opposition to what he considered the narrow world of *Pamela* the wide world of epic with all classes and all manner of locales.[51] His settings are out-of-doors, on roads, in inns, in coaches, on horseback, as well as in the places used by Richardson. Life is not a private relationship between a man and a woman in a closed room but a journey on which one passes through all kinds of experiences and meets a great variety of people.

The experience of Fielding the lawyer travelling from inn to inn as he rode the Western Circuit must have supplemented the stage metaphor of the 1730s with the metaphor of life-as-a-journey. In secular terms this was the metaphor of the picaresque, the uprooted youth surviving by serving whatever master he encounters; in religious terms it was the metaphor of pilgrimage. Pamela's "pilgrimage" led to heaven or hell, based on the assumption of rewards and punishments in the afterlife. One alternative was merely to wander around; Fielding's is a circuit from Booby Hall to London and back, roughly the one he knew in his youth as an annual itinerary and more recently as his professional rounds, with distinctly judicial overtones.

Addison, we have noted, preferred the metaphor of life as "a Theatre, where everyone has a Part allotted to him" and is judged by how well he plays his part, based on the belief in an inscrutable, transcendent god who assigns roles that may be inappropriate. Fielding returns to it and the distinction between character and conduct in a court of law. He adds to a lone protagonist and the mere flow of sequential actions an actor interacting with other actors in a set of specifically provisional situations that seemed much closer to the social reality of the period, especially with the doubts shared by Addison and Fielding about the role of an immanent deity, than the old Puritan teleology. Fielding's personal experience of the journey was, of course, in the context of a series of courtroom scenes of a law case, often plainly theatrical, involving plaintiff, defendant, counsel, judge, and jury.

In the *Craftsman* essays one moment he cited Shakespeare's "the world is a stage and all the men and women merely players," pointing to a "*ministerial Play,* which is somewhat like the *what d'ye call it,* or a *tragi-comical Farce*"; and the next he referred to life as a court of law.[52] One moment he argued that men have "forsaken the noble Roads wherein they were so well enabled to travel on to the highest Degrees of Happiness and Honour" for some byway; the next, in the same essay, he joined the legal and theatrical metaphors in the defense counsel's argument that men are often liable to assume "Characters for which Nature hath rendered them utterly unfit" (*Champion*, 1:14), which will be the burden of his argument in *Tom Jones*. Searching for figures, he slipped from one metaphor to the other, but the discourse remained primarily theatrical because of his abiding interest in role-playing.

In *Joseph Andrews* the journey metaphor dominates, not only as a narrative structure but as a discursive topic. The country inns are particularized, including their signboards, serving also as metaphors for his new "species" of writing. The novelist becomes the coachman (in *Tom Jones* he will be the innkeeper) and the reading of his narrative a journey. "Those little Spaces between our Chapters," he proposes, "may be looked upon as an Inn or Resting-Place, where [the reader] may stop and take a Glass, or any other Refreshment, as it pleases him"; in the same way, the spaces between books can be "regarded as those stages, where, in long Journeys, the Traveller stays some time to repose himself, and consider of what he hath seen in the Parts he hath already past through." The chapter titles are "so many Inscriptions over the Gates of Inns (to continue the same Metaphor,) informing the Reader what Entertainment he is to expect" (2.1.89–90).[53] Fielding urges his reader not "to travel through these Pages too fast: for if he doth, he may probably miss the seeing some curious Productions of Nature which will be observed by the slower and more accurate Reader" – that is, the ideal "reader" he shared with Hogarth.

The chapter divisions, of course, correct the flow of Pamela's letters, unbroken except by the end of one letter and the beginning of another (usually adventitiously). They bring with them the sanction of classical authority – Homer, Virgil, and Milton divided their epics into books. But most pertinent is the fact that the chapter and book divisions show the author's control (his immanence and responsibility for his characters).[54]

The journey is interrupted, or rather punctuated, by dramatic scenes in which Joseph is responded to by diverse bystanders, whose motives are judged. In the matter of Joseph's refusal of Lady Booby's advances, she is figuratively portrayed as judge, Joseph as the accused, and Love his advocate, and this is followed by Fielding's description (obviously from his own experience) of the pointless give-and-take of barristers arguing a case in Westminster Hall (1.9.45), and a bit later by an example of the ribald wit of lawyers (1.12.54). Parson Adams and Fanny are literally judged by a court of law – and other courts of law (where authority comes down hard on the innocent) are burlesqued. If to Richardsdon's closed rooms Fielding opposes the open road, to Richardson's attempt to immerse his reader in his character's consciousness he opposes the metaphor of life-as-theater.

Fielding's narrator is still in one aspect a playwright, a theatrical manipulator. Unlike Cervantes' Sede Hamete Benengeli, who is only a manipulator of the manuscripts he is translating, or even the "historian" or "biographer" he sometimes claims to be, Fielding continues to draw on his stage experience. When an appalling event like the abduction of Fanny by the squire's men takes place, he juggles scenes so that the reader does not lose sight of the overall structure of meaning in his/her concern for Fanny. Instead of closely, pruriently following her fate in the Richardsonian manner, he switches to "a discourse between the Poet and the Player; of no other use in this History but to divert the Reader" (3.10.259). The poet and player, sycophants of the squire who wants Fanny, and participants themselves in the abduction, casually discuss the subject of drama. This scene is followed by a dialogue between Joseph and Adams concerning Fanny, in which Joseph's anguish is counteracted by Adams' insistence on stoic acceptance. Only then is the reader returned to Fanny herself and her predicament. The juxtaposition sets off the narrative and the characters from the reader and emphasizes the author's controlling presence. It exposes the total unconcern of the poet and player about Fanny or any moral issue, as well as Fielding's Augustan analogy between the shoddiness of art and morals, between the stage and life. The effect of the pause after the abduction is essentially to allow contemplation of the action.

Further, all of the typically satiric situations are resolved happily. Having drawn out the full effect of the satire, the narrator cancels it each time with a happy ending. One example is the nightmare situation in which Adams finds himself when he saves Fanny from a rapist and is then accused by the would-be rapist of robbery and attempted murder. (This scene is a more naturalistic version of Justice Squeezum's court in *Rape upon Rape*.) He is brought before a justice and remanded to prison until the next assizes; having reached its satiric climax, after which only pathos can follow, the scene is suddenly interrupted; someone recognizes Adams, and all is saved, except that in the confusion the real culprit slips away. The ending does not cancel the effect of the scene (it preserves the good without altering the fact of the evil), but it does restrain satire from becoming Richardsonian melodrama.

Displacing experience

Although he cites *Don Quixote* on the title page, Fielding does not refer to the book in the preface. Rather he introduces it in the introductory essay to Book 3 as an example of a "History of the World in general," a universal rather than particular "biography." But, as we have seen, he has throughout utilized Don Quixote in a particular, unacknowledged way – as someone who reads a book and acts according to its model, "affecting" its heroism, and so behaving ridiculously.

Fielding begins his preface by citing Aristotle's discussion of a mock epic, Homer's lost *Margites*. But what worries him, he reveals, is Aristotle's assumption that comedy must deal with low people.[55] He remembers Pope's answer in the 1729 *Dunciad* to the accusation that the poor, unsuccessful writers he attacks are not proper objects of satire – that they *are* if they affect show and prosperity.[56] Thus a low type like Pamela can be comic (rather than pathetic) only by affecting or aspiring to the manners of her superiors. By the term low, however, Fielding feels he must, like Pope, justify dealing with the poor; although in *Joseph Andrews* the only poor folk are Adams, Joseph, and Fanny.

"Affectation" is a word with reflexive implications. His example of affectation is "a poor house, . . . a wretched family shivering with cold and languishing with hunger" in which we discover "a grate, instead of coals, adorned with flowers, empty plate or china dishes on the sideboard, or any other affectation or riches and finery either on their persons or in their furniture." It is Hogarth's *Distrest Poet* (1737; republished, December 1740; see plate 14), a more comic work than the *Harlot* or *Rake*, that Fielding alludes to as a case in which poverty can be a legitimate subject of laughter: In a shabby room wife and child are hungry while the poet, who sports the sword of a gentleman, writes a poem on riches.[57]

Concerned as he was with the subject of poverty, Fielding could not have been so obtuse as not to think of himself, fighting off bailiffs (for bills to Henley the coal merchant), permitting his family to suffer in the cold winter of 1739–40. In a February 1739/40 *Champion* he had criticized the rich who "condescend to visit Men of equal or superiour Birth, but infinitely their inferiours in Fortune," who hint "that small grates waste Coals" – or "that Carpets make a Room Warm, that one cannot set his Wig without a Glass"; in short, precisely the position he later assigns to the shivering poor who are affected and are therefore ridiculous. His example of affectation is precisely these large grates, carpets, and mirrors. And yet in March 1739/40 he was sued by Elizabeth Blunt, a stabler, for £15 for the "Coaches, Chariots, Chaizes, Horses, Mares, and Geldings" he had required during just two months in 1739.[58]

This may have been Fielding's own living room, with the flowery show to conceal the pain, a fictive way of dealing with the cold, hunger, and want which he had (as he must have realized) been at least partly responsible, like Hogarth's poet, for imposing upon his family. One side of him finds pathos in the clergyman's daughter who is brought up to greater expectations than she can realize; another side laughs at Mrs. Slipslop, just such a clergyman's daughter,[59] but is this because he feels he must justify Aristotle's dictum that the low are the objects of ridicule, or because he

Plate 14   Hogarth, *The Distrest Poet*, 1737, 3rd state, publ. Dec. 1740, etching and engraving, courtesy of the Trustees of the British Museum.

needs to distance himself, in his comedy, from the sentimentality of his *Champion* essays?

Though his credentials, unlike those of Hogarth's Poet, were real in that he *was* a gentleman, his situation in a sponging house could be regarded either as pathetic, or, in the right reactive mood, as comic.[60] In fact both he and Hogarth may have seen the mixture of comedy and pathos in the poet's situation (Hogarth's family having suffered in debtors' prison). But, as in *The Champion*, when he was writing an essay Fielding set himself off from comedy, and in *Joseph Andrews* Parson Adams, a typical Fielding poor man, is an educated clergyman whose values are unrewarded. It is the woman, Slipslop, who, though she is a clergyman's unfortunate daughter, trying to live up to her father's gentility, affects hard words beyond her small education and so speaks nonsense.

In *Joseph Andrews*, unlike *Tom Jones* and *Amelia*, Fielding includes no self-portrait. Indeed, Joseph, except for Fielding's nose ("a little inclined to the Roman") is his physical antithesis – of medium height, teeth "white and even," with "the most perfect Neatness in his Dress" (though with "an Idea of Nobility" about him) (1.8.38). Whereas, oddly, it is Adams – tall, clumsy, carelessly dressed, pedantic, a tobacco-lover, sociable – who parodies the aspects of Fielding that were most often described by contemporaries.[61] On the other hand, Fielding uses Joseph to express his own ungovernable passion for the one woman (Fanny or Charlotte) and Adams to express the official view that "All Passions are criminal in their Excess" (4.8.241). Fielding would have known about not only Parson Young's pedantry but the rigor of his upholding the morals of his parish; how, on September 20, 1733, he charged two of his parishioners with "incontinency" and getting a bastard; he required the young woman to do public penance in church standing in a white sheet before her fellow parishioners.[62] Adams' doctrine, however, is illustrated by the example of Abraham sacrificing his son Isaac, followed by the news that his son has drowned, which elicits passion. This can be read either as the explosion of Adams' precept by practice or as a justification for Fielding's own passion ("all such brutal Lusts and Affections are to be greatly subdued," Adams has said).

Although it is not likely that Fielding associated himself with the Adams whose figure Mr. Booby "could scarce refrain from Laughter at" (4.5.292), one wonders whether his absentmindedness (in a special sense, of putting off repayment of debts) finds an equivalent in Adams' "shortness of Memory." He has departed the inn forgetting to pay the ostler's reckoning, leaving Joseph to pay it. The bill was so large because he had ordered the horse to be "fed as well as they could feed him" but this was because he had borrowed it from his clerk, and, before leaving, he had divided his last shilling with Joseph (2.2). Continuing to walk away, Adams "fell into a Contemplation on a Passage in *Aeschylus*, which entertained him for three Miles together, without suffering him once to reflect on his Fellow-Traveller." When a passerby responds negatively to his preoccupation, "*Adams* told him he was a *saucy Jackanapes*; upon which the Fellow turned about angrily: but perceiving *Adams* clench his Fist he thought proper to go on without taking any further notice."

In the next chapter (2.3) Adams enters an inn and converses with a pair of lawyers. Two things happen: Their mention of a contention concerning payment for horse feed immediately reminds Adams of Joseph's plight and he determines to return at once. But it rains, and so he stays to listen as the two lawyers offer drastically opposed accounts of a neighboring gentleman – and, when they have left, the innkeeper explains that the truth lies somewhere between and reveals that the two lawyers had just argued a case before this gentleman, the JP of the area. "'God forbid! (said Adams,) that Men should arrive at such a Pitch of Wickedness, to belye the Character of their Neighbour from a little private Affection, or what is infinitely worse, a private Spite.'" In short, their accounts of the gentleman were partisan, as were the accounts of Fielding in the 1730s and the criticisms of needy writers he deplored in his *Champion* essays.[63]

I offer this sequence as an example of how Fielding, ostensibly the objective writer of a comic epic, nevertheless carries out a comic recovery of his own grim past, turning dross into gold. The scene in which Parson Adams turns to his "brother," Parson Trulliber, for aid with his inn reckoning is a comic version of Fielding's feelings, reflected in the *Champion* essays, that his friends should have helped him (2.14).

The other possibility, dross untransmuted, is also occasionally in evidence. The introductory essay to book 2 is about general versus particular character, or rather general versus particular satire *on* a character, along the lines laid down by Addison in the *Spectator*. The introductory essay to book I was on examples, II on chapter divisions. The subject of III, character (first introduced in the preface), is equally important. The discussion, however, only leads up to (or slips into) a tirade against the well-born who condescend to their unfortunate brethren without offering succor: "It is, I fancy, impossible to conceive a Spectacle more worthy of our Indignation, than that of a Fellow who is not only a Blot in the Escutcheon of a great Family, but a Scandal to the human Species, maintaining a supercilious Behaviour to Men who are an Honour to their Nature, and a Disgrace to their Fortune." This, I presume, is an overflow of Fielding's criticism in the *Champion* of the rich who "condescend to visit Men of equal or superiour Birth, but infinitely their inferiours in Fortune" and hint "that small grates waste Coals" (the latter recovered in Fielding's preface).

Joseph and Adams are presented as innocents, mistreated because helpless. Through the satiric fiction of the picaresque they receive all of the punishment Fielding may have felt he had himself received at the hands of cruel critics and creditors. Adams is, of course, something of a joke when he persuades Joseph to wait until he is married to indulge his sexual passion. But the Abraham and Isaac story, the prototypical father–son story, is only funny in the light of its sequel (profession followed by performance).

The problem of religion

The discussion of Adams and the innkeeper continues (2.3): The issue of lying and the innkeeper's admission that he sometimes lies leads into Adams' fear for his "immortal Soul" and his punishment in the "hereafter."

Upon which the Host taking up the Cup, with a Smile drank a Health to
Hereafter: adding, 'he was for something present.' 'Why,' says *Adams* very
gravely, 'Do not you believe another World?' To which the Host answered,
'yes, he was no Atheist.' . . . 'And dost not thou,' cry'd *Adams*, 'believe what
thou hearest at Church?' 'Most part of it, Master,' returned the Host. 'And
dost not thou then tremble,' cries *Adams*, 'at the Thought of eternal Punishment?' 'As for that, Master,' said he, 'I never once thought about it: but
what signifies talking about matters so far off? the Mug is out, shall I draw
another?' (2.3.100)

With this Horatian conclusion (both in the sense of Horace's *Epistle* 2.2
and his dialectic), Fielding recalls his association of the author with both
coachman and innkeeper. There are, of course, good and bad hosts, but
this one seems to represent a sensible secular position as opposed to
Adams' claims to orthodoxy – which were themselves put in question by
the argument with Barnabas at the end of book 1. In Adams and the
innkeeper he dramatizes both the Fielding of the 1730s and the Fielding
who was emerging at this time in the essays of the *Miscellanies*. One of the
things that makes *Joseph Andrews* a uniquely comic triumph is the balance
of these two Fieldings.

Joseph Andrews, though it originated as literary parody, was also an
attempt to resolve the religious tensions raised in the *Champion* essays. The
canonization of Pamela and *Pamela* was, we have noted, a stimulus that
would have brought into play the methods of critical deism; but Pamela's
claims to represent "Virtue Rewarded" also brought attention to bear on
the problem of ethical deism.

The chapter advocating the generality of satiric character opens up the
book, book 3, that is dominated by Mr. Wilson's narrative, the most autobiographical sections of *Joseph Andrews*. Fielding's autobiography, relatively
disguised up to this point, is distanced (or, more probably, *characterized*) by
being put into the form of Hogarth's *Rake's Progress*. Mr. Wilson is a man
who sowed his wild oats, following Rakewell's trajectory downward, fortunately to be saved by the lucky love of a woman.[64]

Mr. Wilson, new to London, joins a freethinking club. The "young Men
of great Abilities" in the club are Shaftesburian deists who profess a commitment to "the infallible Guide of Human Reason" and "the utmost Purity
of Morals," denying "any Inducement to Virtue besides her intrinsic Beauty
and Excellence" – that is, disinterestedness, the center of Shaftesbury's
aesthetics (3.3).

In practice, however, benevolence does not hold passion in check, and
innate virtue is overbalanced by an equally innate but more powerful
"unruly Passion," when one member of the club runs off with another's
wife. This is, on the one hand, Mandevillian, revealing the human desire
under the protestations of deist disinterest; and on the other, it may recall

the personal experience of James Ralph and Benjamin Franklin, when one or the other of these professed deists ran off with the other's lover.[65] Deism at this point serves as another example (as in the *Champion*, 1:233) of passion overcoming virtue. Indeed, the episode's first function is to serve as another variation on the Pamelian discrepancy between profession (however good) and performance: Running off with another member's wife was "so inconsistent with our Golden Rule" that it made Wilson "begin to suspect its infallibility." Whether Fielding identifies with Wilson, as is probable, or simply uses him as a form of expiation necessary at this time, the implication is that ethical deism was a phase through which a youth passes.

The debased practice of the society leads, however, to the remarkable rationalization by one member of the club:

> [1] there was nothing absolutely good or evil in itself; that Actions were denominated good or bad by the Circumstances of the Agent. [2] That possibly the Man who ran away with his Neighbour's Wife might be one of very good Inclinations, but over-prevailed on by the Violence of an *unruly Passion*, and *in other Particulars might be a very worthy Member of Society*. [3] That if the Beauty of any Woman created in him an Uneasiness, he had a Right from Nature *to relieve himself* (3.3.213, emphasis added).

The importance of the passage is evident from the way it breaks into different levels of rationalization, some deist and others Fieldingesque. First, "there was nothing absolutely good or evil in itself" is the ethical deist position, repudiated in *The Champion* and clearly unacceptable, in need of the safeguard of Jesus' teachings. With time, Fielding will increasingly stress the practical impossibility for most people of acting properly only from a "moral sense" without a consideration of rewards and punishments, either in this or the afterlife, that is, without the support of organized Christianity.

The third, "That if the Beauty . . . he *had a Right from Nature* to *relieve himself*," can be divested of the deist postulate "had a *Right* from Nature," and the remainder, including the phrase "*relieve* himself," is the germ of the problem Fielding will explore, without the ethical claims, in *Tom Jones* in the question "Can Black George really love Tom when he steals money from him?" and "Can Tom really love Sophia when he betrays her with Molly, Jenny, and Lady Bellaston?" It is in this context that we read the second proposition, that "the Man who ran away with his Neighbour's Wife might be one of very good Inclinations . . . and in other Particulars might be a very worthy Member of Society."[66]

After abandoning the Freethinkers' Club, Wilson takes to frequenting play-houses, "which indeed was always my favourite Diversion" – a statement that further suggests a parallel with the young Fielding, but which more importantly connects the "Man who ran away with his Neighbour's Wife" with the fiction of the theatrical metaphor. From playhouse and play-writing Mr. Wilson goes to gambling and a lottery within a world governed by chance. But it is his lottery ticket, the symbol of chance, with which Fielding, perhaps fantasizing, has reordered his life, which is now that of a reformed rake. This order is intended to reflect externally the internal order he has achieved, recounted in the "rake's progress" of his early life. "Chance," however, is not the "game of *Hazard,* much more than that of *Chess*" that Fielding had discussed in the *Champion* (Dec. 6, 1739); nor is it divine providence.

The episode of Wilson's freethinking club shows that the deists, however cogent their critique of Christianity, failed to formulate a convincing positive alternative, a version of "natural religion" grounded in the unaided human reason. But if Shaftesbury is wrong, and "natural religion" does not work, the same applies to the externally imposed order of the clergy, which serves only as a hypocritical cloak for such as Barnabas and Parson Trulliber. The latter judges a clergyman's worth solely by the quality of his clothes.

Chapters 13 and 17 of book 1 focus on Parson Barnabas, whose name suggests what he *should* be (a "son of consolation," a companion of St. Paul's in Acts 4.36) first to Joseph and then to Parson Adams. In Chapter 13 while Barnabas invokes doctrine, Joseph invokes a theology of love focused on his beloved Fanny. Thinking he is dying, Joseph says his only sin is "the Regret of parting with a young Woman, whom he loved as tenderly as he did his Heartstrings," and Barnabas assures him "that any Repining at the Divine Will, was one of the greatest Sins he could commit; that he ought to forget all carnal Affections, and think of better things." Barnabas, who has treated the wounded Joseph with anything but Samaritan charity, tells him he must "divest himself of all human passion, and fix his Heart above," which he can only do "by Grace," that is "By Prayer and Faith." Fielding is contrasting Pamelian virtue, grace, clergy, rewards and punishments in the afterlife, and the church with an ethic founded on charity and sexual love.

In chapter 17 Barnabas is brought together with Parson Adams; the subject is sermons, and Adams' religion is defined in terms of the methodist sermons of George Whitefield: "such Heterodox Stuff," as Barnabas says, "levelled at the Clergy. He would reduce us to the Example of the Primitive Ages forsooth! and would insinuate to the People, that a Clergyman ought to be always preaching and praying." Barnabas associates the methodist Whitefield with "the Principles of *Toland, Woolston,* and all the Freethinkers," but Adams says that in fact he agrees with Whitefield insofaras his aim is to strip the Church, or the clergy, of its political authority and to return to a primitive Christianity: "I am as great an Enemy to the Luxury and Splendour of the Clergy as he [Whitefield] can be. I do not, more than he, by the flourishing Estate of the Church, understand the Palaces, Equipages, Dress, Furniture, rich Dainties, and vast Fortunes of her Ministers." However, he does object to Whitefield's doctrine of faith over works and the concomitant "Nonsense and Enthusiasm" – that is, the irrational belief in the direct intervention by God in man's affairs, the existence of ghosts and other superstitions, which were the object of the deist attack on the Church.[67]

Adams' criticism of the principle of faith over works leads him to assert the prototypical deist commonplace (also repeated by Heartfree) that a virtuous heathen is more acceptable to God than a vicious Christian, "tho' his Faith was as perfectly Orthodox as St. *Paul's* himself."[68] When Barnabas and the bookseller cry him down, he responds by citing the authority of Bishop Hoadly's *A Plain Account of the Nature and End of the Sacrament of the Lord's-Supper* (1735), "a Book written (if I may venture on the Expression) with the Pen of an Angel" – a work that has survived the enmity and attacks of the clergy (one of which was to be found in Shamela's library). Barnabas responds by calling Adams a Woolstonian deist, a Hobbesian materialist, a Muslim, and the Devil himself.

Just as Adams asks Barnabas whether he has ever actually read Hoadly's book, there is a great uproar: Mrs. Tow-wouse, who has discovered Mr. Tow-wouse *in flagrante delicto* with Betty, is calling her a bitch. Betty, of course, is the one person in the Tow-wouse household who has shown kindness to the poor, battered Joseph. She objects not to the empirical fact that she was in bed with Mr. Tow-wouse but to being called a bitch – which, in fact, given her history of charity, and the facts of Mr. Tow-wouse's seduction of her, is a matter of dispute. As in *Jonathan Wild*, Fielding suggests a parallel between the mislabeling of Betty by the angry Mrs. Tow-wouse and of Adams and Hoadly by the angry Barnabas.[69]

Bishop Hoadly

Woolston, besides being the referent of deism in Hogarth's *Harlot's Progress*, was, of course, as poor and down-at-heel, as simple and downtrodden, as "misunderstood," as Adams. Hoadly, regarded by many as little better than a deist,[70] enunciated a position on the Bangorian controversy that coincided in important respects with the deist (and was supported by Toland, who saw a chance to cover himself with the cloak of ecclesiastical respectability): "that God's favor depended on sincerity rather than creed, that Christ's supernatural laws were not subject to interpretation by any ecclesiastical body and that, consequently, the church had neither doctrinal nor disciplinary authority."[71]

Hoadly was made a great deal of by Fielding, as by Hogarth (and indeed, Hogarth's deist friend Amhurst). Both made favorable allusions to him, using him as a kind of authorization of orthodox respectability for their heterodox views. Fielding would have encountered Hoadly in person in Salisbury society. Hoadly was bishop of Salisbury from 1723 to September 1734 and would have known Harris as well as the families in which Fielding visited and courted.[72] Hoadly was not, however, a respectable clergyman except with the civil authorities, who rewarded him for his separation of church from state with ever higher preferments. As an establishment clergyman, Hoadly was praised by deists in order to attack Bishop Gibson and other orthodox Church of England clergymen. But among his clerical brethren Hoadly was heartily disliked for what J. P. Kenyon has called his "militant unorthodoxy" and resolute insubordinacy to the ecclesiastical hierarchy.[73] The Hoadly admired by Hogarth and Fielding was not the supporter of Walpole but the Erastian Old Whig who called for a radical disempowering of the clergy.

Adams' description of Hoadly's *Plain Account* of the Lord's Supper was in the following terms:

> for what could tend more to the noble Purposes of Religion, than *frequent cheerful Meetings* among the Members of a Society, in which they should in the Presence of one another, and in the Service of the supreme Being, *make Promises of being good, friendly and benevolent to each other*? (I.17, 65, emphasis added)

What we find when we turn to the *Plain Account* is a redefinition of the Eucharist as just such a society as Adams describes. Like Hoadly's treatise, Adams' description is in effect a homely demystified version, not unlike Woolston's of the miracles of Christ, except without the satire. Hoadly, in turn, makes a case for religion that is remarkably like Fielding's in his *Champion* essays on deism. He wants to protect his parishioners from

> all those uneasy impressions of *Superstition*, which They had a right to be freed from, [and thus] I made it my care to state and explain the Commands peculiar to *Christianity*, from the first Declarations of *Christ* himself, and his *Apostles*, in such a Manner, as that They might appear to Honest Minds to have as little Tendency to create Distress and Uneasiness, as They were designed, in their first Simplicity, to have. (4)

He has eliminated superstition, reduced Christianity to "the first Declarations of *Christ* himself, and his *Apostles*," and his hope is that these doctrines may "appear" to relieve "Honest Minds" of "Distress and Uneasiness": in short, once again, the Mandevillian realist position that religion keeps our minds at ease and happy.

Hoadly focuses on the sacrament of the Lord's Supper, "which had been rendered very Uneasy to Them [his parishioners] by the *Notions* They had, by some means or other, embraced about it." He is interested in "removing any *Error,* or *Superstition,* from this part of *Christianity,*" which means "to shew the *Religion* of *Christ* to the World, as He left it: and . . . to remove from it whatever hinders it from being seen as it really is in itself" (viii). This means that he iconoclasts the Lord's Supper in a conventional Calvinist way, reducing it from an altar to a dining table and from the immediate divine presence in the bread and wine to a commemoration of Christ's sacrifice for men.

Underlying this iconoclasm is Hoadly's belief in the least amount of priestcraft and dogma, and so in the efficacy of works over rituals and ceremonies: follow the command "*love our* Lord Jesus Christ *in sincerity,*" extend this to our fellows, and little more is needed (vii). Such "orthodox" authority permits Fielding to focus morally on love.

While the sacrament that seemed most interesting and problematic to Hogarth was the Trinity, for Fielding (as for Hoadly) it was the Eucharist and the question of the immediate divine Presence. If Hogarth's works plainly deny the possibility of an immanent deity in both art and life, Fielding focuses on the question itself, and its implications, as his central interest. Why he does so is evident in his concern from his plays onward with the relationship between divine and authorial providence in a world dominated by the goddess Chance – by contingencies and epistemological confusions. He combines the notions of the Presence and Christ's love, as does Hoadly, in the Lord's Supper.

The *Champion* that advocated the Horatian "golden Mean" (Feb. 26, 1739/40) based its argument on a dinner – first a quarrelsome inhospitable family, an unpleasant dinner, in a rich household; second a happy family gathered around a congenial table with a contented guest. Fielding used the same model to define "good Breeding" in the "Essay on Conversation." As *Joseph Andrews* is constructed around scenes in inns, it focuses on meals, both good and bad. The "cheerful Meeting" Adams mentions is followed by the meal, the secularized Eucharist, held by Adams, Fanny, and Joseph – the good priest and his two parishioners – in a beautiful meadow with overtones of Eden:[74] They are eating food sent with them by Mrs. Wilson, and they give thanks for the Wilsons' charity and also for the succor of the pedlar who earlier paid Adams' inn bill (3.5). And this good meal is followed by its Corinthian perversion in the meal imposed upon them by the roasting squire and eventually fulfilled in the meal of reunion with Adams' family, where they are all shown "enjoying perfect Happiness over a homely Meal" in Adams' home (4.1.278).

Providence

Adams, refused aid by his brethren of the cloth, is in fact saved by the intervention of a poor pedlar, who has the exact amount to a penny. Fielding announces this windfall by repeating the *Champion* epigraph (Virgil's lines on the luck that permits Turnus to attack the Trojan camp [above, 102]) and this time glossing it in capital letters: "THAT WHEN THE MOST EXQUISITE CUNNING FAILS, CHANCE OFTEN HITS THE MARK, AND THAT BY MEANS THE LEAST EXPECTED" (2.15.133). This could be, in a more general sense, Fielding's awareness of what it meant to his career to have Richardson's *Pamela* published in 1740 (as being offered the editorship of the *Champion* did in 1739). But it also raises the issue of providential intervention. The pedlar appears in *Joseph Andrews* whenever some sort of divine intervention is called for.

The clergyman is followed in the next chapter (2.16) by the squire of the area, who promises Adams a living, a servant and horses, and various other charitable objects, but reneges on every promise. The contrast of clergyman and squire (the religious and secular authorities) that turns out to be a comparison is before the reader as Joseph, the servant, comments that "those Masters who promise the most perform the least; and I have often heard them [other servants] say, they have found the largest Vailes in those Families, where they were not promised any" (176). Significantly it is the "kind host" who brings the chapter to an end with his hospitality – food and drink. He is a figure who corrects "such a Monster" (Adams' words) as the squire. In the next chapter (2.17) he regales Adams with examples of the squire's false promises, including one that in a sentence redacts the story of Hogarth's Harlot, and ends with his own shabby treatment at the hands of the squire.

The stories of the squire lead into a disagreement over the interpretation of physiognomy – the innkeeper's worldly experience (reflecting Fielding's in his "Essay on the Characters of Men") that you can infer nothing from a face versus Adams' reliance on books. The exchange on books/life ends with Adams' metaphor of the clergy's book-learning: they "clothe you with Piety, Meekness, Humility, Charity, Patience, and all the other Christian Virtues," he tells the host, and feed "your Souls with the Milk of brotherly Love," and so on, playing out the metaphor. To which the host responds: "I do not remember ever to have seen any such Clothing or such Feeding" – that is, the priesthood remains theoretical, fictional, limited to books. Fielding is again plainly on the host's side.

This all sounds suspiciously like the traces of modernized allegory in the "comic epic in prose." There is a squire and an innkeeper, figures of authority in the world travelled through by Joseph, Fanny, and Adams. Fielding has already associated himself, as the author, with innkeepers, who at their best appear normative. The one squire central to Fielding's experience (and one who, like this squire, spent most of his time in London not carrying out promises such as the one to the innkeeper and, indeed, seducing the girl he has promised "to make . . . a Gentlewoman") was, of course, Edmund Fielding. But if Fielding faintly recalls his father, his primary purpose is to equate religious and secular figures of authority in the context of providential discourse.

In book 3, providence is linked to the ghosts who prove to be a posse looking for sheepstealers (12 murdered men, 12 sheep [3.2]) – another case of the divine providence of Jonathan Wild's escape from drowning, which was then explained by proverbial wisdom and, finally, by the fact of Wild's pragmatic act of swimming back to the boat. A few chapters later, Joseph, *in extremis*, thinking of his beloved Fanny being raped by the squire, asks Adams if there is nothing he can rely upon – and Adams replies, there is only resignation: "*Joseph*, if you are wise, and truly know your own Interest, you will peaceably and quietly submit to all the Dispensations of Providence; being thoroughly assured, that all the Misfortunes, how great soever, which happen to the Righteous, happen to them for their own Good" (3.11.266).[75]

This is the discourse of providential action (as earlier we observed the models, stereotypes, and affectation of character). When Joseph is being struck in the face, Fanny "invoke[s] all human and divine Power to his Assistance." When Fanny is attacked by Beau Didapper's servant, and "the deity who presides over chaste Love sent her *Joseph* to her assistance," the author is writing the discourse of providence, though careful to invoke Diana or some minor deity (4.7.303–4). The comic resolution with all the right people arriving to expose the truth and right the mistaken identities also partakes of the author's discourse of providence.

Fielding retains the figure and ethic of the New Testament Jesus, embodying them in a few good characters (the pedlar, the postillion, Joseph, and Adams). Against these he reproduces Shaftesbury's picture of priestcraft imposing and obstructing, in the figures of the Pamelas, Cibbers, and Barnabases (as well as the squires of) of society. Fielding puts Joseph and Adams in a world of unequal rewards and punishments (they are good but are punished in this life) but instead of projecting rewards in the afterlife, he gives them a Shaftesburian model in which the author-innkeeper, Fielding himself, endows them with order and meaning, making of them a fiction along the lines of Shaftesbury's "divine example." Joseph, no matter how harmonious a balance of affections he builds within himself, requires a Fielding – not a god who rewards with equal providence – to get him through; thus reminding the reader that, as Joseph Andrews is his own "simile," so Fielding's *Joseph Andrews* is itself the "divine example" available to us in this world, defined by Shaftesbury as the work of art.

Families, fathers, and sons

After Homer and Aristotle, Fielding alludes in the preface to the Abbé Fénelon's *Télémaque*, partly because it was an "epic in prose." To judge by advertisements and references in the London newspapers, the *Telemachus* (first translated in 1699) was one of the most popular foreign fictions in translation of the 1720s into the 1740s.[76]

Another reason to cite the *Telemachus* is that *Joseph Andrews* is not just "The History of the Adventures of Joseph Andrews," but of Joseph "And of his Friend Mr. Abraham Adams." Biography ceases to be the form (as it still is in *Jonathan Wild*) not only because *Joseph Andrews* is episodic, that is, about a segment of a life, but because it is about two people, an interpersonal relationship, a sort of corrective to the strictly amorous relationship of Pamela and Mr. B. (here relatively subordinated in Joseph and Fanny).

The *Telemachus* is a story of travel, education, and a son in search of his father. The instructor is not, however, the father Ulysses, who is thought to be dead, but the wise tutor Mentor, whose body, moreover, has been taken over by Minerva or Wisdom herself. The plot of the *Telemachus* is not (like either the *Odyssey* or *Aeneid*) about a hero trying to return home or trying to find a new home, or even (as we might expect in a romance plot) about the search for reunion with a lover, but about the son's search for his lost father – with, incidentally, his return home educated by his quest.

This prose epic begins with young Telemachus on Calypso's island, where his father had been earlier, telling her how he set out from Ithaca to find his lost father and save his mother from those importunate suitors. Both he and Mentor have by now concluded that Ulysses is dead, and he therefore needs to return home to his besieged mother. The knot here, as described by Andrew Ramsay in his "Discourse upon Epick Poetry" prefixed to the 1720 edition of the *Telemachus*, is "the Hatred of *Venus* against a young Prince, that despises Pleasure for the Sake of Virtue, and subdues his Passions by the Assistance of Wisdom."[77] Venus' surrogate Calypso detains him, having fallen in love with him as she did with his father. Prompted by Venus, Cupid naughtily makes Telemachus fall in love with a young nymph named Eucharis, and Calypso becomes insanely jealous in the fashion of Lady Booby: "her Eyes darted forth Flashes of Fire, her unsteady Looks were thrown at Random round her, they had something gloomy and savage in them; black livid Spots distrain'd her trembling Cheeks, her Colour chang'd ev'ry Moment; a deadly Paleness did o'erspread her Face" (1:144). Her ranting anticipates Lady Booby's: "Where am I! O cruel *Venus*, what Course shall I take? O *Venus*, you have deceiv'd me. . . . O! that I could dye, to put an end to my Sorrows!"[78]

Although Telemachus wants to stay on the island with Eucharis and Calypso wants to detain him, Mentor/Minerva forcibly removes him and they continue their quest. Taking the usual trip to the underworld and expecting to find his father there, Telemachus meets only his grandfather, who tells him that Ulysses is alive and will meet him back in Ithaca. There is a final victorious battle (among many), and he returns to find his father; but the meeting is offstage, after the epic's conclusion.

Joseph Andrews does not know that he has any father other than old Gaffer Andrews. When we first encounter him, as when we encounter Telemachus, he is no longer searching for a father but is only far away from home and (after being expelled from the Booby–Calypso house in London) trying to return. When he gets home, however, he finds his real father. All the way from London he has been accompanied by his Mentor, or Wisdom disguised in the all too human attire of Parson Adams, who, when Joseph encounters the Fanny (Antiope) he loves, keeps urging him to be patient and restrain his passion until they get home and can be married.[79] The narrative of Mr. Wilson serves structurally as the traditional epic descent into the underworld, where the voice from the past can be heard, and where (had Joseph not fallen asleep) he would have heard his father's story. But Joseph discovers his father, who has had his own odyssey, like Ulysses, and in both cases there is a father who has gone travelling and a son who, in some sense searching for his father, reenacts his odyssey and achieves an education.

The tradition of epic commentary interpreted the thematic or allegorical structure of the classical epics as a hero's education.[80] But, as *Telemachus* emphasizes, an education is almost invariably the education of a son, and it implies a family from which he sets out and to which he returns prepared to assume his familial function. The individual is not a lone sojourner, as in picaresque fiction or spiritual autobiographies, but part of a family, of a group. In *Telemachus* and *Joseph Andrews*, with the natural father missing, there is a substitute father, Mentor, and indeed while seeking his father, Telemachus enjoys a whole series of surrogate fathers, each offering a particular moral lesson. They extend from Hazael to Idomeneus to the aged Nestor himself, Ulysses' own preceptor and "father" of his mind.[81]

One of the things Telemachus learns from his quest – from both friends and enemies of Ulysses – is that his father, while a great hero, was far from being a perfect man. The lesson is that he must abandon the idealized image of his father. Then, when he learns that Idomeneus, the surrogate father he loves most, had years before in a momentary passion sacrificed his own son to the gods (an act Parson Adams defends in the case of Abraham and Isaac), Telemachus despairs of ever finding a perfect model of virtue among men. Minerva's advice introduces Telemachus to the subject which Fielding calls "mixed character," opposed to the theatrical "paragon": "You ought not only to love, respect and imitate your father, notwithstanding his imperfections, but you ought very highly to esteem Idomeneus, notwithstanding such parts of his character and conduct which I have shown deserve censure." Another implication of Telemachus' knowledge is that his father's absence has itself been a blessing in disguise, for without it he would never have been permitted to see beyond the illusion of human perfection (to which he would have been blinded at close quarters, at home) to the larger relationship of sons to a world full of "fathers" and tutors.

Fénelon's *Telemachus*, then, shifts the emphasis from the romance plot's search for the reunion of the lovers to the son's search for his father. Adams is of course a travesty Mentor and Joseph, when he falls asleep during Wilson's story, a travesty Telemachus. But even Adams is more than this; he is a contemporary parson whose function in the plot is merely clarified by the parallel with Telemachus' advisor. The personal allegory needs no explication, except that it centers, of course, on the absent father and dead, presumably idealized mother.

Andrew Ramsay, who himself produced a *Travels of Cyrus* (trans. 1727), in his "Discourse upon Epick Poetry" appended to the *Telemachus* distinguishes between the model for a character and for an action, arguing that the characters of Homer's gods, who do not act properly, are below those of Fénelon's heroes. A writer therefore should not use characters uncritically as models for his own, but he can imitate the epic actions of Homer and Virgil and draw upon their undeniable strengths (1:xl–xli). Telemachus himself is above the heroes of Homer precisely because he is not *supposed* to be a perfect hero: Fénelon "stirs up our Emulation, by setting before our Eyes an Example of a young Man, who, with the same Imperfections that every one finds in himself, performs the most noble and virtuous actions." Telemachus – or Joseph – is intended to rub against, jostle with, paragons like Pamela in her way, the biblical Joseph in his, and Adams in his, and come out "with the same Imperfections that every one finds in himself (xl)."

The Crisis *and* The Opposition

In March 1741, while Fielding himself was confined to a sponging house within the Rules of the Fleet, his father, also confined for debt, remarried once again, putting an end to his son's hopes of a patrimony. This symbolic act, and much more resentment, surfaced in April, in *The Crisis: A Sermon*, Fielding's final attack on Walpole. He wrote *Shamela* in the sponging house and probably *The Crisis* as well, and if so perhaps for money to help him through his own crisis. The title is significant. In the form of a sermon, its text *Revelations* XIV, on "If any Man Worship the Beast and his Image," it interprets the sin as "Prostitution for Hire" – at just the time when Fielding was about to change sides, or already had done so. The evil, the prostitution of the soul which is "to worship another for Gain, and do all his vile Purposes for Hire" (4), applies, first, to the follower of Walpole, who "sell[s] the Liberties of his Country" for bribes (7), but, second, to those of "us" who "sell the Liberties of our Children," to which he adds: "The Power of Fatherhood is the power of Preservation, not

Destruction. Let him look to it, who squanders the Patrimony left him by his Ancestors, and entails Beggary upon his Prosperity [i.e., misprint, or Freudian slip, for Posterity]" (8).

Edmund Fielding had just done this by getting himself confined to the Fleet for debt (shortly followed by, as if entailing it upon, his son Henry) and had given away his son's patrimony by profligacy and, finally, by remarrying his servant woman. The next clause shifts back to the Walpole "who prostitutes [his followers'] Liberties for Hire," as if Fielding conflates the Great Man and his father (perhaps a sign that there had been such a conflation all along).[82]

As Battestin notes, Fielding's reference to his father was not lost on the writers of *Old England* when, in 1749, they recalled that Fielding had been *"undutiful to his Father"* and *"impiously stigmatized him in his Old Age and Confinement with opprobrious Language."*[83] But his sister Sarah appears to have suffered as much as he from the financial follies of their father. Early in 1744 in the "Advertisement" to the first edition of *David Simple*, she excused herself from the unladylike occupation of writer by the "Distress in her Circumstances," adding that should her book "meet with Success, it will be *the only Good Fortune* she ever has known."

Edmund Fielding died in debtors' prison in June 1741, just as Fielding was beginning to write *Joseph Andrews*. With this father the son's obedience does not appear to have been an issue, or the son's rebellion against discipline or punishment. With Edmund we hear only of lenience; just "one stroke or two with a whip" was meted out to Henry for spitting in the servants' faces and disrespect to his siblings. What appears fairly obvious is his failure as a model of behavior for his son. There was first the father's absence when Henry's mother died and the children were left and then presented with another, a papist mother. Then there was the father who betrayed the memory of Henry's mother, not once but twice, presumably introduced him to the prodigal ways he himself followed in London, and frittered away Henry's patrimony, finally turning what was left over to his third wife. The moral side of Henry Fielding, which was the conscious and retrospective part, would have felt let down. His own transgressions could be explained away by one who sought self-justification as the result of his father's bad example. And so he writes a novel that begins with a chapter on examples and is structured on the interplay of good and bad examples and models of behavior.

The third admonition in *The Crisis*, however, is addressed to ourselves: "We cannot absolutely sell ourselves. . . . Neither can we give another an Authority over us, sufficient to controul our Religion, our Conscience, our Honour, or our Honesty," by which he means "to deliver ourselves totally and absolutely up to any Man" (8–9). This recalls the *Champion* essay of October 4, 1740 in which Fielding virtually acknowledged taking a bribe to stop publication of *Jonathan Wild*.

The sermon's aim is to "dissuade [its readers] from so black a Crime" as selling themselves: "And first from the Consideration of your own worldly Interest . . . , viewing it in the Light of Prudence only," and second, to "prevent us from bringing such Misery on others: The smallest Degree of paternal Affection, will inspire us to abhor the Thought of bequeathing such a Legacy to our Children" (10, 12). Fielding means the misery of such a government as Walpole's, but he has inextricably mingled the figures of Walpole, his father, himself, and his own children.

In December Fielding published *The Opposition: A Vision* (a sequel to *The Crisis: A Sermon*), his farewell to the opposition and his friends George Bubb Dodington, Lord Chesterfield, George Lyttelton, and Wilham Pitt; his message, that he was now writing for Walpole, unashamedly taking his "bribes."

We must imagine him taking time off from *Joseph Andrews* to write this pamphlet, which also acts as a vent for his long pentup feelings of inadequate reward for his efforts on *The Champion.* Its timing shows: It is good-humored (despite its obvious message, it cannot have offended his late colleagues), high spirited, written in the same mood as *Joseph Andrews.* But it leads back to that work, reminding that *Joseph Andrews*, while very funny, is nevertheless about as despairing a subject as *The Opposition* – about the shaggy asses who are whipped and not fed, and will be turned out to eat thistles; one of whom is "that long-sided Ass they call *Vinegar*, which the Drivers call upon so often to *gee up*, and *pull lustily*, I never saw an Ass with a worse Mane, or a more shagged Coat" (17).[84]

The Opposition, another dream vision, opens with a short account of dream theory, which describes Fielding's method of composition in *Joseph Andrews* as well. "Whatever makes a strong Impression on our waking Minds, either from it's Novelty, or any other Cause, is generally the Subject of our dreams," he begins. "The Object being once laid up in our Memory, Fancy culls it out at her Pleasure, and uses it at her Discretion; *raising, or confounding other ideas with it*, till it at last often *bears very little Resemblance to that, whence it was originally derived*" (emphasis added). This is another, more concise and also more candid explanation of comedy than the one presented in the preface to *Joseph Andrews*, which denied the essentially burlesque nature of Fielding's art. Also candidly, Fielding concludes with the admission that such dreams are "probably owing to nothing more than the quick Succession of Ideas, which it is the Province of Judgment [in the day-light hours] to prevent." That is, comedy is wit not reined in by judgment, that is, essentially farce, or burlesque.

Fielding also starts where *Joseph Andrews* started; he traces "the Chain of Ideas from their first Link, *viz.* from a Player to a Company of Players; from a Company of Players to the comical Romance of *Scarron*; and from thence to any Subject extremely farcical and ridiculous" (2). The player is once again Cibber, whose *Apology* the author has been reading, and the journey on the road follows, indicating the influence of Scarron's *Roman comique*, literally materialized in *The Opposition* with its wagon "extremely heavy laden" and crowded about with actors struggling to reach their next venue.

What, among other things, sets it off from *Joseph Andrews* is the additional figure, "a fat Gentleman . . . [who] appeared to have one of the pleasantest best-natured Countenances I had ever beheld." The benevolent Sir Robert Walpole arrives in a coach, which the driver of the players' wagon demands that he move out of their way and raises a whip to urge on the asses – "when one of them, methought, (such is the Extravagance of Dreams) raised himself on his hinder Legs, and spake as follows"; and this is Fielding uttering a short version of *The Opposition* he has just written ("O thou perfidious Driver!," etc.). Sir Robert, whose smiling aplomb reaches to the margins of burlesque, is the Mr. Wilson of the allegory, and we are tempted to decode him as momentarily at least, and tongue-in-cheek, the true father whom the "long-sided Ass" and Joseph were both seeking.

As we have observed, Fielding had a father who foreshadowed much of his own behavior as well as the consequences of that behavior; a father who can only be judged as a bad example for him to have followed, and who dies as his eldest son is writing *Joseph Andrews*. But why then does Fielding displace his own story of his own youth onto Joseph's father, Mr. Wilson? In a jokey way, Walpole in *The Opposition* is another Mr. Wilson, working toward the counter-model of a father, now that Fielding's father was dead, of the ideal of benevolence – Ralph Allen of Bath (a man of fifty, immensely wealthy, in whom Fielding had recently found a patron and friend).[85]

In his essays Fielding dealt with all the subjects that concerned him most during the troubled years between the close of the theaters and the publication of *Joseph Andrews*. In the essays he used these experiences unguardedly, often exposing himself as self-pitying and obtuse. In the stories he transforms this material into comedy by way of literary fictions. In *Joseph Andrews*, where he works out his problems most satisfactorily, or perhaps transcends them, it is largely because he has found the right fictions; but the reader's experience is that of watching him work through them – the fictions of satire (profession-performance, touchstone), of critical deism (the "living" person concealed beneath the fiction of a god or hero), of Shaftesburian deism (the bad god of rewards and punishments, the "divine example" of order in the work of art), and of Jesus' parables.

On March 26, 1741 a pro-Walpole print was published that shows the opposition in disarray, its leading journals following the "Funeral of Faction" (see plate 15). The figure leading the procession is Nicholas Amhurst, carrying a banner of *The Craftsman*; the second carries *The Daily*

Plate 15 Unknown artist, *The Funeral of Faction,* 1741 (detail of Fielding), etching and engraving, courtesy of the Trustees of the British Museum.

Post; the third is Fielding, carrying a banner or *The Craftsman* inscribed with Hercules' hand holding his cudgel. This is a portrait of Fielding as he looked in the 1740s, closely resembling the one Hogarth made from memory for Arthur Murphy's edition of his *Works* in 1762 (see frontispiece).[86]

5

Author of *Tom Jones,* 1742–1748

CHRONOLOGY

1742   Feb. 22. *Joseph Andrews* published.

HF moves from Essex St. to Spring Garden, in the Verge of the Court, safe from bailiffs.

Mar. 1. The *Champion* partners vote to deprive him of his shares in the *Champion* profits. Daughter Charlotte, not yet six, dies; 9th, buried at some expense (£5.18s.) in St. Martin-in-the-Fields.[1] 27th, borrows £197 from Joseph King (by May 26 he must settle his debt with Allen).[2] He is peddling subscriptions to the *Miscellanies,* collecting and revising materials for inclusion (one guinea a set, two for printed on royal paper).

Apr. 2. *A full Vindication of the Dutchess Dowager of Marlborough: Both with regard to the Account lately Published by Her Grace, and to Her Character in general; against the base and malicious Invectives contained in a late scurrilous Pamphlet, entitled Remarks on the Account, Ec. In a Letter to the Noble Author of those Remarks,* publ. J. Roberts (*DP*), a defense (for which HF received five guineas) of the widow of the duke, his father's commander at Blenheim, and also (as B suggests, 344) a political alignment with the "new Opposition" forming itself around Chesterfield.

May 6. *Miss Lucy in Town. A Sequel to The Virgin Unmasqued. A Farce; with Songs* (begun in 1735), perf. Drury Lane as an afterpiece to *Othello,* seven nights, with a benefit on the 19th with *The Miser;* bought for ten guineas and publ. by Millar, same day (*DA*);[3] successfully revived between Oct. 27 and Dec. 1, when an anonymous attack on its supposed obscenity – *A Letter to a Noble Lord, to Whom alone it Belongs* – brings its run to an end.

31. *Plutus, the God of Riches. A Comedy. Translated from the Original Greek of Aristophanes, with Large Notes Explanatory and Critical. By Henry Fielding, Esq; and the Revd. Mr. Young,* publ. T. Walker (*DP*, May 29), as a specimen of a proposed translation of Aristophanes. Yet another project for making money.

June 5. Announces delay in publishing the *Miscellanies*: "As the Books will very shortly go to the Press, Mr. Fielding begs the Favour of those who intend to subscribe to do it immediately" (*DP*).

10. 2nd. edn. of *Joseph Andrews* with corrections and additions. Lends £199 to one Randolph Seagrim in Dorchester; recovers it with damages, July 8.[4] Seagrim's name is later awarded by HF to Black George and his daughter Molly.

July 7. Court of Common Pleas decrees that HF must settle his debt to King, £197 plus 50s.[5]

July 27–Aug. 28. The Western Assizes; then to Bath.

1743 Feb. 16. *Some Papers Proper to be Read before the R[oya]l Society, Concerning the Terrestrial Chrysipus, Golden-Foot or Guinea; an Insect, or Vegetable, resembling the Polypus, which hath this surprising Property, That being cut into several Pieces, each Piece becomes a perfect Animal or Veg-etable, as complete as that of which it was originally only a Part. Collected by Petrus Gualterus* [i.e., Peter Walter]. *But not Published till after His Death,* a satiric squib, publ. J. Roberts, reprinted, *Miscellanies,* vol. I.

17. *The Wedding-Day. A Comedy. By Henry Fielding, Esq.* (originally drafted in 1729), performed at Drury Lane, six nights, two benefits; publ. Millar, 24th (reprinted, *Misc.,* vol. II). Not a success. Revision interrupted by the illness of Charlotte; cuts of "obscene" lines required by the censor.

Mar. Moves to the Flask Inn, Brompton, for reasons of Charlotte's health.[6]

Apr. 7. *Miscellanies* delivered to subscribers, sold by A. Millar, earning HF upward of £650. Vol. II contains, along with shorter pieces, *A Journey from this World to the Next* and vol. III consists entirely of *The Life of Mr. Jonathan Wild the Great.* 11th, daughter Catharine buried.[7]

Summer and autumn. On the Western Circuit; in Bath and Twerton. Daughter Henrietta Eleanor (called by HF, Harriet) born. Debts continue to accrue.[8]

1744 Jan. Returns to London, leaving Charlotte in Bath; is writing a legal treatise; Bath in the summer, autumn.

June. HF appointed by Charles Hanbury Williams as his attorney in a law suit – his one important case.[9]

July 13. Revises and contributes a preface to the 2nd edn. of Sarah Fielding's *The Adventures of David Simple: Containing an Account of his Travels through the Cities of London and Westminster, in Search of*

*a Real Friend. By a Lady. The second Edition, Revised and Corrected. With
a Preface by Henry Fielding Esq.* (*GA*). In the preface he remarks that
with his legal work (a book he is writing on the "Pleas of the
Crown"), "I have had no Leisure, if I had Inclination, to compose
any thing of this kind," i.e., like *David Simple.* This summer and
autumn are spent in Bath with Charlotte.[10]

ca. Nov. 7. Charlotte dies in his arms;[11] her body is returned
to London and on the 14th buried in St. Martin-in-the-Fields
(beside her daughter Charlotte with equally great expense). In the
interim HF behaves distractedly, spends four days visiting Richard
Owen Cambridge in Gloucestershire before returning for the
funeral.[12]

Moves into one of the more expensive houses in Old Boswell
Court, near Lincoln's Inn Fields. Sarah joins him and his children,
young Henry and Harriet (two and one years old), and the cookmaid Mary Daniel. In Westminster a new "Broad-Bottom" government is formed which includes HF's friends, Lyttelton, Chesterfield,
Dodington, Lord Cobham, the duke of Bedford.[13]

1745 Feb. Announces imminent publication of a legal tome, "An Institute of the Pleas of the Crown," in two folio volumes (never
published).[14]

May 18. Death of Walpole; his doctors blamed.

June. HF is involved in his friend Arthur Collier's attempts to avoid
imprisonment for debt (ensured by Harris).[15]

July 2. *The Charge to the Jury: or, The Sum of the Evidence, on the Trial
of A.B.C.D. and E.F. All M.D. For the Death of one Robert at Orfud, at a
Special Commission of Oyer and Terminer held at Justice-College, in
W[arwi]ck Lane, before Sir Asculapius Dosem, Dr. Timberhead, and Others,
their Fellows, Justices, &c.,* a defense of Dr. John Ranby, who had
accused Walpole's physicians of murder and been attacked by them;
publ. Mary Cooper (*GA*).

July 23. The Young Pretender invades Scotland. HF rides the Circuit,
by this time probably writing *Tom Jones.*

Sept. 17. The rebels take Edinburgh; 21st, win the battle of
Prestonpans and march south.

Oct. 3. At the ministry's urging, Fielding undertakes a number
of patriotic projects: *A Serious Address to the People of Great Britain.
In which the Certain Consequences of the Present Rebellion, are fully
demonstrated* (2nd edn., corrected with additions, ca. Nov. 5); 7th,
the slanted *History of the Present Rebellion in Scotland*; 12th, the
Lucianic *Dialogue between the Devil, the Pope, and the Pretender,* all publ.
Cooper.

17. *The Old Debauchees,* an abridged revival of the anti-papist *The
Debauchees: or, The Jesuit Caught* of 1732, as anti-Stuart propaganda;

afterpiece to Cibber's *Nonjuror,* 25 performances; 2nd edn., publ. Watts.

Nov. 5 (Guy Fawkes Day)–June 17, 1746. Edits *The True Patriot: and the History of Our Own Times,* publ. Cooper, sponsored by HF's friends of the "Broad-Bottom" ministry.

1746 Jan. HF writes to Harris that he has been "imprisoned a Month" with the gout "and am not yet able to stand"; refers to his sister Sarah as "the Woman in the world whom I like best."[16]

Apr. 14. For his services to the government he is awarded by the duke of Bedford the place of High Steward of the New Forest and of the Manor of Lyndhurst, Hants. (£5 per annum plus legal fees).[17]

Summer–autumn, in Bath.

Sept. 13. Mary Hamilton, transvestite, arrested at Glastonbury.

Nov. 12. *The Female Husband: or, The Surprising History of Mrs. Mary, alias Mr. George Hamilton. Who was convicted of having married a Young Woman of Wells and lived with her as her Husband. Taken from Her own Mouth since her Confinement,* publ. Cooper (*DA*).

1747 Feb. 23. *Ovid's Art of Love Paraphrased, and Adapted to the Present Time,* publ. Cooper, Ann Dodd, and George Woodfall (*GA*). HF is trying to sell his interest in his uncle George's bequest and borrow money from Harris.[18]

Apr. 10. Contributes preface and Letters XL–XLIV to Sarah's *Familiar Letters between the Principal Characters of David Simple, and Some Others* (*GA*).

June. Appointed chief magistrate for the City and Liberty of Westminster; the appointment for the County of Middlesex is delayed since he needs to possess property worth £100, which Bedford subsequently gives him.[19]

23. *A Dialogue between a Gentleman of London, Agent for two Court Candidates, and an Honest Alderman of the Country Party. Wherein the Grievances under which the Nation at present groans are fairly and impartially laid open and considered. Earnestly address'd to the Electors of Great-Britain,* publ. Cooper (2nd edn., ca. July).

Sept.–Oct. Bath, writing *Tom Jones.*

Nov. 27. Second marriage, to Mary Daniel, who is already six months pregnant; at St. Benet, Paul's Wharf, where in *Tom Jones* Nightingale, following Tom's advice, marries the pregnant Nancy Miller (11.8). They temporarily move to Back Lane, Twickenham, for the remainder of the pregnancy.[20] Sarah removes to quarters with her sisters, Catherine, Beatrice, and Ursula, in Duke Street, Westminster.[21]

Dec. 5–Nov. 5, 1748. Edits *The Jacobite's Journal. By John Trott-Plaid, Esq.,* defending the Pelham ministry, publ. Cooper.

Dec. 24. *A Proper Answer to a Late Scurrilous Libel, entitled, An Apology for the Conduct of a late celebrated second-rate Minister. By the Author of the Jacobite's Journal,* publ. Cooper (2nd edn., Jan. 2, 1748).

1748   Jan. By this time he is into the third volume of *Tom Jones*.[22]

Feb. 25. Son, William, baptized in St. Mary the Virgin, Twickenham.

Mar. 28. HF opens his "PUPPET-SHEW. . . . With the comical Humours of PUNCH and his *Wife* JOAN, with all the Original Jokes, F-rts, Songs, Battles, Kickings, &c.," in "Madame de la Nash's Breakfasting-Room" in Panton Street, with "Breakfast" served, morning and evening (to avoid the Licensing Act).[23]

Apr. 28. The puppet theater's popularity leads Theophilus Cibber to revive *The Author's Farce* as an afterpiece at Covent Garden with himself playing Henry Luckless. The puppet theater runs through the rest of the season, though HF ends his personal participation May 14.

July 30. Lord Hardwick officially appoints HF to the Commission of the Peace for Westminster.

Sept. First three volumes (nine books) of *Tom Jones* printed.[24]

Oct. 15. Writes to Richardsom commending the first five volumes of *Clarissa*; to Harris, delaying repayment of a loan, complaining of "a very severe Attack" of gout which has "forced" him "to use an Amanuensis" (for the completion of *Tom Jones*).[25]

25. Takes the oath and pays the fees that enable him to act as Justice of the Peace for Westminster.[26]

1749   Feb. 3. The last three volumes printed and *The History of Tom Jones, a Foundling. By Henry Fielding, Esq.,* 6 vols., publ. by A. Millar, who pays HF £600, £100 per volume. 2,000 sets sold before publication date; 2nd ed., 1,500 sets, publ., 28th; 3rd edn., 3,000, in 4 vols., publ. Apr. 12; 4th edn. (revised), Dec. 11, 3,500.

Dec. "Orbilius," *An Examen of the History of Tom Jones, a Foundling . . . In Two Letters to a Friend, Proper to be found with the Foundling,* launches an extended, detailed critique of *Tom Jones*.[27]

MAN OF LETTERS

The Plutus

In February 1741/2, as *Joseph Andrews* was published, Fielding was writing whatever brought in money. In May, as he was putting together works, both old and new, and canvassing for subscriptions to the collection he called his *Miscellanies,* he published a translation of Aristophanes' *Plutus* as a flier for a projected translation of the whole dramatic works. The choice of the play and the gist of the preface are telling: Plutus was the god of riches. The preface ends with a quotation from Addison's précis of the play in *Spectator* no. 464, which may have influenced Fielding's choice: "This Allegory," Addison wrote, "instructed the *Athenians* in two Points, first, as it vindicated the Conduct of Providence in its ordinary Distribution of Wealth; and in the next Place, as it shewed the great Tendency of Riches to corrupt the morals of those who possessed them" (xv).

In the play Chremylus says, "I am persuaded this is universally acknowledged, that good Men are justly entitled to Prosperity; and as certainly, that the base and wicked should suffer a contrary Fate." He therefore recommends that Plutus' sight be restored so that rewards and punishments will be justly distributed. Poverty replies that if they restore Plutus' sight and he gives wealth only to the virtuous, all arts and crafts, all sciences will cease and "Private vices, public virtues" will emerge as the law of life (49–50). The inferences are both public and personal: that Fielding intends a Mandevillian application of the play itself; that the problem of riches, which until recently had been applicable to the corruption of the Walpole ministry, was obviously of pressing interest to Fielding himself; and that he was aware of the way Addison used providence in his *Spectator* essays and followed this model.[28] The gauntlet run by Joseph, Fanny, and Adams could be summed up as the punishment of the innocent; and this was a reflection of Shaftesbury's belief that the Christian god of rewards and punishments is an evil fiction, a creation of priests, and that virtue, to be virtue, has nothing to do with rewards and punishments.

The play embodies the typical Aristophanic hypothesis: Wealth and virtue do not correspond, therefore return sight to the blind Plutus, which should right the situation – but incidentally may have the direst consequences. This is the Aristophanic plot in which a fantastic expedient is invented by a visionary to correct a bad situation, followed by its ridiculous consequences – for example, there is no longer any need to sacrifice to the gods. This is not Fielding's comic structure, either before or after, but the Aristophanic old comedy was the model for Lucian's dialogues, and this particular play interests him because it focuses on the problem of rewards and punishments in this life.[29]

Though the play itself must have been chosen by Fielding and at least touched up by him, he was assisted in the project by William Young. The commentary is heavily interlarded with what appear to be Young's pedantic quibbles, giving us the best traces we have of Parson Adams' prototype. The preface states that if Fielding and Young proceed with the translation they intend to "prefix to it a very large Dissertation on the Nature and End of Comedy, with an Account of its Original, Rise, and Progress to this Day," which sounds like an extension of the preface to *Joseph Andrews*, though also implicitly a defense of the satiric plays of 1736–7, which continued to sully Fielding's reputation. He defends Aristophanes against the old charge that he was the cause of Socrates' condemnation; he argues that the Church Fathers admired him "notwithstanding his Impurities." These impurities he sets against "the Purity of his Diction" in which he surpassed all ancient authors. In the dedication he introduces William, Lord Talbot (a supporter of the "new Opposition" and son of the late Lord Chancellor), to Aristophanes, who, another Henry Fielding, exerted his "Genius in the Service of his Country. He attack'd and expos'd its Enemies and Betrayers with a Boldness and Integrity, which must endear his Memory to every True and Sincere Patriot" (2–3).[30]

The Miscellanies

The gathering of just about all his fugitive writings in a volume of *Miscellanies* can be attributed to Fielding's precarious financial situation, even after the success of *Joseph Andrews*, and presumably also to his wish to demonstrate the breadth of his abilities as a "man of letters." The majority of these writings represent a stage of his development prior to *Joseph Andrews*; there can be little question that some of the material was written as early as the 1720s, though not brought to completion until close to the date of publication in April 1743. The major works are the prose narratives, the *Journey from this World to the Next* and *Jonathan Wild* (the latter taking up the whole of volume three). The poem "Of True Greatness" had been published as recently as 1741. The common theme Fielding finds in most of these works and uses as a unifying thread is greatness, the theme of his plays, the *Champion* essays, the *Vernoniad*, and the attacks on Walpole; but which had been modified by the appearance of the servant girl Pamela.

In this sequence *Jonathan Wild* follows directly from the essays of *The Champion*, the set pieces and orations Fielding had learned and imitated at Eton. One line of development in his prose writing is from the *Champion* essays, the discursive and dramatic histories of Thucydides and Plutarch, the classical oration, satire, and exemplary life, to *Jonathan Wild*. The narrative grows out of these discursive structures, as an illustration expanded. In *Joseph Andrews* there emerges a very different form, in which the essay component is auxiliary, not seminal, as in his model *Don Quixote*. Both strands, the essay-oratorical and the Quixotic, are synthesized in *Tom Jones*, the novel Fielding began to write shortly after publishing the *Miscellanies*.

The new elements appear in volume 1: the preface and the essays. The preface superimposes on the earlier materials and the prevalent topos of greatness a dialectic which appears to have been Fielding's afterthought. To judge by the *Champion* of February 21, 1739/40 Heartfree began as simply the good man who (though not a fool) is exploited by knaves:

Honest and undesigning Men of very good Understanding would be always liable to the Attacks of cunning and artful Knaves, into whose Snares we are as often seduc'd by the Openness and Goodness of the Heart, as by the Weakness of the Head. True Wisdom is commonly attended with a Simplicity of Manners, which betrays a worthy Man to a tricking Shuffler, of a much inferior Capacity. (1:296)

In the preface the merely great is villainy, the merely good the norm but less than wonderful; whereas the great *and* good represent the ideal ("true greatness"). If we apply the dialectic of the preface in volume 1 to *Jonathan Wild* in volume 3, Heartfree is good, Wild is great, and the ideal of greatness *and* goodness is somewhere between. Fielding shades off greatness and goodness on either side: Heartfree occasionally stands up to the world; Wild has occasional weaknesses that distinguish him from the "truly great," an Alexander or a Walpole.[31]

Because the preface offers a Horatian dialectic we expect it to apply in volume 3 when Fielding balances Heartfree against Wild, even if we know he wrote the preface last. We interpret it as Fielding's rationalization of what he had written earlier, less precisely formulated, in the *Wild* narrative.[32] The dialectic is reinforced by the essays in volume 1, which are constructed similarly. In the "Dialogue between Alexander and Diogenes," "greatness" is defined in terms of opposite extremes. The false greatness of Alexander (the conqueror) is opposed to the false greatness of Diogenes (the critic who does nothing positive himself, does not "*do* good").

The dialectic gives rise to an even wittier hypothesis concerning the Heartfrees: Does Mrs. Heartfree therefore represent the middle way between the greatness of Wild and the goodness of Mr. Heartfree in that she learns to manipulate men in order to preserve her fidelity to her husband? In short, do the Heartfrees, as in a satire, only indicate where value lies (therefore need none of the development of Wild, who in the theatrical sense is "the principal Figure" [98]), or are they, as in Plutarch's parallel lives, intended to balance Wild? I think the answer is that Fielding's ideas were developing as he wrote *Jonathan Wild*, then *Joseph Andrews*, the preface to the *Miscellanies* essays and, finally, the essays themselves.

Seen from one perspective, the essays are simply more generic Etonian exercises like many of the poems (the burlesque imitation of Juvenal's Sixth Satire, the Lucian dialogue, the Demosthenes olynthiac, the Martial epigram). The "Essay on Conversation" is a classical oration, moving from general topic ("Man is a social Animal") to definition ("The Art of pleasing or doing Good is therefore the Art of Conversation") to a discussion of the particulars of "Good Breeding," progressing in an orderly manner from "Actions" to "Words."[33] This could be a gloss or retrospective on the procedure of *Joseph Andrews* answering *Pamela.* But the "Essay on Conversation" is, more precisely, a Horatian *epistola* in prose, as the "Essay on the Characters of Men" is a Horatian *sermo* on hypocrites. They herald a new structure, where the public mask guides the reader (often "you") through a maze of good and bad examples, defining a positive and detailed code of proper conduct very much in the manner of Horace. Bad examples are sprinkled along the way, but the objective of the essay is to educate the reader in a decent mode of conduct, not to explore the nature of evil or to examine its universal infiltration. Evil has become individual, what will affect oneself, not all mankind. In the "Essay on Conversation," as in a Horatian *epistola*, the author has an intimate, discursive talk with a reader; "An Essay on the Knowledge of the Characters of Men" is a *sermo* in which he attempts to chart a topology of character set against examples of hypocrisy for the reader to beware of. To say that Fielding plays the moralist in these essays means essentially that he proposes a coherent plan of life and conduct; to the extent that this figure holds the center of the stage, he ceases to be a satirist and becomes a moralist.

In the "Essay on Conversation," to define "good breeding" Fielding cites Jesus' "Golden Rule," "Do unto others as you would they would do unto you,"[34] but he places it in the context of Horace's "Golden Mean" and the works of Chesterfield and Lyttelton. He redefines it in specifically social terms, consonant with rules of deportment for making the other person feel good. (We recall Mr. Wilson's conclusion that running off with another member's wife was "so inconsistent with our Golden Rule.") The consequence is to interpret the teachings of Jesus as both ethical and pragmatic – as an ideal way to live privately *and* socially. The "Essay on Conversation" acts as a bridge between the primitive Christianity that is dramatized in *Joseph Andrews* and polite society, civility, and the more complex world of *Tom Jones.*

Fielding again recalls Shaftesbury, for whom conversation is "what passes in select companies, where friends meet knowingly, and with that very design of exercising their wit, and looking freely into all subjects," to which Shaftesbury added significantly: "I see no pretence for any one to be offended at the way of raillery and humour, which is the very life of such conversations."[35] He is defining an ideal Whig community. As he explains, he is writing "in defence only of the liberty of *the club*, and of that sort of freedom which is taken amongst gentlemen and friends who know one another perfectly well" – well off, therefore disinterested, gentlemen free of religious scruples and monarchical subservience.

"Good breeding" and "liberty" are thus aspects of conversation as opposed to the monological discourse of "men of slavish principles," who "affect a superiority over the vulgar, and . . . despise the multitude," by which Shaftesbury means the Tory-Jacobites, including in particular popish priests (1:53).[36] Ultimately, all such gravity that "is contrary to good breeding is in this respect as contrary to liberty." The Whigs, however superior to the vulgar and the multitude (as proved the case with Shaftesbury's privileged oligarchy), are the "lovers of mankind [who] respect and honour conventions and societies of men." In the Whig "public space," accordingly, conversation implies simply intercourse between equals – not, as among Tories, a grave priest talking down to his congregation.

Politeness was the watchword of *The Spectator*, mediating between the genteel discourse of civic humanism and the middling status of the *Spectator* readers. Addison saw the theater as a prime means of social education, from which it follows that manners and politeness are a function of acting, and proper sociability depends on a true correspondence between inherent virtue and social manner. People act out the manners they see in the playhouse, and a corollary is that manners involve emulation and become a function of role-playing. Manners are "theatrical" both in the sense of originating in the theater and of being parts played in the world-as-a-stage.

The dark side of good breeding was scrutinized in Fielding's earlier work: In *Joseph Andrews* Lady Booby has no "Vice Inconsistant with Goodbreeding" (4.4.226). Earlier, in *Love in Several Masques* "good-breeding" was associated with Lord Formal ("this empty, gaudy, nameless thing" [52, again, 81, 96]). The catch-all term "politeness" is hardly a complimentary term in *The Modern Husband* when Mr. Bellamant chides his foppish son for aping the fashion, and the latter replies: "Lord, sir! you are grown strangely unpolite" (10:29); the most disreputable acts are called "polite," the most candid will have the consequence that "Lady Polite will never forgive you" (42, 77). Politeness fits into the series of analogies between high–low, honest–dishonest, serving as a euphemism (in terms of "Conversation") or hypocrisy ("Characters") for interest. As Trapwit says in *Pasquin*: "Ay, interest, or conscience, they are words of the same meaning; but I think conscience rather the politer of the two, and most used at court" (11:194). Implied is some term that transcends politeness.[37]

In the pendant essay, "The Knowledge of the Characters of Men," Fielding recalls the satiric metaphor of life as "a vast Masquerade, where the greatest Part appear disguised under false Vizors and Habits; a very few only shewing their own Faces, who become, by so doing, the Astonishment and Ridicule of all the rest" (*Misc.*, 1:155). He argues, reflecting the plan of *Joseph Andrews*, that "the Actions of Men seem to be the justest Interpreters of their Thoughts, and the truest Standards by which we may judge them," adding the biblical injunction: "By their Fruits you shall know them." He goes into the subject of "affectation," as he does in the preface to *Joseph Andrews*.[38] But he also notes the various factors that obscure a proper judgment of actions: "when we take their own Words against their Actions" and "when we take the Colour of a Man's Actions, not from their own visible Tendency, but from his public Character: when we believe what others say of him, in Opposition to what we see him do" (163). The first of these is the subject of *Joseph Andrews*; the second, anticipating a new phase of Fielding's thought, becomes the subject of *Tom Jones*, where the reputations of Tom and Blifil render judgment difficult.

By contrast, in the "Essay on Conversation" Fielding suggests both the instability and the means, including benign forms of hypocrisy, by which such instability can be controlled. This situation of course applied with particular intensity to Fielding himself, who was both aware of the discrepancy between actual status and the trappings of it – of his own impecunious situation and the ability of someone with no status to *buy* those trappings and pass himself off for the real thing. This accounts for his great emphasis on the theatricality of hypocrisy in the 1730s and early 1740s, just when his financial situation was most precarious. But, conversely, we should notice the coincidence of the "Essay on Conversation" in the *Miscellanies* and Fielding's experience during 1741–2 in Bath, in the assembly rooms, and in Prior Park as the guest of Ralph Allen: this is the new area of civility from which he takes his examples.

The "Essay on Conversation" stands out as a statement of custom and the utility of belief (parallel to Shaftesbury's acknowledgment of the utility, at least for the lower orders, of religion) as provisional forms that connect at points by way of the theatrical metaphor with hypocrisy – custom's dark side, explored in the "Characters of Men" essay, *Jonathan Wild*, and *Shamela*. Fielding himself, to judge by the essay on conversation, is a negative Wild-Shamela, trying to (advising his readers to) follow rules, models, and such provisional structures as politeness and religion. So the "Essay on Conversation" appears to make a particular statement that requires the co-presence of the essays on "Characters of Men" and "Affliction," and is closest in its assumptions to the last.

Two phenomena that determined what was new in the *Miscellanies* were, first, the profound disillusion he felt in the actions of his old colleagues of the opposition after the fall of Walpole, when they clambered onto the new ministry and continued Walpole's practices; and second, the death of his daughter Charlotte and the illness of his wife Charlotte, foreshadowing eight months after the publication of the *Miscellanies* her death.

The first was already reflected in a footnote to *Plutus*: "TO MAKE USE OF POPULAR INTEREST, AND THE CHARACTER OF PATRIOTISM, IN ORDER TO BETRAY ONE'S COUNTRY, is perhaps the most flagitious of all Crimes" (57n.). In the *Journey*, Julian, in one of his metamorphoses, is leader of the opposition in the reign of King John: "in truth," he says, "I sought nothing but my own Preferment, by making myself formidable to the King, and then selling to him the Interest of that Party, by whose means I had become so" (I.23.103).[39] Most interesting, one chapter that was plainly added to *Jonathan Wild* close to the time of publication shows the inter-changeability of Walpole and the opposition leader William Pulteney:

Fielding turns Wild into Pulteney and Roger Johnson, whom he over-throws, into Walpole.

The essay "Of the Remedy of Affliction for the Loss of Friends," the most directly personal of the essays, is a proposal for dealing with the death of loved ones. After dismissing the "remedies" of philosophy, and focusing on his own bereavement and his wife Charlotte's existential response ("comforting herself with reflecting, that *her Child could never know what it was to feel such a Loss as she then lamented*"), Fielding concludes, in the same language he used in the *Champion* to defend religion against the deists, that

> Religion goes much farther, and gives us a most *delightful* Assurance, that our Friend is not barely no Loser, but a Gainer by his Dissolution. . . . Lastly; It gives a Hope, the sweetest, most endearing, and *ravishing*, which can enter into a Mind capable of, and *inflamed* with, Friendship. The Hope of again meeting the beloved Person, of renewing and cementing the dear Union in *Bliss* everlasting. This is a *Rapture* which leaves the warmest Imagination at a Distance. (emphasis added, *Misc.*, 1:224–5)

Among many other examples, we recall Fielding's joyous reunion with his deceased daughter in the *Journey*: "Good Gods! what Words can describe the Raptures, the melting passionate Tenderness, with which we kiss'd each other, continuing in our Embrace, with the most extatic joy, a Space, which if Time had been measured here as on Earth, could not be less than half a Year" (1.8.37). (Allworthy's *consolatio* for the death of his wife in *Tom Jones* will be another example.)

If there was an aspect of the theology of rewards and punishments that was particularly irrational it was this one. But because of its importance to him, Fielding leaves it unexamined, distinguishing providence in this life from providence in the next; and at the same time he is willing to regard it as the extreme of pragmatic usage. For while he questions in various ways the truth as well as the virtue of rewards and punishments in the afterlife, he accepts the notion of full physical resurrection – not the "light body" model of spiritual embodiment after death, but the "hard body" model, the more commonly accepted one, which in its *reductio ad absurdum* raised questions of how bodily pieces would be reassembled to put together the resurrected self. In graphic sources, there were pictures of beasts of prey spewing back the legs, arms, head, and other parts of those they had devoured.[40] Both the sense of martyrdom and of the power inherent in the dead body of the saint would have underwritten Fielding's extreme devotion to this particular doctrine, while questioning if not rejecting most others. This superstition may suggest a parallel between the belief in resurrection and the endings Fielding imposed on his plays and novels.

We know that Fielding, again drawing on his training in classical rhetoric, tended to adjust his style and views to the person or the occasion he was addressing. When he wrote the essay on bereavement for the *Miscellanies* he had lost his infant daughter Penelope (February 1740), his father (June 1741), and his first child Charlotte (March 1741/2). In April 1743, just four days after the *Miscellanies* were published, daughter Catharine died. Thus he addressed Christian readers and so ended with the belief in an afterlife. Perhaps because of the long series of bereavements he suffered, this "hope" seems to have been Fielding's own entrée to the Christian religion.

In November 1744 the crowning blow was the death of his wife Charlotte. When, immediately following her death, he wrote his "dearest Friend" Harris, he invokes "philosophy" and the classical model of Socrates.[41] It is likely that this was directed to *this* friend, a Shaftesburian deist, with its allusions to Harris's third "Treatise," "On Happiness" with its invocation of philosophy as a "Habit," and his second with its stress on Socrates, models, and again habit. The clergyman Dr. Harrison in *Amelia* (who may owe something to his partial namesake) echoes Harris's words, including the word *habit*, as part of the system of a *Christian* stoic. But in the letter to Harris, when Fielding writes closer to his own heart than to the general public of the sort addressed in the *Champion* and *Miscellanies*, he makes no reference to religion.

In the essays on conversation and affliction Fielding places himself parallel to Wild and Shamela (perhaps Mrs. Heartfree), pragmatically following and utilizing custom; the only difference is that his customs are socially acceptable. But then part of his argument was that Wild and Shamela *are* basing their actions on the socially "fashionable" models.

In his "Essay on the Characters of Men" Fielding raises the subject of virtue, discussed in the *Champion* essays attacking deism. Here he notes that "Nature, which unwillingly submits to the Imposture [of affectation, of hypocrisy], is ever endeavouring to peep forth and shew herself" (1:155). He redefines virtue as "Good Nature," which "disposes us to feel the Misfortunes and enjoy the Happiness of others; and consequently pushes us on to promote the latter, and prevent the former; and that" – he significantly adds – "without any abstract contemplation on the Beauty of Virtue, and without the Allurement or Terrors of Religion" (158).

However, as he had explained in one of his *Champion* essays (March 27, 1740), Good Nature may need the support of one or both of these. In unusually tangled syntax, with ambiguous referents, he says that Christianity is necessary because it "hath taught us something beyond what the Religion of Nature and Philosophy [deism] could arrive at." He goes on, alluding to Tindal's deist tract, which argued that God made the basic tenets of religion available to all men through the use of their reason alone, with no need of assistance from the Bible: "and consequently, that it is *not as old as the Creation,* nor is Revelation useless with Regard to Morality, if it had taught us no more than this excellent Doctrine, which, if generally followed, would make mankind much happier, as well as better than they are."

Sarah Fielding

We can assume that Fielding did not begin writing *Tom Jones* until he had finished putting together his *Miscellanies* (by April 1743).[42] We know that at the beginning of this period he thought he would establish himself in the legal profession, and make some much-needed money, by writing a legal treatise – a work he pursued but never published.[43] By 1746 his gout had made it difficult for him to ride the circuit; setting out from London he complained to Harris that "I cannot yet stand alone," and thereafter there are no more references in his letters to the assizes.[44]

A number of stimuli, beginning with its great success, pointed toward a sequel to *Joseph Andrews.* But the first, literary stimulus appears to have been his continuing dialogue with Richardson: Fielding may have felt that he had not yet completely expressed himself or offered the literary model he was seeking first in *Shamela,* then in *Joseph Andrews.*

In 1742 his sister Sarah contributed a short un-Richardsonian letter (Leonora's reply to Horatio) in *Joseph Andrews* (2.4). In 1743 she contributed a final chapter to *A Voyage from this World to the Next,* an autobiography spoken by Anna Boleyn that demonstrated loyalties divided between her brother and Richardson. A woman's story serves as a supplement to the long story of Julian the Apostate; it is a relatively pious account, which is, in more than one way, a rewriting of *Pamela.* From her brother's point of view, Sarah's heroine is the servant girl upgraded to a gentlewoman attached to the court who catches the eye of the king himself. She exposes precisely the elements that Pamela (as Henry saw it) concealed: "my Mind was too much taken up with Ambition to make room for any other Thoughts," she writes. And while away from court ("I was very jealous that Absence might change the King's Mind") she notes that "my Royal Lover often sent Gentlemen to me with Messages and Letters, which I always answered in the manner I thought would best bring about my Designs, which were to come back again to Court" (*Misc.* 2:123) – though her letters are not, like Pamela's, quoted. The writing is, following the format of the *Journey,* first-person singular; as in *Shamela,* it is to some extent self-exposing. Still, Anna is enough a Richardsonian heroine to suffer a "Struggle in my own Mind" and to be "divided" between love for Percy and ambition for a crown – coincidentally just the situation of her brother's Shamela.

In 1744 Sarah's *David Simple* was published by Henry's publisher, Andrew Millar, obviously with his recommendation, but she was now a member of the Richardson circle at North End. Before the end of the year a second edition was called for, which Henry (who says he was out of town when the manuscript went to press) revised for his sister, contributing a preface that made plain his part in what he referred to repeatedly as her "little Book." His most prominent revision appropriates the book for the author of *Joseph Andrews* (while his preface vigorously disclaims authorship), turning David Simple into a Quixote:

> This was the Fantom, the Idol of his Soul's Admiration. In the Worship of which he at length grew such an Enthusiast, that he was in this Point only as mad as *Quixotte* himself could be with Knight Errantry; and after much amusing himself with the deepest Ruminations on this Subject, in which a fertile Imagination raised a thousand pleasing Images to itself, he at length *took the oddest, most unaccountable Resolution that ever was heard of, viz. To travel through the whole World, rather than not meet with a real Friend.*[45]

Only the emphasized words are Sarah's: Fielding recognized the Quixotic drift of her plot and laid claim to it. In the preface, citing his preface to *Joseph Andrews*, he associates her "little Book" with the *Odyssey* rather than the *Iliad*, epics which "differ principally in the Action, which in the *Iliad* is entire and uniform; in the *Odyssey*, is rather a series of Actions, all tending to produce one great End." The followers of Homer have all observed this principal difference, whether their imitations were serious or comic; and so he notes that just as Pope in *The Dunciad* fixed on one action, "Butler in Verse, and Cervantes in Prose" fixed on a series. His sister's work belongs to the latter category: "the Fable consists of a series of separate Adventures, detached from and independent of each other, yet all tending to one great End." The same, of course, applies to *Joseph Andrews*. The single action of the *Iliad*, needless to say, better describes Pamela's run-in with Mr. B.

David Simple is a Richardsonian Quixote whose madness follows from a disillusionment (with his brother) and leads to an impossible quest for a true friend. Sarah constructs a male protagonist with a delicate feminine imagination who comes into contact with a real, unsentimental world. Yet, following her brother rather than Richardson, who kept his attention on the struggle of Pamela and Mr. B., she in fact lets her emphasis fall decidedly on the sequential examples of the unfeeling world (in *Pamela* the country neighbors who side against her with Mr. B. when she tries to escape) in which the sensibility of the feeling hero is beleaguered if not destroyed.

Fielding recognizes the Richardson influence and, presumably for that reason, emphasizes Sarah's gender and youth – "young Woman,"

unlearned, author of a "little Book," inward-turned, with delicate sentiments: "a vast Penetration into human Nature, a deep and profound Discernment of all the Mazes, Windings and Labyrinths, which perplex
the Heart of Man to such a degree, that he himself is often incapable of
seeing through them" (5). But, as he must have seen, Sarah attaches these
qualities, departing from Richardson, to a masculine subject; he may have
correctly regarded this as a step beyond Joseph Andrews toward a
Richardsonian analysis of his own protagonist.

Even assuming that his remarks are his attempt to assimilate *David Simple*
to his kind of writing, and not merely condescension to a younger and
female sibling (his remarks about women are usually condescending in this
way), the preface is a strange and revealing performance, anticipating in
some ways his commendatory letter to Richardson of four years later.
Whether to further assimilate her work, or simply out of a sense of his own
self-importance, Fielding spends the first quarter of the preface speaking
about himself – how critics have attributed *David Simple* to him (how ridiculous!), but also much worse books, including (the real motive for this out-
pouring) *The Causidicade*, a scurrilous attack on the leading lights of the
legal profession, an attribution that could obviously have done serious
harm to his career. And he makes clear what he will reiterate in *Tom Jones*,
that learning is one of the four muses necessary to the writing of this sort
of history – a quality lacking in his sister's effort. (It is Slipslop's affectation of learning which Fielding, however gently, recalls in his remarks on
Sarah.) He also, as in the novel he was beginning to write, emphasizes the
reader's need to forgive "Faults," primarily the author's "Errors in Style"
which he has attempted to correct. (As in the preface to *Plutus*, he always
stresses the purity of his own style.)

The important story in *David Simple* is the break-up of families, the
replacement of the mother by a step-mother, the closeness of brother and
sister (with the scandalous rumor invented by the bad step-mother, that
they are committing incest), and the fantasy of a reconstituted family. Or
rather, perhaps, a familial society, for there are two intertwined families at
the end who live together as one extended family. The structure, which
appears to be picaresque, proves to be cumulative, the digressive tales all
feeding into the main narrative, contributing characters for the ultimate
"family."

Within the novel the villain, whose despicable behavior starts David on
his quest, is his bad brother, Daniel. Daniel gambles, drinks, and whores,
wasting thousands of pounds on "Women and Sots" (25), and even making
drunken advances to the virtuous Cynthia (180). Sarah's biographer, Linda
Bree, writes that

> For Sarah Fielding drinking and womanizing, far from being [as for her
> brother's Tom Jones] the natural characteristics of an innocent and naive

young man, were symptoms of serious moral faults. Daniel's final reported litany of villainy – an astonishing series of attempts to cheat people out of their money and morals – ends in horror; he dies in mental and physical decrepitude, in the agonies of atheism and, though still a young man, with "all the Infirmities and Diseases incident to old Age."[46]

While this is an "astonishing" anticipation (except for the mental decrepitude) of Henry's own trajectory, in the early 1740s, when Sarah was writing, it was not an unreasonable prophecy, and Henry was certainly the closest example she had of one who wasted thousands of pounds on "Women and Sots." In the 1750s, by which time Henry was securely well off, the elder brother in Sarah's *The Cry* fails to share his wealth with his siblings.

The story of David and his brother Daniel is supplemented by that of Camilla, her infatuated father, and his wife (Camilla's step-mother) Livia, which illustrates another reversal of David's ideal of true friendship. The ideal community David creates at the end is an attempt to reconstruct his family and others' families that have disintegrated as the result of selfishness. The two leading women, Camilla and Cynthia, tell their stories, and these are, as Bree notes, "convincing accounts of the almost insuperable difficulties, in 18th-century society, of a virtuous gentlewoman in adversity" (36).[47] Henry himself writes movingly on this subject, sharing his sister's concern, perhaps based on her experiences. But the conclusion we must draw is that *David Simple* drew to a large extent on Sarah's own experiences with her deeply troubled family, by no means distanced or sublimated to the extent of her brother's comic reenactment.[48]

In the case of Camilla, when she tells how her father, whose passion for the step-mother Livia destroys both family and fortune, "suddenly sprung forward, and struck me," "her Voice faultered by degrees, till she was able to speak no more. . . . She trembled with the agonies, the Remembrance of past Afflictions threw her into; and at last fainted away" (153–4).

Prefixed to the first edition of *David Simple* was an advertisement by Sarah Fielding herself, which calls it a "Moral Romance (or whatever Title the Reader shall please to give it) . . . the Work of a Woman and her first Essay." With the same combination of the serious and flippant she offers her explanation for why she published it: "Distress in her Circumstances: which she could not so well remove by any other Means in her Power." "IF it should meet with Success, it will be the only Good fortune she ever has known; but as she is very sensible, That must chiefly depend upon the Entertainment the World will find in the Book itself." Although her brother would probably have reversed the order of the two points, they share the same tone, balancing self-pity and pragmatism (Bree, 8–9).

Her brother's work may also have shown her how a happy ending was merely a device of human contriving. When David rescues Camilla at her lowest point, she is "'sure he was some *Angel*, who had put on a human

Form, to deliver her from . . . Distress' "; and Valentine claims that "'your Goodness has worked *a Miracle* on me'" (130–1, emphasis added). The irony is plain in this relatively unironic work; but in the sequel, *David Simple: Volume the Last*, published a decade later, reality intrudes, and in a work that asks to be contrasted with her brother's *Amelia* she puts aside the possibility of a happy ending.

Sarah must have partially filled the empty space left by the death of Fielding's wife Charlotte. More moralist than wit, she shared the house with Mary Daniel – almost, perhaps, as Shaftesbury's Virtue and Pleasure vied for the attention of Hercules, not a new paradigm for Fielding.

Clarissa

Unsurprisingly, the reactions of the Richardson circle to *Joseph Andrews* were negative. Within the circle, George Cheyne, whose style Fielding had ridiculed in *The Champion*, called it a "wretched Performance," which "will entertain none but Porters or Watermen," and Richardson himself regarded it as merely "a lewd and ungenerous engraftment" on his *Pamela*.[49] Meanwhile, Richardson was writing *Clarissa* and had finished a draft by the end of 1745, when he was sending it around to his friends for comment.[50] But as early as June 1744 Fielding would have learned, through Sarah or other mutual acquaintances, that such a work was in progress.[51] No one has suggested that Fielding read *Clarissa* before it began to be published on December 1, 1747. He read an advance copy of volume 5 in October 1748, writing his complimentary letter to Richardson on the 15th. *Tom Jones* would have been written with only hearsay knowledge of *Clarissa*. But he would have heard of the size, scope, and ambition of Richardson's new work; probably also that it was the story of another paragon of a woman, in this case forced by her family to marry a monster, Mr. Solmes, who throws her into the arms of a rakish suitor, Lovelace, who abducts and rapes her.[52]

This would have been enough for Fielding to make Allworthy "so averse to the Rigour which some Parents exercise on their Children" (6.3.281) and write a story of a tyrannous father who is forcing Sophia to marry Blifil when she loves Tom; but instead of placing all virtue in a passive/aggressive heroine, and in the sin of sex, Fielding sends her out to pursue Tom and renders his infidelities relatively unimportant to her. He contrasts Sophia's response to familial imprisonment with Clarissa's; her refusal to sacrifice her freedom is an implicit critique of the primacy Richardson gives principle (and Blifil in some ways is Fielding's version of Clarissa's Mr. Solmes).[53]

Throughout the opening chapters of *Tom Jones* (and indeed throughout the whole book) he refers to his work as this "new Province of Writing," "this kind of Writing, of which we have set ourselves at the Head," and "this great Work." It is no coincidence that the two masterpieces were written in parallel and that, toward the end, Fielding was probably hurrying to finish and publish simultaneously for purposes of comparison. Enough volumes of both were in private circulation by the middle of 1748 that the comparison and contrast were in effect accomplished. Both were as popular successes as their authors could have hoped for.

Quite different from *Pamela*, the letters in *Clarissa*, exchanged among the characters, offer diverging perspectives. Clarissa's point of view on an issue, a person, or a scene is supplemented by Anna Howe's and Lovelace's and all the others. Richardson's letters reveal not Hickman, Solmes, or Lovelace but those men as they are seen by Clarissa and Anna Howe, and vice versa. Reality is in fact established, and the truth approximated, by perspectivism, whether Richardson himself likes to think so or not – whatever he may tell us, the editor is in fact only one in a series of perspectives none of which (at least so it would have appeared to Fielding) is privileged.[54] The presentation of reality as not an action but a reflection of an action in a mind is the aspect of the Richardsonian work that seems furthest from Fielding.

But Fielding was also writing a novel about a person (in his case, a male) as he appears to others, and as his actions do. Perhaps he was reacting against the monomania of *Pamela* rather than the polyphany of *Clarissa* – we do not know how much he knew of the multiple letter-writers Richardson was now employing. But while Richardson represents the consciousness that gives back mixed responses to Lovelace, Fielding is interested in the reality of Lovelace; from the attitudes of their observers he tries to piece together the truth about Partridge or Tom or Black George. Bernard Harrison put this very well when he argued that Fielding's unique response to Richardsonian interiority was the "revelation of character by playing off one viewpoint against another":

> For Fielding the contrast between a man's real nature and the surface he presents to the world cannot be identified either with the contrast between inner consciousness and behaviour or with the contrast between what he says and what he does. . . . Rather it is the contrast between what an interlocutor, looking at what a character says and does from a particular viewpoint, might make of him, and what a second interlocutor or a spectator, able to survey both from a second viewpoint, might make of the commerce between them. Fielding's concept of character, in short, is founded in the notion of the coherence of a man's speech and action when seen from different viewpoints.[55]

The "technique of ironically juxtaposing and contrasting points of view, of exposing actions simultaneously to being morally and psychologically construed from more than one direction," projects a world in which "no *one* viewpoint is ever 'guaranteed'; ever wholly adequate as a basis from which to grasp the nature of human reality" (48). This is the position, not that no viewpoint has any but personal validity, but "(1) that no viewpoint reveals *everything* about reality, and (2) that there are some kinds of knowledge, including some kinds of self-knowledge, that can only be acquired by looking at things from two or more points of view at once" (49).

Fielding's response to Richardson in the new novel is an ironic discourse, once satiric but now a more complex instrument that is used to question rather than deny or affirm. In *Joseph Andrews* the irony directed at the lecherous Lady Booby served as both denigration and an indication of her own false picture of herself (her affectation) – a rhetorical and a psychological effect. But there was a third effect, which William Empson characterized when he wrote that Fielding "seems to leave room for the ideas he laughs at."[56] In the sympathetic interpretation, Lady Booby really is, as she claims, heroically battling her passions, just as Quixote's illusions in some sense contain truth. While this is a very slight impression as concerns Lady Booby, it does explain something about our reaction to Parson Adams, who *is* both wise (as he thinks) and foolish. In *Tom Jones* Empson finds what he calls "double irony" to be a controlling principle.[57] This might be called "both/and" irony because it gives some credence to both "the contrary" and "what one means," or to the praise and the blame. When Fielding says that Black George, who has just stolen Tom's money, really does love Tom, he is saying a number of different things – that Black George has persuaded himself by rationalization that he loves Tom, but also that there is a sense in which Black George really does love him, even if at the moment his action shows that he loves money more. While single irony implies the author's grasp of all circumstances and eventualities, with the proper subordination of the false to the true, double irony suggests a greater tolerance, a delicate poise, or mere uncertainty. The effect is an equivalent, in fact an alternative, to the unsubordinated *copia* of Richardsonian realism and suggests Fielding's attempt to achieve (to use Watt's terms) a "realism of presentation" as well as his accustomed "realism of assessment."

The Richardsonian signs are immediately evident in *Tom Jones*: more facts, more information about everything, more extenuating circumstances recorded, and more different motives and attitudes to choose from, all creating a general plenitude which here is encyclopedic. The irony helps to generate this impression; instead of a single statement (such as the one about Lady Booby's passion) Fielding gives two or more possibilities, some very plausible. Mrs. Wilkins' reasons for obeying Squire Allworthy's wishes for the young foundling Tom are: "Such was [1] the Discernment of Mrs. *Wilkins*, and such [2] the Respect she bore her Master, [3] under whom she enjoyed a most excellent Place, that her Scruples gave way to his peremptory Commands" (1.3.41). We are told why Tom avoids a fight with Blifil: "for besides that [1] *Tommy Jones* was an inoffensive Lad amidst all his Roguery, and [2] really loved *Blifil*, [3] Mr. *Thwackum* being always the Second of the latter, would have been sufficient to deter him" (3.4.130). Substantiating the apparent multiplicity of motives is the author's pose of ignorance: "I know not for what reason" Jenny Jones jumps up when Mrs. Partridge enters the room where she and Partridge are studying Latin. Wherever we turn we encounter the word "perhaps" or phrases such as "a matter not so easy to be accounted for," "we will not determine," or "I shall leave the reader to determine" (1.10, 11). All this is the counterpart of the doubt, confusion, and lack of subordination that characterizes the non-ironic Richardsonian verisimilitude.

It is easy enough to take the statement "Black George really loved Tom" as an ambiguity, but in the cases where Fielding lists multiple possibilities and says, "Take them all," one detects the pose of the Socratic ironist. In the examples concerning Mrs. Wilkins and Tom, (1) and (2) are commendable motives, but (3) is prudential and has the effect of exposing the other two as rationalizations. All of the author's alternatives simply point to the ironic recognition that Mrs. Wilkins obeys out of fear for her position and that Tom is shy of the birch. Again, the author's ignorance is plainly a mock-ignorance when he meditates on the motive of Allworthy's friend in recommending Thwackum as a tutor: "doubtless" because of Thwackum's qualifications of learning and religion, "though indeed" the friend was M.P. for a borough controlled by Thwackum's family.

The author is revealing a discrepancy between words (or rationalizations) and deeds that leads up to the exposure of Square behind Molly Seagrim's arras. He asks the reader to pass judgment on Mrs. Wilkins, Tom, and the friend of Allworthy. But the very recording of multiple motives and qualifying clauses invites the reader to embrace them in his assessment; and acceptance of the invitation is made easy in many instances by the fact that the truth, or a missing portion of it, is not revealed until hundreds of pages later.

The basic unit in *Joseph Andrews* was the word contradicted by action or by the revelation of motive, and this same contradiction takes place in *Tom Jones*, eventually. But the latter, unlike *Joseph Andrews*, deals in suspense and surprise, with facts and actions long unknown to the reader; thus the emphasis falls not on the contradiction but on the narrator's speculations of the moment – which, though solidified later, nevertheless give to the novel an air of complexity and doubt which is not swept away by the denouement. When we see Bridget Allworthy showing generosity and kindness to little Tommy Jones (deviating from the pattern of the Wilkins-like harpy we believe her to be), we are led to feel that she is a real person, not a type. And when we eventually discover the "truth" this impression is not altogether lost. Her prudence, like Wilkins', is made to appear no longer a ruling passion but only one aspect of a multifaceted personality.

Fielding is transforming irony from a satiric strategy to a technique for suggesting the complexity of reality and the mitigating forces that make the "mixed" character in whom he is most interested, without succumbing to what he considers the chaos that accompanied Richardson's method, and to do this without abrogating judgment.[58] Fielding's constant aim is to keep the reader from being actually immersed in the action, but to urge him to join the author as an advocate (in the legal sense) who can sympathize with the characters while never losing perspective on their actions.

Tom Jones opens with more anti-*Pamela* structures based on the touchstone form of the Good Samaritan. Tom is a touchstone and throughout the novel characters are judged "as they meet this test."[59] Since socially accepted opinion is against a bastard (legally "nobody," on whom Mrs. Wilkins comments, "it goes against me to touch these misbegotten wretches, whom I don't look upon as my fellow Creatures. Faugh! how it stinks! It doth not smell like a Christian" [1.3.41]), reactions to him tend to be violent and acceptance of him indicates true humanity; as a touchstone he promptly sets up the dichotomy of form and feeling. But if the novel starts with a series of responses to Tom, it soon modulates into a series of actions taken by Tom: he refuses to give away his poaching accomplice; he sells his horse and Bible; and he tries to save Sophia's little bird Tommy. Each of Tom's actions is followed (and in some cases preceded) by commentary, abstract and concrete, delivered by Thwackum and Square, with assistance from Blifil and sometimes Allworthy. The commentary characterizes the commentator, as it did in *Joseph Andrews*. Even after Tom is on the road the form persists, though less obtrusively. The Quaker, for example, shows a spectrum of reactions to Tom: first he is friendly; then he decides Tom is mad; and finally, learning who he really is (a nobody), he becomes indignant; and his reactions are compared with the innkeeper's (7.10).

In *Joseph Andrews* the action – whether Joseph's or Leonora the Jilt's – stands as the norm, good or bad, by which we judge reactions to it. In *Tom Jones* Tom's actions themselves are questionable, as are *all* the actions taken by characters in this novel, and the reader's attention is divided between action and commentary. Indeed, it is through these scenes that Fielding brings about the effect of Tom's greater importance and centrality to his novel than Joseph's or Adams' to his. Fielding has progressed (with the assistance of Richardson) from a villain-centered to a hero-centered plot, and from a hero-centered plot in which motive is exposed in the evil characters who swarm about the hero to a plot that is hero-oriented, with motive being sought in the hero himself. In each episode Tom is hims[elf] by his deeds, and the people around him (protectors and scho[

are specifically judges of his actions rather than persecutors – though physical persecution often follows judgment. Their judgments tell us something about Tom's actions as well as revealing their own characters.

The discrepancies between words and actions come to a head in Book 5, which compares and contrasts two examples: Molly Seagrim, whose words to Tom are belied by the collapse of the arras and the exposure of her affair with Square; and then Tom himself, whose professions of his love of Sophia are followed by his discovery by Square, Thwackum, & Co. in the bushes with the same Molly. Actions are present mostly to highlight Fielding's more subtle and analytic treatment of their wellsprings, and they are seldom allowed to stand and speak for themselves. Even the simple exposure of Square and Molly is not allowed to pass without some mitigating discussion of motives.

Every action is analyzed as to motive and judged by neighbors or chance acquaintances or enemies, whose own motives, of course, appear in their interpretations. When Allworthy is first introduced, the reader is told he "had not the least Doubt" of meeting his late wife in heaven – "Sentiments for which his Sense was arraigned by one Part of his Neighbors, his Religion by a second, and his Sincerity by a third" (1.2.35). These are three kinds of people one must encounter and by whom one's actions are so partially judged. The discovery of Tom in Allworthy's bed is followed by a recounting of the motives assigned to Allworthy by his neighbors – that Allworthy must be the father; that he was cruel in his magisterial treatment of Jenny; and that he probably spirited her away and murdered her – and finally the author's summary of the effect of this talk, that it does no harm to Allworthy and makes the rumor mongers happy.

At the outset Fielding's emphasis is deliberately balanced between the good man who must tread warily in the world to avoid such malicious misinterpretation of his decent actions, and the evil-minded neighbors who are made happy by the misinterpretation. The rumors do Allworthy no harm because he carefully and prudently maintains a proper public image of himself; thus the rumors about Tom's parentage are mere speculation, amusing for the neighbors in part because of their unreality.

But the rumors about Allworthy serve to anticipate Tom's situation. There *are* imprudent people about whom such speculation can be accepted as fact and become harmful. The danger of such misinterpretation is shown soon after Allworthy has ceased to be grist to the mill. Partridge is attacked by his jealous wife and beaten; her women friends enter and believe that he has attacked her; and soon the whole county is ringing with stories of Partridge's cruelty. The story is magnified until Mrs. Partridge has a broken arm and Partridge – when the story of Jenny's maternity becomes known – has a proper motive and two bastards. But the imaginary scene which has usurped reality is not so fantastic as its consequences, each worse than the last, moving toward complete destruction – in this sense, of the Partridge family. Justice goes all awry as the good Allworthy accepts the fabrication as true; Partridge is found guilty of both beating his wife and fathering Tom; his annuity is withdrawn (a backfiring on Mrs. Partridge); he loses his school; and finally Mrs. Partridge dies of smallpox and he leaves the neighborhood. Mrs. Partridge's interpretation of the fight has been accepted, thus making the fantasy effective and ruining herself and her husband. In this case an action is misinterpreted, and the misinterpretation is acted upon and grows to monstrous proportions, the circles of its effect reaching out to innocent people.

As a satiric convention this situation is related to the nightmare injustice that Fielding employs in such scenes as the apprehension of Adams for the crime he had just prevented. In *Tom Jones*, however, the emphasis is not so much on the satiric image of the innocent persecuted as on the perverse or merely mistaken interpretation of actions.

The general drift of *Tom Jones* follows this example, taking little Tommy, the bastard left in Allworthy's bed, and the various fantasies that follow from Bridget Allworthy's original act and developing them into the myth of the Wicked Tom (like Wild, "born to be hanged") and the good Blifil. This leads to Allworthy's misunderstanding of Tom's motive for laughing during his serious illness and consequently to a disaster similar to Partridge's. Thus we are frequently shown the "malicious tongues" that whisper about any behavior that is not immediately understood – "the public Voice, which seldom reaches to a Brother or a Husband, tho' it rings in the Ears of all the Neighbourhood" (3.7.140). The Virgilian Rumor herself makes an appearance amid the confusion of the Pretender's invasion, and Sophia becomes Jenny Cameron, Prince Charles Edward's supposed mistress (8.9.441).[60]

The characters within the novel are paralleled by the kinds of reader Fielding presupposes outside the novel looking in – the "Sneerer" and the "grave Reader," the "virtuous Reader," "Readers of the lowest Class," and the "upper Graduates in Criticism." These readers, like the characters in the book, are considered a more or less prejudiced jury or audience at a play – those two metaphorical equivalents that run through all of Fielding's fiction. The judicial metaphor is the more intense and widespread in *Tom Jones*. Fielding is constantly referring to "Judges" and "Jurisdiction" and to different kinds of justice: Tom's "Mercy" or Blifil's (or Thwackum's) "Justice," a "Court of Conscience" or a "Court of Justice." When Black George is trying to decide whether to take the money Sophia has sent Tom as well as the £500 he has already stolen, his dilemma is described in terms of a courtroom scene with his conscience "a good Lawyer" on one side, Avarice ready to "urge" the other, and Fear stepping in to decide the case (6.13.320).

The motives and causes behind the actions of Black George are as mixed as the various interpretations of them by others. And Black George is, quite simply, a type or foreshadowing of Tom. Fielding gives three motives for Tom's helping Black George and his family – his simple friendship for George; his sense of guilt for George's loss of his job (this is rendered more complex by the fact that George should have admitted his guilt to save Tom a thrashing); and his physical attraction to George's daughter, Molly. "Young Men of open, generous Dispositions are naturally inclined to Gallantry," we are told, and Tom "began now, at Twenty, to have the Name of a pretty Fellow among all the Women in the Neighbourhood" (4.5.166). And Black George, we are also told, "had the Reputation of a loose kind of a Fellow" (4.6.170).

Approaching a crucial action, Fielding marshals all the contributing factors available. Leading up to Tom's betrayal of Sophia with Molly in the grove (5.10), he dwells upon (1) the setting, "so sweetly accommodated to Love." It is "the latter End of June . . . a most delicious Grove . . . the gentle Breezes fanning the Leaves, together with the sweet Trilling of a murmuring Stream, and the melodious Notes of Nightingales." (2) Tom's thoughts of Sophia, memories of their last meeting, in which they realized that they loved each other, and knowledge "that Fortune . . . sets a Distance" between them. (3) Relief at the recovery of Allworthy after despairing of his Life. (4) Drunkeness caused by his celebration of Allworthy's recovery. As Fielding insists of Tom, "the Reader will be . . . pleased to recollect in his Favour that he was not at this Time perfect Master of that wonderful Power of Reason which so well enables grave and wise Men to subdue their unruly Passions" (words that recall the *Champion* essay on passion). Tom, hardly in control of himself to begin with, walks through erotically stimulating scenery thinking of Sophia, whom he can never marry, and sees Molly, who makes advances to him ("Jones probably thought one Woman better than none" [257]).

The consequence of Tom's sin, besides pangs of conscience, is expulsion from *Paradise Hall*. But the connection between the action and the punishment is extremely tenuous, depending on Tom's discovery by Blifil and Thwackum and ultimately on Allworthy's belief that Tom has insulted him. Consequences are not reliable evidence: As Allworthy dismisses Tom for a fancied slight, not for his real crime, Sophia (Fielding insists on the point by giving us authorial comment as well as Sophia's own words) repudiates Tom not because of his affair with Mrs. Waters but because Partridge has manufactured a story about Tom's using her name insultingly in a tavern. As Fielding learns how misleading not only words but even actions and consequences can be, he finds it increasingly difficult to judge actions. He rejects the satirist's simple but commonsensical acceptance of effect as the chief criterion of virtue in favor of the belief that an action can be neither good nor evil in itself, but only, perhaps, as its motive is charitable or self-seeking.

Fielding is saying that actions cannot be isolated and correctly interpreted by anyone – even the author himself – because of their very nature. He has pushed his search beyond motive itself, suggesting that the action, even if understood, is not the basis for a definitive judgment of a man. One must look to the general span of his life. Near the beginning of the book, though admitting that it is an ideal, he argues that character is more important than action (or conduct): "it is a more useful Capacity to be able to foretell the actions of Men, in any Circumstance, from their Characters, than to judge of their Characters from their Actions" (3.1.117). The double irony, in this sense, supports the general meaning of the novel. In both betrayals of Sophia, Tom succumbs to natural instinct, not in the least condoned by Fielding; he has betrayed Sophia but he obviously still loves her, just as Black George in some sense nevertheless loves Tom.

In one sense, Fielding attempts in *Tom Jones* to explore the shadowy Richardsonian realm, but setting out with very different equipment. He has simply moved his tools of assessment into the world of *Clarissa*, pointing out what Richardson never did, that the problem is in fact the opposition between being and actions, justice and law. His progression toward *Tom Jones* can be said to be from law and a study of actions (satire) to justice and an interest in being (novel), brought about perhaps by his intimate contact with the law and his awareness in practice of the discrepancy between law and justice.

ATTORNEY FOR THE DEFENSE

The essay-narrative dichotomy

In the introductory essay to book 5 ("essentially necessary to this kind of Writing, of which we have set ourselves at the Head") Fielding announces as "a Rule necessary to be observed in all Prosai-comi-epic writing" [5.1.209]) the principle of contrast. He means the contrast of the essay with the narrative that follows it. The principle of contrast he draws from the model of Addison's *Spectator* essays, where the abstract principle, the theory (of comedy vs. satire, of true vs. false wit), is presented in an essay; then it is exemplified by a narrative or a character (or an allegory), sometimes within the essay but certainly in later *Spectators*.

Fielding's introductory essays, he tells us, are "Precepts" and "Observations" for which the narrative provides "Exemplification" and "Illustration," the "Mark or Stamp" of "Reflection" and "Learning."[61] One of the features of *Tom Jones*, as of Addison's *Spectators*, that makes it so paradigmatic a work of the 1700s is that it materializes Locke's dichotomy of reflection and sensation, the basis for all understanding: "These two, I say, viz. external material things, as the objects of SENSATION, and the operation of our own

.......s within, as the objects of REFLECTION, are the only originals from whence all our ideas take their beginnings."[62] To which Locke adds: "When the mind turns its view inwards upon itself, and contemplates its own actions, *thinking* is the first that occurs."[63] This sense dominates Johnson's *Dictionary* (1755) definition of reflection as "thought thrown back upon the past, or the absent, or itself," "the action of the mind upon itself," all of which are applicable to the structure of *Tom Jones.*[64]

The bad version of theory and practice remained in *Joseph Andrews* and the early books of *Tom Jones* in the dichotomy of profession and performance: Either you say one thing and do another, or you do one thing (wrong) and then reflect upon it, thus coming to understand, or correct it – and eventually, like Tom, you come to do *and* say the right thing. At the close of *Tom Jones* Tom has "by Reflexion on his past Follies, acquired a Discretion and Prudence very uncommon in One of his lively Parts" (18.13.981). This is Fielding's answer to his rake Ramble in *Rape upon Rape*, who said: "'Tis as I have acted in all Affairs of Life; my thoughts have ever *succeeded* my Actions; the Consequence hath caused me to *reflect when it was too late.* I never reasoned on what I *should do*, but what I *had done*; as if my Reason had her Eyes behind, and could only see backwards" (9:127–8, emphasis added).

Tom has learned to reflect on his life as Fielding's essays reflect on the narrative: he has learned a mode of reflection analogous to the interaction between essay and narrative.[65] Throughout Fielding stresses the virtual homology of character and book and, implicitly, author. Beyond the author's reflection on the narrative which he has already written or at least knows from beginning to end, Fielding is indeed contemplating his own past actions, as Tom is brought around to doing at the denouement.

In the first essay (opening book 1) he gives a slightly different explanation. Each introductory essay is a bill of fare to the banquet that follows (it is hard to imagine Richardson's characters eating), and he announces his plan to begin with plain, solid fare and proceed to French and Italian seasoning. This applies to the movement from the country in the first six books to London with its fashionable affectation in the last six. It also suggests that the introductory essays will tell us how to read the narrative that follows. They are reflexive but also prospective and prescriptive, imposing the author's reading on his story (this too is Addisonian). The effect of the essay, "contrasted" with the narrative, is both explicatory and controlling. Ramble's sad case, of actions followed by thoughts, has been corrected.

Tom Jones, *Tom Jones, and Henry Fielding*

In the Dedication, Fielding makes "two Requests" of the reader, both obsessively repeated in the work that follows: "That he will not expect to find

Perfection in this Work; and Secondly, That he will excuse *some Parts* of it, if they fall short of that little Merit which I hope may appear in others" (8). Shortly after, in book 2, chapter 7, describing Allworthy (and "Men of true Wisdom and Goodness") as "contented to take Persons and Things as they are, without complaining of their Imperfections, or attempting to amend them," he presents the first of a series of statements to this effect:

> For I hope my Friends will pardon me, when I declare I know none of them without a Fault; and I should be sorry if I could imagine I had any Friend who could not see mine. Forgiveness, of this Kind, we give and demand in Turn. . . . The *finest Composition* of human Nature, as well as the finest China, may *have a flaw in it*; and this, I am afraid, in either Case, is equally incurable; though, nevertheless, *the Pattern may remain of the highest Quality.* (2.7.107, emphasis added)

Recalling Fielding's concern in his prefaces to his plays and his *Champion* essays with malicious criticism, we notice the emphasis on forgiveness: First, as was implicit in the Dedication, the mixed quality of the book, and the author's plea for acceptance of it warts and all, applies also to the book's protagonist; and second, more equivocally, in this instance it applies to none other than Captain Blifil (as in *Jonathan Wild* it applied to that villain) and later it will apply to Black George.

Fielding turns the novel he is writing and Tom Jones himself into parallel phenomena. His description of mixed character in the introductory essay to Book 10 is paralleled by the discussion of false critics in the introduction to Book 11, the latter dealing with slanderers of books, the criterion for which is the same as for the slanderers of people. Critics misinterpret Tom's actions because they accept a false character of him. The false critic passes judgment "upon Works he hath not himself read." He may "without assigning any particular Fault, condemn the whole in general defamatory Terms," or, finding "some Faults justly assigned in the Work" (though "not in the most essential Parts, or if they are compensated by greater Beauties"), he yet condemns the whole book (9.1.570). He is like those slanderers who condemn Tom or Black George for one or two mistakes, or those authors who do not believe in mixed characters, but only in paragons. The text and its hero, the public and personal, the aesthetic and moral are one: "Cruel indeed would it be if such a Work as this History, which has employed some thousands of Hours in the composing, should be liable to be condemned, because some particular Chapter, or perhaps Chapters, may be obnoxious to very just and sensible Objection." What we notice here – and which is pursued throughout the novel – is the close association of the "history" with the protagonist Tom and with the author, as "mixed characters" – and with the idea of forgiveness.

Fielding the author of *Tom Jones* is closely related to Fielding the barrister, the defender of malefactors at the assizes on his circuit. More scandalously, his association of himself with Tom has been noted by critics ever since Richardson's jaundiced remark in a 1750 letter to Anne Donnellan that all Fielding's fiction was autobiographical:

> Parson Young sat for Fielding's Parson Adams, a man he knew, and only made a little more absurd than he is known to be. The best story in the piece [*Joseph Andrews*], is of himself and his first wife. In his Tom Jones, his hero is made a natural child, because his own first wife was such. Tom Jones is Fielding himself, hardened in some places, softened in others. His Lady Bellaston is an infamous woman of his former acquaintance. His Sophia is again his first wife. Booth, in his last piece, again himself; Amelia, even in her noselessness, is again his first wife. His brawls, his jarrs, his gaols, his spunging-houses, are all drawn from what he has seen and known.[66]

All of this, despite the malice and the oversimplification, appears to have been essentially true. Even the allegation that Tom is "a natural child, because his first wife was such" could refer to the fact that the identity of Charlotte Cradock's father was a matter of conjecture.[67]

Richardson's "Fielding" is complemented but not contradicted by Arthur Murphy's account written in 1762: "Though disposed to gallantry by his strong animal spirits, and the vivacity of his passions, he was remarkable for tenderness and constancy to his wife, and the strongest affection for his children" (and, he also notes, "never wanted in filial piety").[68] What Murphy suppresses is Fielding's second marriage (Richardson's reference to a "first" wife implies a second).

Fielding cites his own life, especially the death of his daughter, in a journey to the underworld in *The Champion* and, at greater length, in *A Journey from This World to the Next*, where he admits to Minos that he "little expected to pass this fiery Trial. I confess'd I had indulged myself very freely with Wine and Women in my Youth, but had never done an Injury to any Man living, nor avoided an opportunity of doing good; that I pretended to very little Virtue more than general Philanthropy, and private Friendship" (*Misc.* 2:1.7.36). About the same time, in what must be an addition to the original 1729 *Wedding Day* (finally published in the *Miscellanies*), he has Heartfort say to Millamour: "My Practice is perhaps not equal to my Theory, but I pretend to sin with as little Mischief as I can to others; and this I can lay my Hand on my Heart and affirm, that I never seduced a young Woman to her own Ruin, nor a married one to the Misery of her Husband" (5.3; *Misc.*, 2:210).

All of this, suspiciously close to the words of Murphy, could be interpreted as protesting too much. Tom Jones says much the same of himself when he dissuades his friend Nightingale from debauching Nancy Miller: "'I am no canting Hypocrite, nor do I pretend to the Gift of Chastity, more than my Neighbours. I have been guilty with Women, I own it; but I am not conscious that I have ever injured any – nor would I to procure Pleasure to myself, be knowingly the Cause of Misery to any human Being' " (14.4.755).

Battestin's estimate is that "Fielding was something of a rake in his youth; but he always regarded the institution of marriage as inviolable" (129). By the 1750s Fielding had carried this sentiment into the demand for laws punishing adulterers (which would have included Billy Booth). But Battestin's tendency is to read a position Fielding held in the 1750s back into the 1730s.[69] It is more plausible to read Fielding's marriage to Charlotte Cradock in 1734 as the watershed; thereafter marriage *was* "inviolable" in the sense that it was the outward legality that symbolized true love, or the combination of love and lust that Fielding tried to define.

In November 1744 Charlotte Fielding died; and in April 1747 Fielding remarried. The bare facts are suggestive. We know nothing of his married life with Charlotte except what we learn from his references in his fiction and in one or two letters. There is no reason to believe that he did not love her as passionately and singly as he tells us he did. Lady Bute, Lady Mary Wortley Montagu's daughter, wrote that "he loved her passionately, and she returned his affection."[70]

The contradictory accounts of his behavior following Charlotte's death speak for themselves. Lady Bute said his grief was so intense it "approached to frenzy"; and Murphy wrote that his friends feared he was "in danger of losing his reason." But there is Fielding's own account (to Harris) of his four-day visit with Harris's friend Richard Owen Cambridge, a man of letters who lived in Gloucester, a 40-mile detour, while Charlotte's body was being carried to London.[71] One story from Bath places Fielding at a party on the evening Charlotte died. "I am very glad to see you, Mr. Fielding," a friend addresses him, "for there was a report . . . that your wife died this morning." "It is very true," Fielding replies, "and that is the very reason that I have come . . . to join the pleasure party." Another, milder version has him, accompanied by his sister Sarah, explain that he was determined to " 'dissipate,' using the word *dissipate* in the obvious sense of a change of scene – a change from which he would derive solace and comfort, under the care and wise direction of his excellent sister."[72] Though one cannot imagine Fielding not intending the pun on *dissipate*, there is a ring of truth in both stories, and both explain the detour to visit Cambridge, but the frantic nature of his grief is better felt at the party, where one can infer laughter and gaiety. Whereas to Harris he invokes "philosophy" and the classical model of Socrates, he also confesses that, soon after he buried Charlotte, he spent "as pleasant a day . . . as I have known some Months" with Salisbury friends: "Nay, I was so little a mourner that I believe many a Good Woman, had she been present, would have denied the Possibility of my having ever been a good Husband." It was also a funeral of great expense and show (charges of £11.17.2), "a stately funeral of such pomp that only the greatest families in the parish could afford."[73] This was his way of dealing with the great tragedy of his life.

It is noteworthy how casually Tom is introduced in his eponymous novel in a chapter titled "The Heroe of this great History appears with very bad Omems" (3.2); compared with the elaborate introduction of Sophia, which opens book 4, chapter 1, with Flora strewing the stage with flowers, followed in chapter 2 by the elaborate description of her, ending with: "but most of all, she resembled one whose Image never can depart from my Breast" (4.2.156). The high idealizing and the overwrought references to Charlotte indicate something. The central issue in *Tom Jones* is the sexual betrayal of the woman Tom loves; the question is how Tom can sleep with Molly, Jenny, and Lady Bellaston and yet love Sophia; and the ultimate reason given, which also I have no doubt expresses Fielding's worst sense of guilt, is that he has renounced Sophia – is mechanically and physically forgetting her – *because* he knows that if he runs away with her it will ruin her financially and she will be reduced to want and distress of a sort we know Charlotte suffered for living with Fielding. The sexual nature of the betrayals, though part of the donné of the anti-*Pamela* program of Fielding's novels, is so intensely scrutinized that it seems certain that if he did not betray Charlotte in this way he was remembering episodes from his earlier rakish career which he guiltily associated with his marriage to Charlotte or with the years after her death. (Tom describes his waning desire for Molly: "Her beauty was still the Object of Desire, though greater Beauty, or a fresher Object, might have been more so" [4.6.175].)

Whatever the exact circumstances of his married life with Charlotte, these would have been further conflicted by his remarriage two and a half years later to Mary Daniel, who was Charlotte's maid (Fielding was 40, Daniel 26). The interval can be reduced by at least eight months, for he married Daniel far into her pregnancy and made her an "honest woman," precisely as Nightingale does Nancy Miller and only after the intervention of Tom. It seems likely that Fielding was intimate with Charlotte's maid within a relatively short time of Charlotte's death (as, indeed, he would have remembered was the case with his father following his mother's death). This in itself invites various interpretations: she would have been a surrogate, another Charlotte, as Molly Seagrim and Jenny Waters were substitutes for Sophia, and would have constantly reminded him of Charlotte; she would have been a convenient vent (a term to which I shall return) for a lusty widower – not of his class, a mistress; but she would also have reminded him of any earlier transgressions, she would in an important sense have been a betrayal of Charlotte, and he utilized his sense of duty to both women when he made Mary an "honest woman."

This personal problem was, I believe, central to Fielding's feelings in the

1740s. Aside from the fact that he was in his prime, with all the experience of his plays, his essays, and his prose narratives to draw upon, he also experienced a unique intersection of crises, public and private, literary and political, that made possible a particular kind of fiction. This was a comic fiction in which Fielding indulges in a proto-Byronic poeticizing of himself; and, parallel with it, a half-ironic exaltation of his new kind of writing of which he is mock-monarch and also personal embodiment, blemishes and all. Beneath the comic hubris lies an argument based on special pleading.

The theological defense

Tom Jones opens with a fairly close description of Fielding's earliest memories of the Sharpham and Glastonbury landscape and goes on to present what it must have felt like to grow up in a family with step-brothers and sisters, contesting mothers, and a father who misjudges crucial events. Edmund Fielding, however, can have had little in common with Mr. Allworthy other than being a local magistrate. Allworthy, master of Paradise Hall, contains an allusion to the deity and, once that is said, more than a touch of Shaftesbury's Judeo-Christian God. It is surely significant that Tom's first two crimes are robbing an orchard and selling a Bible. It is also significant for Tom's story, which argues that his sexual promiscuity is an aspect of his good nature, that Allworthy is first praised for his charity (demonstrated in his taking in the little bastard) and then shown delivering a very orthodox and pompous sermon to Jenny Jones on "the Violation of your Chastity. A crime, however lightly it may be treated by debauched Persons, very heinous in itself, and very *dreadful in its Consequences*" – that is, God's "highest Vengeance" (1.7.52, emphasis added). First he presents Jenny with the religious consequence, second with the social – ostracization and commitment to the house of correction (recalling the bad magistrate's commitment of Fanny in *Joseph Andrews*). Allworthy is a magistrate, in both public and private capacities (constantly passing judgment on Tom), who is presented as the God of rewards and punishments – related, in his first example of judgment, to sexual freedom. Whatever we decide about the degree to which his speech is undercut (in the next book he passes an erroneous and damaging judgment on Partridge), his speech sets up a standard against which Tom's sexual promiscuity has to be, in the sequel, defended.[74] I mean that Fielding, worrying as he clearly does about the issue, intends Allworthy's as the official view which has to be answered. Allworthy speaks the harsh Old Testament judgment but, as mitigation, supplements it with New Testament mercy. He will send Jenny away, out of the reach of punishment – with a stipend if she will identify "the wicked Man that seduced you; for my Anger against him will be much greater than you have experienced" (that is, Jones's crime will be worse than Molly Seagrim's). Like Tom, in the parallel scene concerning poaching with Black George, Jenny refuses to name her accomplice and is sent off without the stipend.

Like Shaftesbury's monstrous deity, Allworthy begins with, but then elides, the personal affront – that Jenny appears to have, as he tells her, "laid your Sins at my Door." The procedure is repeated when he passes judgment against Tom, ignoring the sexual encounter with Molly and condemning Tom because he has supposedly shown Allworthy disrespect during his illness (and Blifil, following the news of his mother's death). Nevertheless, Allworthy seems to regard sexual incontinence as about the worst crime, as when he commits the pregnant Molly to the house of correction: "A Lawyer may, perhaps, think Mr. *Allworthy* exceeded his Authority a little in this Instance. And, to say the Truth, I question, as there was no regular Information before him, whether his Conduct was strictly regular" (4.11.192).

A Christian reading of *Tom Jones* depends upon the line from *Paradise Lost,* "The world lay all before him" (7.2.331), heralding Tom's expulsion from Paradise Hall by Mr. Allworthy.[75] Blifil (rhymes with Devil) invents the lie of disrespect for Allworthy which leads this figure of the deity to expel Tom. And Allworthy is influenced by (his authority replaced by) his delegated representatives such as Thwackum and Square. Whether or not he carries signs of the monster God, Allworthy is certainly related, at the end of the novel, to the father in the parable of the Prodigal Son. But the roles are reversed, and he must beg forgiveness of his son.

The significant detail in Tom's story is the asymmetry of the Fall and the Expulsion. Book 9, as in *Paradise Lost* the book of the Fall (his Fall at Upton), is the central book, rather than 6, the Expulsion itself; and this is because in *Tom Jones* the Expulsion does not follow from, is not a consequence, of the Fall. The ostensible reason is the *amour propre* of Allworthy, compromised by lies based on the hatred (or jealousy) of Blifil and his henchmen Thwackum and Square. Tom is expelled for one reason (Allworthy's), but what matters to Allworthy and later to Sophia (respect for their good names) does not matter to Fielding. He focuses on Tom's betrayal of his love for Sophia – *and* explains and justifies it.

Allworthy, as if expressing the views of the "Essay on Conversation," equates prudence and religion as Tom's desiderata (5.8.244). The positive sense of good breeding in the "Essay" reappears in the context of Tom's experience in the real world; Tom's actions, he is told, must not only be "intrinsically good, you must take Care they shall appear so." And Fielding's message, I presume to himself and to the enemies (the "mob") who have maligned him, is "That no Man can be good enough to enable him to neglect the Rules of Prudence; nor will Virtue herself look beautiful, unless she be decked with the outward Ornaments of Decency and

Decorum" (3.7.141). Fielding's irony is underlined two chapters later when young Blifil is called "a very prudent Lad" (2.9.144). The occasion is Tom's selling his Bible to alleviate the want of the Seagrims – an act Thwackum calls "Sacrilege," a "monstrous Crime, as it appeared to him" (145); an act defended by the deist Square.

These are the reactions of the Levites and Pharisees to Jesus' teachings. Now, however, rather than citing Jesus' words, "Love thy neighbor as thyself" (employed in the "Essay on Conversation"), he is citing the text of Corinthians 13, which ends with "Faith, hope, and charity, and the greatest of these is charity," which Fielding, like many commentators, equated in the *Champion* with "love."[76] Faith to Fielding is the opposite of works, the doctrine Parson Williams teaches Shamela; hope is based on Shaftesbury's *bête noire*, the church doctrine of rewards and punishments; and only charity/love serves Fielding in his major fictions.

The philosophical defense

Empson was the first critic to take seriously Fielding's remark about "the great, useful and uncommon Doctrine, which it is the Purpose of this whole Work to inculcate" (12.8.652). He saw it as the engine driving that great machine *Tom Jones*, and made a stab at defining it: "If good by nature, you can imagine other people's feelings so directly that you have an impulse to act on them as though they were your own; and this is the source of your greatest pleasure as well as of your only genuinely unselfish actions."[77]

Bernard Harrison, a professional philosopher, picked up Empson's brilliant but unsystematic discussion, arguing that in *Tom Jones* Fielding is not merely a moralist (certainly not a religious spokesman) but a moral theorist.[78] Harrison argues that the "great doctrine" of *Tom Jones* is Fielding's presentation in fabular terms of a philosophical position which modulates between the Shaftesburian and Mandevillian views of virtue, in important ways correcting Joseph Butler's solution to the dichotomy (in his *Analogy of Religion* [1736]). The solution is Fielding's sense of love as governed not by inclination alone (this is merely lust), however important this is, but by the sense of responsibility for the person loved: Tom's inability to simply run off with Sophia because of his awareness (via honor or duty or whatever) of how this would affect her.[79] It would, of course, have rendered Sophia vulnerable to precisely the sort of life he imposed on Charlotte by his careless living, which ended in a sponging house, the death of children (however unconnected with their neediness), and the death of Charlotte herself.

The theme of love-lust begins to emerge after his marriage. In 1741 this is the subject of the conversation Fielding had with James Harris "concerning the clear Distinction between Love and Lust"; one suspects that he was learning this from Harris, the disciple of Shaftesbury.[80] Shaftesbury's central term "disinterestedness" is focused in the religious context on the distinction between a disinterested love of God and an interested one based on "belief in a future reward and punishment": he concludes that "to serve God by compulsion, or for interest merely, is service and mercenary."[81] Fielding's own moral program, however, is devoted to justifying the "interestedness" of virtue: Tom's benevolence is based on neither the religious principles of Thwackum nor the Shaftesburian "natural Beauty of Virtue" advocated by Square. It is based on a "love" of the *other* which, though extended to a general sympathy, is posited on physical desire. This "love" is qualitatively different when addressed to Molly, Jenny, and Lady Bellaston, but only because with them it remains at the level of physical hunger (one of Shaftesbury's terms for interestedness), whereas "love" leads Tom to give up Sophia when he knows that it will be harmful to her if he does not.

Such relationships are distinguished not by Shaftesbury's ascending scale of body and mind but by appetite, in Harrison's words "a desire for some goal which can be fully specified without at all mentioning the consicous states of other people" ("a desire to use somebody's body, without the slightest concern for any mental state of the person concerned"); as opposed to human needs, or "desires for goals which cannot be specified without mentioning the conscious states of other people." Human needs lead us "into connexion with each other, and out of that solitary egoistic self-absorption" of mere appetite.[82] Human needs include both an internal sense of empathy and an external sense of duty to the loved one.

In *Tom Jones* Fielding is morally opposed both to Mandeville, who sees humans as all appetite, *and* to Shaftesbury, who sees them as all human needs but of a single sort, based on the model of the disinterested country gentleman in a coffee house or in Mr. Spectator's club. Fielding's human needs are based unashamedly on heterosexual desire. Even Tom's "friendship" with Black George, it is strongly hinted, is based at least partly on his sexual attraction to his daughter Molly. Tom's refusal to betray George can be taken as parallel to his later sense of duty to Molly when he thinks he is the father of her child and offers to give her "a Sum of Money."[83]

Fielding's position derives from the Mandevillian exposure of interest beneath Shaftesbury's disinterestedness. Fielding marginalizes the economic aspects of interest which are Mandeville's focus, leaving primarily sexual desire – but not entirely, since it is precisely Sophia's economic dependence on her father that weighs heavily with Tom in his decision to leave off his courtship. By narrowing egoism to the primary role of sexual desire he can replace Shaftesbury's distinction between lust for an individual body and general benevolence with a more realistic psychology. He can contrast the *pleasure* Tom gets from Sophia as an end in itself (Sophia is only a means to that end) with Sophia herself, whose happiness and well-being give him pleasure.

What Fielding has produced out of the Shaftesburian principles of order and harmony, mind over body, and "disinterested" pleasure is an alternative ethics (or aesthetics) of pleasure centered on the body of a real woman. While he probably draws upon Hogarth's *Strolling Actresses dressing in a Barn* (the real woman who emerges from the actress's role of the goddess of chastity) he differs in significant ways from Hogarth for whom it is the pursuit itself that gives the pleasure. Tom takes no "pleasure" or "love" in the "pursuit" or "chase" of Sophia for its own sake.

Theatrical and legal defenses

Fielding ends *Tom Jones* (18.1) with "the last Stage of our long Journey," with the author "an entertaining Companion." The metaphor of journey, he suggests, functions as a means of explaining the process of living, writing, and reading the unfolding romance, with its clear-cut beginning, middle, and end; while the metaphor of theater must be resorted to in order to examine objectively and understand the problematic actions of both living and writing. The journey metaphor remains associated with the subject, who sees himself as a pilgrim (as both writer and protagonist), while the theatrical metaphor emerges when it is necessary to explain something about these figures in relation to the world – that is, in terms of custom, roles, and disguises. This is the metaphor they unconsciously live by.

In the introductory essay to book 7 Fielding points out that in the past the resemblance between life and the theater has been "taken from the Stage only"; now he turns to "the Audience of this great Drama," "the Behaviour of her Spectators" as well as "that of her Actors." The focus is still on Black George's action, and Fielding sketches in the various reactions of the upper gallery, the pit, and the boxes to his deed, each censuring Black George in its characteristic way. Then he adds that

> we, who are admitted behind the Scenes of this great Theatre of Nature . . .
> can censure the Action, without conceiving any absolute Detestation of
> the Person, whom perhaps Nature may not have designed to act an ill Part
> in all her Dramas; for in this instance Life most exactly resembles the Stage,
> since it is often the same Person who represents the Villain and the Hero.
> (7.1.327)

However, this is not enough because, as he adds, "the Passions, like the Managers of a Playhouse, often force Men upon Parts without consulting their Judgment, and sometimes without any Regard to their Talents." The passions, he says, "are the Managers and Directors of this Theatre (for as to Reason, the Patentee, he is known to be a very idle Fellow and seldom to exert himself)."

As Addison suggested in his *Spectator* essay on the metaphors of life as journey and theater, there may be new roles assigned in heaven commensurate with our performance in the assigned roles on earth – once again Fielding's emphasis is on the happy afterlife:

> The great Duty which lies upon a Man is to act his Part in Perfection. We may, indeed, say that our Part does not suit us, and that we could act another better. But this (says the Philosopher [Epictetus]) is not our Business. All that we are concerned in is to excell in the Part which is given us. If it be an improper one the Fault is not in us, but in him who has cast our several Parts, and is the great Disposer of the Drama.

It is thus Epictetus' god, the playwright, who is replaced in Fielding's formulation by Nature, or human nature, and the Passions. We are actors assigned roles by a playwright or stage manager or author – not a deity but the ruling, policing order of his surrogates on earth who take little interest in the appropriateness of role to actor. The clergy promise at some distant time a reward for the way we play the role assigned to us – and this keeps us comforted and operational. Like the imitation of the upper orders, this permits Fielding to shift responsibility, at least partially, from the individual to society.[84]

Theater offers the essential element for an understanding of Tom – in the sense of role-playing. Tom finds himself in situations where he adopts roles that are not necessarily true to his "character." It is the metaphor most appropriate for a society such as the one Fielding describes, at its best based on "good breeding" and at its worst on hypocrisy. To supplement the theater, the court of law adds a depth of seriousness, of consequences, that is lacking in the theater. Real or putative crimes have real punishments, as do guilt and innocence, the words of plaintif and defendant; this is a world of good and evil rather than only appearance and reality; or rather, it turns the world as theater into a world of right and wrong. The jury carries a more positive charge than a theater audience (which, moreover, by the time he quit the theater, Fielding regarded as quite unreliable). For one thing, the jury represents the very heart of the English tradition: not trial by ordeal, which meant appealing to God for his miraculous intervention, but by jury; and a jury whose decision must be unanimous – based on "the unanimous consent of twelve of [the defendant's] neighbours and equals." As Blackstone would put it: "the trial by jury ever has been, and I trust ever will be, looked upon as the glory of the English law." In the jury trial the judge is subordinated, responsible for law not facts, to the barrister. A defendant is judged by his peers, not by the judge, who should not meddle with questions of fact, should not directly examine the witness or unduly influence the jury.

In *Joseph Andrews* Fielding was primarily concerned with the contrast of an unreliable or interested "witness" and the circumstantial narration of a barrister. In *Tom Jones* it is the trial of a "mixed character," Tom, whose crime was the betrayal of the woman he loves, and whose legal defense was the argument that judgment should be based on his overall character rather than one or two cases of bad conduct (or inapproprite roles); the form was essentially the brief of a barrister for the defense. Again, the theatrical and legal contexts come together. Lillo's *London Merchant* had established for Fielding an assumption that would be supplemented by his law studies and play a large part in *Tom Jones* – the distinction between character and conduct, between the whole course of a virtuous lifetime and the single culpable act, exemplified by George Barnwell's murder of his uncle. In Lillo's final act once the evil is punished the characters can go on to admire the good; Maria and Trueman praise Barnwell's character ignoring his one significant piece of conduct. Lillo dispenses with the legal question, the guilt, trial, and punishment of Barnwell for his criminal acts, and turns to the question of his overall stretch of life and its many good qualities. The difference, of course, will be between Barnwell's theft and murder and Tom Jones's sexual betrayal of Sophia; but the issue will be the relationship of character (real and by reputation) and conduct.

The physiological explanation

Tom Jones opens its first chapter with a "bill of fare," introducing the metaphor of eating with the author as chef and innkeeper, the readers as the diners at his feast which is the work itself – *Tom Jones* (e.g., chapter divisions are like the cutting of joints of meat).[85] The metaphor is used to distinguish from true love the need to satisfy bodily hunger. In the introductory essay to book 7 he distinguishes true love from "the Desire of satisfying a voracious Appetite with a certain Quantity of delicate white human Flesh," and this prepares us for Tom's defection with Molly. Blifil's desires, such as they are, tend toward appetite alone – in Sophia he experiences only "the same Desires which an Ortolan inspires into the Soul of an Epicure" (7.6.346).[86]

The form the Lord's Supper took for Bishop Hoadly (see above, 172) relied on St. Paul's Second Epistle to the Corinthians (chaps. 10 and 11), where he attacks the Corinthians for their handling of the Lord's Supper. Hoadly made the distinction "between the *eating* and *drinking* in memory of their *Master*, and their eating and drinking indecently at a Common Meal." Hoadly's "Corinthian Sinners," those who "place the least hope in their partaking of the *Lord's Supper*, whilst they continue in the practice of their Sins" and are "guilty of *eating and drinking Unworthily*" (84, 85), serve as a gloss on Tom's dinner with Jenny Waters (9.5). Fielding is distinguishing between love and lust, the proper supper and the improper, as focused on his central question of whether Tom can love Sophia and yet betray her with Molly, Jenny, and Lady Bellaston. The sequence begins with Tom's fascination with Jenny's bare breasts, a parody of the iconography of Charity, which sets in motion the lust that is at first satisfied with the food placed before him but, when that is used up, finds satisfaction in Molly herself, another "choice morsel."[87]

The metaphor of appetite is closely related to a larger model of the body along the lines of fluid mechanics. Only when Tom finishes filling his stomach can he evacuate into Mrs. Waters; which might be read as saying that the love and frustration concerning Sophia find vent in a hearty meal, but when this outlet is insufficient there remains enough for Mrs. Waters, another (parallel) natural outlet.[88]

In book 5 Tom sets out on a warm June night, drunk and ebullient because Allworthy is recovering, but thinking "on his dear *Sophia*," from whom fortune has irrevocably separated him. When Molly passes he promptly disappears into the bushes with her – because (among other reasons) he "probably thought one Woman better than none" (5.10.256).[89] In the contrasting scene that began book 5, Fielding's explanation for Molly's affair with Square, for whom she had no great fondness, was "the Absence of *Jones* during his Confinement" with a broken arm (231). This model pervades *Tom Jones*; at one point Fielding generalizes, quoting Roger L'Estrange to the effect that "if we shut Nature out at the Door, she will come in at the Window."[90]

The physical explanation is incidentally applied to Sophia herself earlier in book 5. She has fallen in love with Tom but she restrains herself from any show of her feelings:

> Notwithstanding the nicest Guard which *Sophia* endeavoured to set on her Behviour, she could not avoid letting some Appearances now and then slip forth: For Love may again be likened to a Disease in this, that when it is denied a Vent in one Part, it will certainly break out in another. (5.2.218–19)

And so Sophia blushes and turns alternately hot and cold, symptoms repeated in Tom when he realizes he has fallen in love with her. When he ascertains the truth about Molly and Square, "His Heart was now, if I may use the Metaphor, entirely evacuated, and *Sophia* took absolute Possession of it" (5.6.235).

The mechanical, iatrohydraulic model is used for lust, or whatever falls short of "love." Even thoughts of Sophia can be driven out by concern for Allworthy's health (5.7.242). Tom's relief over Allworthy's recovery gives vent to joy – amorous songs, augmented by drinking toasts to his recovery; following which, Tom and Blifil, "prevented from executing present Vengeance on each other [by the interposition of Thwackum and the physician], . . . vented their Wrath in Threats and Defiance." These outlets for the love of Sophia then lead to Tom's sexual interlude with Molly; which is followed by the introductory essay to Book 6 on love as distinguished from hunger.

In *Joseph Andrews* Joseph rebuffs Betty the chambermaid, who has fallen in love with him; shortly after, she gives herself to Mr. Tow-wouse when he makes an advance, although she is not attracted to him and has until now consistently fended off his embraces. We are told that her "Passions were already raised, and . . . were not so whimsically capricious that one Man only could lay them, though perhaps, she would have rather preferred that one." And of Tow-wouse himself: "for as the Violence of his Passion had considerably abated to Mrs. Tow-wouse; so like Water, which is stopt from its usual Current in one Place, it naturally sought a vent in another" (1.11.87–8). The point is that the hydraulic model is applied not to Joseph but to Betty, who would have, in Joseph's position, settled for Lady Booby. But Joseph, a simpler case than Tom, can love only Fanny.[91] In *Tom Jones* Fielding levels the distinction he made in *Joseph Andrews* between Joseph and Betty; for here it applies to almost everyone.

Allworthy, a lusty man in youth who married for sex as well as "love" (in the sense of the opening chapter to book 5), has lost his beloved wife and sublimates the loss by his faith in an anticipated meeting in the afterlife and by service and charity in this life. Allworthy's sublimation is embodied in his adjustment from a lusty husband to a widower who "hungers after Goodness" – a meal which thoroughly satisfies him and affords him more repose than that "occasioned by any other hearty Meal" (1.3.41). Allworthy may be thought of as a positive projection of this aspect of Fielding himself – how he would have *liked* to act.

The model also explains Tom's immediate responses (his charity) to the beggar, the highwayman, Mrs. Miller, Nancy Miller, and the rest. Perhaps we have to go back to the melancholic model and those who do *not* respond as Tom does, those who do *not* find a vent. Fielding's version seems to accept the assumption that evil people are those who repress and therefore allow (or direct) their sexual urges toward perverted intellectualized ends. Even Bridget and Square eventually find vents. A page before the account of Sophia's "disease," Square is shown in Tom's sickroom arguing with Thwackum. He gets so excited that he bites his tongue, which gives Thwackum the opportunity of carrying the argument, and leaves Square furious: "as he was disabled from venting his Wrath at his Lips, he had possibly found a more violent Method of revenging himself," had the discussion not been brought to an end (5.2.217). It is following the frustrations of argument and repression of emotion in Tom's sickroom, we learn three chapters later, that Square vents himself in his affair with Molly.

Only Blifil and Thwackum remain relentlessly costive. Blifil is the prime example of those who retain or control their vapors, which then are diverted into plotting and sedition, like the vapors of Swift's Aeolists. Blifil – whose father the captain was a melancholiac – has "not the least Tincture" of true love in his composition, and his sexual appetite is "so moderate, that he was able by Philosophy or by Study, or by some other Method, easily to subdue [it]." While "some other Method," in Fielding's language, may refer to masturbation as well as sublimation, what he means is that Blifil was "altogether as well furnished with some other Passions," namely "Avarice and Ambition." Sexual attraction for Sophia is translated into lust for the power and fortune to be gained by possessing her (6.4.284).

A variant appears when Squire Western is hunting Sophia, has lost her trail, and the sound of hunting horns reaches his ear: he is off after the pack, and we are told that "if we shut Nature out at the Door, she will come in at the Window," for Fielding insists again that "we are not to arraign the Squire of any Want of Love for his Daughter: For in reality he had a great deal; we are only to consider that he was a Squire and a Sportsman" (12.2.623). Western really loves Sophia, but this spiritual object is not present, and the stimulus to his animal nature – his instinct – sends him off after the hounds.

Even Sophia, near the end, once victory is in sight, lets us see in her own realistic but discrete way what might have happened if she had been forced into marriage with Blifil. She says to Allworthy:

> to lead our Lives with one to whom we are indifferent, must be a State of Wretchedness. —— Perhaps that Wretchedness would be even increased by a Sense of the Merits of an Object to whom we cannot give our Affections [i.e., Tom]. If I had married Mr. *Blifil* —— (18.9.953)

She does not finish her sentence, but given the physical structure presupposed throughout *Tom Jones*, we can imagine the rest.

In Jones's case, when he is preparing to go to the masquerade, where he hopes to meet Sophia, love offers "delicious Repasts" to some of his senses, but "it can afford none to others"; it can offer Tom such "delicacies" as "the Hopes of seeing Sophia" but he nevertheless begins "to languish for some Food of a grosser Kind" (13.6.710–11). The final temptations, however, show him achieving a balance of humors. In his moment of deepest despair about the possibility of a physical reconciliaton with Sophia, he turns down the alternative of Arabella Hunt: there is the usual list of reasons for accepting her, parallel to those he had for accepting Molly Seagrim, but they no longer overbalance his love for Sophia (15.11.827). Finally, he refuses Mrs. Fitzpatrick's suggestion that he woo Mrs. Western in order to get at Sophia (to "make sham Addresses to the older Lady, in order to procure an easy Access to the Younger" – Mr. Fitzpatrick's stratagem for getting at his future wife): "his whole Thoughts were now so confined to his *Sophia*, that I believe no Woman on Earth could have now drawn him into an act of Inconstancy" (16.9.867–71).

Laughter and the body

While "love" is Shaftesburian benevolist and (via Hoadly and the Eucharist) Christian *caritas*, the basic model is Hobbesian-mechanist, the Rochester-libertine model of Fielding's early comedies. What in Rochester was a pessimistic view of man, summed up in his "Imperfect Enjoyment," in Fielding becomes a statement of how nature operates, especially when constrained by some form of "art," and a defense for human frailty of a certain sort.

The satiric model appears in Swift's "Digression on Madness," where, for example, (A) Henry IV of France lusts after (B) a pretty girl but cannot obtain her, and so the semen generated, having lost its normal outlet, mounts to his brain and makes him mad, leading to (C) war, unless evacuated by (D) a "state-Surgeon's [the assassin Ravaillac's] Knife." "Nature shut out at one passage," as Swift puts it in *The Mechanical Operation of the Spirit*, "was forc'd to seek another." The medical model behind both Swift and Fielding is explained by Robert Burton in *The Anatomy of Melancholy*: if there is no evacuation of the sexual vapors, melancholy and madness will follow. Melancholy is implicitly what is avoided by Tom – by Booth and Betty, and in their different ways by Molly and Square, when they open another vent. These are lusty characters: as the doctor notes of Tom after his wounding by Northerton, "the Pulse was exuberant and indicated [i.e., called for] much Phlebotomy" (7.13.381). Swift used this model but associated it with Hobbesian materialism and atheistic moderns, believing that the humour might be controlled by religious forms; the more optimistic Fielding believed in release – in laughter or in innocent sexual play (though not always so innocent in its consequences, as he acknowledges – and as Tom significantly acknowledges when he makes his decision *not* to pursue Sophia).

In his vindication of laughter in *Craftsman* no. 612 (Apr. 1, 1738) Fielding cited the Democritean definition of man as the creature who laughs: "my *Humanity*, I mean my *Laughter*" (*New Essays*; 287). This, the therapeutic purpose of laughter, implies the release of melancholy vapors by the venting of laughter and is probably Fielding's ultimate source (along with the analogy of body politic and body private) for his hydraulic explanation of human actions.[92]

For the tradition of positive laughter – a secular, philosophical tradition, beginning with Hippocrates and associated with the laughing philosopher

Democritus – Fielding naturally invokes Shaftesbury.[93] In the preface to
Joseph Andrews he cited Shaftesbury's comment on burlesque as a bad reaction to "spiritual tyranny," the diversion of a good reaction and not to be
found in the politer ages, in which free discourse was encouraged. This
citation is in proximity to his remark that burlesque can "contribute more
to exquisite Mirth and Laughter than any other; and these" – he adds, substituting the cathartic for the satiric explanation – "are probably more
wholesome Physic for the Mind, and conduce better to purge away Spleen,
Melancholy and ill affections, than is generally imagined" (5).[94]

In *Sensus Communis* Shaftesbury cited an "ancient sage" to the effect "that
humour was the only test of gravity; and gravity of humour. For a subject
which would not bear raillery was suspicious; and a jest which would not
bear a serious examination was certainly false wit" (1:52).[95] Moreover,
Sensus Communis is the locus of Shaftesbury's case against the central
Christian doctrine of rewards and punishments, which he associated with
the "gravity" of priestcraft. It is significant for Fielding that this argument
appears in the essay on the "Freedom of Wit and Humour" and so probably was his way into both subjects, with which he wrestled.

Shaftesbury's model for both virtue and beauty is the balanced and harmonious system, his version of the Whig idea of the English body politic
as a harmonious balance between monarch, aristocracy, and people. The
worst restraint upon liberty, the straitjacket which distorts the body into
grotesque shapes, is "gravity." On the basis of his ideal of the balanced body
Shaftesbury develops the hydraulic metaphor:

> There are certain humours in mankind which of necessity must have vent.
> The human mind and body are both of them naturally subject to commo-
> tions: and as there are strange ferments in the blood, which in many bodies
> occasion an extraordinary discharge; so in reason, too, there are heteroge-
> neous particles which must be thrown off by fermentation. Should physicians
> endeavour absolutely to allay [subdue] those ferments of the body, and strike
> in the humours which discover themselves in such eruptions, they might,
> instead of making a cure, bid fair perhaps to raise a plague, and turn a spring-
> ague or an autumn-surfeit into an epidemical malignant fever.

Shaftesbury's metaphor is the same as the one Swift uses in his "Digression
on Madness"; both are applied to religious enthusiasm. In Swift's scenario,
liberty (sexual energy) blocked will rise to find an outlet in the brain and
through the mouth in enthusiasm – that is, in "new" philosophies, religions,
and politics which lead to insurrection. In Shaftesbury's scenario, "the
natural free spirits of ingenious men" permitted their natural exit will
produce laughter – and a test of truth. Blocked they will be diverted into
civil insurrection or vicious Tory satire.

Although a great admirer of Swift, Fielding follows Shaftesbury in each
of these particulars. For him this comic catharsis is parallel to Shamela's

inability to withhold her passion, beginning with her mother's admonition, "Why will you give way to your Passion?" (23), and ending with her inability to restrain her lust for Parson Williams, which from one point of view is her downfall, from another is the humanizing of her. The surest sign is Shamela's exclamation after frightening "the poor booby ... out of his Wits": "O what a Difficulty it is to keep one's Countenance, when a violent Laugh desires to burst forth" (27).

In *Tom Jones* it is Punch who bursts out when nature is repressed; whether to send Sophia on her pursuit of Tom or to expose the gravity of a Cibberian "comedy," the phallic figure of Punch is liberating. The episode that sums up this assumption gives us Tom's argument with the puppet master for the inclusion of Punch, the comic element, in Cibber's *Provok'd Husband*. This is Fielding's homage to Quixote and the puppet show and his final word on the conflict between farce and five-act comedy he had struggled with in the 1730s. It is the Punchless production of Cibber's comedy that led the landlady's maid into sex with the Merry Andrew: "If I am a Wh – e," she cries, "my Betters are so as well as I. What was the fine Lady in the Puppet-show just now?" In her arms the Merry Andrew stands in for Punch and so for Tom himself, carrying for the reader memories of the moment when a phallic Punch, a surrogate Tom, was invoked by Sophia's muff (7.9.360; 12.6.641).

Tom's sympathy for the Merry Andrew's plight may be partly fellow-feeling for another Tom caught *in flagrante delicto*. But at the same time that Tom laments the absence of Punch in *The Provok'd Husband*, Fielding was advertising (March 1747/8) his revival of "the comical Humours of PUNCH and his *Wife* JOAN," which "hath been of late Years, for I know not what Reason laid aside."[96] Although only descriptions have survived, it appears that these were satiric reviews along the line of his *Pasquin* and *The Historical Register*. The sort of show can be inferred from the advertisement of April 14 (for the 18th): "a Comical Puppet-Show Tragedy, call'd FAIR ROSAMOND. With the Comical Humours of King *Henry II.* and his Queen. And likewise the Comical Humours of the Town, as Drums, Routs, Riots, Hurricanes, Hoops, Plaid Wastecoats [i.e., Jacobites], Criticizing, Whisk [whist]-Learning, Muffle-Boxing, Mimicking, &c."[97] This exactly echoes the old announcements for shows at Bartholomew Fair, but it also illustrates what Tom means: with Punch comes the burlesque of a love story burlesqued, farce intermingling with tragedy, and the therapeutic release of laughter, which prevents worse evacuations.

The "great, useful, and uncommon Doctrine"

Chapter 8 of book 12, the chapter in which Fielding uses the term "great Doctrine," begins with Tom stopping the puppet master's beating of the Merry Andrew: an act of spontaneous good nature, based on sympathy for

the Merry Andrew, associated as he is with sexual transgression by his exposure in coitus with the maid, indeed on the puppet master's stage.

   This particular act is rewarded with welcome news of Sophia, elicited
from the Merry Andrew's angry response to the brutal puppet master.[98]
From Partridge's point of view, the Merry Andrew's news of Sophia is an
act of Providence, significantly a word in the mouth of a superstitious
papist: "'two such Accidents could never have happened to direct him after
his Mistress,' Partridge says, 'if Providence had not designed to bring them
together at last.' And this was the first Time," the author adds, "that Jones
lent any Attention to the superstitious Doctrines of his Companion." It is
also the first of the two references to "Doctrine" in this chapter: one "superstitious," the other "great, useful, and uncommon."

   Partridge's charitable act leads to a boy's reminding Tom of the one time
he took Sophia's name in public "from the Overflowing of his Heart" in
the presence of the officers, "where he thought it was impossible she should
be known," and therefore to the transgression of naming Sophia as
opposed to the sexual betrayal of her. We had first heard that it was the
bantering of her name which caused Sophia to leave her muff on Tom's
bed in book 9 (5.545). The author now states as a fact that Sophia was
"much more offended at the Freedoms [with her name]" than "with the
Person of another Woman," "and not without good Reason (i.e., while Tom
was not guilty, Partridge's indiscretion had made it seem that he was)." At
this point it appears that Sophia represents an anti-Puritan point of view
(Punch's), which, however, subordinates the sexual peccadillo to good
breeding or the public appearance of things (supported later by the ease
with which she accepts Tom's repentance and Tom himself).

   Returning to his theater-courtroom metaphor, the author notes that
some ("wise and good") will regard Sophia's abandonment of Tom as "just
Punishment for his Wickedness, with Regard to Women, of which it *was
indeed* the *immediate* Consequence"; while others ("silly and bad") will
attribute his abandonment to sheer accident. The first can only be taken
as the orthodox position – by which here he must mean Puritan,
Richardsonian; the second applies to freethinkers and deists. But he con-
tradicts both of these responses and argues that

> these Incidents contribute only to confirm the great, useful and uncommon
> Doctrine, which it is the Purpose of this whole Work to inculcate, and which
> we must not fill up our Pages by frequently repeating, as *an ordinary Parson*
> fills his *Sermon* by repeating his Text at the End of every Paragraph.

In this one instance Fielding does not give us an introductory essay or any
essay at all. The "great Doctrine" (versus Partridge's "superstitious
Doctrines") is presumably to be found demonstrated, or illustrated, rather
than stated, in the foregoing chapter; in which case it must be summed up

in the episode of the Merry Andrew. It would seem to suggest that Tom's natural overflow of feeling is related to, or follows from, the love for Sophia illustrated back in book 6 (12.312), when Tom, having left Paradise Hall, debated with himself (parallel to similar debates by Black George and Honour) as to whether he should follow his immediate inclination and pursue Sophia and elope. But "Honour at last, backed with Despair, with gratitude to his Benefactor, and with real Love to his Mistress, got the better of burning Desire, and he resolved rather to quit *Sophia*, than to pursue her to her Ruin."[99]

It is the "chance" of Sophia's accidentally hearing Partridge's story of Tom's bandying about her name which makes "providential" acts necessary. *Providence, Sophia*, and such *Names*, including *prudence* and *discretion*, are simply the way people – whether Sophia herself, or Partridge – control transient gusts of hunger or sexuality. *Providence* equals, on the one hand, the word in Partridge's mouth, and on the other, the result of Tom's generous act. With Sophia, we have, in effect, the muff itself (Tom's fetish of her, a clearly sexual object, which says that the sexual act caused her to leave it in his bed) and her words which substitute, purify, and elevate what it represents. It also says, Don't lose hope.

We can now see that Tom's sense of "love" – his decision "rather to quit *Sophia*, than to pursue her to her Ruin" – proves in retrospect to have been an aspect of good breeding, based on prudence and discretion *for the other*.

Gout

In the contemporary medical controversy over fluid mechanics, the "iatro-hydro-dynamicists" saw the body as a complex of canals through which fluids pass; the ease or difficulty with which the fluids moved caused the various symptoms associated with diseases. Thomas Sydenham, the seventeenth-century physician who (like so many others) specialized in gout, explained that gout was a disease in which fluids are trying to find an outlet and descend into the great toe; and, he noted that "the natural outlet for the disorder became obstructed, and it would migrate to other regions, turning into 'irregular gout.' " George Cheyne, the prominent gout expert of the eighteenth century, pursued the same mechanistic theory focused on the vascular system. Indeed, as Roy Porter and G. S Rousseau point out in their *Gout: The Patrician Malady*, "it was believed that gout was not a destructive invasion or a mere breakdown but an integral, protective systematic response: a kind of overflow pipe, Nature's means of evacuating poisons."[100] Ancient wisdom was that gout is good for you – "that a fit of gout clears the system," and that to attempt to cure it is "to 'bottle up' the gout in the system."[101] One wonders if this explains the increasing emphasis Fielding gives the iatrohydraulic metaphor, as his gout becomes disabling. He suffered from gout which culminated in dropsy, both thought of as diseases in which body fluid accumulates, is congested, and its outflow obstructed.

This model also explains one common element noted in attacks of gout – stress, attached (in more recent times) to elevated blood pressure.[102] The onslaught of Fielding's gout followed the close of the theaters and the onset of his financial troubles; his most serious and debilitating attacks followed the encroachment of poverty and debtors and the illness of Charlotte (and her and young Charlotte's deaths). Gout, thought to be the result of excesses of eating and drinking (though perhaps hereditary), involved long stretches of exquisite agony – gout and kidney stones were considered the most painful of diseases. The pain in Fielding's case centered on the big toe but moved to the heel, ankle, and up the leg, incapacitating the sufferer and causing extreme (often, to judge by the literary references, comic) irritability: the least movement or touch was agony. The only treatment during an attack was some form of opium, Dr. Sydenham's being laudanum. The irony for someone like Fielding was the common assumption that it was a disease of the aristocracy and the rich. It was only the elite, Cheyne explained, "whose nervous systems were sufficiently refined to be susceptible to nervous complaints [like the gout]; those in whom surfeit assumed a gouty form were hale and hearty sorts."[103]

PATRIOT AND HISTORIAN

The Forty-Five: love and war

If *Tom Jones* began as another response to *Pamela* and to the plot and perhaps the epistolary form of *Clarissa*, it took a second impulse from the events of June 1745. Battestin believes that Fielding had taken Tom to the brink of his travels, was interrupted by the responsibilities put upon him in 1745, and returned to the novel in book 7 by having Tom join a company of soldiers marching against the rebels, and by utilizing, in the following books, the events of the Forty-Five.[104] It would be nice to think that Fielding had begun *Tom Jones* before the Forty-Five, but if he did so it was between bouts with his "Institute of the Pleas of the Crown," which occupied him into 1745.

In any case, the central paradigm of *Tom Jones* is the historical event of the Forty-Five. What *Pamela*, the parable of the Good Samaritan, and Fénelon's *Télémaque* meant to *Joseph Andrews* the historical Rebellion of 1745 meant to *Tom Jones*. And this fact indicates a fundamental difference between the narrative modes of the two novels, the one with a literary and the other a historical nexus. A major difference between the Fielding and the Richardson novel is that Fielding introduces the public sphere, on both a national and international scale.

In the contrast between the Jacobite's absolute monarchy and the disorderly but very English parliamentary system of government that was staggering along under the Hanoverians the Forty-Five offered (or supported Fielding's existing plan for *Tom Jones* with) a metaphor for a clash between ideals of order and stability. Absolute and limited (constitutional) monarchies represent the same oppositions that appear in the contrasts between a theoretical paragon (Blifil, Pamela, Clarissa) and the "mixed" Tom Jones, between rigorous judgment and mercy, between Roman canon law and the principles of the English Common Law – the same principles on which Fielding constructs the new species of writing called *Tom Jones*.[105]

The moral of both macrocosm and microcosm (the stories of the Forty-Five and of Tom–Sophia) is summed up in the simile: "As a conquered Rebellion strengthens a Government, or as Health is more perfectly established by Recovery from some Diseases; so Anger, when removed, often gives new Life to Affection" (18.5.933). Fielding applies this simile to Allworthy's regard for Blifil after his first suspicions, and it represents the false calm before the storm: the rebellion is going to destroy, not strengthen, Blifil's government. But the simile is a peripheral sign which describes the central, unrepressed characters for whom rebellion conquered may indeed strengthen the government; a disease cured may strenghten health; and anger vented may strengthen affection.

In *The Opposition: A Vision* of 1741, as Fielding had shown, the crucial discovery of the 1740s was that the system of political patronage and electoral corruption developed by Walpole was not simply a case of his personal regime but a public and ongoing system, one that (in the pamphlets of 1747) he could argue was a reasonable *modus vivendi* for England. This insight is reflected in *Tom Jones* in the contrast between the univocal Jacobite government and the confused system of corruption in which Tom has to operate, foregrounded by the Forty-Five, but which Fielding, speaking for the Pelham ministry, now supports.

In a sequence of public events, Walpole died in May 1745, and Fielding joined the controversy over diagnosis and cure with his *Charge to the Jury: or, The Sum of the Evidence, on the Trial of A.B.C.D. and E.F. All M.D. For the death of one Robert at Orfud*, published in July, satirizing the confusion of cures that probably helped to kill Walpole; and this sequence of events ends in the scene early in *Tom Jones* (2.9) in which the doctors Y and Z conduct "a learned Argument, each in Favour of his own Cause of Death" of the defunct Capt. Blifil. The scene reflects the doctors in Hogarth's *Harlot* 5 who argue over their respective cures while the Harlot dies, but it also follows from the more powerful personal sequence of events involving the death of Fielding's daughter Charlotte and his wife Charlotte in 1742 and 1744 respectively.

The intersection of the personal and the public appears in an early essay in *The True Patriot* (no. 3, Nov. 19, 1745), Fielding's journal supporting the government against the Jacobite threat. He was living at the time in Boswell Court, an elegant quarter largely occupied by lawyers, and he describes himself "sitting in my Study, meditating for the Good and Entertainment of the Public, with my two little Children (as is my usual Course to suffer them) playing near me." He mentions "my little Boy," apparently his namesake (then aged three).

The fantasy sequence that follows is of Jacobite victory, repression, and terror. (It should be contrasted with the dream in *The Opposition: A Vision.*) While the terror is centered around these two children, the other image he introduces is of "a young Lady of Quality, and the greatest Beauty of this Age, in the Hands of two *Highlanders*, who are struggling with each other for their Booty." This "lovely Prize" is characterized by her "dishevelled and torn" hair and marks of blood on her face "and her breast, which was all naked and exposed." He adds the question "whether perfect Beauty loses or acquires Charms by Distress" (it is only "matter of Entertainment" to the Jacobites).

She is, publicly, the familiar figure of Britannia, often represented in distress during the Walpole years. In the second, revised edition of *Joseph Andrews* (June 10, 1742), Fielding had added to book 2, chapter 10, Fanny's "dreadful Apprehensions," in the dark and silence of the night, that Adams, having rescued her from the arms of a rapist, "had rescued her out of the hands of one Rifler, in order to rifle her himself." This is Fielding's allegory of the change of government after the fall of Walpole in February of that year. But it also places the first stone in the bridge from *Joseph Andrews* to the writings that led up to *Tom Jones*, and the merger of political and sexual rape.

On the association of patriotism and love, Fielding writes in *The True Patriot*: "It is certain that no Man can love his Country, who doth not love a single Person in it" – who does not love "in private as in public Life" – by which he means that he excludes both Hobbesian misanthropes *and* those who love mankind only on principle (no. 2, 117). The Forty-Five, however, gives a bizarre twist to the subject of love.

Fielding's reputation for lewdness was said to be the reason for the failure of his play, *The Wedding-Day*, in February 1742/3, which he attributed to the malicious reports by his "Enemies" of its "Indecency."[106] In December 1742 the production of his *Miss Lucy in Town* was said by the anonymous author of *A Letter to a Noble Lord* to have made "a *Play-house* and a *Bawdy-house* . . . synonimous Words." Reporting the obscene responses of the audience, the author claims to have overheard one "sober Person" say, "Faith *Fleetwood* [the manager of Drury Lane] had better have hired *Mother Heywood*, and her Company, personally to have appeared."[107]

All this (as Fielding thought) malicious misrepresentation contributed to the thematics of *Tom Jones*. The fact is that he followed the Forty-Five with a sequence of works on sexual passion – *The Female Husband* in the autumn of 1746, his translation *Ovid's Art of Love* in February 1747 (and his marriage to Mary Daniel in November) – while he was writing *Tom Jones*, his major work on the subject of *amor*. The most vivid image in *The Female Husband* is the whipping of the naked female body of the transvestite Mary Hamilton.

The Female Husband, an account of a notorious case of lesbian cross-dressing, may be, as Battestin believes, "the shoddiest work of fiction he ever wrote," but it is not "almost wholly the product of the darker fancies of his imagination." Terry Castle calls it a "piece of antifeminist propaganda" concerning the subversion of "gender, the most basic 'essential' human qualities."[108] One could argue that political issues are coded as gender issues; Jill Campbell has drawn attention to the caricature of Jacobite women as Amazons, and this would apply to Mary Hamilton with her male disguise and her dildo.[109]

Surely significant to a contemporary was the fact that Mary "alias Mr. Charles Hamilton" was arrested September 13 and sentenced October 7, 1746, and on October 6 in York George Hamilton, a captain of Hussars accused of participating in the Forty-Five, was tried. Fielding calls Mary Mr. *George* Hamilton, either intentionally or because one source conflated the names of the Jacobite and the woman.[110] The wording of the verdict passed on Mary, quoted by Fielding, based on the new Vagrancy Act, is that she is condemned "for having by false and deceitful practices endeavoured to impose on some of his Majesty's subjects"; which further supports an analogy with the treason of the Jacobite Hamilton (49).

Mary also makes an appearance in *Ovid's Art of Love* in the story of Pasiphae: "a Passion worse, if possible, than that of Mrs. *Mary Hamilton*." This "Paraphrase, . . . adapted to the present Time" is not the disreputable hack work described by Battestin; not something Fielding "took time off from *Tom Jones*" to do.[111] Fielding puffed it in his *Jacobite's Journal*, no. 15 (March 23, 1748), as an extended analogy between the "art of love" and Jacobitism.[112] It is essentially a political erotics, which changes Rome to London and Caesar to the duke of Cumberland, and introduces the context of the Forty-Five and its suppression. At the appropriate point, in his invocation, Fielding adapts Ovid's contrast of war and love by changing the cast: the schoolmaster Chiron was to Achilles as Ovid is to Cupid; now the tutor Pointz is to the young duke of Cumberland as Fielding is to Cupid, and the Trojan War is replaced by the war with France and the Forty-Five.

The places where women are to be found, according to Ovid, are the law courts, the theater, the race track, and the state triumphs.[113] In these settings Ovid makes his most explicit statement of the connection between love and politics (implicit throughout the *Metamorphoses*). In his account of the theater he places the origins of Rome not in duty and *pietas* (the *Aeneid*'s Aeneas vs. Dido, Octavius vs. Cleopatra, the wench who succeeded in seducing Antony), but rather in *amor*, in Romulus' seizure of the Sabine women and his men's rape of them. Virgil showed the fulfillment of Rome, begun by Aeneas with the lares and penates of Troy, in the order established by the Emperor Augustus, but for Ovid the "Triumphs" of the Caesars turn out to be no more than occasions for assignations, as the origin of Rome was in love and sexual play. Fielding replaces Ovid's race track with the London masquerades and pleasure gardens (Vauxhall, Ranelagh, and the Mall) and, under state triumphs, he focuses on that of the duke of Cumberland and concludes with his victory at Culloden (10).

The *Art of Love*, though it is a manual of seduction, is about Fielding's subject in *Tom Jones*, love, and it is based on the premise that "Art [is] required to drive the Chariot of Love well" (5), arguably a comic equivalent of the prudence required of Tom. Ovid's intention, at the outset, is to instruct the "raw recruit, [his] inexperienced soldier" in how "to find the girl whom you really can love," "how to win her," and how "to make sure mutual love will endure."[114] This is not exactly fulfilled in the sequel, which merely tells where to find women (in the plural) and how to seduce them. But it *is* the poem's statement of purpose.

Following Ovid's disavowal of "stern looks" and modesty, Fielding adds: "Good natured Girls are all I write to, and such I promise them may read my Works without a Blush" (6); which echoes the apology of *The Female Husband* that "not a single word occurs through the whole, which might shock the most delicate ear, or give offense to the purest chastity" (51). The sentence also adds girls to the seducing men as his addressees, which is certainly the effect of joining Sophia's to Tom's subjectivity as necessary for the latter's sense of "love."

The Female Husband shows Fielding's interest (going back to the casting of his plays) with cross-dressing,[115] but it also anticipates the mixture of the Ovidian focus on the details of sexual activity (in this case of a lesbian who to satisfy her desires must pass as a woman and marry another woman) and the proper moral outrage called for by the transgressions that we find in Fielding's ambivalence toward Tom's sexual transgressions. In *The Female Husband* Fielding, in his morality and his prurience, is both Allworthy and Tom.

Fielding, or one aspect of him, may have seen Ovid and his *Art of Love* as in some way the equivalent of his own enterprise in *Tom Jones* vis-à-vis Richardson's great rival work. Recall Parson Tickletext's introductory letter in *Shamela*: "The Comprehensiveness of his [Richardson's] Imagination must be truly prodigious! It has stretched out this diminutive mere Grain of Mustard-seed (a poor Girl's little *&c.*) into a Resemblance of that Heaven, which the best of good Books has compared it to."[116] In plain

English (as Fielding would say), Fielding sees Shamela's "etcetera" (or Keyber's Conny) as only one among other subjects, related to true *love* for example; and in the same way Tom's sexual transgressions are, among other things, placed, explained, and subordinated in *Tom Jones*. Subordinated but always cropping up again like Master Punch in the puppet show. Against the principles of Virtue, Chastity, Piety, and the rest of the Virgilian canon, Fielding places *amor, eros,* and (Christian) *agape* – and, waving it like a red flag, the name of Ovid, a name in fact invoked by the novels of amorous intrigue to which Fielding was responding in *Tom Jones*.

At the outset of his dedication of *Tom Jones* to Lyttelton Fielding informs his reader that there will be "nothing prejudicial to the Cause of Religion and Virtue; nothing inconsistent with the strictest Rules of Decency, or which can offend even the *chastest Eye in the Perusal*" (7). Perhaps this is to ward off the reputation of having recently published *Ovid's Art of Love* and *The Female Husband*; but the "Example" he gives connects with a strand in his work that goes back at least to *The Champion*: "a Kind of *Picture*, in which Virtue becomes as it were an Object of Sight, and *strikes us* with an Idea of that *Loveliness*, which Plato asserts there is *in her naked Charms*." The allusion is to the *Phaedrus*, but as "Orbilius," in his tediously circumstantial attack on *Tom Jones*, noted: "Could one imagine, that after this solemn Declaration, the Author cannot, in the same Paragraph, forbear giving a loose Picture of VIRTUE itself, by *his Idea of that Loveliness which* Plato *asserts there is in her naked Charms?* . . . I have put on my Spectacles; but cannot see here any Word answering the adjective NAKED." True, in the *Phaedrus* (250d) we find the idea of a clear image through sight but no "naked Charms" – a mistake Fielding makes every time he cites the Platonic source.[117]

The notion, which begins with his discussion in the *Champion* of Virtue (religious versus deist),[118] crops up again in *Tom Jones* book 8, chapter 8, when the Merry Andrew reveals that his master had "wished to have [Sophia] alone in a Wood to strip her, to strip one of the prettiest Ladies that ever was seen in the World" (649).[119] When we read of Virtue "in her naked Charms" we therefore envisage Sophia stripped, as well as a great deal of Molly and Jenny revealed to the eye of Tom and others.[120]

Foundlings and the family

Tom Jones was advertised up to publication as *The History of the Foundling*, which at the time would have registered primarily as a reference to the Foundling Hospital, its ideal of charity, and a certain kind of outcast figure – someone like the poor postillion in *Joseph Andrews*. From the novel itself it is clear that Fielding meant the title to start the analogy which runs throughout *Tom Jones* between the eponymous hero and the book itself. The title – eventually the subtitle – draws attention to the equivocal status of this "new Province of Writing," a bastard of epic, romance, and satire.[121]

But "Foundling" also marks the connection with "my friend Hogarth" (as he calls him in one of his many references in *Tom Jones*). A year after the publication of *Tom Jones* the Reverend James Townley, another friend of Hogarth's, wrote the artist: "I wish I were as intimate with you . . . as your friend Fielding."[122] By the autumn of 1746 Hogarth's *Moses brought to Pharaoh's Daughter* was hanging in the board room of the Foundling Hospital, along with paintings by Joseph Highmore, Francis Hayman, and James Wills. Like the *Pool of Bethesda* and *Good Samaritan* of St. Bartholomew's Hospital, these were paintings in a public building seen by crowds of people on their Sunday walks. By 1746 Fielding may have been far enough along in his novel that he inspired Hogarth; or Hogarth's work in progress may have inspired Fielding. But the fact remains that Hogarth's painting was as much a departure as Fielding's novel: he had chosen for his painting (quite unlike the pious, straightforward works of his fellow-artists) the moment in which the puzzled-looking boy Moses confuses his mother with his nurse and his adoptive mother with his real mother. Fielding opens *Tom Jones* with an equivalent of the bulrushes scene (the one painted by Hayman) but focuses on the confusion over whether this foundling's mother is Jenny Jones or Bridget Allworthy, a situation in which Tom, as he grows up, is as helpless and divided as Hogarth's young Moses.

But while Fielding may have started with a foundling and the context of Coram's charitable hospital, the subject of questionable parentage arose in its acutest form and at the highest level with the invasion of the Young Pretender. While in the Restoration the subject of plays and poems had been the succession, the question of patrimony, and royal potency, in the 1740s, we have seen, the literary imagination had been turned (by Jacobite-inclined, or rather antiministerial artists) away from the monarch to his upstart prime minister, and so to upwardly mobile characters such as the Harlot and Rake, Pamela and the anti-Pamelas. In 1745 the invasion of the young prince Charles Edward highlighted the absence of a clearly legitimate, traditionally accepted monarch and the legitimacy of the royal line. In the historical context of the Forty-Five in Fielding's genuinely "historical" work, England has to decide between an unkingly Blifil with apparent legitimacy and an admirable Tom Jones with a bend sinister. In 1748 "Foundling" would have carried a resonance of the dynastic struggle, from the title page onward, but the Forty-Five itself is not mentioned until book 7, at which point it becomes a central governing paradigm of the novelistic action.

Courts in the first half of the century were concerned primarily with matters of private rather than public issues, and in particular criminal offenses and matters involving property law; which fact draws attention to the sense in which *Tom Jones* is about the ownership and inheritance of the Allworthy estate (that is, England in the Forty-Five). This property is a significant part of the definition of Tom and, morever, of the national myth (state and church, state and law) that Fielding is creating in terms of the Protestant Succession and the conflicting families of Hanover and Stuart.[123]

Fielding sets up a bewildering variety of families and heritages for the supposed bastard Tom, and to do so he begins the novel with the period before the hero actually makes his appearance and presents at great length the relatives and neighbors who are influences on his character.[124] It takes two books (or 23 chapters) for Tom to make his appearance, during which time we get to know the Allworthys, the Blifils, the Partridges, and the scandalmongering Somersetshire community in general. Allworthy, despite a few half-hearted rumors as to Tom's paternity, is, in fact as well as practice, his uncle. Under his benevolent gaze move Tom's real mother, Bridget (his real father, the scholar Summer, is dead), and his stepfather Captain Blifil, who also soon dies; Benjamin Partridge, his putative father, and Mrs. Partridge, who suspects Partridge of the paternity, causes him to be expelled from the region, and herself dies; Jenny Jones, his putative mother, who is also expelled as a result of Mrs. Partridge's jealous accusations; and Tom's half-brother Blifil. So we have a real mother but only a very shadowy father, and a putative mother and father with whom Tom will have complex relations later in his history. In fact, Tom's history consists largely of his discovery of his true relationship to his mother, father, uncle, step-brother, and, not least, his beloved Sophia.

There is an interesting bifocality to these early books. This is partly the result of all those constructions that imply uncertainty and complexity. At first Tom the "natural" child is a blank among these hypothetical genealogies, the point being that he is *without* the name, relatives, and fortune that would place him socially. One of the remarkable features of *Tom Jones*, however, is that Fielding deposits ambiguities along the way which have to be reconsidered by the reader when he finally sees the whole narrative in a true light. Scene after scene means one thing on first reading, and something different on second reading; the "sagacious reader" knows and does not know that Bridget is Tom's real mother and that Mrs. Waters is Jenny Jones, who is supposed to be Tom's mother but in fact is not. Knowing and not knowing, the reader experiences some very curious ironic effects in the scenes between Tom and his "mothers."[125] In book 3, chapter 6, the narrator tells us of the stories being circulated about Bridget's "degree of intimacy" with Square, to which "we will give no credit, and therefore shall not blot our Paper with them," which is usually Fielding's signal that where there is smoke we may expect fire. When the narrator then explains that upon Tom's growing up to be a handsome and gallant youth,

> at last she so evidently demonstrated her Affection to him to be much stronger than what she bore her own Son, that it was impossible to mistake her any longer. She was so desirous of often seeing him, and discovered such satisfaction and delight in his company, that before he was eighteen years old he was become a Rival to both *Square* and *Thwackum*; and what is worse, the whole Country began to talk as loudly of her Inclination to *Tom* as they had before done of that which she had shown to *Square*. (3.6.139–40)

Fielding gives this inclination as another motive for Square's dislike of Tom (as later in the parallel case of Square's and Tom's rivalry for Molly Seagrim). Yet it is hard to imagine why Fielding lumps together in just this conjunction what we suspect of Bridget's inclinations (and of Square's) with her affection for Tom. At the moment, we read this as sexual attraction; in retrospect, it refers to Bridget's motherly love; but the former to some extent remains in the retrospect.

One explanation can be inferred from another irony, implicit in Mrs. Wilkins' remark that it would be better for such creatures as Tom "to die in a state of Innocence, than to grow up and imitate their Mothers; for nothing better can be expected of them" (1.3.41). Tom may be thought to have inherited his propensity for the other sex, or at least his acquiescence, from his mother, as Blifil presumably inherited his mother's *and* father's worst qualities of hypocrisy and gloomy ill nature. The mother–son relationship haunts Tom through the climactic books of the novel, in the figures of both true and false mothers, until the final revelation that his real mother had in fact acknowledged him on her deathbed. Clamoring against the disasters at Upton and London is the less directly inherited blood of Squire Allworthy. The family becomes another significant context which helps to explain Tom's character and conduct.

Another explanation is that the constructions of uncertainty ("whether . . . or") project a shadow narrative and shadow relationships. This returns us to the notorious issue of incest in *Tom Jones*, which Battestin has attached to a supposed liaison between Fielding and his sister Sarah. There is certainly a shadowy relationship that is incestuous in the innuendos about Tom and Bridget in the early books; and the same is true of Tom and Jenny Waters in the later. For Fielding the idea of incest would have had far more resonance associated with his mother than with his sister. It was his mother he lost before he was 11. We have noticed from his earliest plays how he presents as rivals for his hero's affection a younger and an older woman (in one instance the younger woman's mother). Bridget and Jenny – but also Lady Bellaston – are older women. When Fielding actually shows the reader a woman's "naked Charms" he focuses on her breasts. Tom's erotic obsession with full-breasted women – Molly, Jenny, and Sophia herself – has an obviously maternal dimension. Nor is the obsession limited to Tom; Fielding gave to Joseph Andrews, and before him the rake Ramble in *Rape upon Rape*, the same focus of attention (Ramble: "Oh! Sotmore, I could die ten thousand millions of times upon them——").[126] We recall how Sophia's little bird Tommy, a surrogate for Tom, used to "lie contented in her Bosom, where it seemed almost sensible of its own Happiness" (4.3.159).[127]

The staunch Richardsonian reading of *Tom Jones* by Frank Kermode focuses on the incest chapter (18.2) and sees Fielding fudging the one real test of Tom's sexual license – the ultimate taboo of incest. But for Fielding incest offered the ultimate in mock tragedy, accompanied by a momentary return to the diction of *Tom Thumb*. Incest caps the theatrical sequence of events set in motion by Tom's response to the tragedy of *Hamlet*, a play interpreted in Fielding's time as about the duty of sons to fathers.[128] If the fiction of the Fall is one in which Fielding sees Tom's (and obviously his own) experience, another – which he had glancingly broached in *Joseph Andrews* – is the fiction of Oedipus, which carries with it the most blatant form of the theater metaphor (with Aristotle's blessing) that Fielding has used since his earliest writings. Its most striking feature is its theatricality. Partridge's reaction ("his face paler than Ashes, his Eyes fixed in his Head, his Hair standing on End, and every Limb trembling") recapitulates his reaction at the performance of *Hamlet* (which in those days was read as Oedipal) when he "fell into so violent a Trembling, that his Knees knocked against each other" (18.2.915; 16.5.853).[129] The most Oedipal moment comes when, contemplating Sophia, Tom repudiates *any* other woman: "'But why do I mention another Woman? could I think my Eyes capable of looking at any other with Tenderness, these Hands should tear them from my Head" (5.10.256). Which is not to settle the deeper question of Fielding's surrounding Tom's relationship to Jenny Jones with his other shadows of incest – the reputation for a similar intimacy with his aunt Bridget and his involvement with older women (an attraction mostly from *their* direction, as we noted in *The Author's Farce* and other earlier works). As one scholar has put it, Fielding introduces incest "to mock it – as if, perhaps, by flaunting the comic artist's mastery even of life's tragic possibilities, he could in this way exorcise whatever demons the theme may have had for him."[130]

As we have seen, Fielding persistently stocks his plots with father as well as mother figures. And if the mothers tend to double as prospective lovers, the fathers double as the protagonist, whether Joseph or Tom. In *Tom Jones* the Old Man of the Hill is another double. In Wilbur Cross's words, the Old Man of the Hill "is a Mr. Wilson of darker fibre; each has had his experience of the world; and each, becoming disenchanted, has retired from it into seclusion."[131] He tells Tom his story, as Wilson did his: "I was high-mettled, had a violent Flow of animal spirits, was a little ambitious, and extremely Amorous" (8.11.453). Like David Simple's brother Daniel, he is dissipated and falls into debt, gambles and drinks, and takes up with a loose woman. His European travels may even recall Fielding's while at Leiden.[132] He saves the life of his father, suffers, and goes to prison, where repentance sets in, with words that are repeated when Tom is in prison and realizes that "I am myself the Cause of all my Misery" (18.2.916): words that echo Aristotle on Oedipus' *anagnorisis*.

In book 8 the Old Man of the Hill recalls how as a youth he chose the path of Pleasure, which he thoroughly exhausted before turning to the path of Virtue – which however led him to the sort of pleasureful virtue that leads to the same end, a disinterestedness that permits him to stand by, though holding a firearm, while Jenny Waters is being strangled by Ensign Northerton.[133] In book 9 Tom, who rescues Jenny, is attracted by her bare breasts and eventually succumbs (after a hearty meal) to her blandishments. Here is Tom's Herculean choice, at the centerpoint of the novel, between Sophia and Jenny (the usually languid, underdressed, gourmandizing Pleasure figure).

The sequence of events leading to Upton seems to be, among other things, Fielding's attempt to place his novel within the history-painting tradition of the Shaftesbury–Hogarth narrative of choice: Certainly Fielding places at the center of *Tom Jones* a Choice of Hercules. This is a public "choice" between Stuart and Hanover, between Roman Catholicism and Protestantism, and between absolute monarchy and parliamentary government.

The Forty-Eight and euhemerist history

There was, of course, no "Forty-Eight" but there was the fictionalizing of another Jacobite-threatened uprising by Fielding and his patrons in the Pelham Ministry. Three years after, with the Forty-Five quite dead but the unpopularity of the Hanoverians growing and with the need to defend the ministry's policies at home and abroad, Fielding spent the year 1748 issuing weekly attacks on opponents from the right and left who, he claimed, sought a change in the sovereign and the form of government. The journal he published for this purpose was called *The Jacobite's Journal* (December 1747–November 1748), in which he adopted the ironic persona of a Jacobite sympathizer.[134]

The satiric designation "Jacobite" was perhaps not so purely propagandistic as has sometimes been thought; for every five portrait prints of Charles I advertised in 1747 there was one of William III and none of George II. *The Jacobite's Journal* (for which Hogarth contributed the design for the headpiece; see plate 16) spends much of its time contrasting the

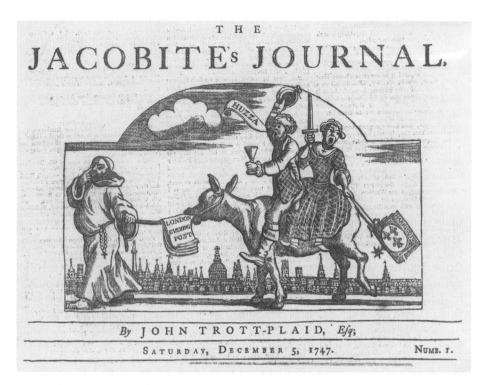

Plate 16 After Hogarth, Headpiece for *The Jacobite's Journal*, 1747, woodcut, courtesy of the Trustees of the British Museum.

Jacobite mythology with the plain historical facts of 1688, 1715, and 1745.[135] For Fielding this myth becomes the embodiment of the larger controversy, in which his work (and his friend Hogarth's) was embroiled, of the foreign, Roman Catholic, hieroglyphic iconography that had replaced the original object or sign with a second system of signs, and perhaps a third, which totally obscured (in terms of his Dedication, "veiled") the original truth.

He begins with the mythology of the Stuart family as a type of mythic falsification but goes on to all sorts of verbal misunderstandings. Some readers, he notes, take his ironic mask literally; the Opposition press casts lies and slanders at him and his ministerial friends, analogous to the Jacobite lies about Stuart genealogy and the succession. Fielding's essays in the *Journal* once again treat such subjects as slander (nos. 8, 26, 28) and personal attacks on himself (from serious slanders to the comic mimicry of Samuel Foote [nos. 20, 22]) and on his friends (e.g., no. 18 on

Lyttelton, the dedicatee of *Tom Jones*). The equation between the slandering of the man and his writing, which Fielding develops so strikingly in *Tom Jones*, is laid out in the pages of *The Jacobite's Journal*. The application Fielding makes is equally to a *Paradise Lost* and to a Socrates or Brutus: "to condemn a Work or a Man as vicious, because they are not free from Faults or Imperfections" is contrasted to the alternative, a paragon or "faultless Monster" (no. 8) of the sort treated in the apparent paragon (according to his reputation) of, say, Blifil.

False history is the subject of *The Jacobite's Journal*, and so it is of *Tom Jones*, where Jacobite rumors lead to the identification of Sophia with Jenny Cameron, the Young Pretender's mistress, and the Jacobite rumors act as an acute symptom of the chronic fabrications that surround Allworthy, Partridge, and especially Tom, re-creating "character" in the forms of the personal fantasies of the rumor-mongers. By book 8 (8.432–33) rumor has Tom getting a servant maid with child, breaking Thwackum's arm, snapping a pistol at Blifil, and beating a drum while Squire Allworthy is sick. Book 8 continues with Partridge's story of a man's fight with a ghost (a drunk encountering a whitefaced calf) and ends with the Man of the Hill's conclusion that men must be mad to entertain the possibility of the Stuarts' return. The climax, of course, is Upton, where, we are told, "they talk, to this Day, of the Beauty and lovely Behaviour of the charming *Sophia*, by the Name of the Somersetshire Angel" (10.8.554); and at the Bull's Head at Meriden, the rumor is that 10,000 Frenchmen have landed in Suffolk and that Sophia is Jenny Cameron (11.3). In this atmosphere, Rumor herself appears, and a toast to Sophia becomes a toast to the Pretender (8.9.441). The Liars' Club's lie that Tom has been killed in a duel is only the last and most perfectly unfounded rumor (15.3).

The narrator of *Tom Jones* is himself in the limited, though privileged, position of a historian who is trying to extricate the true from the false. In chapter 1 of book 8, as he nears the center of the narrative, he talks about the historical origins of fictions, telling us that remarkable deeds of humans "gave Birth to many Stories of the Antient Heathen Deities (for most of them are of poetical Original)." It was the poet who carried out this transformation, whereas "the Historian will confine himself to what really happened, and utterly reject any Circumstance, which, tho' never so well attested, he must be well assured is false" (8.1.397, 401).

The source for the historiography employed in *The Jacobite's Journal* is the Abbé Antoine Banier's *Mythology and Fables of the Ancients, Explain'd from History* (translation, 1739–40). Fielding singles out Banier's volumes (republished in 1748) for praise in the "Court of Criticism," and we know that he owned a copy himself.[136] In *Tom Jones* Fielding cites Banier by name only (12.1.619), but, as in the passage I quoted above, Banier's approach is discernible in much of the historical analysis he carries on. Banier's euhemerist analysis of myths is the basic methodology Fielding brings to bear on the Jacobites' constructions in nos. 6 and 12, first as a parallel or comparative mythology linking the story of Bacchus to the Jacobite ethos of hunting, drinking, and dipping into politics, and second as a pursuit of the sources or motivations for such fabulating (vanity, illiteracy, and the lies of travelers).

There is, of course, a close relationship between euhemerism or the reduction of mythology to history, the travesty mode Fielding had practiced in the 1730s, and the demystification of critical deism. Banier's explanation, "that the *Minotaur* with *Pasiphae*, and the rest of that Fable, contain nothing but an Intrigue of the Queen of *Crete* with a Captain named *Taurus*" (1:29), could almost, but not quite, have appeared in *Tumble-Down Dick*.[137] The difference is between finding the source of the god in a great man and in a bumpkin. With Banier Fielding replaces the last traces of deist controversy with a more fashionable and safer demystification applied to classical myths, though (as the French *philosophes* realized) applicable to Christian as well. But besides being safer, Banier carries a more complex and far-reaching sort of analysis than critical deism. Fielding's real subjects in *Tom Jones* are the demonizing and apotheosizing of real human acts, both Tom's and the author's.

The euhemerist Banier, for example, to "fully unravel the History of this God" Mars, relates him to several possible sources: first to the king Belus (the scriptural Nimrod), "to whom *Diodorus* attributes the Invention of Arms, and the Art of marshalling Troops in Battle," or perhaps Ninus or Thutas; second to an ancient king of Egypt; third to a king of Thrace named Odin; fourth to a Greek named Ares; and finally to a Roman named Mars, a brother of Amulius Numitor (2:316). His researches seek a correspondence in dignity to the god, which would explain the magnitude of the fable; no discrepancy is sought, though one of course emerges; and the mode is scholarship of the historian, not travesty of the satirist.[138] Unlike travesty (or its sister, the mock heroic), this mode is concerned with causality and historical relationships, in some sense genealogy and etymology: How *did* the historical ur-Tom become the rake, the Adonis, the "Angel from Heaven," or the "murderer"? And what exactly is the relationship, and does it tell us something about the reality, or is it an element without which the reality itself does not signify?

Let us take two battle scenes, Joseph Andrews and the fox hounds (3.6) and Tom Jones and the attackers of Molly Seagrim in the graveyard (4.8). In the first, Fielding is merely demonstrating the inadequacy of heroic analogues as literary forms to characterize the real heroism of Joseph: he tells us that no simile, no figure from literature, is "adequate to our Purpose," that Joseph is himself a simile for heroism. Tom's battle against Molly's attackers begins as a travesty: Echepolus is in fact a Somersetshire sow gelder and Myrdon is Kate of the Mill; but there is an additional dimension, already established by all the lies and fabrications that from the start have surrounded Tom, Allworthy, and the others. There is no longer the same kind of adverse comment on the heroic level itself. For there to be, Tom and even Molly would have to be acting foolishly to fight, and they are not (except insofar as Tom is deceived about his relations with Molly); only perhaps the villagers, these pious folk who are outraged by the sight of Molly in Sophia's finery and flaunting her pregnancy in church, retain something of the pretensions we associate with the mock heroic. But the villagers are primarily myth makers, and the narrator is showing that this local scuffle in a graveyard is "the real truth" or "what really happened" beneath the stories the villagers will spread, as beneath the Homeric description of the Greeks and Trojans in battle (or, we might add, under the New Testament "Miracles" analyzed by Woolston). Mars is really Alexander the Great, or the bull is really Captain Taurus; Achilles is a mythologized version, fabricated by the villagers to assuage their wounded self-esteem, of Tom Jones in the graveyard fighting off the mob that is after Molly; and the real Tom can only be known through the myths surrounding him. We are seeing history in the making and in the process of being mythologized, as earlier, in the more literal way, when Partridge's battle with Mrs. Partridge was promptly mythologized by their neighbors. What distinguishes such a scene from those in *Joseph Andrews* is the sense of a myth being simultaneously created and analyzed.

The analogy with war engendered by the skirmish in the graveyard leads to the real war with the Pretender's army. On his way with the troops to meet that army, Tom and some soldiers are supping at an inn (7.12.372–6). Tom compares these soldiers to the Greeks on their way to Troy; Ensign Northerton shows his ignorance of the classical allusion; and one of the soldiers identifies the Greeks and Trojans as "dey fight for von Woman." Shortly after, Tom toasts Sophia, Northerton mythologizes her into a notorious whore (the truth about Helen), Tom calls him a rascal, and he knocks Tom senseless with a bottle: "The Conqueror perceiving the Enemy to lie motionless before him, and Blood beginning to flow pretty plentifully from his Wound, began now to think of quitting the Field of Battle, where no more Honour was to be gotten." Sophia has been turned into a kind of Helen and the inn table into a "Field of Battle." The effect is very different from that of Joseph's battle with the hounds, but it is an extension of Tom's with Molly's attackers, and so quite naturally the battle of Upton is based on "no very blameable Degree of Suspicion" among the people at the inn as to Tom's relations with Mrs. Waters, who is a "poor unfortunate Helen, the fatal Cause of all the Bloodshed" (9.3.504).[139]

There is another battle in the inn just prior to the "battle" over dinner; and the "drubbing" Partridge receives is later called a "hearty Meal." Chapter 5 then opens presenting Banier heroes with "more of mortal than divine about them." We can presume that in Banier's terms battle equals meal. The battles progress toward the single combat of Tom and Mrs.

Waters at the dinner table, introduced by an allusion to Pasiphae and the bull (a memory perhaps of Banier's amusing euhemerist account), which is presented as an elemental struggle that will be mythologized as a battle – and is literally mythologized in the conversation of the servants in the kitchen.

The fundamental point Banier makes is that the stories of the gods are not fables, "Tales of mere Invention," but "ancient Facts" (or "Truths of Importance") "embellished" with "numbers of Fables" (1:21, 26). The form he describes is "ancient Histories, mix'd with several Fictions": "those which speak of *Hercules, Jason,* &c. instead of telling us in the simple way, that the latter went to recover the Treasures which *Phrixus* had carried to *Colchis,* they have given us the Fable of the Golden Fleece" (1:30). As Banier describes it, however much "the Truths of ancient History . . . may be disguised by the great number of Ornaments mixed with them, it is *not absolutely impossible* to unfold the historical Facts they contain" (1:20; emphasis added).

"The most perplexing Difficulty in the way of a Mythologist consists in unravelling the Intricacy of different Opinions about one and the same Fable, which is told in so many ways, and so different from one another, that it is impossible to reconcile them all" (1:18). For example, the fable of Tom, Black George, and Molly, as told by Thwackum, Square, Blifil, and Tom, and interpreted by Allworthy, the narrator, and the reader – or by the critical, judicious, or good-natured reader – is a complex knot perhaps never completely capable of being untied. The method "observed by our best Mythologists," says Banier, is never to adopt a fable "without having first enquired what might have given rise to it," and in both *The Jacobite's Journal* (e.g., no. 12) and *Tom Jones* Fielding's emphasis falls upon the searching out of motives.

As opposed to either David Hume, who tries to present demythologized facts for history, or his opposite, the Christian weaver of the providential pattern, the Banier sort of euhemerist requires three roles: poet, historian, and mythologist.[140] It is assumed that the poet mythologizes historical facts, the historian tries to establish what really happened, and the mythologist analyzes the myth in the light of history. The product is a rich complex of the three stages with the emphasis on the process itself. This is a stage well beyond the role of the travesty poet or the critical deist, "to strip it of the Marvellous" (1:17), which in *Tom Jones* is conveyed by repeated phrases like "This was the true Reason why," "To say the Truth," "the real Truth," or "what really happened." But Fielding is showing the simultaneous construction and explanation of myth, showing how it is produced by poets out of historical events.

The historical fact does not exist without its embellishment in fable. Banier asks "What would the *Aeneid, Iliad,* or *Odyssey* be, was it not for the . . . perpetual mixture of Truths of small concern, with the most interesting Fictions" (1:39). The "truth of small concern," that Ulysses and his crew loiter debauching at Circe's court, is augmented by the "interesting fiction" that Circe is a sorceress who transforms men into swine. Thus we may regard such fictions "as so many Metaphors and figurative Ways of speaking," and the distinction applies equally to imaginative leaps like the connecting of Captain Taurus (a name only) with a bull. In general, Banier is describing what Cassirer called the "mythico-religious Urphenomenon" in which the primitive man is confronted by a new and strange thing, and to come to terms with it *names* it, designates it metaphorically, perhaps calling it a god or a spirit. The function of this activity in *Tom Jones* is both instrumental and ontological, partly to express the vanity and other motives of the fabulator and partly to approximate the thing's essential being in the only way possible. There is a sense in which Sophia *is* Jenny Cameron, just as there is one in which Black George *does* love Tom, and Tom *is* both "so terrible a Rake" and "an Angel from Heaven" (as Enderson calls him [13.8.720]) and Bridget is both his mother and lover.

We come to understand Tom Jones or Sophia Western by a number of these "errors,"[141] much as we do a woman having an affair with a Captain Taurus by the mistake of the story of Pasiphae and the bull. Perhaps this is only a more carefully worked out version of the construction of character Fielding undertook in *Joseph Andrews*. What he has in *Tom Jones*, that was only glimpsed in *Joseph Andrews*, is the knowledge that the reality of Tom or of Molly in the graveyard, or of Sophia – called Jenny Cameron – is the historical figure plus the poeticized one plus the mythologist's relation of the two. Any one of these is inadequate without the others.

Roughly speaking, we can say that Fielding presents the following types of mythologizing: (1) The true character of Tom (perhaps ultimately unknowable) is related to the fables of his enemies and others, reaching from the extreme cases of mistakes (Mrs. Fitzpatrick's thinking he is Blifil) to the gradual equation of him with "so terrible a Rake," "so very fine a Figure," or "an Angel from Heaven."

(2) "Fables of the Historical Kind," writes Banier, "are easily distinguished, because mention is made in them of People we know elsewhere" (1:31). One such group would include Lady Ranelagh, painted by Kneller, and the duchess of Mazarin by Lely, who are given to us by Fielding as approximations of what Sophia looked like; Hogarth's Bridewell warder for Thwackum, the old lady in *Morning* for Bridget, and the servant woman in *A Harlot's Progress* plate 3 for Mrs. Partridge. Fielding may have recalled Banier's statement that "the Painters working upon Poetical Fancies, may be reckoned instrumental in propagating some Fables. . . . They have even frequently promoted the Credit of fabulous Stories, by representing them with Art, a thing so true . . . that the Pagans owed the Existence of many of their Gods, to some fine Statues, or Pictures well done" (1:44). Ultimately we come to the scene or character that has no precedent, and he can only

specify: "O, *Shakespear*, had I thy Pen! O, *Hogarth*, had I thy Pencil!" (10.8.555). This is not the exclamation of the author of *Joseph Andrews*, demonstrating the discrepancy between the real and the literary, who at last threw up his hands ("not from the inimitable Pencil of my Friend *Hogarth*"), but an attempt to approximate as best one can the unformulable reality.

(3) On another level are Ralph Allen and Lord Lyttelton, the actual historical figures of whom Allworthy is a poetic version; Charlotte Cradock Fielding for Sophia; and perhaps Fielding himself for Tom. Fielding is creating his own myth as he analyzes those of other mythographers, while at the same time admitting the fabrication.

The public dimension of "historical truth" shades off into the private, and this applies especially to the Forty-Five itself, the ultimate fact in process of being mythologized by the Jacobites. The confusion of Tom and Sophia wandering about searching for each other in the wilderness, of families broken up, lovers separated, and allegiances mixed, is the historical reality of the Forty-Five. *The Jacobite's Journal* and Abbé Banier come together in Partridge, the garrulous, superstitious Catholic-Jacobite, who believes in the Jacobite "Mysteries" (e.g., that a popish king would defend a Protestant church) as he believes in prodigies and old wives' tales; and although he concludes of Tom's own story "that the whole was a Fiction" (8.7.427), he proceeds to construct his own on the basis of his fecund self-interest. As in the *Journal*, the time is one of rumors and lies and myths, the greatest being concerned with the virtues of an absolute monarch (vs. a constitutional or mixed form of government) and an absolute paragon (vs. at best a "mixed character," at worst a scoundrel).

We are reminded of the parallels from the outset with the two heirs to Paradise Hall, both as ambiguous as "the famous [Jacobite] Story of the Warming-Pan" and as "the no more unaccountable Birth of *Bacchus*" Fielding tells in his *Jacobite's Journal* parody of Banier (no. 6, 125). Tom is a bastard, but Blifil is himself conceived out of wedlock, though legally born within. What is clear is that Blifil, despite his technical claim to inheritance, is morally disqualified from his right to carry on the Allworthy-Western line, while Tom demonstrates his right to the title of successor. The parallels extend from the elaborate lies and plots of Blifil to his behavior after his exposure, which recalls that of the Stuart prince reported by unsympathetic observers during the rout of Culloden.[142]

(4) Another kind of myth is also in process of construction by Fielding the narrator. The similes from book 5 onward push unobtrusively toward the materials of country folklore. In the second battle scene, with Tom defending Molly from the interruption of Blifil and company (5.9.259–60), the simile links Tom's response to the ritual mating of a stag in "the Season of Rutting," and Tom becomes the defender of a "frighted Hind": "fierce and tremendous rushes forth the Stag to the Entrance of the Thicket; there

stands the Centinel over his Love, stamps the Ground with his Foot, and with his Horns brandished aloft in Air, proudly provokes the apprehended Foe to Combat." The simile remains implicit in the battle that follows, modifying the stated epic terms, and thereafter extends from Partridge's story of the drunk's encounter with a white-faced calf that grows into a battle with a ghost, to the simile with which book 10, chapter 2, opens, with frolicking hares, hooting owls, a half-drunk clown in terror of hobgoblins and robbers on the prowl while watchmen are asleep: "in plain English it was now Midnight." We have left behind alien classical similes and are in the true world of native English country superstitions and folklore, where the absence of Punch and Joan in the puppet show is noticed and the presence of the gypsies' encampment comes as no surprise. This is the world of jests, practical jokes, and Skimmingtons; of Addison's "Strange" and *faerie* in *The Spectator*; ultimately of Fielding's childhood in Glastonbury and Somersetshire.

It is in this world that the major characters also function most suggestively. As Pasiphae's bull was a captain named Taurus, so God is in fact a benevolent country squire named Allworthy who lives in Paradise Hall. By Allworthy's errors and pomposities, Fielding makes it clear that he is *not* God; but mythologically the relationship is meaningful. We might say that Fielding never loses sight of the historical reality while mythologizing him – just as his neighbors also mythologize him as atheist, old fool, father of Tom, and persecutor of Jenny Jones. Besides Allworthy of whom God is the fable, there is Tom of whom Adam (expelled from Eden and sent out, in Milton's words, into the world) is the fable, and Sophia of whom Wisdom is the fable, and so on to Molly, the latter-day Eve, and Blifil, associated with the Devil.[143]

The question of the "Devil" and his existence is answered in book 9 with a memory of Northerton's "hellish Intention" to murder Mrs. Waters (9.6 and 7.516 and 521). Here, in the book of the Fall, the devil makes his appearance (in his earlier appearance, when Northerton nearly kills Tom, he is distinguished by his wanton lie about Sophia – the devil being the prince of liars). But, as Ensign Northerton, he is a euhemerized devil, and his attempted murder of Mrs. Waters is explained by the fact that he thinks he has already committed one murder.

In the case of Tom, all the contemporary "poetry" to the effect that he is the son of Jenny Jones and Partridge is swept away and we are left with the fact that he is the son of Bridget (Allworthy) Blifil and, as it happens, a man named Summer. Bridget herself, as her alliance with Hogarth's old woman in *Morning* and Fielding's identification as "an Emblem of Winter" suggest, is as real and yet projective of myth as her early lover named Summer, who is remembered by Mrs. Waters (Tom's suppositious mother, whose own married name has the same ambience) as "a finer Man, I must say, the Sun never shone upon" (16.7.940).[144] Blifil, on the other hand, is the son of Winter – and whatever we are to make of the swarthy, rough, calculating, ungrateful, melancholic Captain Blifil. Fielding uses as his example, in the opening chapter on "contrast" (5.1.212): "Thus the Beauty of Day, and that of Summer, is set off by the Horrors of Night and Winter," and this is roughly the scheme of the novel's own myth: the vigor and fertility in the native Englishman of somewhat confused blood lines – his release of erotic energy in a repressed civilization – versus the paragon of melancholy, the saturnine, self-enclosed, and unvented Blifil, as the historical reality of the whole imbroglio of 1745.

The hero as nature deity had been broached more straightforwardly in Joseph Andrews, who was employed to serve as scarecrow to keep off birds, "to perform the Part the Antients assigned to the God *Priapus.*" His cathexis is as ambiguous as Priapus', for his voice "rather allured the Birds than terrified them," as do his protestations of chastity to Lady Booby (1.2.21). Tom at times recalls one of the gods analyzed by Banier. To take, not quite at random, the one Fielding himself analyzes in *Jacobite's Journal* no. 6, we notice that Bacchus too came of an obscure liaison: "the antients had formed a Design to throw a Veil of obscurity over the true History of this Prince's Birth and Education," and what follows (2:437–53) is the analysis of whether he comes of a human or immortal father, and after that of the myths of Bacchic celebration – all those women dancing "to celebrate the Memory of his Conquests" and carrying aloft the phallus. The main point of debate, indeed, is the nature and meaning of the strange ceremonies that accompanied him wherever he traveled, characterized by "Debauchery, Lewdness, and Prostitution being carried to the greatest Extremity." Bacchus was "commonly represented like a young Man, without a beard," rendered enthusiastic by too deep a use of the vine, and known for his generosity – spreading his mysteries to the world, especially to women. He carried about with him "a Kind of ambulatory Seraglio," Banier wrily remarks. Tom, there can be no argument, attracts both men and women of all kinds, and only repulses sterile figures like Blifil.

As a referent Bacchus (whose *Jacobite's Journal* caricature is the Jacobite country squire) draws attention to the possibility that Fielding has reversed the "popular" characteristics of the Jacobite myth, making Tom the life force which Bonnie Prince Charlie was portrayed as being, while Blifil has all the Hanoverian-Whig traits attributed by the Jacobites – as by many objective Englishmen.[145] It is certainly the case that the names with which Jacobite pamphlets commemorated Charles Edward – the Wanderer, the Young Adventurer, the Young Chevalier, and Ascanius (pamphlets with which Fielding was very familiar) – apply to Tom, not to Blifil.[146] The sort of song the loyalists were singing about Prince Charles (parodying a Jacobite song) is a song that Blifil and his friends might have sung about Tom:

Over the water and over the lea,
   And over the water to Charley.
Charley loves good ale and wine,
   And Charley loves good brandy,
And Charley loves a pretty girl
   As sweet as sugar candy.[147]

Fielding himself had had a difficult task demythologizing the prince in 1745, first in *The True Patriot* and then in his *History of the Present Rebellion in Scotland*. In the latter, where we could juxtapose passages from newspapers and contemporary accounts, what Fielding did was to turn the dashing prince into a Blifil, the spontaneity and expansive gestures into calculation, prudence, and vanity.[148] When the real prince leads his soldiers across the Forth, his Rubicon, dashing ahead into the historic waters, Fielding's prince does it to show off:

> Here Charles attempting to give an extraordinary Instance of his Bravery by passing the Water first, and mistaking the Ford, very narrowly escaped drowning, from which he was preserved by Lieutenant *Duncan Madson*, who at the Hazard of his own Life rescued him from the Waves.[149]

Fielding's most egregious fabulating of the Forty-Five, however, had been in the pages of *The True Patriot*, where he exaggerated the dangers of rape, burning, looting, and terror to the civilian population (including in a dream vision, we recall, threats to his own children and a woman who sounds like his late wife – whose situation is duplicated in the dreams of the puppet master's treatment of Sophia). And yet even there, true to his own character and preoccupations, Fielding carefully distinguished by headlines between "The Present History of Great Britain" and an "APOCRYPHA. Being a curious Collection of certain true and important WE HEARS from the News-Papers." And once the rebellion was over, in his final apology for his work on *The True Patriot* (no. 33) he expressed something of a sense of guilt: "for the Paper principally intended to inflame this Nation against the Rebels, was writ whilst they were at *Derby*, and in that Day of Confusion, which God will, I hope, never suffer to have its equal in this Kingdom." His valedictory was to urge not justice but mercy, human understanding, and a spirit of tolerance toward the defeated – sentiments echoed in his attitude toward Tom throughout the narrative and in Tom's toward Blifil at the denouement.[150]

It would be good to know more about Fielding's response to the undeniably romantic boy who landed in a remote corner of the kingdom with only a few men to win back his father's crown. Presumably Fielding had begun *Tom Jones* before the prince's landing.[151] But without Squire Western nearby as the pure Jacobite country squire, Tom might have reminded readers of the prince. Either Fielding turned the myth upside down, or he found that, in an ironic way, the myth of the gallant young prince was closer to the one he had already sketched in *Joseph Andrews*, and for that matter to his own story, or one aspect of it. That is not to suggest that he was in any way more sympathetic with the prince's cause than he was in *The Jacobite's Journal*, but only that a common myth of alienation from one's true home and wandering as exile or fugitive unites these two heroes. Perhaps Tom is the true historical figure beneath the Jacobitish myth, as Sophia is beneath Jenny Cameron.

Jacobite mythology treated with Banier's euhemerism was a safe version of Woolston's critical deism, contributing to a dynamic of delusion, slander, and lies, historically grounded in the Forty-Five. The facts are, however, that the alternatives of Anglicanism and deism of *Joseph Andrews* do reappear in *Tom Jones*, materialized in equally bad opposites, those Allworthy substitutes, Thwackum and Square; but that Roger Square the deist (a lusty man who shares Molly with Tom, who does show other-directed passion) is capable of reformation. He is converted on his deathbed to religion, specifically to belief in an afterlife. Battestin points to the influence on Fielding of Lyttelton's *Observations on St. Paul*, published at about the time he was writing the concluding books of *Tom Jones*. Clearly Square's conversion is an analogue to Tom's success at controlling his potentially anarchic impulses. But, knowing he is dying, Square needs consolation as well as control. It is Square who is converted and condemned to die – which, together, lead him to confess the truth he knows about Tom. Thwackum, the clergyman, remains cold-hearted, self-righteous, self-seeking, and hypocritical to the end. This says, as Fielding has said from the beginning, that deist morality of the Shaftesbury sort can be corrected – as both control and consolation – by a pragmatic belief in Christian examples and eschatology; the Christian clergy, although there is an occasional Parson Adams, is hopeless. Parson Supple, the best the clergy can show in *Tom Jones*, is summed up in his name (he cannot control the violent impulses of Squire Western) and his ultimate marriage to Jenny Waters.

Like St. Paul, Square was a persecutor and is now converted. But he has no Pauline vision, no divine intervention (nor is the receiving of his sight a miracle), only the same pragmatic belief advocated by Fielding at the end of his essay on bereavement. This is a matter of some importance because Lyttelton's aim in his book is no less than to prove, on the strength of this Pauline text, that Paul's conversion and its aftermath "did all really happen, and therefore the Christian religion is a divine revelation."[152] Fielding was not attempting to subvert his friend's pious tract, but *Tom Jones* represents a generic form which, as defined by Fielding, cannot advocate both divine presence *and* belief in the divine: the one is, as the deists taught him, not historical; the other is necessary for human survival.

By book 7, however, with the news of the Pretender's invasion (which coincides with Tom's departure from Paradise Hall, his descent into the fallen world of history), Fielding no longer permits himself to be equivocal in his respect for the clergy and belief in Protestant Christianity. The Anglican cloth and patriotism are at this time and place in history of necessity equated.[153] This event decidedly changes his attitude toward religion, albeit still in a pragmatic way.

Rewards and punishments: Clarissa *and* Tom Jones

Three volumes of *Tom Jones* (Books 1–9) were in print by September 1748; in October five volumes of *Clarissa* were in print, and on 15 October Fielding wrote a letter of praise to Richardson. Richardson (while continuing to denigrate Fielding and his *Tom Jones*) saved the letter, had at least two copies made of it, and sent the first part (the part that praised *Clarissa*) to disciples.

The letter is remarkable for Fielding's enumeration and description of his responses, stage by stage, to the rape of Clarissa – presented in the Aristotelian terms of pity and terror, but so hyperbolic that one at first suspects irony and then, when that explanation is abandoned, a more subtle strategy: that his experience of reading describes an aesthetic, not a moral experience. At the same time, it cannot help recalling the hypothetical image of Sophia stripped and raped, or the figure of Virtue in the dedication stripped, and so on to Mary Hamilton, and the young lady in Fielding's dream in the *True Patriot* who is fought over by the Young Pretender's Highlanders: "Indeed, it may be questioned whether perfect Beauty loses or acquires more charms by distress."[154]

Fielding's description of a tragic or sublime drama is curiously sandwiched between praise of Richardson's "humourous" characters (hardly a central issue in *Clarissa*) and a digression on his own fame. In the *Jacobite's Journal* piece in praise of *Clarissa* (no. 5, Jan. 2, 1747/8) he had juxtaposed his correspondent's (i.e., his own) praise with the unjust criticism of *Clarissa* by others and, immediately after, with another correspondent's praise of his own (in the context contrasting) art of humor. It seems significant that here, in his public utterance on the subject of *Clarissa*, he emphasizes its negative reception – a common way writers have of deflecting their sensitivity to attacks on their own works. The introduction of himself, half way through the letter (and the part Richardson omitted when he sent it out to friends), implies that his work is not as well received as Richardson's, that he himself desires and deserves as much or more fame.

Fame is designated, not surprisingly, as Mrs. Fame, *his* mistress, whom he pursues erotically, a strange parallel under the circumstances to the

Clarissa of the rape drama to which he has just described so vividly his responses (unless, as in *Tom Jones*, he is contrasting rape with consensual sex). He justifies this digression only as proof that he is not envious of Richardson (with a brief consideration of "envy") and that his compliments are sincere. But what is stressed, on the most conscious level, is the rivalry of Fielding and Richardson, which will still be evident at the very end of his preface to his last work, *The Journal of a Voyage to Lisbon.*

The traces of the actual book *Clarissa* are felt in the later volumes of *Tom Jones.*[155] In book 15 letters begin to play an important role in the plot, showing presumably the way letters *should* be used, embedded in the narrative, as part of "a nice Train of little Circumstances" (916), rather than uncontested witnessing, and written with point and wit rather than prolixity and repetition. Sarah's *Familiar Letters from the Characters in David Simple* had appeared in 1746 with some letters contributed by Fielding and an introduction with his comments on epistolary writing. This form was not, he wrote, "adapted to the Novel or Story-Writer; for what difference is there, whether a Tale is related this or any other way? And sure no one will contend, that the epistolary Style is in general the most proper to a Novelist, or that it hath been used by the best Writers of this Kind." A writer's models, he says, should be Ovid's *Heroides* and Lyttelton's *Persian Letters.*

Another point of contact between the rivals comes in Richardson's Postscript to the final volume, which Fielding cannot have seen before he finished the relevant parts of *Tom Jones* and before he wrote his letter to Richardson. Richardson says his intention was to produce not a "History" but a "Dramatic Narrative"; he means the letters are to be read as speeches in a play, and that his genre (not a Puritan diary, spiritual autobiography, or saint's life – although of course it *is* all of these) is tragedy. Tragedy is implicitly contrasted with comedy, and the further distinction insisted upon is between a happy (in that sense, Fielding's comic) and a tragic ending; in terms of "poetic justice," immanent providence, in the one, and in the other: "good and evil happen alike unto ALL MEN on this side the grave: And as the principal design of Tragedy is to *raise commiseration and terror* in the minds of the audience, we shall defeat this great end, if we always make Virtue and Innocence happy and successful" (emphasis added) Richardson uses the equation of tragedy with unequal providence in this world but equal providence in the next, as his reason for preferring the tragic disproportion of justice in the fate of Clarissa to the "comic" and trivializing happy ending of Fielding's novel. His intention is to produce not the relief of a happy ending and poetic justice, but the catharsis produced by pity and terror (he cites Aristotle) of tragedy.[156]

In the introductory essay to book 15 on "Virtue," which introduces Fellamar's design on Sophia, Tom's misfortunes, and Nightingale's dilemma, Fielding tells us, speaking for experience, that virtue is not accompanied

254 Author of Tom Jones, 1742–1748

by "happiness" (by which he means reward) in this life but only in the hoped-for afterlife. He has seen so many "exceptions" that "we chuse to dispute the Doctrine on which it is founded, which we don't apprehend to be Christian, which we are convinced is not true, and which is indeed destructive of one of the noblest Arguments that Reason alone can furnish for the Belief of Immortality" (15.1.784). But then Fielding proceeds to give his story a happy ending anyway.

Book 17 takes up the subject of tragic and comic plots, applied to the fate of Tom: the author will not use supernatural means to extract Tom from his troubles, as happens in the classical myths, the tales of the Arabs and Persians, which were based on belief and articles of faith; he will use only natural means based on *our* system of beliefs. It is not clear whether he means religious or literary here. The crucial passage appears in this chapter:

> This I faithfully promise, that notwithstanding any Affection, which we may be supposed to have for this Rogue, whom we have unfortunately made our Heroe, we will lend him none of that supernatural Assistance with which we are entrusted, upon Condition that we use it only on very important Occasions. If he doth not therefore find some natural Means of fairly extricating himself from all his Distresses, we will do no Violence to the Truth and Dignity of History for his Sake; for we had rather relate that he was hanged at *Tyburn* (which may very probably be the Case) than forfeit our Integrity, or shock the Faith of our Reader. (1.1.874)

This passage, "of amazing complexity" as Melvyn New remarks, tells us that in one sense Tom's history is still historically in progress, the end of the book has not been written, the author does not yet know the conclusion. In this sense, Tom is an independent agent, whose conduct *will* determine both his character and his end. But of course, "the finished work is already in the reader's hand, the author, who has never bothered to conceal himself, is quite involved in bringing events to pass, and . . . he admits the supernatural is available if the occasion is important enough."[157]

Providential events begin to happen following the essay on the marvelous which opens book 8; in effect they coincide with two events, the news of the Forty-Five and Tom's rendezvous in Upton, mostly reported by the superstitious Partridge; but these "providental" events are motivated by Tom's benevolent acts to the beggar, Merry Andrew, Enderson, the Endersons, and the Millers in books 10 to 15; after which the notion of providence and the author's duty, as they focus on the fate of Tom, carry some ambiguity.

The only direct statement on the subject made by the narrator is the one at the beginning of book 15: "There are a Set of Religious, or rather Moral Writers, who teach that Virtue is the certain Road to Happiness, and

Vice to Misery in this World. A very wholesome and comfortable Doctrine, and to which we have but one Objection, namely, That it is not true" (15.1.783). If we equate happiness/reward and misery/punishment, we may conclude that when providence shows itself it is either in defiance of the laws of the real world or is a coincidence or somehow helped along by the characters themselves: sometimes, as with Mrs. Miller, the direct consequence of Tom's good-natured actions; sometimes, as with the beggar and the Merry Andrew, a combination of sheer accident and Tom's good action (without the latter, he would not have learned of the coincidence). The word "Providence," in fact, is used only by the characters (and most strikingly by the superstitious Partridge), while the narrator refers to "fortune," its visible or apparent form with which the characters have to deal.[158] When the narrator does use the word, he refers, speaking of Tom's arrival in time to prevent Northerton's strangling of Jenny Waters, to the murder "which the *providential* Appearance of Jones did so *fortunately* prevent". This is related not only to chance but, considering the alternative response of the Old Man of the Hill in this situation, to what Addison called "Discretion" or the "Under-Agent of Providence."[159]

Tom *tells* Jenny Waters

> he was highly pleased with the *extraordinary Accident* which had sent him thither for her relief, where it was so improbable she should find any; adding that *Heaven* seemed to have designed him as the *happy Instrument* of her protection. 'Nay,' answered she, 'I could almost conceive you to be some good Angel.'

– extending the discourse of providence into the discourse of the erotic, which is maintained until Tom's "fall" (9.2.496, emphasis added). Divine providence itself (as in the metaphor of life-as-theater) is too distant to matter much except as a topic for conversation among men and women in society. While his characters or "very good and grave Men" (or "wise and good Men") talk of providence, *he* talks of fortune.[160] He cites Isaac Barrow and Nathaniel Wanley, but the word providence does not happen to be that of the narrator of *Tom Jones*.

The implied contrast of explanations, one superstitious, the other pragmatic, reflects the author's repeated "either [or whether] this . . . or that" constructions. In book 1, for example, Dr. Blifil, encumbered with a wife, does not consider a mere sexual encounter with Bridget. "This was owing either to his Religion, as is most probable, or to the Purity of his Passion, which was fixed on those Things, which Matrimony only, and not criminal correspondence, could put him in Possession of, or could give him any Title to" (1.10.62).[161] We infer also Bridget's relatively unattractive figure.

The construction in all probability derives from Virgil's *Aeneid*, as when the Trojan horse is discovered outside the gate of Troy, one Trojan, Thymoetes, advises that it be brought inside: "sive dolo deu iam Troiae sic fata ferebant" (II.34) – "whether in treachery, or because / The fates of Troy so ordered," or when Laocoön's spear fails to break open the horse because "something / Got in his way, the gods, or fate, or counsel" (II, Rolfe Humphries trans.). More generally, Aeneas tells us that "[Panthus'] words, or the gods' purpose, swept me on / Toward fire and arms."[162] But Fielding also carries it from Banier's history to *The Jacobite's Journal*, where he writes on the articles of the peace of Aix-la-Chapelle: "Whether we are to impute these Articles (if they are true) to the Intervention of Providence, to the reasonable Disposition of our Enemies, or to the Wisdom and Watchfulness of our own Ministers, I will not determine" (278).[163] In *Tom Jones*, the "Whether . . . or . . . I will not determine" construction, an example of the classical figure of *aporia* or the doubtful, becomes a virtual refrain of historical probability.

Providence is on the same level of reality as Joseph's image of himself as the biblical Joseph or Adams as the biblical Abraham, or Allworthy's of himself living in Paradise Hall as God the Father. Fielding is certainly denying the miraculous nature of events; he may, however, be arguing that what is *perceived* as providential (conveyed in the discourse of providence) is achieved "by a nice Train of little Circumstances" such as "we may frequently observe in Life" (18.2.916, 815).

What of rewards and punishments in the afterlife? In the *Champion* of March 4, 1739/40 Fielding referred to the "noble Argument for the certainty of a future State," and asked how "can the Heart of Man be warmed with a more ecstatic Imagination, than that the most excellent Attribute of the great Creator of the Universe is concerned in rewarding him?" In *Tom Jones* as early as the second chapter of book 1, Allworthy expresses his widower's comfort in the belief that "his Wife [has] only gone a little before him, a Journey which he should most certainly, sooner or later, take after her; and that he had not the least Doubt of meeting her again, in a Place where he should never part with her more" (1.2.35). Battestin's note records this as a devotional commonplace, a *consolatio*; but we have seen Fielding's own particular concern with this – as in his essay on affliction for his deceased daughter and his meeting with her in *A Journey from this World to the Next*, both in the *Miscellanies*. But here, in the world of *Tom Jones*, these are "Sentiments for which [Allworthy's] Sense was arraigned by one Part of his Neighbours, his Religion by a second, and his Sincerity by a third." If belief in an afterlife is introduced as belief and custom, as opposed to reality, a form of Banier's euhemerism, it recurs in the literary context of the genre of comedy – and so in the *literary* nature of the work itself.

Richardson and Fielding share the emphasis on the reward of virtue only in the afterlife. They clearly do not disagree on this point, but they arrive at a solution by different routes: Richardson by the belief of all his characters, himself, and presumably his audience in the afterlife to which, in their different ways, Clarissa and Lovelace are destined; Fielding, by no means so certain, and addressing himself to a more sophisticated audience that would not accept in such a fiction such certainty, arrives by substituting a harmonious, beautiful fiction in this life which will lead *his* readers to better behavior through the "happiness" of a hope in that life.

Richardson would say that Fielding is a sentimental artist, and he himself a hardbitten tragic artist. This is true in the sense that Fielding, generically and professionally constrained by the assumptions and conventions of a comic artist, requires a happy ending, even if it often carries with it an unseemly irony. But if so, it must also be acknowledged that Richardson is sentimental in both the sense of permitting excessive response (of the sort Fielding, in his letter, is either enjoying or parodying) and of in fact presupposing a happy ending (the reward in the afterlife) that conceals his pretensions to a tragic one.

In short, Richardson defines his genre in terms of, and as a reaction to, what he takes to be Fielding's generic and moral assumptions. His followers, from Lady Bradshaigh to Samuel Johnson, did the same. Johnson's "character of manners," which he claimed Fielding produced as opposed to Richardson's "characters of nature," refers to characters patterned on social stereotypes; and this is what Fielding does, but with the awareness that these stereotypes are external to the characters, roles assigned or taken up, found in fashion or in books, but also based on slander and rumor. Fielding sees people as largely determined by their sets and subsets of manners and discourses, taken up by themselves or seen and misinterpreted by others; and he maps the differences in his "deep" characters like Tom and Sophia. This – a social placement – was Fielding's way, rather than diving "into the recesses of the human heart," which Johnson associated with Richardson, but which Richardson himself wished to narrow and simplify into stark moral polarities.[164]

The "great Creation"

Fielding could have been thinking of Shaftesbury when he declared repeatedly in *Tom Jones* that this work of art (like his hero Tom) may appear to some observers flawed but is nevertheless a "great Creation." Shaftesbury writes of the "moral artist who can thus imitate the creator, and is thus knowing in the inward form and structure of his fellow-creature...."[165] He describes a world that seems to religious bigots as well as atheists fallen and flawed but to him a perfect harmonious "system" made up of other systems, parts subordinated to a unified whole. Some men "find fault, and imagine a thousand inconsistencies and defects in this wider constitution," but others ("you, my friend, are master of a nobler mind") "are conscious of better order within, and can see workmanship and exactness in yourself and other innumerable parts of the creation" (2:62).

Fielding gives art the primary didactic importance it carried for Shaftesbury. As a unique power for influencing those who have not yet reached a state of virtuous equilibrium, this more than any other formulation sums up Fielding's sense of his audience, his persuasive function, and his "new Province of Writing." It proclaims that the representation of a perfectly well-ordered world will produce similar order in the minds of men; that, though a fiction, the representation of the world as a beautiful and harmonious construction is on the one hand the greatest work of art and on the other the most powerful agency for improving morals.[166] It is, of course, a formulation intended primarily for an elite, whom Fielding will designate in *Tom Jones* as his "sagacious Readers" (as opposed to those who require the hope and fear of rewards and punishments in this life).

Most important, he follows Shaftesbury in not presuming to assert (with Anglican clergymen) that this providential order corresponds to reality. I am distinguishing between the providential assumptions of the clergy, attributed to Fielding by Battestin and Williams, and the deists' view that providential design, however essential to our happiness and social stability, is a human fiction. This is not so much to claim that Fielding is any longer himself a deist as that he accepts the consequences of deism; he recognizes the providential order as having been rendered by the deists no longer valid except as a fiction – as "Dreams of purling Streams, and shady Groves" (in the *Champion*) or "poetic justice" and a happy ending (in *Joseph Andrews* and *Tom Jones*).[167]

Tom Jones is, after all, as Fielding suggests, his "Creation," precisely the sort of "system" on which Shaftesbury bases his philosophy of harmony and order.[168] *Tom Jones* is all about the fictions people create in order to live in the world, which become equated with the larger fiction of Fielding's novel (both foundlings, both maligned for small flaws within larger virtues) which controls and orders the "Doctrine" of Tom's selfless love. These constitute a spectrum that reaches from the travestied order of Blifil and Bridget to the no less fictional order of virtue and beauty of Tom and of Fielding himself, which are repeatedly equated. The narrator is himself a substitute deity in a world of substitute forms, fictions, customs, which include religion – for the reality which, deity absent, is governed by chance, with good punished and bad rewarded.

These are the provisional social structures of roles, names, words ("love," "honor"), emphasized for example in the essay which is "A Comparison of the World and the Stage" which opens book 7; the classical myths and Arab stories, the Christian religion and "providence," but especially the rewards and punishments of the afterlife. This is the "system"; the "history" is: block one passage, it comes out another, which is the mechanist, materialist reality of the actual world, underlying the fictions.[169]

In *Tom Jones* he acknowledges that he is constructing a flawed world – a good pattern, he tells us in the dedication and often thereafter, which may contain some incidental flaws. This is presented as a duplication of the actual world: Tom as opposed to the paragon Pamela (Blifil) and *Tom Jones* as opposed to weak, small, conventional works of art. But this also modifies radically Shaftesbury's distinction between the contingent world and the beautiful world of art. Presumably it is a realistic step beyond Shaftesbury toward the real, "mixed" character *and* the "mixed" fictional model of the world. Balance and harmony of the Shaftesburian sort, yes; but not ideal perfection, not a paragon.

At the same time he enacts a fantasy of omniscience in his narrator: "Reader," he announces early in book 1, "I think proper, before we proceed any farther together, to acquaint thee, that I intend to digress, throughout this whole History, as often as I see Occasion: Of which I am a better Judge than any pitiful Critic whatever" (1.2.37). He provides and withholds information, often in a seemingly wilful way, and he repeatedly tells us that *his* world corresponds to the real, as it does to his hero, in being flawed and yet basically good.

The *historical* reading (centered on the Forty-Five), however, suggests that perhaps it is not a flawed world so much as one that is not, like the political world, governed by a tyrant, an absolute monarch; but, as in England, by a balanced government of Lords, Commons, and Monarch (demonstrated by the central paradigm of the Forty-Five); in his case, of author, actors, and audience.

Fielding, in *Tom Jones*, posits the actual world of change, accident, and disorder – evil rewarded, good punished; the ideal, comic, simulated world of *Tom Jones*, with its clockwork structure and good rewarded, evil punished; and the false, parody order of Blifil's "system," which is illusory as against the Good Nature, the love and charity, of Tom. Fielding could easily have suggested that the real world, in which the evil is only an encrustation on the good, blown away by the breath of ridicule, is exactly congruent with the fictional. But through all of the devices we have noticed he wards off this possibility.

In the long eighteenth century the great English books share a quality of being great *basic* works, the dictionaries or principias or mythographies. The religious-political-literary myth of the Fall and Redemption was written at the end of the seventeenth century in Milton's *Paradise Lost*; the myth of natural philosophy in Newton's *Principia Mathematica* and Locke's *Essay concerning Human Understanding*. All three of these texts were attempts to order the cosmos, nature, and the human mind, especially following the great cataclysm of the 1640s; they ushered in, and characterized, a century of search for order – or rather *re*-order after trauma, public and, by extension in each of these cases, personal. These are cosmologies related not only to Blackstone's *Commentaries of the Law*, or Adam Smith's *Wealth of Nations* (or Johnson's *Dictionary of the English Language*), but to Pope's *Essay on Man* and its dark brother, *The Dunciad*, Fielding's *Tom Jones*, and Gibbon's *Decline and Fall of the Roman Empire*.

　　Pope's *Essay on Man* seeks to "vindicate" (a more desperate verb than Milton's "justify") the ways of God to man, but *The Dunciad* is attempting, among other things, to vindicate Pope himself, as man, satirist, and poet. Gibbon's *Decline and Fall*, an anti-theodicy, places the blame for Rome's fall on the Christian God Pope vindicated. Fielding's *Tom Jones* shares with these encyclopedic works the attempt to place a problematic human act in a universal system of order that centers on, subordinates heterogeneity to, the understanding of that single act.[170]

6

Magistrate, 1748–1754

CHRONOLOGY

1748 Nov. 2. Begins to hold court as Chief Westminster Magistrate at the Bow Street court; 5th, concludes *Jacobite's Journal*. Within the last several months he has moved his residence from Twickenham to Brownlow Street, to Meard's Court, and finally to Bow Street.

1749 Jan. 6. Daughter Mary Amelia baptized, St. Paul's, Covent Garden (died Dec. 17).[1]

11–12. Takes the oaths for the commission of the peace for Middlesex County (and resigns the stewardship of the New Forest). 13th, begins acting in the Middlesex commission. All of this the benefaction of Bedford.

Sarah Fielding's novel, *The Governess, or Little Female Academy*, published, printed by Richardson; also her *Remarks on Clarissa*.

Feb. 3. *Tom Jones* published.

Mar. 29. Elected Chairman of the Westminster Quarter Sessions.[2]

June 29. *A Charge delivered to the Grand Jury, at the Sessions of the Peace held for the City and Liberty of Westminster, &c. . . . by Henry Fielding, Esq., Chairman of the said Sessions*, delivered; publ. Millar, July 21.

July 1–3. Penlez Riot: Sailors riot in the Strand, burning brothels. Attacks on HF and the government for their handling of the affair by "Argus Centoculi" in *Old England*.

21. HF submits to Lord Chancellor Hardwick a "Bill" to reform the police.[3]

Sept. 6. At the Quarter Sessions at the Old Bailey, Penlez is convicted and sentenced to hang. Lord Chief Justice Willes refuses to commute and on Oct. 18 Penlez is hanged.

Nov. 18. *A True State of the Case of Bosavern Penlez, Who suffered on Account of the late Riot in the Strand . . . by Henry Fielding, Esq; Barrister at Law, and one of his Majesty's Justices of the Peace for the County of Middlesex, and for the City and Liberty of Westminster*; publ. Millar; 2nd edn., Dec. 16 (*GA*).

Dec. HF is "very dangerously ill with a Fever, and a Fit of the Gout."[4] He appears to have been some way into the writing of *Amelia.*[5]

1750   Jan. 12. Another daughter, Sophia, baptized at St. Paul's, Covent Garden.[6]

29. HF's deputy, Saunders Welch, High Constable of Holborn, begins a series of raids on gangs of street robbers and house-breakers.[7] The events of this year are largely centered in the Bow Street court.

Feb. 19. Opening, with his brother John, of the Universal Register Office.

Mar. 31. Samuel Johnson's *Rambler* essay contrasting HF and Richardson to the latter's advantage.[8]

July 5. Death of sister Catherine (sister Ursula followed on Dec. 12, Beatrice on Feb. 24, 1750/1). Sarah now lodges with Jane Collier, the most sympathetic of the Collier family, friends from Salisbury.[9]

Aug. 3. His son Henry, dead in his eighth year, is buried in St. Martin-in-the-Fields, with another expensive funeral.[10] Takes off Aug. from the Bow Street court.[11]

1751   Jan. 2. Hogarth's *March to Finchley* delivered to subscribers (*LEP*).

19. *An Enquiry into the Causes of the Late Increase of Robbers, &c. with some Proposals for Remedying this Growing Evil . . . by Henry Fielding, Esq.* (identified as above), publ. Millar; 2nd edn., Mar. 6 (*GA*).

Feb. 14. Hogarth publishes his prints, *Beer Street* and *Gin Lane* and *The Four Stages of Cruelty* (*LEP*).

Feb. 21. *A Plan of the Universal Register-Office, Opposite Cecil Court in the Strand.*

July 27. John Fielding takes the oath and on the 30th is appointed to the Commission of the Peace for Westminster.[12] Leaving him in charge, HF retires to Bath and Glastonbury for his health.[13]

Sept. 12. Back in London, resumes business of the court (*LDA*).

Nov. 21. John marries Elizabeth Whittingham.[14]

Sarah, in financial straits, is sued for debt.

Dec. 19. *Amelia. By Henry Fielding, Esq.* (misdated 1752), 4 vols., publ. Millar, in an edition of 5,000, for which he pays HF £800; "2nd ed." publ. ca. Jan. 1752; 2nd edn. revised, in *Works* (1762). A chilly response leads HF, by the 23rd, to refer to *Amelia* to Harris as "my damned book (for so it is)"; by the 28th, another friend of Harris's wrote that it "does not answer people's expectations in reading, or the bookseller in selling. . . . [But] as to Fielding himself he laughs, & jokes, & eats well, as usual."[15]

1752 Jan. 4–Nov. 25. Edits *The Covent-Garden Journal. By Sir Alexander Drawcansir, Knt. Censor of Great Britain,* twice weekly, on Tuesday and Saturday; publ. Dodd (and probably Millar).

Apr. 13. *Examples of the Interposition of Providence in the Detection and Punishment of Murder, Containing, above thirty Cases, in which this dreadful Crime has been brought to Light, in the most extraordinary and miraculous Manner; collected from Various authors, antient and modern. With an Introduction and Conclusion. Both written by Henry Fielding, Esq.*; publ. Millar; 3,000 copies printed, 1s., 10d. per dozen "to those who give them away"; advertised, *Covent-Garden Journal.*

June 27. Proposes the publication by subscription of a new translation of Lucian's works, "With Notes Historical, Critical, and Explanatory," in two large quarto volumes, at two guineas. "Every Thing which hath the least Tendency to the Indecent will be omitted in this Translation."[16]

July 4. *Covent-Garden Journal* cut back to Saturdays only; last issue is Nov. 25.

Dec. 1. HF continues his reports of the Bow Street court and the Universal Register Office in the *Public Advertiser.* 3rd, his daughter Louisa is christened at St. Paul's, Covent Garden.[17]

1753 Jan. 29. *A Proposal for Making an effectual Provision for the Poor, for Amending their Morals, and for Rendering them useful Members of the Society. To which is added, A Plan of the Building proposed, with proper Elevations. Drawn by an Eminent Hand. By Henry Fielding, Esq.*; publ. Millar, 2,000 copies.[18]

Feb. 1. Has leased Fordhook, a "handsome house" and 44 acres at Ealing.[19]

Feb. 6. HF interviews Elizabeth Canning and hears her account of her abduction; in the days following HF arrests and questions the principles and charges Mary Squires and Susannah (Mother) Wells.

Mar. Sir John Hill's "Inspector" column in the *LDA* appears between March 9 and 14, attacking Fielding and Canning's credibility; Fielding announces his reply on the 13th. 20th, *A Clear State of the Case of Elizabeth Canning, Who hath sworn that she was robbed and almost starved to Death by a Gang of Gipsies and other Villains in January last, for which one Mary Squires now lies under Sentence of Death. By Henry Fielding, Esq.*; publ. Millar; "2nd ed." publ. Mar. 22.

Sarah publishes *David Simple: Volume the Last,* the gloomy sequel to *The Adventures of David Simple.*

May 10. Louisa is buried at St. Paul's Hammersmith, with HF's sisters.[20]

Sept. HF takes lodgings for a month in Bath, hoping to recover his health, but in mid-Sept. is detained by an outbreak of crime – "five different murders, all committed within the space of a week, by different gangs of street robbers."[21] He is summoned by the duke of Newcastle to provide a plan; his plan, based on "quick notice and sudden pursuit,"[22] is approved and carried out.

Dec. 1. Hogarth's *Analysis of Beauty* delivered to subscribers (*LEP*). Also, like *Amelia*, "damned" by hostile critics, in this case the artists whose plan for a state academy he opposed.

7. HF announces in the *PA* that since the implementation of his plan "no one Robbery, or Cruelty hath been heard of in the Streets, except the Robbery of one Woman, the Person accused of which was immediately taken." 14th: "With great Pleasure we can assure the Public, that since the apprehending the great Gang of Cutthroats, not one dangerous Blow, or Shot, or Wound has been given either in the Roads or Streets in or near this Town."

31. HF's finances once again in disarray, he borrows £1,892 from Millar, unpaid at his death.[23]

1754 Dec. Withdraws to the country to recuperate. In Jan. his brother John takes his place as Court Justice.[24]

Feb. Back in London, continuing to serve in Bow Street.

Mar. 6. Bolingbroke's posthumous *Works* published, including "Fragments or Minutes of Essays" expounding deist principles; HF undertakes to refute these.

19. Revised edition of *The Life of Mr. Jonathan Wild the Great. A New Edition with considerable Corrections and Additions. By Henry Fielding, Esq.*; publ. Millar (*PA*). *The Cry*, by Sarah Fielding in collaboration with Jane Collier, publ.

Apr. 6. Son Allen (named after Ralph Allen) christened at St. Paul's, Covent Garden.[25]

May. Returns to his house in Ealing; tries the tar water cure – unsuccessful; decides to try the mild climate of Portugal. John has now taken his brother's place in Bow Street.[26]

June 12. Engages passage to Lisbon on the *Queen of Portugal*. Writes his will.[27]

22. HF's death erroneously reported, and the *PA* responds that he is in better health than "for some Months past."

26. Sets out for Gravesend with Mary, Harriet (his surviving daughter by Charlotte, now 11), Margaret Collier, and the servants Isabella Ash and William; sails to Lisbon, keeping a journal.

Aug. 7. Arrives in Lisbon. Begins a history of Portugal. Complains of the behavior of Margaret Collier. Believes his health has improved and goes on outings. Settles in Junqueira, outside Lisbon.[28]

Oct. 8. Death; burial in Lisbon.

Dec. 2. *The Journal of a Voyage to Lisbon, by the late Henry Fielding, Esq.*, concluding with *A Fragment of a Comment on L. Bolingbroke's Essays*; publ. Millar, 2,500 copies. Announced (*PA*) but withheld while a second edition (omitting critical references to living people, changing Mrs. Francis to Mrs. Humphrys) is printed by Millar, publ. Feb. 25, 1755 (*PA*).

Dec. 26–7. Auction of house and furniture at Fordhook (*PA* 20th). The property bought by HF's friend Dr. Ranby for £800.[29]

1755 Feb. 10. Sale of HF's library at Samuel Baker's, Covent Garden, ca. £365.[30]

1762 *The Works of Henry Fielding, Esq; with The Life of the Author*, issued by Millar in 4 vols. quarto and in 8 vols. octavo; frontispiece by Hogarth; "An Essay on the Life and Genius of Henry Fielding, Esq;" by Arthur Murphy.

1778 Nov. 30. *The Fathers; or, The Good-Natur'd Man. A Comedy. By the late Henry Fielding, Esq.*, Drury Lane, publ. Dec. 12, T. Cadell (*PA*).

Reformer

The reformation of society

In October 1748 Fielding was appointed magistrate of the Bow Street court. As such he presided over the crimes of the lower orders, and it was their problems to which he devoted himself professionally for the last five years of his life. Thus after *Tom Jones*, as Westminster Magistrate and official spokesman for the government, Fielding speaks for orthodoxy without his usual irony and ambivalence. If earlier, his reliance on rewards and punishments in the afterlife had seemed to satisfy a personal need, in his later years it satisfied a social one. We can speculate that his becoming a magistrate changed his attitude toward crime, judgment, and mercy, as his marriage and the subsequent deaths of loved ones had changed his attitude toward religion.

Lady Mary Wortley Montagu noted that "the highest of his preferment [was] raking in the lowest sinks of vice and misery" and thought it would have been "a nobler and less nauseous employment to be one of the staff officers that conduct nocturnal weddings."[31] Westminster Magistrate (the position held by Justices de Veil and Squeezum) was not a position of great status, as Lady Mary's remark suggests (and there were far less sympathetic comments than hers). Essentially Fielding ran a police court and had the power to arrest, question, and commit, and in that sense pass judgment, but not to try and sentence. The latter, of course, depended on a jury; but in that sense he had more latitude and independence than the superior judges.[32]

However, holding both the Westminster and Middlesex County magistracies, Fielding was a "court JP," described as "a specially-appointed urban magistrate with a heavier workload and correspondingly higher level of government financial support and judicial power than his gentleman-amateur counterparts [such as his father, for example, had been] in the country."[33] And, whatever the exact status conferred, Fielding's enemies were correct when they noted that this was a position well suited to the author of *Jonathan Wild* and *Tom Jones*, as it was, certainly, to a moralist and satirist. As satire was often referred to by satirists (including Fielding) as extra-legal action, the police court offered him an opportunity to propose if not put into practice legal innovations; unsurprisingly, he found many opportunities to criticize the limitations of the law.

He was in a position to suggest and draft legal proposals with direct access to the ministry. As the reports of the daily activity of his court, printed in his *Covent-Garden Journal*, show, he was also in daily contact with the lowest orders of society, spending long hours questioning the accused and witnesses (not infrequently as long as eight hours at a stretch), his principle being to examine witnesses separately in order to catch inconsistencies and disagreements.[34] The chief experience – though one that Fielding would have known well enough from his years as a barrister – was to observe and judge the interplay of the credibiliity of eye-witness testimony and the probability of the circumstantial narrative, what in the first chapter of *Amelia* he referred to as "observing minutely the several Incidents which tend to the Catastrophe . . . and the minute Causes whence those Incidents are produced" (1.1.17). Beyond the judicial function, however, Fielding created the modern London police force; he greatly expanded the function of anticipating crimes and waylaying criminals, working out the logistics of such problems as how to retrieve within 24 hours the trunk of an East India Company man, with all his crucial papers, stolen on the way to the ship that would take him to India (*Enquiry*, 398–9). All of this represented a rich and various experience shared by no other writer of the time. The irony is that despite this wider area of experience, the judicial function in fact narrowed Fielding's responses and cramped his comic style.

In May 1749, in his first year as magistrate, he was chosen chairman of the Quarter Sessions of the Peace, and on June 29 delivered the annual charge, which was published three weeks later. While stocked with learned precedents and legal references, it was as much a charge to the citizens of Middlesex as to the law enforcement officers. Trying to anticipate crime at its source, he spends much time on minor offenses, and locates its roots in the brothels and dance halls, "where idle Persons of both Sexes meet in a very disorderly Manner, often at improper Hours, and sometimes in disguised Habits."[35] The familiar Fielding term "masquerade" is supplemented by "idleness," a term that recalls his dismissal of beggars as proper objects of charity in the *Champion*.

The term "idleness" would also have been significant for his old friend Hogarth. Both had turned their attention to the lower orders and correspondingly popular forms of expression at about the same time. Fielding had launched his puppet theater in Panton Street in 1748; a year earlier Hogarth had published *Industry and Idleness*, ostensibly addressed in style, form, and content to apprentices and their masters. We do not know exactly what went on in Fielding's puppet theater, but Hogarth still works the *Beggar's Opera* fiction that notes the similitude between the high and low except for the hanging of the latter. Hogarth the satirist could still imply the similarities between the trajectories of Tom Idle and Francis Goodchild, whereas Fielding the magistrate could no longer afford to indulge in such ironies.[36] He had to deal day after day with men and women in practical circumstances. Of course, a magistrate continues to see them in the terms he has always known, and Fielding was no exception. He always looked down from above, whereas Hogarth, himself once a struggling apprentice, saw things from below, not always excluding the perspective of the criminal. But after 1750 it is safe to say that from Hogarth's point of view, Fielding had lost his sense of humor; from Fielding's point of view, Hogarth was no longer acting responsibly.

The Penlez riot: the mob and prostitution

In 1749–50 Hogarth painted his homage to *Tom Jones*, *The March to Finchley* (plate 17), which places a handsome grenadier – the way Tom would have looked in uniform – in a Choice of Hercules pose flanked by Virtue and Pleasure. (Here Pleasure is the older woman, as ill-favored as Jenny is said to be; she gestures toward the house of pleasure, the brothel on her side of the choice.) These are the same poles upon which Hogarth constructs *The March to Finchley*, and they take the form of the same historic struggle that sundered families, confused loyalties, and led to egregious misunderstandings. Like Fielding's, Hogarth's context is not the patriotism of 1745–6 but the later discontent in an unhappy England ruled by an unpopular foreign family and swarming with dissident elements.

The old mythology of continental history-painting and heroic behavior, of the Jacobites *and* the Hanoverians, is replaced in *The March to Finchley* by a new one based on English folk skimmingtons and charivaris and their particular brand of disorder. This is Hogarth's attempt to show what really happened when the troops marched north to meet the Young Pretender – not the Jacobite or Hanoverian myths of it. The "natural" actions of these

Plate 17 Hogarth, *The March to Finchley*, 1750, engraving by Luke Sullivan, courtesy of the Trustees of the British Museum.

people simply exceed (parody) the topoi of the old master paintings of the Good Samaritan, Hercules at the Crossroads, Adam and Eve, and the Madonna and Child which dot the scene.[37]

Published at the beginning of 1751, *The March to Finchley* raised another issue, the divergence of Hogarth's and Fielding's views between the writing of *Tom Jones* and his administration of the Westminster magistracy. The confused but efficacious mixed government of 1745 had become by 1750 the object of discontent as a result of the 1749 attempt by the victor of Culloden, the duke of Cumberland, to bring the British army up to a German standard of discipline. *Finchley*, in its immediate context, juxtaposes an English "liberty" and disorder with the imposed order of Cumberland's "Mutiny Bill." The print is dedicated to "his Majesty the King of Prussia and Encourager of the Arts and Sciences!" – as usual an ambiguous dedication, but one that, in conjunction with the mob in the foreground, was a commentary on the Mutiny Bill which was being violently and spectacularly debated in the Commons during 1749–50. Characteristically, the print could be read by Cumberland's supporters as admonitory, with the thin column of marching troops in the distance the satirist's indication of the ideal; and by the supporters of the prince of Wales as a comment on the duke as the incarnation of "Prussianism," treating his soldiers "rather like Germans than Englishmen." The testimony of George II and John Wilkes, as well as Hogarth's other prints of the 1750s, supports the second interpretation.[38]

But the brothel of Hogarth's print did not figure in the story of the Mutiny Act. It figured rather in another conjunction of the British armed forces and its treatment of a riot, moreover one in which Fielding played a central and controversial role in his first year as magistrate. On July 1, 1749 some sailors of H.M.S. *Grafton* felt they had been cheated in a London brothel and started to riot. Joined by their comrades and many nonsailors, they destroyed three brothels and much adjacent property before the vigorous intervention of Fielding brought the trouble to an end. Fielding then prosecuted a few of the rioters, including the riot's hero/scapegoat, a young man named Bosavern Penlez. The anti-Fielding journal *Old England* represented the mob as "honest tars who, having served their country gallantly on the high seas, wanted now, in an access of patriotic zeal, to rid the capital of vice."[39] Fielding was represented as protecting the brothels (probably taking bribes from the bawds) against the armed forces of Britain.

He replied on November 18 in *A True State of the Case of Bosavern Penlez* that they were "a licentious, outrageous Mob, who in open Defiance of Laws, Justice or Mercy, committed the most notorious Offences against the Persons and Properties of their Fellow-Subjects":

> The Clamour against Bawdy-Houses was in them a bare Pretence only. Wantonness and Cruelty were the Motives of most, and some, as it plainly appeared, converted the inhuman Disposition of the Mob to the very worst of Purposes, and became Thieves under the Pretense of Reformation.

But as to the brothels: "The Law, clearly considers them as a Nuisance, and hath appointed a remedy against them; and this Remedy it is in the Power of every Man, who desires it, to apply."[40] In his *Charge to the Grand Jury*, delivered just before the riots on June 29, Fielding spoke out strongly against brothels as tending "directly to the Overthrow of Men's Bodies, to the wasting of their Livelihoods, and to the indangering of their Souls" (23). Hogarth, the author of *A Harlot's Progress* and Fielding's old friend, would have been bemused by such effusions (as, we might suppose, would also the Fielding who wrote *The Covent-Garden Tragedy*).[41] In his attacks on prostitutes, in his legal pamphlets as well as in *The Covent-Garden Journal* of two years later, Fielding sounds rather like Squire Allworthy addressing Jenny Jones, except that he invariably singles out as the exception the 16-year-old girl (Hogarth's Harlot?) who has been suborned into a life of prostitution. The age is invariable (see below, 310).

One consequence of Fielding's stand was the trial and capital conviction of the supposed inciters of the riot. The villain of the affair, in the public view, was the judge, Lord Chief Justice Sir John Willes, who rejected the jury's plea for mercy and thrice refused to advise the king to grant a pardon (based on public petitions to the duke of Newcastle) on the grounds that the condemned men must be made an example.[42] Bosavern Penlez and 14 others were hanged for the crime on October 18, the antiministerial reaction was strong, and Fielding, whose pamphlet of November 18 defended the executions, came in for his share of opprobrium.

We can only speculate on where Hogarth stood on these issues, but we do know that he included the grim visage of Chief Justice Willes as the hanging judge in his *Analysis of Beauty*, Plate 1 (1753), and among the judges of *The Bench* (1758), where erroneous judgment is at issue and their motto is "semper eadem" (always the same). From the evidence of *Industry and Idleness*, he would have agreed with the ironic "Monumental Inscription intended for PENLEZ" that was published in late October in the *Gentleman's Magazine* and ends:

And think thyself happy under that Government
'That doth *truly* and *indifferently* administer Justice,
    'To the Punishment of Wickedness and Vice,
  'And to the Maintenance of God's True Religion and
Virtue.'[43]

The Penlez Riots were also conflated in the public consciousness with the unruly Westminster election of November–December, one of the longest and most riotous, bitterly fought Westminster elections on record, and one in which Fielding was again castigated by the opposition: this time as a magistrate who used his power to support the candidacy of the ministry's candidate, Granville Leveson-Gower, Lord Trentham.[44] Trentham was opposed by Sir George Vandeput, second baronet of Twickenham. The election race was made more bitter by the support the duke of Cumberland gave Trentham and the prince of Wales gave Vandeput. The mobs were appropriately (given the reputation of "Butcher" Cumberland at this time) against Trentham. The chief accusations leveled at Trentham were that he had been responsible for the king's ignoring the public desire that Penlez be pardoned and that he sponsored "the French Stollers," who performed at the Little Theatre in the Haymarket, at a time when anti-French feeling ran especially high in England in the wake of the war that had just come to an unsatisfactory end. The attempt to prevent the French players from performing led to a riot in the theater on November 14, four days before Fielding's Penlez pamphlet appeared.

Reading Fielding's long account of riots, the law, and the Riot Act, which takes up almost the whole text of the *Penlez* pamphlet, Hogarth would have noted with interest that a "public" riot is "High-Treason within the Words Levying War against the King," and (Fielding quotes Coke) "is levying War within the Purview of the above Statute" (37). In the accompanying note Fielding adds that such a group is "called an Army" by Coke. In *The March to Finchley* Hogarth simply equates *riot* and *army*. From his (and Fielding's own) experience in the 1730s the Riot Act was a repressive Hanoverian weapon used against the liberties of a free people. Given the evolution during these years of Hogarth's morality in the direction of an aesthetics, it is also possible to see the crowd, moving as it does within the geometrical forms of the nursery and brothel, as embodying the formal principle of the operation of variety – the utmost variety possible – within unity, which he was to enunciate as a theory in *The Analysis of Beauty* three years later. He must have read Fielding's words as expressing a position quite different at this point from his own, and his print, which he announced early in 1750, both pays homage to the author of *Tom Jones* and questions the author of the *Penlez* pamphlet. Fielding would himself become increasingly aware of the dichotomy of morality-law and aesthetics.

The Enquiry

At the beginning of 1751 Fielding and Hogarth coordinated their verbal and visual programs for the last time. In mid-January Fielding published *An Enquiry into the Causes of the Late Increase of Robbers*, addressing the "reigning Vices peculiar to the lower Class of People," and a month later were published "Two large Prints, design'd and etch'd by Mr. Hogarth call'd BEER-STREET and GIN-LANE" and, "on Thursday following will be published four Prints on the Subject of Cruelty." They were 1 shilling each, though for 1*s*. 6*d*. "the Curious," that is, the connoisseurs, could secure the prints on better paper.

One can imagine Fielding, with the sense of urgency he expresses in the *Enquiry*, seeking the assistance of Hogarth: first the words, then the images. Since Hogarth's prints address the "reigning Vices peculiar to the lower Class of People" and represent, almost point for point, the issues of Fielding's *Enquiry*, he must have read the manuscript and begun his plates by the time the *Enquiry* was published. The differences, however, show how far the friends at this point diverged on the subject of the London poor.

In his *Charge to the Grand Jury* Fielding had distinguished between the poor and the rich: it is the poor who lose most through gambling, he argues, whereas "for the Rich and Great, the Consequence is generally no other than the Exchange of Property from the Hands of a Fool into those of a Sharper, who is, perhaps, the more worthy of the two to enjoy it" (26). The imitation of the "great" becomes in the *Enquiry* the basic cause of crime in London. Each rank in society, Fielding says, is now imitating the expensive pleasures of the next rank above. He is not, however, much disturbed by the nobleman who "will emulate the Grandeur of a Prince" nor by the gentleman who "will aspire to the proper State of the Nobleman"; but there is reason for concern when (as he remarks, still employing the key words "affect" and "idleness")

> the Tradesman steps from behind his Counter into the vacant Place of the Gentleman. Nor does the Confusion end here; it reaches the very Dregs of the People who aspiring still to a degree beyond that which belongs to them, and not being able by the Fruits of honest Labour to support the State which they affect, they disdain the Wages to which their Industry would entitle them; and abandoning themselves to Idleness, the more simple and poor-spirited betake themselves to a state of Starving and Beggary. While those of more Art and Courage become Thieves, Sharpers, and Robbers. (75–8)

Seeking practical solutions, Fielding has turned his attention to "the lower Order of People," but the *Enquiry* does not imply that the rich are without vice. Its point is that they can afford their vices, unlike those who are ruined by imitating them – and there is legally nothing to be done. In *Rape upon Rape* Fielding had included the speech: "Well, Sir, if you cannot pay for your transgressions like the rich, you must suffer for them like the poor." "Let the Great therefore answer for the Employment of their Time to themselves," he says in the *Enquiry*, "or to their spiritual Governors" (83). The poor, who threaten our daily existence, can and must be dealt with, and so his subject is the poor fools who, like Hogarth's Hackabout and Rakewell, try to imitate their superiors. His aim, Fielding says in his preface, is "to rouse the Civil Power from its present lethargic State" by focusing on practical measures that might conceivably alleviate the problem of crime among the emulative poor.

If his first chapter (as in *Joseph Andrews*) is on imitation, his second is on idleness, or the poor's primary way of escaping from the burdens of productive labor in a "New Kind of Drunkenness . . . which, if not put a Stop to, will infallibly destroy a great Part of the inferiour People" – that is, gin drinking, which he has "great reason to think, is the principal Sustenance (if it may be so called) of more than a hundred thousand People in this Metropolis" (88–9). Giving examples of the consequences of this "diabolical Liquor," he sounds as if he is recalling the gin-seller's baby in Hogarth's

March to Finchley, emaciated and evidently nourished only on its mother's wares: "What must become of the Infant who is conceived in *Gin?* with the poisonous Distillations of which it is nourished both in the Womb and at the Breast" (176). In *Gin Lane* (see plate 18) Hogarth shows one mother pouring gin into her baby's mouth and another (the central figure) with exposed breasts that suggest she has been feeding her child; the child is falling from her relaxed grip to its death (in a later state Hogarth gave the child a gin-ravaged face).

Fielding shows that one of the causes of the poor's thievery lies with the churchwardens and overseers of the poor (discussed in his fourth section) who "are too apt to consider their Office as a Matter of private Emolument, to waste Part of the Money raised for the Use of the Poor in Feasting and Riot" – a point Hogarth illustrates in *Gin Lane* and the *First Stage of Cruelty*. The parish insignia on the arms of two young girls drinking gin and of the young Tom Nero draw attention to the conspicuous absence of the parish officers who should be looking after them.

But in the terms of Fielding's *Enquiry*, "looking after" is just one thing, and that is keeping the children employed and out of mischief (110–11, 122). Fielding's chief recommendations are for finding ways "to force the Poor to Industry," and so for stopping the supply of cheap gin in order "to put a Stop to the Luxury of the lower People," that is, their idleness (171). In his later *Proposal for Making an effectual Provision for the Poor*, he prescribes punishments for the idle – not only "a Fasting-room" but cells for solitary confinement, and for all, hours scheduled for worship and moral instruction in a room with iron grates which looked into a chapel.[45] However much he damns the various strata of the governing class, Fielding is offering small comfort to – and certainly not reasoning with – the governed.

He is, after all, with his genteel ironic tone, writing to the superior sort, not the inferior. Reading the pamphlet is beyond their scope, as its cost is beyond their means. And so he must employ his irony to get at the rich while proposing stronger laws for limiting the potentials for mischief in the poor, who *can* be affected by legislation. The laws must prevent the poor's excessive gin drinking and make them settle down to safe, industrious behavior.

The effect on Fielding the author is, however, narrowing and simplifying. The mob is no more than the poor out of control (and will continue so into his *Journal of a Voyage to Lisbon*); whereas in *Tom Jones* he wrote: "Whenever this Word [mob] occurs in our Writings, it intends Persons without Virtue, or Sense, in all Stations, and many of the highest Rank are often meant by it" (1.9.59).

While Fielding does not omit the horrible consequences to the gin drinkers, he emphasizes the consequences to other citizens – the thefts and

Plate 18 Hogarth, *Gin Lane*, 1751, etching and engraving, courtesy of the Trustees of the British Museum.

murders the gin "emboldens them to commit." In *Gin Lane,* however, Hogarth offers no signs of crime, only the terrible accidents and self-destruction the gin-drinkers bring upon themselves and their families. Human and architectural decline is plainly the consequence of drinking gin, but if we peruse the scene to see what led to the gin drinking, we find (besides the distiller) only the pawnbroker who permits, indeed encourages, these people to drink themselves to death. The only hints of authority are a man holding a staff who is assisting in the burial of a woman killed by gin and the remotely distant church spire. Nor do the poor depicted by Hogarth emulate the next class higher up the social scale but are simply exploited or ignored by that class, which should oversee and (Hogarth implies) protect them.[46]

The fact, certainly understood by Fielding, is that the government encouraged distillation and sales of gin to support the landed interest (to encourage the production of spirits distilled from homegrown cereals) and provide itself with revenues. As one historian of gin has concluded, "the rise and decline of gin drinking can be related directly to taxation and legislation."[47] In 1743 Parliament repealed the 1736 Gin Act and adopted a more moderate one, drafted by a prominent distiller of the time. Lord Bathurst's argument was that since it was impossible to prevent the retailing of spirits, it would be better to license it instead, as this would reduce usage by increasing expense and also provide money for England's European wars. The new law, known as the Tippling Act, increased the price of gin, granted licenses only to alehouse license holders, and forbade distillers to retail. But in 1747 the distillers petitioned for the right to retail, and the act was modified accordingly. Once this right was restored to the distillers, gin consumption, which had waned slightly since 1743, rose markedly; drunkenness increased, population declined, and in 1750 a commission reported that in some parts of London one in every five houses was a gin shop.

Hogarth would seem to be illustrating this fact when he includes the spire of St. George's (capped by the statue of the monarch, George I) in *Gin Lane* and juxtaposes with this print of the emaciated gin drinkers the prosperity of the fat merchants and George II's urge to greater commerce in the pendant, *Beer Street.* The basic cause-and-effect relationship would be understood by the poor: not that beer drinking leads to prosperity and gin drinking to want, but the reverse.

Fielding's point about industry is illustrated in Gin Lane by the carpenter who pawns his saw, the housewife who pawns her kettle, saucepan, and fire tongs, to buy gin. Significantly, however, Hogarth shows the prosperous folk of Beer Street no more at their labor than the dregs of Gin Lane. He has chosen the moment when they are relaxing with their mugs of beer *following* labor, as those of Gin Lane "relax" with their gin *in place of* labor. Even the workmen repairing the building have climbed up on the roof to rest. Only the needy artist is actually working, at a signboard (the painted equivalent of the sort of popular print Hogarth has produced).

Two of the three tailors in the adjacent building, high above Beer Street, are also working. One of the tailors holds a beer mug while the other two sew: a detail that refers to "those wretched emblems of death and hunger, the Journeymen Taylors,"[48] and more specifically reflects the troubles between the master tailors and their journeymen (some 7,000 of them in London) over wages and working conditions. Hogarth uses the beer drinking to distinguish the master from his journeymen, whose oppressive working conditions, long hours, and miserably low wages (from 6 a.m. to 8 p.m., with half an hour for lunch and an hour for dinner, at less than 2*s.* a day) may suggest that journeymen labor while their masters idly drink.

This dispute finally went into arbitration at the July 1751 Quarter Sessions. Fielding was one of the magistrates who decided in favor of raising the journeymen's wages.[49] In practice, when he could, he showed his sympathy; but in the directed discourse of his *Enquiry* he did not have the leisure for Hogarthian play.

While Fielding's address reaches down as far as the middling sort of people, Hogarth extends his to the inferior sort, the poor wage-earners if not the indigent poor – the journeymen and apprentices and indeed the gin-drinkers themselves, the denizens of Gin Lane. Fielding questions only an occasional particularly brutal law, but Hogarth's visual images undermine the structure of authority itself – of the legislator's authority if not, as Fielding may have thought, the magistrate's, which permitted him to interpret the laws, as in the case of the journeymen tailors. Hogarth had, working for him, the greater potential for doubleness of interpretation in visual forms. Fielding's audience was of the superior sort, and verbal irony was his only weapon against them (or method for instructing them).

The happy effect of Fielding's and Hogarth's campaign was the passage of the Gin Act of 1751 (24 Geo. II, cap. 40) which, in a relatively short time, reduced the annual consumption of gin in England from 11 million to less than 2 million gallons.[50]

Punishment

There was, however, another aspect to Fielding's *Enquiry*: the argument for increasingly severe laws. In Section 10, which presents the case against royal "Pardons," Fielding derides the efficacy of "mercy": "To speak out fairly and honestly, tho' Mercy may appear more amiable in a Magistrate, Severity is a more wholesome Virtue; nay Severity to an Individual may, perhaps, be in the End the greatest Mercy" (164).

In *Tom Jones* he had argued that governing the passions was done from within, but now he has given up that line of argument and demonstrated that it can be governed only from without, by religion or government, essentially by fear of punishment: "the Passions of the Man are to give Way to the Principles of the Magistrate"; and the great variety of examples now comes down to one: "The Terror of the Example is the only Thing proposed, and one Man is sacrificed to the Preservation of Thousands" (*Enquiry*, 164, 166). He believes in the exemplary nature of punishment – which he sums up in the last months of his life in the *Journal of a Voyage to Lisbon*: "Example alone is the end of all public punishments and rewards," citing the judge who told a convicted felon who complained that it was hard to hang for only "stealing a horse," "You are not to be hanged, Sir, . . . for stealing a horse, but you are to be hanged that horses may not be stolen" (36). He recommends a reform, what he calls "the Dread of a sudden and violent Death" without any hope of a pardon that would encourage criminals to commit more crimes. With no possibility of pardon, in Section II of the *Enquiry*, he turns to the "terrors" of the execution, which, for maximum effect on the prisoner but especially on the public, should be carried out without delay and witnessed only by the magistrates who condemned him.

His image of the current state of public executions – the wrong sense of spectacle – is that of Hogarth's scene of Tyburn in plate 11 of *Industry and Idleness* (see plate 19), showing "the Diversion of the Populace" and illustrating "the little Force which such Examples have on the Minds of the Populace" (*Covent-Garden Journal*, 416, 447). It is not strange that Fielding the magistrate disapproves of precisely the element that Hogarth played upon for his irony, the execution as a subculture crowd ritual – "a Holyday to the greatest Part of the Mob about Town". Fielding's critique of the holiday aspect of the public execution draws upon the long line of mock-heroic references to criminals in his work going back to Gay's *Beggar's Opera*: "The Criminals themselves behaved with the wonted Affectation of Mock-Heroism"; "No Heroes within the Memory of Man ever met their fate with more Boldness and Intrepidity, and consequently with more felonious Glory," and this is "to the great Encouragement of all future Heroes of the same Kind" (416, 428). Hogarth's point, comparing the execution with the celebration (in the pendant, plate 12) of the Lord Mayor's inauguration, was that they came down to the same thing.

Behind closed doors, where it could be seen only by the immediate participants, the execution, Fielding believed, would be far more terrible in the imagination of the multitude. Indeed, he invokes a "poor Wretch, bound in a Cart, just on the Verge of Eternity, all pale and trembling with his approaching Fate" who recalls Hogarth's Idle on his way to the gallows. But if not spectacular, Fielding's execution *is* theatrical, based on the off-stage murder of Duncan in Shakespeare's *Macbeth* (an Englishman's play

Plate 19 Hogarth, *Industry and Idleness*, Plate 11, 1747, etching and engraving, courtesy of the Trustees of the British Museum.

about dynastic problems which could allude back to the Forty-Five) acted by Garrick.[51]

The most controversial terms of his *Enquiry* centered on "cruelty" and capital punishment. Fielding piously refuses to accept "the general Charge against the People of *England*" of a "natural inbred Cruelty":

> that we are cruel to one another is not, I believe, the common, I am sure it is not the true Opinion. Can a general Neglect of the Poor be justly charged on a Nation in which the Poor are provided for by a Tax frequently equal to what is called the Land-Tax, and where there are such numerous Instances of private Donations, such Numbers of Hospitals, Alms-houses, and charitable Provisions of all Kinds? (98–9)

But cruelty and neglect are emphatically the subject of Hogarth's six prints. In *Gin Lane* the cruelty is the result of gin drinking, but in the *Four Stages of Cruelty* it originates in the neglect of Tom Nero, who (in Fielding's terms) without work to keep him busy sets the cycle in motion which ends with his own "cruel" end. Cruelty is what defines not just Nero but "the People of England" in Hogarth's *Stages of Cruelty*. Indeed, Fielding may have been acknowledging Hogarth's prints a year later in the *Covent-Garden Journal* of March 3, 1751/2 ("Modern History"): "*If something be not done to prevent it, cruelty will become the Characteristic of this Nation*" (471).

The first stage of cruelty is defined by the absence of the St. Giles Parish officers, who should have looked after these boys; the second is defined by the very bulky presence of lawyers whose weight is responsible for the collapse of the horse Nero is consequently beating to death. They have crowded in to save a fare – the Thavies Inn sign indicates the farthest shilling fare from Westminster Hall, the lawyers' destination.[52] The third stage is dominated by the grimly threatening constabulary and the fourth by the surgeon-magistrate – the representatives of the law, the forces from above for whom Nero serves merely as someone who is not (to use Fielding's phrase) "beyond the reach of . . . capital laws."

Hogarth's final plate, *The Reward of Cruelty* (see plate 20), presents the chief surgeon in the pose of a magistrate presiding over a condemned malefactor. The Company of Surgeons has made off with Tom Nero's body from the gallows. Only a year later, in March 1752, the law settled the matter by making dissection a part of the official penalty the judge could impose upon certain, though not all, criminals. This law, the "Murder Act," was framed as an immediate response to the Penlez Riots of 1749 in which Fielding had played a major role. It is not without significance that the dissector in Hogarth's picture has been traditionally identified as Dr. John Freke, the surgeon who was prevented from dissecting Penlez's body in the cause célèbre that followed his execution – but who did dissect many other criminals.[53]

Plate 20 Hogarth, *The Reward of Cruelty*, 1751, etching and engraving, courtesy of the Trustees of the British Museum.

Hogarth sets up this scene as if it were a theatrical performance, as if recalling Fielding's call for spectacle. But he has shifted his emphasis from Nero to the Overseers of the Poor and to government in general, which not only permits Nero to commit his first act of cruelty but enjoys this final drama of *lex talionis*. There is no other conclusion to be drawn than that Hogarth is submitting Fielding's terms – "mercy," and the Aristotelian "pity" and "terror" – to analysis, asking us to regard them not in Fielding's

Plate 21 Unknown artist, *Henry Fielding* (?), drawing, ca. 1751, courtesy of the Trustees of the British Museum.

legal context but in the context of contemporary literary works (also in the shadow of the Forty-Five) such as Collins' odes to Mercy, Pity, and Fear (1747), and of Fielding's own earlier literary works and of all Hogarth's graphic works. Hogarth is criticizing the idea of capital punishment as vengeance but also as salutary admonition, as advocated in all its theatricality by Fielding. Fielding recommended a quick, private, symbolic execution; and in that sense Hogarth could be caricaturing a process both he and Fielding opposed.

Fielding was widely regarded by contemporaries as a stern magistrate, quite at odds with the advocate of good nature and forgiveness who wrote *Tom Jones.* The caricatures of him as magistrate, as Battestin notes (529), included "his stern and arrogant demeanor on the bench, his habit of declaiming with his jaws crammed with tobacco, his way of favoring the rich and great while bullying the lower classes." If we are to accept Battestin's identification of a profile in pencil and red chalk (see plate 21) as Fielding at this time (and the resemblance to Hogarth's authentic portrait of the young Fielding [see frontispiece]), we must note the close resemblance between its features and those of Hogarth's chief surgeon, whom he presents in the position and pose of a magistrate: the same long overhanging nose, the same receding, probably toothless mouth and protruding jaw.[54] James Field, a pugilist and ex-sailor, whose name appears above one of the displayed dissected skeletons on the wall, had been examined by Fielding before being tried, sentenced, and hanged for robbery; and his skeleton (like the other, James Macleane's) could be construed as pointing to the surgeon-magistrate.[55]

There is also the contemporary evidence of Samuel Johnson's response to Fielding's *Enquiry* in *Rambler* no. 114 (Apr. 20, 1751), though characteristically he does not name names. He is referring to Fielding when he says that "some are inclined to accelerate the executions; some to discourage pardons; and all seem to think that lenity has given confidence to wickedness, and that we can only be rescued from the talons of robbery by inflexible rigour, and sanguinary justice." Johnson's argument is for mercy in the particular sense that crimes of theft and murder should not equally deserve capital punishment. But the Johnsonian sentiment comes in his reference to Herman Boerhaave's remark that "he never saw a criminal dragged to execution without asking himself, 'Who knows whether this man is not less culpable than me?' On the days when the prisons of this city are emptied into the grave, let every spectator of the dreadful procession put the same question to his own heart" (*Rambler*, 2:242–4).

Although Hogarth does have Nero commit murder as well as theft, it is presumably to focus on capital punishment while avoiding the complicating issue of murder or theft. He is nevertheless closer to Johnson, whose wisdom he was praising in the 1750s, than to his old colleague Fielding – possibly now that Fielding was, of all things, a magistrate.[56] And in this sense, his engraving of *Paul before Felix*, announced in May, could be seen as a seventh plate following *Beer Street, Gin Lane,* and *The Four Stages of Cruelty*: here the magistrate is wicked, the accused is innocent, and the accusers are corrupt. The story of Paul and Felix was conventionally used to show the tables turned on the magistrate as the innocent defendant directs the accusation against his judge (Paul, interestingly, was charged with inciting to riot, the cause of the Penlez case). The magistrate will reappear in 1753 in the first plate of *The Analysis of Beauty*, with the face of Justice Willes, joining the severity of capital punishment with stupid judgments of taste, embodied in the "square," both a symbol of correct form and a gallows.

There is no indication of friction between the two friends. Fielding had a copy of the *Analysis* in his library, and he continues to cite Hogarth. In *Amelia* he compares Hogarth to Shakespeare (although including Kitty Clive as his third figure may have moderated the effect), and Dr. Harrison, who has never "read a word of" either Dryden or Pope, knows and reveres Hogarth's graphic works. But Harrison's significant remark is that Hogarth's prints are worth more than *The Whole Duty of Man*: Fielding now reads Hogarth's prints as graphic *Amelia*s, anticipating the solemnity of Trusler's *Hogarth Moralized* (1768). In any case, friendly remarks continue to appear in the *Covent-Garden Journal* and, in the last months of Fielding's life, *The Journal of the Voyage to Lisbon*. If Hogarth's six prints were in some sense a critique of Fielding, it was of Fielding the "magistrate," only one aspect of the "man" (Fielding's own term) who wrote *Tom Jones* and was writing *Amelia*. And if the stern visage of the presiding surgeon was meant to suggest Justice Fielding, Hogarth's ultimate image of his old friend was the younger, smiling face of *Characters and Caricaturas*, which he remembers in the drawing he made as frontispiece for Fielding's *Works* of 1762 (see frontispiece).

A detail Fielding fails to mention in the *Enquiry* is that one of the worst gangs was headed by Thomas Jones, who was dramatically rescued by his gang from the Gatehouse in January 1749, recaptured by one of Fielding's Bow Street constables in October, committed by Fielding to trial, and hanged at Tyburn the following March.[57] The historical Tom Jones tauntingly and parodically called his gang "The Royal Family," a detail we might imagine the young Fielding having inserted in one of his plays; but the ludic possibilities of actually hanging Tom Jones one year after having vindicated his life in a prolonged narrative trial were not, so far as we know, explored by Fielding. If the novelist had been at pains to reveal the innocence of the purported criminal Tom Jones, the magistrate offered his tract to expose the criminality that lurked behind the "disguises," including that of a "Gentleman," which Jones wore "in most Companies."

That Fielding was changing with his role as magistrate was recognized by his contemporaries, especially by old friends. We have seen Hogarth's reaction to the Penlez pamphlet and his role in the Westminster election of 1749. But these changes were picked up by other old friends, most significantly by his former deist associates Ralph and Cooke.[58] Especially the latter, who in the *Craftsman* for April 7, 1750 assumed the old mask of Martinus Scriblerus to depict the court of Folly:

> A Lawyer next stands Candidate for *Fame*;
> For now the Queen's amphibious Justice came:
> The Part he acts still changing with the Year;
> Now Whig, now Tory, *Trotplaid, Vinegar*!

Battestin characterizes Cooke as "a man quick to take offense and unforgiving, who would suffer no rivals in wit" (494), but he seems to be just another of the friends of Fielding's youth who remark the change in their old chum. Like Hogarth, Cooke refers to the snuff habit: "his Snuff-strown Chin" and the rather run-down look of the magistrate; but he mourns the loss of the old Fielding, having him address Folly's throne:

> "Forgive each *Pasquinade*;
> Forgive my antient, merry, honest Trade;
> Forgive the Sallies of ungovern'd Youth;
> Forgive, good Queen, my early love of Truth.
> Ah! let this leaden Journal [i.e., *Covent-Garden*] of your own
> The Wit of *Joseph* or of *Jones* attone."

As Shaftesbury had noted of the despised doctrine of rewards and punishments: "the principle of fear of future punishment, and hope of future reward, how mercenary or servile soever it may be accounted, is yet in many circumstances a great advantage, security, and support to virtue." And:

> Thus in a civil state or public we see that a virtuous administration, and an equal and just distribution of rewards and punishments, is of the highest service, not only by restraining the vicious, and forcing them to act usefully to society, but by making virtue to be apparently the interest of every one, so as to remove all prejudices against it, create a fair reception for it, and lead men into that path which, afterwards they cannot easily quit.

Finally, he extended punishments in the afterlife to public executions in this life in which

> we see generally that the infamy and odiousness of their crime, and the shame of it before mankind, contribute more to their misery than all besides; and that it is not the immediate pain of death itself which raises so much horror

either in the sufferers or spectators, as that ignominious kind of death which is inflicted for public crimes and violations of justice and humanity.[59]

Here, in a nutshell, is the trajectory followed by Fielding's views of religion from the 1730s to his death in 1754: from beautiful order (the world is a work of art), to pragmatic and provisional order based on fear and hope, to grim necessity in order to hold together a collapsing society.

Hogarth, it seems likely from all the evidence,[60] still espoused the view of Shaftesbury's opponent, Mandeville: "The Chief Thing, therefore, which Lawgivers and other wise Men, that have laboured for the Establishment of Society, have endeavour'd, has been to make the People they were to govern, believe, that it was more beneficial for every Body to conquer than indulge his Appetites"; and "That virtue and religion were inventions of politicians to awe the mob."[61]

Author of *Amelia*

Richardson once more

In October 1748 Fielding wrote his letter to Richardson praising *Clarissa*. The letter (and his references to *Clarissa* in the *Jacobite's Journal*) shows the impact Richardson's novel had on him *in the reading* (as opposed to what he had heard about it as he was writing *Tom Jones*). One's first reaction is that the impact was such that it turned him around and led him to produce *Amelia*. Certainly this is one explanation for Fielding's radical and unexpected departure from his own mode in *Tom Jones*.

Further, the solemn voice of Samuel Johnson announced in *Rambler* no. 4 (March 31, 1750) that the novelist, recognizing the power he wielded over his reader, must make his protagonist a paragon:

> if the power of example is so great as to take possession of the memory by a kind of violence, and produce effects almost without the intervention of the will, care ought to be taken, that, when the choice is unrestrained, the best examples only should be exhibited; and that which is likely to operate so strongly, should not be mischievous or uncertain in its effects. (*Rambler*, 1:22)[62]

Johnson is criticizing Tom Jones, Fielding's "mixed character," whose good qualities seduce the reader into accepting his bad. In the right hands, Johnson believed, the novel could be a transcendent force for moral reform; the reader, sympathizing with the good man, would then go out and behave in the same way. But Fielding, seeing more danger than

Johnson did in the example of a Pamela, believed that with such an instrument in the hands of a bourgeois like Richardson, the paragon will be no paragon but an incentive to wicked behavior. Now, in *Amelia*, he seems to be experimenting with his own version of a female paragon.

A reader of *Amelia* would have noticed the use of a woman's first name as title – Amelia for Clarissa; the much greater use of first-person narrative, as experienced in Richardson's epistolary form but presented as oral recountings (in *Tom Jones* only the Old Man of the Hill and Mrs. Fitzpatrick had served this function). These flashbacks were an equivalent of the letters in *Clarissa* but only shifted the emphasis from the letter to a character talking, the dramatic form Richardson himself had laid claim to in his Postscript, but with the greater unity and coherence Fielding had cited in his preface to Sarah's *Familiar Letters*. His model there had been Ovid's *Heroides*, which, unlike the *Clarissa* letters (or at least Richardson's understanding of them), were specifically love letters.

Fielding the narrator accordingly plays a much smaller part, and his irony and mock-heroic diction are displaced to the speeches and conversations of the characters. The introductory chapters, which Fielding had claimed as a sign of his new form, are omitted, adding to the dramatic effect, which in terms of the reader tends to be immersive, recovering one of the problems that had been raised for him by *Pamela*.

Amelia, the epitome of goodness, represents a remarkable reversal of her author's values. As the central symbol of value she is presented as the object of seducers, and the evil under consideration becomes the violation of sexual fidelity. Indeed Amelia is another Clarissa, whose problem is treated within the marriage relation, and who is ultimately successful in maintaining her integrity: she represents the "virtue rewarded" ending that Fielding, according to Richardson, wished to accord Clarissa. Mrs. Bennet's exclamation after the "fatal Consequence" of the Noble Lord's attack on her virtue, "happy had I been had this been the Period of my Life" (7.7.295), exactly echoes Pamela's "May I never survive, one moment, that fatal one in which I shall forfeit my innocence!" While Mrs. Bennet does not altogether escape Fielding's irony, in this instance her own sad fate is a warning to Amelia.

This is not to say that Fielding has adopted the Puritan ethic. Sexual intemperance in both *Tom Jones* and *Amelia* is a serious offense only when, as Tom tells Nightingale, it injures someone, when it betrays Sophia or Amelia. Booth, driven by passion and seduced by Miss Matthews, is clearly less culpable than Colonel James, who is driven by passion to destroy his friend and an innocent woman; even worse are the Ellisons and Trents, who betray for pay, or the Noble Lord, who betrays for his own amusement (the equivalent of Lord Richly in *The Modern Husband*). Nevertheless, in *Tom Jones* the sexual is only one of many kinds of violation; in *Amelia* it is the central one, with Booth's various misfortunes merely leading toward or away from the potential seduction of Amelia.

Fielding apparently felt that this aspect of *Amelia,* among others, needed justification. Not long after *Amelia*'s publication he wrote defenses of his "favourite Child" in his *Covent-Garden Journal.* One of these essays (although not mentioning *Amelia* by name) discusses the idea of evil in those men "by whom [women] are deceived, corrupted, betrayed, and often brought *to destruction, both of Body and Soul.*"[63] The crime as he outlines it is Satanic – evil hating and wishing to destroy the good. In *Amelia* Satan, the seducer of mankind, becomes more specifically the Noble Lord, the seducer of women. He has all the Satanic trappings, both satiric and melodramatic, of Lovelace. He is "the handsomest and genteelest Person in the World," a consummate actor, who carries out his seductions with masks; he corrupts his victims and then leaves them – corrupting is all that interests him. "What is that Appetite," cries Mrs. Bennet, one of his victims, "which must have Novelty and Resistance for its provocatives, and which is delighted with us no longer than while we may be considered in the light of Enemies?" (7.9.303).

If in his earlier work Fielding tried to establish some perspective on sexual evil, opposing the trivial evil of Pamela's situation to the real evil in ordinary social relationships, in *Amelia* he accepts the assumption of sexual evil, but since sexual evil is no laughing matter, the seduction must receive the overtones of Juvenalian indignation and melodramatic complaint. The most remarkable fact about Fielding's solution to the Richardsonian challenge is the alternation of satiric and satiro-melodramatic scenes with visions of the good which are idealized and sentimentalized. A scene in Fielding's best satiric manner will be followed by a depiction of goodness painted in sharply contrasted colors. While Fielding leaves the reader to react to the satiric exposure, in the sentimental scenes he lets his characters do the reacting: Booth "stopped, and a torrent of tears gushed from his Eyes – such Tears as are apt to flow from a truly noble Heart at the hearing of anything surprisingly great and glorious" (2.1.67). Virtuous behavior is also as stylized as the grotesque wambling of satiric characters: fearful for the safety of her son, Amelia "staggered toward him as fast as she could, all pale and breathless, and scarce able to support her tottering Limbs" (4.7.181).

Smollett

Besides Richardson, the only novelist that challenged Fielding was the Scotsman, Tobias Smollett, who had published *Roderick Random* at the beginning of 1748, between *Joseph Andrews* and *Tom Jones.* Shortly after the publication of *Amelia* Smollett (or someone close to him) published a satire called *Habbakkuk Hilding* (1752) which accuses Fielding of having stolen Partridge from Strap and Miss Matthews from Miss Williams in

Roderick Random.[64] The resemblance between Partridge and Strap was probably coincidental, cowardice being a characteristic of the stock fictional
servant which either writer might have obtained independently from
Sancho Panza. But Miss Matthews is surprisingly like Miss Williams in character and utterance; the theme of seduction and the emotionalism of her
rhetoric, indeed the alternation or merger of satire with melodrama and
sentiment, could have been learned from Smollett's practice in *Roderick
Random. Amelia* as a whole is a departure for Fielding that might draw attention to similarities in *Peregrine Pickle* (Feb. 1751). It is safe to say that once
the two novelists became aware of each other as the chief practitioners of
the comic novel, strange parallels began to occur.

In the long run, Smollett owed more obvious debts to Fielding than the
other way around: there are suggestive echoes of *Joseph Andrews* in *Roderick
Random*, the opening of *Ferdinand Count Fathom* (1753) appears to derive
from *Jonathan Wild*, and the idea of *Sir Launcelot Greaves* (1760–1) is perhaps
related to *Don Quixote in England* and Fielding's other mediating versions
of the Cervantean hero.

But characteristic of each author, Smollett's Miss Williams is pure victim
and her storyline follows a singleminded intensification of physical abuse,
while every word and act of Miss Matthews is fitted into a character and a
plot, into a network of past and future actions, as well, of course, as a classical analogy in the story of Dido and Aeneas.

A more interesting and profound parallel occurs in *Peregrine Pickle*, which
followed *Tom Jones* by two years. What had set apart *Roderick Random* from
Joseph Andrews was its first-person narrative, which in effect created a
Richardsonian version of the picaresque, applying the Richardsonian sensibility to a picaro. Now in *Pickle* Smollett abruptly adopts the third-person
narrator, and with it assessment, distancing, and a more discursive effect,
all emulating Fielding's more successful example.

Pickle also follows *Tom Jones* by beginning with the period before the hero
actually makes his appearance and by presenting at great length the relatives and neighbors who are influences on the hero's character. Both novels
open at a time before the birth, or at least the sentience, of their heroes.
In *Tom Jones* it takes two books or 23 chapters for Tom to make his appearance, during which time we get to know the Allworthys, the Blifils, the
Partridges, and the gossipy Somersetshire community in general. In *Pickle*
it takes 11 chapters to bring Peregrine on stage (whereas Roderick Random
was in charge by chapter 2). There is no earlier English novel in which the
appearance of the hero is so long delayed, and it does not happen again
until *Tristram Shandy*, where the idea of late entry is pursued with a
vengeance, and Tristram does not emerge as an actor until the seventh
volume.

On the other hand, in *Peregrine Pickle*, Smollett establishes a precedent
for the alternation of satiric and sentimental scenes. His villains even tend

to weep when confronted by the goodness they are in the process of destroying. Peregrine, when he attempts to ravish Emilia, finds "the tears gushing from his eyes," which recalls his earlier attempt on Amanda, when "the tears ran down his cheeks."

Public and private life

In *Tom Jones* Fielding had responded to the domestic relations of the patriarchal family in *Clarissa*; both novels were about courtship and enforced marriages. One innovation of *Amelia* is that it shows people *after* marriage, instead of in courtship. But Fielding begins with Booth and Miss Matthews, an unmarried couple, has them recall their different past histories – one a complicated courtship and idealized marriage, the other a disastrous seduction and non-marriage – and then commit adultery. With marriage comes the new, darker subject: not promiscuity as in *Tom Jones* but adultery. The former, as Robert Alter has noted, involves "an individual's moral responsibilities *to himself*," the latter "the individual's responsibilities *to others and to society*," which destroy the basic unity of the family.[65]

In terms of his own experience of a family, from *Joseph Andrews* and *Tom Jones* to *Amelia*, Fielding progresses from the search for a father, to the construction of a family (mother and father, as well as others), to the merger of son and father in a married protagonist in a plot about the reconstruction of a disintegrating family. He chooses a conjugal rather than a patriarchal family for various reasons. For one, as magistrate and public man, he wants to envisage the state not as a patriarchal tyranny but as a balanced, mixed government, one constantly threatened by interlopers with money and power. He begins *Amelia* with the parallel of the Ancient Constitution and the Body Politic and the Family.

The significant fact at the time Fielding wrote *Amelia* was, of course, his profession, and this goes far toward explaining his position in the novel. If in *Tom Jones* he assumed the role of an advocate, a defense attorney, here he is a stern and realistic magistrate. Part of his realism is the pragmatic demand, if society is to be held together, for stringent laws upheld by a strong and efficient police force on the one hand, and for belief in the Christian religion on the other, especially its system of rewards and punishments. The public Fielding is now responding to his duty (the brutal experience) as a magistrate, a member of the criminal courts, and of the politics that placed him there (he is a political follower of Bedford, Richmond, and Lyttelton).

In his dedication to Ralph Allen Fielding says that he is going "to expose some of the most glaring Evils, as well public as private, which at present infect the Country"; that the satire will be general, not personal. Yet, as Fielding adds, the evils are "as well public as private." In *Amelia* he presents the legalism of the magistrate who wrote the *Enquiry* but, at the same time, retains the search after meaning of *Tom Jones*, though in a divided world of private (in which he still acts as advocate) and public (on which the magistrate passes strict judgment).

The literary form on which Fielding draws is the Juvenalian satire in which the evil men are entrenched and the good man is isolated. It is centered in London and recalls in many respects Juvenal's "Rome" (*Satire III*), depicting an un-Roman Rome where money now controls preferment, justice, and of course chastity and honor. It begins with Booth in a version of the story Umbricius tells of the innocent man who stands up to hoodlums, is beaten up, and subsequently committed to jail for assault, and ends with Booth and Amelia retiring, like Umbricius, to a house in the country.[66] But what Fielding also takes from Juvenal is the situation of a degraded patronage (degraded from the ideal of the Augustan Age) in which the patron and his client interact in a symbiotic relationship of knave and fool.[67] Booth is a neat modernization of the Juvenalian "client": raised as a gentleman, he may not become a tradesman, cannot make a living as a farmer or as a half-pay lieutenant, and thus is trapped in a social situation in which he is utterly dependent on the men in power (Juvenal's patrons). On all sides are the fools who have compromised themselves, men such as Trent, who tells Booth: "if you have no other Pretensions than your Merit, I can assure you would fail, if it was possible you could have ten times more Merit than you have" (10.7.441). Trent has sold the favors of his own wife (like Mr. Modern of *The Modern Husband*) and suggests to Booth (parallel to Bellamant) that he do the same. Money, lust, and sheer restless vice are the motive forces of this world – from Sister Betty's greed to Colonel James's passion and the Noble Lord's sinister destructiveness. The Trents and the Booths can either pander to Noble Lords or starve and suffer for their virtue.

Evil in the Juvenalian world is pervasive. *Amelia* makes monotonously regular all the isolated evils of the earlier books: whenever a good sergeant appears there is bound to be a 15-year-old colonel to countermand his wise order; if a man does a good deed, he will certainly be thrown into prison by the police. Every person to whom one turns is prepared to betray him or her, and whenever she leaves home a sister is bound to forge a will and take the family fortune herself. Friends are potential corruptors of one's wife, philosophers are sharpers, and religious pretenders are pickpockets.

The good are relentlessly persecuted and appear to be in a dwindling minority. But a few good people have become *very* good: as Booth says of that paragon Sergeant Atkinson ("the Tears bursting from his Eyes"), "I scarce ever heard of so much Goodness" (5.4.206). The acts of young Atkinson are unambiguously good: while Tom Jones was caught poaching and would not implicate his confederate, Atkinson is caught restoring baby birds to their nest and accepts punishment for attempting to steal them rather than implicate the boy who did steal them (5.3.201).

In the scenes with which the novel opens a series of Fielding's profession-performance structures convey the anatomy of a prison (1.4). There is the girl with "great Innocence in her Countenance" who damns Booth's eyes and discharges "a Volley of Words, every one of which was too indecent to be repeated"; there is the innocent-looking girl who is held as a dangerous criminal on the word of her father-in-law; and there is the Methodist who says that crimes do not jeopardize the saved and proceeds to pick Booth's pocket.

The aspect of *Amelia* that is based on Juvenalian conventions is, one assumes, Fielding's literary equivalent of the legal discourse of the *Enquiry*. The anatomy of a prison is as much exposé as satire. Even Fielding's usual contrasts of appearance and reality, as in the innocent-looking girl who damns Booth's eyes, are simply reported. The footnote that explains the technicality by which perjurors may escape punishment under English law is symptomatic. The whole has the weary tone of the magistrate who has seen much injustice and suffering and must tell somebody about it. Fielding the public man has emerged and is saying: Now, at once, we must change certain laws.

These incidents, however, which are experienced by Booth as he tours the prison, prepare the reader for the entrance of Miss Matthews (1.6). She is clearly not what she appears to be. She looks innocent but has just attempted to kill an ex-lover. This crime was one of passion, not calculation. "Indeed sir," she says, "one subornation of Perjury would sit heavier on my Conscience than twenty such Murders as I am guilty of" (1.10.64). And yet the reader follows her as she carefully exploits Booth's doctrine of passions as the only human motivation, playing upon his weaknesses until eventually she seduces him.

The climax of the first third of the novel is, as it was in *Tom Jones*, a betrayal – Amelia's by Booth and Miss Matthews. Everything leading up to it has, once again, been presented to explain Booth's action. As in Tom's betrayal of Sophia with Molly, Fielding explains:

> Let the Reader set before his Eyes a fine young Woman, in a manner a first Love, conferring Obligations and using every Art to soften, to allure, to win, and to enflame; let him consider the Time and Place; let him remember that Mr. *Booth* was a young Fellow, in the highest Vigor of Life; and lastly, let him add one single Circumstance, that the Parties were alone together; and then if he will not acquit the Defendant, he must be convicted; for I have nothing more to say in his Defence. (4.1.154)

When Fielding precedes this recital with an obvious reference to Booth's own self-justification, that "Fortune seemed to have used her utmost Endeavors to ensnare poor *Booth*'s Constancy," he is condemning Booth's rationalization but not quite condemning his action. As with Betty the chambermaid and with Tom, Booth falls from a combination of circumstances, some internal and some external, including his persistent thoughts of Amelia combined with her inaccessibility. Indeed, Fielding virtually duplicates Tom's situation: Booth meets Miss Matthews, an old flame who is still in love with him, although he has married Amelia, the only woman he really loves. Miss Matthews feeds him rack punch, gets him to talk about and think about his absent Amelia, and at length he goes to bed with her. In both cases the narrator is at pains to explain the hero's seeming infidelity, including many reasons clustered around the physiological center, based on the hydraulic model. In Booth's case the hydraulic system is related to his theory of the predominant passion, excess corrected by a balance (Shaftesbury's harmonious order). The reader is not allowed to forget that, like Tom Jones, he "probably thought one Woman better than none"; that his thoughts are on Amelia while he sleeps with Miss Matthews; and that this is a casual affair, and Booth really loves Amelia.

Miss Matthews' conduct is also explicable in terms of causality: her recent disappointment in the man she loved; the meeting with Booth, who was her first and perhaps continuing love; the talk about love and Amelia, her retelling of her own story, and the details of love that she elicits from Booth to inflame him. All of these do their work on her as well.

In short, Fielding emphasizes the relationship between character and conduct at least as much in *Amelia* as in *Tom Jones*. But he is dealing here with two kinds of experience, more widely separated than they were in *Tom Jones*. Miss Matthews is introduced as the climax of a series of profession-performance contrasts, but her own case is much too complex to fit into this shorthand form. Since we are not led to conclude that Robinson and the rest are also, if we could know them, similarly complex, we tend to accept both the caricatures and the character study as true but unrelated facts, one concerning a general public theme, the other a private. The two areas again come into conflict as Booth and Miss Matthews tell their stories.

These narratives retain Fielding's action-commentator form with which we are now well acquainted, but in each case it is the listener who acts as commentator correcting the reader's possible misapprehensions about the speaker and his story. Booth smiles at Miss Matthews' excesses, Miss Matthews gives the woman's view on Booth's errors of interpretation, and occasionally Fielding himself intervenes. The tone of Miss Matthews' narrative tends to make the reader take it (as she offers it) as an attack on vice, in this case on the seducer Hebbers. The melodramatic style corresponds to Hebbers' actions as the sentimental style does to Amelia's. But, as the commentary of the listener and her own unconscious slips demonstrate, Miss Matthews is in fact not satirizing but producing bitter personal reminiscence, and her story is a scheme for seducing Booth. The reader is left with the impression that Fielding wants her story to do two things – present a lesson *and* depict Miss Matthews. Because these are so far apart, one very general and the other very particular, the reader is never sure to what extent she represents moral truth and to what extent psychological.

Much more than in any of Fielding's earlier works two kinds of writing exist side by side, the satiric incidents of Justice Thrasher and the prison and the stories of Miss Matthews and Booth, merging at times as in the story of Hebbers. The treatment of setting and minor characters is satiric in a way that goes back to the farces, while the main characters are treated as private lives and searched for motive and character, as in *Tom Jones.* Some of the later episodes, especially concerning Mrs. Bennet (whose narrative is less a parody and therefore more convincing than Miss Matthews'), show a distinct advance in subtlety and penetration.[68] Public evil (from Thrasher to the Noble Lord) becomes much easier to see and private character is even more difficult to judge. The old pre-*Tom Jones* system of judging by a single action (conduct) applies to the public characters, while the private characters are judged by the general sweep of their lives. For the satirically regarded characters Fielding shifts away from motives; indeed, the conventionality or absence of motive is part of his characterization of evil in *Amelia.* In *Joseph Andrews* the squire who "roasts" Adams indicates a momentary plunge into a kind of motiveless evil nowhere else present in that novel; when Blifil's lust for Sophia turns (with the knowledge of how she loathes him) to the sheer desire to make her suffer, he too is approaching the malevolent. In *Amelia,* however, there is the sinister Noble Lord (rendered more sinister by the generic designation), whose villainy is the same as Sempronius' in Addison's *Cato*: "I long to clasp that haughty maid, / And bend her stubborn virtue to my passion; / When I have gone thus far, I'd cast her off" (3.7). Captain Trent, Mrs. Ellison, and even Miss Matthews (once we lose sight of her in the flesh) carry out their evil deeds for pure malice, with selfish motives as only secondary inducements. The emphasis in their actions is no longer on motive or self-deceit or hypocrisy, but on effect – the injustice manifested in imprisoning Booth and other "poor wretches" and freeing the wicked. While the reader could, in *Joseph Andrews,* react with laughter at Parson Trulliber or Mrs. Tow-wouse, here, where the effects of actions are emphasized, he reacts with indignation.

The happy ending is quite different from *Tom Jones's,* where the weakness of Blifil's schemes are evident from the first and the denouement is carefully prepared. The end of *Amelia* is miraculous – or, to use Battestin's word, providential (a word that here, in *Amelia,* finally seems justified): Robinson thinks he is dying and confesses at exactly the right time and place so that the one person who can understand and utilize his confession is present. Colonel James' decision to give up his pursuit of

Amelia is almost as providential. But the happy ending, far from having any effect at the public level, is only in terms of Amelia and Booth. As George Sherburn wrote, "Obviously, if the fears of political and social degeneracy were not to be justified, what was really needed was the conversion, not of Booth, but of some noble lord, who acting from pure desire to secure an able officer for the guards would get the long-coveted commission for Booth."[69] The society remains as corrupt at the end as at the beginning.

The case of Colonel James is rendered particularly interesting by the ending. More than anyone else James effectively bridges the two areas and the two plots. He begins as an example of character opposed to conduct, who does good deeds for Booth but then, under certain circumstances, tries to ruin him and seduce his wife. The evil act reveals the motive that informed the good act and thus renders it less good. Yet at the end James goes unpunished, like Tom at the end of *Tom Jones*. As part of the public action, his being accepted is ironic, a parody *komos* as the Booths and Jameses eat dinner together; the point is pessimistic and Juvenalian. But as part of the private action, it suggests that James too is enough of a mixed case that his few bad acts (the reasons for which have been made clear) do not outweigh his acts of friendship, that though a weak, passion-driven man (and his friendship is only one of those passions), he has always in some sense, like Black George, loved the man he attempted to betray.

The two plots function most effectively as a statement of Fielding's awareness, in the 1750s, of the discontinuity between public and private areas of experience, or of the importance of a personal, as opposed to a social, solution.

Classical and Christian models

Fielding goes to some length to call upon a classical model. The novel begins with a parody of "arma virumque," the opening of the *Aeneid*, and draws attention to the parallel in *The Covent-Garden Journal* no. 8 (Jan. 28, 1752, 65) where he calls it the "noble Model" for his novel.[70] But this also draws further attention to the difference between *Amelia* and the earlier novels. In the earlier novels the epic story, the mystery of religion, was demystified or secularized. Joseph and Tom were the contemporary reality under the biblical Joseph or Adam, the Homeric Telemachus, and even the contemporary myth of the Young Pretender. The Virgilian parallels in *Amelia* are used to elevate the domestic (marriage) plot and to connect it with public issues of a degenerating society and nation. Much of the sense of hyperbole and hype in the diction of the characters and, from time to time, of the narrator of *Amelia* comes from this attempt to "redeem banality through art," which also here becomes, reversing the whole procedure of the earlier novels, as if acceding to Richardson's wishes, redeeming *life* through *religion*. The *Aeneid* was, of course, an appropriate epic for Fielding's purpose because it was interpreted as a proto-Christian poem. But also, given the downside associations of Augustan Rome, the parallels in *Amelia* might suggest to Fielding and his readers Christians trapped in the *un*Christian society of an imperial, Juvenalian Rome. As Dr. Harrison puts it: If British society is corrupt, "I think it is high Time to amend it. Or else it is easy to foresee that *Roman* and *British* Liberty will have the same Fate; for Corruption in the Body Politic as naturally tends to dissolution as in the Natural Body" (11.2.460).

The story of Dido and Aeneas (book IV) was the crux in the *Aeneid*, the great epic of duty, where love and duty collide and duty wins, where private experience is subordinated to public. A form of *pietas* remains to inform the civic ideal, but beginning with the classical context, following the *arma virumque* opening with a discussion of Virgil's *Fatum* as Booth's "Fortune," Fielding replaces Dido, the pagan Fanny Matthews, with the Christian Amelia and the Christian virtue of *caritas*.[71]

Amelia is about the Christian religion, education, and the necessity of belief on the one hand; about a strong and honest judiciary and police force on the other. In the *Enquiry* and the other legal tracts of 1751 and later in *The Covent-Garden Journal* Fielding shows that to keep order in a disintegrating society religion is as essential as the law; in *A Charge to the Grand Jury* he draws attention to the statutes against irreligious writings. Fielding begins in *Amelia* an argument he carries on in *The Covent-Garden Journal* against deist tracts as perhaps having had some validity for the few in the 1730s but now pernicious; though now largely forgotten, they must be corrected with sincere religious belief. He makes his hero a deist – first a critical deist, but also in the freedom of his actions (sexual with Miss Matthews, financial with James and others), an ethical deist, who believes in a world governed by chance; and at the end he converts him with a reading of Barrow's sermons. Square's conversion was in the face of death; Booth's is less interested or pragmatic but also much less probable.

Paradoxically, in this novel in which the reader is asked to admire the emotional displays of Amelia and Booth, the message is that feeling allowed to go unchecked by religion – or some external restraint (laws and social custom obviously should but do not work) – will lead for Booth to disaster and for James to the commission of evil deeds.

Thus Booth praises Bob James for his good nature in spite of his atheism; and we can attribute no other motive than good nature to James's friendship for Booth, his loans to him, and his sitting up with him during his illness. For these scenes take place before he becomes aware of Amelia's charms; and so he is no hypocritical Blifil – his motive is real charity and friendship. But his passion for Amelia, when it comes, shows us what good nature or charity unguided by religious precept can come to: charity turns into lust, and nothing is allowed to stand in its way. Only a matter of degree separates Tom's betrayal of Sophia with Molly or Jenny Waters from James's attempt to betray Booth by seducing Amelia. It is strange and salutary to see this sort of awareness on Fielding's part. Booth himself represents the other possibility: good nature without prudence, which comes to be defined by Amelia and Harrison as something filled in by religion. Without "religion" (which means belief in an immanent God and the Bible) one's actions, however virtuously inspired, are not good – or at least trustworthy – guides as to one's conduct. A final mention of rewards and punishments comes from Dr. Harrison, the grim successor to Parson Adams: He believes that religion is useful *because* it "applies immediately to the strongest of these Passions, Hope and Fear, chusing rather to rely on its Rewards and Punishments, than on that native Beauty of Virtue" advocated by the deists and Shaftesbury (12.5.511–12).

Fielding has shifted his emphasis from the value of feeling (now embodied in the weathercock James) to the value of prudence – but even prudence is no longer common sense as it was in *Tom Jones*; it is specifically the guidance of religion. Tom found wisdom by gradually experiencing the fruits of imprudence; Booth's conversion is a literal one, attained (precisely as in *Pamela*) by reading a text.

Among other things, *Amelia* (as well as the *Enquiry* and then *The Covent-Garden Journal*) shows Fielding performing an act of conversion or of refashioning. While not ruling out the possibility of a "conversion" like Booth's (perhaps down to the specifics of reading Isaac Barrow), I see deism and orthodoxy as coexisting for Fielding on different levels of belief; but, for both personal and professional reasons, orthodoxy gained the final ascendancy. Even then one can imagine the aging, ailing Fielding still joking while the official voice proclaimed whatever was necessary to maintain order. In *Amelia*, as in *The Covent-Garden Journal*, the reversal of his position on Shaftesburian ridicule of gravity is evident; and yet: Booth is converted in prison by reading Barrow's sermons on the Apostle's Creed (vol. 2 of the *Works*). If this had been in a work of Fielding earlier than *Amelia* I would have thought it was the author's little joke to suggest that Booth could have applied himself in prison to these dense and endless sermons let alone have been converted by them to Christianity. *Anything*, the implication would have been, would have converted Booth at that moment.

Autobiography

Fielding expresses his "conversion" in *Amelia* by placing its action in 1733, when he was in his rakish prime, by making its hero Billy Booth a deist or freethinker, and giving him Fielding's own physical description: his nose, his learning in the classics, his love of snuff, and also of gaming, his friends and physicians (who are named). From specifics of his work as magistrate to mentions of his Universal Register Office and translation of Lucian to descriptions of debtors' prisons and sponging houses, *Amelia* can be regarded as another very personal work. In this case the aim is not justification but the exorcism in the deist Booth of the Fielding of the 1730s, of "the dreadful Idea of having entailed Beggary on my *Amelia* and her Posterity" (9.4.368), and with it the correcting of these facts with a happy ending in which she survives.

The heroine is plainly based on his wife Charlotte and their courtship is placed in Salisbury and, married, they live in London, but he gives her someone closer to his father than himself as lover and husband, and he gives her the surname of his closest friend James Harris. He gives Booth his father's profession, the army, not his own; and not only his father's profession and exploits, but his courtship of Sarah Gould and the articles of their marriage settlement; the farming that follows reduction to half pay; and the episode when he was cheated at cards. Battestin optimistically sees this as Fielding's coming to terms with his father (541); by conflating the generations, recalling the parallel acts of his father in the particular context of the family, he can equally be seen as blaming it all on the father, pushing his own situation back to his parentage.

As interesting is the extended family in which the Booths live and its association with Fielding's own household in the 1740s. The idea of a family or household was based on the close relationship of Henry and Sarah, at a time when they lived together – Sarah in the same house as Henry and his mistress, wife-to-be, Mary Daniel, with the memories of Charlotte. One wonders whether Sarah, when she read *Amelia*, made the connection between Edmund and Henry and their second wives.

Tom Jones was concerned with family in the sense that it was about Tom's construction of a family for himself; but *Amelia* is closer to *David Simple*, putting together characters into families and so into larger social units: Booth and Amelia, Atkinson (her half-brother, who also loves her) and Mrs. Bennet (her lookalike and dark alter ego). Sarah's *Final Volume*, which was published the year of Fielding's death, depicts a world closer to the disintegrating one of *Amelia* in which the family is decimated. Reflecting the pessimism of *Amelia*, perhaps of her own experience of Henry's disintegrating family, Sarah dismantles the society that had been accreted in the first part of *David Simple* into the vestige of a family, but without her brother's happy ending.

Battestin is right to draw attention to the strange episode in *Amelia* where Booth suddenly takes off, just as he is about to marry Amelia, to visit his sick sister. In fact, the incident involving Amelia's sister could have been inserted when, in July 1750, Fielding's sister Catherine died, simply because it happened. Fielding seems to have put things into *Amelia* for no other reason than that they happened to him. The real significance of the digression on the death of his sister may be that Booth can only have Amelia once his sister has died, and the trip has momentarily cost him Amelia herself, whose mother has in the meantime agreed to the proposal of another, richer man. Amelia, in turn, can only recover her fortune and rehabiliate Booth once her own sister is discredited and exiled, and Charlotte Cradock had such a sister though the circumstances were different.

The notable issue in *Amelia*, parallel to "Can Tom love Sophia and yet sleep with Molly, Jenny, etc.?" in *Tom Jones*, involves the same question, now "How can Booth love Amelia and sleep with Miss Matthews?" But, though activated by the fall in Newgate, as the novel proceeds other questions arise. Mrs. Bennet/Atkinson speaks of Atkinson's love of her *and* Amelia, asking whether a man can love *another* woman after he has lost the important one or she is unattainable:

> I only hope I have changed the Object: For be assured, there is no greater vulgar Error, than that it is impossible for a Man who loves one Woman, ever to love another. On the contrary, it is certain, that a Man who can love one Woman so well at a Distance, will love another better that is nearer to him. (7.10.306)

Earlier there was talk of bigamy and second marriages. Tom's situation has graduated to Booth's, as Fielding's situation has from marriage to Charlotte to marriage to Mary Daniel, this new, more up-to-date version of Tom-Sophia-Molly. Fielding had not been permitted to forget his second marriage to his maid and its duplication of his father's action (as so many of his transgressions had done). In *Old England*, September 24, 1748, he would have read:

> When erst the *Sire* resided *near* the Fleet,
> In Want of something, like the Son, to eat,
> For Fifty Pounds in Hand, prime Fortune! paid,
> Before the Priest he led his Servant Maid.
> *Curse on the Scoundrel* for the Deed he's done,
> *How I'm disgrac'd!* cried out his *pious* Son.
> . . . Another Way did operate the Curse,
> In it's own Kind; *for better or for worse,*
> The Kitchen Maid is coupl'd with the *'Squire,*
> Who copy'd that for which he curs'd his Sire.
> Just Retribution! for, by Heaven scons'd,
> He makes the *Scoundrel* he himself pronounc'd!
> This Diff'rence only 'twixt the Sire and Son,
> The first had Money but the other none.[72]

Lady Mary simply noted that his "natural Spirits gave him Rapture with his Cookmaid."[73] Lady Louisa Stuart reported Fielding's version:

The maid had few personal charms, but was an excellent creature, devotedly attached to her mistress, and almost broken-hearted for her loss. In the first agonies of his own grief, which approached to frenzy, he found no relief but from weeping along with her; nor solace, when a degree calmer, but in talking to her of the angel they mutually regretted. This made her his habitual confidential associate, and in process of time he began to think he could not give his children a tenderer mother, or secure for himself a more faithful housekeeper.

"At least this was what he told his friends," she concludes.[74] To be noted are the facts that "what he told his friends" corresponded to the explanation he gives for Booth and Miss Matthews and that, combining love and prudence, "he could not give his children a tenderer mother, or secure for himself a more faithful housekeeper," though, of course, we have to recall that this is Lady Mary's witty daughter recounting his story.

Indisputably, Fielding's actions corresponded to a pattern with which we are familiar, in his life and his writing. He cannot control his passions and commits what members of his class considered a transgression and folly; but he corrects the consequences of his passion in an honorable way that few of his peers would have done, by marrying Mary Daniel. He still appears to include both a Malvil and a Merital, a Valentine and a Veromil, within a single frame. And now, in *Amelia*, the question is whether you can love a second person (wife) if you loved a first one better than all else.

There are other complications such as Atkinson's dream in which he dreams that Col. James is about to stab Amelia and, to protect her, he takes James by the throat – and this turns out to be Mrs. Atkinson, his Amelia-substitute and alternative. In order to defend – which may mean also *have* – the woman he really loves he must dispose of her substitute. But then Atkinson is Amelia's half-brother, and in that sense recalls Booth's choice at a crucial moment of his sister over Amelia; which can also be read, as I have said, as his having to kill off his sister before he can marry Amelia.

It should be obvious that the story of bigamy and displaced love is moved from Booth to Atkinson and the sibling situation. Initially Atkinson steals the picture of Amelia, in place of the unreachable woman herself, and he keeps it until he finds Mrs. Bennet, who resembles Amelia in height, general appearance, and voice (at the masquerade she is mistaken for Amelia), and marries her. She has replaced the portrait, which he can then give up. But it is the portrait, with its close "likeness," which, recognized by Robinson, begins the unwinding of the happy denouement.

It is impossible not to recall as well Miss Matthews' seduction by Hebbers, which means in fact her falling in love with him, which followed her sister's wedding. We have recalled the reappearance in Booth's liaison with Miss Matthews of Fielding's materialistic, bodily model in *Tom Jones*, but here, for female characters at least, jealousy is the agent, not displacement. This seems to be Fielding's female version of the male hydraulic model. It is another woman who stimulates the first woman's passion, a mediated desire among the women. The same explains the behavior of Amelia's sister Betty following the advent of Booth and especially his and Amelia's marriage.

Virtue and beauty; morality and aesthetics

The most notorious example of the autobiographical insertion of fact was Amelia's damaged nose. Richardson noted the common "noselessness" of Amelia and Fielding's "first wife"; and Lady Mary Wortley Montagu recalled "a frightful overturn, which destroyed the gristle of her nose."[75] The detail was included because it happened – because it was a part of Fielding's memory of Charlotte which he was not willing to relinquish – and, presumably, because he felt that it embodied something important about her that could not be otherwise expressed (and perhaps something that needed justification, either for him or for her). As it originally appeared in the first edition, the accident is presented as a test of Amelia's moral fiber. It only brings out the best in her, and it does not preclude Booth's love for her.

When the first readers of *Amelia* noticed that Fielding had forgotten to include the detail that a surgeon had repaired Amelia's nose, they had a field day making fun of the slip. Samuel Foote's *Taste* (published in Jan. 1752) showed a noseless bust (of Praxiteles' Venus of Paphos) on its frontispiece which clearly referred to Amelia. In Smollett's *A Faithful Narrative of the base and inhuman Arts that were lately practised upon the Brain of Habbakuk Hilding* (Jan. 15, 1751/2) Hilding (Fielding) is described:

> riding up to a draggle-tail Bunter, who had lost her Nose in the Exercise of her Occupation, he addressed himself to her by the Appelation of the adorable *Amelia*, swore by all the Gods she was the Patern of all earthly Beauty and Perfection; and that he had exhausted his whole Fancy in celebrating her Name – To this Compliment she answered in a snuffling Tone, "Justice, you're a comical Bitch; I wish you would treat me with a Dram this cold Morning." (18)

The idea that the situation was "ridiculous" prompted Fielding to add more and more theory about the "ridiculous" in *The Covent-Garden Journal*, but it also led him in the second edition to insert the successful surgery and the argument that the scar actually increased Amelia's beauty.[76] Mrs. James (who has been called by her husband "tall," "a tall awkward Monster") responds that Amelia is neither tall nor short, in a middle area between the "pretty" and the "fine," as she says, burlesquing Addison's "Pleasures of the Imagination":

"There is such a Thing as a Kind of insipid Medium – a Kind of something that is neither one Thing or another. I know not how to express it more clearly; but when I say such a one is a pretty Woman, a pretty Thing, a pretty Creature, you know very well I mean a little Woman; and when I say such a one is a very fine Woman, a very fine Person of a Woman, to be sure I must mean a tall Woman. Now a woman that is between both, is certainly neither the one nor the other." (11.1.454–5)

Mrs. James' formulation is intended to be negative, but Fielding's response is not. He had already had Col. James, defending Amelia's appearance, describe Booth's nose – "a Nose like the Proboscis of an Elephant," asking: "He handsome?" The reference is Fielding's to his own nose – which, in the absence of a reference to Amelia's makes one wonder if unconsciously there was not an aesthetic dimension to Amelia's disfigurement from the outset which linked it with his own.

The idea of imperfection goes back to Jonathan Wild's "Blemish" that sets him off from the ideal of the great, the flaw that does not invalidate a work of art, the character who is "mixed." The blemish introduces the aesthetic dimension to Mrs. James' critique of Amelia's appearance, which relies on Addison's three terms of Beautiful, Great, and Novel. Amelia's "beauty" falls precisely into the area of the Novel, which Hogarth was redefining in 1752–3 in his *Analysis of Beauty* as the Beautiful. (Both *Tom Jones* and the *Analysis*, works written within four years of each other, are about judgment, true or erroneous, based on experience or hearsay, on common sense or some arcane authority.) Fielding owned a copy and we can assume that he made his corrections to Amelia's nose soon after publication, but it supposes give and take with Hogarth. What he adds – which will not see print until the first collected edition of his works in 1762, but which has to be read in the context of Hogarth's *Analysis* – is Mrs. James' remark that (as well as her neck, "too protuberant for the genteel Size," "her Eyebrows . . . too large") "her Nose, as well proportioned as it is, hath a visible Scar on one Side" (454). And earlier he adds the remark, which is significantly the author's and not Booth's: "I know not whether the little Scar on her Nose did not rather add to than diminish her Beauty" (4.7.184). This is precisely Hogarth's argument, concerning the contingencies without which Beauty cannot exist, that a face which is a perfect oval is more alluring if broken, as by a lock of hair. Hogarth's central claim is for an aesthetics of living as opposed to one of art, of the living woman preferred to the most perfect antique Venus.

In Sophia as well as in Amelia Fielding expressed (in Angela Smallwood's words) his "own image of female virtue";[77] but the figure has to be understood in relation to the Shaftesbury tradition of morality-aesthetics. As Fielding knew, Shaftesbury posited "the absolute opposition of pleasure to virtue." This would have fitted into his idea of Richardson's Pamela, representing institutionalized (religiously orthodox) virtue, to which he responded with a contrary type, first the reality of desire underneath in Shamela, and then an alternative, most fully worked out in Sophia. It also should explain why he never hides Amelia's many amorous interludes with her husband, as well as why Hogarth centers, shortly after, in his *Analysis*, the Venus de' Medici (to whom Fielding had alluded in both *Tom Jones* and *Amelia*) as not only pleasure but wantonness.

For structurally Amelia is not in the Sophia but the Tom position – misread and misrepresented in one way or another by all the characters (except Atkinson, who idolizes her) *and* the reader. The characters, good and bad, including both Booth and Dr. Harrison, see her through "misogynist assumptions," and (as Smallwood notes) "The reader's concern about the unfair treatment of the heroine in *Amelia* is thus much more widely diffused than in *Tom Jones*, and more comprehensive than the concern of any of the characters who surround her" (159). She is, in short, both moral and aesthetic object.

So on the public level Amelia is a love object for all the men; on the personal, a muse for the author, a wife for Booth, a mediator between Booth and the world (the role both Fielding and Hogarth had given their women in the later 1730s–1740s), above all a Charlotte Cradock. In Amelia Fielding conflates beauty, morality, and love. Beginning with Shaftesbury's equation of beauty and virtue, Fielding complicates the relationships. "Beauty" before Amelia makes her appearance is embodied in Newgate, characterized by appearance disguising an unbeautiful (immoral) reality; associated with sexual attraction, seduction, betrayal, jealousy, revenge, and "murder." So, presumably, a false beauty, corrected with Booth's memories of Amelia, anticipating her actual arrival. Initially these seem to be throwbacks to *Joseph Andrews*, satiric structures exposing the reality under appearances or disguises. But with the retelling of his courtship of Amelia, Booth seems to be contextualizing her in a series which includes not only the "very pretty Girl" whose looks do not correspond to her morality but also the two pretty but pathetic young women, leading up to Miss Matthews, whose beauty conceals "murder." These are examples of beauty versus or minus goodness or plus seduction. For Miss Matthews' and Booth's narratives (the latter of Amelia herself) do serve to seduce Booth – and under the protestations of conjugal love reveal misdirected, adulterous desire of the sort Hogarth associates with Beauty in his *Analysis* plates. In plate 1 Venus turns her back on Hercules to dally with Apollo in a romantic, adulterous triangle; in plate 2 a young wife, behind the back of her elderly husband, receives a note from a handsome young man. Both women are defined by the serpentine lines with which they are drawn as beautiful; as he writes in *The Analysis*, they are aesthetic objects of the "pleasure of pursuit" or "the chase."[78]

The libertine metaphor of the chase (common in Fielding's plays) is echoed in the words of Miss Matthews at the masquerade (disguised as a shepherdess) applied to James: "You are a true Sportsman, . . . for your only Pleasure, I believe, lies in the Pursuit." She translates this to mean: "He gets every handsome Woman he can" (10.2.412). Later Captain Trent is described as the Noble Lord's pointer or setter, on the "Scent of Amelia," for whom Amelia is the "Game" (11.3.471).[79] The metaphor came easily to the lips of Fielding's comic rakes. Mondish in *The Universal Gallant* (1734) remarked:

> I was weary of the affair, and she has found out the only way to renew my eagerness [i.e., by making him jealous] – the whole pleasure of life is pursuit:
>
>> Our game though we are eager to embrace,
>> The pleasure's always over with the chase.
>>> (Henley edn., 11:95)

There is a residuum of libertinism in Addison's aesthetics of the Novel or Uncommon (also based on the chase, pursuit, an "insatiable Thirst after Knowledge," and "Curiosity") that informs the outlook of both Hogarth and Fielding.[80]

Though it is Colonel James who most fully embodies the libertine aesthetics in *Amelia*, Booth himself in his own way hunts, tests, and mistreats Amelia. His behavior in book 2, turning his attention to Miss Osborn, telling Amelia he loves another, causing her intense suffering, is rationalized as another Tom Jones situation: he loves her so much he gives her up rather than ruin her (much later we hear the same refrain: "the dreadful Idea of having entailed Beggary on my Amelia and her Posterity"). But this explanation is both obscurely put and incommensurate with the strangeness of his strategy (as compared with Tom's more straightforward one with Sophia). It seems rather a vestigial association of beauty, the aesthetic experience, and the "chase."

In the opening books, where Booth tells the story of Amelia to Miss Matthews, *both* take an erotic pleasure in the sexual "chase" – Booth's of Amelia, Miss Matthews' of Booth. There is a patient Griselda aspect as well, taking its place in the larger plot in a series of tests of Amelia's virtue – threats that are also tests – by the Noble Lord and Colonel James, but also by Booth himself as errors and stupidities and attempts at cover-up for the originating act of adultery with Miss Matthews.

Booth's treatment of Amelia has also to be related to the Noble Lord's behavior to *his* women. Mrs. Atkinson says: " 'Good Heavens! what are these Men! What is this Appetite, which must have Novelty and Resistance for its Provocatives; and which is delighted with us no longer than while we may be considered in the Light of Enemies' " (7.9.303) – words which could apply to Booth's behavior in book 2, to his abrupt departure to his beloved sister without saying a word to Amelia, and, to some degree, throughout.

His fecklessness almost – as if he wanted it to – permits Amelia's dishon-
oring. The old plot of *The Modern Husband* is not only projected in the
Trent plot but is implicit in Booth's obtuseness, which allows the reader to
enjoy the same antithetical games of the chase Booth plays with Amelia in
courtship and then permits to be played by the seducers in London. Fielding, Booth, the reader – all on some level find aesthetic experience in the
erotic possibilities that extend from seeing Amelia, with her scarred nose,
dressed in rags, to wearing a disguise at a masquerade (in fact, it is Mrs.
Atkinson).

All of this evokes the principle of Hogarth's aesthetics. First, with variety,
surprise, and pursuit goes curiosity. But the other side of the coin, in a
tragic rather than comic context, appeared in George Lillo's *Fatal Curiosity*, which Fielding produced at the Little Haymarket in 1736. Young Wilmot
defers the announcement of his return home in favor of the "surprise" and
"astonishment" of his parents and his own "curiosity." His need for
"improv[ing] . . . pleasure by surprise" leads to his murder at the hands of
his parents and their suicides.

Second, contrast – not only Booth's quick turns vis-à-vis Amelia but the
abrupt turns and surprises of character and plot. Contrast is most frequently associated with that puzzling character Dr. Harrison, who one
minute is for and the next against the Booths, having Booth arrested or
freeing him; but also with Mrs. Harris, who agrees one moment to Booth's
proposal and, while he is away with his sister, accepts another suitor – and
apparently turns on Amelia, repudiating her and cutting her out of her
will. These contrasts include the social cuts and snubs of Colonel and Mrs.
James, as well as the quick turnabouts of Miss Matthews. It is only partly
explained by "changes of fortune," "Surprising Accidents."[81]

In *Tom Jones* Fielding put it this way:

> This Vein is no other than that of Contrast, which runs through all the Works
> of the Creation, and may probably have a large Share in constituting in us
> the idea of all *Beauty*, as well natural as artificial: For what *demonstrates the
> Beauty* and Excellence of anything *but its Reverse*? Thus the Beauty of Day, and
> that of Summer, is set off by the Horrors of Night and Winter. And I believe,
> if it was possible for a Man to have seen only the two former, he would have
> a very imperfect Idea of their *Beauty*. (5.1.212, emphasis added)

In *Tom Jones* this included all the foils set off against Sophia and Tom, but
in *Amelia* it is focused only on Amelia and is much more prominent – as
with so much in this novel, eccentrically so. Here it suggests not that something can only be defined by its opposite or negative but that there is a
beauty in sheer contrast. Amelia's virtue – her lovableness, "so amiable and
great a Light" – is *set off by* Booth's "own Unworthiness" (12.2.498).

If the question in *Tom Jones*, and at the outset in *Amelia*, is how can Tom or Booth be judged in terms of character and conduct, by shifting attention from Booth to Amelia – placing, as I have said, Amelia in the Tom Jones position – Fielding sets up a new problem, an aesthetic-moral issue: how to get at her, how to represent her virtue, her beauty, how to win her, how to represent her virtue *after* marriage, how to *relate* her beauty and virtue. And the answer seems to be: deviously, through contraries, through flaws, and ultimately (in the largest sense) through her flawed, erring husband, as well as her would-be seducers, and all of those who fail to understand her virtue-beauty.

The portrait of Amelia, which was Atkinson's surrogate for her, is recognized by Robinson and leads to the fortunate conclusion of the story. This is because of its strong "likeness" which was earlier said to be beyond even Hogarth's ability (3.4.109). Throughout *Amelia* Fielding is saying that he cannot find words to express Amelia but neither can he find graphic analogues. In book 1, chapter 1, he opposes the "Art of Life" to the statue of a Venus; which recalls the very different description of Sophia in *Tom Jones* (4.2.155) by means of the Venus de' Medici and the Hampton Court "Beauties" *and* (for the privileged few) Charlotte herself.[82] Fielding the widower, recently remarried, needs to recreate Charlotte exactly as she was, "nose and all." But the Venuses and "Beauties" return in his hyperbolic discourse of response, expression, gesture, which evokes an aesthetics at odds with Hogarth's – closer to Addison's Great or, later, Burke's Sublime. The two discourses, visual and verbal, join in Robinson's recognition of Amelia's portrait. Elsewhere, however, they jar.

In fact, Fielding expresses Amelia through Booth and Booth's treatment of her. Fielding the magistrate is making a dramatic spectacle of Booth's crimes against Amelia, extending them from betrayal with Miss Matthews back to pre-marital cruelty. He shows that a deist-libertine like himself can be converted and live happily ever after with a fantasized wife who also survives; but Booth, like Wilson and Square and Fielding (if not Tom), leaves behind casualities. In the presentation of Booth Fielding records in lively colors, though indirectly, the unforgiving rigor of the magistrate.

IN THE WAKE OF *AMELIA*

The Covent-Garden Journal

There is no doubt that the *Covent-Garden Journal* was, as Fielding's critics claimed, an advertising medium for his Universal Register Office, for his activities in his court, and for his literary activities of the time. But primarily it drew attention to the Universal Register Office, his business scheme *and* social project for bringing together producers and consumers in one central place, solving a serious problem of communication and balancing the market of sellers and buyers in a utopian scheme; and one where, once again, Fielding stresses, it is a way to save young girls from the country from being led into a life of prostitution ("secured from dangerous Snares").[83] Again, he takes off time to defend *Amelia* and he puffs his "little Book against Murder," *Examples of the Interposition of Providence*, whose aim corresponds to the public aspect of his court and his legal pamphlets.

The public and private strands of *Amelia* are materialized in *The Covent-Garden Journal* in magistrate and moral censor. In many ways the most interesting parts of the *Covent-Garden Journal* were the "Covent-Garden" columns relaying news of Fielding's court, attributed to Fielding's clerk Joshua Brogden but often showing signs of Fielding's hand. The lead essays (as well as the "Court of Censorial Enquiry") are the work of a censor. To begin with, they are on literary subjects and then, intermixed, on general moral issues. The moral issues supplement and correct the legal pragmatism of the *Enquiry*, *Proposal*, and Fielding's other pamphlets; in them he makes it plain that the laws controlling the poor advocated in those pamphlets did not tell the whole story – that the poor are in fact the victims of society, in much the way Hogarth presented the situation in his prints of 1751 that accompanied the *Enquiry*.

Every once in a while the author (probably Fielding *in propria persona*) stops to show his concern with the inadequacies of the existing laws (401, 409–10). The lead essays, however, set out to deal with the subject of literature – bad literature in the old Scriblerian sense. The allegory of a "paper war" is a weak opening for the new journal. The references to his publisher Andrew Millar, David Garrick, and the rest set off a rather silly in-joke about friends, enemies, and his own books – pointing up the advertising aspect of the enterprise and the many directly personal aspects (which his enemies at once noticed). Though he opens the "paper war" as a general subject, soon it turns out to be a defense of *Amelia* from (predictably) malicious attacks. The "ridicule" of *Amelia* leads him to discuss at length – in important essays, both satiric and critical-theoretical – ridicule, humor (and humor characters), and other aspects of satire. And, given his current "official" position on these matters, he must carefully delimit ridicule and, turning upon Shaftesbury's view of ridicule as a test of truth, rehearse once again in essay form the issues of his novel: the Christian religion, prostitution, and adultery.

In no. 10 he identifies his favorite authors (for wit and humor at least) as Lucian, Cervantes, and Swift in that order; and this is a significant retrospect, for we recognize in that order the models for Fielding's works of the 1730s, the 1740s, and now the 1750s.[84] may be turning to Swift as an English equivalent of Juvenal, but the two names he cites are Swift and Lucian, at one point asserting that the best impression a reader can get of

Lucian in Greek is to read Swift in English. He now repudiates Aristophanes and Rabelais as instances of *dulce* over *utile*. Although there is a comic violence in these two lacking in Lucian, the fact remains that the Lucian who was a rationalist and skeptic, suspicious of the supernatural, gods and providence, priestcraft and oracles, was the literary model for his farces of the 1730s. To recover him now in the 1750s, and put the blame on Aristophanes, can only be a way of saying that his own demystifications were, like Lucian's, more interested in comic contrast and juxtaposition (of gods and men, of the dead and alive, of fable and truth) than in subversion of religion and society. He recalls the official position awarded Lucian for his service by Marcus Aurelius.

This reading of Lucian, emphasizing his civic office, must also explain how Fielding misreads Swift. To him at this time Swift represented the ecclesiastical authority of the Dean of St. Patrick's, the Drapier who stood up against England and Walpole's government, a figure not unlike Fielding himself as Bow Street Magistrate, whose views were bold and untrammeled but supported order and orthodoxy; and a satirist who, in the works of those later years, could be interpreted as speaking out in his own dark, disillusioned voice to condemn the corrupt society and offer final alternatives. This had never been Fielding's pose, which was always closer to the cheerful irreverence of Lucian. Fielding always had Swift in his mind, but it was as the master of irony and seldom or never a particular satire or fiction. Swift is another pose utilized to accomplish the particular end he sees himself carrying out – as in the *Examples of the Intervention of Providence* he chooses the voice of the popular preacher.

Fielding either had a copy of Swift's *Tale of a Tub*, which included *The Battle of the Books*, at his elbow; or, what is quite as likely, he knew Swift's works so well that all it took was to decide that Swift was to be his model in this new journal. He begins by adapting Swift's satire on modern writing in the *Tale*, imitating the "Preface" in the essays of nos. 1 and 2 (in 1 he invokes Swift, Pope, and Juvenal by name), followed by the beginning of his "Paper War" based on the *Battle of the Books*. A contemporary critic noticed the allusions to the *Tale* when he wrote that Fielding was using the *Covent-Garden Journal* "as a Barrel thrown out from the Ship of Adminstration to some . . . Whale of the Country Interest," that is, to divert public attention from the blunders of the Pelham ministry.[85] In no. 3 Fielding follows Swift's "Digression on Critics," and in 6 his "Dedication to Prince Posterity." But with nos. 8 and 9, turning to religion in his satire on the heterodox Robin Hood Society, he begins to imitate the *Argument against Abolishing Christianity* and, at one moment, the *Modest Proposal*.[86] He approaches as close as he can to the Swiftean rigor, compression, anger, and intensity, but these are weak, popular versions of Swift that show a slackening of Fielding's own particular kind of writing without finding a substitute in Swift.

One explanation is that he was now ill, overworked, tired, and discouraged (over the reception of *Amelia*, over his magistracy and the apparent decline of society) and it was easy to slip into literary imitations (as he had learned to do with Latin models at Eton). The effect, however (and this may have been intentional), is to muffle, or distance, the moral issues – or even deflect attention from these now disturbing issues to the imitations of known literary works. He seems unwilling to deal as directly as Swift would have done with the fact that the ultimate problem is not the poor but their betters; in fact, he is now treating the old *Beggar's Opera* theme once more but under the disguise of Swift. His imitation is, in fact, of works parallel with his own, whose *saeva indignatio* he draws upon and makes second-hand – not the anti-models of *Hurlothrumbo* and *Pamela* that inspired his best work. In *Joseph Andrews*, where he attacked literary models, he was seeking a form that exceeded or superseded the literary formulae; whereas in the *Covent-Garden Journal* he is using Swift's *Argument* or *Modest Proposal* as a conventional form, a crutch for a message which at best seems more Swift's than Fielding's.[87]

Although he now makes plain his allegiance in Swift's "Battle," Fielding had not always been so clearly an "ancient." In the 1730s the *Grub-Street Journal* attacked him as a modern. To "surprise" an audience with the "new" and "uncommon" is to be a modern. But he wanted to write under the aegis of the Scriblerians and so adapted for himself the name Scriblerus Secundus. The *newness* of *Joseph Andrews* (a form "never before attempted") made Fielding a "modern" in the Scriblerian sense; and although he added Scriblerian parodies to classical and biblical models, these were not, as in *The Battle of the Books* and *The Dunciad*, normative models. In *Amelia*, where the *Aeneid* serves a normative function, indicating the importance of these apparently mundane events, the Scriblerian tests, perhaps discredits, but does not cancel the world of wit, novelty, chase, curiosity, and surprise. In *The Covent-Garden Journal* Fielding simplifies the message of *Amelia* into a contrast of ancient and modern as rigid as the law.

"Religion" he ironically defines in the "modern Glossary" as "A Word of no Meaning; but which serves as a Bugbear to frighten Children with" (38). No. 6, an imitation of Swift's "Dedication to Prince Posterity," takes up the uses to which forgotten books are put: Too great a dissemination (e.g., through use of pastry cooks) of deist tracts is dangerous because these were meant for "the Use and Inspection of the few" but "are by no means proper Food for the Mouths of Babes and Sucklings" (49).[88]

The more free-ranging play of Fielding's mind in the 1730s – in, for example, his Lucianic theatrical pieces – was, indeed, open to censure by the Scriblerians whose name he had appropriated; it *was* the position of the modern rather than the ancient which saw the classical ideal as ill-fitting and inappropriate. Now he exorcises that position, associating it in a new war of Ancients and Moderns with the Moderns:

there are certain Arcana Naturae, in disclosing which the Moderns have made great Progress; now whatever Merit there may be in such denudations of Nature, if I may so express myself, and however exquisite a Relish they may afford to *very* adult Persons of both sexes in their Closets, they are surely too speculative and mysterious for the Contemplation of the Young and Tender, into whose Hands Tarts and Pies are most likely to fall. (50)

I read this passage as a retrospect on his imagination in the 1730s seen from the vantage of the magistrate of the 1750s.

But, as so often with Fielding's particular use of irony (quite unlike Swift's), his repudiation expresses a hard Mandevillian truth: not only that deist tracts are now unread, used by trunk-liners and pastry cooks, but that there was in those days (when Fielding was a deist) a distinction between the thinking few, who were entitled to play around with these skeptical, freethinking ideas, and the public as a whole who *must* be guided and guarded by religion. In the *Enquiry* and the other legal tracts and in the *Covent-Garden Journal* he shows that to keep order in a disintegrating (in literary terms, Juvenalian) society religion is as essential as the law;[89] and in *Amelia* he also shows that this includes the character who is his own surrogate. But the passages in the *Covent-Garden Journal* draw our attention back to the way Fielding felt before he had responsibility for public order, before he saw society as dangerously degenerate, and to the pragmatic function religion has in public life, together with (as in the matter of grieving) in his own private life. And the reference to children (which inevitably recalls Locke on the simplicity of children) exposes, at least to the "few," his realistic appraisal of the public, as his portrait of Booth exposes his realistic appraisal of himself in middle age.[90]

He ends No. 6 with what must now appear the ambiguous conclusion (which also recalls the ambivalence of his model, the "Dedication to Prince Posterity"): "How melancholy a Consideration must it be to a modern Author," because his writings are "liable to so many various Kinds of Destruction," but also, implicitly, because they have such a deleterious effect on the childlike public.

Children

With Fielding's career as magistrate also goes a strange intensification of the fictionality, even fabular quality, of religion. In its most extreme and revealing form, in *Examples of the Interposition of Providence in the Detection and Punishment of Murder* (1752), Fielding literalizes the "interposition of providence" in crimes that are exposed by supernatural means. Where pragmatism ends and belief begins is impossible to say; but the old Fielding connects with the new in his advertisement for this "little Book" in *The Covent-Garden Journal* no. 30 (Apr. 14, 1752):

> No Family ought to be without this Book, and it is most particularly calcu-
> lated for the Use of those Schools, in which Children are taught to read: For
> there is nothing of which Children are more greedy, than Stories of the Trag-
> ical Kind; nor can their tender Minds receive more wholesome Food, than
> that which unites the Idea of Horror with the worst of Crimes, at an Age when
> all their Impressions become in great Measure, a Part of their Nature

– for which he invokes, presumably for his more sophisticated audience, Locke's *Essay on Human Understanding*. It is important that children believe in these divine interpositions. Whether Fielding does himself is irrelevant. Fielding the magistrate does.[91]

We might, for example, ask how we are to take Dr. Harrison's comment in *Amelia* that Hogarth's prints are worth more than *The Whole Duty of Man*. Does he mean this as a comment on how Hogarth's prints (perhaps those of 1751) should be used by the simple childlike readers of such works as his own *Examples of the Interposition of Providence?* or as another embedded joke like Booth's reading of Isaac Barrow, which can be taken two ways and indicates the level or residue of Fielding's comic sense in the 1750s?

A contrast between Fielding and Samuel Johnson is useful. Johnson accepted the orthodox position – a benevolent god, a fallen man (by his own choice), divine redemption – but he worried about God's mercy and justice. His emphasis falls on the terror of the Last Judgment and the sus-picion that he has not fulfilled the promise of his talents and will be damned. Fielding never hints at such a notion. Fielding always looked at orthodox Christianity from the outside; he accepted its morality but not revealed religion except as (in Hume's sense) custom or belief. Both needed to believe, but Johnson did believe and worried about himself within the belief system, while Fielding worried about himself outside it. He functioned within the deist position – and found it expedient for sur-vival to "believe" in rewards and punishments, specifically in the afterlife, but more for other people (the Shaftesburian formula) than for himself.

A subject that naturally preoccupies Fielding the magistrate is prostitution. It is interesting, given what we have said about the aesthetic dimension of *Amelia*, to see what "Beauty" is in the "modern Glossary": "The Qualifica-tion with which Women generally go into Keeping" (35). Again, the irony says that *in this society* beauty only qualifies a woman for whoredom; but also that beauty is of course the basis for sexual attraction; and that beauty inevitably involves this complex of ideas.

In the reports printed in *The Covent-Garden Journal*, while there is no sym-pathy for prostitutes and especially for bawds and pimps, Fielding shows great sympathy for the girl "who seemed younger and less abandoned than the rest," "very pretty, under 17 Years of age, and had been 3 Years by her own Confession upon the Town." These "young, thoughtless, helpless, poor Girls, who are as often betrayed, and even forced into Guilt, as they are bribed and allured into it," are invariably 16 years old (382–93).[92]

Sixteen would have been the age of his daughter Charlotte had she lived (Harriet, his surviving daughter by his wife Charlotte, was nine). In some ways Fielding was frighteningly, willfully transparent.

In the *Covent-Garden Journal* for January 28, 1752, at the "Trial of Amelia" for dulness, Fielding speaks for the defense:

> If you, Mr. Censor, are yourself a Parent, you will view me with Compassion when I declare I am the Father of this poor Girl the prisoner at the Bar; nay, when I go farther, and avow, that of all my Offspring she is my favourite Child. I can truly say that I bestowed a more than ordinary Pains in her Education. (65)

Because, like his favorite daughter, *Amelia* had "died."[93]

The metaphor of the book as Fielding's offspring began in *Tom Jones*. In the introduction to book 11, where he brought up again the old business of the slanderer of a man's writings, equating character, book, and author, he added the circumstance that "we consider a Book as the Author's offspring, and indeed as the Child of his Brain":

> The Reader who hath suffered his Muse to continue hitherto in a Virgin State, can have but a very inadequate Idea of this Kind of paternal Fondness. To such we may parody the tender Exclamation of *Macduff. Alas! Thou hast written no Book.* (11.1.568–9)

He pursued the metaphor, describing "the Uneasiness with which the big [pregnant] Muse bears about the Burden, the painful labour with which she produces," but left the book with its father, noting "the Care, the Fondness, with which the tender Father nourishes his favourite, till it be brought to Maturity, and produced into the World." "These Children may most truly be called the Riches of their Father; and many of them have with true filial Piety fed their Parent in his old Age." (At a later point in *Tom Jones* he writes that he "regard[s] all the Personages of this History in the Light of my children" [16.6]).

The origin at this point in his career is the sexual, as in his reference in the 1748 letter to Richardson to his pursual of Mrs. Muse. He depicts writing as a sexual act between the male author and his female muse; but he also stresses his "paternal Fondness" for the product. Once the muse has given birth to the child/book, he, the father, cares for her and, as he notes in the *Covent-Garden Journal*, educates her and teaches her the rules (of Homer and Virgil). *Amelia* is, again, like *Tom Jones* (and its protagonist): "I do not think my Child is entirely free from Faults. I know nothing human that is so; but surely she doth not deserve the Rancour with which she hath been treated by the Public." From *Tom Jones* to *Amelia*, however, Fielding has progressed from comedy to pathos. Defending "this poor Girl the Prisoner at the Bar . . . my favourite Child," he replaces "Defense" with "a Compromise": "I do, therefore, solemnly declare to you, Mr. Censor, that I will trouble the World no more with any Children of mine by the same Muse." (He did, however, produce two more children by Mary Daniel, one in December 1752, the other in April 1754.)

Then, though Fielding has this "Declaration . . . received with a loud Huzza," he ends (recalling the dead children of "Affliction" and the *Journey*) with Amelia "delivered to her Parent, and a Scene of great Tenderness passed between them." The shifts of tone, the protective irony of the huzzas, do not completely cover the self-exposure. "Child" is what Dr. Harrison calls Amelia; Amelia is consistently Booth's "Child," and *Amelia* is Fielding's own "Child." His child Charlotte was, of course, named after his wife; Harriet, his favorite surviving daughter, was given a version of his own name (which he had given earlier to Harriot Moneywood, Harry Luckless's lover in *The Author's Farce*, and to Harriet Hearty, who saved Mr. Wilson and married him, in *Joseph Andrews*). He named his daughter by Mary Daniel, Sophia, and their son William, called Billy, a name later given to Booth.

Elizabeth Canning

In January 1753 Fielding became involved in the case of Elizabeth Canning, one of the most celebrated criminal cases of the century. He was about to leave for a vacation in the country when Canning's solicitor appeared: What caused him to stop and immediately hear the case? Canning, a young servant girl of "upwards of eighteen years of age, pitted with the small pox, a high forehead, fresh coloured, light eyes and eye brows, dark hair, about five feet [tall],"[94] had left her master's house to dine with an uncle and aunt, and failed to return. Twenty-eight days later she appeared at her mother's house, weak and emaciated. The story she offered to explain her absence was that on her way back to her master's house that evening she had been abducted by men who robbed and beat her and took her to a bawd's house, intending to sell her into prostitution. She refused the bawd's blandishments and was locked in an attic room and fed nothing but bread and water until, 28 days later, she escaped through a window. Her outraged master and his neighbors made her lead them back to the house, where she identified the women and the room where she was confined. There were many inconsistencies in her account of the house and women, as later noted, and many of the details which supported her identification of the house were garnered from others (one of her neighbors had pointed her toward a known bawdy house, run by Mary Squires and Susannah

Wells). Another difficulty in Canning's story was that more than one witness testified that the woman she accused, the gypsy Mary Squires, was 150 miles away on the day in question.

As it happened, on February 6 Canning's solicitor Mr. Salt went to Justice Fielding for advice on how to proceed with the case. As Fielding wrote, "besides those Importunities [of Salt], some Curiosity, occasioned by the extraordinary Nature of the Case, and a great Compassion for the dreadful Condition of the Girl, as it was represented to me by Mr. *Salt*" led him to put off his vacation and hear the case immediately (298).

He interrogated Canning and also Virtue Hall, a servant girl in Squires' house, who at length corroborated Canning's story. The case went to trial, the two women, Squires and Wells, were found guilty, and Squires was sentenced to death. But Canning was in fact a young woman, however plausible (and everyone agreed on how convincing her testimony was), who had made up the whole story in order to cover for some other story which she presumably did not want her family to hear – and which has not to this day emerged. Squires and Wells were pardoned, and in a second trial, a year later, Canning was found guilty of perjury and transported.

A contemporary print (plate 22) shows Canning on the left and Squires on the right of a magic circle in which stand the three "conjurors" who contest the contradictory stories. Fielding is on the left, closest to his authority, Canning; Sir Crisp Gascoyne, the Lord Mayor of London who presided at the first trial and questioned the truth of Canning's story following it, is in the middle; and Sir John Hill, the journalist who took Squire's side and accused Fielding of bullying the witnesses into giving false evidence, is on the right, closest to Squires.

The attacks on Canning's credibility following the first trial, and in particular the personal attacks by Sir John Hill, led Fielding to dash off a reply, *A Clear State of the Case of Elizabeth Canning*. Fielding seems to have been visualizing another novel along the lines of *Amelia*. As he wrote in the *Clear State*, "there is something within myself which rouses me to the Protection of injured Innocence" from such "wild beasts" as the men who abducted her and the women who tried to prostitute her; and to "the defence of a poor little Girl whom the many have already condemned" (286) – by which he means have disbelieved her story.[95] His aim in writing the pamphlet was "to prevent them [the public, reading the accusers of Canning] from forming a very rash, and, possibly, a very unjust Judgment" (286). The attraction is obvious: Here is the plot of *Tom Jones* and, with the disbelieved hero feminized, of *Amelia* – also the plot projected by the first plate of Hogarth's *Harlot's Progress* and his source, the story of Ann Bond, lured by Mother Needham and raped by Colonel Charteris. As Malvin Zirker and others have noted, Fielding was particularly susceptible to certain types – "figures of pathos" like the 16-year-old prostitutes he pitied, and the daughters of poor clergymen (who often ended in prostitution).[96] And Fielding had spent his career writing such fictions.

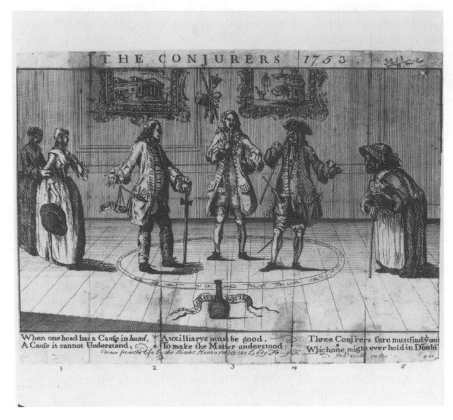

Plate 22   Unknown artist, *The Conjurers, 1753*, etching, 1753, courtesy of the Lewis Walpole Library, Yale University.

One of the *Covent-Garden* reports just a year earlier (Jan. 24, 1752) could have been a rehearsal for Canning's story:

> Among the women taken at this House, was one Mary Parkington, a very beautiful Girl of sixteen Years of Age, who, in her Examination said, That she was the Daughter of one Parkington a Hatter, in the Parish of St. Catharine's; that her Father dying, her Mother married again. . . . about three Weeks ago she was seduced by a young sea-Officer, who left her within a Day or two; that being afraid and ashamed to go Home to her Mother, and having no Money, she was decoyed by a Woman to this Bawdy-House, where she was furnished with Clothes; for which she gave a Note for Five Pounds; that she was there prostituted to several Men for Hire; and all the Money, except a few Shillings, she was obliged to pay over to the Mistress of the House . . . [and she] was kept a Prisoner there, against her Will and Consent, and the Doors always locked, to keep her and other Women within the said House. (400–1)

Thus when Fielding described Elizabeth Canning

> before Noblemen, and Magistrates, and Judges, Persons who must have inspired a Girl of this kind with the highest Awe. Before all these she went through her Evidence without Hesitation, Confusion, Trembling, Change of Countenance, or other apparent Emotion. As such a behaviour could proceed only from the highest Impudence, or most perfect Innocence, so it seemed clearly to arise from the latter, as it was accompanied with such a Shew of Decency, Modesty, and Simplicity. (294)

he may have had overly impressed upon his memory the case of Mary Parkington.

He was also perhaps overly proud of his powers of interrogation and his ability to unravel the most complicated circumstantial narrative. He does not, he admits, "pretend to Infallibility," but "I can at the same time with Truth declare, that I have never spared any Pains in endeavouring to detect Falsehood and Perjury, and have had some very notable Success that Way" (310). He was able to lead (if not, as some claimed, coerce) Virtue Hall, the one witness whose testimony corroborated Canning's and so led to the conviction of the women.

His error was to conclude "that the truth lay with an utterly compelling witness who told an improbable story"[97]: which offers the irony that Fielding had *not* believed the story of Richardson's Pamela. In this case, 13 years later he overthrew the logic of his pre-*Amelia* fiction, which was based precisely on the belief that the testimony of the most plausible witness must be tested against the probability of a circumstantial narrative, as in the case of Pamela.

The most balanced response to Fielding's pamphlet was by Allan Ramsay, the young painter, who responded to Hogarth's *Analysis of Beauty* with an equally balanced criticism.[98] He writes that "perhaps there are none of his [Fielding's] performances that more discover the ingenuity of the man of wit, the distinctness of the lawyer, or the politeness and candour of the gentleman" than the Canning pamphlet; however, he follows this with a critique worthy of Fielding himself of the improbabilities of this contemporary Pamela.

RETIREMENT AND DEATH

Preparations for retirement

The first edition of *Jonathan Wild* was written in the spirit of Fielding's journalistic writings; its original intention was in general political ("those who employ Hands for their own Use only ... *Conquerors, absolute Princes, Prime Ministers,* and *Prigs*" – 1.14.48). Whatever the bias for or against Walpole, the sense was political satire, and Walpole was the Great Man when we can presume Fielding began writing. The second edition he published in 1754 generalizes Walpole out of the picture: in the chapter on parties the two factions of Whigs become Whig and Tory; "Prime Minister" becomes "Statesman"; "a complete ministerial Tool" becomes "Tool of State," and the whole chapter on hats is dropped. The revision attempts a greater verisimilitude in line with the three novels that have intervened – it tries to move *Wild* as far as possible from farce. Fielding attempts to make the duping of Heartfree more believable by filling in his past life, particularly the hint given in the 1743 edition that he "had formerly been his [Wild's] School-fellow," and adds another passage converting Heartfree's suspicion and Wild's explanation concerning the fact that he escaped while Heartfree's wife did not and a few lines to strengthen the probability of the perjured evidence of Wild and Fireblood against Heartfree. And of course he drops the whole chapter in which fabulous travel books are burlesqued.

When, after unsuccessful efforts to improve his health, he knew he was leaving for Portugal, he wrote his will, which stipulates that his shares in the Universal Register Office are to be divided between his wife and Harriet (his surviving daughter by Charlotte), as well as the sale of his property. A certain amount was to be used by the two sons when they were 23; to be handled by Ralph Allen.

Some indication of Fielding's life-style can be gathered from the auctions following his death; and of the extent to which he lived beyond his means by the debts he left behind. His Fordhook "farm" included outhouses, gardens, and 40 acres of land, with "two large Ricks of Hay, two of Wheat, one of Oats, and one of Pease; about eighty Sheep, seven Cows (four of them Alderney)[,] five Hogs, three Sows, three Asses, a Monkey [brought back by his widow from Portugal], seven Coach and Cart-Horses, two Saddle Horses, three Carts, and other Farming Utensils," and "his Landau and Harness, Plate, Wines, and other [household] Effects."[99] The library – only the part put up for auction – has been called "the largest working library possessed by any man of letters in the eighteenth century."[100]

In the *Journal* he kept of the voyage he records his farewells to the children and friends he left behind at Fordhook, convinced as he was at this point that he would probably not see them again.

Early in 1754, when he had just finished revisions of *Jonathan Wild*, Fielding would have read Bolingbroke's posthumous "Fragments or Minutes of Essays." He undertook a reply, and quite possibly carried the books with him to Portugal.[101] Fielding's draft, which does not go beyond Bolingbroke's first point, was published at the end of Millar's edition of *The*

Journal of a Voyage to Lisbon. His approach in the fragment that survives is to assume that so clever a man as Bolingbroke, sheer wit incarnate, must have been joking: "That, as the temporal happiness, the civil liberties and properties of Europe, were the game of his earliest youth, there could be no sport so adequate to the entertainment of his advanced age, as the eternal and final happiness of all mankind" (Henley edn., 16:315). Inevitably, the phrase "his advanced age" referred to Bolingbroke jesting on the brink of the grave; while "his earliest youth" sounds the personal note, his own youthful folly when he was in fact associated with Bolingbroke's deist friends of the opposition, looked back upon by a man near his own death. With a certain nostalgia, he writes that "novelty, boldness, and even absurdity, as they all tend to surprize, do often give a poignancy to wit, and serve to enhance a jest" (315). This was, of course, the source of Fielding's most brilliant comedy.

In the few pages of his essay Fielding picks out for quotation Bolingbroke's reprise of the deist theatrical metaphor of life-as-theater which he had himself used in ways that could be interpreted as similar:

The sensitive inhabitants of our globe, like the dramatis personae, have different characters, and are applied to different purposes of action in every scene. The several parts of the material world, like the machines of a theatre, were contrived not for the actors, but for the action: and the whole order and system of the drama would be disordered and spoiled, if any alteration was made in either. The nature of every creature, his manner of being, is adapted to his state here, to the place he is to inhabit, and, as we may say, to the part he is to act. (314–15)[102]

Fielding remarks that he has "somewhere in an English dramatic writer, met with one so nearly resembling the above, that his lordship might be almost suspected to have read it likewise"; but, he adds now, such "similes" and "conceits" "are inconsistent with any (even the least) pretence to philosophy." Thus he offers the final repudiation of his youth, the years in which he also "put on the jack-pudding's coat" (317) and expressed the libertine ethos.

But Fielding had not lost his wit. As he set out, James Harris recalled, probably at their last meeting,

Two Friends made him a visit in his last Illness, when his Constitution was so broken, that twas thought he could not survive a week. To explain to them his Indifference as to a protraction of Life, he with his usual humour related them the following story. A Man (sd. He) under condemnation at Newgate was just setting out for Tyburn, when there arrived a Reprieve. His Friends who recd. ye news with uncommon Joy, prest him instantly to be blooded; they were feard (they said) his Spirits on a change so unexpected must be agitated in the highest degree. Not in the least (replied the Hero) no agitation at all. If I am not hanged this Sessions, I know I shall ye next.[103]

This is perhaps the most revealing example of a Fielding joke – as defensive as Bolingbroke's. Harris contrasts the witty man who in adversity abandons his wit and the man like Fielding "whose Wit, though it might have had perhaps its intensions and remissions, yet never deserted him in his most unprosperous hours, nor even when Death itself openly lookt him in ye face."

The voyage to Lisbon

Only 47, Fielding is toothless, asthmatic, jaundiced, and dropsical. Dropsy, the condition to which he most often refers, can be interpreted either as a terminal stage of other ailments or, more probably, as the sign of cirrhosis of the liver. In the prevalent contemporary view Fielding was "a poor, emaciated, worn-out rake, whose infirmities have got the better of his buffoonery"; "visited by his sins," writes one acquaintance, and even the testimony of friends was that "intemperance" was "the cause" of his decline in his forties and he was "visited for his sins."[104]

In his own account of how he came to make the voyage to Lisbon he attempts to correct these stories. This work, he writes as he nears Lisbon, "if I should live to finish it, (a matter of no great certainty, if indeed of any great hope to me,) will be probably the last I shall undertake"; and again, he writes that he is "satisfied in having finished my life, as I have, probably, lost it, in the service of my country, from the best of motives" (Pagliaro edn., 105, 107). Not the consequences of libertinism, Fielding tells us, but of devotion to civic duty explain his physical decline. And he relates his duty to the state to his love for his family (35): the *Journal's* purpose was at least as much to provide a support for his family after his probable death as self-justification or self-expression.

He presents his illness before writing the "plan" for Newcastle as merely "a lingering imperfect gout," which he hopes to rid himself of in Bath; following the execution of the "plan" he suffers from "a jaundice, a dropsy, and an asthma, altogether united ... in the destruction of a body so entirely emaciated, that it had lost all its muscular flesh" ("no longer what is called a Bath case") (33).

As he introduces his *Journal of a Voyage to Lisbon*, Fielding turns the facts into a story. He, the chief police magistrate of Westminster and Middlesex, is about to leave for recuperation in Bath when the duke of Newcastle asks him for a plan to cope with the crime and the criminal gangs that are plaguing London. He stays in London, produces a plan, and carries it out successfully, though it affects his health beyond the point where a stay in Bath can be of any help, and so he leaves for a warmer climate in Lisbon (he is too weak for the overland trip to the Mediterranean).

Formally the *Journal* is a continuation of the *Covent-Garden Journal*: It makes explicit the personal events of each day that presumably gave rise to the "lucubrations" of the *Covent-Garden Journal* (which also included the designation of day and month). In both cases we can imagine Fielding experiencing his journey or his grim law court and then writing an essay for the day, deriving from that experience; which gives a sense of either his professional *modus* (as a journalist) or his way of thinking, moving from a personal event or observation to a general statement of morals and, usually, its materialization in the law. And indeed, one thing the *Journal* shows is how the *modus operandi* of his journalism was by this time his *modus vivendi* as well. Near the end of the journey he remembers the moment on the Downs when he knew he must write this journal (122); this means that his recording of the experience was accompanied, presumably soon after, by the reflections it elicits.

These are the same elements that produced the form of *Tom Jones* but reversed: Fielding himself acts and reflects, whereas the author set up a framework of reflection and then fitted Tom's actions into it, explaining them. The *Journal* is perhaps a perspective on personal experience that (as, in a different way, in *Amelia*) draws closer to the sort of witnessing he once deplored in his counter-example, *Pamela*; yet it retains the distancing of Fielding's irony and, as in his own version of the correspondents in *Clarissa*, the awareness of different viewpoints. Richardson makes a final appearance in his preface as one of those "authors, who often fill a whole sheet with their own praises, to which they sometimes set their own real names, and sometimes a fictitious one"; who seek to reform "a whole people, by making use of a vehicular story, to wheel in among them worse manners than their own"; and who believe that "entertainment . . . be but a secondary consideration in a romance" (29–30).

The Fielding who placed the story of Booth and Amelia in the context of the *Aeneid* uses the epic parallel a last time in *The Journal of a Voyage to Lisbon*. Although he has dissociated himself from the epic in favor of the plain prose of history (as he insists in the preface, history, not romance or epic),[105] he recalls the classical norms: "I had vanity enough to rank myself with those heroes who, of olden times, became voluntary sacrifices to the good of the public" (i.e., a Curtius who cast himself into the abyss to preserve Rome) (34). But he complements this with the example of Don Quixote, whose travels invoke the image of an old and decrepit and exploitable person like Fielding, helpless and ridiculous as he is carried in his chair or litter, but able to stand up to the ship's captain when he is pushed far enough.

He does not draw attention to the parallels with the *Odyssey*, though he names it more than once and alludes to the Circe episode. And his most explicit reference is a recovery of Banier's euhemerism: "By this allegory then I suppose Ulysses to have been the captain of a merchant-ship, and Circe some good alewife, who made his crew drunk with the spirituous liquors of those days" (100).[106]

But the *Odyssey* is in his mind, supporting the public aspect of his narrative. Fielding and London correspond to Odysseus and Troy. The Greeks, after their ten-year struggle, are ready to give up their siege; Odysseus conceives the plan of the wooden horse, and after its success (Fielding's description of the destruction of the London gangs sounds as decisive as the Greeks' defeat of the Trojans) he sets out for well-deserved rest in Ithaca – but has many delaying adventures on the way: Thus Odysseus' plan for taking Troy, and then the delays along the way, in particular the bad innkeeper Mrs. Francis, who is a particularly euhemeristic Circe or Calypso.

More prominent is an allegory of the struggle between the captain and the wind; and, with the wind, allusions to Aeneas, Aeolus, and Neptune's *Quos Ego.* The fact that the *Journal* closes with the line from the *Aeneid,* "*Egressi optata Troes potiuntur oerena*" (the Trojans gain the welcome beach of Carthage; *Aeneid* 1.172) turns around the *Odyssey* parallel: Fielding is in fact not Ulysses but Aeneas, the defeated Trojan who is seeking his ancient mother and reaches a stop-over in Lisbon (on his way to Italy, like Odysseus' return to his homeland Ithaca a voyage with unconscionable delays, but this one based on civic duty, not nostalgia) – ending, as we have come to expect, "with a good supper, for which we were as well charged, as if the bill had been made on the Bath road, between Newbury and London" (131).

As early as his arrival at the ship Fielding introduces the Juvenalian convention of the last good man, in this case helpless and confined to his chair, carried onto the ship, running the gauntlet "through rows of sailors and watermen, few of whom failed of paying their compliments to me, by all manner of insults and jests on my misery" (44). His pain and despair find one outlet in Juvenalian forms: Life has become essentially the gauntlet he describes himself running. This fiction in the *Voyage* corresponds in much the same way to Fielding's early work as *The Epilogue to the Satires* and *The Dunciad*'s fourth book did to Pope's, Gulliver's fourth voyage to Swift's, and *Finis; or The Tailpiece* will to Hogarth's in 1764. These are terminal satires, final self-defenses.

But we have the facts and what Fielding makes of them, in the gauntlet he saw himself running as he first entered the ship: what must have been disorienting was the fact that people could jeer at a complete stranger in a helpless state – *because*, he surmises in the journal, they are of the lower orders and without "good breeding," that is, they are a mob; because they are sons of Adam, fallen and without the good breeding that would lift them above the state of nature. And so he places them in a Juvenalian fiction, but also relates himself to an aesthetic effect, the pathos he described himself feeling when he read Richardson's account of Lovelace's rape of Clarissa, with himself now in the Clarissa (or Amelia) position.

The sea, the ships on the sea, the fish (to eat), and the final sights in the Lisbon harbor are more intense, less abstract than in the essays of *The Covent-Garden Journal* – and the essays of the *Journal* dwindle as the wind finally turns and guides the travellers into the Bay of Biscay. The personal details are what we remember – how Fielding cannot survive without conversation, how he must have his tea chest, how he cannot chew tough old duck meat or hard biscuits (his bad teeth are contrasted with Mary's aching back molar, which no one will try to extract because it is so rotten it would break off at the root). And of course the excruciating tappings for his dropsy. The central fact (which he acknowledges often) is that he is sick and dying, though in un-Richardsonian fashion this is offset by the cheerfulness of his discourse. It is also offset by the tacit assumption that this cripple was once the tall vigorous rake Harry Fielding. It is true (as Harold Pagliaro notes [9]) that he seems to assume the friendship and familiarity of his readers. Certainly he offers a reprise of his old spectrum of readers and his uncertainty as to their interpretations: "Some of my readers will, perhaps, . . . Others will as probably regard it . . . I will not decide either way; but will content myself with observing . . ." (129). The uncertainty at this point is purely rhetorical.

The body, politic and personal

The particulars of illness, tappings, tooth-aches, and seasickness, the helpless limbs, the humiliations, and the continuing appetite for good food are precisely the things of interest only to the traveller which he says he will not write about. He does because they are not finally personal but invoke the metaphor of the body politic, for which it is also important that his ailments were the result of duty to the state rather than intemperance.

To begin, although Fielding calls the book *A Journal of a Voyage to Lisbon*, it is in fact a voyage around the coast of England, with only the most fleeting look at Lisbon. His preoccupation with land- and sea-scape shows Fielding continuing the nationalizing of England he carried out in the *Covent-Garden Journal*. His own experience always opens out into comments on English trade, the English navy, and so on; and this is, of course, a moral discourse, distinguishing evils from goods.

England, and not Portugal, figures in the *Journal*. It ends with a description of the scene as one approaches Lisbon from the sea and makes a final aesthetic judgment of it – at a distance it impresses, but up close it is ugly, confused, and chaotic; but, since he is keeping a journal and not writing an allegory, Fielding is last seen being carried up the hill and into a tavern where he has a "good supper" which he compares with one "on the Bath road, between Newbury and London."

Fielding's use of his own body goes far beyond the scene of his running the gauntlet of the mob. In his *Charge delivered to the Grand Jury* he had talked of the diseased body politic: the mob's "Fury after licentious and luxurious Pleasures" produces "chronical [rather] than epidemic Diseases," "which have so inveterated themselves in the Blood of the Body Politic, that they are perhaps never to be totally eradicated" (14, 25). And in *Amelia* Dr. Harrison commented that "Corruption in the Body Politic as naturally tends to dissolution as in the Natural Body" (11.2.460).[107] Now Fielding's body serves as an equivalent of the body politic in that his limbs no longer obey the commands of his head – the mob and its elevation of liberty (license) will not obey the law of magistrates and monarch (described in the longest of the "essays" in the *Journal* [82–5]). Fielding's body is a part of as well as a site of (a consequence of) the process of breakdown in society.

The same disequilibrium dogs him in every phase of his journey. As Terence Bowers puts it, "In the same way that his head seems to have little control over his limbs, Fielding has little control over those below him on whom he depends to serve as his limbs. Thus, just as Fielding's paralyzed legs refuse to carry him, watermen and dock workers repeatedly refuse to carry him or fetch provisions. Servants and inn-keepers either ignore or disobey his commands, leaving Fielding without hands to perform basic tasks for him (such as cooking)."[108] Similarly his wife Mary suffers seasickness, vomiting, and toothache – other forms of the head's loss of control over the body amounting to the disruption of the natural bodily as well as civil hierarchies.

The general theme Fielding follows in the *Journal* is degeneration: of his body (implicitly as a consequence of trying to deal with London crime), of its chief social equivalent, conversation, and of sustenance. The latter is centered, with conversation, on the meal, the significance of which Fielding had made much of in *Joseph Andrews* and *Tom Jones* (which we traced back to its sacralization in Hoadly's version of the Eucharist). On his voyage Fielding insists that his meals be social, that his meat is "dressed" properly, the "cloth to be laid," and that they be "seated in one of the most pleasant spots, I believe, in the kingdom" (73) – and, of course, that the conversation be pleasant. By contrast, his meals are constantly late, bad, interrupted, and disorderly. The disorder, as with his bodily troubles, comes from the lower members of the social hierarchy.

The metaphor of the body is centered on Fielding's dropsy – on his frequent need to tap the water from his stomach cavity; the humor must find release – "I find myself, since my tapping, much lighter and better" (52). But the fluids of his body relate to the unreliable tides and winds of the ocean, with the common element of the relief of pressure to permit movement, of getting out to sea for the ship: a final memory of the hydraulic model through which he had conceived the operations of nature from his earliest works.[109]

Fielding's body finds its locus in the ship, which is supposed to transport and supply his needs in transit. What is perhaps most revealing in the personal way is Fielding's confession of his absolute need for conversation. He says he cannot appreciate an experience unless he is conversing about it. His worst times are when Mary and Charlotte are seasick, the captain deaf and uncommunicative, and he is isolated. Implicitly the need to communicate, that is, socially share the experience, means that if not with Mary then with the reader, whom he occasionally addresses: the author must "make himself, in some degree, an agreeable, as well as an instructive companion" to his reader (24). He is, unlike the Richardsonian heroine, always addressing an other in a social situation. The *Journal* presents itself as social event, and its locus is the ship.

As in Smollett's *Roderick Random* the ship serves as a microcosm of society; but Fielding has a powerful pair of metaphors – the body politic *and* the ship of state, an anticipation of Smollett's final materialization of the body metaphor in Matthew Bramble in *Humphry Clinker* (in 1771).

If in one sense the captain serves as a model for the overturning of hierarchy, in another (in which he takes on the role of tyrant) he is the absolute monarch whose power over his sailors keeps them in line as long as they are on his ship – but once off, they become the Penlez rioters (99–100, 121–2). So long as sailors are on shipboard they are obedient and orderly; it is only when they are released on shore, beyond the command of their captain, that they produce riots like the Penlez one.

This permits Fielding to develop the two chief themes of the *Covent-Garden Journal*, liberty (excess) and the mob – that is, the lower parts take over the body, crippling it and isolating the still active head. He now revises his opinion about the English as a cruel nation. His experience running the gauntlet "was a lively picture of that cruelty and inhumanity, in the nature of men," adding "that this barbarous custom is peculiar to the English," but, he further adds (parting from Hogarth's *Stages of Cruelty*, which otherwise he seems to be recalling): "and of them only to the lowest degree," which he associates with the mob's "uncontroul'd licentiousness mistaken for liberty," an excess that "never shews itself in men who are polish'd and refin'd" – that is, the well-bred gentlemen who carry on polite conversation and properly dress their meat at meals (45). His image is of fallen man redeemed to some extent by culture, both civic and religious.[110]

For the diseased Fielding, recalling also the "Fielding" of earlier years, food is of the greatest importance. One of his symbols of nationalism was roast beef, which he wrote into the sub-national anthem "The Roast Beef of Old England" (in *The Welsh [Grub-Street] Opera* and materialized in Hogarth's print of 1749).[111] But when he arrives on shipboard, "A sirloin of beef was now placed on the table [which was] little better than carrion" (45) – indeed not unlike his own condition as he has just described it. Mr. and Mrs. Francis, the egregious innkeepers, serve Fielding as little food as possible – he expresses his "hunger" and concern at being "starved"; and the food they do produce is the same sort of rotting food he was served on the ship – "some stale beer and moldy cheese."

Thus the arcadian scene, produced in the middle of Mrs. Francis's meanness, is in the "dry, warm, oaken floored barn, lined on both sides with wheaten straw, and opening at one end into a green field, and a beautiful prospect," where the family gathers to enjoy "the best, the plesantest, and the merriest meal, with more appetite, more real, solid luxury, and more festivity, than was ever seen in an entertainment at White's" (72–3). This is Fielding's reprise of the (literally) edenic dinner of Joseph, Fanny, and Adams, in *Joseph Andrews.*

In retrospect, the life recorded by the *Journal* has to be seen through different perspectives, the different accounts of Mrs. Francis, Fielding and Margaret Collier (as told to Richardson).[112] Collier says he invented the scene in the barn; indeed, the story of the dinner in the doorway of the barn becomes the ideal sacramental meal of the sort Fielding had described Joseph, Adams, and their friends enjoying in a countryside recalling Milton's Eden. On the other hand, that he invented the barn seems unlikely. Collier's account seems (with the exception of the matter of the barn) to be merely an alternative interpretation from one less sympathetic with Fielding – by the time she reported they had had their falling out, Fielding must have raged at her (as he did in his letter to his brother John), he was now dead, and she was writing to Richardson, who always liked to hear the worst about Fielding (and, by this time, would have read Fielding's final remark in his preface). It is true, nevertheless, that Mrs. Francis may have been herself ill and Fielding's description of her was doubtless exaggerated, as was Pamela's of Mrs. Jewkes. His ill temper, intensified by his illness and helplessness, must be seen in the contexts of both the earlier fracases with Bennet and others and what is known of the agonies of gout and dropsy.

In the case of the captain Fielding embodies the contradiction of perspectives in a character. The captain (unlike Mrs. Francis, unnamed, but in fact Richard Veal), though a "tyrant" and blustery, nevertheless "was one of the best natur'd fellows alive," who cared tenderly for his crew and cats (116) – deaf but loud-voiced, harsh but kindly. The result is a captain who, in relation to his "cargo" is a tyrant and in relation to his sailors (themselves tyrannous to Fielding but admirable "in their own element") a just taskmaster, and yet tenderhearted to a fault with the kitten who falls overboard. We notice, as Fielding does, that his initial peremptoriness – and the first appearance of tyranny – is partially explained when Fielding learns he is deaf. Fielding fits him, however, into the *Joseph Andrews* model of affectation: he is pretending to be a gentleman.

The captain who ought to be serving his passenger treats him as a "subject" who "becomes bound in allegiance to his conveyer"; indeed, the passenger is "under the dominion of that tyrant, who, in this free country, is as absolute as a Turkish bashaw" (49). Moreover, he tries to pass himself off as a gentleman before the true gentleman, Fielding.

In his final letters from Portugal to his brother John it is possible to understand Fielding's overreaction to the threat of what he had always called petticoat government that alarmed him now, touching as it did on his comfort and well-being in extremis in a strange country. Equally understandable is the desire of Margaret Collier, an old maid, to catch the Rev. Williamson – a Jane Austen situation that Fielding saw from the perspective of Mr. Collins. But Fielding is also asking John to dispatch hams and other delectables from his Fordhook farm for his table and for his new friends.

As I have said, the *Journal of a Voyage to Lisbon* could be better called a tour of the southern coast of England and in one sense a celebration of the country and in particular the views of the sea and the ships on it; but also of the indigenous products, mutton and cider, and, above all, fish. In fact, though he experiences it from the sea (and experiences the sea from on it rather than from the shore), this is the country in which he grew up; and the focus on the sea might recall his first love – Sarah Andrews – in Lyme Regis.

One of the most striking, and surprising, revelations of Fielding himself is his love of landscape, and in particular seascape. Near the book's end, on the high seas, he writes:

> But here, tho' our voyage was retarded, we were entertained with a scene which as no one can behold without going to sea, so no one can form an idea of any thing equal to it on shore. We were seated on the deck, women and all, in the serenest evening that can be imagined. Not a single cloud presented itself to our view, and the sun himself was the only object which engrossed our whole attention. He did indeed set with a majesty which is incapable of description, with which while the horizon was yet blazing with glory, our eyes were called off to the opposite part to survey the moon, which was then at full, and which in rising presented us with the second object that this world hath offered to our vision. Compared to these the pageantry of theatres, or splendor of courts, are sights almost below the regard of children. (124–5)

Many of these comments on his appreciation of nature couch morality in terms of aesthetics; the word "beauty" appears with increasing frequency, and Fielding experiences the morning as "fair and brighter" and the "fine ships" are "noble sights," in part at least because of "the great perfection to which we are arrived in building those floating castles."

We can read this as a continuation of the discourse of beauty in *Amelia*, written in the context of Hogarth's *Analysis of Beauty*, which he would have read during the preceding year. His final reference to Hogarth accompanies the noise of the seamen, watermen, and the fish wives which composes "a greater variety of harmony than Hogarth's imagination hath brought together" (46) – a reference specifically to his *Enraged Musician* (1741) but one that strongly implies a reading of the *Analysis*, where Hogarth sets forth the principle of his aesthetics as the discovery of the maximum variety in apparent unity.[113]

In the preface his distinction between the poetry of Homer and the "humble prose" of the "true history" of Herodotus, Thucydides, and Xenophon is given an aesthetic emphasis: The former causes "more admiration and astonishment," the latter "more amusement and more satisfaction" (26). The first is Addison's Great, the second his Novel, New, or Uncommon, around which Hogarth built his aesthetics in the *Analysis*.

Thus Fielding writes: "A fleet of ships is, in my opinion, the noblest object which the art of man hath ever produced; and far beyond the power of those architects who deal in brick, in stone, or in marble" (91). The principle invoked for men of war and merchant-men is utility (Hogarth's "fitness").[114] But, he adds, drawing our attention to the discrepancy between beauty and morality (the equation Shaftesbury had made between beauty and virtue, which Hogarth had put in question in his prints and in the *Analysis*, and which Johnson was to note in his journey to the northern islands): These "men of war, which seem so delightful an object to our eyes" are also "the support of tyranny, and oppression of innocence, carrying with them desolation and ruin wherever their masters please to send them." Resolving the dilemma, he contrasts the "superior beauty" but evil of the man of war with the "superior excellence of the idea" of a merchant-man, "engaged in the daily improvements of commerce, to the mutual benefit of all countries, and to the establishment and happiness of social life" (91–2).

Finally, there is the abrupt breaking off – the voyage is over and they have arrived in Lisbon – and, with a final bow to his learning, he ends with a couple of Latin quotations. (He has made a final nod to Walpole as well – "one of the best of men and of ministers" [91].) He lived a few weeks longer, during which he must have written the introduction and revised the journal; and then he died and was buried in the English Cemetery.

Birch reports, from a letter Fielding wrote to Millar from Lisbon, that he called the *Journal* "the best of his performances." He was, of course, offering the manuscript to Millar and hoping for an advance, and he had referred to *Amelia* as his "favourite Child." But that phrase implied fondness, probably for its picture of Amelia-Charlotte. The *Journal*, if not his very best performance, was an important departure; it was Fielding's final masterpiece, comparable to *Joseph Andrews* and *Tom Jones* in its power and originality. If *Amelia* maps out an area that will be explored by Victorian fiction, the *Journal of the Voyage to Lisbon* foreshadows the "travel" books of D. H. Lawrence, Graham Greene, and Evelyn Waugh.

Birch also reports that he was writing a history of Portugal. Otherwise, after the completion of the *Journal*, Fielding continues to focus on food – the pleasures of the senses in these final weeks. The concern with food picks up at the point when he is convinced that he has improved, is able to get around a little, at least ride around in his coach for extended periods. And as Donald Thomas notes, it includes a need for wine that was hardly conducive to recovery if he was suffering, as is assumed, from cirrhosis of the liver. Then there is the food and wine he disburses to his friends back in England (from the Isle of Wight as well as from Portugal) and which he secures for himself, his family, and retainers; and his final request that John ("Jack") send him Stilton and Cheshire cheeses, pork, and other plainly English food. And, of course, as on the voyage, the meal is a social event with conversation (he asks John to send him as his amanuensis a conversable man). Here are the physical equivalents, the remaining vestiges, of what Fielding had successfully embodied in his writings.

Lady Mary Wortley Montagu's comment on hearing a report of Fielding's death goes straight to his sensuous pleasures: "no Man enjoy'd life more than he did, tho," she adds,

> few had less reason to do so. . . . His happy Constitution (even when he had, with grat pains, halfe demolish'd it) made him forget every thing when he was before a venison Pasty or over a Flask of champaign, and I am perswaded he has known more happy moments than any Prince upon Earth.[115]

The personal and the public aspects of Fielding's life enjoy a happy synthesis in the *Journal of a Voyage to Lisbon*, concluding with the topos of an imagined retirement. This picture of illness overcome, or at least survived, conceals the imminent death and the feeble bequest awaiting his widow and family back in England, where they found themselves deeply in debt. And yet to some extent counterbalancing Fielding's prodigality was the assistance extended by his devoted friends: the other side of Fielding was his charm, wit, and ability to make and hold friends. Then there was the professional Fielding, the dedicated public magistrate, the assiduous keeper of public order – sometimes, one might think, overcompensating for his own less than orderly example. Finally, there was the author – his extraordinary mind, in knowledge, memory, scope, and invention, in power of concentration and application; though often, at his most creative,

he employed these to understand and justify the depredations of the falli-
ble man.

His bequest to English literature – not even now, I believe, sufficiently
appreciated – was not only the comic novel, an essentially English phenomenon (found where else but in *Don Quixote* itself?), but also the powerful architectonic form of *Tom Jones* and its hard intellectual core. At the
center of that great "clockwork" (as Coleridge called it), as also in the best
of Austen, Eliot, Conrad, and others, was the personal issue of conduct
(love, marriage, honor, courage) embodied in a flawed character, point-
edly not a paragon. Fielding made explicit what was only accidental and
incidental in the novels of Defoe and Richardson: that evil is not religious,
not Adam's disobedience (as Allworthy judged it), not the breaking of laws
(although in the 1750s, as magistrate, he said so), but the injuring of
another person, especially if loved, but in the end any neighbor.

Given Fielding's great concern about reputation and his "character," his
death surrendered him up to his detractors. While his novels were never
without enthusiastic readers, his reputation fell into the hands of Christian
moralists and Richardsonian sentimentalists for 150 years (the reputations
of Pope and Swift suffered similarly), only to be turned around in the 1950s
by a generation of scholars who remade him into a virtuous Christian
apologist.

In a *Champion* essay (March 4, 1739/40) Fielding distinguished a man
with "a Consciousness in [his] true Merit, which renders [him] careless of
the Reception it meets with," from one whose worldly success brings with
it reputation ("Had Alexander been entirely defeated in his first Battle in
Asia, he might have been called a Robber only by Posterity"), but since this
is a world of unequal rewards, he adds, "the virtuous Man" whose merit
goes unrewarded "may rejoice" and "be warmed with a more exstatic
Imagination" of the reputation awaiting him in heaven (1:329–31).

In fact, I have no doubt that when Fielding died he looked with some
confidence toward the vindication of this third alternative, the reward of
his virtue in the afterlife, but he had spent his life worrying in his writings
about the discrepancies between what he felt to be his true merit and those
actions that thwarted due recognition. His procedure was to behave carelessly of his reputation and then reexamine that behavior, trying to explain
it to a "sagacious reader," and perhaps to himself.

Notes

NOTES TO PREFACE

1 Toland, *Amyntor; or a Defence of Milton's Life* (London, 1699), 6.
2 Battestin, *Life*, 583.
3 See my chapters on Fielding in *Satire and the Novel* (1967) and *Popular and Polite Art in the Age of Hogarth and Fielding* (1979) and my books on Hogarth (1971, 1991–3); more recently, *The Beautiful, Novel, and Strange: Aesthetics and Heterodoxy* (1996) and *Don Quixote in England: The Aesthetics of Laughter* (1998). I have included passages from the earlier works which I don't believe I can improve on.

NOTES TO CHAPTER 1

1 Baptized May 6, St. Benedict's, Glastonbury; affidavit sworn by HF, Oct. 26, 1728 (PRO C41.43.1030); B 3 n. 1. Edmund was b. Jan. 20, 1679/80; Sarah, Dec. 28, 1682.
2 Register, St. Benedict's, Glastonbury.
3 *Magna Brittania et Hibernia Antiqua & Nova* (1720), the "Seat" of "Ed. Fielding, Esq." receipt, offices of Dodson, Harding & Reed, Solicitors, Bridgewater, Somerset; for PRO, see B 12 n. 45.
4 Battestin cites the documents relevant to Edmund's regiment (628 n. 47).
5 Register of Christ's Church, East Stour.
6 His housekeeper, Marie Bentham, sued for £600 in Trinity Term, 1721 (PRO KB122.99, Roll 572); his neighbor, Thomas Freke, £100 (PRO C11.2171/12); his wife's aunt, Katherine Cottington, £700 (PRO C33.337, Pt. 2, p. 377).
7 C. Dalton, *George I's Army* (London, 1912), 2:141; *Feilding v. Midford*, PRO C11.2726/91.
8 Buried on the 18th, Register of Christ's Church, East Stour.

9 Poor Rate Books, St. James's, Gt. Marlborough Div. (B 18 n. 71). His regiment had been reduced in Nov.

10 Based on the birth of Edmund's first child by his new wife (George, baptized Oct. 18, 1719, register of St. James's Piccadilly). A second son, John, who would grow up to be HF's assistant in the Bow Street court and the Register Office, was b. Sept. 16, 1721.

11 C. Dalton, *English Army Lists and Commission Registers 1661–1714* (London, 1904), 5, pt. 2: 43 n. 8.

12 The quotation and the information that follows concerning HF's movements, etc., are from the records of Lady Gould's complaint against Edmund for custody of the children (PRO C11 259/37).

13 Again, the Chancery records supply this information.

14 *Index of Fines*, 1–7 Geo. I, Trin. 7 Geo.I.Dorset, p. 199v (PRO CP25 [2]), which indicates the amount as £2,000 (the original purchase price for his part was £1,750; for the losses in the South Sea stock, see Edmund's letter of Oct. 4, 1720, giving reasons he cannot repay Freke (PRO C11.2171/12).

15 I prefer this explanation for Henry's departure from Eton to Battestin's that "he had fled to escape the birchings at Eton" (93).

16 See above, n. 6.

17 PRO C11.2283/45; responding to Lady Gould's ejectment proceedings to remove him from the farm to prevent his appropriating rents and selling off property (PRO KB122.99, Roll 302).

18 The case and judgment against Edmund: PRO C33.337 Pt. 1, p. 377; KB122 99/302, 572.

19 The exact dates are not known. The Eton School Lists are missing for 1719–24 (R. A. Austen-Leigh, *The Eton College Register, 1698–1732* [Eton: Eton College, 1927]). For the house in Upton Grey, see *Misc.*, 1:53; and J. Heathcote papers, Hampshire Record Office, Winchester, 58M71M.E/B44; Edmund's house, Westminster History Collection, Buckingham Palace Road: D26–32.

20 C. Wanklyn, *Somerset and Dorset Notes & Queries*, 20 (Mar. 1930), 166–7, and *Lyme Leaflets* (Colchester: Spottiswoode, Ballantyne, & Co., 1944), 68–9.

21 Dobson, *Fielding* (1907), Appendix I; Wanklyn, *Lyme Leaflets*, 69–71; "Fugitive Pieces," Dorset County Record Office: B7/N23/4, f. 25.

22 PRO KB Crown Side IND 1/6672, Michaelmas Term, 1726, 13 George I, No. 127, Middlesex, ffielding, Henricus; KB10.19/37, Pt. 1, Indictments; KB29.386, Middlesex, CXXVII.

23 PRO SP44.180, p. 99; HF was receiving cash from his father's account in Drummond's bank.

24 *DP* and *DJ*, Nov. 10, 1727. Thomas Lockwood found another advertisement, in the *St. James's Evening Post* of the 11th, which also includes the epigraph, some lines from Virgil on Octavian (i.e., applied to George II): "Early Poems by – and not by – Fielding," *PQ*, 72 (1993):177–8.

25 *Monthly Chronicle*. It was attributed to Fielding when published as an appendix to the authorized edition of *The Grub-Street Opera* in 1755.

26 *DP*. The dates for the plays are based on the data collected in the *London Stage*, Pt. 3.

27 "16 Martii 1728 Henricus Fielding, Anglus, annor. 20 Litt. Stud., bot nog toe in het Cast. van Antw" (B 63). Summarized in Dobson, *Fielding*, Appendix IV; transcription by P. J. Blok, Professor of History at the University of Leiden,

included among the correspondence of Dobson at the Senate House, Univ. of London (ADC MS. 810/VI/10 [ii]).

28 Although attribution is not universally accepted, I believe both of these are by Fielding. See Battestin, "Four New Fielding Attributions: His Earliest Satires of Walpole," *Studies in Bibliography*, 36 (1983):69–109; and B 67–9.

29 B 634 n. 46.

30 For the debts, see B 72–3 and notes. For *Don Quixote*, see Fielding's preface to the play; *Wedding Day*, H. K. Miller's preface, *Misc.*, 1:4–5.

31 For the facts and the text of the poem, see Isobel Grundy, *PMLA*, 87 (1972): 213–45.

32 Preface to *Don Quixote in England*; preface to *Misc.*

33 *DP* Feb. 2, 1730.

34 Letter to Harris, Oct. 5, 1745, in *Corresp.*, 51.

35 See J. H. Round, *Studies in Peerage and Family History* (London: A. Constable, 1901), 216 ff.; B 7–8.

36 Following Blenheim, his ascent was rapid: from captain in Marlborough's campaigns to major, April 12, 1706, and lieutenant colonel, August 31 (B 11).

37 Dalton, *English Army Lists*, 5, Pt. 2: 43 n. 8.

38 Richard Warner, *An History of the Abbey of Glaston; and the Town of Glastonbury* (1826), plate 1.

39 PRO C11.259/37 fol. 2.

40 PRO PCC 1710; proved, May 5, 1710; *Notes & Queries*, 3rd series, 2 (1862): 199.

41 B 15. For records of Edmund as JP, see the Museum of the Gillingham Local History Society.

42 Testimony of Frances Barber, PRO C24.1396/29; B 14 and n. 53.

43 PRO C11.259/37 fol. 1; C41.37 Trinity Term 1721 nos. 15, 16.

44 Ibid., no. 17.

45 Ibid., nos. 404, 405 (Thomas Grafton).

46 Ibid., no. 403.

47 B 23–30. For a good rebuttal of Battestin in this matter, see Thomas, 30–1.

48 Letter to the *DP*, July 31, 1732 (for the whole text, see B 142–3). It is Dr. Harrison's opinion in *Amelia* that "a Boy in the fourth Form at *Eton* would be whipt, or would deserve to be whipt at least, who made the *Neuter Gender* agree with the *Feminine*" (10.1.410).

49 *TP* no. 1, 112. One of the authors he thinks he may be mistaken for in this regard is the much admired Bishop Hoadly.

50 On Bland, see B 40.

51 In *The Covent-Garden Journal* (July 25, 1752), near the end of his career, Fielding expresses the opinion that "Much the greater Part of our Lads of Fashion return from School at fifteen or sixteen, very little wiser, and not at all the better for having been sent thither," but the context here is the way boobies can emerge uneducated from public schools and universities – and, at this point, he thinks more in terms of how the schools can be reformed.

52 Battestin thinks he was in London in May 1725 and witnessed the execution of Jonathan Wild. Although it would be nice to think that his interest in Wild (and in judicial punishment) began with Wild's actual hanging, the only evidence is a letter to the *Craftsman* (June 5, 1736; 152) which Battestin

attributes to Fielding. Even if Fielding wrote this letter, he need not have himself attended the execution of Wild, which had virtually passed into folklore and is used here to set off the allegorical execution of Mother Gin.

53 Written by Horace Walpole in the margins of his copy of Cibber's *Apology* (pp. 164–5), now in the King's School, Canterbury; noted by W. B. Coley, "Henry Fielding and the Two Walpoles," *PO*, 45 (1966): 166, n. 45.

54 Donald Thomas has beautifully evoked the landscape of Somersetshire, the levels from Glastonbury to the sea, and the rolling hills from Sharpham Park to the farm at East Stour, especially their liminal quality.

55 PRO C24.1396/29.

56 Henley ed., 9.239–40.

57 *The Times*, Aug. 31, 1736; cited, Thomas, 41, who notes that Fielding claimed he was set upon by Joseph Channon, the servant of a local miller called James Daniel, assuming that Daniel was in Tucker's employ. Battestin simply notes that Fielding appears in the records lodging a complaint before a magistrate against a local miller (49).

58 PRO KB28.133/22; James Davidson, *The History of Newenham Abbey* (London, 1843), 166; J. Paul de Castro, "Henry Fielding," *Somerset and Dorset Notes and Queries*, 20 (1930): 18.

59 He finally spelled his name ffielding or Ffielding as well as Fielding. He notes that Jonathan Wild spelled his name with both *i* and *y*, though this is because he cannot spell.

60 See above, n. 22.

61 Probyn, *Sociable Humanist*, 305.

62 Murphy, 1: 47.

63 To Lady Bute, July 23, 1754; *Complete Letters of Lady Mary Wortley Montagu*, ed. Robert Halsband (Oxford: Clarendon Press, 1965–7), 3: 66.

64 Walpole and Skerritt were lovers by the autumn of 1724 (an illegitimate daughter was born in 1725); they possibly met through Lady Mary (Plumb, *Walpole*, 2: 112–13).

65 *Corresp.*, 3.

66 Gulliver is referred to again around the same time in *Love in Several Masques* (8:55).

67 As Wycherley had done in *The Country Wife* and Etherege in *The Man of Mode*, both of which employed characters based on Rochester.

68 See Robert Hume, *Henry Fielding and the London Theatre, 1728–1737* (Oxford: Clarendon Press, 1988), 31. Although Hume's account of Fielding's theater and its context is the best informed and fullest we have, it tends to distort the plays. Hume focuses influence on the performance history and popularity of particular contemporary plays, on minor authors and details of their plots. Minimizing the general lines of filiation with the types of comedy written by the great English dramatists, he reduces Fielding's plays to the level of successful intrigue comedies; he does not ask what makes Fielding's plays, even the slightest and least "successful," special and his own.

69 Alberto Rivero gives a useful account of Cibber's reputation and the evidence of Fielding's writing against his comedies at the outset of his career (*The Plays of Henry Fielding: A Critical Study of his Dramatic Career* [Charlottesville: University of Virginia Press, 1989], chap. 1).

70   The situation was repeated in his next play, *The Temple Beau*, in Sir Avarice Pedant's comment on his niece: "if we are not expeditious, the stock will be sold to another purchaser . . . for in dealing with women (contrary to all other merchandise) the way to get them cheap is to cry them up as much beyond their value as possible" (8:114).

71   Lady Matchless, also from the country, warns Vermilia, "in the country our ideas are more fixed and more romantic," a situation more dangerous than an assembly or playhouse in the city (8:31) – though Lady Matchless, having vowed never to remarry after the experience of her late husband, has fled back to the safety of London after falling dangerously in love with Wisemor.

72   Dryden, preface to *An Evening's Love* (1671), *Works* (Berkeley and Los Angeles: University of California Press, 1961–), 10:203–4.

73   Dryden, dedication to *The Spanish Friar*, in *Works*, 14:102.

74   Probyn, *Sociable Humanist*, 305.

75   See Battestin, *New Essays*, 510–11; and Battestin, "Four New Fielding Attributions," 69–109.

76   *Daily Journal*, 24 July; *London Journal* and *British Journal*, 27 July; in *New Essays*, 510–11.

77   *An Historical View of the Principles, Characters, Persons, &c. of the Political Writers in Great Britain* (1740), 49–50.

78   *Daily Journal*, 1, July 17, 1728.

79   *New Essays*, 512–16.

80   For Shaftesbury and the hydraulic model of laughter, see below, chap. 5.

81   *New Essays*, 514–15.

82   *Misc.*, vol. 1

83   See Halsband, *Lady Mary Wortley Montagu* (New York: Oxford University Press, 1960), 130–1.

84   See letter to Harris, Sept. 24, 1742, *Corresp.*, 24.

85   This is not to deny that he imitated the *Spectator* dream allegories when they served his purpose.

86   See George Sherburn, "*The Dunciad*, Book IV," *University of Texas, Studies in English*, 24 (1945), 174–90.

87   There seems to be more than duty involved in the Horatian epistle he wrote defending Sappho in 1733 – which is about slander and reputation; but this too was not published, remaining among Lady Mary's MSS.

88   See W. R. Irwin, *The Making of "Jonathan Wild": A Study in the Literary Method of Henry Fielding* (New York: Columbia University Press, 1941), 189.

89   John Loftis, *Comedy and Society from Congreve to Fielding* (Stanford: Stanford University Press, 1959), 108; also, for general background, Loftis, *The Politics of Drama in Augustan England* (Oxford: Clarendon Press, 1963).

90   See Paulson, *Hogarth* (New Brunswick: Rutgers University Press, 1990), 1: 172–88.

91   See Harold Weber, *The Restoration Rake-Hero* (Madison: University of Wisconsin Press, 1986); Warren Chernaik, *Sexual Freedom in Restoration Literature* (Cambridge: Cambridge University Press, 1995), esp. chs. 1 and 2.

92   Murphy, 1:10. Murphy's account of Fielding's youth is on pp. 7–11.

93 The set pieces Fielding learned at Eton and Leiden are associated with Young Pedant (144, 149, 156).

94 *The Wedding Day* was finally produced in 1743, with a splendid cast including David Garrick, Charles Macklin, and Peg Woffington. The failure has been attributed (by Murphy among others) to Fielding's inability in 1743, due to his wife's serious illness, to revise the original play of 1729; but a clearer picture of what that failure involved can be inferred from the remark of a Mrs. Russell, who observed that "Fielding's Play had a fair hearing last night, first and second Acts tolerable but from thence every one grew worse to the End." There is a slackening in the last two acts, and Millamour's reformation may be unconvincing, but the unfavorable response probably had to do with the transgressive situations, particularly that of incest in the denouement (though Kitty Clive was upset at having to play the role of the bawd Mrs. Useful). Prostitutes and incest apparently could, if presented in a way the audience brought up on Collier's Puritanism regarded as indelicate, offend an audience. Speaking of indelicacy, I am aware of nowhere else in comedy of the period in which a character excuses himself to use the toilet, as Sir Harry does in *The Temple Beau*: "I'll first obey a certain call that I find within me" (8:142).

95 Robert Hume thinks this is poor stuff, a great falling off from Thomas Durfey's popular *Comical History of Don Quixote* (three parts, 1694–5), which was still in repertory in the 1730s. What Hume means is that Durfey's play was a success. Aside from the distinction of having a musical score by Henry Purcell, it simply dramatized (in effect, illustrated) highlights from Cervantes' novel, mixing the comic and romantic elements. Hume's query "Why Fielding set his hand to *Don Quixote in England* is hard to guess" (47) is itself radically puzzling. It would be surprising if he had not.

96 Quixote notes, like the Beggar of *The Beggar's Opera*: "Then indeed knight-errantry were of no use; but I tell thee, caitiff, gaols in all countries are only habitations for the poor, not for men of quality. If a poor fellow robs a man of fashion of five shillings, to gaol with him: but the man of fashion may plunder a thousand poor, and stay in his own house" (17).

97 The possibility of a "comic epic in prose" is raised by the curate in the discussion of romance near the end of Part I.

98 See Alexander Welsh, *Reflections on the Hero and Quixote* (Princeton, 1981); Paulson, *Don Quixote in England: The Aesthetics of Laughter* (Baltimore: Johns Hopkins University Press, 1997).

NOTES TO CHAPTER 2

1 See B 80 and below, 58.

2 Fielding received a percentage of the profits rather than benefits. See B 83 n. 67; Hume, "Henry Fielding and Politics at the Little Haymarket 1728–1737," in J. M. Wallace, ed., *The Golden and the Brazen World: Papers in Literature and History 1650–1800* (Berkeley and Los Angeles: University of California Press, 1985), 81. For publication, see *DP*.

3   Thomas Davies, *Memoirs of the Life of David Garrick* (1784), 2:209; cited, B
    164.
4   See B 87.
5   *DP*; the date is on the page following the title page ("This Day is Publish'd").
    For this and the many subsequent edns., see L. J. Morrisey (ed.), *Fielding's
    "Tom Thumb" and "The Tragedy of Tragedies"* (Edinburgh, 1970), 11–12.
6   *LEP*, June 4–6; 3rd edn., July 11, *LEP*, 11 July 9–11.
7   *DP*, June 12, 1730 advertised for June 15, but illness of an actor caused the
    play to be postponed until the 23rd.
8   Letter HF to Lady Mary Wortley Montagu, Sept. 4, 1730; in Halsband ed.,
    Complete Letters of Lady Mary Wortley Montagu, 2:93; Fielding, *Corresp.*, 4.
9   Announced as "The City Politician: or, The Justice Caught in His own Trap"
    (*Daily Post*, Nov. 28, 1730); when performed, *The Coffee-House Politician*. HF's
    signed denial was published in the *Daily Journal*, Nov. 30. "The Battle of the
    Poets" is usually attributed to Thomas Cooke. In one of the editions of
    Thomas Cooke's *The Bays Miscellany, or Colley Triumphant* (n.d. [1730]) is
    included the playlet, *The Battle of the Poets; or, the Contention for the Laurel* – "as
    it is now Acting At the New Theatre in the Hay-Market; introduced as an intire
    New Act to the Comical Tragedy of Tom Thumb. Written by Scriblerus Tertius
    [a name assumed by Cooke]." The reference is on p. 179. On November 30,
    the day Cooke's playlet was performed, Fielding thought it necessary to print
    a notice in the *Daily Journal* denying authorship, signed with his name. This
    does not indicate anything about his relationship with Cooke, only at most
    the suggestion that the management of the Little Haymarket had commis-
    sioned the extra scene without consulting him (he was, at the moment,
    working at Lincoln's Inn Fields).
10 *LEP*, Dec. 1–3. See W. J. Burling, "Fielding, His Publishers and John Rich
    in 1730," *Theatre Survey*, 26 (1985): 41; J. A. Masengill, "Variant Forms of
    Fielding's *Coffee-House Politician*," *Studies in Bibliography*, 5 (1952): 178–83.
11 Announcement of performances, *DP*, Feb. 12, 1730/1; Mar. 19; publication,
    DP, Mar. 22.
12 *GSJ*, April 22.
13 The linkage drew attention to the politics of *The Welsh Opera*: the actor Mullart
    played both Mortimer and Robin. On *The Fall of Mortimer*, see Cross, 1: 107f.
    and Loftis, 105f.
14 *DJ*; HF's denial, *DP*, June 28.
15 B 118–23.
16 *GSJ*. The authorized ed., *The Grub-Street Opera. By Scriblerus Secundus* (with *The
    Masquerade, a Poem*), with the imprint of Roberts and the date 1731, was prob-
    ably not published until 1755 in Andrew Millar's ed. of HF's *Dramatic Works*.
    See Edgar V. Roberts, introduction, *The Grub-Street Opera* (Lincoln, Neb.,
    1968). For the cancellation, see xv–xvi; and B 118–23.
17 *DJ*. There was a benefit for HF on the 21st (B 125). Hume says HF was paid
    a flat fee plus this one performance (H 118–20).
18 *DP*; a second ed. in Aug.
19 See Paulson and Lockwood, 31–65.
20 *LS* 213.
21 *DP*, June 13 and 23; H 129, 133.

22 *DP*, June 16 and 26, 1732; and pirated Aug. 4; 2nd edn. with additional songs and alterations, publ. ca. Nov. 1732 (*LEP*, Nov. 30–Dec. 2, 1732).
23 Quoted in full, B 140–3.
24 *DP*, Sept. 6, 1732; *Daily Advertiser*, Sept. 8–9.
25 *LS* 247.
26 Ibid. 252.
27 *DP*, Jan. 26, 1732/3.
28 B 163 and n.
29 *DP*, Mar. 12, 1732/3.
30 Ed., Isobel Grundy, "New Verse by Henry Fielding," *PMLA*, 87 (1972): 240–5.
31 *DP*, Mar. 14, 1732/3; *DA*, April 6; see E. V. Roberts, "Henry Fielding's Lost Play *Deborah, or A Wife for You All* (1733), Consisting Partly of Facts and Partly of Observations upon Them," *Bulletin of the New York Public Library*, 66 (Nov. 1962): 576–88; H 154–5.
32 B 167.
33 Ibid.; H 155–69, 173–8.
34 *DA*, Oct. 29, 1733.
35 *DA*, Dec. 8, 1733.
36 The reference in the title is to Jean-François Regnard's *Le Retour imprévu; The Intriguing Chambermaid* was announced, *DJ*, Jan. 16, 1733/4; publ. Watts (*GM*). *The Author's Farce* enjoyed eight performances (an additional four by the rebels), one benefit; H 169, 172. Watts reissued the second edition (*LEP*, Jan. 10–12, 1733/4); but the text of the revised *Author's Farce* did not appear until 1750, "The Third Edition . . . Revised, and greatly Alter'd."
37 H 179–80.
38 HF's preface to the published *Don Quixote in England*.
39 *LEP*, April 11–13, 1734.
40 See B 173 and Battestin's *New Essays*, where he dates HF's earliest contribution to the *Craftsman* 16 Mar.
41 B 185–6; Aaron Hill, review of *Pasquin*, *Prompter*, Apr. 2, 1736.
42 Register at the church of St. Mary the Virgin, Charlcombe. See B 178–9.
43 PRO SP41.9, f.317.
44 No benefit advertised; H speculates £50–£60 cash payment. Publ. announced, *GSJ*, Jan. 23.
45 H 265; B (145) suggests that *Miss Lucy* was intended as an afterpiece in 1735, but heavily revised in 1742, probably drawing on Garrick's *Lethe: or, Esop in the Shades*, itself a kind of sequel to *The Virgin Unmask'd* (346). In the preface to the *Miscellanies* HF says he had only "a very small Share" in writing the piece.
46 B 182, 186.
47 PRO KB.122.164, Roll 658; De Castro, *Somerset and Dorset Notes & Queries*, 20 (Mar. 1930): 130–2. The date of his plea was July 26, 1737 (index, Books of Judgment, No. 9633).
48 Aaron Hill, see above, n. 40.
49 PRO KB.122.160, Roll 457; with much more, quoted by B 190. Judgment was finally entered on Nov. 3, 1736 in HF's favor (PRO KB.125.144, Rule Book).

50 See HF's preface to the *Miscellanies* and B 191 n. 219. *The Good Natured Man* was not performed until 1778.
51 H 211, 216; *LDP*, April 6–7, 1736.
52 PRO SP.47 and Ind.6899.
53 Registers, St. Martin-in-the-Fields; B 191.
54 H 214, 216; *LEP*, April 29–May 1.
55 Publ. April 1737 (*GM*).
56 Charles Fielding, PRO KB.IND.4583; Hugh Allen, PRO KB.122.189 (Pt. 2), Roll 689; James Gascoigne, PRO CP.40.3502, Roll 1792; Bennet, PRO KB.125.144 and KB.122.164, Roll 658. See B 210–11, who speculates that the money might have been needed to settle old debts; also, perhaps, to initiate his ambitious plans for the Little Haymarket.
57 *DA*, Feb. 2, 1736/7. See E. L. Avery, "Proposals for a New London Theatre in 1737," *Notes & Queries*, 182 (1942): 286–7; H 225–6.
58 H 222.
59 Published in *Misc.* 2.
60 Ad, presumably by HF, *Grub-Street Journal*, Feb. 24, 1736/7.
61 *DA*, Mar. 8, 1736/7.
62 Ibid., Mar. 10, 1736/7; PRO KB.28.144.20. Cf. Aaron Hill's letter to HF, urging him to suppress the play, which Hill had read (*Corresp.*, 5).
63 Thirty-four performances according to Hume, 36 according to Battestin (H 233, B 218); 16 benefits for the 42 performances between Mar. 14 and May 23 (not clear how many for the *Historical Register*).
64 H 237, B 220; *DP*.
65 MSS. Folger Library (MS. T.b.3/3); Ce Castro, *Notes & Queries*, 182 (June 20, 1942): 346.
66 *Craftsman*, July 30, Aug. 6, 13, Sept. 3, 17, Oct. 1, 1737; see B 236–37 and n. 414.
67 See V. J. Liesenfeld, *The Licensing Act of 1737* (Madison, Wis.: University of Wisconsin Press, 1984).
68 H 36.
69 B 82–3.
70 James Miller, *Harlequin-Horace: or, the Art of Modern Poetry* (1731; 4th edn., 1741), note to l. 120; *Biographical Dramatica*, 2:315; *DNB*. On the fiddle, see Fielding's remark, *Tom Jones*, 4.1.151.
71 *Hurlothrumbo*, 1st edn., dedication to Lady Delves; Bailey, *Dictionary* (1755), and *DNB*.
72 Fielding could also be drawing upon the sort of happy ending Molière attached to *Tartuffe*. The situation is so bad, Molière says, that only a *deus ex machina* can remedy things; and the intervention of the king only tends to point up the impossibility of survival in France for normal virtue.
73 Fourteen years later, in the preface to his *Miscellanies*, he notes that the translation was "originally sketched out before I was Twenty, and was all the Revenge taken by an injured Lover" (*Misc.*, 1: 3, 117). Unless we are to suppose that Fielding was also pursuing around the same time another girl, Sarah herself may have been the cause of the elopement's failure, against whose fickleness he turned in Juvenal's Sixth Satire.

74 Dryden, preface to *An Evening's Love* (1671), *Works*, 10:203–4.

75 *Spectator* no. 249.

76 See "Mr. Congreve to Mr. Dennis, Concerning Humour in Comedy" (1695), in Joel Spingarn, ed., *Critical Essays* (Bloomington: Indiana University Press, 1957), 3:252.

77 *Hurlothrumbo*, 14.

78 See Noel Malcolm, *The Origins of English Nonsense* (London: Harper Collins, 1997), and Michael Dobson's review, *London Review of Books*, Nov. 13, 1997, 28.

79 Archer remarks to Aimwell that " 'tis still my maxim, that there is no scandal like rags, nor any crime so shameful as poverty." To which Aimwell replies: "The world confesses it every day in its practice, though men won't own it for their opinion" (1.1.354).

80 Cf. Pope's powerful realization of the topos seven years later in his *Epilogue to the Satires* I.

81 *The Modern Husband*, 2.2; *Works*, ed. Henley, 10:27.

82 Pope's mock epic is about "dulness," perhaps because Dryden had preempted nonsense (and because its point of origin was the supposed pedantry of Lewis Theobald); but dulness only serves Pope's purpose when it becomes nonsense.

83 Tom's relations with the giantess were part of a Danish version, which treated "Svend Tomling, a man no bigger than a thumb, who would be married to a woman three ells and three quarters long." In a German version, "Danmerling," or Little Thumb, was swallowed by a cow. In this and other ways (Tom is also carried away by a raven, dances on the queen's hand), Thumb may have been a source for Gulliver's adventures in Brobdingnag. See *Chap-books of the Eighteenth Century*, ed. John Ashton (London, 1882).

84 The ballad of Tom Thumb was printed for John Wright in 1630; the second and third parts were written around 1700.

85 *Chap-books*, 209, 210, 213.

86 Why, Hume asks, should Fielding in *Tom Thumb* "flog so sickly a horse as heroic tragedy?" Though some of the old plays he parodies were still revived, and of course permit him to satirize pseudo-scholarship in *The Tragedy of Tragedies*, the most cogent reason is that they, better than any other literary form, embodied – illustrated – the bombast he associated with false greatness, in this case of a specifically *heroic* (Herculean) sort (to cite the title of Eugene Waith's *Herculean Hero* [New York: Columbia University Press, 1962]).

87 See *Dunciad*, esp. Book I; but also Dryden's *MacFlecknoe*, ll. 91–3.

88 For *The Beggar's Opera* as a world-turned-upside-down, see Ian Donaldson, *The World Upside-Down: Comedy from Jonson to Fielding* (Oxford: Clarendon Press 1970).

89 Bertrand A. Goldgar, *Walpole and the Wits: The Relation of Politics to Literature, 1722–1742* (Lawrence: Univ. of Kansas Press, 1976). See also T. R. Cleary, *Henry Fielding: Political Writer* (Waterloo, Ontario: Wilfred Laurier University Press, 1984), and Brian McCrea, *Henry Fielding and the Politics of Mid-Eighteenth-Century England* (Athens, Ga.: University of Georgia Press, 1981).

Hume's assertion that there is "no evidence that Fielding wished to write political satire" in the early 1730s, that "none of his early plays was genuinely political" (115), offers too narrow a sense of political, meaning simply *for the Opposition.* The problem with Hume's statement that "nowhere before 1737 does [Fielding] display fundamental disapproval of Walpole, either moral or ideological" (118) is that we have to define what we mean by "Walpole" and how this relates to the topos of "greatness."

Cross and Dudden see *The Tragedy of Tragedies* as an attack on Walpole; Goldgar as "innocent of political innuendo" in both versions; Cleary as innocent in the first text, political in the second. *The Tragedy of Tragedies*, of course, added "the Great" in the subtitle, the description of the dramatic personae, and the performance *with The Welsh Opera* in 1731 (the connection of royal families).

90 Though *Polly* would have shown him how not to carry on in a more specific form that may be censored.

91 See Michael McKeon, *The Origin of the English Novel 1600–1740* (Baltimore: Johns Hopkins University Press, 1986).

92 Percival, *Ballads*, 15; also *A Miscellany of Court Songs* (1728).

93 I have discussed the matter in these terms in *Breaking and Remaking: Aesthetic Practice in England, 1700–1820* (New Brunswick: Rutgers University Press 1989), 94–8.

94 See below, 125, 144.

95 This he learned from Shaftesbury; see below, 75.

96 In II.2 Molly assumes the roles of Polly Peachum between father and lover: "Oh! unhappy wretch that I am: I must have no husband, or no father – What shall I do – or whither shall I turn?" (9:236); which directly echoes the scene in which Macheath pivots back and forth between Polly and Lucy, followed by Polly's doing the same between Macheath and Mr. Peachum.

97 Fielding may have picked up the analogy between government and family from *Fog's Weekly Journal,* Aug. 15, 1730 (B 114).

98 This may be partly as a contrast and comparison with his mother (Prince Frederick with Queen Caroline), a supporter of religion who admired such controversial divines as Samuel Clarke.

99 Laetitia Pilkington, *Memoirs,* 3 (1751):155.

100 I think this explanation carries more weight than Battestin's that "modern critics have strained too hard to attribute the play's success to timely political satire" (B 88; citing Goldgar, *Walpole and the Wits,* 104–5).

101 Walpole "three Times graced with his Presence that sublime *Drama* call'd the History of *Tom Thumb,* acted at the little House in the *Haymarket*" (*Fog's Weekly Journal,* Aug. 1, 1730). "Orator" Henley, in *The Hype-Doctor* of June 10, 1740, associates the play with *Pasquin* and *The Golden Rump* as anti-ministerial propaganda; again, the *DP*, March 29, 1742.

102 *Fog's Weekly Journal,* Aug. 1, 1730; *Craftsman,* Aug. 22, 1730; *Grub-Street Journal,* Nov. 18, 1731.

103 Giles Jacob, *The Mirrour: or, Letters Satyrical, Panegyrical, Serious and Humorous, on the Present Times* (1673), 3, 13.

104 Anon., *Observations on the Present Taste for Poetry* (1739).

105 As early as April 1731 he sided with the critics in the epilogue he wrote to Lewis Theobald's *Orestes,* affirming its "variety" to those "who come / From the *Italian Opera,* and *Tom Thumb.*" Battestin is probably right that he (or some

part of him) felt that he had been "reduced to making a living by scribbling farces and burlesques for the worst of the London theatres" with "the reputation of a writer of drolleries" (B 127).

106 Dryden, *Works*, 10:206, 209, 207. Harold Love gives a good example of the dramatic operation of wit in Congreve's *Old Batchelour* (*Congreve*, Oxford: Blackwell, 1974, ch. 2).

107 To Lady Mary Wortley Montagu, Sept. 4, 1730, *Corresp.*, 4.

108 *Misc.* 1:57.

109 Greater London Record Office (Middlesex): MDR/Bundle 474, No. 386; B 80.

110 *The Connoisseur: A Satire on the Modern Men of Taste* (1735), 20.

111 See Alvin Kernan, *The Cankered Muse* (New Haven: Yale University Press, 1960).

112 Which probably recalls Swift's "Progress of Love" (1719).

113 See B 181–3.

114 The parallel with *The Old Debauchees* and *The Covent-Garden Tragedy* suggests itself.

115 Preface to *Love of Fame* (2nd edn., 1728), sig. a verso. Collins, on the other hand, cites Lucian's dialogues as a model in his *Discourse concerning Ridicule and Irony in Writing* (1729), connecting Lucian's impious dialogues with Erasmus' *Colloquies*. On Lucian, see Levi R. Lind, "Lucian and Fielding," *Classical Weekly*, 29 (1936): 84–6; Christopher Robinson, *Lucian and his Influence in Europe* (Chapel Hill: University of North Carolina Press, 1979), 211–23; Miller, *Essays*, 366–86. These pages originated in Paulson, *The Fictions of Satire*, 31–42; and re Fielding, *Satire and the Novel*, 132–8.

116 *Covent-Garden Journal*, no. 52, 288.

117 Fielding has Billy Booth remark in *Amelia* that Swift excelled every writer except Lucian (bk. 8, chap. 6); cf. *Covent-Garden Journal*, Feb. 4 and June 30 1752. Fielding's Lucianic imitations include a vision of Charon's boat in the *Champion*, May 24, 1741), based on Lucian's tenth. The *Dialogue between Alexander the Great and Diogenes* is based on Lucian's thirteenth *Dialogue of the Dead*; the *Interlude between Jupiter, Juno, Apollo and Mercury* and *Tumble-Down Dick* owe a general debt to the *Dialogues of the Gods*. *The Journey from This World to the Next* derives from the *Dialogues of the Dead*, the *True History*, *Menippus*, and *The Cock*; the voyage of Mrs. Heartfree in *Jonathan Wild* derives in a general way from the *True History*. For an interesting account of Lucian's influence on Fielding, see H. K. Miller, *Essays*, 366–86.

Nancy A. Mace (*Henry Fielding's Novels and the Classical Tradition* [Newark, Del.: University of Delaware Press, 1996]) bases her agument that Lucian was not, as Fielding claimed, of great importance to him, on the number of Fielding's quotations from Lucian's works. But of course quotations are going to be more frequent from Horace, Juvenal, and Martial; but the presence of the Lucianic travesty as a central mode of Fielding's satire, as well as direct imitations such as those mentioned (*pace* Mace, the *Journey* owes more to Lucian than to Plato), argue against her position.

118 The action-commentary was discussed by, among others, F. W. Bateson in *Comic Drama, 1700–1750* (Oxford: Clarendon Press, 1929), 121–42; Paulson, *Satire and the Novel*, 85–95; J. Paul Hunter, *Occasional Form: Henry Fielding & the*

Chains of Circumstance (Baltimore: Johns Hopkins University Press, 1975), 50–6.

119   *Spectator* no. 415; Bond ed., 3:541. Addison extended novelty into a further area he called the Strange, the land of *faerie*, the subject matter of English folklore. In *Tom Thumb* the mock similes represent the area of the novel, that is, the new as satirized by Buckingham and the Scriblerians; but with the subject of little Thumb, the giants and cows, he represents the Strange; both areas, for Fielding like Addison, despite their pedigree in Augustan satire, contain a positive valence. See Paulson, *Beautiful, Novel, and Strange*, ch. 2.

120   The politicians discussing a tax are followed by the ladies discussing Farinelli (the opera star) dolls; and Medley comments: He has already noted

> that there was a strict resemblance between the states political and the-
> atrical; there is a ministry in the latter as in the former; and I believe
> as weak a ministry as any poor kingdom could ever boast of; parts are
> given in the latter to actors, with much the same regard to capacity, as
> places in the former have sometimes been . . . ; and though the public
> damn both, yet while they both receive their pay, they laugh at the
> public behind the scenes; and if one considers the plays that come from
> one part, and the writings from the other, one would be apt to think
> the same authors were retained in both. (Henley edn. 11:257–8).

And this introduces Apollo and the theater to balance the politicians, Walpole (the silent politician) and Ground Ivy the theater manager (Cibber).

121   B 233.

122   See *LS*, 1:lxxxvi–lxxxvii, cxlii–clxiv; B 233.

123   According to the account of Thomas Davies, ed. Lillo's *Works* (1775), 1:xv–xvii.

124   Harris, "Essay" on Fielding, in Probyn, 306–7.

125   See Vincent J. Leisenfeld, *The Licensing Act of 1737* (Madison: University of Wisconsin Press, 1984).

126   John, Lord Hervey, *Memoirs of the Reign of George the Second*, ed. J. W. Croker (London, 1848), 2:341–2.

127   Chesterfield, *Miscellaneous Works* (1777), 1:228ff.

128   B 236.

129   Earl of Egmont, Historical MSS. Commission, *MSS. of the Earl of Egmont. Diary of Viscount Percival* (London: Historical Manuscript Commission, 1920–3), 1:97.

130   Aaron Hill[?], *See and Seem Blind: Or, A Critical Dissertation on the Publick Diversions, &c. . . . In a letter from the Right Honourable the Lord B—— to A—— H——*, Esq. (June 1732), 7–8; ed. Robert Hume, Augustan Reprint Society Publication no. 235 (Los Angeles: Clark Memorial Library, 1986).

131   See also James Miller in *Seasonable Reproof* (1735), ll. 46–52.

132   Lady Mary Wortley Montagu to her daughter, Lady Bute, Sept. 22 [1755]; in Halsband, ed., *Complete Letters*, 3:88. See also Murphy, 1:27–8.

133   Quoted, B 103.

134   *Dramatick Sessions*, 11–12. Fielding shares Mr. Apshinken's love for tobacco (we know from later satires that he was addicted to tobacco, and in his last

year he will recreate Mrs. Apshinken as the mean hostess Mrs. Francis in *Journal of a Voyage to Lisbon.*

135 *Daily Gazetteer,* July 30, 1740, admittedly a ministerial journal responding to Fielding's *Champion.* He was recalled by the ministry journal *The Gazetteer,* Oct. 9, 1740: "one whose Private Conduct on many Occasions, is charitably pass'd over, lest it should make his Readers (those at least who are sincere in the Cause of Virtue) blush."

136 T 104.

137 *Universal Spectator,* July 6, 1734; in *The Connoisseur: A Satire on the Modern Men of Taste* (1735), 20.

138 *Spectator* no. 412; ed. Bond, 3:540.

139 This discussion of deism originated in Paulson, *Beautiful, Novel, and Strange,* ch. 5.

140 *Champion,* Jan. 22, 1739/40. Even Battestin acknowledges that Fielding may have had deist inclinations in his early years. But to Battestin deists were the egregious sinners depicted by clergymen in the sermons that are his primary source for religious thought in the period. Although in Fielding's day latitudinarian meant to many no more than a safe deist, Battestin applies the term to Fielding in order to emphasize his orthodoxy, and in Aubrey Williams's account Fielding can be mistaken for an Anglican divine. See James A. Work, "Henry Fielding, Christian Censor," in *The Age of Johnson: Essays Presented to Chauncey Brewster Tinker* (New Haven: Yale University Press, 1949), 139–148; Battestin, *The Moral Basis of Fielding's Art: A Study of "Joseph Andrews"* (Middletown, Conn.: Wesleyan University Press, 1959); Aubrey Williams, "Interpositions of Providence and the Design of Fielding's Novels," *South Atlantic Quarterly,* 70 (1971): 265–86.

141 See Paulson, "Life as Journey and as Theater: Two Eighteenth-Century Narrative Structures," *New Literary History,* 8 (1976): 43–58, reprinted in R. Paulson, *Popular and Polite Art in the Age of Hogarth and Fielding* (Notre Dame: University of Notre Dame Press, 1979), ch. 2. 2.

142 *Comedian* no. 1 (April 1732), 4. For the continuation of this metaphor, see below, 317.

143 For the history of deism, see John Orr, *English Deism: Its Roots and Fruits* (Grand Rapids, Mich., 1934) and – for our purposes, the most useful source – Roland N. Stromberg, *Religious Liberalism in Eighteenth-Century England* (Oxford: Oxford University Press, 1954).

144 As the deist John Toland wrote, "Popery in reality is nothing else, but the Clergy's assuming a Right to think for the Laity" ("A Word to the Honest Priests," in *An Appeal to Honest People against Wicked Priests* [1713], 38; see Stephen H. Daniel, *John Toland: His Methods, Manners, and Mind* [Kingston and Montreal: McGill-Queen's University Press, 1984], 28–9.)

145 *Library,* G75–7, S31, S37, S48–9.

146 According to Battestin and Probyn in *Corresp.,* 12–13. The Fielding–Harris correspondence only began in 1741 with a letter that refers to itself as "a first Visit, which gives you a Power either to encourage or reject the Acquaintance," but Fielding seems to be referring to their situation that summer, with himself in Bath and Harris in Salisbury, which called for epistolary correspondence.

147 See Probyn, 38–41. Battestin mentions that Harris's mother was the daughter of the *second* earl, but does not mention the third, and instead of mentioning deism writes that "it was Harris's keen mind and kind heart that drew Fielding to him" (310).

148 Probyn, 64, 62–3. Shaftesbury dissociated himself from the name of deist, attacking those he referred to as deists. See Robert Voitle, *The Third Earl of Shaftesbury* (Baton Rouge: University of Louisiana Press, 1984), 347. Fielding may have been ambivalent about Harris's extreme classicism which led him to revise the classical philosophical sources and efface "contemporary references and, more importantly, the insights which were both new and original to himself" – that is, precisely the opposite of Fielding's procedure. Indeed, as Probyn puts it, Harris was convinced "that the collective cultural memory of mid-eighteenth-century England [of classical culture] has become parochial, insular, obsessed with its own present..." (79). This aspect of Shaftesburian thought Fielding rejected.

149 "This ... is certain," he wrote in his *Inquiry concerning Virtue and Merit* (1699, 1711), "that the admiration and love of order, harmony, and proportion, in whatever kind, is naturally improving to the temper, advantageous to social affection, and highly assistant to virtue, which is itself no other than the love of order and beauty in society" (Shaftesbury, *Characteristics of Men, Manners, Opinions, Times, etc.*, ed. John M. Robertson [New York: E. P. Dutton, 1900], 1: 279).

150 They illustrate certain important subjects in which Fielding as well as Harris and Shaftesbury were interested – primarily charity; and the fact that Fielding owned the fifth edition of Isaac Barrow's *Works* and quoted him shows that he read the sermons; something of Barrow's phrasing, his homiletic formulations, and even perhaps the form comes across in some of Fielding's essays. One suspects, in fact, that Fielding may not have read Barrow until he acquired the 1741 edition, possibly in the reprint of 1751. The earliest suggestions that he may be echoing Barrow are in Battestin's notes to *Tom Jones*, but there is no similarity in phrasing, only similar ideas; or when there may be, it is to Barrow's biblical source not Barrow's sermon that Fielding has turned. See, e.g., *Tom Jones*, 567 n., the "sword." The reference to Epicures/ Epicurus in 96 (cf. Battestin's note) is the closest, since Fielding does quote the Barrow passage later in the *CGJ* – but significantly *not* the part about Epicurus. Beginning in *Amelia* and the *Covent-Garden Journal* Fielding does cite and quote Barrow with approval. But this coincides with his need (personally and as magistrate) for religious texts and citations of ecclesiastical authority.

He does quote "the witty" South in the earlier years: the same quotation in *An Essay on Knowledge of the Characters of Men* and in the *Champion* for March 6, 740; again in *A Dialogue* and *A Proper Answer* and the *Jacobite's Journal* ("The fatal Imposture and Force of Words").

151 And probably Benjamin Franklin as well. Battestin notes with horror Franklin's youthful deist tract (152). Ralph and Cooke were deists and at the same time supporters of the Walpole ministry: significant because this indicates the different paths by which one arrived at deism – Hogarth by way of radical protestantism, others by way of libertinism or Hobbesian (and Tory) rationalism.

152 His attacks on Pope immediately preceded Fielding's, as did his first dramatic production, *Penelope, a dramatic Opera* (1728, assisting John Mottley). In 1731 *The Triumph of Love and Honour* was performed at Drury Lane, and in 1737 a musical farce based on Terence's *Eunuch*. See Sir Joseph Maubey's life of Cooke in *GM* for 1791, 92 and 97; xli, pt. 2, 1089, 1178; lxii, pt. 1, 26, 215, 313; lxvii, pt. 2, 560; *DNB*.

153 *Comedian* no. 2. Subsequent papers are on the immortality of the soul and a future state (no. 5), on liberty, necessity, and the freedom of the will (no. 6), on the origin of evil (no. 7), and climactically on God, Providence, and Nature (no. 8). See B 156.

154 Cooke, ed., *The Works of Andrew Marvell, Esq.* (1726), 17. He describes Marvell, an Old Whig, as "a Defender of Truth, when it was almost a capital Crime to assert it" (8). He emphasizes Marvell's independence and the constant threats to his life – no one is named, but it is implicitly the high church and the court party. The verses on Marvell he quotes open with another attack on the clergy:

> While Lazy Prelates lean'd their mitred Heads
> On downy Pillows, lull'd with Wealth and Pride,
> Pretending Prophecy, yet Nought foresee, . . . (37).

155 *Touch-Stone*, 22, 25–6. See Helen S. Hughes, "Fielding's Indebtedness to James Ralph," *Modern Philology*, 20 (1922): 19–34. On Ralph and deism, cf. B 152.

156 *DP*, Feb. 1, 1726/7.

157 See John Burke Shipley, *James Ralph: Pretender to Genius* (Columbia Univ. doctoral diss., 1963), 81, citing H. N. Fairchild that *The Tempest* "is the only overt expression of Ralph's contempt for orthodox religious belief" (*Religious Trends in English Poetry* [New York: Columbia University Press, 1939], 1:373).

158 Battestin thinks the puff in the *Craftsman* might show that Amhurst "believed that Fielding was drifting into the Opposition camp" (100). If Fielding wrote the "Thomas Squint" piece for *Fog's Weekly*, July 25, or the "Harry Hunter" essay for the *Craftsman* of Oct. 10 (with its characteristic *Craftsman* analogy between fox-hunters and politicians) this would support Battestin's speculation (*New Essays*). But significant links already existed, and it is easy to suppose that over drinks Fielding was as *Craftsman-* and Opposition-oriented as Amhurst and Hogarth.

159 L. P. Goggin was the first to draw attention to *The Masquerade*'s debt to Hogarth's print ("Fielding's *The Masquerade*," *Philological Quarterly*, 36 [1957]: 475–87).

160 See Addison's account of the "Men of greater Penetration" in the hierarchy of readers of allegory, *Spectator* no. 315.

161 However, Fielding had opened his first comedy with *ut pictura poesis*, the poetry-painting analogy, and he continued throughout his work to compare his writing with Hogarth's graphic images.

162 Gildon's book was *The New Metamorphosis* (1725), a modernization and burlesque of Apuleius' *The Ass* (see Paulson, *Hogarth's Graphic Works* (New Haven: Yale University Press, 1965; 3rd edn., London: The Print Room, 1989) nos. 45–50.

163   The reversal of roles in Justice Squeezum and the hero Ramble recall Hogarth's paintings, *Falstaff examining his Recruits* and *Committee of the House of Commons* (1727, 1729).

164   Hogarth had contributed to the Opposition satire in 1726–7, but in 1728 he accepted a commission from Walpole to engrave the Great Seal of England he had relinquished upon the death of George I and painted close relatives of Walpole's; in 1731 he was praised by the Walpole supporter, Joseph Mitchell in a poetic epistle and was friendly with other Walpole supporters. But he continued to glance at Walpole in the *Harlot* in the analogical way of the *Craftsman*. See Paulson, *Hogarth*, 1 (New Brunswick: Rutgers University Press, 1992), ch. 8, and *Hogarth's Graphic Works*, nos. 120–6.

165   *Champion*, June 10, 1740 (2:317). He adds, "I almost dare affirm that those two Works of his, which he calls the *Rake*'s and the *Harlot's Progress*, are calculated more to serve the Cause of Virtue, and for the Preservation of Mankind, than all the *Folio*'s of Morality which have been ever written; and a sober Family should no more be without them, than without the *Whole Duty of Man* in their House."

166   In the actress unsuccessfully playing the goddess of chastity Hogarth may have remembered Fielding's lines

> But had Diana thro' her clan,
> (To try how far th' infection ran)
> Forc'd all her followers to tryal
> Of chastity, by ordeal;
> Who knows (tho' it had rag'd no higher)
> What pretty feet had swell'd by fire?
> (*Masquerade*, ll. 243–8)

167   Cf. my different accounts in *Breaking and Remaking*, 149–55, and *Hogarth*, 2 (New Brunswick: Rutgers University Press, 1992) 97–103.

168   See Paulson, *Hogarth*, 1, and *Beautiful, Novel, and Strange*, passim. While the images are most easily traced to the Dürer prints, they are found in numerous paintings and prints of the fifteenth to seventeenth centuries.

169   This was a method Woolston picked up from Anthony Collins's *Discourse on the Grounds and Reasons of the Christian Religion* (1742), which argues that only through allegory could the argument from Old Testament prophecy for the divine origins of Christianity be supported, and carried to a satiric (or lunatic, depending on the point of view) extreme.

170   See Paulson, *Hogarth*, vol. 1, ch. 9.

171   In 1725 Woolston had published his *Moderator between an Infidel and an Apostate*, which focuses on the suspicious "miracle" of the Virgin Birth, one story being the Jewish slander that she was seduced by a soldier named Panthera (53). For this he was charged by Bishop Gibson with blasphemy and arrested in the autumn of 1725, though the charges were finally dropped. In Hogarth's *Cunicularii: Or the Wise Men of Godlimen* of 1726, ostensibly a reportorial print, the "Wise Men" of the title draw attention to the echo of an "Adoration of the Magi" composition; Mary Toft's husband stands at the left, gaping at the miracle, in the position of Joseph. The Virgin Birth was always, among freethinkers, the miracle that evoked the most mirth.

172   Aaron Hill, *Prompter*, April 2, 1736.
173   The allusion to the betrayal of Christ when Jenny points him out to the police could have been dramatized by the gestures of the actors, as was certainly the case in the "Choice of Hercules" scene (Macheath between Polly and Lucy). The opening scene of the act in which Macheath is betrayed could have been staged as a mock Last Supper. For contemporary awareness of Hogarth's practice, see the attacks by Paul Sandby in the 1750s, in particular *The Burlesquer Burlesqued.*
174   The influence went both ways. In *Harlot* 4 Hogarth illustrates the constable's prediction to Mrs. Novel in *The Author's Farce* that she will have "been in Bridewell a week; / Have beaten good hemp, and been / Whipt at a post" (8:254); or, in both detail and sentiment, the simile in *Tom Thumb.*

> So, when some wench to Tothill Bridewell's sent,
> With beating hemp and flogging she's content,
> She hopes in time to ease her present pain,
> At length is free and walks the streets again.

Plate 5 echoes the two doctors who argue about their respective cures over the dead Tom Thumb. And perhaps plate 2 recalls the line, "take a dress'd Monkey for a Man" (Hillhouse edn.: New Haven: Yale University Press, 1918, 61, 68, 69).
175   Though not produced until June, Fielding's play may have been ready as early as April 4, but in any case Fielding would have seen the paintings as early as the subscriptions in March 1731.
176   There may also have been allusions in Fielding's sets and costumes. The *Grub-Street Journal* (June 8, 1732) noticed the similarity when, in its unsympathetic discussion of Fielding's new play, it linked Stormandra with "Hackabouta" as whores Fielding paraded on his stage; and in his introduction to the printed text of his play, Fielding added "A Criticism on the Covent-Garden Tragedy, originally intended for The Grub-Street Journal," in which he refers to "several very odd names in this piece, such as Hackabouta, &c." Either the *Grub-Street Journal* introduced the Harlot's name as a hint that Fielding was playing on Hogarth's popularity, or Fielding had actually used the name on his stage but changed it in the printed text.
177   Hogarth absorbed the effect Mother Needham's death must have had into his meaning: She became another sacrifice, like the Harlot, to society's "greatness" (i.e., sins).
178   Both Hogarth and Fielding are following their common source, Gay's *Beggar's Opera*, in this respect.
179   Returning to the model of *The Beggar's Opera* (his opening recalls Peachum's first song), Fielding substitutes a brothel for Gay's prison setting. He had been successful when he placed *Tom Thumb* in a fairy tale setting and *The Welsh Opera* in the English countryside; a brothel offended.
180   Quoted, B 141.
181   Cited, B 135. From Battestin these plays elicit the outrage he always expresses at signs of deism (a "tasteless attempt").

182 B 142. For the *Grub-Street Journal's* attack on Fielding's irreligion, see "Marforio," May 6, 1736, aimed at Firebrand in *Pasquin*; also *A Letter to a Noble Lord, to whom Alone it Belongs* (1742), 2 (B 199). *On Religious Disputes*, a poem of 1736, equates Fielding and Hoadly (pointed out, B 200).

183 See Peter Lewis, "Fielding's *The Covent-Garden Tragedy* and Philips' *The Distrest Mother*," *Durham University Journal*, 37 (1976): 33–46.

184 In retrospect, it is even arguable that in the 1731 *Tragedy of Tragedies; or The Life and Death of Tom Thumb the Great*, which sported Hogarth's frontispiece, Fielding offered something resembling a safer version of Hogarth's *Cuniculario; or, The Wise Men of Godlimen*. Fielding added to Doodle's speech on the birth of Tom Thumb in the 1730 text: "Some God, my *Noodle*, stept into the Place / Of Gaffer *Thumb*, and more than half begot, / This mighty *Tom*." To which Noodle adds, "Sure he was sent Express / From Heav'n, to be the Pillar of our State" (Hillhouse, 92). The publication was in the last week of March 1731, just as Hogarth launched his subscription for the *Harlot*.

185 Unless the lost *Deborah: or, A Wife for You All* was possibly a burlesque of the Old Testament story (or of Handel's *Deborah* of 1733).

186 "Some Accounts of PLAY-HOUSES," in *The Usefulness of the Stage to Religion, and to Government* (2d edn., 1738), 16–17.

187 *LS*, xlv. PRO LC.5.160.318. Warrant Book (Mar. 10, 1736/7). According to John Mottley, the dramatic historian, Cibber, reading his "New Year's Day Ode," was performed by none other than Charlotte Chark, his own daughter, well known for transvestite roles: "what was shocking to everyone who had the least Sense of Decency or good Manners," wrote Mottley (Mottley, "List of all the Dramatic Authors," appended to Thomas Whincop, *Scanderbeg* (1747), 235.

188 Thomas (coming from the direction of Sadean libertinism) detects a "whiff of political nihilism" in Fielding's satire; accepting the ministry propagandists' accusation that Fielding's satire was aimed at all political parties (ix). G. B. Shaw saw Fielding the playwright as a "*Herculean* Satyrist . . . that seem'd to knock all Distinctions of Mankind on the Head" (preface to *First Volume of Plays: Pleasant and Unpleasant* [1906]).

189 Hogarth's *Four Times of the Day* and its pendant, *Strolling Actresses dressing in a Barn* of 1737–38 (see plate 5, 84), recover many of the details of *Tumble-Down Dick* of 1736. Having carried his modernizing (or demythologizing) of the Christian story as far as or farther than it could be carried, he turns to the safer area of classical mythology in specifically the terms of a stage performance. Fielding's *Tumble-Down Dick* appeared at the Little Haymarket in April 1736; Hogarth's prints were announced as "in great forwardness" in May 1737 (all five were published together in March 1738), by which time *Strolling Actresses* carried – an obvious last-minute insertion – a notice of the Licensing Act that forbade future performances of strolling actresses.

190 B 124.

191 See 8: 277, 288.

192 In his earlier plays the low were viewed as analogues of the great, but Fielding made no attempt to suggest that these characters behave as they do in imitation of the royal family or the prime minister. This idea becomes explicit

only in *The Covent-Garden Tragedy* with the bawds, whores, and their clients assuming the poses and diction of epic heroes. Whether Fielding is puffing the *Harlot's Progress* or, more likely, benefiting from its thematization of imitation, the presence is felt, but Fielding's imitation drags down only classical heroes (their inappropriateness as models for contemporaries) and not, as in the *Harlot*, social superiors.

193 Though, in *The Welsh Opera* Sweetissa sings: "valets, who learn their lords' wit, / Our virtue a bauble can call" (234). Trapwit's *"Election"* comedy was picked up 20 years later by Hogarth in his *Election*, especially plate 2. *Pasquin* also contained a hint Hogarth picked up and illustrated in *Strolling Actresses*, when Mrs. Mayoress, yearning for city ridottos, complained that, "confined these twelve months in the country[,] we have no entertainment, but a set of hideous, strolling players" (179).

194 See Jill Campbell, *Natural Masques: Gender and Identity in Fielding's Plays and Novels* (Stanford: Stanford University Press, 1995).

195 In Hogarth's paintings of *The Beggar's Opera* he shows Polly mediating between her father and Macheath; this is the configuration he builds on in his works following the *Harlot*.

196 *Comedian*, no. 5 (Aug. 1732), 37 and n. Thomas Lockwood accepts the poem on internal evidence, and Battestin agrees (161).

NOTES TO CHAPTER 3

1 *Daily Gazetteer*, Oct. 12, 1737.
2 Middle Temple: "Admissions to House and Chambers, 1695–1737," f. 574.
3 *Corresp.*, 7.
4 B 250–1.
5 For the whole transaction, see B 248–9.
6 Walter was not, however, the purchaser of the property, as Hanbury Williams suggests in his "Dialogue between Peter Walters & Henry Fielding" (Aug. 1743). B cites the evidence on both sides (248–9). For Walter's (Peter Pounce's) interest rate, see *Joseph Andrews*, 1.10.47.
7 PRO Kempson vs. Fielding, KB.122.178, Roll 253; Gascoigne vs. Fielding, PRO Ind.6501 (Docket Books) and CP.40.3502, Roll 1592; recounted, B 252.
8 Where in August the deaths of his stepmother Eleanor and his aunt Mrs. Cottington took place (B 252).
9 The house is a comfortable one at a yearly rent of £50. See the letter to Nourse, July 9, 1739, *Corresp.*, 8–9; N. Maslin, "Henry Fielding's Homes," *Notes & Queries*, 30 (Feb. 1983): 50.
10 For the "proprietors," see B 259.
11 Fielding v. William Deards, PRO KB.122.175, Roll 522, Michaelmas term. HF's thrusts at Deards appear, before, in *The Temple Beau* 4.6 and *The Miser* 2.1, and after, *The Vernoniad* (1741, 30 and n. 58), *Joseph Andrews* 3.6, *Jonathan Wild* 2.3 and 3.6, *A Journey from This World to the Next* 1.1, *Tom Jones* 12.4, and *Covent-Garden Journal* Jan. 4, 1752.

12   PRO CP.40, Roll 362; KB.docket Book. Hil., 14 Geo. II, 1740, Special Remem-
      brances, No. 697; and KB.125.147, Rule Book, Easter, 14 Geo. II, 1741; and
      another, Brien Janson, PRO CP.Docket Book, Ind.6173. For Henley's and
      other debts coming due and going unpaid, see B 265–6. For Penelope,
      see St. Clement Danes burial registers, Westminster History Collection,
      Buckingham Palace Road (B 234, 650 n. 411).

13   B believes "There is little reason to doubt that Fielding wrote the whole of the
      translation" (654 n. 25, citing M. and J. Farringdon, "A Computer Aided Study
      of the Prose Style of Henry Fielding and its Support for his translation of the
      Military History of Charles XII," in D. E. Ager, F. E. Knowles, and J. Smith [eds.],
      Advances in Computer-Aided Literary and Linguistic Research [Birmingham, 1979],
      95–105). All this proves is that HF corrected the whole translation.

14   Elizabeth Blunt, PRO KB.122.178/253, Roll 255; and Ind.6173, May 1740; also
      CP40 3502/1592; KB122 187/604; KB122 189/689.

15   See Godden, 115, 138–9; John F. Speer, "A Critical Study of the *Champion*,"
      Ph.D. dissertation, University of Chicago, 1951.

16   Middle Temple, "Orders of Parliament" (June 20, 1740), 467. HF takes cham-
      bers in Pump Court, Middle Temple, but probably only pro forma; obtained
      on June 20 for £2 and relinquished on November 28 for the same fee (Middle
      Temple "Day Book" for June 20 and Nov. 28, 1740).

17   Edmund, who committed John to Wilkie's care on March 10, sued Wilkie for
      gross negligence and incompetence and won damages of £500 (PRO
      KB.122.183, Hil., 14 Geo. II, 1740, Pt. II, Roll 778; B 655 n. 28).

18   Letter to Davidge Gould, July 15, 1740, *Corresp.*, 9.

19   *LDP*, Dec. 15, 1739; for Oct. 10, 1740, *DG*. HF's receipt for payment of the
      £45 from Nourse for the translation is dated Mar. 10, 1739/40 (Yale, MSS.
      Vault: Fielding).

20   B 299.

21   For all of the records of General Fielding's trial and commitment (including
      earlier cases), see B 299 n. 64.

22   PRO Plea Rolls, KB.122.189, Pt. 2, Roll 689; KB.122.187, Roll 604; Palace
      Court, 2/34, Plaints, p. 379. To take this one example: HF first borrows £25
      from Charles Fielding, Esq., and the note is subsequently transferred to Allen.
      Then in Dec. HF borrows another £170. The suit is continually postponed
      (ten or so reschedulings), until finally on April 24 Allen is called on to settle
      a final amount. The other debts had been separated from Allen's, reducing
      the amount from £200 to £28.16s (PRO KB122 189/689). The charge for
      Allen's court costs is £35.9.8. At the very finish of the record, Fielding and
      Giles Taylor appear on the record not only denying the charges but suggest-
      ing they be reversed (and that judgment be annulled).

23   See the *Champion* partners' minute-book, Mar. 1 [1741/2]: HF has "withdrawn
      himself from that Service for above Twelve Months past and refused his Assis-
      tance in that Capacity since which time Mr. Ralph has solely Transacted the
      said Business" (Godden, 128–39).

24   B 295–6.

25   Lambeth Palace Library: Faculty Office Calendar of Marriage licences, Mar.
      7, 1740/1; married on the 9th in St. Bride's Church (Guildhall Library, MS.
      6542/1, Mar. 9).

26   PRO Palace Court 1/37, Bail Book, pp. 61, 63.

27   Anon., *The Young Senator. A Satyre, With An Epistle to Mr. Fielding, on His Study-
      ing the Law* (Mar. 1738), 16.

28   Anon., *The Church Yard: A Satirical Poem* (May 1739), 14–15.

29   *Craftsman* No. 650, Dec. 23, 1738 (*New Essays*, 386).

30   Battestin's attributions are controversial, but I find enough of them convinc-
      ing to tend toward accepting the others as well. Though Bolingbroke had
      returned to the continent, *The Craftsman* was still heavily subsidized by the
      Opposition magnates.

31   He had promised a "paper" to match the *Gazetteer* in the dedication to *The
      Historical Register*; at the time it may have been rhetoric, but it is also possible
      that something like *The Champion* had been proposed to him and later came
      to fruition.

32   Advertisements in *Craftsman, Common Sense*, and *London Evening Post*, Nov. 10,
      1739 (B 260).

33   One wonders why Fielding, considering his own experience of the army in
      his immediate family, has Hercules add the gratuitous information that "I
      entered upon the Title of *Captain*; this I did without the Consent of any One
      Person living, or without any other Commission or Authority than what imme-
      diately derived from myself."

34   B 261.

35   First number, Nov. 15, 1739; first collected edition, 1741.

36   In the essay for Nov. 20, on our misunderstanding of our talents, Fielding
      cites the "Humour of a Father in an *English* Comedy [i.e., his own *Temple
      Beau*], who is determined at all Events to breed his Son a Lawyer" (1:14).

37   One of the latter is described in *Joseph Andrews*, 1:9.

38   Harris's "Essay" on Fielding, Probyn, 308. See also Murphy, 1:28.

39   See J. H. Baker's *An Introduction to English Legal History* (London: Butterworth,
      1979), 148 and chap. 11.

40   Anon., *The Young Senator. A Satyre, With An Epistle to Mr. Fielding, on His Study-
      ing the Law*, 16–17.

41   *Champion*, 2: 199; Apr. 22, 1740, 2: 127; Aug. 19, 1740, Sackett, 24.

42   We may assume that Fielding sat in on assize courts before he was admitted
      to the bar, as he did on the courts of Westminster Hall.

43   *LDP*. Cf. the account in *The Prompter*, Feb. 18.

44   *Champion*, 1: 32–4. "*O!*," Vinegar exclaims at one point, "*they are hunting an
      Author*" (1:89).

45   Quite characteristically he designates the "conversation" of relations and
      acquaintances as what is most missed.

46   *Covent-Garden Journal*, 312.

47   Poverty is another of his subjects. One of his first essays was a dream-vision of
      the Palace of Wealth, in which he finds "a vast Gallery, which surrounded a
      huge Pit so vastly deep, that it almost made me giddy to look to the Bottom."
      This is "the Cave of *Poverty*," which he describes as a terrifying "Abyss" (Dec.
      29, 1739; 1:140).

48   Battestin points out Fielding's slip, which he thinks is significant, when in his
      registration in the Middle Temple he identifies his father as a Brigadier
      General, when he had been promoted to Major General two years earlier.

49 Battestin could also be correct that *Eurydice* produced back at Drury Lane could have been a flirtation with Walpole, a beginning of Fielding's anxiety about turncoats and party writing for money; he refers to "this demeaning equation of Walpole and himself" (221).

50 *Champion* (1740 edn.), 208–9.

51 Swift, "Digression on Madness," in *A Tale of a Tub* (1704), ed. A.C. Guthkelch and D. Nicholl Smith (2nd edn., Oxford: Clarendon Press, 1958), 173–74. The passage also includes a sentence condemning *"Unmasking,* which I think, has never been allowed fair Usage, either in the *World* or the *Play-House,"* which connects "Delusion" with the important strand of theatrical metaphor in Fielding's works.

52 Addison's knight errant in his "Pleasures of the Imagination" further recalls his discussion of the reasonableness of belief in his justification of the Christian religion in no. 465: "A Man is quickly convinced of the Truth of Religion, who finds it is not against his Interest that it should be true. The Pleasure he receives at present, and the Happiness which he promises himself from it hereafter, will both dispose him very powerfully to give Credit to it, according to the ordinary Observation that *we are easie to believe what we wish"* (4:143). In the phrases "against his Interest" and the "Pleasure" and "Happiness" promised from the faith "hereafter," not to mention the final complacent clause, Addison offers essentially the same argument as Fielding.

53 Fielding's passage invites comparison with Cooke's non-satiric *Demonstration,* where he wrote of "that *Power* to which Man owes his Desire of Happyness, and his Aversion to Misery, which Power is *God."* Cooke claims that obedience to "the rule of Right [vs. Christianity] advances our Happyness here; and consequently every Deviation from it is a Deviation from the Road which leads to Happyness" (xiii). The discussion of providence (8–11) concludes that Nature is "that *Power* to which Man owes his Desire of Happyness, and his Aversion to Misery, which Power is *God"*: in short, Nature, God, and Happiness are one.

54 *Enquiry,* I.ii.3, in *Characteristics,* 1:279.

55 In *Tom Jones* he cites Shaftesbury's objection to "telling too much Truth," a reference to "defensive Raillery," which Shaftesbury explained as "when the Spirit of Curiosity wou'd force a Discovery of more Truth than can conveniently be told. For we can never do more Injury to Truth, than by discovering too much of it, on some occasions" (*An Essay on the freedom of Wit and Humour* (1709), in *Characteristics,* 1:45; *Tom Jones,* 14.12).

56 For a corrective, cf. Melvyn New, "'The Grease of God': The Form of 18th-Century English Fiction," *PMLA,* 91 (1976): 235–43.

57 Fielding frequently uses, and alludes to, the passage in Plato's *Phaedrus* (250d); for the dedication to *Tom Jones,* see below, 235.

58 These essays Battestin sees as simply a reflection of the low standing of the clergy at the time – "contempt of the clergy" being "a stock phrase of the time," words he quotes from an ecclesiastical history of 1885 (J. H. Overton, *Life in the English Church (1660–1714),* 1885, 302; B 130). But the key word of the deists was "priestcraft": John Toland, author of *Christianity not Mysterious,* argued that a clergy maintained itself by focusing on the mysterious activity of God and arguing that they alone understood the mysteries of religion. Like

Fielding, Toland distinguished bad priests from good – "an Order of Men not only useful and necessary, but likewise reputable and venerable" (he started a work called "Priesthood without Priestcraft"). See Toland, "A Word to the Honest Priests," in *An Appeal to Honest People against Wicked Priests* (1713); cited, Stephen H. Daniel, *John Toland: His Methods, Manners, and Mind* (Kingston and Montreal: Mc Gill-Queen's University Press, 1984), 26.

59 Fielding's sense of bad clergy in the clergy essays is implicitly related to the bad stewards (lawyers, ministers, Walpole) of Opposition satire (see *Champion* for Feb. 12, 1739/40; cf. Howard Erskine-Hill, *The Social Milieu of Alexander Pope* [New Haven: Yale University Press, 1975], 243–59).

60 Fielding's positive touchstones, based on the Gospels, are humility and charity, which allow him to emphasize the spirit versus the letter of the law. He quotes Luke 20.46, 47: "to beware of the Scribes which desire to walk in long Robes, and love Greetings in the Markets, and the highest Seats in the Synagogues, and the chief Rooms at Feasts, which devour Widows' Houses, and for Show make long Prayers."

61 See S. J. Sackett, ed. and introduction *Voyages of Mr. Job Vinegar.*

62 Sackett, 7.

63 Sackett, 11.

64 Letter to Harris, Sept. 24, 1742; *Corresp.*, 23.

65 *Joseph Andrews*, 3.3.217.

66 Harris, Probyn, 308. Murphy comments that "He attended with punctual assiduity both in term-time and on the Western circuit, as long as his health permitted him; but the gout soon began to make such assaults upon him, as rendered it impossible for him to be as constant at the bar as the laboriousness of his profession required" (Murphy, 1: 51–2).

67 For example, when in June 1739 he borrowed £23.10s. from Walter Barnes, agreeing to repay in five months, Barnes on the same day (the 6th) signed the promisory note over to John Kempson, a pharmacist to whom Fielding already owed "divers other Sums of Money" due to illnesses in his family. Soon after, James Gascoigne sued Fielding for a note for £30 signed over to him by Charles Fielding, going back to 1736, for which he now demanded payment. With further promises and delays the case dragged on until August when he was ordered by the court to pay £38.10s. (See above, n. 22.)

68 Thomas, 159.

69 Lockwood, 4. See also Lockwood, "New Facts and Writings from an Unknown Magazine by Henry Fielding, *The History of Our Town Times*," *Review of English Studies*, s.s. 35 (1984): 463–93.

70 He will pick up this strand of Swift imitation again ten years later in *The Covent-Garden Journal.*

71 Fielding also alludes to the famous lantern at Houghton ("A huge dark lantern hung up in his hall, / And heaps of ill-got pictures hid the wall," 41), which recalls the fledgling satire of 1727.

72 An earlier paper is an imitation of a Lucian dialogue written as a narrative; but the narrative element is only sufficient to support another of Fielding's allegories.

73 The death of his daughter Charlotte was, of course, one of the details added in his final revision of the MS. in 1743. (She died in that year.)

74 He was reading Petronius as he wrote to Harris in 1742 (Sept. 24, *Corresp.*, 24). Peter Burmann's 1709 edition was in his library; which could mean that he acquired it during his stay at Leiden. Later, in his more pious days, in the *Covent-Garden Journal*, he dismissed Petronius.

75 Cumberland, *Memoirs* (1806), 146.

76 One *Champion* provides evidence that what became the chapter "Of Hats" in *Jonathan Wild* may have been in circulation in April 1740 (Apr. 24, 1740, cited B 284).

77 Sept. 16, 1740; also a leader on "Reputation" refers to Wild, Mar. 4, 1740.

78 *Tumble-Down Dick*, 12:16. And when in *Eurydice* Mr. Spindle arrived in a Lucianic hell, ready to recommend himself to the devil by the fact that he was hanged, Captain Weazel warned him: "No, hanged, no; then he will take you for a poor rogue, a sort of people he abominates so, that there are scarce any of them here. No, if you would recommend yourself to him, tell him you *deserved* to be hanged, and was too great for the law" (11:274). As Fielding pointed out regarding punishment in *The Champion* (Jan. 8, 1739/40), "It is not being hanged, but deserving to be hanged, that is infamous."

79 Imitation is distinguished from emulation in the emblem books: one is represented by an ape (who never gets it quite right), the other by two cocks competing.

80 Nor does it matter whether it is specifically Walpole – plainly, by 1743 this is an irrelevant issue; as in *Tom Thumb*, it is the Walpole type of "greatness," which dominates the writing leading up to *Jonathan Wild*.

81 Cf. the opening section of Defoe's biography of Wild (1725).

82 *Champion*, Feb. 26, 1739/40, on Lillo's death.

83 B notices the parallel, 207.

84 Mar. 26, 1748; in *Jacobite's Journal*, 211.

85 *Covent-Garden Journal*, no. 11.

86 "Soliloquy; or, Advice to an Author" (1710), in *Characteristics*, 1:222–3.

87 Hugh Amory has commented somewhere (though not in the Wesleyan edition he coedited) that any judge would know that she has made it all up. David Nokes notes that "the jokes at Mrs. Heartfree's delicacy rather undercut her pose of resilient chastity" (ed. *Jonathan Wild* [Harmondsworth: Penguin Books, 1982], 276).

88 Hogarth, in *Industry and Idleness*, plate 11, in 1747, certainly looks as if he is illustrating the Wild-Ordinary chapter, with Idle being comforted by the dissenter preacher while the Ordinary is ensconced in his coach, placed just above the declaiming ballad-woman vending a life of Idle, a contrast between her demotic and the official, moralizing "life" that the Ordinary will write.

89 Lord Byron thought *Jonathan Wild* more powerful than the Jacobin satire of his day ("Detached thoughts," no. 116 [1821], in *Works*, ed. R. E. Prothero [London, 1901], 5:465).

90 B 282–5.

91 B 281. The quotation is also B's.

92 Blackstone, *Commentaries on the Laws of England* (1765), 3:293. Blackstone, who began to deliver his lectures on the common law at Oxford in the later 1740s, defined the court somewhat differently: as having "three constituent parts, the *actor, reus,* and *judex*: the *actor,* or plaintiff, who complains of an injury

done; the *reus*, or defendant, who is called upon to make satisfaction for it; and the *judex* or judicial power, which is to examine the truth of the fact, to determine the law arising upon the fact, and, if any injury appears to have been done, to ascertain and by it's officers to apply the remedy. It is also usual in the superior courts to have attorneys, and advocates or counsel, as assistants" (3: 25). Besides Blackstone, I have found very useful J. H. Baker's *An Introduction to English Legal History*. See above, n. 39.

93 Cicero, *Murder Trials*, tr. Michael Grant (1975), 73.

94 Blackstone, 1: 17.

95 Ibid., 1: 6.

96 Baker, 144.

97 Brian Abel-Smith and Robert Stevens, *Lawyers and the Courts: A Sociological Study of the English Legal System 1750–1965* (Cambridge, Mass.: Harvard University Press, 1967), 8.

98 See, e.g., Edwin Jones, *The English Nation: The Great Myth* (Thrupp, Gloucester: Sutton, 1998).

99 See S. E. Rasmussen, *London, The Unique City* (Harmondsworth: Penguin, 1960).

Notes to Chapter 4

1 For the case for the attribution, see B 657 n. 57.

2 PRO Pris.1.8. Commitment Books, Fleet Prison, for 1740, Case 194, f. 253.

3 In October Allen visited in London and returned to Prior Park on the 27th with Pope, who spent the winter there. This is probably when HF first visited Prior Park, meeting Pope (if the reference in *JA* can be trusted – B 316). If so, then HF was in Bath at least through October.

4 Authorship acknowledged in the preface to *Miscellanies*.

5 See T. C. Duncan Eaves and Ben D. Kimpel, "Henry Fielding's Son by His First Wife," *Notes & Queries*, n.s. 15 (June 1968):212.

6 P. T. P., "Woodfall's Ledger, 1734–1747," *Notes & Queries*, 1st ser., 11 (2 June 1855):419.

7 *An Apology for the Life of Colley Cibber*, ed. B. R. S. Fone (Ann Arbor: University of Michigam Press, 1968), 155–6.

8 *Champion* Apr. 22, 1740.

9 He also attacks Cibber's style in the essay of Apr. 29.

10 Laura Brown, *English Dramatic Form* (New Haven: Yale University Press, 1981), 123.

11 This applies to both *Love's Last Shift*, which Vanbrugh corrected with *The Relapse*, and *The Provok'd Wife*, in which Cibber "corrected" Vanbrugh's unfinished play with another of his pleasing endings. See Rivero, *Plays of Henry Fielding*, 12–15.

12 *History of the Works of the Learned*, 2 (1740):433–9; *GM*, 11 (Jan. 1741):56.

13 On Mar. 3 a third edition of *Pamela* appeared; and immediately after Fielding's publication of *Shamela* on Apr. 2, other attacks followed – *Pamela Cen-*

sured on Apr. 25 and *Anti-Pamela* and *The True Anti-Pamela* in June. It seems doubtful that he had already conceived the parody and only added the frame of the clerical commentary.

14   *Pamela,* ed. T. C. Duncan Eaves and Ben D. Kimpel (Boston: Houghton Mifflin, 1971), 67.

15   *Shamela,* ed. Baker, 53.

16   He had made Wisemore respond in *Love in Several Masques* to a surprising revelation ("news") with, "What novel's this?" (8:69). The word "novel" appears in Steele's *Spectator* no. 254 as part of the pair "Romance and Novels," that is a genre defined by its opposition to romance by its sense of the "new," in fact a synonym for *news.*

17   Jose Ortega y Gasset, "Notes on the Novel," in *The Dehumanization of Art and Other Writings on Art and Culture* (Princeton: Princeton University Press, 1948; reprinted, New York, 1956), 87.

18   William B. Warner uses the term "absorption," from Michael Fried's dichotomy of absorption and theatricality; I believe that Ortega's term comes closer to the effect Fielding recognized in *Pamela* (see *Licensing Entertainment: The Elevation of Novel Reading in Britain, 1684–1750* [Berkeley and Los Angeles: University of California Press, 1998]).

19   Welsh, *Strong Representations,* 25–6. Relevant to *Tom Jones,* Welsh notes Fielding's fundamental turn from a prosecutorial use of circumstantial evidence (as in a criminal biography) to the management of evidence in order to vindicate the accused. See also Douglas Lane Patey, *Probability and Literary Form: Philosophic Theory and Literary Practice in the Augustan Age* (Cambridge: Cambridge University Press, 1984), which traces the changing sense of "probability" from authority, i.e., expert witness, to likelihood (*vraisemblance*) or our modern sense of probability.

20   Blackstone, *Commentaries,* 3: 370–1.

21   As Baker puts it, "Systems of justice which depended on general oaths and supernatural tests had no need of pleading in any refined sense, because God could not be interrogated" (*English Legal History,* 62).

22   We could relate the judicial model equally well to that of critical deism. Plate 2 of the *Harlot,* we recall, revealed the "truth," the existential reason for the miraculous birth of the child, alluded to by the New Testament parallels of the other five plates.

23   See Bertrand Bronson's types of personification, restrictive and non-restrictive. The poet starts with an abstraction and personalizes it, and the more personal detail the more non-restrictive ("Personification Reconsidered," in *Facets of the Enlightenment: Studies in English Literature and Its Contexts* [Berkeley and Los Angeles: University of California Press, 1968], 119–52).

24   Cf. the contrast he makes in *Tom Jones,* 6.1.

25   *Champion,* no. 340, also 217.

26   As Rebecca Parkin has noted, it "implies a sophisticated reader and a sophisticated poet, together with an awareness and acceptance, on the part of both, of their sophisticated status" (*The Poetic Workmanship of Alexander Pope* [Minneapolis: University of Minnesota Press, 1955], 31).

27   Ian Watt, *The Rise of the Novel* (Berkeley and Los Angeles: University of Los Angeles Press 1956).

28 Slipslop is also defined, when first described, in relation to Cervantes' Maritornes (and perhaps the similar, but subjective descriptions of Jewkes and Colbrand in *Pamela*): see Paulson, *Satire and the Novel*, 103–4.

29 On the page following Pope's accounts of "rational beings . . . represented above their real character," he adds: "The use of pompous expressions for low actions or thoughts is the *true Sublime* of *Don Quixote*" (Postscript to *The Odyssey*, Twickenham edn., 10:388).

30 *The Gray's-Inn Journal*, no. 96, Aug. 17, 1754.

31 Maynard Mack pointed out this effect in his introduction to *Joseph Andrews* (New York: Rinehart, 1948), 6.

32 Battestin originally pointed this out in "Pictures of Fielding," *ECS*, 17 (1983):9–13; see also *Hogarth*, 1: 207ff.

33 At Mr. B's advance Pamela faints but exposes her stratagem by the words of her text: "I sighed, and scream'd, and fainted away. And still he had his Arms about my Neck"; on which Mr. B. comments: "As for *Pamela*, she has a lucky Knack at falling into Fits, when she pleases." Fielding's analysis of *Pamela* seen from one direction is libertine (Mr. B's analysis of Pamela's fainting fits), from another rationalist and deist. (See *Pamela*, 67, 68.)

34 Although Fielding plainly disagrees with Mandeville's view of human nature as unredeemably selfish, these disavowals divert attention from a fundamental indebtedness to Mandeville in the "new" mode of discourse he initiates in *Joseph Andrews* and *Tom Jones*. See *Covent-Garden Journal*, Mar. 14, 1752; also *Amelia* 3.5. Without being named, Mandeville is with Hobbes the villain of the attack in the *Champion* for Jan. 22, 1730/40. Cf. also Battestin's view of Mandeville's lack of influence on Fielding in *Providence of Wit*, 160.

35 See Herbert Davis, "The Augustan Conception of History," in *Reason and the Imagination: Studies in the History of Ideas, 1600–1800*, ed. J. A. Mazzeo (New York: Columbia University Press, 1962), 213–29. See also Robert M. Wallace, "Fielding's Knowledge of History and Biography," *Studies in Philology*, 44 (1947):89–107. My remarks on history are condensed from *Satire and the Novel*, 151–6.

36 Pierre Le Moine, *Of the Art of Both Writing and Judging History* (Paris, 1690; trans., London, 1695), 32–110, 117; cited, Davis, "Augustan Conception," 218. Cf. Swift's explanation of his role in *The Examiner* and *History of the Four Last Years of Queen Anne's Reign* (*The Prose Writings of Jonathan Swift*, ed. Herbert Davis [Oxford: Blackwell, 1939], 3: 141; 7:1–2). See also *Spectator* nos. 136, 170, 420, 483.

37 *Library*, B13.

38 Battestin, *The Moral Basis of Fielding's Art: A Study of "Joseph Andrews"* (Middletown: Wesleyan University Press, 1959), 41, 48.

39 J. Paul Hunter's argument that Fielding is *refuting* Morgan is unconvincing; following Battestin, he sees the Joseph–Abraham analogies as normative (*Occasional Form: Henry Fielding and the Chains of Circumstance* [Baltimore: Johns Hopkins University Press, 1975], 101–5; Battestin, *The Moral Basis of Fielding's Art*, 30–43).

40 See Hugh Blair, Lecture XXXVI, in *Lectures on Rhetoric* (publ. 1783).

41 See *The Works of M. de Voltaire*, trans. T. Francklin, Tobias Smollett, and others (London, 1779), 6:168.

42 Hogarth, *The Analysis of Beauty* (1753), ed. Paulson (New Haven and London: Yale University Press, 1997), 59.

43 Hoadly, Sermon XVI in *Twenty Sermons* (London, 1755), 332; noticed by Battestin, *Moral Basis*, 22.

44 See Paulson, *Hogarth*, 2:91; Paulson, "Models and Paradigms: *Joseph Andrews*, Hogarth's *Good Samaritan*, and Fénelon's *Télémaque*," *MLN*, 91(1976): 1186–1207; rpt. *Popular and Polite Art*, 157–71.

45 *Twenty Sermons*, 320.

46 For Hogarth's use of Woolston's demystification of the miracle of the Pool of Bethesda in his painting, see Paulson, *Hogarth*, 2: 87–97.

47 In the *Champion* (Dec. 11, 1739) Fielding argued that "The only Ways by which we can come to any Knowledge of what passes in the Minds of others, are their Words and Actions; the latter of which, hath by the wiser Part of Mankind been chiefly depended on, as the surer and more infallible Guide" (1.79). Faces, he added, are no more reliable than words. This discussion, which is used to introduce a hypocrite's letter-to-the-editor, is transformed into the theme of *Shamela*. Reminiscent of Pamela, Shamela tells us (what she has learned from Parson Williams) "That to go to church, and to pray, and to sing psalms, and to honour the clergy, and to repent, is true religion; and 'tis not doing good to one another." For the Methodist Parson Williams the maxim is "That 'tis not what we do, but what we believe, that must save us" (40).

48 The coach scenes in *Wild* and *Andrews* show the difference: In the former the encounter in the coach simply served as grist to Wild's mill, the raw material for a plot to steal money, therefore further evidence of his "greatness"; in the latter it offers a spectrum of response to Joseph in his extreme plight.

49 These forms are not, of course, honest searches for truth or reality. Even if their extremely schematic structure did not argue against their objectivity, it would be clear that their purpose is a satiric one – to support Fielding's general premise about the relationship between his heroes and Cibberian and Pamelian society. As A. D. McKillop put it, in Fielding's novels the discrepancy between appearance and reality "is not treated as an ultimate metaphysical problem, as in *Don Quixote*. Fielding is not trying to present or to pluck out the heart of a mystery; he is continuously corroborating a position which he has made clear from the first" ("Some Recent Views of *Tom Jones*," *College English*, 21 [1959]:19). Nevertheless, Fielding's basic unit, in his next novel, will have outgrown its satiric origin.

50 The *Odyssey* is only implied in the preface (Fielding refers to the lost "Margites"), an omission that he rectified in his preface to Sarah Fielding's *David Simple* (1744). See below, 198.

51 Although, as I have argued, Hogarth's *Harlot* provided Richardson with precisely the claustrophobic closed rooms that are so important a part of the effect of *Pamela* (*Hogarth*, 1:330–6; see also Robert Folkenflik, "A Room of Pamela's Own," *ELH*, 39 [1972]:585–96).

52 *Craftsman* no. 624 (327), no. 627 (*New Essays* 339–40).

53 Already in the *Champion* essays he introduces the metaphor: the paper is "a Sort of Stage Coach, a Vehicle in which every one hath a Right to take a Place" (1:173).

54 Shifting the metaphor to the gustatory (what is eaten in the inn), Fielding
    says that the dividing of meat into joints "is of great Help to both the Reader
    and the Carver."

55 The most Aristotelian element in *Joseph Andrews* is, of course, the faux-Oedipal
    denouement – the discovery that Fanny and Joseph could be siblings.

56 *Dunciad*, Twickenham edn., 10:387–8. On the subject of Fielding and the
    poor, see Judith Frank, "'What You Seek is Nowhere': The Comic Novel and
    Lower-class Literacy," in *Common Ground: Eighteenth-Century English Satiric
    Fiction and the Poor* (Stanford: Stanford University Press, 1997), 30–62.

57 Shortly after the publication of *The Distrest Poet* Fielding had alluded to the
    Poet in *Craftsman* no. 612 (Apr. 1, 1738): "for is it not *ridiculous* to see a poor,
    meagre Wretch drudging in a Garret, for a little hungry Fame, and sacrificing
    all the Advantages of this Life to the vain Hopes of Popularity hereafter?"
    (*New Essays* 288; emphasis added). He also refers to *The Distrest Poet* in *On True
    Greatness*, published in January 1740/1.

58 Blunt accused him of intending "artfully and subtilly to deceive and defraud."
    See above, chap. 3 n. 14.

59 He also joked in *Rape upon Rape* about the daughters of clergymen who
    become prostitutes (9:100–1).

60 But a page earlier Fielding had cited "the solemn Figure of an *Ass*, or an *Owl*,"
    and "the *same forked Animals* acting their several Drolleries, distinguish'd by
    different Habits, whether of *Ermin, Fur*, or *Lawn, Robe'd, Wigg'd, Ribbon'd*, or
    Garter'd," which could have been in Hogarth's mind when he wrote the pages
    on comedy in his *Analysis of Beauty* in the 1750s.

61 E.g., "*Adams*, who liked his Seat [by the fire], his Ale, his Tobacco and his
    Company" (3.2.200). Also for his love of tobacco, 2.16.

62 Wiltshire County Record Office: Diocesan Records, "Acts of the Court, 1733–"
    [Archdeacon's Court of Dorset], f. 5v; cited, B 188 n. 66.

63 The subject of reputation, slander, and back-biting in this scene (Leonora is
    another case, Miss Grave-airs another) will take on greater proportions in *Tom
    Jones* and the paranoid allegory of Sarah Fielding's *The Cry*.

64 The following pages are adapted from my *Beautiful, Novel, and Strange*,
    110–18.

65 See above, 78.

66 See below, on the hydraulic metaphor, 221–5.

67 In 1738 John Wesley had begun preaching salvation by faith alone – one corol-
    lary being that even gross sinners might believe in an instant, as on the scaf-
    fold, and be saved. This part of the Methodist doctrine Fielding clearly and
    emphatically rejects, associating it with Parson Williams' preaching to
    Shamela. In early 1739 George Whitefield's preaching in the open air to
    crowds in Bristol and Bath had drawn much attention, followed by similar
    gatherings in London itself. Wesley was also preaching in the Bristol-Bath
    area, in April–June 1739; and in London in September 1739 and the summer
    of 1740. This, the preaching to the poor, is the aspect of Methodism that
    Adams respects. See Stanley Ayuling, *John Wesley* (London: Collins, 1979),
    chap. 6.

68 Deist admiration for Mohammedanism was related to the smaller role it gave
    church and clergy. The topos that Christians were morally inferior to non-

Christians was, of course, deployed by Latitudinarians as well as deists. (See Isabel Rivers, *Reason, Grace, and Sentiment: A Study of the Language of Religion and Ethics in England, 1660–1780* [Cambridge: Cambridge University Press, 1991], 8–12.)

69 The meaning of the word "Christian" varies with its context. After Adams' battle with the Tow-wouses, a lawyer advises him to take them to court: "if your Jury were Christians, they must give swinging Damages" (2.5.121). Mrs. Trulliber, "seeing [her husband] clench his Fist, interposed, and begged him not to fight, but shew himself a true Christian, and take the Law of him" (2.14.168). Earlier Trulliber has told Adams that a Christian's "Treasure" is not in acts of charity but in the Scriptures, and when Adams chides him, he accuses him of being a freethinker, and Adams has to remind him that charity is advocated *in* the Scriptures. From the clergy's point of view, a "Christian" has gold in his pocket, wears respectable clothes, and takes you to law rather than beating you himself; in the special Adams sense, a "Christian" may not know the difference between the sexes but is charitable.

70 For example: "View here the pourtrait of a faction's priest, / Who (spight of Proverbs) dares defile his nest; / And when he shou'd defend the Church's cause, / Barely deserts her, and arraigns her laws" (quoted Redwood, 175). Hoadly's mentor was Samuel Clarke, whose works he edited in 1738. Whitefield, distinctive among many other critics only for his Calvinist perspective, saw the doctrine of the Latitudinarians as "only Deism refined" ("Sermon 1, "The Folly and Danger of Being Not Righteous Enough," *Works*, 5:126).

71 Sullivan, *Toland*, 35. As Leslie Stephen has written, Hoadly was a "clergyman who oppose[d] sacerdotal privileges"; one who "supported the political pretensions of the dissenters"; and was therefore "the best-hated clergyman of the century amongst his own order" (*History of English Thought in the Eighteenth Century*, 2:129).

72 It is possible that Hogarth first met Hoadly through Fielding. If, with Battestin, we read the "very eminent Physician of this age" (who accompanied Fielding when he read *The Wedding Day* to the managers of the Lincoln's Inn Theatre) as a reference to Benjamin Hoadly the younger, who wrote plays himself, then Fielding also knew the bishop's son by the autumn of 1730 – another close friend of Hogarth's (Preface to the *Miscellanies*; Battestin, 104).

73 Kenyon, *Revolution Principles: The Politics of Party, 1689–1720* (Cambridge: Cambridge University Press, 1977), 116.

74 Jill Campbell notes how Fielding invokes Milton's *Paradise Lost* 4.131–43 in this passage (*Joseph Andrews*, 3.5), Campbell, *Natural Masques: Gender and Identity in Fielding's Plays and Novels* (Stanford: Stanford University Press, 1995) 90–1.

75 The sentence was added in the second edition.

76 The other was LeSage's *Diable boiteux*. My text is the London edition of 1720 in 24 books. This section is a condensation of my essay, "The Pilgrimage and the Family: Structures in the Novels of Fielding and Smollett," in *Tobias Smollett: Bicentennial Essays Presented to Lewis M. Knapp*, ed. G. S. Rousseau and P.-G. Boucé (New York: Oxford University Press, 1971), 57–78; also appearing in *Popular and Polite Art*, chap. 3.

77   "Discourse upon Epick Poetry; Particularly on the Excellence of the Poem of
       Telemachus," in *Telemachus*, 1:xxx.
78   473. J. Paul Hunter has noticed a relationship between Fielding and the
       Telemachus, but only in *Tom Jones* (*Occasional Form*, 133–5).
79   The parallel here is with Antiope, daughter of Idomeneus, whom Telemachus
       is destined to marry *after* he has delivered Penelope from the suitors, and so
       Mentor stands between them, despite her father's stratagems. The point of
       the temptation of Antiope, Fénelon tells us, is that "he was not now the same
       Telemachus who had been such a slave to a tyrannical passion in the island
       of Calypso" (2.312).
80   Joseph's education is as stylized as Telemachus', beginning in book 1 with his
       confrontation by the prudential world of London and Lady Booby. He rejects
       both, though the second more emphatically than the first. After his expul-
       sion by Lady Booby, he finds that the opposite, his pure simplicity and chastity,
       is vulnerable to the robbers and the coachload of respectable Lady Boobies.
       Next he encounters Parson Adams, who is at the other extreme of pruden-
       tiality from Lady Booby. But he learns in book 2 that pure simplicity is also
       folly: Mentor is discredited or at least subordinated. If Fielding opposes in a
       general way the old virtue/vices of Prudentia and Simplicitas in, respectively,
       books 1 and 2, then in 3 Joseph begins to build his own structure out of their
       ruins: he begins to instruct Parson Adams. See Dick Taylor, Jr., "Joseph as
       Hero in *Joseph Andrews*," *Tulane Studies in English*, 6 (1957):91–109, and Jessie
       R. Chambers, "The Allegorical Journey in 'Joseph Andrews' and 'Tom
       Jones,'" (doctoral dissertation, Johns Hopkins University, 1960), chap. 3.
81   For the background of *Telemachus* and English educational theory of the
       period, see Jay Fliegelman, *Prodigals and Pilgrims: The American Revolution
       against Patriarchal Authority, 1750–1800* (New York: Cambridge University
       Press, 1984).
82   One obvious aspect shared by Edmund and Walpole was embodied in Robin
       in *The Welsh Opera*.
83   *Old England*, Nov. 25, 1749; cited B 300; which I take to support the attribu-
       tion of *The Crisis* to Fielding.
84   He is accompanied by another shaggy ass, named Ralph. In *Joseph Andrews*
       Fielding also expresses his disillusionment with the Opposition in the man
       who talks bravery in battle, whose cowardice is exposed at Fanny's cry of rape.
       His opinion of the soldiers at Carthagena reconstructs from a different per-
       spective the argument of *The Vernoniad*; this man was presumably in the
       Walpole Opposition. Then the analogy between a man who saves Fanny from
       one rapist only to attempt to ravish her himself recalls the sense Fielding had
       of the Opposition leaders following Walpole's fall.
85   Battestin notes that *patron* derives from the Latin *pater* (454).
86   It is worth considering the possibility that it was this print that served
       Hogarth as the source for his 1762 profile of Fielding. The traditional anec-
       dotes sound dubious. According to Murphy's story, Hogarth could not
       summon up an image of his old friend until "[a] lady, with a pair of scissars,
       had cut a profile, which gave the distances and proportions of his face suffi-
       ciently to restore his lost ideas of him" (*Works*, 1:48). The lady has been

identified as Margaret Collier (see below, 324–5). The other story, that Garrick, the great mimic, impersonated Fielding for Hogarth (including variants in which he surprised and terrified Hogarth as Fielding's ghost), is recounted by W. T. Whitley (*Artists and their Friends in England* [1928; repr., New York: Benjamin Blom, 1968], 1:152–3). (See *Hogarth's Graphic Works* no. 241 [248].)

NOTES TO CHAPTER 5

1   Burial Account Books (1735–44), St. Martin-in-the-Fields (Westminster History Coll., Buckingham Palace Road: 419/264).
2   PRO CP.40.3524, Roll 522, where King asks for damages of £98.12s. in addition to the £197; July 7 HF is charged only 50s.
3   See above, chap. 2, n. 44.
4   The debt was contracted on June 1 in Dorchester. PRO KB.122.192, Pt II, Roll 963; for the details, see B 352.
5   B 660 n. 114.
6   Letter to Harris, Mar. 14, *Corresp.*, 29–30.
7   St. Margaret's, Westminster (B 234, 650 n. 411). No record of her birth.
8   Harriet: B 650 n. 410. Debts: May 13, Charles Malson (PRO Ind.9761); autumn, William Goffe (PRO CP.40.3533); see B 369 and 662 n. 168.
9   For details and HF's ingenious defense, see B 391–2.
10 *Corresp.*, 31–4.
11 Lady Louisa Stuart, "Introductory Anecdotes," in Lord Wharncliffe, ed., *The Letters and Works of Lady Mary Wortley Montagu*, rev. M. Moy Thomas (1861), 1:106.
12 Letter to Harris, from London, Nov. 24, 1744 (*Corresp.*, 39–40). For the burial, see below, 214.
13 Poor Rate Books, St. Clement Danes Parish, Shire Lane Ward (Westminster History Collection, Buckingham Palace Road: B154–9, 1743–8); J. P. de Castro, "Fielding at Boswell Court," *Notes & Queries*, 12th ser., 1 (Apr. 1, 1916):264–5. A satiric pamphlet, which Battestin attributes to HF, *An Attempt towards a Natural History of the Hanover Rat*, published Nov. 23, seems to be an unlikely attribution. Cf. Coley, "Did Fielding write the Rat?," *Papers of the Bibliographical Society of America*, 88 (1994):1, 13–35.
14 Ad., *General Evening Post*, Feb. 26–8, 1744/5, and repeated in papers until early April. See W. B. Coley, "Henry Fielding's 'Lost' Law Book," *MLN*, 76 (1961):408–13.
15 B 393–4.
16 Letter to Harris, Jan. 2, Jan. 11, 1745/6, in *Corresp.*, 54, 55.
17 Bedford Record Office: R5/6457A, R4/6140; B 666n.246.
18 Letter to Harris, Feb. 19, 1746/7, *Corresp.*, 59.
19 Greater London Record Office (Middlesex): MJP/CP/124, ff. 1–2.
20 Daniel Lysons, on the authority of Horace Walpole, in *Environs of London*, 3 (1795):598 and n. 160; B 667 n. 273.

21 She is there by Oct. 25, 1748; see letter from Ursula to Mrs. John Barker of Salisbury, *Corresp.*, 182.
22 Thomas Birch, letter to Lord Orrery, Jan. 19, 1747/8, in *The Orrery Papers*, ed. Countess of Cork and Orrery (London, 1903), 2:14.
23 The reference is to Beau Nash, the master of ceremonies of Bath.
24 Sept. 17, letter from Birch to Philip Yorke, BL Add. MSS. 35397, f. 164.
25 *Corresp.*, 70–4, 69.
26 See B 669 n. 324.
27 Selections from this extraordinary attack are in Paulson and Lockwood, 187–212.
28 In fact, *Spectator* no. 454 is immediately preceded by an essay on the heavenly balance – the "golden balance" in which true weights are measured – and followed by Addison's creed of a Christian rationalist (which followed from no. 459, of the week before, on faith). The whole sequence would have interested Fielding and, in many ways, corresponded to his own views.
29 Fielding may have seen Aristophanes' play as a comic illustration of Shaftesbury's principle of disinterestedness: Once everyone is rich there is no need for religion.
30 The fiction was picked up by William Robinson in *The Champion*, June 29, 1742, applying it to Walpole, the Patriots, priests, kings, and lawyers, with a complimentary reference to Parson Adams.
31 See Alan Wendt, "The Moral Allegory of *Jonathan Wild*," *ELH*, 24 (1957):306–20.
32 In the *Champion* of Feb. 21 where Fielding describes good men who are *not* fools, he is primarily concerned with those who *are*, and these more closely resemble Heartfree: "How comes it that Servants get at the Secrets of Families? How do Lawyers get Possession of Men's Writings? Priests of their Minds, and Physicians of their Bodies, and by these Means all four of their Purses? . . . Why have a whole People often lost their Liberties, or indeed why have Kings desir'd to take them away . . . but for the above Reason. — . . . THAT FOOLS WERE THEN IN THE LAND" (1:294).
33 Miller, intro., *Misc.*
34 Matt. 22.39; Mark 12.31; Luke 10.27; and Romans 13.9.
35 *Characteristics*, 1:53.
36 For Shaftesbury on Hobbes, see *Characteristics*, 1:61ff.
37 One wonders if Fielding does not base his ambivalence about hypocrisy – especially in the "Essay on Conversation" – upon his reading of Swift's "Project for the Advancement of Religion" (1709), where he makes the case for the pragmatic value of hypocrisy in society: "Hypocrisy is much more eligible than open Infidelity and Vice: It wears the Livery of Religion, it acknowledgeth her Authority, and is cautious of giving Scandal" (*Works*, ed. Herbert Davis, 2:59–60). See also, Claude Rawson, "Gentlemen and Dancing Masters," in *Henry Fielding and the Augustan Ideal Under Stress* (London: Routledge and Kegan Paul, 1972), 3–34.
38 He covers much of the ground of the preface to *Joseph Andrews*, 159–62.
39 Also I.vii.
40 Caroline Walker Bynum, *The Resurrection of the Body in Western Christianity, 200–1336* (New York: Columbia University Press, 1995).

41 *Corresp.*, 47–8.

42 Battestin supposes that Fielding began work on *Tom Jones* in the spring of 1745 (391); Thomas, in January 1745 (241); Cross (2:100) and Duddon (585) thought it was in the summer of 1746, *after* Fielding had finished *The True Patriot.*

43 The MS. passed on to his brother John and was lost in the fire of 1780 during the Gordon Riots that destroyed the Bow Street court.

44 Letter to Harris, Jan. 11, 1745/6, *Corresp.*, 55.

45 *David Simple*, ed. Malcolm Kelsall (Oxford, 1969), 1.3.27.

46 Linda Bree, *Sarah Fielding* (New York, 1996), 33. She notes how "sexual desire is often portrayed by [Sarah] Fielding not as an aspect of romance but as a destructive passion, closely allied to other destructive passions involving loss of self-command, like greed and envy" (43).

47 Camilla: "there is no Situation so deplorable, no Condition so much to be pitied, as that of a Gentlewoman in real Poverty" (3.2.170).

48 Battestin draws attention to the story of Camilla and her brother Valentine, whom the step-mother Livia accuse of incest. I take this to be, at most, a reflection of the sort of scandal (later developed in the eponymous Cry of that novel) that may have been heard in the divided camps of the Fielding family in the 1720s.

49 Cheyne to Richardson, Mar. 9, 1741/2, in Mullett, ed., *Letters of Dr. George Cheyne*, 88; Richardson to Lady Bradshaigh, Nov. (?) 1749, in John Carroll, ed., *Selected Letters of Samuel Richardson* (Oxford: 1964), 133. For the range of responses, see Paulson and Lockwood.

50 T. C. Duncan Eaves and Ben Kimpel, *Richardson*, Boston: Houghton Mifflin, 207, 213.

51 Sarah Fielding was introduced to Richardson by her childhood friends the Colliers "sometime in 1744 or 1745" (Eaves and Kimpel, *Richardson*, 202; B 415).

52 See Battestin, edn., *Tom Jones*, 793, 850, and 955 notes.

53 We should also mention Hogarth's work-in-progress from 1743–5, when it was published: *Marriage-à-la-mode*, which presents the same story of a family imposing an arranged marriage, in this case one that is carried through with disastrous results. The early volumes of *Clarissa* show evidence of Richardson's knowledge of *Marriage à-la-mode*; for his friendship with Hogarth, see Paulson, *Hogarth*, 2:239–40; 3:263–4.

54 See William B. Warner, *Reading Clarissa: The Struggles of Interpretation* (New Haven: Yale University Press, 1979).

55 Harrison, *Henry Fielding's "Tom Jones": The Novelist as Moral Philosopher* (Sussex: Sussex University Press, 1975), 40, 44–5. Harrison takes off from Empson's "double irony." In an essay, "The Pictorial Circuit" (1971), I argued that "The pictorial circuit set up different discrete views of an object which was itself various, its different aspects revealed by different contexts," a form reflected in other art forms ("The Pictorial Circuit & Related Structures in 18th-Century England," in *The Varied Pattern: Studies in the 18th Century*, ed. Peter Hughes and David Williams (Toronto: A. M. Hakkert, Ltd., 1971), 169.

56 *Some Versions of Pastoral* (New York: New Directions n.d.), 197.

57 "Tom Jones," *Kenyon Review,* 20 (1958):217–49; reprinted, Paulson, ed., *Fielding: Twentieth-Century Views* (Englewood Cliffs, N.J.: Prentice Hall, 1960), 123–45 (with Empson's revisions).

58 Fielding's irony also serves simpler purposes in *Tom Jones,* for example, as a euphemism when he says "but something or other happened before the next Morning [after the fight over Jenny], which a little abated the Fury of Mrs. *Partridge*" (2.3.85). It is also a way of saying that the motive is obvious: why so-and-so did this "must be left to the judgment of the sagacious reader," Fielding says when the answer is quite evident, "for we never choose to assign Motives to the Actions of Men, when there is any possibility of our being mistaken" (5.10.258). Yet even in these cases, Fielding has drawn attention to the problematic nature of motives.

59 A. McKillop, *Early Masters of English Fiction* (Lawrence: University of Kansas Press, 1956), 212.

60 A few years later in *The Cry* (1754) Sarah Fielding picks up on the conflicting voices that sully and distort reputation. Already in her contribution to the *Miscellanies,* however, she had presented Anna Boleyn in the context of the conflicting accounts (the protestant and the papist) of her life. She is, she says, "the continual Subject of the Cavils of contending Parties; the one making me black as Hell, the other as pure and innocent as the Inhabitants of this blessed Place" (she ends in heaven) (113).

61 *Tom Jones,* 9.1.487–8. Sometimes Fielding refers to them ironically as "digressive Essays" that "dressing" and "garnishing" the narrative by "interspersing through the whole sundry Similes, Descriptions, and other kinds of poetical Embellishments," and sometimes as "Interruptions" and "ornamental Parts" (5.1.212; 1.1.33; 4.1.151–2).

62 *An Essay concerning Human Understanding,* Bk. II.i.rev., edn. A. C. Fraser, vol. 1 (Oxford, 1894):124.

63 *Essay,* 2.1.15.

64 These are followed by "attentive consideration" and "censure," equally relevant to *Tom Jones.*

65 This is Scott Black's formulation, developed in his chapter, "*Tom Jones,* Essays, and the Novel," in "Social and Literary Form in the Eighteenth Century: Civil Society and the Essay" (unpublished doctoral dissertation, Johns Hopkins University, 1999). Black argues that there is a progression from the simple profession-performance structure of the country books to the social situations and interactions of the city books.

66 Paulson and Lockwood, 335. For Amelia's nose, see below, 300.

67 B 98; 637n.112.

68 Murphy, in *Works* (1762), 1.11.

69 Battestin makes a simple equation, which ignores chronology, between Allworthy, Fielding the author, and Fielding the magistrate writing in his *Enquiry into the late Increase in Robbers* of 1751 (see Battestin, ed. *Tom Jones,* 102n., on Allworthy's judgment of Partridge and Jenny).

70 Lady Louisa Stuart, "Introductory Anecdotes," 1:105–6.

71 Letter to Harris, Nov. 24, 1744, *Corresp.,* 42–8.

72 R. E. M. Peach, *Historical Houses in Bath,* 2nd semes(1884), 37–8; cf. Battestin's comments, 384–5.

73 Letter to Harris, Nov. 24, *Corresp.*; B 385. "Until Sep. 1745, when there was an equally expensive funeral, the next highest amount recorded for such a service is £3.13.8" (B, 664, n. 199, citing St. Martin-in-the Fields, Burial Account Books, 1744–9: Westminster History Collection, Buckingham Palace Road (419/265).

74 The Partridge case brings in his lack of vigilance as to corroborating evidence – he takes the word of witnesses of dubious authority.

75 Fielding refers to *Paradise Lost* in *True Patriot* no. 1 as "the best Poem which perhaps [the world] hath ever seen" (106); and in *Jacobite's Journal* no. 8 he writes that "*Paradise Lost*, the noblest Effort perhaps of human Genius, *hath its Blemishes*" (138, emphasis added).

76 *Champion* Apr. 5, 1740, on 1 Corinthians 13, the word *agape*, "which some versions render Charity, is better rendered by others Love" (2:73).

77 Empson, Paulson, ed., *Twentieth-Century Views*, 128–9.

78 Harrison, *Tom Jones.*

79 In fact, the love is mutual; both think of the ruin to be brought on the other (6.8.299, and 12.312).

80 *Corresp.*, 15.

81 *Characteristics*, 2:55.

82 Harrison, *Tom Jones*, 80–1.

83 Fielding's position is related to, but not the same as, Isaac Barrow's Latitudinarian doctrine that Nature has "made the conjunction of benefits to others to be accompanied with a very delicious relish upon the mind of him that practises it; nothing indeed carrying with it a more pure and savoury delight than beneficience. A man may be virtuously voluptuous, and a laudable epicure by doing much good" (Sermon 31, *Theological Works*, 2 [Oxford, 1830], 225).

84 Fielding himself, when he develops the metaphor in *Tom Jones* (7.1) quotes Samuel Boyse's poem, *Deity* (1740), which calls the world "the vast Theatre of Time": "Perform the Parts thy Providence assign'd, / Their Pride, their Passions to thy Ends inclin'd." This is the Epictetus version, which Fielding applies to Black George's confusion of roles assigned him – however, not by the divine playwright but by the passions within himself.

85 The opening chapter of book 2 of *Joseph Andrews* refers to the book as first a commodity (paper and binding), then a journey, and finally a meal. Adams then narrativizes the metaphor when his "insatiable curiosity" for the story of Leonora the Jilt is described as hunger ("his Ears were the most hungry Part of him") and when, listening to Wilson's story, he licks his lips (2.4.118).

86 Blifil's seeing Sophia as no more than a succulent piece of roast beef was adumbrated by Jonathan Wild's response when he first sees Mrs. Heartfree.

87 Next, Partridge is once again led by hunger to eat, and on this occasion Tom too eats "a very hearty Breakfast," but though he fills his stomach he grows "uneasy" thinking of Sophia. We are reminded of the earlier scene in which both look at the moon, Tom thinking of Sophia, while Partridge thinks only of a hearty repast (8.9.436). Tom is at this point confusing physical hunger and Sophia, but privileging the latter. We are meant to see this as a development beyond the dinner with Jenny Waters when he had put Sophia out of his mind.

88   It is instructive to compare Tony Richardson's film version of *Tom Jones*, where the food *led to* sexual appetite and was the means of seduction employed by Mrs. Waters. In the novel, eating and sex are linked as two forms of appetite, with hunger being the stronger, and sex following (despite Mrs. Waters' attempts at seduction) only after Tom has satisfied the first.

89   This section is based on Paulson, *Popular and Polite Art*, 172–89.

90   *Tom Jones*, 12.11.623; citing L'Estrange's *Fables of Aesop* (1692), fable 61.

91   In a letter to *The Champion* a hypocrite confesses his hypocrisy and concludes: "Believe me, it is a great Comfort to me, to *unburthen myself* thus, without any Possibility of being discovered. And, perhaps, I shall take future Occasions of *giving myself vent* in the same Manner; for to a Man who lives under such a continual *Constraint* as myself, *these Evacuations* must be extremely pleasant" (Dec. 11, 1739; 1:79; emphasis added).

92   Again, *Champion*, Mar. 25, 1740; and at the very beginning of his career, above, 21.

93   As early as the essay on laughter and the prologue to *The Author's Farce* ("Bred in *Democritus* his laughing schools"), Fielding cites Democritus. The "Hippocratic novel," an addendum to "Hippocrates' Aphorisms," comments on the "madness" of Democritus as expressed in his laughter – "directed at the life of man and at all the vain fears and hopes related to the gods and to life after death" (cited, Mikhail Bakhtin, *Rabelais and his World*, tr. Helene Iswolsky [Cambridge, Mass.: Harvard University Press, 1968], 67). See, e.g., Hippocrates, *Humours*, 6; in *Hippocrates*, tr. W. H. S. Jones, 4 (*Loeb Classical Library*: Cambridge, Mass.: Harvard University Press, 1931), 74–7. Aristotle's own formula in *De Anima* ("Of all living creatures only man is endowed with laughter") interpreted laughter as man's highest spiritual privilege, inaccessible to other creatures (*De Anima*, bk. 3, ch. 10; see Bakhtin, *Rabelais and his World*, 167).

94   Shaftesbury, *Sensus Communis*, 1.5; Robertson, 1:52. See Paulson, *Don Quixote in England* (Baltimore: Johns Hopkins University Press), 121–5.

95   As Ramble says in *Rape upon Rape*, "I see gravity and hypocrisy are inseparable" (9:112).

96   *True Patriot*, Feb. 11–18, 1745/6; announced, *General Advertiser*, Mar. 7, 1747/8, and *Jacobite's Journal*, Mar. 12.

97   *General Advertiser*, Apr. 14, 1748.

98   Besides learning that Sophia had passed this way, Tom hears that the puppet master had planned to waylay, strip, and rape her; an act which, among other things, contrasts the violence of the projected rape with the consensual sex for which the puppet master was punishing his Merry Andrew.

99   At the moment in book 7 when he decides that he cannot solicit "such a creature to consent to her own Ruin," "Here Passion stopped his Mouth, and found a Vent at his Eyes" (7.2.331).

100 Sydenham, *Tractatus de podagra et hydrope* (1683), tr. and abridged, Comrie, ed. (1922), 70; Cheyne, *Observations Concerning the Nature and Method of Treating the Gout* (1720); Roy Porter and G. S. Rousseau, *Gout: The Patrician Malady* (New Haven: Yale University Press, 1998), e.g., 13, 52, 55–6, who show the connection between the classical etiology of gout and humoral theory.

101 J. M. Fothergill, *Indigestion, Biliousness, and Gout in its Protean Aspects*, pt. 1: *Indigestion and Biliousness* (1883), 149–50; I quote Porter and Rousseau, 193.

102 Porter and Rousseau, 194, 200.
103 Cheyne, *The English Malady*, paraphrased by Porter and Rousseau, 56–7.
104 7.11.368; B 409. Although it could, of course, have been added later, the contrast in book 2, ch. 1, of Carthage and Rome (parallel to Blifil and Tom) already indicates the parallel with the Stuart and Hanoverian dynasties. The context is the discussion of Fielding's "new Province of Writing" and his own role as ruler, law-giver, constitutional monarch.
105 See Battestin, "Tom Jones and 'His *Egyptian* Majesty': Fielding's Parable of Government," *PMLA*, 72 (1967):68–77; also Lennard J. Davis, *Factual Fictions: The Origins of the English Novel* (New York: Columbia University Press, 1983), 196.
106 *Misc.*, preface, 1:6.
107 See B 361–2.
108 B 411; Castle, "'Matters Not Fit to be mentioned': Fielding's *The Female Husband*," in *The Female Thermometer: Eighteenth-Century Culture and the Invention of the Uncanny* (New York: Oxford University Press, 1995), 67–81.
109 Campbell, *Natural Masques*, 56–8.
110 As Sheridan Baker noticed, "the papers in general followed the trial. Captain George Hamilton and others were drawn and quartered, their hearts cut out and thrown in the fire on Nov. 1, at York. This news reached the London papers at the very time the two reprints about Mary Hamilton did. The *St. James's Evening Post* of Saturday, Nov. 8, prints the account of the execution on p. 2, under 'COUNTRY NEWS': immediately under this, also with no specific headline, is the piece on Mary Hamilton, just half as long." (Sheridan Baker, "Henry Fielding's *The Female Husband*: Fact and Fiction," *PMLA*, 74 [1959]:213–24.)
111 Both works were published by Mary Cooper. *Ovid's Art of Love Paraphrased, and adapted to the present Time* was published February 1747 (*GM*, 17 [1747]: 108); the 1756 Dublin edition puts Fielding's name on the title page; it was reissued in 1759 and 1760 as *The Lover's Assistant, or New Art of Love*.
112 Fielding's advertisement in the *Jacobite's Journal* was alongside a political satire in which Ovid's *Art of Love* is transposed into the "Art of Jacobitism." In the prologue the reader is told "he will find all the Precepts of the Original modernized, and rendered agreeable to the present Times, and . . . he will be better enabled to relish the Beauties of this Performance." The satire is presented as the first book of "a Translation of a *Latin Poem*, intitled, *De Arte Jacobitica*," sent by M. O. A. J. (suggested by Coley to stand for "Master of the Order of Ancient Jacobites"), an instruction manual for Jacobites on where to find potential proselytes and how to seduce them. The primary rubric under which all of the suggestions fall, and echo Ovid, is deception. The Jacobite is to "learn the Art of Lying, and Misrepresenting," and so on – like Proteus he will learn to "transform himself into what monstrous Appearance he pleased."
113 Ovid's comparison of the art of controlling love to a charioteer controlling his horses (plural) becomes in Fielding's version a coach-driver and the coach is his argument about love. This is of course one of the metaphors used to describe the writing and reading experience of *Tom Jones*.
114 *Ovid's Metamorphoses*, Humphries tr. (Bloomington: Indiana University Press, 1955), 106.

115 See, chap. 1, Campbell, *Natural Masques*, esp. 55–60.

116 Cf. Pope's "On gilded clouds in fair expansion lie, / And bring all Paradise before your eye" ("Epistle to Burlington," ll. 147–8).

117 *An Examen of the History of Tom Jones, a Foundling* (1749), Paulson and Lockwood, 189. The words appear in neither the *Phaedrus* nor its paraphrases by Cicero, Seneca, and Sir Philip Sidney.

118 *Champion*, Jan. 24, 1739/40; again in "An Essay on the Knowledge of the Characters of Men," in *Misc.* 1:173. See Alan Wendt, "The Naked Virtue of Amelia," *ELH*, 27 (1960):131–48.

119 See *Champion*, "Essay on Conversation" and "Characters of Men" in *The Miscellanies*.

120 The "Stripping and Whipping" began with Fanny, who "trembled at that Sound; but indeed without reason, for none but the Devil himself would have executed such a sentence on her" (*Joseph Andrews* 4.5.227).

121 For a discussion of the reference, see Homer Obed Brown, "*Tom Jones*: The 'Bastard' of History," *Boundary* 27 (1979):201–33.

122 *Tom Jones*, 2.3; J. Ireland, *Hogarth Illustrated*, 3 (1798):lxxxiii. (One wonders whether son William, b. Feb. 1748, was named after Hogarth; as his next son, Allen, was named after Ralph Allen.)

123 See James Thompson, *Models of Value: Eighteenth-Century Political Economy and the Novel* (Durham: Duke University Press, 1996), chap. 4. In terms of the law, the actionable "crime" of *Tom Jones* was Blifil's tampering with the law in order to secure his inheritance of the property of Paradise Hall.

124 This passage is taken from Paulson, *Popular and Polite Art*, 143–4.

125 John Preston raised this issue in "Plot as Irony: The Reader's Role in *Tom Jones*," *ELH*, 35 (1968):365–80; repr. in *The Created Self* (London: Heinemann, 1970).

126 Fanny's breasts: "the Ravisher had tore her handkerchief from *Fanny*'s Neck, by which he had discovered such a Sight; that Joseph hath declared all the Statues he ever beheld were so much inferior to it in beauty, that it was more capable of converting a Man into a statue, than of being imitated by the greatest Master of that Art" (*Joseph Andrews*, 4.7.239); and Ramble: "and for her breasts, not snow, marble, lilies, alabaster, ivory, can come up to their whiteness; but their little, pretty, firm, round form, no art can imitate, no thought conceive – Oh! Sotmore, I could die ten thousand millions of times upon them – "(*Rape upon Rape*, Henley edn., 9:117).

127 Also the oceanic names – Waters and Seagrim, noted by Peter Rudnetsky. I am indebted for this argument to Rudnetsky's chapter, "The Transcendental Subject of *Tom Jones*," in *Fielding and the Masculine Subject*, which he was kind enough to let me read in MS. (forthcoming). Rudnetsky gives a full Freudian reading of *Tom Jones* as fulfilling the classic plot of patriarchy: (1) "That Molly, Mrs. Waters, and Lady Bellaston are all alternatives to Sophia is clear; and it involves only one further substitution to see that they are likewise a composite image of 'the three forms taken by the figure of the mother in the course of a man's life'" (MS., 30). (2) "The plot of *Tom Jones* thus adumbrates the 'plot' of Freud's 'The Dissolution of the Oedipus Complex,' which holds that the son must renounce his incestuous attachment to the mother, confront his ambivalent feelings toward his father, internalizing the latter's castration

threat in the form of conscience, and finally find a suitable substitute for the mother in order to reach emotional maturity" (36). See also Christine van Boheemen, *The Novel as Family Romance: Language, Gender, and Authority from Fielding to Joyce* (Ithaca: Cornell University Press, 1987).

128 See Kermode, "Richardson and Fielding," *Cambridge Journal*, 4 (1950):106–16. For the Oedipal interpretation of *Hamlet* in the eighteenth century, see Manuel Schonhorn, "Heroic Allusion in *Tom Jones*: Hamlet and the Temptations of Jesus," *Studies in the Novel*, 6 (1974):218–27.

129 I owe this point to Rudnetsky.

130 William Park, "Tom and Oedipus," *Hartford Studies in Literature*, 7 (1975):215 (207–15). For the Oedipus allusion as burlesque (Oedipus thought himself innocent and was guilty; Tom just the reverse), see Barry D. Bort, "Incest Theme in *Tom Jones*," *American Notes & Queries*, 3 (1965):83–4. For Fielding's playing out of the incest theme, which obviously includes his innuendos about Tom and Bridget as well as Jenny Waters, see also Sheridan Baker, "Bridget Allworthy: The Creative Pressures of Fielding's Plot" (1967), rept. in Baker's edition of *Tom Jones* (New York: 1973), 908. Battestin's theory is spread through his *Life* but concentrated in "Henry Fielding, Sarah Fielding, and 'the dreadful Sin of Incest,'" *Novel*, 13 (1979):6–18.

131 Wilbur Cross, *The History of Henry Fielding* (New Haven: Yale University Press, 1918), 3 vols., 2:205–6.

132 B 74–5.

133 See Maren-Sofie Røstvig, "*Tom Jones* and the Choice of Hercules," in Røstvig, *Fair Forms: Essays in English Literature from Spenser to Jane Austen*, (Cambridge: Cambridge University Press, 1975), 147–77. The Choice of Hercules was also suggested in the figure of Moses in *Moses brought to Pharaoh's Daughter*; actually, however, Hogarth implies in that case the more somber topos of a Judgment of Solomon, the child divided between its two "mothers."

134 This section draws upon Paulson, "Fielding in *Tom Jones*: The Historian, the Poet, and the Mythologist," in *Augustan Worlds: Essays in Honour of A. R. Humphreys*, ed. J. C. Hilson, et al. (Leicester: Leicester University Press, 1977), 175–87; rpt. *Popular and Polite Art*, chap. 6.

135 The drawing, a rough sketch, is in the Royal Library. See *Hogarth's Graphic Works* no. 229 for the woodcut; A. P. Oppé, *Drawings of William Hogarth* (London: Phaidon, 1948), cat. no. 67, pl. 40, for the drawing.

136 *Library* no. B6. In the "Court of Criticism" it is ordered "that the said *Mythology* be strongly recommended to the Public, as the most useful, instructive, and entertaining Book extant" (no. 9, 146). We know that he had read Banier as early as 1741, when he and/or Parson Young wrote an extensive review of it for their journal, *The History of Our Own Times*. I cite the 1739 edition. Cf. Thomas Blackwell's attack on Banier in his *Letters concerning Mythology* (1748), 207–60.

137 Taken from, for example, Natale Conti, *Mythologiae sive explicationis fabularum libri decem* (1616 edn.), 305.

138 See Frank Manuel's explanation of the eighteenth-century euhemerist mode in *The Eighteenth Century Confronts the Gods* (Cambridge, Mass.: Harvard University Press, 1959), 105; and on Banier, 104–7.

139 By 7.3. Fielding is beginning to show that the Blifil–Sophia "alliance" or "treaty" of marriage on the level of personal history is the equivalent of the alliances and treaties in the War of the Austrian Succession that in 1748 was just being brought to a close (333). The mythmaker is Mrs. Western, who sees the Blifil–Sophia negotiations in precisely this way (see 334).

140 I am suggesting an alternative meaning of "history" in *Tom Jones* to that offered by both Leo Braudy and Martin Battestin, the one based on Hume's *History of England* and the other on the pattern of divine providence. See Braudy, *Narrative Form in History and Fiction* (Princeton: Princeton University Press, 1970), esp. Parts III and IV, and Battestin, *The Providence of Wit* (Oxford: Clarendon Press, 1974), chaps. 5 and 6.

141 Walker Percy, *Message in a Bottle* (New York: Farrar, Straus and Giroux, 1975), 72, 81. Cf. Aristotle's distinction between poet and historian, *Poetics*, 8:1451.

142 There are the stories that Elcho found Charles in a hut by the river Naim after the battle "in a deplorable state," "prostrate and without hope, and surrounded only by his Irish friends," believing the Scots officers were going to betray him, and speaking to none of them, etc. See Chevalier de Johnstone, *Memoirs concerning the Affairs of Scotland* (London, 1820), 186 and n.; David Elcho, *A Short Account of the Affairs of Scotland*, ed. Evan Charteris (Edinburgh, 1907), 94–5, 435–6. Fielding discusses Charles's behavior during and after the battle in *True Patriot* no. 27, 1–2.

143 For Molly-Eve, see 4.6.175. Cf. Henry Knight Miller's argument for the "romance tradition," the creation of "archetypal figures who remain true to generalized human experience, transcending variations in local cultural detail, but who are nevertheless rendered in terms of personal idiosyncracies that make them unique beings." *Tom Jones*, he argues, draws upon that tradition: "Tom Jones's 'character' is better conceived in terms of his 'public' role as *adulescens* and of the typological and allusive roles (Adam, Aeneas, Adonis, and so on), which place him in a tradition of *literary* character, than in modern terms of non-fictive individual psychology – a language that does not adequately 'translate' or 'decode' the language of which romance characters are made and within whose ambience they 'live'" (*Henry Fielding's 'Tom Jones' and the Romance Tradition*, English Literary Studies, monograph series, no. 6 (Victoria, B.C.: University of Victoria Press, 1976), 63.

144 The importance of names was of course equally thrust upon Fielding by the tradition of epic commentary with its etymological methods. See Thomas Maresca, *Epic to Novel* (Columbus: Ohio State University Press, 1974), 33–35.

145 More than once Fielding compares Tom to Adonis (9.5 and 15.7).

146 See *Jacobite's Journal*, no. 6, 125; Rubert C. Jarvis, *Collected Papers on the Jacobite Risings* (Manchester, 1972), 2, chaps. 16–18.

147 Iona and Peter Opie, *The Oxford Dictionary of Nursery Rhymes* (Oxford: Oxford University Press, 1951), no. 96, 115–16.

148 Fielding's emphasis is on Charles Edwards' bigotry and such stories as how he executes a Protestant sheep stealer and pardons a Catholic rapist of an eleven-year-old girl. The refrain is "Such is the spirit of Popery" or "Such are the Terrors of arbitrary Power." See also Jarvis, 2:134.

149 *History* (London, 1745), 35; cited in Jarvis, 137.

150 See *True Patriot*, no. 33, June 17, 1746, 309.

151 See also Peter J. Carlton, "*Tom Jones* and the '45 Once Again," *Studies in the Novel*, 20 (1988):361–70; and John Allen Stevenson, "*Tom Jones* and the Stuarts," *ELH*, 61 (1994):571–95.

152 Lyttelton, *Observations on the Conversion and Apostleship of St. Paul*, in *The Works of George Lord Lyttelton* (1776), 2:10.

153 In *The True Patriot* he had used Roman Catholicism to sum up all the worst in priestcraft, the determination "to extirpate Heresy by all Methods whatever" and "inevitably destroy [England's] Civil Liberties" – which he opposes to "the Temper of Protestants." And, in the dangerous situation of the Forty-Five, he also lumps "the most noble Party of Free-Thinkers, who has no Religion" with the Jacobites (*True Patriot*, no. 2, 124–5, 137). But the same reference to one bad clergyman as opposed to the order (in *Champion*, Feb. 23, 1740, 1:259) reappears in *True Patriot* no. 14, Jan. 28–Feb. 4, 1746 (207–8), where it is extended from clergy to writers. Cf. *Tom Jones*, 9.6.516–17; see also 373.

154 *True Patriot*, no. 3 Nov. 19, 1745. His daughter, little Harriet, we recall, was "prostituted even in her infancy to the brutal lust of a ruffian" of the Young Pretender. Cf. Fielding's opinion, in Adams' mouth, of the "pathetic" in Homer – the example being Andromache and Hector (*Joseph Audrews* 3.2.199).

155 The contrasts between Sophia and Clarissa also intensify in the last volumes: 15.3, 16.5, 18.9.

156 Revision of the Postscript (3rd edn., 1750, 8:281). Richardson's irony is heavy-handed, his reference obvious: "Others, and some gentlemen, declared against tragedies in general, and in favour of comedies, almost in the words of the libertine Lovelace, who was supported in his taste by all the women at Mrs. Sinclair's, and by Sinclair herself" (278). The sentence also connects with the story he liked to tell that Fielding, on the basis of his reading of volumes one through five, had begged him to preserve Clarissa and give her a happy ending. The happy ending Richardson envisions is to reform Lovelace and marry him to Clarissa, which sounds very like his interpretation of the conclusion of Tom and Sophia's romance:

> To have a Lovelace for a series of years glory in his wickedness, and think that he had nothing to do, but as an act of grace and favour to hold out his hand to receive that of the best of women, whenever he pleased, and to have it thought, that Marriage would be a sufficient amends for all his enormities to others, as well as to her; he [the author] could not bear that.

The author, he writes, "had a great end in view," for "He has lived to see Scepticism and Infidelity openly avowed, ... The great doctrines of the Gospel brought into question, ... And taste even to wantonness *for out-door pleasure and luxury*, to the general exclusion of *domestic as well as public virtue*, industriously promoted among all ranks and degrees of people" (179). That too obviously is aimed at the author of *Tom Jones*.

157　New, "'The Grease of God': The Form of Eighteenth-Century English Fiction," *PMLA*, 91 (1976):235–44.

158　On Fortune, see 14.8.771: "certain it is there are some Incidents in Life so very strange and unaccountable, that it seems to require more than human Skill and Foresight in producing them." The reference is to the fortuitous moment at which Tom encounters Mr. Nightingale, but of course the sequel depends not on this lucky moment but on Tom's skillful handling of the old man; and as such recalls Fielding's comment in *The True Patriot* no. 8 of Dec. 24, 1745: "What we call ill Luck, is generally ill Conduct," and he uses the example of chess: "those who lay the Blame on Fortune, talk as absurdly as the passionate bad Player at Chess, who swore he had lost the Game by one d-n'd unlucky Move, which exposed the King to Cheque-mate" (161). Cf. *Amelia* 1.1.16, where the same argument is used; but in *Champion* Dec. 6, 1739: "Human Life appears to me to resemble the Game of *Hazard*, much more than that of Chess."

159　*Spectator* no. 225, Bond edn. 2:375.

160　Aubrey Williams, who uses this example, argues that "the discovery of the deepest and most secret villainy by 'accidents' and 'strange chances' of an 'extraordinary kind' was considered one of the surest marks of the Hand of Providence by almost everyone who argued the subject, either as preacher or as author of such works as those cited by Fielding in his own *Examples of the Interposition of Providence in the Detection and Punishment of Murder*" (1752; Williams, 280).

161　Also on Deborah Wilkins' searching out Tom's father (2.2.81) or Partridge's not offering Tom any of his money (12.7.712).

162　This passage is followed a few pages later in book 2 by the death of Rypheus ("he was first among the Teucrians for justice and / observing right; the gods thought otherwise"), which had worried Fielding in one of his *Craftsman* essays, suggesting his abiding interest in the role of the deity in human affairs.

163　An early version of the "whether . . . or . . . or . . . I will not determine" structure appeared in *Champion* May 24, 1740 (2:254).

164　Boswell, *Life of Johnson*, ed. Hill, 2:48–9.

165　*Characteristics*, 1:136.

166　For Cooke too beauty "is that which arises to the Mind in exact Proportion, and which gives that Pleasure which the Mind enjoys from Propriety of Action" (*Demonstration*, xii).

167　Wayne Booth has noted that the narrator's presence in *Tom Jones* creates for the reader "a kind of comic analogue of the true believer's reliance on a benign providence in real life"(Booth, *Rhetoric of Fiction* [Chicago: University of Chicago Press, 1961], 217).

168　For a demonstration of *Tom Jones'* Palladian structure, its Shaftesburian order, see F. W. Hilles, "Art and Artifice in *Tom Jones*," in *Imagined Worlds: Essays on Some English Novels and Novelists in Honour of John Butt*, ed. Maynard Mack and Ian Gregor (London: Methuen, 1968), 91–110.

169　I would not want to rule out the possibility that Fielding regards this as yet another fiction.

170　Sterne fits into this company, writing *Tristram Shandy* to explain the flaws of his own "small hero," but *Tristram Shandy* is also a parody of the Fielding effort, refusing to subordinate the heterogeneity of experience to any explanation.

NOTES TO CHAPTER 6

1 Registers of St. Paul's, Covent Garden: Harleian society, vol. 33 (Births), vol. 4 (Burials).
2 GLRO[M]: WJ/SBB/1062, p. 81. HF was apparently regularly reappointed chairman until Oct. 9, 1751 (B 672n. 31).
3 See B 477 and Appendix I.
4 *GA* Dec. 28, 1749.
5 Richardson to Lady Bradshaigh, *Selected Letters*, 133–4.
6 Register of Births, St. Paul's, Harleian Society, vol. 33.
7 B 500–1.
8 Johnson, *The Rambler*, ed. W. J. Bate and Albrecht B. Strauss (New Haven: Yale University Press, 1969), 1:19–25.
9 Burial Register, St. Paul's, Hammersmith, July 1750 (Shepherd's Bush Branch Library: Archives, DD/71/7 and 9). See the reference HIF inserted in *Amelia*, 2. 4–5. Jane Collier was author of *The Art of Ingeniously Tormenting* (1753) and HF's favorite, to whom he gave an inscribed copy of Horace when he left for Lisbon.
10 Burial Book, St. Martin-in-the-Fields, Aug. 3, 1750 (Westminster History Collection, F2466); Burial Accounts Book, Aug. 1750 (419/266); Eaves and Kimpel, *Notes & Queries*, n.s., 15 (June 1968):212.
11 For an account of the upward turn of HF's finances during this period, see B 508–9.
12 PRO C.193.45, C.2a34.25.
13 *LDA* Aug. 8, Aug. 24.
14 *LDA* Nov. 22, 1751.
15 HF to Harris, Dec. 23, *Corresp.*, 98; John Upton to Harris, Dec. 23, cited B 533. For the responses to *Amelia*, see Paulson and Lockwood, nos. 106–20.
16 *Covent-Garden Journal*, June 27, 1752; and for July 4.
17 Harleian Society, Registers, vol. 33.
18 The printer William Strahan's ledger, BL. Add. MSS. 48800, f. 96v.
19 Poor Rate books, Ealing Central Library; B 682 n. 338.
20 Burial Register, St. Paul's, Hammersmith (Shepherd's Bush Branch Library: Archives, DD/71/11).
21 *Journal*, 31. See *DA* from Sept. 17–Oct. 19.
22 John Fielding's words, *Plan*, 1.
23 Hugh Amory, *Huntington Library Quarterly*, 35 (1971), 80, n. 39.
24 PRO C.193.45; GLRO MJ/SBB/1107, p. 53.
25 Harleian Society, Registers, vol. 34.
26 *PA*, June 10, 1754.
27 PRO. Prob.10/2161; P.C.C. Nov. 1754.
28 To John Fielding, ca. Sept. 10–14, 1754 and ca. Sept. 20, *Corresp.*, 109–18.
29 B 682 n. 338.

30 *PA* Dec. 20; cat. publ. Feb. 6. For the catalogue and commentary, see *Fielding's Library: An Annotated Catalogue*, ed. Frederick G. Ribble and Anne G. Ribble (Charlottesville: University of Virginia Press, 1998).

31 *Letters of Lady Mary Wortley Montagu*, ed. W. Moy Thomas (London, 1861), 2:282–3.

32 As J. M. Beattie explains, it was the magistrate's duty "to bring the parties in conflict before [him], to take depositions of the complainant and his witnesses, to examine the accused, and to ensure that they appeared at the next sitting of the appropriate court." In time "the magistrate's examination ceased being simply a means of assembling the best evidence against the prisoner and took on some of the characteristics of a judicial hearing. Magistrates began to feel more obligation to make some assessment of the evidence being presented and to assume more right to dismiss charges when they thought the case too weak to justify a trial" (Beattie, *Crime and the Courts in England, 1660–1800* [Princeton: Princeton University Press, 1986], 36, 274; also 59–67).

33 Lance Bertelsen, "Committed by Justice Fielding: Judicial and Journalistic Representation in the Bow Street Magistrate's Office," *ECS*, 30 (1997):338; citing Norma Landau, *The Justices of the Peace, 1679–1760* (Berkeley: University of California Press, 1984).

34 See *CGJ*, 392, 394, 402. Lance Bertelsen analyzes these *Covent-Garden* columns ("Committed by Justice Fielding," 337–63).

35 *A Charge Delivered to the Grand Jury*, in *Enquiry*, 23–24.

36 In fact, Hogarth could have taken the inspiration for the parallels of plates 11 and 12 from Fielding's line in *The Modern Husband* of 1732: "How happy is that country, where pimping and whoring are esteemed publick services, and *where grandeur and the gallows lie on the same road*" (emphasis added; Capt. Merit's line; Henley edn., 10:20).

37 The parody of a Good Samaritan group in the right foreground refers back to Fielding's quotation of Hogarth's St. Barthomew's paintings in *Joseph Andrews*. It is now marginalized: What the biblical parable of the Good Samaritan had meant to that novel the historical rebellion of the Forty-Five meant to *Tom Jones*. Perhaps he recalls how Fielding reverses the parable of the Prodigal Son, having the father seek the forgiveness of the son.

38 George II thought the print satirized his troops (Paulson, *Hogarth*, 3:13).

39 *Old England*, July 15, 1949; B 475.

40 *Enquiry*, 58–9.

41 In the year after Fielding's death Hogarth undertook his greatest church painting, a 17 foot by 51 foot altarpiece for St. Mary Redcliffe, Bristol, representing the Resurrection. The principal figure of the central panel (the Ascension) is a harlot, Mary Magdalen (the figure of Christ is very high, small, and distant). She is, like the women of *The Analysis of Beauty*, announcing to the disciples the miracle of the new dispensation. Unlike Fielding, Hogarth had no conversion, even when his patron was the clergy. His views on priestcraft are still reflected in the priests of the left panel checking out Christ's tomb to be sure there is no "miracle" such as resurrection.

42 See *Newgate Calendar*, ed. Andrew Knapp and William Baldwin (London, 1824), 2:61.

43   *GM*, Oct. 1749, 465.
44   B 479.
45   See in particular Sections XXVI and XXX. Section XXVII assesses the use-
     fulness of religion on the idle (he quotes Tillotson) to "make them obedient
     to Government, and peaceable towards one another" (269).
46   For further analysis of Hogarth's position in these prints, see Paulson,
     Hogarth, 3:20–3.
47   T. G. Coffey, "Beer Street, Gin Lane: Some Views of 18th-Century Drinking,"
     Quarterly Journal of Studies on Alcohol, 27 (1966):669–92; see also Sidney and
     Beatrice Webb, *History of Liquor Licensing in England* (London, 1903), 20–2,
     29; and Brian Inglis, *Forbidden Game: A Social History of Drugs* (London, 1975),
     67.
48   Quoted, Peter Linebaugh, *The London Hanged: Crime and Civil Society in the
     Eighteenth Century* (London: Allen Lane, 1991), 241, and, more generally on
     the plight of journeymen tailors, 241–3.
49   See B 524.
50   See Coffey, "Beer Street."
51   It is not, as Battestin suggests (518) and I echoed in *Hogarth*, 3:449n. 24 in
     any sense aesthetic or anticipatory of Burke's sublime.
52   Hogarth could be dramatizing Sir Avarice Pedant's remark to Sir Harry
     Wilding, whose son is studying to be a lawyer: "how comes it that your son
     pays four shillings for a coach to Westminster, when four lawyers go thither
     for one?" (*Temple Beau*, 1.4.8:113).
53   See John Ireland, *Hogarth Illustrated* (1791), 2:72n.
54   BM 1892.8.4.5; Battestin, "Pictures of Fielding," *ECS*, 17 (1983):1–13. The
     identification of Fielding is made in the BM acquisitions log as well as by
     Battestin in the *ECS* essay, and seems possible. It is considerably more doubt-
     ful that the artist is (as the BM entry tentatively proposes and Battestin
     believes) Joshua Reynolds.
55   *General Advertiser*, Dec. 8, 15, 1750; *Penny London Post*, Dec. 7–10, 12, 12–14,
     1750; see B 511 and n. 154.
56   See Hester Lynch Thrale's account, *Hogarth*, 3:263.
57   See OBSP, Feb.–Mar. 1749/50, no. 169; B 464, 501–2 and n. 120.
58   See B 493ff.; Battestin also identifies Cooke as author of the *Craftsman* cited.
59   *Characteristics*, 1:270–3.
60   These were the years he and John Wilkes became close friends and frater-
     nized with the Medmenham Monks of Sir Francis Dashwood's "Hell-Fire
     Club."
61   Mandeville, "An Enquiry into the Origin of Moral Virtue," in *Fable of the Bees*,
     1:42, 47. In *Tom Jones* Fielding gave a very Humean representation of provi-
     dence. He owned a copy of Hume's *Philosophical Essays on Human Under-
     standing* (1748), which included the two essays (chaps. 10 and 11) disposing
     of miracles and rewards and punishments in the afterlife that came to a con-
     clusion very close to Fielding's. Once he is a magistrate, Fielding begins to
     speak and act out a discourse of religious rewards and punishments that
     recalls Shaftesbury's pragmatic proposal for the utilization of religion to
     control the lower orders. But it also recalls the words of the Humean
     spokesman that philosophy, "denying a divine existence and consequently a

providence and a future state, seems to loosen in a great measure the ties of morality, and may be supposed, for that reason, pernicious to the peace of civil society." Hume's retention of *belief*, "based on *faith*, not on reason," with its provisional and pragmatic nature, describes Fielding's probable position in the 1750s. (See *Fielding's Library*, H42, no. 539; Hume, *Enquiry*, ed. L. A. Selby-Bigge [Oxford: Clarendon Press, 1966], 143, 140.)

62   Battestin draws attention to Johnson's appearance in court before Fielding earlier in the same month to post a bond for the wife of one of his assistants on the *Dictionary*. He suggests that Johnson's remark that such authors (implicitly Fielding) "confound the Colours of Right and Wrong" could reflect his opinion of Fielding's action in this case (B 504–5). Something of the sort may have happened in the courtroom on that occasion.

63   *Covent-Garden Journal*, no. 20, Mar. 10, 1752 (136).

64   This was attributed to Smollett on the strength of a *GM* statement that it was "supposed to be written by the author of *Peregrine Pickle*" and the earlier attack on Fielding in *Peregrine Pickle* (see H. S. Buck, *A Study in Smollett* [New Haven: Yale University Press, 1925], 109–21; Lewis M. Knapp, *Tobias Smollett* [Princeton: Princeton University Press, 1949], 131).

65   Robert Alter, *Fielding and the Art of the Novel* (Cambridge, Mass.: Harvard University Press, 1968), 153; emphasis added. As Alter notes, in *Tom Jones* "all the sexual liaisons, with the single exception of Mrs. Fitzgerald's, are merely promiscuous, not adulterous."

66   We recall the role of Juvenal in Fielding's earliest poems and such comedies as *Love in Several Masques*.

67   See Satires V and VII, among others.

68   See John S. Coolidge, "Fielding and the 'Conservation of Character,'" *Modern Philology*, 57 (1960):245–59.

69   Sherburn, "Fielding's *Amelia*: An Interpretation," *ELH*, 3 (1936):14.

70   See Sherburn, op. cit., 3–4; L. H. Powers, "The Influence of the *Aeneid* on Fielding's *Amelia*," *MLN*, 71 (1956):330–6; Maurice Johnson, *Fielding's Art of Fiction* (Philadelphia: University of Pennsylvania Press, 1961), 139–56.

71   Alter also sees dueling, an important subject in *Amelia*, as "a pagan conception of honor, or love and honor, [which] must be exorcised before an authentically Christian hero can come into being" (146).

72   See also, suggesting the notoriety of the event: stories by Horace Walpole in *Old England*, April 23, 1748; Smollett in *Peregrine Pickle* (1751), and Bonnell Thornton in the *Spring-Garden Journal*, Nov. 16, 1752.

73   Lady Mary to Countess of Bute, Sept. 22 [1755], in Halsband, ed., *The Complete Letters of Lady Mary Wortley Montagu* (Oxford: Clarendon Press, 1966), 3:87.

74   J. A. S. Wortley Mackenzie, Lord Wharncliffe, ed. *Letters and Works of Lady Mary Wortley Montagu* (Philadelphia, 1837), 1:106.

75   Richardson, letter to Anne Donnellan, 1750, in Paulson and Lockwood, 335; and cited, B 97. Lady Mary told her daughter, Lady Bute, that in *Amelia* Fielding had "given a true picture of himself and his first Wife in the Characters of Mr. and Mrs. Booth (some Complement to his own figure excepted) and I am persuaded several of the Incidents he mentions are real matters of Fact" (letter of July 23, [1754], Halsband, edn., 3:66).

76 His obsession with noses led him to include in the *Covent-Garden Journal* a strange account of a witness who identifies a man just by his nose – a nose nobody else finds at all unusual (404).

77 Angela Smallwood, *Fielding and the Woman Question* (New York: St Martin's Press, 1989), 126; see chap. 8.

78 *Analysis of Beauty*, ed. Paulson, chap. 5, "Of Intricacy."

79 At the extreme of this line of argument, the rankness of the guilt adds zest to the sin (10.2.415). On Hogarth's title page the serpentine Line of Beauty is given the form of Eve's serpent and accompanied by an epigraph from *Paradise Lost* describing the seduction. In the chapter that opens book 6 of *Amelia*, Amelia's beauty is similarly evoked in a series of quotations from *Paradise Lost* in which Adam describes Eve's beauty (230), but as she appears not to Booth but to Colonel James, arousing his passion.

80 The quotations are from *Spectator* no. 1, but they reappear in the "Pleasures of the Imagination" essays and throughout the *Spectator*. See Paulson, *Beautiful, Novel, and Strange*, chap. 3.

81 See 9.6.353; cf. explanation, 357–8; and then 360.

82 In the autobiographical "Dream" of Lucian, Fielding's favorite satirist at this time, Lucian figures a Herculean choice between a woman representing sculpture, mechanical and laborious, and literature (education, words vs. pictures, etc.).

83 Advertisement, *London Daily Advertiser*, Nov. 9, 1751/2 (also June 3).

84 This view of Swift was substantiated in Orrery's *Remarks on the Life and Writings of Dr. Jonathan Swift*, published early in 1752. Drawcansir, the "author" of the *Covent-Garden Journal*, refers back to the mock-hero of Buckingham's *Rehearsal* (see above, chap. 2), an influence also on Swift's *Tale of a Tub*.

85 *Craftsman*, Jan. 25, 1752; *Old England*, Dec. 21, 1751, Jan. 11 and 18, 1752.

86 An essay on "lies" recalls Swift's *Examiner* nos. 14 and 18 on champaign and perry, though Fielding attributes *Peri Bathous* to Swift, is obviously drawing upon the imagery of Swift's *Tale*, which Pope later used in *Peri Bathous*; and no. 16 recalls the *Mechanical Operation of the Spirit*.

87 For example, in the imitation of the *Modest Proposal* in no. 11 he takes the proposition that the only way to support the poor Irish is to make them eat their children (this is Fielding's misreading of Swift – actually the children were to provide money for their parents when they were sold for the dinner tables of the Anglo-Irish ruling class) and "improves" upon it, that is, removes the verisimilitude that Swift used to catch his reader, raising the economic into a religious action. Fielding proposes (incorporating an aspect of the *Argument against Abolishing Christianity* imitation from No. 8) that since the English have no Christianity now, they should become heathen idolworshipers and sacrifice the poor to their god. The satire is too literary, too secondary, and too allegorical to be taken altogether seriously.

88 In the process, he alludes to Hogarth's *Beer Street*, one of the prints of 1751 issued following upon the *Enquiry*.

89 In *A Charge to the Grand Jury* he had drawn attention to the statutes against irreligious writings.

90 See no. 9, 68, the ironic but truth-telling account; and on the *Providence* book, 422; and cf. *Enquiry*, 172, on parents and children.

91   In the Christian tradition "baby talk" was a metaphor for God's conde-
     scension when he spoke to man in Scripture. It was a favorite metaphor
     of Calvin's ("God lisps, as it were, with us, just as nurses are accustomed
     to speak to infants"). See Calvin, *Institutes of the Christian Religion*, 2 vols.,
     ed. John T. McNeill, trans. Ford Lewis Battles (London: S.C.M.P., 1958),
     1.xii.1.
92   Noted, B 550–2.
93   Cf. Fielding's letter to Harris, referring to *Amelia* as "my damned Book (for
     so it is)" (to Harris, Dec. 23, 1751; *Corresp.*, 98).
94   *Daily Advertiser*, Jan. 20, 1753; quoted, Zirker, *Enquiry*, xcvii.
95   Again, he concludes that he is finally convinced "that *Elizabeth Canning* is a
     poor, honest, innocent, simple Girl, and the most unhappy and most injured
     of all human Beings" (311).
96   *Enquiry*, xcix.
97   Zirker, *Enquiry*, cxiv; Zirker notes the parallel with Allworthy's judgments
     guided by "*a priori* considerations of credibility or incredibility."
98   "A Letter to the Right Honourable the Earl of —— Concerning the affair of
     Elizabeth Canning," in *The Investigator* (London, 1762), 2–3; first published
     as "By a Clergyman" in 1753 (Paulson and Lockwood, 360).
99   *PA* Dec. 20, 1754.
100 Cross, 3:77.
101 Battestin notes that since they did not appear in Fielding's library sale, it
     seems likely that he took them with him to Portugal and, given their hereti-
     cal nature, they were confiscated by the censors of the Inquisition.
102 He is citing Bolingbroke, *Works*, 5:377. Cf, Fielding's Job Vinegar's descrip-
     tion of a sect whose religion "seems the best drawn from human Observa-
     tion": "They believe Men to be Comedians, or rather Puppets, who are
     created only to act on the Theatre of this World for the Entertainment of the
     Gods. That the World every where represents a vast Theatre, on which trag-
     ical and comical drama's are exhibited, some of shorter Duration, as a Farce
     of one act; some of longer, as a Play of five. That, as in a Play-House, the
     Talents of some Actors are confin'd to one Part, while there are others, whose
     Genius seems universal; so it happens in Life, . . ." (*Voyages*, 24).
103 Harris, "Fielding," Probyn, 312–13.
104 Richard Hurd, cited in F. Kilvert, *Memoirs of the Life and Writings of Bishop Hurd*
     (1860), 45; Edward Moore to the Rev. John Ward, undated letter, probably
     1748–52; Joshua Toulmin, "A Delineation of the Character of the late Rev.
     John Ward, of Taunton," *Protestant Dissenter's Magazine* (July 1797), 242. For
     the view that his dropsy was a sign of cirrhosis of the liver, see B 577.
105 In the preface he argues that Homer and Hesiod "and the other antient poets
     and mythologists," whatever their intention, did "pervert and confuse the
     records of antiquity": "and, for my part, I must confess I should have hon-
     oured and loved Homer more had he written a true history of his own times
     in humble prose, than those noble poems that have so justly collected the
     praise of all ages; for though I read these with more admiration and aston-
     ishment, I still read Herodotus, Thucydides, and Xenophon, with more
     amusement and more satisfaction" (26).

106 Also "the gang of Captain Ulysses," on the next page (101) and Circe again on the next (102).
107 In the *Enquiry* he wrote of the disabling of the body hierarchy (227): "As there is no Part . . . admitted in the Body that doth not work and take Pains, so ought there no Part of her Commonwealth to be, but laboursome in his Vocation. The Gentleman ought to labour in the Service of his Country; the Serving-man ought to wait diligently on his Master; the Artificer ought to labour in his Work; the Husbandman in tilling the ground; the Merchant in passing the Tempests." To which he adds, "but the Vagabonds ought clearly to be banished, as is the superfluous Humour of the Body; that is to say, the Spittle and Filth; which, because it is for no Use, is put out by the Strength of Human Nature." The vagrants have now replaced the spirit of comedy or love or sheer energy of Fielding's old hydraulic model.
108 Bowers, "Tropes of Nationhood: Body Politic and Nation State in Fielding's *Journal of a Voyage to Lisbon*," *ELH*, 62 (1995):575–602.
109 Something of the sense of heroism implicit in Fielding's tappings can be seen in an epitaph in Bunhill Fields Cemetery in London: Dame Mary Page (wife of Sir Gregory), who died in 1728, is memorialized on a large square monument on the side of which is inscribed: "In 67 months she was tap'd 66 Times / Had taken away 240 gallons of water / without ever repining at her case / or ever fearing the operation."
110 To the subjects of liberty and the mob he adds, unsurprisingly, another discussion of exemplary punishment (36).
111 Cf. the author of the "Essay on Eating" (probably Fielding) in the *Universal Spectator*, Aug. 21, 1736, on his preference for plain, heartily English food – for beef and plum pudding, venison and beans, chines of bacon and joints of mutton, chicken and roast pig (a "Dish I am particularly fond of"); *Champion*, Feb. 26, 1739/40, but repeated in the *Journal of a Voyage*; see B 149–51.
112 Margaret Collier to Richardson, Oct. 3, 1755; in A. L. Barbauld, ed., *Correspondence of Samuel Richardson* (Oxford, 1804), 2:77–8.
113 He also invokes Hogarth on the next page when he refers to dedicating his journal to the king of Prussia, precisely what Hogarth had done to his print of *The March to Finchley* (47).
114 In the same way fish, he notes disapprovingly, are used by the rich when they should feed the poor (106).
115 *Complete Letters*, ed. Halsband, 3:87.

Bibliography

I   Principal Works Cited

Note: The principal works of Fielding published so far in the Wesleyan Edition are cited with short title, book, chapter, and page numbers. Exceptions are cited in the W. E. Henley edition, with volume and page number. When not in the Henley edition, and in a few cases when they are, I cite separate editions, indicated below.

Amelia: ed., Martin C. Battestin, Wesleyan Edn. Oxford: Clarendon Press, 1983.
Champion: *The Champion*, 2 vols., first collected Edn. London: J. Huggonson, 1741.
Corresp.: *The Correspondence of Henry and Sarah Fielding*, ed. Martin C. Battestin and Clive T. Probyn. Oxford: Clarendon Press, 1993.
Covent-Garden Journal: *The Covent-Garden Journal and A Plan for the Universal Register-Office*, ed. Bertrand A. Goldgar, Wesleyan Edn. Oxford: Clarendon Press, 1988.
Enquiry: *An Enquiry into the Causes of the Late Increase of Robbers and Related Writings*, ed. Malvin R. Zirker, Wesleyan Ed. Oxford: Clarendon Press, 1988.
Female Husband: *The Female Husband and Other Writings*, ed. Claude E. Jones. English Reprint Series, No. 17. Liverpool: Liverpool University Press, 1960.
Grundy: Grundy, Isabel. "New Verse by Henry Fielding." *PMLA*, 87 (1972):213–45.
Henley edn.: *The Complete Works of Henry Fielding, Esq.*, ed. W. E. Henley, 16 vols. London: William Heinemann, 1902, 1903; rpt. New York: Barnes & Noble, 1967.
History: *The History of Our Own Times*, ed. Thomas F. Lockwood. Delmar, N. Y.: Scholars' Facsimiles, 1985.
Jacobite's Journal: *Jacobite's Journal and Related Writings*, ed. W. B. Coley, Wesleyan Edn. Oxford: Clarendon Press, 1974.
Joseph Andrews: ed., Martin C. Battestin, Wesleyan Edn. Oxford: Clarendon Press, 1967.
Journal: *Journal of a Voyage to Lisbon*, ed. Harold E. Pagliaro. New York: Nardon Press, 1963.

Journey: *Journey from This World to the Next*, in *Miscellanies, Vol. 2*.

Jonathan Wild: in *Miscellanies*, vol. 3.

Misc. 1: *Miscellanies, Volume One*, ed. Henry Knight Miller, Wesleyan Edn. Oxford: Clarendon Press, 1972.

Misc. 2: *Miscellanies, Volume Two*, ed. Bertrand A. Goldgar and Hugh Amory, Wesleyan Edn. Oxford: Clarendon Press, 1993.

Misc. 3: *Miscellanies, Volume Three*, ed. Bertrand A. Goldgar and Hugh Amory, Wesleyan Edn. Oxford: Clarendon Press, 1997.

New Essays: *New Essays by Henry Fielding: His Contributions to the Craftsman (1734–1739) and Other Early Journalism*, ed. Martin C. Battestin. Charlottesville: University of Virginia Press, 1989.

Ovid's Art of Love: *The Lovers Assistant, or, New Art of Love*, ed. Claude E. Jones. Augustran Reprint Society, no. 89. Los Angeles: Clark Memorial Library, University of California Press, 1961.

Plutus, the God of Riches. A Comedy. Translated from the Original Greek of Aristophanes. London: T. Walker, 1742.

Shamela: *Shamela*, ed. Sheridan Baker. Berkeley and Los Angeles: University of California Press, 1953.

Tom Jones: ed., Martin C. Battestin, Wesleyan Edn., 2 vols. Oxford: Clarendon Press, 1974; 2nd Edn., 1975, 1 vol.

The Tragedy of Tragedies, ed. James T. Hillhouse. New Haven: Yale University Press, 1918.

True Patriot: *The True Patriot and Related Writings*, ed. W. B. Coley, Wesleyan Edn. Oxford: Clarendon Press, 1987.

Voyages: *The Voyages of Mr. Job Vinegar* (from *The Champion*), ed. S. J. Sackett. Augustan Reprint Society, no. 67. Los Angeles: Clark Memorial Library, University of California, 1958.

The Wesleyan Edition of the Works of Henry Fielding. Oxford: Clarendon Press, 1967–. Unnumbered volumes; see above under individual titles.

The Works of Henry Fielding, Esq.: with the Life of the Author, 4 vols. quarto (8 octavo). London: A. Millar, 1762.

II Biographical Studies

Amory, Hugh. "Fielding's Lisbon Letters," *Huntington Library Quarterly*, 35 (1971):65–83.

——. "Henry Fielding and the Criminal Legislation of 1751–2," *Philological Quarterly*, 50 (1970):175–92.

Battestin, Martin C. "Fielding and 'Master Punch' in Panton Street," *Philological Quarterly*, 45 (1966):191–208.

B: Battestin, Martin C., with Ruthe R. Battestin. *Henry Fielding: A Life*. London and New York: Routledge, 1989.

Coley, William B. "Fielding's Two Appointments to the Magistracy," *Modern Philology*, 63 (1965):144–9.

——. "Henry Fielding and the Two Walpoles," *Philological Quarterly*, 45 (1966):157–78.

——. "Henry Fielding's 'Lost' Law Book," *Modern Language Notes*, 76 (1961):408–13.

Cross: Cross, Wilbur. *History of Henry Fielding*, 3 vols. New Haven: Yale University Press, 1918.

Dobson: Dobson, Austin. *Fielding*. English Men of Letters. London, 1883; rpt. New York: Harper, 1883.

Duddon: Duddon, F. Homes. *Henry Fielding, His Life, Works, and Times*, 2 vols. Oxford: Clarendon Press, 1952.

Godden: Godden, Gertrude M. *Henry Fielding: A Memoir*. London: Sampson Low, Marston, 1910.

Jones, B. M. *Henry Fielding: Novelist and Magistrate*. London: Allen & Unwin, 1933.

Murphy: Murphy, Arthur. "An Essay on the Life and Genius of Henry Fielding, Esq.," in *The Works of Henry Fielding, Esq.: with the Life of the Author*. 1762, vol. 1.

Pagliaro, Harold. *Henry Fielding: A Literary Life*. New York: St. Martin's Press, 1998.

Paulson and Lockwood: *Henry Fielding: The Critical Heritage*, eds. Ronald Paulson and Thomas Lockwood. London and New York: Routledge & Kegan Paul, 1969.

Probyn: Probyn, Clive T. *The Sociable Humanist: The Life and Works of James Harris, 1709–1780* (Oxford, 1991), which includes Harris' memoir of Fielding.

Rogers, Pat. *Henry Fielding: A Biography*. New York: Charles Scribners, 1979.

T: Thomas, Donald. *Henry Fielding*. London: St. Martin's Press, 1990.

III   Selected Interpretive Studies

Alter, Robert. *Fielding and the Nature of the Novel*. Cambridge, Mass.: Harvard University Press, 1968.

Amory, Hugh. "*Shamela* as Aesopic Satire," *ELH*, 38 (1971):239–53.

Baker, Sheridan. "Fielding's *Amelia* and the Materials of Romance," *Philological Quarterly*, 41 (1962):437–9.

——. "Henry Fielding's Comic Romances," *Papers of the Michigan Academy of Science, Arts, and Letters*, 45 (1960):411–19.

——. "Fielding and the Irony of Form," *Eighteenth-Century Studies*, 2 (1968):138–54.

——. "Fielding's Comic Epic-in-Prose Romances Again," *Papers of the Michigan Academy of Science, Arts, and Letters*, 58 (1979):63–81.

Battestin, Martin C. "Fielding's Definition of Wisdom: Some Functions of Ambiguity and Emblem in *Tom Jones*," *ELH*, 35 (1968):188–217; rpt. in *Providence of Wit: Aspects of Form in Augustan Literature and the Arts*, 164–92. Oxford: Clarendon Press, 1974.

——. "Lord Hervey's Role in *Joseph Andrews*," *Philological Quarterly*, 42 (1963):226–41.

——. *The Moral Basis of Fielding's Art: A Study of Joseph Andrews*. Middletown, Conn.: Wesleyan University Press, 1959.

——. "Tom Jones and 'His Egyptian Majesty': Fielding's Parable of Government," *PMLA*, 82 (1967):68–77.

——. "*Tom Jones*: The Argument of Design," in *The Augustan Milieu: Essays Presented to Louis A. Landa*, eds. Henry Knight Miller, Eric Rothstein, and G. S. Rousseau, 289–319. Oxford: Clarendon Press, 1970; rpt. in *The Providence of Wit: Aspects of Form in Augustan Literature and the Arts*, 141–63. Oxford: Clarendon Press, 1974.

Beasley, Jerry C. "Fiction as Artifice: The Achievement of Henry Fielding," in *Novels of the 1740s*, 184–209. Athens: University of Georgia Press, 1982.

Bell, Ian A. *Henry Fielding: Authorship and Authority*. New York: Longman, 1994.

Blanchard, Frederic T. *Fielding the Novelist: A Study in Historical Criticism*. New Haven, Conn.: Yale University Press, 1926.

Boheemen, Christine van. *The Novel as Family Romance: Language, Gender, and Authority from Fielding to Joyce*. Ithaca: Cornell University Press, 1987.

Booth, Wayne C. "Fielding in *Tom Jones*," in *Rhetoric of Fiction*, 215–18. Chicago: University of Chicago Press, 1961.

Braudy, Leo. "*Joseph Andrews*: The Relevance of Facts" and "*Tom Jones*: The Narrative Stance," in *Narrative Form in History and Fiction: Hume, Fielding, and Gibbon*, 95–121, 144–80. Princeton, N. J.: Princeton University Press, 1970.

Brooks, Douglas. "Richardson's *Pamela* and Fielding's *Joseph Andrews*," *Essays in Criticism*, 18 (1967):158–68.

Brown, Homer Obed. "*Tom Jones*: The 'Bastard' of History," *Boundary* 27 (1979):210–33.

Brown, Laura. *English Dramatic Form, 1660–1760: An Essay in Generic History*, 173–209. New Haven: Yale University Press, 1981.

Butt, John. *Fielding*. Writers and Their Work, no. 57. London: Longmans, Green, 1954.

Campbell, Jill. *Natural Masques: Gender and Identity in Fielding's Plays and Novels*. Stanford: Stanford University Press, 1995.

Castle, Terry. "Masquerade and Allegory: Fielding's *Amelia*," in *Masquerade and Civilization: The Carnivalesque in Eighteenth-Century English Culture and Fiction*. Stanford: Stanford University Press, 1986.

——. "Matters Not Fit to Be Mentioned: Fielding's *The Female Husband*," *ELH*, 49 (1982):602–22; rpt. *The Female Thermometer: 18th-Century Culture and the Invention of the Uncanny*, 67–81. New York: Oxford University Press, 1995.

Cauthen, I. B., Jr. "Fielding's Digressions in *Joseph Andrews*," *College English*, 17 (1956):379–82.

Cleary, Thomas R. *Henry Fielding: Political Writers*. Waterloo, Ontario: Wilfred Laurier University Press, 1984.

Coley, William B. "The Background of Fielding's Laughter," *ELH*, 26 (1959):229–52.

Coolidge, John S. "Fielding and the 'Conservation of Character,'" *Modern Philology*, 57 (1960):245–59.

Craik, T. W. "Fielding's 'Tom Thumb' Plays," in *Augustan Worlds*, ed. J. C. Hilson et al., 165–74. New York: Harper and Row, 1978.

Crane, R. S. "The Plot of Tom Jones," *Journal of General Education*, 4 (1950):112–30.

Cruise, James. "Fielding, Authority, and the New Commercialism in *Joseph Andrews*," *ELH*, 54 (1987):253–76.

Davis, Lennard J. "Fielding: Politics and Fact," in *Factual Fictions: The Origins of the English Novel*, 193–211. New York: Columbia University Press, 1983.

Digeon, Aurélien. *The Novels of Fielding*. London: Routledge, 1925. Originally pub. in French, Paris, 1923.

Ducrocq, Jean. *Le Théâtre de Fielding: 1728–1737 et ses prolongements dans l'oeuvre romanesque*. Etudes Anglaises 55. Paris: Didier, 1975.

Ehrenpreis, Irvin. *Fielding: Tom Jones.* London: Edward Arnold, 1964.

———. "Fielding's Use of Fiction: The Autonomy of *Joseph Andrews*," in *Twelve Original Essays on Great English Novels,* ed. Charles Shapiro, 23–41. Detroit: Wayne State University Press, 1960.

Empson, William. "*Tom Jones*," *Kenyon Review,* 20 (1958):217–249; rev., rpt., in *Fielding: A Collection of Critical Essays.* ed. Ronald Paulson. Twentieth Century View Series. Englewood Cliffs, N.J.: Prentice-Hall, 1962.

Erzgräber, Willi. "Das Menschenbild in Henry Fieldings Roman *Amelia*," *Die Neueren Sprachen,* 6 (1957):105–16.

Farrell, William J. "The Mock-Heroic Form of *Jonathan Wild*," *Modern Philology,* 63 (1966):216–26.

Folkenflik, Robert. "Purpose and Narration in Fielding's *Amelia*," *Novel,* 6 (1973):168–74.

———. "Tom Jones, the Gypsies, and the Masquerade," *University of Toronto Quarterly,* 44 (1975):224–37.

Frank, Judith. "'What You Seek is Nowhere': The Comic Novel and Lower-Class Literacy," in *Common Ground: Eighteenth-Century English Satiric Fiction and the Poor,* 30–62. Stanford: Stanford University Press, 1997.

Gautier, Gary. "Henry and Sarah Fielding on Romance and Sensibility," *Novel,* 31 (1998):195–214.

Goggin, Leo P. "Development of Techniques in Fielding's Comedies," *PMLA,* 67 (1952):769–81.

Goldberg, Homer. *The Art of Joseph Andrews.* Chicago: University of Chicago Press, 1969.

Golden, Morris. *Fielding's Moral Psychology.* Amherst: University of Massachusetts Press, 1966.

Han, Jiaming *Henry Fielding: Form, History, Ideology.* Beijing: Peking University Press, 1997.

Harrison, Bernard. *Henry Fielding's Tom Jones: The Novelist as Moral Philosopher.* Sussex, England: Sussex University Press, 1975.

Hassall, Anthony, J. "Fielding's *Amelia*: Dramatic and Authorial Narration," *Novel,* 5 (1972):225–33.

Hatfield, Glenn W. *Henry Fielding and the Language of Irony.* Chicago: University of Chicago Press, 1968.

Hilles, Frederick W. "Art and Artifice in *Tom Jones*," in *Imagined Worlds: Essays on Some English Novels and Novelists in Honour of John Butt,* eds. Maynard Mack and Ian Gregor, 91–110. London: Methuen, 1968.

H: Hume, Robert. *Henry Fielding and the London Theatre, 1728–1737.* Oxford: Clarendon Press, 1988.

Humphreys, A. R. "Fielding's Irony: Its Methods and Effects," *Review of English Studies,* o.s. 18 (1942):183–96.

Hunter, J. Paul. *Occasional Form: Henry Fielding and the Chains of Circumstance.* Baltimore: Johns Hopkins University Press, 1975.

Hutchens, Eleanor Newman. *Irony in "Tom Jones."* University: University of Alabama Press, 1965.

Irwin, Michael. *Henry Fielding: The Tentative Realist.* Oxford, England: Clarendon Press, 1967.

Irwin, William Robert. *The Making of Jonathan Wild: A Study in the Literary Method of Henry Fielding.* New York: Columbia University Press, 1941; rpt. Hamden, Conn.: Archon Books, 1966.

Iser, Wolfgang. "The Role of the Reader in Fielding's *Joseph Andrews* and *Tom Jones*," in *The Implied Reader: Patterns of Communication in Prose Fiction from Bunyan to Beckett*, 29–56. Baltimore: Johns Hopkins University Press, 1974. Originally pub. in German, 1972.

Johnson, Maurice. *Fielding's Art of Fiction: Eleven Essays on Shamela, Joseph Andrews, Tom Jones, and Amelia.* Philadelphia: University of Pennsylvania Press, 1961.

Kermode, Frank. "Richardson and Fielding," *Cambridge Journal*, 4 (1950):106–14.

Kern, Jean B. *Dramatic Satire in the Age of Walpole, 1720–1750.* Ames, Iowa: University of Iowa Press, 1976.

Kettle, Arnold. "*Tom Jones*," in *Introduction to the English Novel*, 1: 76–81. London: Hutchinson, 1951.

Knight, Charles A. "*Tom Jones*: The Meaning of the Main Design," *Genre*, 12 (1979):379–99.

Kraft, Quentin G. "Narrative Transformation in *Tom Jones*: An Episode in the Emergence of the English Novel," *The Eighteenth-Century: Theory and Interpretation*, 26 (1985):23–45.

Kropf, Carl R. "Educational Theory and Human Nature in Fielding's Works," *PMLA*, 89 (1974):113–20.

Lamb, Jonathan. "Exemplarity and Excess in Fielding's Fiction," *Eighteenth-Century Fiction*, 1 (1989):187–207.

Levine, George R. *Henry Fielding and the Dry Mock: A Study of the Techniques of Irony in His Early Works.* The Hague: Mouton, 1967.

Lewis, Peter. *Fielding's Burlesque Drama: Its Place in the Tradition.* Edinburgh: Edinburgh University Press, 1987.

Lockwood, Thomas. "Matter and Reflection in *Tom Jones*," *ELH*, 45 (1978):226–35.

Loftis, John. "The Displacement of the Restoration Tradition, 1728–1737," in *Comedy and Society from Congreve to Fielding*, 101–32. Stanford: Stanford University Press, 1959.

——. "Fielding and the Stage Licensing Act of 1737," in *The Politics of Drama in Augustan England*, 128–53. Oxford: Clarendon Press, 1963.

London, April. "Controlling the Text: Women in *Tom Jones*," *Studies in the Novel*, 19 (1987):323–33.

Lynch, James J. *Henry Fielding and the Heliodoran Novel: Romance, Epic, and Fielding's New Province of Writing.* London and Toronto: Associated University Presses, 1986.

McCrea, Brian. *Henry Fielding and the Politics of Mid-Eighteenth Century England.* Athens: University of Georgia Press, 1981.

McKeon, Michael. "The Institutionalization of Conflict: Fielding and the Instrumentality of Belief," in *Origins of the English Novel, 1600–1740*, 382–409. Baltimore: Johns Hopkins University Press, 1987.

McKillop, Alan D. "Henry Fielding," in *The Early Masters of English Fiction*, 98–146. Lawrence: University of Kansas Press, 1956.

Mace, Nancy A. *Henry Fielding's Novels and the Classical Tradition.* Newark: University of Delaware Press, 1996.

Mack, Maynard. Introduction to his edition of *Joseph Andrews*, pp. ii–xxiv. Rinehart Edn. New York: Holt, 1948.

Maresca, Thomas E. "Fielding," in *Epic to Novel*, 181–234. Columbus: Ohio State University Press, 1974.

Miller, Henry K. *Essays on Fielding's Miscellanies*. Princeton: Princeton University Press, 1961.

——. *Henry Fielding's "Tom Jones" and the Romance Tradition*. English Literary Studies Monograph Series no. 6. Victoria, B.C.: University of Victoria Press, 1976.

Moore, Robert Etheridge. "Hogarth's Role in Fielding's Novels," in *Hogarth's Literary Relationships*, 107–62, Minneapolis: University of Minnesota Press, 1948; rpt. New York: Octagon, 1969.

Morrissey, LeRoy J. "Henry Fielding and the Ballad Opera," *Eighteenth-Century Studies*, 4 (1971):386–402.

Park, William. "Fielding *and* Richardson," *PMLA*, 81 (1966):381–88.

——. "Tom and Oedipus," *Hartford Studies in Literature: A Journal of Interdisciplinary Criticism*, 7 (1975):207–15.

——. "What Was New about the 'New Species of Writing'?" *Studies in the Novel*, 2 (1970):112–30.

Poovey, Mary. "Journeys from This World to the Next: The Providential Promise in *Clarissa* and *Tom Jones*," *ELH*, 43 (1976):300–15.

Preston, John. "The Ironic Mode: A Comparison of *Jonathan Wild* and *The Beggar's Opera*," *Essays in Criticism*, 16 (1966):268–80.

——. "*Tom Jones* (i): Plot as Irony," "*Tom Jones* (ii): The Pursuit of True Judgment," in *Created Self: The Reader's Role in Eighteenth-Century Fiction*, 94–132. London: Heinemann, 1970.

Price, Martin. "Fielding: The Comedy of Forms," in *To the Palace of Wisdom: Studies in Order and Energy from Dryden to Blake*, 286–312. Garden City, N.Y.: Doubleday, 1964.

Rabb, Melinda Aliker. "Confinement and Entrapment in Henry Fielding's *Journal of a Voyage to Lisbon*," *Studies in the Literary Imagination*, 17 (1984):75–89.

Rawson, Claude J. *Henry Fielding*. Profiles in Literature Series. London: Routledge & Kegan Paul, 1968.

——. *Henry Fielding and the Augustan Ideal Under Stress: "Nature's Dance of Death" and Other Studies*. London: Routledge & Kegan Paul, 1972.

Richetti, John. "Fielding: System and Satire," in *The English Novel in History 1700–1780*, 121–61. London and New York: Routledge, 1999.

Rivero, Albert J. "Figurations of the Dying: Reading Fielding's *The Journal of a Voyage to Lisbon*," *JEGP*, 93 (1994):520–33.

——. *The Plays of Henry Fielding: A Critical Study of his Dramatic Career*. Charlottesville: University of Virginia Press, 1989.

Roberts, Edgar V. "Eighteenth-Century Ballad Opera: The Contribution of Henry Fielding," *Drama Survey*, 1 (1961–2):71–85.

Rogers, Katharine M. "Sensitive Feminism vs. Conventional Sympathy: Richardson and Fielding on Women," *Novel*, 9 (1976):256–70.

Rogers, Winfield H. "Fielding's Early Aesthetic and Technique," *Studies in Philology*, 50 (1943):529–51.

——. "The Significance of Fielding's *Temple Beau*," *PMLA*, 55 (1940):440–4.

Rothstein, Eric. "Amelia," in *Systems of Order & Inquiry in Later Eighteenth-Century Fiction*, 154–207. Los Angeles and Berkeley: University of California Press, 1975.
——. "The Framework of *Shamela*," *ELH*, 35 (1968):381–402.
Sacks, Sheldon. *Fiction and the Shape of Belief: A Study of Henry Fielding with Glances at Swift, Johnson, and Richardson*. Berkeley: University of California Press, 1964.
Scheuermann, Mona. "Henry Fielding's Images of Women," *Age of Johnson: A Scholarly Annual*, 3 (1990):231–80.
Schonhorn, Manuel. "Fielding's Ecphrastic Moment: Tom Jones and His Egyptian Majesty," *Studies in Philology*, 78 (1981):305–23.
Sherburn, George. "Fielding's *Amelia*: An Interpretation," *ELH*, 3 (1936):1–14.
——. "Fielding's Social Outlook," *Philological Quarterly*, 35 (1956):1–23. rpt. in *Eighteenth-Century English Literature*. ed. James L. Clifford. New York: Oxford University Press, 1959.
Shesgreen, Sean. *Literary Portraits in the Novels of Henry Fielding*. Dekalb: Northern Illinois University Press, 1972.
Simpson, K. G., ed. *Henry Fielding: Justice Observed*. London: Vision and Barnes & Noble, 1985.
Smallwood, Angela J. *Fielding and the Woman Question: The Novels of Henry Fielding and Feminist Debate, 1700–1750*. New York: St. Martin's Press, 1989.
Spilka, Mark. "Comic Resolution in Fielding's *Joseph Andrews*," *College English*, 15 (1953):11–19.
Stevick, Phillip. "Fielding and the Meaning of History," *PMLA*, 79 (1964): 561–68.
Taylor, Dick, Jr. "Joseph as Hero in *Joseph Andrews*," *Tulane Studies in English*, 7 (1957):91–109.
Thompson, James. "Fielding and Property," in *Models of Value: Eighteenth-Century Political Economy and the Novel*, 132–55. Durham: Duke University Press, 1996.
Thornbury, Ethel M. *Henry Fielding's Theory of the Comic Prose Epic*. University of Wisconsin Studies in Language and Literature, no. 30. Madison: University of Wisconsin Press, 1931; rpt. New York: Russell & Russell, 1966.
Van Ghent, Dorothy. "On *Tom Jones*," in *English Novel: Form and Function*, 65–81. New York: Rinehart, 1953; rpt. New York: Harper, 1961.
Varey, Simon, *Henry Fielding*. Cambridge: Cambridge University Press, 1986.
——. *Joseph Andrews: A Satire of Modern Times*. Boston: Twayne, 1990.
Wanko, Caryl. "Characterization and the Reader's Quandary in Fielding's *Amelia*," *JEGP*, 90 (1991):505–23.
Warner, William B. "The Elevation of the Novel in England: Hegemony and Literary History," *ELH*, 59 (1992):577–96.
——. "*Joseph Andrews* as Performative Entertainment," chap. 6 in *Licensing Entertainment: The Elevation of Novel Reading in Britain, 1684–1750*. Berkeley and Los Angeles: University of California Press, 1998.
Watt, Ian. "Fielding and the Epic Theory of the Novel," in *Rise of the Novel: Studies in Defoe, Richardson, and Fielding*, 239–59. Berkeley: University of California Press, 1957.
——. "Shamela." Introduction to his edition of *An Apology for the Life of Mrs. Shamela Andrews*, 1–11. Augustan Reprint Society, no. 57. Los Angeles: Clark Memorial Library, 1956.

Weinbrot, Howard. "Chastity and Interpolation: Two Aspects of *Joseph Andrews*," *Journal of English and Germanic Philology*, 69 (1970):14–31.

——. "Fielding's *Tragedy of Tragedies*: Papal Fallibility and Scriblerian Satire," *Harvard Library Bulletin*, 7 (1996):20–39.

Welsh, Alexander. "False Testimony about Jones," in *Strong Representations: Narrative and Circumstantial Evidence in England*. Baltimore: Johns Hopkins University Press, 1992.

Wendt, Allan. "The Moral Allegory of *Jonathan Wild*," *ELH*, 24 (1957):306–20.

——. "The Naked Virtue of Amelia," *ELH*, 27 (1960):131–48.

Williams, Aubrey. "Interpositions of Providence and the Design of Fielding's Novels," *South Atlantic Quarterly*, 70 (1971):265–86.

Work, James A. "Henry Fielding, Christian Censor," in *The Age of Johnson: Essays Presented to Chauncey Brewster Tinker*, eds. Frederick W. Hilles and Wilmarth S. Lewis, 139–48. New Haven, Conn.: Yale University Press, 1949.

Wright, Andrew, *Henry Fielding: Mask and Feast*. Berkeley: University of California Press, 1965.

Zirker, Malvin R. *Fielding's Social Pamphlets*. Berkeley and Los Angeles: University of California Press, 1966.

IV   Bibliographical Studies

Hahn, H. George. *Henry Fielding: An Annotated Bibliography* [to 1977]. Metuchen, N. J., & London: Scarecrow Press, 1979.

Library: Fielding's Library: An Annotated Catalogue, ed. Frederick G. Ribble and Anne G. Ribble. Charlottesville: Bibliographical Society of the University of Virginia, 1998.

LS: The London Stage 1660–1800, Pt. 3: 1729–47, ed. Arthur H. Scouten. Carbondale: University of Southern Illinois Press, 1961.

Morrissey, L. J. *Henry Fielding: A Reference Guide* [to 1977]. Boston: G. K. Hall, 1980.

Stoler, John A., and Fulton, Richard D. *Henry Fielding: An Annotated Bibliography of Twentieth-Century Criticism, 1900–1977*. New York & London: Garland, 1980.

V   Contemporary Journals Frequently Cited

DA: *Daily Advertiser*
DJ: *Daily Journal*
DP: *Daily Post*
GM: *Gentleman's Magazine*
GSJ: *Grub-Street Journal*
LDA: *London Daily Advertiser*
LEP: *London Evening Post*
PA: *Public Advertiser*

Index